UGARITIC VOCABULARY IN SYLLABIC TRANSCRIPTION

Revised Edition

HARVARD SEMITIC MUSEUM PUBLICATIONS

Lawrence E. Stager, General Editor
Michael D. Coogan, Director of Publications

HARVARD SEMITIC STUDIES

W. Randall Garr, Jo Ann Hackett, and John Huehnergard, editors

Syriac Manuscripts: A Catalogue — Moshe H. Goshen-Gottstein
Introduction to Classical Ethiopic — Thomas O. Lambdin
The Songs of the Sabbath Sacrifice — Carol Newsom
Non-Canonical Psalms from Qumran: A Pseudepigraphic Collection — Eileen M. Schuller
An Exodus Scroll from Qumran — Judith E. Sanderson
You Shall Have No Other Gods — Jeffrey H. Tigay
Ugaritic Vocabulary in Syllabic Transcription — John Huehnergard
The Scholarship of William Foxwell Albright — Gus Van Beek
Features of the Eschatology of IV Ezra — Michael E. Stone
Studies in Neo-Aramaic — Wolfhart Heinrichs, Editor
Lingering over Words: Studies in Ancient Near Eastern Literature in Honor of William L. Moran — Tzvi Abusch, John Huehnergard, Piotr Steinkeller, Editors
A Grammar of the Palestinian Targum Fragments from the Cairo Genizah — Steven E. Fassberg
The Origins and Development of the Waw-Consecutive: Northwest Semitic Evidence from Ugaritic to Qumran — Mark S. Smith
Amurru Akkadian: A Linguistic Study, Volume I — Shlomo Izre'el
Amurru Akkadian: A Linguistic Study, Volume II — Shlomo Izre'el
The Installation of Baal's High Priestess at Emar — Daniel E. Fleming
The Development of the Arabic Scripts — Beatrice Gruendler
The Archaeology of Israelite Samaria: Early Iron Age through the Ninth Century BCE — Ron Tappy
A Grammar of Akkadian — John Huehnergard
Key to A Grammar of Akkadian — John Huehnergard
Akkadian Loanwords in Biblical Hebrew — Paul V. Mankowski
Adam in Myth and History: Ancient Israelite Perspectives on the Primal Human — Dexter E. Callender Jr.
West Semitic Vocabulary in the Akkadian Texts from Emar — Eugen J. Pentiuc
The Archaeology of Israelite Samaria, Volume II: The Eighth Century BCE — Ron E. Tappy
Leaves from an Epigrapher's Notebook: Collected Papers in Hebrew and West Semitic Palaeography and Epigraphy — Frank Moore Cross
Semitic Noun Patterns — Joshua Fox
Eighth-Century Iraqi Grammar: A Critical Exploration of Pre-Ḫalīlian Arabic Linguistics — Rafael Talmon
Amarna Studies: Collected Essays — William L. Moran
Narrative Structure and Discourse Constellations: An Analysis of Clause Function in Biblical Hebrew Prose — Roy L. Heller
The Modal System of Old Babylonian — Eran Cohen
Studies in Semitic Grammaticalization — Aaron D. Rubin
Markedness in Canaanite and Hebrew Verbs — Paul D. Korchin

Acknowledgments

It is a pleasure to express my sincere thanks to the individuals who have given of their time and expertise in the development of this study.

An earlier draft of Part I was read by Delbert R. Hillers, Piotr Steinkeller, and Gernot Wilhelm, each of whom offered numerous suggestions for improvement and corrected many errors. The treatment of several topics throughout the volume also profited from discussions with Frank M. Cross, Thomas O. Lambdin, William L. Moran, and Wheeler M. Thackston, Jr.

Prof. Cross also has my gratitude for publishing the study in the Harvard Semitic Studies series.

I am grateful as well to David Dalton, who provided unlimited access to his Apple LaserWriter, and to John Cheng, Theodore J. Lewis, Charles Merkle, Ronald A. Simkins, and Prof. Thackston for help with other computer-related issues.

Finally, the study and its author are most indebted to Jo Ann Hackett, who created the laser font in which the volume is printed, and whose counsel on matters of Northwest Semitic philology and English style appears on nearly every page. Without her unfailing wisdom and encouragement, this book would not exist. It is dedicated to her, with love.

UGARITIC VOCABULARY IN SYLLABIC TRANSCRIPTION

Revised Edition

by

John Huehnergard

EISENBRAUNS
Winona Lake, Indiana
2008

UGARITIC VOCABULARY IN SYLLABIC TRANSCRIPTION
(revised edition)
by
John Huehnergard

Printed in the United States of America

www.eisenbrauns.com

Library of Congress Cataloging-in-Publication Data

Huehnergard, John.
Ugaritic vocabulary in syllabic transcription / by John Huehnergard — Rev. ed.
p. cm. — (Harvard Semitic Museum publications) (Harvard Semitic studies)
Includes bibliographical references and index.
ISBN 978-1-57506-933-3 (hardback : alk. paper)
1. Ugaritic language—Dictionaries—English. 2. Ugaritic language—Grammar. I. Title.
PJ4150.Z5H84 2008
493′.67321—dc22
2008035682

The paper used in this publication meets the minimum requirements of the American National Standard for Information Sciences—Permanence of Paper for Printed Library Materials, ANSI Z39.48-1984.⊗™

for Jo

Contents

Abbreviations

A. Bibliographical

A	lexical series á A = *nâqu* (Civil, MSL 14).
AAAS	*Annales archéologiques arabes syriennes* (Damascus).
AASF	*Annales Academiae Scientiarum Fennicae* (Helsinki).
AASOR	*Annual of the American Schools of Oriental Research* (New Haven).
ABAW (NF)	Bayerische Akademie der Wissenschaften, Philosophisch-Historische Klasse: *Abhandlungen,* Neue Folge (Munich).
AbB	F.R. Kraus, ed. *Altbabylonische Briefe.*
ABZ[2]	R. Borger. *Assyrisch-babylonische Zeichenliste,* 2nd ed.
AcAntHung	*Acta Antiqua Academiae Scientiarum Hungaricae* (Budapest).
AcOr	*Acta Orientalia* (Oslo).
AfK	*Archiv für Keilschriftforschung* (Berlin).
AfO	*Archiv für Orientforschung* (Berlin/Graz).
AHw	W. von Soden. *Akkadisches Handwörterbuch.*
Ai	lexical series ki.KI.KAL.bi.šè = *ana ittīšu* (Landsberger, MSL 1).
AION	*Annali.* Istituto Orientale di Napoli (Naples).
AJSL	*American Journal of Semitic Languages and Literatures* (Chicago).
ANLR	*Atti* della Accademia Nazionale dei Lincei - Rendiconti - Classe di Scienze Morali, storiche, e philologiche (Rome).
AnOr	*Analecta Orientalia* (Rome: Pontificium Institutum Biblicum).
AnOr 48	L.R. Fisher, ed. *The Claremont Ras Shamra Tablets.*
AnOr 48 26,27	M.C. Astour. "A Letter and Two Economic Texts."
Antagal	lexical series an-ta-gál = *šaqû* (M. Roth, MSL 17).
AOAT	*Alter Orient und Altes Testament* (Kevelaer/Neukirchen-Vluyn).
AOAT 1	W. Röllig, M. Dietrich, eds. *lišān mitḫurti: Festschrift von Soden.*
AOATS	*Alter Orient und Altes Testament — Sonderreihe* (Kevelaer/Neukirchen-Vluyn).
ARM(T)	*Archives royales de Mari (Textes)* (Paris).
ArOr	*Archiv Orientální.* Journal of the Czechoslovak Oriental Institute (Prague).
AS	*Assyriological Studies* (Chicago).
AS 16	H.G. Güterbock, T. Jacobsen, eds. *Studies Landsberger.*
AS 16 29ff., 31ff.,33ff.,39	J. Nougayrol. "'Vocalises' et 'syllabes en liberté' à Ugarit."

AS 21	I.J. Gelb, et al. *Computer-Aided Analysis of Amorite.*
AS^3	W. von Soden, W. Röllig. *Das akkadische Syllabar,* 3rd ed.
ASJ	*Acta Sumerologica* (The Middle East Culture Center in Japan).
ASOR	American Schools of Oriental Research
AulaOr	*Aula Orientalis.* Revista de estudios del Próximo Oriente Antiguo (Barcelona).
BA	*Beiträge zur Assyriologie und semitischen Sprachwissenschaft* (Leipzig/Baltimore).
BASOR	*Bulletin of the American Schools of Oriental Research* (Baltimore/ New Haven/Philadelphia).
BDB	F. Brown, S.R. Driver, C.A. Briggs. *A Hebrew and English Lexicon.*
BE	The Babylonian Expedition of the University of Pennsylvania, Series A: Cuneiform texts (Philadelphia: University Museum).
Biblica	*Biblica* (Rome).
BiOr	*Bibliotheca Orientalis* (Leiden).
BN	*Biblische Notizen* (Bamberg).
BZ	*Biblische Zeitschrift* (Paderborn).
CAD	I.J. Gelb, et al. *The Assyrian Dictionary of the Oriental Institute of the University of Chicago.*
CH	*Codex Ḫammurabi: Textus Primigenius* (3rd ed., E. Bergmann).
CRAIBL	Académie des Inscriptions et Belles-Lettres, *Comptes rendus* des séances de l'année ... (Paris).
CTA	A. Herdner. *Corpus des tablettes en cunéiformes alphabétiques.*
Diri	lexical series diri DIR *siāku* = *watru.*
Ea	lexical series ea A = *nâqu* (M. Civil, MSL 14).
EA	J.A. Knudtzon. *Die El-Amarna-Tafeln.*
Erimḫuš	lexical series erimḫuš = *anantu* (A. Cavigneaux, MSL 17).
ErIs	*Eretz-Israel.* Archaeological, Historical and Geographical Studies (Jerusalem).
GAG	W. von Soden. *Grundriss der akkadischen Grammatik.*
GHL	F.W. Bush. "Grammar of the Hurrian Language."
GLECS	*Comptes rendus du groupe linguistique d'études chamito-sémitiques* (Paris).
GLH	E. Laroche. *Glossaire de la langue hourrite.*
Ḫḫ	lexical series ḪAR-ra = *ḫubullu* (= B. Landsberger, E. Reiner, MSL 5-11).
HSM	Harvard Semitic Monographs (Cambridge, Mass.).
HSS	Harvard Semitic Studies (Cambridge, Mass.).
HTR	*Harvard Theological Review* (Cambridge, Mass.).
IEJ	*Israel Exploration Journal* (Jerusalem).
IH	E.A. Speiser. *Introduction to Hurrian.*

IOS	*Israel Oriental Studies* (Tel Aviv).
Izi	lexical series izi = *išātu* (M. Civil, MSL 13).
JANES	*Journal of the Ancient Near Eastern Society of Columbia University* (New York).
JAOS	*Journal of the American Oriental Society* (New Haven).
JCS	*Journal of Cuneiform Studies* (New Haven).
JESHO	*Journal of the Economic and Social History of the Orient* (Leiden).
JNES	*Journal of Near Eastern Studies* (Chicago).
JNSL	*Journal of Northwest Semitic Languages* (Leiden).
JQR	*The Jewish Quarterly Review* (Philadelphia).
JSS	*Journal of Semitic Studies* (Manchester).
KAR	E. Ebeling. *Keilschrifttexte aus Assur religiösen Inhalts.*
KBo	Keilschrifttexte aus Boghazköi (Berlin).
KTU	M. Dietrich, O. Loretz, J. Sanmartín. *Die keilalphabetischen Texte aus Ugarit.*
Lĕšonénu	*Lĕšonénu.* Quarterly for the Study of the Hebrew Language and Cognate Subjects (Jerusalem).
Lú	lexical series lú = *ša* (M. Civil, MSL 12).
MAD	I. J. Gelb. *Materials for the Assyrian Dictionary.*
MAOG	*Mitteilungen der Altorientalischen Gesellschaft* (Berlin).
MEE 4	G. Pettinato. *Materiali epigrafici di Ebla 4: Testi lessicali bilingui.*
MSL	B. Landsberger, et al. *Materials for the Sumerian Lexicon.*
MVAG	*Mitteilungen der Vorderasiatisch(-Ägyptisch)en Gesellschaft* (Berlin).
OA	*Oriens Antiquus* (Rome).
OLP	*Orientalia Lovaniensia Periodica* (Leuven).
OLZ	*Orientalistische Literaturzeitung* (Leipzig).
Or.	*Orientalia* (Nova Series, Rome).
PBS	Publications of the Babylonian Section, University Museum, University of Pennsylvania (Philadelphia).
PRU 2	C. Virolleaud. *Le Palais royal d'Ugarit 2.*
PRU 3	J. Nougayrol. *Le Palais royal d'Ugarit 3.*
PRU 4	J. Nougayrol. *Le Palais royal d'Ugarit 4.*
PRU 5	C. Virolleaud. *Le Palais royal d'Ugarit 5.*
PRU 6	J. Nougayrol. *Le Palais royal d'Ugarit 6.*
PSD	A. Sjöberg, ed. *The Sumerian Dictionary of the University Museum of the University of Pennsylvania.*
QS	*Quaderni di Semitistica* (Florence).
RA	*Revue d'assyriologie et d'archéologie orientale* (Paris).
RA 38 5,12	C. Virolleaud. "Cinq tablettes accadiennes de Ras-Shamra."
RA 63 83f.	J. Nougayrol. "Nouveau 'Silbenvokabular A' d'Ugarit."
RHA	*Revue hittite et asianique* (Paris).

RlA	E. Ebeling, et al. *Reallexikon der Assyriologie.*
RS	Ras Shamra excavation/tablet number.
RSO	*Rivista degli Studi Orientali* (Rome).
S^a	lexical series Syllabary A (R.T. Hallock, MSL 3 1-45).
S^a Voc.	lexical series Syllabary A Vocabulary (B. Landsberger, R.T. Hallock, MSL 3 47-87).
SEb	*Studi Eblaiti* (Rome).
SEL	*Studi Epigrafici e Linguistici sul Vicino Oriente Antico* (Verona).
Silbenvokabular A	lexical series.
ŠL	A. Deimel. *Šumerisches Lexikon.*
StBoT	Studien zu den Boğazköy-Texten (Wiesbaden).
StOr	*Studia Orientalia* (Helsinki).
Syllabary u-a-i	lexical series.
Syria	*Syria.* Revue d'art oriental et d'archéologie (Paris).
Syria 10 pl. 77	C. Virolleaud. "Les inscriptions cunéiformes de Ras Shamra."
Syria 12 228ff., 231ff.,236ff. pl.46ff.,pl.49	F. Thureau-Dangin. "Vocabulaires de Ras-Shamra."
Syria 13 234, 235, 237	F. Thureau-Dangin."Nouvelles fragments de vocabulaires."
Syria 16 194	E. Dhorme. "Petite tablette accadienne de Ras Shamra."
Syria 18 249f., 251ff.,253f.	F. Thureau-Dangin. "Trois contrats de Ras Shamra."
Syria 28 173f.	C. Virolleaud. "Six textes de Ras Shamra."
Syria 59 199ff.	D. Arnaud. "Les textes cunéiformes suméro-accadiens des campagnes 1979-1980."
TA	*Tel Aviv* (Institute of Archaeology, Tel Aviv).
TA 8 7f.	D. Owen. "An Akkadian Letter from Ugarit at Tel Aphek."
UF	*Ugarit-Forschungen* (Kevelaer/Neukirchen-Vluyn).
UF 11 479	E. Laroche. "RS 20.189."
Ug. 3	C.F.A. Schaeffer, ed. *Ugaritica 3.*
Ug. 4	C.F.A. Schaeffer, ed. *Ugaritica 4.*
Ug. 5	J. Nougayrol et al. *Ugaritica 5.*
Ug. 5 1 - 173	J. Nougayrol. "Textes suméro-accadiens des archives et bibliothèques privées d'Ugarit."
Ug. 6	C.F.A. Schaeffer, ed. *Ugaritica 6.*
Ug. 6 394ff., 401ff.,403b, 404	J. Nougayrol. "La Lamaštu à Ugarit."
Ug. 7	C.F.A. Schaeffer, ed. *Ugaritica 7.*
Ug. 7 pl. 1-68	C.F.A. Schaeffer. "Epaves d'une bibliothèque d'Ugarit."

UT	C.H. Gordon. *Ugaritic Textbook.*
VT	*Vetus Testamentum* (Leiden).
WO	*Die Welt des Orients* (Göttingen).
WZKM	*Wiener Zeitschrift für die Kunde des Morgenlandes* (Vienna).
ZA	*Zeitschrift für Assyriologie und Vorderasiatische Archäologie* (Berlin).

B. Other

acc.	accusative.
adj.	adjective.
Akk.	Akkadian
alphab.	alphabetic (text, form).
Arab.	Arabic.
Aram.	Aramaic.
C	consonant.
c(.)	common (gender).
cf.	compare.
ch.	chapter.
conj.	(verbal) conjugation.
D	verbal stem with doubled middle radical.
DN	divine name.
du.	dual.
econ.	economic (text).
Eth.	Ethiopic.
f(.)	feminine.
f.	following line, page.
fem.	feminine.
ff.	following lines, pages.
G	basic stem of the verb; guttural (consonant).
gen.	genitive.
GN	geographical name.
Gt	basic verbal stem with infixed *-t-*.
Heb.	Hebrew.
Hur.	Hurrian.
infin.	infinitive.
JAram.	Jewish Aramaic.
LB	Late Babylonian (Akkadian).
legal	legal (text).
lex.	lexical (text).
lit.	literary (text).
m(.)	masculine.
MA	Middle Assyrian (Akkadian).
masc.	masculine.
MB	Middle Babylonian (Akkadian).
MHeb.	Mishnaic Hebrew.
MN	month name.
N	verbal stem with prefixed *n-*.
n.	noun, nominal; (foot)note.
NA	Neo-Assyrian (Akkadian).
NB	Neo-Babylonian (Akkadian).
nn.	notes.
no.	number.
nom.	nominative.
nos.	numbers.
num.	numeral.
NWS	Northwest Semitic.
OA	Old Assyrian (Akkadian).
OAkk.	Old Akkadian.
OB	Old Babylonian (Akkadian).
obl.	oblique.
obv.	obverse.
OSA	Old South Arabian.
p(.)	page; plural.
pl.	plural; plate.

PN	personal name.
P(NW)S	Proto-(Northwest) Semitic.
pp.	pages.
PS	Proto-Semitic.
ptcpl.	participle.
r.	reverse.
RN	royal name.
s(.)	singular.
s.v.	sub voce, under the word in question.
SB	Standard Babylonian (Akkadian).
Sem.	Semitic (language(s)).
sg.	singular.
Sum.	Sumerian.
syll.	syllabic (writing, text).
Syr.	Syriac.
Š	verbal stem with prefixed *š*-.
Targ.	Targum(ic Aramaic).
tD	verbal stem with doubled middle radical and prefixed *t*-.
Ugar.	Ugaritic.
v	vowel.
v.	verb(al).
v. adj.	verbal adjective.
v. n.	verbal noun.
vocab.	vocabulary (text).
WPA	Western Peripheral Akkadian.
WSem.	West Semitic.

1	first person (verbal form).
2	second person (verbal form).
3	third person (verbal form).
:	transliterates cuneiform "gloss sign" ("Glossenkeil").
!	indicates correction of scribal error.
< >	enclose scribal omission.
« »	enclose scribal plus.
*	precedes reconstructed or unattested form.
/ /	enclose phonemic normalizations of Ugaritic forms attested in syllabic transcription.
*/ /	indicates vocalizations of Ugaritic forms attested only in alphabetic spelling.
{ }	enclose graphemes, specifically, alphabetic signs.
[roman]	enclose phonetic normalizations.
[*italic*]	enclose damaged sign(s).
⌜ ⌝	enclose partially damaged sign(s).

INTRODUCTION

The essentially unvocalized nature of the alphabetic script used to write Ugaritic is, of course, a major hindrance in our attempts to understand the language and its texts. For without a clear picture of the vocalism of the language, we are unable to form a clear picture of its word structure, and thus of its morphology. There are, fortunately, several sources of information about the vocalization of Ugaritic, which may be classified in terms of their linguistic validity into two levels of significance. The more important sources are

1. the three aleph signs; and
2. Ugaritic words written in syllabic cuneiform.

In both of these sources, native scribes provide our only contemporary witness, and hence our only reliable data, about the vocalization of the local language. Other sources of vocalization are

3. writings in Sumero-Akkadian texts of personal and geographical names, which, for reasons to be taken up below, should generally not be used for linguistic description; and
4. comparative Semitic philology, which can furnish only an abstract reconstruction, not a linguistic reality.

The present monograph is an investigation of the second of these sources. Its primary goal is to provide an analytical glossary of all Ugaritic words attested in syllabic cuneiform (Sumero-Akkadian) texts. In the course of compiling such a glossary, it has also been necessary to prepare a new edition of the famous polyglot vocabulary texts from Ras Shamra, most of which were first published by J. Nougayrol in Ugaritica 5. A final objective is a summary of the orthographic conventions governing the representation of Ugaritic phonemes in syllabic cuneiform, and of the phonological processes and morphological elements discernible in this collection of Ugaritic vocabulary. The polyglot vocabulary texts are presented in Part I, the glossary in Part II, and the analyses of orthography, phonology, and morphology in Part III.

The monograph is intended primarily for Ugaritologists and other students of Northwest Semitic philology, rather than for Assyriologists. The glossary, therefore, is arranged by Ugaritic root, in the consonantal order used in most modern Ugaritic lexicons.

The Corpus of Ugarit Akkadian Texts

The corpus of Akkadian texts from which the Ugaritic words in this study are culled is restricted to those that were actually written, i.e., composed or copied, by scribes in the ancient city-state of Ugarit proper. All but a very small number of these were unearthed at the site of Ras Shamra during the French excavations there since 1929. The exceptions are five letters found at el-Amarna in Egypt, two of them (EA 45, 49) certainly, and three (EA 46-48) very probably, sent from Ugarit; one letter found at Tel Aphek, sent by a prefect of Ugarit (TA 8 7f.); and the two economic dockets among four texts taken illicitly from Ras Shamra, later published in AnOr 48 (pp. 26, 27). Thus, not all of the texts in our corpus were found at Ras Shamra. More important, not all of the 700-800 Sumero-Akkadian texts found at Ras Shamra are included in our corpus. Many of those texts are letters or treaties written elsewhere[1] and sent to Ugarit.[2] Although all are written in a type of Akkadian generally referred to as Western Peripheral, it has become clear as a result of recent research that texts written at different sites exhibit small but significant orthographic and grammatical differences. For linguistic purposes, therefore, what is important is not the find-spot of a text, but rather its provenance. Texts found at Ras Shamra but sent from Ḫattusas, for example, must be considered together with other texts written at Ḫattusas found at Boğazköy and at el-Amarna. In this way we may isolate several sub-dialects within the general framework of Western Peripheral Akkadian, including, among others, the Akkadian of Amurru,[3] of Byblos,[4] of Carchemish,[5] of Emar,[6] of Ḫattusas,[7] of Jerusalem,[8] and, of course, of Ugarit.[9]

Since certainty regarding the provenance of a given text is not always possible, and there is occasionally some scholarly disagreement, a summary of my own criteria for the inclusion of a text in the Ugarit Akkadian corpus is in order here.[10] These

[1]E.g., Alašiya, Amqu, Assyria, Beirut, Carchemish, Ḫattusas, Mukiš, Parga, Qadiš, Sidon.

[2]A very helpful list of all Ras Shamra Akkadian texts published through 1974 was presented by Kühne in UF 6 129-56 (Nachträge, UF 7 515-16); the list, arranged by RS number, includes provenance, genre, date, find-spot, and place of publication.

[3]See Izre'el, "The Akkadian Dialect of the Scribes of Amurru"; idem, UF 16 83-92.

[4]See, e.g., Moran, "Syntactical Study"; JCS 4 169-72; JCS 5 33-35; Or. 29 1-19; "The Hebrew Language."

[5]Described in my doctoral dissertation, "The Akkadian Dialects of Carchemish and Ugarit."

[6]See, provisionally, Huehnergard, RA 77 11-43, esp. 35-43.

[7]Durham, "Studies in Boğazköy Akkadian."

[8]See Moran, "Syrian Scribe."

[9]See further below, and the next note.

[10]The present monograph is an outgrowth of a more general study of the grammar of Ugarit Akka-

criteria vary according to the genre of the text:

> The provenance of all *economic* texts, since they are the internal records of the Ugarit court, and could therefore hardly have originated elsewhere, is assumed to be Ugarit unless there is a specific reason to doubt it.[11]
>
> For *legal* texts, the mention of the action of a particular king of Ugarit, or that an action took place "in the presence (*ana pānī*)" of a particular king, or the presence of a royal seal of Ugarit, is sufficient indication of origin.
>
> *Letters* are the most difficult texts to assign a provenance, since the senders usually did not feel obliged to report their location at the time of writing. And since at least some letters must have reached their destination, the find-spot of a letter should generally not be equated with its provenance, an equation that will be true only for copies of letters and for letters that were never sent. I take a rather "minimalist" approach to letters, therefore, and include in the corpus of Ugarit Akk. only those in which the sender may be identified as a king, queen, or prefect of Ugarit.[12]
>
> The *lexical* and *literary* texts, unlike the other genres, were for the most part not composed at Ugarit, but are rather copies of originals from Mesopotamia or elsewhere (e.g., Ḫattusas). Copies that are the work of Ugarit scribes exhibit errors or other idiosyncracies that betray the scribes' local substrate dialect, and similar features (e.g., a Ugaritic month name in the colophon of MSL 10 37ff./107ff. A; see MSL 10 37 n. 1).

For reference, a complete list of the texts that, in my opinion, were written by

dian, the results of which will soon appear in a separate volume entitled The Akkadian of Ugarit (Harvard Semitic Studies). For the sake of brevity and to avoid excessive repetition of information (without, I hope, causing excessive frustration), the reader is referred to the latter throughout the present study, here for a more detailed description of the corpus, elsewhere, e.g., for new readings, and for matters concerning the orthography and grammar of the Akkadian texts in which the Ugaritic words, our present topic of investigation, occur.

[11]Similarly Kühne, UF 6 131.

[12]In one instance, a double letter—Ug. 5 55—half of which is from one Rapʾānu, who is known to have lived at Ugarit, is also included.

Here it should be noted that the provenance of EA 46-48, which I also include in the Ugarit Akk. corpus, is suggested by features such as palaeography and clay type, rather than by content (see Albright, BASOR 95 30-31); thus, their Ugaritic provenance, while highly likely, is not certain.

The Ugarit Akk. letters, by these criteria, number only seventeen: EA 45-49; PRU 3 4b; PRU 4 294; PRU 6 3, 8; TA 8 7f.; Ug. 5 21, 24, 28, 29, 49, 54, 55.

scribes at Ugarit appears at the end of this study as Index A 1. (For the number of texts in the corpus by genre, see further below.) It is in these texts that the forms that constitute the subject of the present monograph are found.[13]

The reason for restricting our sources to texts written at Ugarit proper is straightforward. Foreign, i.e., non-Akkadian, words appear in the texts of nearly all peripheral Akkadian dialects; these "intrusive" words, generally speaking, reflect substrate languages that are, in most cases, the native local idiom of the scribe. In many instances in Late Bronze texts from Syria-Palestine, such forms, and the substrate idiom they reflect, may broadly be labeled Northwest Semitic. But we may not assume that Late Bronze Northwest Semitic constituted a dialectal unity; rather, the area represented by the provenances of those texts displays considerable dialectal diversity in all subsequent periods,[14] and a similar diversity, a dialect continuum, undoubtedly existed in the Late Bronze period as well (and is, in fact, evidenced for several linguistic features in the forms themselves).[15] A consistent linguistic description of a particular substrate language, therefore, is possible only if all of the evidence for it is derived from sources written in the locale where that language was spoken. If our goal is to review the evidence in Akkadian texts for the phonology and morphology of Ugaritic, and to compare that evidence with the alphabetic evidence,[16] only forms in texts written at Ugarit may be considered, since only with those forms may we be relatively (though not entirely) confident that we are dealing with the same dialect, i.e., with actual Ugaritic forms, rather than similar (or even identical) forms in a related dialect.

The Akkadian dialect of Ugarit[17] belongs to the northern variety of WPA,

[13]Although it is likely that the same, or a similar, group of scribes are responsible for some of the Sumero-Akkadian texts discovered in recent years at Ras Ibn Hani (see Arnaud-Kennedy, Syria 56 317-24; Arnaud, Syria 61 15-23), it has seemed best, provisionally, to exclude them from the Ugarit Akk. corpus.

[14]See, e.g., Garr, Dialect Geography.

[15]See also §B of my review of Sivan, Analysis, forthcoming in JAOS 107/4.

[16]The issue of chronology is also important. The Ugarit Akkadian texts found at el-Amarna are from the reign of ᶜAmmiθtamru I, in the first half of the 14th century; all others date to the reigns of Niqmaddu II through Niqmaddu III, the second-last king of Ugarit, i.e., roughly, the second half of the 14th through the end of the 13th century. The alphabetic tablets are contemporaneous with this majority of Sumero-Akkadian texts, although the actual date of composition of some of the literary alphabetic texts may be somewhat earlier, so that their grammar may on occasion be relatively more archaic than that of other genres.

[17]For descriptions of the grammar, see Nougayrol, PRU 3 pp. xxxv-xxxvi; Swaim, "Grammar"; Arnaud, "La culture suméro-accadienne" 1349-54. All of these fail to distinguish the various provenances of the texts found at Ras Shamra. Only those written at Ugarit are considered in my forthcoming The Akkadian of Ugarit (see above, n. 10).

variously called "Reichsakkadisch,"[18] "Ḫurro-Akkadian,"[19] or, as I would prefer, "Syro-Anatolian Akkadian."[20] As such, it exhibits, among other features, a certain orthographic confusion in the representation of stops and sibilants,[21] forms with an enclitic particle *-mê*,[22] and a relatively larger amount of influence from the contemporary Middle Babylonian and Middle Assyrian dialects of Mesopotamia than is exhibited by southern WPA texts.[23] Also like other northern WPA dialects, Ugarit Akk. exhibits virtually none of the pervasive Northwest Semitic verbal morphology that characterizes the so-called "Canaanizing" southern WPA dialects, such as those of Byblos and Gezer.[24] Nevertheless, the substrate Ugaritic idiom does make its presence known in other features: e.g., nouns in construct frequently bear a case-ending, contrary to normative Akkadian morphology; the curious word order, which is predominantly Subject-Verb-Object but has many permutations, was undoubtedly influenced to some degree by that of Ugaritic (although the details are elusive).[25] But the clearest evidence of the underlying language of the scribes lies in the vocabulary, for Ugaritic words occur, with varying degrees of frequency, in all genres of the Akkadian texts.

The Identification of Ugaritic Forms

The process of isolating Ugaritic vocabulary in Akkadian texts and the accuracy of the result of that process in any given instance depend on several factors, including the genre of the text in question, the presence or absence of a gloss mark, and features

[18]See Landsberger, JCS 8 54.

[19]Cf. Wilhelm, Ḫurro-Akkadisch.

[20]I.e., texts written at Alalaḫ, Carchemish, Egypt, Emar, Ḫattusas, Mittanni, and some texts written in Amurru.

[21]See below, Part III, ch. 1 §A 1-2.

[22]Instead of or in addition to *-ma*, e.g., *mi-nu-um-me-e* "whatever" Ug. 5 55 r.8'; *ki-i-me-e* "as" Syria 18 253f.:10.

[23]For the general isogloss between northern and southern WPA, "roughly ... a line from Ṣumur on the coast to Qatna inland," see Moran, "Syrian Scribe" 158 n. 5. All of the features just enumerated are exhibited by Ugarit Akk. to a lesser degree than by some other northern WPA dialects, such as those of Carchemish, Ḫattusas, and Mittanni; i.e., if all WPA dialects, northern and southern, were arranged along a continuum line, Ugarit Akk. would be on the northern side, but relatively close to the center.

[24]See, e.g., Moran, "Syntactical Study"; Or. 29 1-19; "The Hebrew Language"; Rainey, IOS 1 86-102; UF 5 235-62; UF 7 395-426; Izre'el, IOS 8 13-90.

[25]Other features, such as the prefixes *ta-* and *ti-* for 3fs verbs, the use of *ištu* for expected *ina*, and the *u* of apodosis, may result from substrate influence, but they are common to several WPA dialects. For a more detailed discussion of substrate influence in Ugarit Akk., see my forthcoming monograph.

of morphology. The conditions under which forms in this study were isolated as Ugaritic are the following, listed in decreasing order of reliability.

1. Forms in the last column of the four-column exemplars of the polyglot Syllabary A Vocabulary (abbr. S^a Voc.),[26] viz., UF 11 479, Ug. 5 130, 131, 137, 138,[27] are Ugaritic equivalents of the Sumerian sign and Akkadian word appearing in the first and second columns (the third column is Hurrian).

In other texts:

2. It is assumed that a "gloss mark" (see below, Part III, ch. 1 §C) that does not serve as a word divider, line connector, or indicator of the reading of a logogram marks the word that follows as non-Akkadian, even if the word in question is attested in the Akkadian lexicon. In all but one instance, a Hurrian form, the non-Akkadian word is Northwest Semitic and therefore, in these texts, Ugaritic.
3. A form that is otherwise unattested in Akkadian, or differs in one or more significant features from the expected Akkadian,[28] is interpreted as Ugaritic if such an interpretation is plausible on formal grounds, i.e., if it conforms to what is otherwise known about Ugaritic phonology and morphology.[29]
4. Similarly, a word that can be interpreted orthographically and

[26]See below, Part I.

[27]Also four-column exemplars of the S^a Voc. are Ug. 5 133, 134, 136, but the Ugaritic column in each of these is unfortunately completely broken. Ug. 5 135 is also an S^a Voc. text, but a three-column version, without a Ugaritic column.

[28]I have in mind here especially the few forms culled from the various Ugarit Akk. exemplars of Mesopotamian lexical series (other than the fourth column of the S^a Voc. texts). Several of these exemplars exhibit a rather large number of curious spellings vis-à-vis their canonical Mesopotamian counterparts. Most of these odd writings are simply "Hörfehler," and make no sense as Ugaritic forms. A few, however, may be seen as mistakes in which the scribe wrote a Ugaritic form rather than the somewhat different Akkadian form: */lašānu/* "tongue" for Akk. *lišānu* (see the Glossary under LŠN); */sug/kuru/* "bolt" for *sikkūru* (SGR a); */ᶜuṣṣūru/* "bird" for *iṣṣūru* (ᶜṢR). (For other probable or possible Ugar. forms in these texts, see the Glossary under BRḤ, DRQ, RDM.) I have included these examples in this study, but it should be kept in mind that some or all of them may simply be part of the larger group of "Hörfehler."

A set of forms that pose a rather different problem are the divine names in Ug. 5 18 and Ug. 5 170, for which see further below.

[29]While it is not inconceivable that an Akkadian word that has failed to appear in all other Akkadian texts would make its only appearance in a text written at Ugarit, the possibility is considerably more remote than that an unidentified form is part of the Ugaritic lexicon, our knowledge of which, given the far smaller number of texts, and their rather limited range of content, is much less complete than our knowledge of the Akkadian lexicon.

formally as Akkadian, but the meaning of which, in the relevant context, does not conform to the established meaning of the Akkadian, may also be identified as Ugaritic if that is formally plausible.[30]

5. Forms that exhibit distinctively Northwest Semitic (here, of course, specifically Ugaritic) phonology or morphology,[31] such as initial /y/ and post-consonantal /w/ or /y/,[32] the masculine plural morpheme /-ūma, -īma/ on nouns and adjectives,[33] certain nominal and verbal patterns, such as the N verbal noun *naqtal*[34] and the D suffix-conjugation *qattila*.[35] The danger in identifying all such forms as Ugaritic, of course, is that it is conceivable that the scribes would on occasion furnish strictly Akkadian lexemes with Ugaritic morphological features;[36] for example, not all of the bound forms that bear a case-ending, in Ugaritic fashion, are Ugaritic words.

6. Still other forms that may not be isolated as Ugaritic words on the basis of any of the preceding criteria are nevertheless identified as such in this study because they appear in contexts that are the same as, or analogous to, contexts in which other Ugaritic forms occur; specifically:

   (a) The terms that occur *passim* in the legal texts to designate particular plots of land in the vicinity of Ugarit, when they are not names of villages, are assumed to be Ugaritic, including those that could under other circumstances also be intrepreted as Akkadian;

[30]An example is the common form *ṣa-mi-ID*, which may be read as Akk. *ṣamid*, but which does not conform, in the Ugarit Akk. texts, to the known meanings of Akk. *ṣam(ā)du*, and is thus better taken to reflect the Ugaritic root *ṣ-m-t*. Another example is the form *a-ši-ib*, which if Akk. is either a bound form participle or a predicative adjective, 3ms, neither of which makes sense in context; see the Glossary under YΘB a.

[31]In some instances, this criterion is better stated in the negative, i.e., forms that exhibit distinctively non-Akkadian phonology or morphology. For example, the nominal pattern *maqtal* is not specifically Northwest Semitic, but a *maqtal* form containing a labial root consonant in which the prefix remains *ma-* (see the Glossary under MṢR, ᶜBR, RKB) is not Akkadian, in which *na-* would appear.

[32]See below, Part III, ch. 2 §E 2.

[33]See below, Part III, ch. 3 §C 1 d (1).

[34]See the Glossary under ᵓBD and PṬR c.

[35]See the Glossary under ŠLM b.

[36]This is the normal situation in many of the southern WPA dialects, such as that of Byblos; these are pidgins in which the vocabulary is almost exclusively Akkadian, while the morphology and syntax are predominantly Northwest Semitic.

these terms are considered in more detail further below.

(b) The economic texts contain, after the S^a Voc. texts, the largest number of individual Ugaritic words (see below). In several instances, forms may be interpreted with equal reason, on both formal and semantic grounds, as either Akkadian or Ugaritic, and it is difficult, if not impossible, to determine which was intended by the scribe, or even, if the Akkadian and Ugaritic words are identical, whether one or the other was specifically intended. In some cases, I have opted for the Ugaritic interpretation because all other forms written syllabically in the texts in which they occur are Ugaritic.[37] Other forms are listed in the Glossary, and cited where relevant in Part III, with a caveat that they may reflect either language.[38]

Proper nouns, i.e., personal and geographical names, have been omitted from consideration in this study,[39] for several reasons. The most basic problem associated with names is that they bear no semantic relationship to their surrounding linguistic context; that is, the meanings of elements in names have nothing to do with the texts in which they occur, and must accordingly always be established in isolation from their context. Because those meanings are often uncertain, the formal analysis of the elements of names, which proceeds from our understanding of their meanings, must likewise often remain unclear. Another significant difficulty encountered, if one is

[37]E.g., */su'nu/* in PRU 6 126; */gallābu/* and */māḫiṣu/* in PRU 6 136; */nē/īru/*? and */saplu/* in PRU 6 168 (see the Glossary under GLB, MḪṢ, NW/YR, S'N, SPL).

Loanwords into Ugaritic, especially loans from Akkadian, pose a special problem in a study of this kind, since they will obviously be difficult to isolate in Akkadian contexts. Essentially, loanwords are included in our list of Ugaritic forms under the same conditions as apply to other words: (1) words in the Ugaritic column of the S^a Voc. texts (e.g., */nādu/*, */pilakku/*; see the Glossary under ND, PLK^1); (2) words marked as "non-Akkadian" by a gloss mark, regardless of whether they are attested in alphabetic form (e.g., perhaps, */tarbaṣu/*; see under RBṢ); (3) words in economic lists in which all other words written syllabically are Ugaritic (e.g., perhaps, */gallābu/* [see above]). Other forms that we have reason to suspect to be Ugaritic, however, are included only if they are also attested in alphabetic form (see, e.g., under 'LḪN, PWT in the Glossary). Loanwords are collected in Part III, ch. 3 §C 3.

[38]This is a less-than-perfect solution to a dilemma presented by two conflicting goals of this study: (a) presentation and analysis of a linguistically uniform corpus of forms, which require that only forms that may be labelled Ugaritic with a fair degree of certainty be included; and (b) presentation of *all* forms in the Ugarit Akkadian texts that *might* be Ugaritic, so that other students might have access to them, especially as new alphabetic texts come to light.

[39]Personal and geographical names are cited at various points throughout the monograph in reference to issues of orthography. While the precise dialects that such names represent are generally unknown (see below), clear examples of the same name in both alphabetic and syllabic form can be helpful in ascertaining the orthographic principles employed by the scribes of the Akkadian texts to represent in syllabic form the sounds corresponding to the various alphabetic graphemes.

attempting to present a consistent linguistic description of a particular dialect at a particular point in time, is the tendency of names to resist contemporary linguistic processes, and so to retain archaic or non-local features. Further, certain names, especially favorite personal names, may be intentionally archaistic, similarly unrepresentative of the dialect of the community in which their owners reside.[40] Geographical names, the age and history of which are often unknown, present the additional problem of folk etymology: local reinterpretation of a place name may only approximate the assumed etymon and the morphological structure of the adopting dialect, and thereby provide us with misleading data.

More important than these, however, is still another consideration. As has been stated earlier, the aim of this study is a list and analysis of forms that may be considered with a fair degree of certainty to reflect a specific dialect, Ugaritic. But the specific dialect represented by the elements of any given personal or geographical name, unlike the case with common forms occurring in a given linguistic context, is ultimately unknowable, since we do not normally know precisely the individuals who named a given person or locality. Even when such information is available, we have no guarantee that the elements of any given name reflect the spoken dialect of those individuals or whether that dialect differed from the local dialect of the area in which the person or place in question was situated.[41]

The conclusion to be drawn from each of the above considerations, in my opinion, is that the elements of any given personal or place name, even if they conform formally to what is known from other sources about the phonology and morphology of Ugaritic, that is, even if they "look like" or "could be" Ugaritic, may not be shown with certainty to *be* Ugaritic, and may not, therefore, be included as part of the evidence for the structure of the contemporary language.[42]

Exceptions to the exclusion of proper nouns from this study are several divine names found in three lexical texts: Ug. 5 18, Ug. 5 137 iii 33"ff., Ug. 5 170.[43] Ug. 5 137 is one of the polyglot S^a Voc. texts; appended to the end of the S^a Voc. series, lines iii 33"ff., is the beginning of another lexical series, the Weidner god-list An,[44]

40Examples are some of the royal names at Ugarit, such as ᶜAmmiθtamru and Niqmepaᶜ; these are extremely old, as evidenced by their occurrence in Old Babylonian texts from Mari (*am-mi-iš-ta-mar*) and Alalaḫ (*ni-iq-mé-pa*), respectively, and by their repetition in the Ugaritic king list KTU 1.113.

41Pace de Moor, QS 2 84 n. 2, who recommends the inclusion of names in a study of this type.

42To return to the example of the Ugarit royal names cited above in n. 40: such names go back to one or more of the bundle of dialects collectively referred to as "Amorite," several centuries earlier than the time of the last kings to bear those names. They are, accordingly, useless as evidence for the morphology and syntax of contemporary Ugaritic. It is possible that many of the personal names attested in texts from Ugarit (and elsewhere, for that matter) are likewise relics of earlier, and not even necessarily directly ancestral, languages.

43These are collected, for convenience of reference, in an appendix to Part III, ch. 3 §C.

44Weidner, AfK 2 1-18, 71-82; see also Lambert, RlA 3 474. In addition to the polyglot exemplar

also in a polyglot format, with Hurrian and Ugaritic equivalents of the gods in the second and third columns, respectively. Since the forms in each column are language specific, I have felt obliged to consider those in the last column to be part of the Ugaritic lexicon, and to include them in this study.

Ug. 5 18 and 170 are syllabic exemplars of the so-called "Pantheon of Ugarit." These texts are god-lists compiled at Ugarit proper (rather than in Mesopotamia, like the Weidner god-list An at the end of Ug. 5 137), and also exist in alphabetic exemplars (KTU 1.47, 1.118); the same gods in the same order also appear in an alphabetic ritual text (KTU 1.148).[45] Some of the god-names in the syllabic exemplars are written with logograms, the intended forms of which are therefore unclear. Of the syllabically written names, some are clearly Mesopotamian or Hurrian (e.g., ^{d}*sa-sú-ra-tu*$_4$ corresponding to alphabetic *kθrt*; ^{d}*al-la-tu*$_4$ to *arṣy*; ^{d}*ḫé-bat* to *pdry*) or at least clearly Akkadian in form (e.g., DINGIR^{meš} *til-la-at* ^{d}IM = *il tᶜðr bᶜl*), while one clearly represents a Ugaritic name ($^{d.giš}$*ki-na-rù* = *knr*). It is therefore difficult to be certain which of the other forms in which the syllabic writing corresponds formally to the alphabetic are intended as Akkadian and which as Ugaritic. I have included as probably Ugaritic, besides $^{d.giš}$*ki-na-rù* (see the Glossary under KNR), only *a-mu-q*[*u*] of ^{d}ḪUR.SAG *u a-mu-q*[*u*] (see ᶜMQ^2), ^{d}*a-na-tu*$_4$ (ᶜNT), and ^{d}*SA-li-mu* (ŠLM a), since these forms differ in one feature or another from their expected Akkadian counterparts; other possibly Ugaritic examples that have been noted in the Glossary and elsewhere in this study are ^{d}*aš-ra-tu*$_4$ (ʾθR) and ^{d}*ma-lik*^{meš} (MLK c). ^{d}*da-gan* (Ug. 5 18:3, 170:17'), corresponding to *dgn* in the parallel alphabetic exemplars, and ^{d}*pu-ḫur* DINGIR^{meš} (Ug. 5 18:28), corresponding to *pḫr ilm*, have been assumed to be Akkadian since they lack an expected Ugaritic case-ending.[46]

A large group of forms that may on a certain level be considered geographical names has also been included in our list of Ugaritic lexemes. Throughout the legal texts there occur phrases of the type A.ŠÀ$^{(meš/ḫi.a)}$ *X*, literally "field(s) (of) X,"[47] which designate areas or parcels of land that are either the objects of transactions or the locations in which the objects of transactions are situated. It is likely that such designations would normally reflect one of three semantic categories: (i) the name of the owner of the land;[48] (ii) the name of a nearby village; or (iii) a common word in the local language referring to a prominent geographical or similar feature. The

---

in Ug. 5 137, several single-column exemplars of this list are attested in Ugarit Akk: Ug. 5 texts 120-129 and 172 [note also 119, probably from Ḫattusas], for which see Nougayrol's comments in Ug. 5 pp. 211-12; and Arnaud, Syria 59 204ff.

[45]See Xella, Testi rituali 91-100.

[46]See Part III, ch. 3 §C 1 e, f.

[47]Such designations generally appear in alphabetic texts as *gt X*; see below, n. 51.

[48]Occasionally, the title or rank of the owner, rather than his or her name; e.g., A.ŠÀ$^{ḫi.a}$ LUGAL-*ri* "fields of the king" (PRU 3 47a:8); these are either Akkadian or written with logograms, and so not relevant for our investigation.

examples in the first category, personal names, have of course been omitted from consideration in this study. Examples that contain the name of a village are marked as such with the determinative ^{uru}, which is used with great consistency in this regard in Ugarit Akk.;[49] they too are true proper nouns, and have likewise been excluded from this study.

The forms in the third category are more difficult. Many of them are preceded by the gloss mark, which does not otherwise accompany proper nouns in these texts, and must therefore be considered common words in the local dialect, i.e., Ugaritic. Since there is no obvious criterion according to which still finer distinctions may be made among them, I have assumed, for the sake of consistency, that all of the forms in this group are, in origin at least, common words in the Ugaritic lexicon. The problem remains, however, that such forms are, to an extent, still names, without a real semantic connection to the clauses in which they occur; thus, it is often difficult to establish their meaning with any certainty. Nevertheless, as words that could be applied to identify parcels of land, they ought generally to exhibit a relatively restricted semantic range—trees, soil descriptions, prominent geographical features, and so on[50]—that can guide us to some extent in our attempts to identify them.[51]

One tablet, Ug. 5 153, was identified by Nougayrol[52] as a unique example of a continuous Ugaritic text in syllabic cuneiform. It is clearly difficult to read the text as Akkadian. It is unfortunately so badly broken, however, that it is also difficult to be certain that it is to be read as Ugaritic, although that seems the most likely possibility. In most of the 14 lines preserved, at most four or five signs in succession may be read with certainty; further, the ends and most of the beginnings of the lines are missing. Thus, the genre and context are quite unclear, and that in turn means that even the division of words is in most cases uncertain. I hesitate, therefore, to include any of the forms in this text in the present study with any confidence. Nevertheless,

[49]See the section on determinatives in my Akkadian of Ugarit.

[50]Cf. in English, e.g., "Twelve Oaks," "Central Park," "the Black Hills," "Division Street," "Market Square," "Long Island," "Cold Spring Road," etc.

[51]Forms in this group attested in both alphabetic and syllabic texts are the following (for the alphabetic, see UT 382 no. 627): *gt gwl* = A.ŠÀ^{meš} *gu-wa-⸢li⸣* = */guw(w)ǎli/* "circuit(?)" (see the Glossary under GWL); *gt dprnm* = A.ŠÀ$^{\text{ḫi.a}}$ *: dì-ip-ra-ni-ma* = */diprānīma/* "junipers" (DPRN); *gt knpy* = A.ŠÀ *: ka(-an)-na-BI-PI* = */kannǎpīyv/*? "?" (KNP b); *gt nb/pk* = (A.ŠÀ$^{\text{(meš)}}$) *(:) NAB/na-AB/ba/bá-ki-ma* = */nab/p(a)kīma/* "springs" (NBK); *gt nḫl* = A.ŠÀ^{meš} *na-ḫa-li* = */naḫal(l)i/*? "wadi" (NḪL); *gt ǵl* = A.ŠÀ$^{\text{ḫi.a}}$ *: ḫu-li* = */ǵōli/*? "low ground(?)" (ǴWL); perhaps also *gt ṣb⸢r?⸣* (KTU 4.400:2) = A.ŠÀ$^{\text{(meš/ḫi.a)}}$ *(:) ṣí(-ib)-bi-ri* = */ṣibbīri/* "collective land(?)" (ṢBR); *gt rb⸢t?⸣* (KTU 4.125:16) = A.ŠÀ *ra-ba-ti* = */rabbati/* "great" (RBB). In a few instances, the logogram that corresponds to alphab. *gt* is $^{\text{(é)}}$AN.ZA.GÀR (normally Akk. *dimtu* "tower, settlement"); three of these occur in one text, Ug. 5 96: *g⸢t⸣ tgbry* (?; see KTU 4.271:7,9; 4.296:13) = ^{é}AN.ZA.GÀR *ta-ga-bi-ra(-yv)* = */tagabbir-/*? "?" (GBR); *gt sknm* = ^{é}AN.ZA.GÀR *ZI-GA/QA-ni-ma* = */sikānīma/*? "statues(?)" (SKN b); *gt mᶜbr* = ^{é}AN.ZA.GÀR *ma-ba-ri* = */maᶜbari/* "pass" (ᶜBR); note also *gt ᶜmq* = [AN.ZA].GÀR *: am-qa* = */ᶜamqa/* "stronghold(?)" (ᶜMQ^{1}) in PRU 3 118:12.

[52]See Ug. 5 p. 257-58 with n. 1.

because of the likelihood that the text is Ugaritic, the few forms I believe can be identified are cited where appropriate below as parenthetical additions, for the sake of completeness. *Caveat lector*, however, that both the identification of these forms as Ugaritic and the interpretations given are suspect. For reference, my (very tentative) reading of the text is as follows:

Obverse

1 [*i]a(-)ab-ṣi-ru ar-zi-ma[*

2 [*i]v(-)šu-bi-lu ša-⸢BI?⸣ x[*

3 [*]⸢x⸣-ni e-⸢nu? x⸣[*

4 [*]a la[*

5 [*]ra x[*

6 [*]⸢x⸣[*

Reverse

1' *⸢da??⸣ [x (x)]-ru-B[I? d]a-mu[*

2' *la ⸢x-⸣[š]i?-ḫi-ni la kiš-š[a*

3' *[d]a?-mu TI-ru da-mu la TI-r[u*

4' *[l]a-ša-na-ia ar-⸢nu? x šu/la⸣ [*

5' *la iv-ši-?⸢x-x⸣ PI ⸢x⸣ [ ]i ru ⸢x⸣ [*

6' *[P]I BI(-)šu-l[a]⸢x⸣ ša-TI-i pa(-)TI-⸢x⸣ [*

7' *[P]I la-a BI(-)ḫa-te/li?[(x?)] da-m[i*

8' [ ] *ni ka ZU m[u*

☛ p. 376

Possible identifications of Ugaritic forms:

Obv. 1. */yabṣiru/* "he will cut off" or */-ya ʾabṣiru/* "...of mine, I will cut off" (see the Glossary under BṢR);

/ʾarzīma/ "cedars" (oblique; see under ʾRZ).

2. */yvšōbilu/* "he will have brought" or */-ya šōbilū/* "of mine, have brought (imperative, pl.)" (see under YBL c).

3. */ʿēnu/* "eye" (nom.; see under ʿYN).

Rev. 2'. */lā/* "not" (bis; also lines r.3',5', *la-a* r.7'; see under L[1]).

3'. */damu/* "blood" (nom.; also */dami/* gen.; line r.7'; see under DM);

/dīru/ "hateful, foul(?)" (nom.; see under DYR);

4'. */lašāna-ya/* "my tongue" (acc.; see under Y[2]; LŠN);

5'. *PI* = */wa-/* "and" (also lines r.6',7'; see under W).

6'. *BI* = */bi-/* "in" (also line r.7'; see under B);

ša-TI-i = */šadî/* "field" (gen.; see under ŠDW).

The texts in the corpus of Ugarit Akkadian (including Ug. 5 153), by my reckoning, number 565.[53] Of these, 168, or roughly 30 per cent, contain one or more Ugaritic forms. The latter are distributed among the various genres as indicated in the following chart, which lists numbers of Ugaritic roots, of discrete words or forms, and of occurrences of Ugaritic forms:

[53]See Index A 1 for a complete list. The number of tablets is actually 557; eight tablets contain two separate lexical texts each: RS 17.03 (= MSL 8/2 96ff. [RS b] and MSL 10 149ff. [B]); 20.32 (= MSL 8/2 96ff. [RS a] and MSL 10 149ff. [A]); 20.123+ (= Ug. 5 137 i 1 - iii 32" and ibid. iii 33"ff.); 20.125 (= AS 16 29ff.:1-37 and AS 16 31ff.:11-54,...), 20.155 (= AS 16 29ff.:27-44 and AS 16 33ff. D 21-32); 22.220 (= AS 16 31ff.:40-48,... and AS 16 33ff. B 1-40,...); 22.337 (= MSL 10 37ff. [D] and MSL 10 107ff. [D]); 22.346+349 (= MSL 10 37ff. [A] and MSL 10 107ff. [A]).

Genre	Roots	Words	Occurrences
Economic	95	97	173
Legal	79	82	208
Letters	3	3	6
Lexical:			
Sª Voc.	113	114	137
god-list An[54]	16	16	18
"pantheon of Ugarit"[55]	6	6	6
other lexical texts	10	11	16
Literary:			
Akkadian texts	4	4	4
Ug. 5 153 (Ugaritic?)	12	12	22
(attested in 2 or 3 genres:	-45	-30)	
Totals:			
all forms	293	315	590
identifications proposed	263	285	554
unidentified	30	30	36

Once a form has been isolated as certainly or probably Ugaritic rather than Akkadian, it is of course still another matter to identify that form, i.e., to establish its form and meaning. The Mesopotamian writing system allows for ambiguity in several important features: vowel length is not consistently indicated;[56] and the indication of consonant gemination is optional.[57] Thus, for example, it is uncertain whether the writing [*ḫ*]*a-ra-š*[*u*] "deaf(?)"[58] represents /*ḫarašu*/, /*ḫarāšu*/, /*ḫarrašu*/, or /*ḫarrāšu*/. In addition, Ugarit Akkadian, like other northern WPA dialects, does not consistently distinguish voiced, voiceless, and emphatic sounds in the signs used for stops and for sibilants.[59] Several Ugaritic phonemes do not occur in Akkadian: the fricatives /*ð*/ and /*θ*/; the emphatic sibilant /*ẓ*/; the gutturals /*h*/, /*ḥ*/, /*ᶜ*/, /*ǵ*/; and the vowel /*ō*/. Signs for related phonemes were of necessity pressed into service for the representation of these as well, thereby increasing the polyvalency, and the ambiguity, of those signs.[60] The writing *: ḫa-ar-ZA-ti*,[61] for instance, may, theoretically, at

54Ug. 5 137 iii 33"ff., appended to the end of an Sª Voc. exemplar.
55Ug. 5 18 and Ug. 5 170.
56See below, Part III, ch. 1 §F.
57See below, Part III, ch. 1 §D.
58See under ḪRŠ in the Glossary.
59See below, Part III, ch. 1 §§A 1-2, E 1-2.
60See below, Part III, ch. 1 §§A 2, 4, G 3.
61See the Appendix to the Glossary.

least, reflect any of the following roots: *ḥ-r-ð, ḥ-r-z, ḥ-r-ẓ, ḥ-r-s, ḥ-r-ṣ; ḫ-r-ð, ḫ-r-z, ḫ-r-ẓ, ḫ-r-s, ḫ-r-ṣ; ǵ-r-ð, ǵ-r-z, ǵ-r-ẓ, ǵ-r-s, ǵ-r-ṣ*. The distributions of other Ugaritic phonemes—/ʾ/, /w/, /y/, and the vowel /ē/—differ from their Akkadian counterparts, and the writing system was not well equipped to represent them clearly; the PI sign, for example, may represent either /w/ or /y/ plus any vowel.[62]

Despite the difficulties outlined above, we may nevertheless discern a relatively consistent set of orthographic principles employed by the scribes to represent the individual Ugaritic phonemes.[63] Once these principles have been delineated, on the basis of Ugaritic words whose form and meaning are well established, they should, of course, be applied with rigor in attempts to ascertain the identity of words whose form and meaning are less obvious. Having identified the possible forms that a given writing may represent, one may then check the lexicon of Ugaritic words in alphabetic form to discover whether any correspond semantically to the syllabic writing. If no alphabetic Ugaritic correspondence is found, of course, one must then check the other Semitic languages for possible cognates.[64] Given our limited knowledge of the Ugaritic lexicon, it is largely irrelevant, in my view, whether a form that we propose to identify as Ugaritic is attested in the alphabetic texts. Some of the most certain identifications among the syllabic transcriptions are words that do not as yet occur in alphabetic form:[65] e.g., in the S^{a} Voc. exemplars: /*dakaru*/ "male," /*ḥēqu*/ "lap," /*ḫinnīṣu*/ "piglet," /*riglu*/ "foot," /*tiʾnatu*/ "fig," /*tibnu*/ "straw."[66]

Because of the ambiguities of the writing system it is often impossible to be certain about the precise phonological or morphological shape of a word even when its root and meaning are relatively clear, as the example [*ḫ*]*a-ra-š*[*u*] cited above demonstrates. For the most part, we must rely here on comparative evidence from other Northwest Semitic languages, provided such evidence is consistent with what can be established a priori about Ugaritic phonology and morphology on the basis of the Ugaritic forms themselves, both in alphabetic texts and in syllabic transcription. The evidence of the syllabic transcriptions taken as a whole, in other words, should be given precedence over that of the cognate languages. Since some forms obviously

62See below, Part III, ch. 1 §E 3 c.

63Described in detail below in Part III, ch. 1 §§E, G.

64I have generally tried first to locate Northwest Semitic cognates (particularly, of course, Hebrew and Aramaic dialects), then Akkadian, and finally Arabic, Ethiopic, and the Old and Modern South Arabian languages. In a few cases, non-Semitic loanwords have been proposed; see below, Part III, ch. 3 §C 3.

65Of the 285 words for which identifications are suggested in this study, approximately 69 per cent correspond to attested alphabetic forms, and another 9 per cent reflect roots that occur in alphabetic texts; fewer than one-fourth (22 per cent) are words for which no corresponding alphabetic form is attested.

66See the Glossary under DKR1, ḤYQ, ḪNṢ, RGL, TʾN, TBN, respectively.

differed from their cognates in other languages,[67] such as *a-du-rù* vs. Hebrew *ʾaddîr,* and *da-ab-ḫu* vs. **ðibḥ-* in Aramaic, Hebrew, and Arabic, the possibility of differences must also be allowed in less obvious cases, when positing such differences is necessary for a consistent interpretation of the Ugaritic data: e.g., *ṭu-ú-ru* for */ṭuhūru/,* originally **ṭahūru* rather than **ṭahuru* as in Hebrew; *⸢ba⸣-aḫ-ḫu-rù* for */baḫḫuru/* rather than **baḫ(ḫ)ūru* as in Hebrew; *ma-ad-da-tù* for */maddatu/,* vs. Hebrew *middâ* and Akkadian **middatu.*

A small group of forms among the syllabic transcriptions, the identification of which as Ugaritic lexemes or verbal roots is certain or probable, do not conform to the patterns of phonology and morphology discernible in the majority of forms, but rather to Akkadian patterns. These few examples thus represent the inverse of the Akkadian words that appear in these texts furnished with Ugaritic morphological features, and will be referred to throughout as "Akkadianized forms."[68]

Previous Work

The existence of two fairly recent studies devoted entirely or in part to Ugaritic vocabulary in Akkadian texts prompts a legitimate question about the necessity of another volume on the subject. In his excellent 1975 dissertation, which unfortunately remains unpublished, J. L. Boyd III collected and analyzed all the forms he considered to be Ugaritic in the Akkadian letters, economic texts, and legal texts found at Ras Shamra.[69] He did not, however, include the large number of words in the polyglot S^a Voc. texts, or the few forms that occur in other lexical texts and in literary texts. D. Sivan has recently published an impressive study that is intended as a comprehensive collection and analysis of all Northwest Semitic forms attested in Akkadian texts from Syria-Palestine in the Late Bronze period.[70] Sivan included proper names in his study, although he generally considered them separately from other evidence.[71] Both of these investigations suffer, in my opinion, from their

[67]Similar differences are also obvious in alphabetic forms, of course: e.g., *ṣat* = **/ṣiʾatu/* "emergence" vs. Heb. *ṣē(ʾ)t* < **ṣiʾt-*; *mit* = **/miʾtu/* "hundred" vs. Heb. *mēʾâ* < **miʾat-*; etc.

[68]Of the four Ugaritic forms in Akkadian literary texts, the three verbs all exhibit Akkadian morphology (see the Glossary under DBQ, PḤ/ḪD, RðY). Examples are proportionately far less common in other genres. The "Akkadianized forms" are collected in Part III, ch. 3 §G.

[69]"A Collection and Examination of the Ugaritic Vocabulary contained in the Akkadian Texts from Ras Shamra" (University of Chicago, 1975).

[70]Grammatical Analysis and Glossary of the Northwest Semitic Vocables in Akkadian Texts of the 15th-13th C.B.C. from Canaan and Syria (AOAT 214, 1984).

[71]Notice should also be taken here of the earlier study of F. Gröndahl, Die Personennamen der Texte aus Ugarit (Rome, 1967), in which only personal names were considered. As noted by Sivan, Analysis 2, a grammatical study of such a diverse corpus cannot yield linguistically reliable results for a specific dialect.

failure to take adequately into account the diverse provenances of their textual sources.[72]

The present study differs from those of Boyd and Sivan in drawing its data from a linguistically uniform corpus of texts, those written by scribes at Ugarit. This is not only a sounder approach methodologically, as argued above; it also affords a more consistent comparison with the other, larger source of evidence at our disposal for the study of Ugaritic, the alphabetic material. Another, admittedly less significant, difference, is the arrangement of its glossary by consonantal root, in the order used in modern Ugaritic lexicons, for convenience of reference.

A major impetus for a new presentation of the Ugaritic vocabulary in syllabic transcription is that a fresh investigation of the orthographic principles involved in the transcriptions and a thorough re-examination of the polyglot S^{a} Vocabulary texts have yielded a significant number of new readings. Roughly one-third of the Ugaritic forms collected and analyzed here are either presented or identified for the first time or given new interpretations, always with reference to the cuneiform copies.

Method of Citation

Texts

Ugarit Akkadian texts:

These are cited according to the place of publication of the *transliteration*;[73] if no transliteration is extant, a text is cited by the place of publication of the copy.[74] Texts in *Ugaritica 7,* most of which have not yet been edited, are cited by the numbers of the plates (between pages 406 and 475) on which the photographs of the relevant texts appear.

A cross-index of the texts by RS number appears below as Index A 2.

Texts in *PRU 3* and *PRU 4* are cited by *page numbers,* in a fashion that is intended to eliminate ambiguity; each text is consistently cited throughout the volume as illustrated by the following examples:

[72]See further the remarks in §B of my review of Sivan's study, forthcoming in JAOS 107/4.

[73]There are two reasons for citing these texts by the location of the transliteration: first, the transliteration is probably consulted before the copy by most people; second, to cite a Ugarit Akkadian text only by RS number invariably involves at least one extra step on the part of the reader to find the text, since a cross-index must be consulted. Citing a text by both place of publication and RS number requires an unnecessarily large amount of space.

[74]A number of lexical texts have not yet received formal publication, but are cited in the notes to editions of the Mesopotamian versions in MSL 4 - 8; they are cited in the present study by MSL volume, page, and note numbers.

PRU 3 78: the text is the only one on page 78;
PRU 3 35a: the text appears at the top of page 35, but one or more texts follow on the same page;
PRU 3 4b: the entire text appears on page 4, but another text or part of a text appears before it on the same page;
PRU 3 36c: third text on page 36; two or parts of two texts precede;
PRU 3 32f(f).: begins on page 32, but continues on the following page(s).

Texts in *PRU 6* and *Ugaritica 5* are cited by *text number*. Note that an otherwise unspecified reference "Ug. 5 1" through "Ug. 5 173" invariably indicates an Akkadian text edited by Nougayrol. References to page numbers in these volumes are specifically indicated as such.

Texts published in journals and elsewhere are cited in the fashion used for PRU 3 and 4: by volume and page number of the transliteration.

The vast majority of the Akkadian texts from Ugarit were published by J. Nougayrol; some, however, have been published by other scholars; full references for the publications may be found in the Bibliography below as follows:

Publication:	*see under:*
AnOr 48 26,27	Astour
AS 16 29ff. - 39	Nougayrol
EA 45-49	Knudtzon
KTU	Dietrich-Loretz-Sanmartín
MSL	Landsberger et al.
PRU 3; PRU 4; PRU 6	Nougayrol
RA 38 7ff. - 12	Virolleaud
RA 63 83f.	Nougayrol
Syria 10 pl. 77	Virolleaud
Syria 12 226 - 236ff., pl. 46ff., 49; Syria 13 234 - 237+	Thureau-Dangin
Syria 16 194	Virolleaud
Syria 18 249f., 251ff., 253f.	Thureau-Dangin
Syria 28 173f.	Virolleaud
Syria 59 201 - 220f.	Arnaud
TA 8 7f.	Owen
UF 11 479	Laroche
Ug. 5 1 - 173	Nougayrol
Ug. 6 394ff. - 404	Nougayrol
Ug. 7 pl. 1 - 64	Schaeffer

p. 376

Other Akkadian texts:

Cited according to standard Assyriological convention; abbreviations of publications appear above in the list on pages xiii-xviii.

Alphabetic Ugaritic texts:

Cited by KTU number = M. Dietrich, O. Loretz, J. Sanmartín, Die Keilalphabetischen Texte aus Ugarit (AOAT 24/1, 1976).

Forms

Alphabetic Ugaritic forms:

For convenience, these are normally cited, if possible, with reference to their listing in the most comprehensive lexicon of Ugaritic published to date, chapter 19 of UT = C.H. Gordon, Ugaritic Textbook (AnOr 38, 1965), by page and entry number.[75]

Ugaritic forms in syllabic transcription:

To save space and, it is hoped, for convenience of reference, the texts in which the syllabic transcriptions occur are cited only in the primary discussions of them, in Part I for forms in the S^a^ Voc. texts, in the main entries in the Glossary (Part II) for other forms. Elsewhere, forms are usually keyed to the Glossary entries; citations normally consist of four parts:

a sign-by-sign *transliteration,* followed by

an "equals" sign and a *phonemic normalization,* in italics between slashes, followed by

a *translation* of the form, between quotation marks, followed by

the *root* under which the form is listed in the Glossary, in upper case roman between parentheses;

e.g., *ar-ṣu* = */ʾarṣu/* "earth" (ʾRṢ).

Occasionally, a *phonetic normalization* instead of a phonemic one is appropriate; phonetic normalizations appear in lower case roman letters between brackets, e.g., *ḫe-e-ia* = [ḫēya] "vacant" (ḪWY).

A question mark in the transliteration indicates that the sign it accompanies is uncertain; transliteration of a sign in upper case letters indicates that no specific value of that sign is intended: e.g., TU in *ma-ar-⌜TU?⌝*[76] may have the value *tu, ṭú,* or *dú.*

[75]Throughout this study there is frequent reference to a few standard works on Ugaritic, including Gordon's UT and A. Caquot, M. Sznycer, A. Herdner, Textes ougaritiques 1: Mythes et légendes (Paris, 1974); in addition, the series of articles "Zur ugaritischen Lexikographie" by M. Dietrich and O. Loretz (and sometimes J. Sanmartín), most of which have appeared in Ugarit-Forschungen, are often cited. Reference to these works does not always imply agreement with their interpretations, and differing opinions, including my own, will of course be noted where appropriate; rather, because of their comprehensiveness, they serve as convenient summaries, up to the time of their publication, of the vast research literature on Ugaritic texts, lexicography, and language.

[76]Listed in the Appendix to the Glossary.

A question mark following the phonemic normalization indicates that either the interpretation of the form or meaning of the word or the status of the word as Ugaritic is uncertain.

A lower case letter after the root indicates that more than one word derived from that root is attested among the syllabic transcriptions; e.g., lú*na-ḫi-ru* = /*nāǵiru*/ "guard" (NǴR a); *ni-iḫ-rù* = /*niǵru*/ "to guard" (NǴR b).

A superscript accompanying a root indicates that more than one root with the same consonants is attested among the syllabic transcriptions; see, e.g., DKR^1 and DKR^2 in the Glossary.

To distinguish them from normalizations of the syllabic transcriptions, vocalizations of Ugaritic forms attested only in alphabetic spelling are preceded by an asterisk: e.g., *ulp* = */*ʾullūpu*/ "chief."

Forms preceded by an asterisk, but not between slashes, are either reconstructions of earlier (proto-)forms (e.g., **śadawu* in *ša-du-ú* = /*šadû*/ < **śadawu* (ŠDW)) or unattested forms.

An italic colon (*:*) transliterates a gloss mark when the latter occurs to indicate that the following form is non-Akkadian; see Part III, ch. 1 §C.

Note on Transliteration

Throughout this study, the cuneiform signs that appear in Ugaritic words will be transliterated with the values that most closely reflect the Ugaritic sounds represented, from among the values attested for those signs in *Akkadian* words in texts written at Ugarit.[77] No new values have been assigned to any of the signs to account for Ugaritic phonemes that do not occur in Akkadian, viz., /*ð*/, /*θ*/, /*ẓ*/, the gutturals /*h*/, /*ḥ*/, /*ᶜ*/, /*ǵ*/ (signs exist for ʾ and *ḫ*), and the vowel /*ō*/.[78] Thus, for example, /*tabaᶜa*/ appears in transliteration as *ta-ba-ʾa*, /*maqqaḥā*/ as *ma-qa-ḫa*, /*ᶜiðirtu*/ as *i-zi-ir-*[*tu4*], /*ǵōli*/ as *: ḫu-li*, etc. Although the representation of the consonants in transliteration will be essentially phonemic (e.g., *de4* for TE when the latter has the value

[77]Values of signs follow von Soden-Röllig, AS3. The Ugarit Akkadian syllabary is presented in detail, with a complete sign-list, in my forthcoming Akkadian of Ugarit.

[78]Dietrich-Loretz-Sanmartín, in UF 5 109-10, recommend that the ʾ sign, when used to represent Ugar. /*ᶜ*/, be assigned, and transliterated with, the values *ᶜ(a)*, *ᶜ(e)*, *ᶜ(i)*, *ᶜ(u)*. But if we were to accept this proposal, we would for the sake of consistency need to transliterate, e.g., ḪA when used for /*ḥ*/ with the value *ḥa* (and in the rare instances of ḪA for /*ᶜ*/, as *ᶜá*?), ZI when used for /*ð*/ with the value *ði*, ŠA for /*θ*/ as *θa*, etc., and even, perhaps, A in *ta-a-ma-tu4* = /*tahāmatu*/ as *ha*, in d*a-na-tu4* = /*ᶜanatu*/ as *ᶜa* (*ᶜà*?). The list could, of course, be multiplied considerably (even to include *vC* signs such as AB in *ab-du* = /*ᶜabdu*/ with the value *ᶜab*). The system that has evolved over the last century and more for the transliteration of syllabic cuneiform is already overly complicated, and there is little to be gained, I would suggest, by burdening that system with still more values applicable to such a relatively small group of forms. (See also Gelb, Or. 39 525-26.)

/dĭ/ or */dē/*), the vowels, especially *e* and *i,* will be transliterated according to the basic value of the signs, since it appears that the scribes maintained a phonetic distinction between those vowels.[79]

The signs used to represent the glides */w/* and */y/* will be transliterated as follows:[80]

> the PI sign (Deimel, ŠL no. 383, von Soden-Röllig, AS^3 no. 223) as *wa, we, wi, wu* and *ya, ye, yi, yu*;
>
> the IA sign (Deimel, ŠL no. 142a, von Soden-Röllig, AS^3 no. 104) as *ia, ie, ii, iu.*

For details of usage, see below, Part III, ch. 1 §E 3 c.

[79]See below, Part III, ch. 1 §G 2.

[80]Following Gelb, Or. 39 536-40, rather than the cumbersome system espoused in AS^3.

PART I

THE POLYGLOT S^a VOCABULARY TEXTS

In Ug. 5, J. Nougayrol published as numbers 130-138 nine cuneiform texts and fragments belonging to the Mesopotamian lexical series *Syllabary A Vocabulary* (abbr. S^a Voc.),[1] as well as ten texts, numbers 109-118, belonging to the simple *Syllabary A* (S^a) series from which the former is derived. The series S^a is a list of 211 cuneiform signs in a fixed order; the known exemplars were edited by R. T. Hallock in MSL 3 1-45.[2] The series S^a Voc. in Mesopotamian exemplars consists of the same 211 signs in the same order, but augmented by a second column in which one or more Akkadian words as equivalents of each sign appear; these were edited by B. Landsberger and Hallock in MSL 3 47-87.

The exemplars of S^a Voc. from Ugarit resemble their Mesopotamian counterparts in that, with rare exceptions, they follow the same fixed order of Sumerian signs, and in that they frequently give the same Akkadian correspondences. But they differ from the Mesopotamian version in having in one instance (Ug. 5 135) three columns (Sumerian sign - Akkadian - Hurrian), in the others four columns (Sumerian sign - Akkadian - Hurrian - Ugaritic).[3] The importance of these texts for our knowledge of both Hurrian and Ugaritic vocabulary was immediately obvious. But so, too, was their significance for our understanding of Ugaritic vocalism and word structure: the S^a Voc. texts list some 114 vocalized Ugaritic words in syllabic cuneiform; because of their equation with well-understood Sumerian and Akkadian forms, their meanings, and thus their forms, are often more secure than those of other Ugaritic words in syllabic transcription.[4]

[1]The small, fragmentary texts Ug. 5 139-142 do not obviously belong to the S^a Voc. (see Nougayrol's comment, Ug. 5 p. 250 n. 1), and are not included in the present study.

[2]The ten Ugarit Syllabary A exemplars contain the following sections (cf. MSL 3 pp. 15-41): 15-18, 25-41, 43-48, 50-78, 80-107, 110-130, 150-151, 160-164, 170-195, 203-211.

[3]As Nougayrol pointed out (Ug. 5 p. 231), no standard, two-column exemplars of the S^a Voc. were found at Ugarit. The same is true of the S^a Voc. texts from Boğazköy, which are three-column exemplars in which the last column is Hittite; see MSL 3 49-87, texts B_1 - B_8.

[4]This is frequently true even when the Sumerian and Akkadian columns are broken, thanks to the fixed order of the entries in the S^a series. There are, however, a couple of difficulties presented by the equations in the Ugarit exemplars. One problem is that the scribes on occasion gave correspondences for the signs on a *pars pro toto* basis; i.e., a sign was taken to represent the first sign of a complex logogram: e.g., NA for $^{(na4)}$NA.ZÀ/ZA.ḪI/AḪ.LI(.A) (no. 25.1); NA for NA.RÚ/DÙ.A (25.4); IGI for IGI.GÁL (41.6); perhaps also UD for UD-*ma* (63.4) and UD for ud+du = È (63.6). A more disturbing difficulty is the scribes' tendency to mistake a given sign for a homophone (or

Despite the unfortunate fact that each of the Ugarit S^a Voc. texts is fragmentary, Nougayrol in his admirable edition was able to place most of the fragments within the well-known S^a sequence of signs, and to offer sound and insightful proposals for the interpretation of many of the Ugaritic words. Yet many difficulties and uncertainties remained (see n. 3), and two of the texts, Ug. 5 131 and 138, could not be placed.

Since the original publication of these texts, several scholars have made suggestions concerning individual entries. In a note in RA 63 (1969) 172, R. Borger placed Ug. 5 138 as nos. 61, 63, in the S^a series. In UF 11 (1979) 477-80, E. Laroche published a fragment, curiously overlooked by Nougayrol, which joins Ug. 5 132 and contains some 15 new Ugaritic words. Yet the texts as a whole have not, to the best of my knowledge, received a thorough re-examination. Such a new study is merited, I believe, because of a number of factors. The publication of the new fragment in UF 11 477-80 makes possible the placement of Ug. 5 131 at nos. 46-53/54 in the S^a sequence, since the two fragments have three lines in a row in common (see nos. 46.2, 47.1, 47.2 below). Words in the Hurrian column, even when not understood fully, indicate in a few instances that forms taken by Nougayrol and others to be verbal infinitives must instead be nouns or adjectives, or vice versa (e.g., nos. 184.2, 190.2 below). In other instances, a slight movement of a fragment permits new correspondences to emerge (e.g., nos. 176-179 below). And, finally, there has been progress in our understanding of Ugaritic vocabulary and word structure, and of Ugarit Akkadian spelling practices. These factors have led me to offer below new suggestions or alternatives for not a few of the entries in the vocabularies.

Since the originals of the individual texts are easily accessible, it has seemed best, for ease of comparison and reference, to present them on the following pages in a synoptic edition, according to the S^a sign sequence, with subsection numbers when a sign has more than one entry. In the commentary that follows, therefore, entries will be referred to by S^a sign number rather than by text and line number.

☛ p. 376

Texts

a. Trilingual (Sumerian - Akkadian - Hurrian):
   Ug. 5 135 (RS 21.062): S^a nos. 49/50-65, 141/142-161.

b. Quadrilingual (Sumerian - Akkadian - Hurrian - Ugaritic):
   UF 11 479 (RS 20.189A+B; 20.189B = Ug. 5 132): S^a nos. 24-32, [33-40],

---

even worse, a near homophone): the clearest example, perhaps is the equation of I with (Akk.) *nāru* "river," properly I_7 (ÍD) in no. 56; other probable or possible instances include ZU (SÚ) for SU (21); UR for UR_5 (47.1-47.3); BÍL (GIBIL) for BÌL (49.1); LÁL for LAL (142); DAG for ZAG (151.2); URU_8 (ÚR) for URU_3 (ŠEŠ) (158.2); TIL for TI.LA (173.3); KAR for KA/KIR_4 (183.3). The existence of these tendencies increases considerably the uncertainty of any reconstruction in a number of broken entries.

41-48;
Ug. 5 130 (RS 20.149): Sª nos. 20-25, 32-40/41;
Ug. 5 131 (RS 20.426G+201G): Sª nos. 46-53/54;
Ug. 5 132: see UF 11 479;
Ug. 5 133 (RS 23.493A): Sª nos. 39-46, 170-174b;
Ug. 5 134 (RS 20.426D): Sª nos. 41-44;
Ug. 5 136 (RS 21.063): Sª nos. 66-68/69;
Ug. 5 137 (RS 20.123+): Sª nos. 150-160/162, 173-211;
Ug. 5 138 (RS 20.426B): Sª nos. 61, 63.

Of the eight quadrilingual exemplars, only in the following five are Ugaritic forms preserved: UF 11 479; Ug. 5 130; Ug. 5 131; Ug. 5 137; Ug. 5 138. The Ugaritic column of the remaining three tablets is completely broken.

Sections of the Sª Vocabulary Preserved in Ugarit and Mesopotamian Texts

Sª Section	RS Text (Ug. 5)	Sª Section	MSL 3 47ff.
		4-9	pp. 51-58
		13-14	pp. 58-61
20-23	130		
24-25	UF 11 479; 130		
26-32	UF 11 479		
32-38	130		
39-40	130; 133		
41-44	UF 11 479; 133; 134		
45-46	UF 11 479; 131; 133		
47-48	UF 11 479; 131		
49-53/54	131; 135		
55-60	135		
61-62/63	135; 138	63-64	p. 61
64-65	135		
66-68/69	136		
		112-120	pp. 62-64
141/142-149	135	129-143	pp. 64-72
150-160/162	135; 137	148-149	pp. 72-73
		163-170	pp. 73-75
170-172	133		
173-174b	133; 137	173-178	pp. 75-78
175-211	137	181-193	pp. 78-83
		195-209	pp. 84-87
		(200)	p. 58

The synopsis of entries in the Ugarit texts follows immediately, pages 24-45. The commentary on individual entries begins on page 46.

	S^a Voc. No.	Sign	Akkadian	Hurrian
	20.1	[LU]M	⸢*x*⸣[	]-⸢*e*?⸣
	20.2	LUM	*qa-an-nu-nu*	*ḫí-iš-la-e*
	21	[Z]U	*ši-i-ru*	*ú-zi*
☛ p. 376	22.1	ZA	*at-ta*	*ši-ni-*⸢*bi*⸣
	22.2	ZA	*a-mi-lu*	*tar-*⸢*šu-wa-an*⸣*-ni*
☛	23	SU	*ma-aš-ku*	*aš-ḫé*
	24.1	NU NU	*la-a* *la-*[	*ma-nu-ku*
	24.2	NU	*a-mi-lu*	*tar-šu-wa-an-ni*
	24.3	NU	*a-bu*	*at-ta-ni*
	25.1	NA NA	*ur-ṣú* *ur-*[	*it-ki*
	25.2	[N]A	*na-a-du*	*na-di*
	25.3	[NA	*l*]*a-a*	*ma-nu-ku*
	25.4	[NA	*x-x*]*-lu*	*an-*[ ]*-ni*
	25.5	[NA	*a*]*-me-lu*	*t*[*ar?-šu-wa-an-ni*
	25.6	NA	*na-*[*x*]-⸢*x-x*⸣	[
☛	26	⸢BA?⸣	*zu-*[ ]-⸢*x*⸣	⸢*x-x*⸣[
☛	27?	[ZI(?)		]-⸢*x*⸣[
☛	28?	[GI(?)	*qa?-nu?*]*-ú*(?) [	]-⸢*x*⸣[
	[29	GI$_4$ missing?]		
☛ p. 377	30.1?	[GIM?	(*bānû*/*itinnu*?)]	*i-*⸢*x*⸣-[*x*]-⸢*e*⸣
	30.x/30a.x	[GIM/BAN?	(?)]	⸢*x-x*⸣[ ]
	30a.y	[BAN	(*qaštu*)	]
	31	[MA	(*tittu*)	]
☛	32.1	[MU [	*š*]*a-*⸢*at?*⸣*-t*[*u*]	⸢*x-x-x*⸣[ ]

Ugaritic		Meaning	Reference
x-x⸣-[	]	?	Ug. 5 130 ii 1'
qu-u[*n*?]-*n*[*a*?-*nu*?]		coiled?	Ug. 5 130 ii 2'
⸢*ši-i-ru*⸣		flesh	Ug. 5 130 ii 3'
at-ta		you	Ug. 5 130 ii 4'
: bu-nu-⸢*šu*⸣		man	Ug. 5 130 ii 5'
[*ú*?]-*ru*		hide, skin	Ug. 5 130 ii 6'
[*l*]*a-a*	]	not	Ug. 5 130 ii 7' UF 11 479 1
[*b*]*u-nu-šu*		man	Ug. 5 130 ii 8'
a-da-nu		father	Ug. 5 130 ii 9'
ik-tu$_4$	]	mortar	Ug. 5 130 ii 10' UF 11 479 2
na-du		stela	Ug. 5 130 ii 11'
l[*a*]-*a*		not	Ug. 5 130 ii 12'
⸢*x-x*⸣-[	]	?	Ug. 5 130 ii 13'
bu-nu-šu (?)	]	man	Ug. 5 130 ii 14'
	]	?	UF 11 479 3
	]	to divide?	UF 11 479 4
	]	?	UF 11 479 5
	]	reed?	UF 11 479 6
ḫa-ra-⸢*šu*?⸣		artisan	UF 11 479 7
ri/tal-GI-⸢*mu*?⸣		?	UF 11 479 8
⸢*qa*⸣-*aš-tu*$_4$		bow	UF 11 479 9
ti-[*n*]*a*?-*tu*$_4$		fig	UF 11 479 10
 ša?-*na*!?-[*t*]*u*$_4$	]	year	Ug. 5 130 iii 1' UF 11 479 11

	S^a Voc. No.	Sign	Akkadian	Hurrian
	32.2	[MU] [	*zi-ik-ru* [	]]
	32.3	[MU	*z*]*a-ka*$_4$*-ru* [	]
	32.4	[MU	*n*]*u-ḫa-ti-mu*	*is-ḫa-*⸢*ri-ni*⸣
	32.5	[MU]	*a-na*	*i-di-da*
	32.6	[MU]	⸢*i*?⸣-[*n*]*a*	*i-gi-da*
	33	[DAḪ	*re*]-⸢*e*?⸣-[*ṣ*]*ú*?	*ma-zi-ri*
☛ p. 377	34	[GIŠ	(*iṣṣū*?)]	*ta-li*
☛	35/36.1	[MAL/GÁN	(*kakkabu*?)]	*zu-zu-ḫé*
	35/36.2	[MAL/GÁN]	⸢*ša*?⸣-[*ka*?-*nu*?]	*ke-um-mi*
	35/36.3	[MAL/GÁN	*e*]*q*?-[*lu*?]	*a-wa-ar-re*
	35/36.4	[MAL/GÁN]	*a-na-*⸢*ku*⸣	*iš-te-en*$_6$
	37.1	[EN	*ša*]*r-ru*	*i-wi-ir-ni*
	37.2	[EN	*be*]*-lu*	*e-wi-ri*
☛	37.3	[EN	*z*]*é*?*-ru*	*tu-ur-bi*
	37.4	[EN	*a*?*-r*]*a*?*-ru*	*ši-da-ar-ni*
	38	[IN	*ti-i*]*b-nu*	*ti-ib-ni*
	39	[URU?] [URU	⸢*a*?⸣[*-lu*? (*ālu*)]	 *ar-de-na*
	40.1	[EL?] [EL	*el-*[*lu*? (*ellu*)]	 *ši-ḫa-la-e*
	40.2	[EL?	(*tēliltu*?/*ebbu*?)]	⸢*x-x-x-ni*⸣*-ḫi*
	40.3	EL	AN[	
	40.x/41.x	[EL/IGI(?)		
	41.1	IGI	*e-nu*[	
	41.2	IGI	*pa-nu-*⸢*ú*?⸣[	
	41.3	⸢IGI⸣	[*m*]*aḫ-r*[*u*(*-ú*)	

Ugaritic		Meaning	Reference
⸢x⸣[*ú*-[*w*]*a*!?-[*t*]*u*$_4$	]	utterance	Ug. 5 130 iii 2' UF 11 479 12
ra-g[*a*?-*mu*?]		to speak	Ug. 5 130 iii 3'
: *⸢a⸣*-[*p*]*í*?-[*yu*?]		baker	Ug. 5 130 iii 4'
le-⸢e⸣		to(ward)	Ug. 5 130 iii 5'
⸢bi⸣-i[	]	in	Ug. 5 130 iii 6'
i-zi-ir[-*tu*$_4$?]		help	Ug. 5 130 iii 7'
iṣ-ṣú-[*ma*?]		wood, trees	Ug. 5 130 iii 8'
ku-ku-bá-t[*u*$_4$?]		vase? (star??)	Ug. 5 130 iii 9'
ši-tu[	]	to place	Ug. 5 130 iii 10'
: *ša-d*[*u-ú*	]	field	Ug. 5 130 iii 11'
a-na-ku		I	Ug. 5 130 iii 12'
ma-al-ku		king	Ug. 5 130 iii 13'
ba-a-lu-ma		lord	Ug. 5 130 iii 14'
e-bu		enemy	Ug. 5 130 iii 15'
: *ṣi-il-yv*[*(-tu*$_4$*?)*	]	curse	Ug. 5 130 iii 16'
ti-ib-nu		straw	Ug. 5 130 iii 17'
 qa-ri-t[*u*$_4$]	]	town	Ug. 5 133 i 1' Ug. 5 130 iii 18'
 ṭu-ú-ru	]	pure	Ug. 5 133 i 2' Ug. 5 130 iii 19'
: *rap-⸢ú?⸣*[	]	purification?/holy?	Ug. 5 130 iii 20'
	]	?	Ug. 5 133 i 3'
]*⸢x⸣*[	]	?	Ug. 5 130 iii 21'
	]	eye	Ug. 5 133 i 4'
	]	former	Ug. 5 133 i 5'
	]	previous	Ug. 5 133 i 6'

	S^a Voc. No.	Sign	Akkadian	Hurrian
☛ p. 377	41.4	[IGI?	(*maḫāru*?)	
	41.5	⌜IGI⌝	*a-ma-r*[*u*	
		⌜IGI	*a-ma*⌝[*-ru*	
	41.6	IGI	*da-*[*ga?-lu* (?)	
	[42	IGI-*gunû* missing]		
	43.1	ḪI	*ba-*[*la?-ṭu?/lu?*	
		⌜ḪI⌝	*ba-la-ṭu?*[	
		[		]
	43.2	ḪI	*ṭa-a-bu* [	
		ḪI	*ṭá-*[*(a-)bu*	
		[		]
	43.3	ḪI	*la-*[	
	43.4	ḪI	*tu-*[	
	44.1	KAM	*di-qa-ru* [	
		KA[M		
		[		]-⌜*x*⌝
☛	44.2	KAM	*mé-re-él-t*[*u*	
		[		]⌜*x*⌝*-še*
☛	45.1	[A]N	*ša-mu-*⌜*ú?*⌝[	
		[		*ḫa-b*]*ur-ni*
☛	45.2	AN	*e-nu* [	
☛	45.3	AN	*i-lu* [	
		[		]⌜*e*⌝*-ni*
☛	45.4	[A]N	*šar-ru* [	
		[AN?	(*šarru*?)]	*ta-ni*
☛	45.5	[A]N	*šar-ra-nu* [	
		[AN?	(*šarrānū*?)]	*zi-ia-ni*
☛	46.1	[ḪA]L	*ḫal-l*[*u*	
☛	46.2?	[ḪAL?	(*zittu*?)]	*pu-ru?-da-ni*
		[		*p*]*u-ru-d*[*á*]*?-n*[*i?*
☛	47.1?	[UR?	(*kabattu?/ qar(rā)du?*)]	*ir-bi*
		[		*i*]*r-wi* [

Ugaritic	Meaning	Reference
la?-q]a?-ḫu	to receive?	UF 11 479 24
]	to see	Ug. 5 133 i 7'
]		Ug. 5 134 1'
]	to look	Ug. 5 134 2'
]	life?/to mix?	Ug. 5 134 4'
]	life	Ug. 5 133 i 8'
ḫi-[i]u?-ma	life	UF 11 479 25
]	sweet, fine	Ug. 5 133 i 9'
]		Ug. 5 134 3'
ṭa-bu		UF 11 479 26
]	?	Ug. 5 134 5'
]	?	Ug. 5 134 6'
]	bowl, jar	Ug. 5 133 i 10'
]		Ug. 5 134 7'
di-[k]a$_4$-ru		UF 11 479 27
]	request	Ug. 5 133 i 11'
i-[r]i?-iš-[tu$_4$?]		UF 11 479 28
]	sky	Ug. 5 133 i 12'
[š]a!?-[m]u?-ma?		UF 11 479 29
]	priest/Anu?	Ug. 5 133 i 13'
]	god	Ug. 5 133 i 14'
⌜i?-lu?⌝	god, El	UF 11 479 30
]	king	Ug. 5 133 i 15'
ba!?-a-[lu?]	lord	UF 11 479 31
]	kings	Ug. 5 133 i 16'
[b]a?-a-[lu?-ma?]	lords?	UF 11 479 32
]	crotch	Ug. 5 133 i 17'
pu-ru-s[à?-tu$_4$?]	division?	UF 11 479 33
]		Ug. 5 131 1'
ka-bi-[du?]	liver?/ hero?	UF 11 479 34
]		Ug. 5 131 2'

	S^a Voc. No.	Sign	Akkadian	Hurrian
p. 378	47.2	UR [	*⸢ba?⸣[-a?-šu* (?)	]⸢*x*⸣ *i]n-ni*
	47.3	UR	*mi-it-[ḫ]a-ri-i[š*	]
	48.1	NE	*i-ša-tu* [	
	48.2	[NE?		*(x-?)p]í-ir-ri*
	49.1	[GIBIL	*(perʾu)*	*ḫ]í?-iš-ši*
	49.2/50.x	[GIBIL/KA]	⸢*x*⸣[	]
	50.1	[KA]	*ši-⸢in⸣-nu* [	]
	50.2??	[KA??	(??)	*š]u-ḫu-ur-ni*
	51.1	[SAG]	*qa-qa-du*	*pa-[a-ḫi*]
	51.2?	[SAG?	*(amīlu?)*	*tar]-š[u-w]a-an-ni*
	52	[ŠÚ]R	*ez-zu*	*še?-[*]
	53.1	[D]U	*a-la-ku*	*uš-[*]
	53.2	[D]U	*iz-zi-zu*	*u[m?]-x-[*]
	53.3	[D]U	*ken^{en}/ke$_x$-en-nu*	*mu-u[š?*]
	53.4/54	[DU/SUḪUŠ	*(išdu)*	]⸢*x*
	55	K[A]Š$_4$	*la-sà-mu*	*e?-b[i?*]
	56	I	*na-a-ru*	⸢*x*⸣[ ]
	56a	[I]A	*ma-ṣa-ar-t[u$_4$*	]
	57.1	ŠU	*qa-t[u$_4$*	]
	57.2	[Š]U	*gi-mi-l[u*	]⸢*x*⸣
	58	[ŠÀ]	*li-ib-bu* [	]
	59	[Š]A	*pí-it-nu*	[ ]
	60	[Ù]Ḫ/[Ú]Ḫ	*ru-uʾ-tu$_4$*	[ ]
	61.1	[A]Š [	*it-te-tù*	[ ]
	61.2	AŠ	*e-de$_4$-nu*	[ ]

Ugaritic	Meaning	Reference
ḫe-bu *ḫé-b*[*u*?]	shame?	UF 11 479 35 Ug. 5 131 3'
bi-ru/šub/p[ ]	equally?/likewise?	UF 11 479 36
]⌜*i*⌝-*ši-t*[u_4]	fire	UF 11 479 37
[*i*]*r-KU*	?	Ug. 5 131 4'
šap-ḫu	sprout, scion	Ug. 5 131 5'
	?	Ug. 5 135 1'
	tooth	Ug. 5 135 2'
ḫé-yu-ma	life	Ug. 5 131 6'
	head	Ug. 5 135 3'
: bu-nu-šu	man	Ug. 5 131 7'
	furious	Ug. 5 135 4'
	to go	Ug. 5 135 5'
	to stand	Ug. 5 135 6'
	true, just	Ug. 5 135 7'
:⌝ *iš-*du_4	lower extremities	Ug. 5 131 8'
	to run	Ug. 5 135 8'
	river	Ug. 5 135 9'
	garrison	Ug. 5 135 10'
	hand	Ug. 5 135 11'
	favor	Ug. 5 135 12'
	heart	Ug. 5 135 13'
	box, case	Ug. 5 135 14'
	saliva	Ug. 5 135 15'
 a-ḫ]*a-du*	one, first	Ug. 5 135 16' Ug. 5 138 1'
	alone	Ug. 5 135 17'

S^a Voc. No.	Sign	Akkadian	Hurrian	
(62	$ERIN_2$ after no. 63)			
63.1	UD [	*u-mu*	[	]]
63.2	[UD	(*šamšu*/*Šamaš*)		]
63.3	UD [	*pé-eṣ-ṣú*	[	]]
63.4?	[UD?	(*anumma*?)		]
63.5?	[UD?	(*bēlu*?)		
63.6?	[UD??	(*aṣû*??)		
62.1	[ER]IN_2	*nam-ru* [		]
62.2	[ER]IN_2	*ṣa-a-b*[*u*		]
64	[A]D	*a-b*[*u*?		]
65?	[D]A?[			]
. . .				
66.1?	T[A?			
66.2	TA [			
66.3	TA	*i*[*t*?-*ti* (?)		
67	TI	*l*[*a-ba*/*bi-ru* (?)		
68	UM [			
68/69	U[M/D[UB			
. . . (no entries preserved between numbers 68/69 and 141/142)				
141/142	[Ú/LÁL	-*m*]*a*?[		]
142	[LÁL?	*m*]*a-ṭ*[*u-ú* (?)		]
143	[LÀL]	*di-*⌜*iš*(EŠ)?⌝*-pu*	⌜*ni*?⌝[	]
[144	ID missing?]			
145?	[ZÉ?]	*me-er-tù*	*aš*-[	]
[146	$MURUB_4$ missing?]			

☛ p. 379 (at 63.4?); ☛ (at 63.6?)

Ugaritic	Meaning	Reference
	day	Ug. 5 135 18'
PI-mu		Ug. 5 138 2'
ša-ap-šu	sun (god)	Ug. 5 138 3'
	white	Ug. 5 135 19'
la-ba-nu		Ug. 5 138 4'
al-li-ni-ya	now (then)	Ug. 5 138 5'
b]*a*?-*a-lu*	lord?	Ug. 5 138 6'
z]*u*?-*ut-ta-ru*	to go out??	Ug. 5 138 7'
	bright	Ug. 5 135 20'
	troop	Ug. 5 135 21'
	father	Ug. 5 135 22'
	?	Ug. 5 135 23'
]	?	Ug. 5 136 1'
]	?	Ug. 5 136 2'
]	with?	Ug. 5 136 3'
]	(to be) old?	Ug. 5 136 4'
]	?	Ug. 5 136 5'
]	?	Ug. 5 136 6'
	?	Ug. 5 135 r. 1'
	to diminish?	Ug. 5 135 r. 2'
	honey	Ug. 5 135 r. 3'
	gall bladder?	Ug. 5 135 r. 4'

	S^a Voc. No.	Sign	Akkadian	Hurrian
	147	[U]Š	*zi-ik-ru*	*tù?-r[u?-ḫi* (?)]
	148	KUŠ$_6$	*ma-at-qu*	*ni?-šu?-[*]
	149	SUM	*na-da-nu*	*a-ru-[um-me]*
	149a	NAGA	*uḫ-ḫu-NU*	*uḫ-[ḫ]u?-ur-r[i?]*
	150.1	KID [	*ki-i-tu* *ki?]-⸢i?⸣-[tu* (?)	*n[a?]-ḫ[al?]-bi[*]
	150.2	KID KID	*zi-qí-qú* *za-qi-q[ú!*	*⸢zi?⸣-[*]
	151.1	[DA]G	*[š]a-ad-du*	*[a]r?-g[i?*]
	151.2	DAG	*pa-aṭ-ṭ[u?*	
	151.3	DAG	*pu-uḫ-r[ù*	
	152	E [ ]	*i-ku* *e-ku* [	*⸢x⸣-ib?-[*]
	153	É [ ]	*[b]i-tu* *bi-tu*$_4$ [	*⸢pu?-ur?-li?⸣[*]
	154	[KISAL	*k]i-sà-lu* [	

[154, 155 missing in Ug. 5 135; 3-4 line break in Ug. 5 137]

	S^a Voc. No.	Sign	Akkadian	Hurrian
☛ p. 379	156	AR	*na-ma-rù*	*ḫi-⸢x-x-x⸣[*]
☛	157	⸢MUŠ⸣ [	*ṣi-i-ru*	*ap-ši?-[*]]
☛	158.1	[Ú]R [	*[s]u?-nu*	*⸢ḫu?⸣-zi-[*]]
☛	158.2	⸢ÚR⸣	*⸢na?⸣-[ṣ]a!?-ru*	*⸢x⸣-ru-[*]
☛	158.3	⸢ÚR⸣ [	*pè-nu*	*ip-⸢x⸣-[*]]
☛	159.1	[Š]EŠ	*a-ḫu*	*še-e-n[i?*]
☛	159.2	[Š]EŠ [	*na-ṣa-r[u*	]]
☛	159.3	[Š]EŠ	*ma-r[a-ru*	]
☛	160.1	IB	*ú-l[a?-pu* (?)	]

Ugaritic	Meaning	Reference
	male	Ug. 5 135 r. 5'
	sweet	Ug. 5 135 r. 6'
	to give	Ug. 5 135 r. 7'
	(a plant)	Ug. 5 135 r. 8'
	reed mat	Ug. 5 135 r. 9'
]		Ug. 5 137 i 1
	phantom, wind	Ug. 5 135 r. 10'
]		Ug. 5 137 i 2
	extended	Ug. 5 135 r. 11'
]	boundary?	Ug. 5 137 i 3
]	assembly	Ug. 5 137 i 4
	dike	Ug. 5 135 r. 12'
]		Ug. 5 137 i 5
	house	Ug. 5 135 r. 13'
]		Ug. 5 137 i 6
]	courtyard	Ug. 5 137 i 7
	to be bright	Ug. 5 135 r. 14'
	serpent	Ug. 5 135 r. 15'
tu-un-na-nu		Ug. 5 137 i 8'
	lap	Ug. 5 135 r. 16'
ḫ̮é-qu		Ug. 5 137 i 9'
	to guard?	Ug. 5 135 r. 17'
	foot	Ug. 5 135 r. 18'
ri-i[g]-lu		Ug. 5 137 i 10'
	brother	Ug. 5 135 r. 19'
	to guard	Ug. 5 135 r. 20'
ni-iḫ̮-rù		Ug. 5 137 i 11'
	to be bitter	Ug. 5 135 r. 21'
	bandage?	Ug. 5 135 r. 22'

	Sª Voc. No.	Sign	Akkadian	Hurrian	
	160.2	IB	*g[a?*		]
	160.3	[IB?	(*nēbettu*??)		]
	160.4	[IB?	(*tubuqtu*?)		]
	160-162?	[IB/TAG/SAL			
	160-162?	[IB/TAG/SAL			
	161?	[TA]G? [			]
	. . . (no entries preserved between numbers 160/162 and 170)				
	170.1	K[UR			
	170.2	⸢KUR⸣ [			
	171	⸢SILA$_3$⸣ [			
	172.1	T[AR			
	172.2	TAR [			
	172.3	TAR [			
☛ p. 380	173.1	BAD [B]AD [	⸢*bi/pí*⸣-[		
	173.2	BAD [			
☛	173.3	BAD BAD	*ba-l[a?-ṭu* (?) TIL-*la-ṭu*	 *šu-ḫ[u-ur-ni*	]
☛	173.4	BAD	*ka-ta-mu*	*ḫu-x[*	
	173.5	BAD BAD	*ga-ma-rù* ⸢*ga?*⸣-*m[a-rù*	⸢*x*⸣[	
☛	173.6	BAD	*la-b[i?-ru* (?)		
	173.7	BAD BAD	*mu-tu$_4$* [⸢*mu*⸣-*t[u$_4$?*		
	173.8	[B]AD BAD	*da-m[u* *d[a?-mu* (?)		
	173.9	[BA]D?	*ši-i[r-*		
	173.x?	[BAD??			

Ugaritic		Meaning	Reference
		?	Ug. 5 135 r. 23'
ḫe?-e[*-ru?*	]	enclosure?	Ug. 5 137 i 12'
pí-⸢*i?*⸣*-*[*tu*$_4$*?*	]	corner, edge?	Ug. 5 137 i 13'
]⸢*x*⸣*-ri-*[	]	?	Ug. 5 137 i 14'
]⸢*x-x*⸣[	]	?	Ug. 5 137 i 15'
		?	Ug. 5 135 r. 24'
	]	?	Ug. 5 133 r. 1'
	]	?	Ug. 5 133 r. 2'
	]	?	Ug. 5 133 r. 3'
	]	?	Ug. 5 133 r. 4'
	]	?	Ug. 5 133 r. 5'
	]	?	Ug. 5 133 r. 6'
	]	?	Ug. 5 133 r. 7'
	]		Ug. 5 137 i 18"
	]	?	Ug. 5 137 i 19"
	]	life	Ug. 5 133 r. 8'
⸢*ḫé-yu-ma?*⸣			Ug. 5 137 i 20"
l]*i?/UZ?-ZU*		to cover?	Ug. 5 137 i 21"
	]	to finish	Ug. 5 137 i 22"
	]		Ug. 5 133 r. 9'
	]	old?	Ug. 5 133 r. 10'
	]	death	Ug. 5 137 i 23"
	]		Ug. 5 133 r. 11'
	]	blood	Ug. 5 137 i 24"
	]		Ug. 5 133 r. 12'
	]	ligament?	Ug. 5 137 i 25"
	]	?	Ug. 5 137 i 26"

	Sª Voc. No.	Sign	Akkadian	Hurrian
	174.1	KUG	*e*[*l?-lu* (?)	
		[		*ši-ḫ*]*a-al-e*
	174.2	[KUG	(*kaspu?*)	*uš-ḫ*]*u?-ni*
	174a	KUG.BABBAR	*k*[*a-as-pu* (?)	
		[		]⌜*x*⌝
	174b	⌜GUŠKIN⌝	*ḫ*[*u-ra-ṣú* (?)	
		[		]
	175	[GIŠIMMAR?	*gišimmaru* (?)	]
	[175-176:	four lines in Ug. 5 137 ii, all signs obliterated; Nougayrol did not count		
	176.x?	[TUR??		]
☛ p. 380	176.y?	[TUR??	(*šerru??*)	*z*]*u?-*[*k*]*i!?*
	177.1	U[N	(*nišū*)	*x*]*-lu-ʾV-*[*x*]
	177.2	U[N	(*mātu*)	*u*]*-mi-*in_4*-n*[*i*
	178	G[Ú	(*šubtu?*)	*x* (*-x*)]*-a-ri*
	179?	D[UR	(*markasu??*)	*x* (*-x*)]*-*⌜*a?*⌝
☛	180.1?	[SIG?	(*ṣeḫru??*)]	⌜*ga?*⌝*-al-gi*
	180.2?	[SIG?	(*enšu??*)	*z*]*i* /*m*]*u-na-ar-ḫi*
☛	180.3/181?	[SIG/SIG$_5$?	(?)	*t*]*ap-ša-ḫal-še*
☛	182	[TE?	(*simtu?*)]	*ḫa-*[*a*]*ḫ?-li*
☛	183.1	KA[R	(*eṭēru?*)]	*eḫ-lu-um-me*
	183.2	KAR	*la-sà-mu*	*i-z*[*u*]*-ri*
	183.3	KAR	*ap-pu*	*pu-u*[*ḫ*]*-ḫi*
	183.4	KAR	*šu-zu-bu*	⌜*a*⌝*-bu-uš-ku-me*
	183.5	KAR	*ka-a-ru*	*ma-ḫa-*[z]*i*
	184.1	BAL	*pí-la-ak-ku*	*te-a-ri*
	184.2	BAL	*na-bal-ku-*tu_4	*tap-šu-ḫu-um-me*
	185	ŠUL	*eṭ-lu*	*uš-ta-an-ni*

Ugaritic		Meaning	Reference
	]	pure	Ug. 5 133 r. 13'
ṭu-ú-ru			Ug. 5 137 ii 1
kàs-pu		silver	Ug. 5 137 ii 2
	]	silver	Ug. 5 133 r. 14'
ka-as-p[*u*]			Ug. 5 137 ii 3
	]	gold	Ug. 5 133 r. 15'
ḫu-r[*a-ṣu*]			Ug. 5 137 ii 4
ta-[*ma?-ru?*]		date palm	Ug. 5 137 ii 5

three of these lines in his numbering.]

Ugaritic		Meaning	Reference
⌜*na/ta/ša*⌝-[	]	?	Ug. 5 137 ii 7'
P[*I?-al/la?-d*]*u?*		child??	Ug. 5 137 ii 8'
⌜*na*⌝-[*š*]*u-*⌜*ma*⌝		people	Ug. 5 137 ii 9'
ḫ]*u-wa-tu*$_4$		country	Ug. 5 137 ii 10'
⌜*ḫu*⌝*-du-rù*		room?	Ug. 5 137 ii 11'
ma-a-al-tu$_4$		bolt?	Ug. 5 137 ii 12'
d[*a*]*-aq!?-qú*		small?	Ug. 5 137 ii 13'
da-al!?-⌜*lu*⌝		weak, poor	Ug. 5 137 ii 14'
ma-aš-⌜*x*⌝[	]	?	Ug. 5 137 ii 15'
la-ḫa-m[*u?*]		suitable?	Ug. 5 137 ii 16'
ḫu-PI-ú		to save	Ug. 5 137 ii 17'
⌜*ma*⌝*-al-sà-mu*		course?/courier?	Ug. 5 137 ii 18'
ap-pu		nose	Ug. 5 137 ii 19'
pu-la-ṭu[	]	to save	Ug. 5 137 ii 20'
ma-aḫ-ḫa-[*du*]		quay	Ug. 5 137 ii 21'
pí-lak-ku		spindle	Ug. 5 137 ii 22'
tu-a-pí-[*ku?*]		to be upset	Ug. 5 137 ii 23'
⌜*ba*⌝*-aḫ-ḫu-rù*		youth	Ug. 5 137 ii 24'

	S^a Voc. No.	Sign	Akkadian	Hurrian
☛ p. 380	186.1	[ŠA]Ḫ	*še-ḫu-ú*	*ú-ḫi*
☛	186a?	[ŠAḪ.TU]R?	*kur-ku-za-nu*	---
☛	186.2?	[ŠAḪ??	*x*]-⌜*x*⌝-*rù*	*šu-ra-at-ḫi*
☛	187.1	[LÚ	(*šu-ú*?)]	*ma-an-ni*
☛	187.2	[LÚ	(*ša*?)]	*a-PI*
☛ p. 381	187.3	[LÚ	(*bēlu*)	]⌜*e*?⌝-*wi-ri*
☛	187.4	[LÚ	(*amīlu*)	*tar-š*]*u-wa-ni*
☛	188.1	[LUGAL	(*šarru*)	*e-wi-i*]*r-ni*
☛	188.2	[LUGAL	(*bēlu*)	(*ewiri*)
☛	189.1	[MAḪ	(*ṣīru*)	]⌜*x*⌝
☛	189.2	[MAḪ	(*ṣēru*)	*a-wa-a*]*r-re*
☛	189.3	[MAḪ	(*mādu*/*maʾdu*)	]-*ši*
☛	190.1	[ḪUL?	(*sarru*?)	]-*ri*
☛	190.2?	[ḪUL?	(*zapru*/*ṣabru*?)	]-*ba-di*
☛	190.3?	[ḪUL?	(*zāmânu*?)	]⌜*x*⌝
☛	190.4?	[ḪUL?	(*šulputu*?)	*šu*(?)]-*bi*
☛	190.5?	[ḪUL??	(*zīru*?)	*TA*]*R*?-*du-bar-ri*
☛	191.1?	[GUL?	(*šulputu*?)]	*šu-bi*
☛ p. 382	191.2?	[GUL??	(*abātu*/*naqāru*?)]	*na-ak-di*
☛	191.3?	[GUL??	(*nābutu*/*ḫepû*/ *pašāru*)]	*pí-i-ri*
☛	192.1	[ÁŠ	*ku-na*]-*šu*	*ut-te*
	192.2	[ÁŠ	*a*]*r-ra-tu*$_4$	*ši-da-ar-ni*
	192.3	[Á]Š	*ṣi-bu-tu*$_4$	*ma-gu-un*?[
	192.4	ÁŠ	*mur-ṣu*	*ma-ru-*⌜*ši*?⌝
	193.1	ÍL	*še*!-*qu-ú*	*ḫi-*[*i*]*l-da-e*
	193.2	ÍL	*ma-aš-*⌜*šu*⌝-*ú*	*p*[*a-b*]*ar-ra*

Ugaritic	Meaning	Reference
ḫu-zi-rù	pig	Ug. 5 137 ii 25'
ḫe-en-ni-ṣu	piglet	Ug. 5 137 ii 26'
qi-i-lu	(a tree?)	Ug. 5 137 ii 27'
ú-wa	he	Ug. 5 137 ii 28'
du-ú	(relative pronoun)	Ug. 5 137 ii 29'
ba-a-lu-ma	lord	Ug. 5 137 ii 30'
bu-nu-šu	man	Ug. 5 137 ii 31'
ma-al-ku	king	Ug. 5 137 ii 32'
b]*a-*⸢*a-lu-ma*⸣	lord	Ug. 5 137 ii 33'
a-du-rù	mighty	Ug. 5 137 ii 34'
: ša-du-ú	plain, field	Ug. 5 137 ii 35'
ma-a-du-ma	much, many	Ug. 5 137 ii 36'
sar-rù	false	Ug. 5 137 ii 37'
ba-ṭá-lu	false(hood)?	Ug. 5 137 ii 38'
ḫa-ri-mu	foe?	Ug. 5 137 ii 39'
ḫa-ri-mu	desecrated?	Ug. 5 137 ii 40'
ma-aš-nu-ú?	enemy?	Ug. 5 137 ii 41'
ḫa-ri-mu	desecrated?	Ug. 5 137 ii 42'
i-pu-ú	destruction?	Ug. 5 137 ii 43'
pí-rù	flight?/separation?	Ug. 5 137 ii 44'
⸢*ku*⸣*-sú-m*[*u*]	emmer	Ug. 5 137 ii 45'
: ṣ[*i-il-yv(-tu*$_4$*?)*]	curse	Ug. 5 137 ii 46'
]	desire	Ug. 5 137 ii 47'
⸢*x* ⸣[ ]	pain, disease	Ug. 5 137 ii 48'
[*:*]	high	Ug. 5 137 ii 49'
m[*a*?]	(a basket)	Ug. 5 137 ii 50'

	Sa Voc. No.	Sign	Akkadian	Hurrian
	193.3	ÍL	*na-gi-rù*	[*n*]*a-gi-ri*
	193.4	ÍL	*za-b*[*i*]-⸢*lu*$_4$?⸣	(*x*-?)]*di-ia-ši*
☛ p. 382	194.1?	G[AB?	(*irtu*?)]	⸢*a*?⸣-*ḫé-er-ni*
	194.2	GAB	*gaba*-[*ru*]-*ú* (?)	*pa-at-pí-ri*
	194.3	GAB	*pa-ṭá*-[*r*]*u*	*zu-lu-du-me*
	194.4	GAB	*tu-uḫ-ḫu*	*šu-ḫu-li*
	195.1	ÌR	*ar-du*	*pu-ra-mì*
	195.2	ÌR	*zi-ka-rù*	*tu-ru-ḫi*
	[196	IR$_{11}$ (ìr x še) missing]		
	197.1	EZEN	*i-sí-nu*	*e*-⸢*li*?⸣
	197.2	EZEN	*za-am-ma-rù*	*ḫal-mi*
☛	198.1	IDIM	*na*[*b-qu* (?)]	⸢*tar*⸣-*m*[*a-n*]*i*
	198.2	IDIM	[(?)	]
	198.3	[IDIM	(?)	]
	198.4	[IDIM	(?)	
☛	198.5	[IDIM	(*šegû*?)	
	198.6	[IDIM	(*šamû*)	*ḫa-bur*]-*ni*
	198.7	[IDIM	(*erṣetu*)	]
☛	198.8?	[IDIM?	(*ekletu*?)	]
	198.9?	[IDIM?	(*nakbatu*?/*balāṭu*?)	
☛	198.10?	[IDIM?	(*kabtu*?)	]
	198.11?	[IDIM?	(*sebû*?)	
	199?	[ŠE?	(*šeʾu*?)	
	?	[		
	?	[		
	?	[		

Ugaritic		Meaning	Reference
m[*u*?	]	herald	Ug. 5 137 ii 51'
da-[	]	porter?	Ug. 5 137 ii 52'
i-r[*a*?-*tu*$_4$?	]	chest?	Ug. 5 137 ii 53'
⸢*x*⸣[	]	copy?	Ug. 5 137 iii 1
pí-iṭ-r[*ù*?]		to loosen	Ug. 5 137 iii 2
šu-ḫu-ut-t[*u*?]		bran, residue	Ug. 5 137 iii 3
ab-du		slave	Ug. 5 137 iii 4
da-ka-rù		male	Ug. 5 137 iii 5
da-ab-ḫu		festival/sacrifice	Ug. 5 137 iii 6
ši-i-ru		song	Ug. 5 137 iii 7
NAB-ku		spring	Ug. 5 137 iii 8
DINGIR-*lu*$_4$		god, El?	Ug. 5 137 iii 9
⸢*x-x*⸣[	]	?	Ug. 5 137 iii 10
	]	?	Ug. 5 137 iii 11
r]*a*-[*g*]*a*?-[*zu*?]		to be enraged?	Ug. 5 137 iii 12'
ša-mu-ma		sky	Ug. 5 137 iii 13'
ar-ṣu		earth	Ug. 5 137 iii 14'
ḫu-ul-ma-tu$_4$		darkness?	Ug. 5 137 iii 15'
ḫ]*u-ul-ma-t*[*u*$_4$]		strength?	Ug. 5 137 iii 16'
ma!?-*al-ku*[	]	noble, king?	Ug. 5 137 iii 17'
ḫ]*a-ra-š*[*u*	]	deaf?	Ug. 5 137 iii 18'
š]*i*?-*i-ru*[	]	barley?	Ug. 5 137 iii 19'
x]-⸢*i*?-*x*⸣[	]	?	Ug. 5 137 iii 20'
t]*u*$_4$		?	Ug. 5 137 iii 21'
l]*u*?		?	Ug. 5 137 iii 22'

S^{a} Voc. No.	Sign	Akkadian	Hurrian	
?	[			
?	[			
?	[			
. . . (3-4 lines broken)				
206?	[KAB?	(*kappu*?)		
207?	[KIB?			
208?	[TIR?	(*atmānu*?)		
209?	[TUK?	(*birku*?)		
210?	[KÍD?	(*karṣu*?)		
211	[BARAG	(*mūšabu*)		]

Ugaritic	Meaning	Reference
l]*u*?	?	Ug. 5 137 iii 23'
]-*mu*	?	Ug. 5 137 iii 24'
d]*a-mu*	?	Ug. 5 137 iii 25'
ka?-*n*]*a*?-*pu*	wing?	Ug. 5 137 iii 27"
x-š]*i*?-⸢*ku*?⸣	?	Ug. 5 137 iii 28"
é?]-⸢*qi*?-*id*?-*šu*?⸣	sanctuary?	Ug. 5 137 iii 29"
bi?]-*ir*?-*ku*	knee?	Ug. 5 137 iii 30"
q]*à*?-*ar-ṣú*	piece/pinch?	Ug. 5 137 iii 31"
mu-ša-bu	seat	Ug. 5 137 iii 32"

Commentary

20.1

Sign: The traces of the end of the sign conform to no. 20 LUM, but not to no. 19 LA.

Ugar.: Not enough remains to suggest a reading.

20.2

Sign/Akk.: *qannunu* is apparently Assyrian (vs. Bab. *qunnunu*), a D verbal adjective (rather than infinitive; cf. the Hurrian) of *kanānu/qanānu* "to coil, twist." For the lexical equation, cf. LUM.LUM = MIN *(ka-na-nu) ša BU-x,* LUM$^{lu\text{-}um}$LUM = MIN *(ka-na-nu) ša* LÚ, both cited in CAD K 142b (*kanānu* lex.).

Hur.: The ending *-ae* of *ḫišlae* is adverbial; see Laroche, Ug. 5 p. 460.

Ugar.: The reading is uncertain; both *qu-u*[*n*]-*n*[*u-nu*] and *qu-u*[*n*]-*n*[*a-nu*] are possible. In view of the *quttal* pattern for D infinitives elsewhere in the Ugarit S^a Voc. (e.g., *pu-la-ṭu*; see no. 183.4 below), the latter, i.e., */qunnanu/,* is perhaps more likely as an adjective related to the D stem (note also, perhaps, *tu-un-na-nu* = */tunnanu/* "serpent" in S^a Voc. no. 157). The only NWS cognate to Akk. *k/qanānu* appears to be MHeb. *kānan* "to encircle, protect," in the D "to wind around" (Levy, Wörterbuch II 351-52). Since the Ugar. word in question is not attested in alphab. texts, it is unclear whether the root here is *q-n-n* as occasionally in Akk. (thus, a loanword from Akk.?), or *k-n-n*; strongly militating against the latter alternative is the fact that KUM with the value ku_{13} (i.e., ku_{13}-*u*[*n*]-*n*[*a-nu*] = */kunnanu/*) is otherwise unattested in the Ugarit Akk. syllabary.

21

Sign/Akk.: Nougayrol, Ug. 5 p. 232 n. 1, suggested that ZU here is for UZU = *šīru* "flesh." More likely, however, ZU represents SÚ, for SU (note that ZU is used for syllabic *sú* passim in Ugarit Akk.); SU is also equated with *šīru* in lexical texts (pointed out by P. Steinkeller, oral communication; see AHw 1248-49, *šīru* LL). (For SU = KUŠ = *mašku,* see no. 23.)

Hur.: For *uzi* "flesh," see Laroche, GLH 291.

Ugar.: Probably for */šiʾru/* = alphab. *šir* "flesh" (KTU 1.96:2, 1.101:13; cf. Hebrew *šəʾēr* < **šiʾr-*, by hypercorrection). Much less likely is alphab. *θir* (the Arabic cognate of which is *θa*ʾ*r*), for which see, e.g., Loewenstamm, Comparative Studies 190-1; Caquot-Sznycer-Herdner, Textes ougaritiques 505 n. j. On the use of a vowel sign to indicate a syllable-closing aleph in the syllabic transcription of Ugar., see Part III, ch. 1 §E 4 b (3 b ii).

22.1

Sign/Akk.: ZA = *atta* "you."

Hur.: The form *ši-ni-bi* as a second person pronoun is difficult (see Laroche, Ug. 5 p. 461-62); the pronoun is otherwise attested with stem *fe-* (Speiser, IH 76 §109; Bush, GHL 106 §6.2212; Wilhelm, Or. 54 496).

Ugar.: /*ʾattă*/ = alphab. *at* "you."

22.2

Sign/Akk.: ZA = *amīlu* "man."

Hur.: For *taršuwanni* (*tarzuwani*), see Laroche, Ug. 5 449-50, GLH 258; Wilhelm, Or. 54 495, notes that the form does not mean "humanity" (so Laroche), but rather "man."

Ugar.: /*bunŭšu*/ = alphab. *bnš* "man." The consistent spelling of the form in these texts as *bu-nu-šu* suggests that the *n* is not doubled, thereby ruling out a derivation from **bun-(*ʾ*)nāš* "son of man" (as in Aramaic *bar nāšā*; see Aistleitner, Wörterbuch 54 no. 539; Gordon, UT 373b no. 486), which is difficult in any case since **ā* does not become *ō* in Ugar. (see Part III, ch. 1 §G 1). Gordon's alternative suggestion, a derivation from **bunu-šv*, in which the second element originally would have meant "man" (note in this connection Egyptian *s* "man"), is perhaps more plausible, although the vocalization of "son" as */*bunu*/ would be quite unexpected (despite Punic *bun*; Gordon, UT 373 no. 481).

Cf. also nos. 24.2, 25.5, 51.2, 187.4.

23

Sign/Akk.: SU = KUŠ = *mašku* "skin, hide."

Hur.: Laroche, GLH 59, lists *ašḫe* here separately from another noun (or nouns) *ašḫi*.

Ugar.: The suggested reconstruction is Nougayrol's, for /ᶜ*ōru*/, unattested in alphab. texts as yet; note also, in an economic text, ^túg^*ú-ra-tu* (PRU 6 126:6), probably for the pl. /ᶜ*ōrātu*/ "hides" (see the Glossary under ᶜWR). The root of this word and of the Hebrew cognate *ᶜôr,* whether *ᶜ-w-r* or *ᶜ-r-r,*[1] is uncertain, but the writing of the pl. form with initial *ú* rather than *ur* probably indicates the former.

24.1

Sign/Akk.: NU = *lā* "no(t)."

Hur.: On the derivation from *mann-* "to be," see Laroche, Ug. 5 p. 452-53, GLH 165-66; for *mann-* , see also Wilhelm, Or. 54 493.

Ugar.: */lā/* = alphab. *l* "not."

Cf. also no. 25.3.

24.2

Sign/Akk.: Cf. NU = *a-wi-lum* in MSL 14 118 no. 7 i 4 (Proto-A).

Cf. nos. 22.2, 25.5, 51.2, 187.4.

24.3

Sign/Akk.: NU probably reflects graphic confusion for PAB = *abu* "father" (Nougayrol, Ug. 5 p. 232 n. 2).

Hur.: For *attai* "father," see Laroche, GLH 63-64.

Ugar.: */ʾadānu/* = alphab. *adn* "father, lord" (cf. Hebrew *ʾādôn*).[2]

[1]It seems unlikely that alphab. *ǵr* ever means "skin, hide," as has been suggested by some scholars (see, e.g., Aistleitner, Wörterbuch 250 no. 2165). The spelling of the pl. ^{túg}*ú-ra-tu* indicates initial */ʾ/, /h/*, or */ᶜ/*, but not */ǵ/*, since the latter is invariably represented by Ḫ-signs in the syllabic transcriptions; see Part III, ch. 1 §E 4.

[2]I am not convinced by the suggestion of Weippert, UF 6 415-19, that Ugaritic distinguished **/ʾaddānu/* "father" from */ʾadānu/* "lord." Weippert's main formal evidence is the writing ^{lú}AD. DA.A.NI in EA 287:26; 288:13,15, letters from Jerusalem, which he would read syllabically as ^{lú}*ad-da-a-ni* = **/ʾaddānī/* "my father." Several factors militate against this: since WSem. forms in the Jerusalem letters exhibit the Canaanite **ā* > *ō* shift (as in *a-nu-ki* = *ʾanōkī* < **ʾanākŭ* EA 287: 66,69; *zu-ru-uḫ* = */ðorōᶜ/?* < **ðirāᶜ-* EA 286:12; 287:27; 288:14,34; *ú-bi-il/li-mi* = */(y)ōbil(īmi)/* < **yābil-* EA 287:55; 288:13), the writing in question cannot be considered Canaanite, for which **ʾaddōn-* would be expected; the writing of an extra vowel-sign in *-da-a-ni,* even for a long vowel, would be unusual; although a normalization of our S^a Voc. form *a-da-nu* as */ʾaddānu/* is not impossible, the latter would be much more likely to be written **ad-da-nu* in these texts. Thus, ^{lú}AD.DA.A.NI should be read as a logogram, like DUMU.MUNUS.A.NI-*ia* in EA 3:7 from Babylon (so also Moran, "Syrian Scribe" 163 n. 52); Ugar. *adn* reflects a single word */ʾadānu/*, which means both "lord" and "father."

25.1

Sign/Akk.: NA for ^{na4}NA.ZÀ/ZA.ḪI/AḪ.LI(.A) = *urṣu* "mortar"; note ^{na4}ZÀ.ḪI. LI.A = *er/ur-ṣú* in MSL 10 37ff.:253 (cf. also 254), a Ugarit lexical text (Ḫḫ XVI).

Hur.: Only here; apparently not connected with the common *itki* "sacred" (for which see Laroche, GLH 129-30). G. Wilhelm, in a private communication, reports that E. Neu, in a recent conference paper handout, derives *itki* "Mörser" from *id-* "(zer)schlagen."

Ugar.: No Semitic cognate or etymology presents itself for the Ugar. *IG-TU*$_4$ (*qitl* of *ʾ/h/*^{c}*-g/k/q-d/ṭ/t*; less likely, *qīl-t* or *qil-t* of *ʾ/h/*^{c}*-(w/y-)g/k/q* or *w-ʾ/h/*^{c}*-g/k/q*). Thus, unless the form contains a scribal error, it is probably a loan of the Hurrian *itki,* with metathesis of the dental and velar, i.e., */ʾiktu/*; cf. the metathesis of similar sounds in the borrowing of Hurrian *kešḫi* as Ugar. *kḥθ* "seat, throne" (see Friedrich, AfO 14 329-31), the latter written *ka-aḫ-šu* in EA 120:18 (from Byblos).

25.2

p. 382

Nougayrol suggested NA for NÁ "se soucier de" (i.e., *naʾādu/nâdu*), but the Hur. is a noun or adjective. Hillers, BASOR 200 18, proposes "waterskin"? (cf. Hebrew *nô(ʾ)d*), but Sum. for Akk. *nādu* "waterskin" is ^{kuš}A.EDIN(.LA), etc., not NA.

Probably we should understand NA for NA.RÚ/DÙ.A =*nādu* B = *nadû* A "stela" (alternate readings of NA.RÚ/DÙ.A = *narû*; see Steinkeller, JCS 35 249-50); note in a Ugarit lexical text ^{na4}NA.RÚ/DÙ.A = *na-du* MSL 10 37ff. A 243 (vs. *na-ru-ú* in ibid. text B; Ḫḫ XVI). Akk. *nādu* B would thus be a loan into both Hur. (*nadi*) and Ugar. (*/nādu/*).

25.3

Sign/Akk.: Nougayrol, Ug. 5 p 232 n. 5, suggested that the equation NA = *lā* was probably from a grammatical text (cf., e.g., MSL 4 145f.:416); note also, however, *nu-u* NA = *la-a* in MSL 14 359:107 (Ea IV).

Hur., Ugar.: Cf. no. 24.1.

25.4

Sign/Akk.: Nougayrol, Ug. 5 232 n. 6, proposed NA for NÁ = [*na-a*]-*lu* "lie down?"; the Hur. form is probably not an infinitive, however. Another possibility is NA for ^{na4}NA.BUR = *pīlu* "limestone" (e.g., MSL 10 37ff. B 244 [Ḫḫ XVI], from Ugarit; cf. no. 25.2 above, where NA is for NA.DÙ.A).

25.5

Cf. nos. 22.2, 24.2, 51.2, 187.4.

25.6

Akk.: The signs do not conform to *na-a-du* as in no. 25.2, according to Laroche, UF 11 479.

26

Sign/Akk.: Apparently for BA = *zâzu* "to divide," but here a derived form (D *zuzzu*/*zu*ʾʾ*uzu*?).

28

Sign/Akk.: Perhaps GI = *qanû* "reed."

[29]

Note that GI_4 is present in the Ugarit Sª, in Ug. 5 110.

30.1

Sign/Akk.: If the Ugar. column is understood correctly, we may restore no. 30 GIM = DÍM/ŠITIM = *bānû* or *itinnu* "house builder."

Ugar.: The only one of several orthographically possible Ugar. words that fits at this point in the Sª Voc. is */ḥarrāšu/* = alphab. *ḥrš* "artisan" (cf. Hebrew *ḥārāš*; see Loewenstamm, Comparative Studies 78-80).

☛ p. 382

30.x/30a.x

If the preceding and following lines are correctly interpreted, either no. 30 GIM or no. 30a BAN is expected here. Yet neither of these offers a key to the meaning of Ugar. *ri/tal-GI-mu*; the value of the second sign is probably either *gi* or *kí*, since GI = *qì* is rare in Ugarit Akk. apart from writings of *leqû* (no examples of GI for */qĭ/* or */qē/* are attested among the syllabic transcriptions of Ugar. words; see Part III, ch. 1 §E 1 b).

30a

Sign/Akk.: For the presence of BAN = *qaštu* "bow" in a S[a] text, cf. MSL 3 18 n. to line 55 (2).

(Hur.: For Hurrian words for "bow," *kašti, ḫaštiyati,* see Haas-Wilhelm, Or. 41 5-6.)

Ugar.: /*qaštu*/ = alphab. *qšt* "bow" (cf. Hebrew *qešet,* Aramaic *qaštā,* etc.).

31

p. 383

Sign/Akk.: We may reconstruct MA = PÈŠ = *tittu* "fig"; note, e.g., MIN (pe-eš) MA = *ti-it-tú* as the first value given for MA in MSL 14 360:120 (Ea IV).

Ugar.: The traces in Laroche's copy, UF 11 478, conform well to a reading *ti-*[*n*]*a-*[*t*]*u*4, for /*tiʾnatu*/ (or /*tīnatu*/?) "fig" (alphab. unattested); cf. Syriac *tē(ʾ)ttā* (pl. *tē(ʾ)nē*), Hebrew *təʾēnâ* (hypercorrection for [tēnâ] < **tiʾnatu*), Arabic *tīn,* Akk. *tittu* (pl. *tīnātu*), Eblaite gišPÈŠ*ti-ì-tum/du* (MEE 4 240 no. 368a; see Krebernik, ZA 73 14). Since the word is not attested in alphab. texts, it is impossible to know with certainty whether the original middle aleph of the root was preserved. The spellings of the Hebrew and Aramaic cognates indicate that it was present at least in Proto-NWS; further, syllable-final /ʾ/ seems generally to be preserved in Ugaritic.[3]

32.1

p. 383

Sign/Akk.: MU = *šattu* "year."

Hur.: Nougayrol read [*š*]*a*(?)-*a*[*l*(?)-]*w*[*a*(?)-*an-ni*(??)]; cf. *šawali* "year" in Laroche, GLH 221.

Ugar.: Laroche, UF 11 479, reads *da-an-*[*t*]*um,* but this yields no satisfactory word. Since the copy does not rule out *ša* for the first sign, a more likely reading is *ša-na*!-*tu*4, for /*šanatu*/ = alphab. *šnt* "year."

A less likely alternative is ⸢*ša-ap*⸣-[*t*]*u*4 for /*šaptu*/ "lip" (alphab. *špt*), although /*šapatu*/ is perhaps expected on the basis of Hebrew *śāpâ*;[4] further, MU "speech, utterance" → "lip" is difficult.

Still another possibility is MU for MUN = ⸢*ṭa- ab*⸣-[*t*]*u*4 "salt" as in Akk. But Ugar. "salt" is *mlḥ*; further, /*ṭābatu*/ is expected.

[3]See further Part III, ch. 1 §E 4 b (3 b i).

[4]Note, however, other instances in which Ugar. has the fem. allomorph /-*t*/ where Hebrew has **-at*; see n. 67 in the Introduction to the present study.

32.2

Sign/Akk.: MU = *zikru* "word, speech, utterance."

Ugar.: Probably *ú*-[*w*]*a*!-[*t*]*u*4 for /*huwătu*/ < **hawătu* = alphab. *hwt* "word" (cf. Akk. *awātum* [> *amātu*]). For the use of the Ú sign in Ugarit Akk. to represent Ugar. /*hŭ*/, see Part III, ch. 1 §E 4 b (3 a). The /*u*/ of the first syllable is the result of the raising (assimilation) of the original **a* to the following /*w*/; see Part III, ch. 2 §A 1 e.

32.3

Sign/Akk.: MU = *zakāru* "to speak, mention."

Ugar.: Nougayrol suggested *ra-a*[*m*(?)-*mu*(?)] "s'élever??"; but MU does not correspond to Akk. *zaqāru* "to raise, build high"; further, double -*mm*- for the root *r-w-m* is difficult.

Read instead probably *ra-g*[*a-mu*] for the G infinitive /*ragāmu*/ = alphab. *rgm* "to speak," corresponding to the Sign/Akk.

32.4

Sign/Akk.: MU = MUḪALDIM = *nuḫatimmu* "baker."

Hur.: The word *isḫarin(n)i* apparently occurs only here (Laroche, GLH 125). For the pattern, G. Wilhelm, in a private communication, compares *itt=ar=a=nni* "courier," for which see von Schuler, RHA 19 (68) 21-22.

Ugar.: Cf. alphab. *apy*, pl. *apym*, i.e., /*ʾāpiyu*/ (pl. */*ʾāpiyūma*/) "baker." Nougayrol read *a-p*[*u-ú*], which, if correct, would reflect contraction of the final triphthong.[5] A preferable reading, which the copy does not rule out, is ⌜*a*⌝-[*p*]*í*-[*yu*],[6] conforming to the alphab. spellings.

32.5

Sign/Akk.: MU = *ana* is unexpected; as Nougayrol suggested, Ug. 5 p. 232 n. 7, the equation is probably from a grammatical text.

Hur.: *edi*/*idi* "person, body" + postposition-*da* "at, for" = *idi-da* "to(ward), for,

[5]Final /*-iyv*/ does not normally contract in Ugar. nominal forms; for a discussion of final triphthongs, see Part III, ch. 2 §E 3.

[6]For BI in the same text, see Ug. 5 130 iii 15', Hurrian column (no. 37.3).

concerning"; see Laroche, GLH 73f.

Ugar.: Apparently *le*-⌜*e*⌝ for /*li*-/ = alphab. *l* "to, for (etc.)." This form and that of the next entry, ⌜*bi*⌝-*i* = /*bi*-/ "in," require some discussion. The writing of an extra vowel sign in Ugarit Akk. is almost invariably an indication either of the presence of one of the Ugaritic gutturals /ʾ/, /*h*/, /ᶜ/ or of vocalic length; thus, it seems that the pronunciations [lē] and [bī] are intended in these examples. But it should not therefore be concluded that these prepositions had long vowels normally, a feature that would be very difficult to explain historically.[7] Rather, it may be suggested, they were pronounced long in this particular context specifically, since only in a lexical list (or other "grammatical" discussion) would they not be proclitic to another word.[8] As to the vowel of *le-e*, it is not necessary to postulate the contraction of **ay* or a similar process.[9] The Ugarit scribes used the syllabic signs *Ci* and *Ce*, and *iC* and *eC*, quite consistently when transcribing Ugaritic words; the transcriptions indicate strongly that the Ugaritic phoneme /*i*/ was pronounced [e] in the environment of the sonorants /*l, m, n, r, y*/.[10] Thus, the writing *le-e* simply reflects the pronunciation [lē] for the morpheme /*li*-/, with its vowel lengthened outside of a normal speech context.

32.6

Sign/Akk.: Same comment as in no. 32.5 (preceding entry).

Hur.: *egi/igi* "in" + postposition *-da* "at, for, toward" = "to the inside of"; see Laroche, GLH 74.

Ugar.: See the commentary on the preceding entry. For /*bi*-/, see also no. 47.3.

33

Sign/Akk.: DAḪ = *rēṣu* "help."

Hur.: On the form *maziri*, see Laroche Ug. 5 p. 456.

Ugar.: Since a form without a case-vowel would be unique in these texts, we should

[7]Dietrich-Loretz-Sanmartín, UF 5 86, state, without further comment, that the vowel of *bi-i* is short, despite the spelling.

[8]Cf., in Mesopotamian lexical lists, the spelling of the precative marker *li*-, in which the vowel was almost certainly short, as *li-i* (see CAD L 224a, s.v. *lu*, lex.), and the writing of the determinative pronoun *ša*, undoubtedly unstressed [šă] in context, as *ša-a* (see AHw 1116a, s.v. *ša* LL, for examples).

[9]See, e.g., Blau and Greenfield's proposal, BASOR 200 16, that *lē* reflects **la-* + *ʾilay*.

[10]See Part III, ch. 1 §G 2.

undoubtedly read *i-zi-ir*[*-tu*$_4$] rather than Nougayrol's *i-zi-ir* (there appears on the copy to be room after the break for another sign); cf. alphab. ^{c}*ðrt* in KTU 1.140:8 (omens; context damaged, but see Herdner's comments, Ug. 7 pp. 61-62 with n. 180);[11] further, Byblos Canaanite *i-zi-ir-ta*$_5$ "assistance" (EA 87:13); Hebrew ^{c}*ezrâ* (alongside ^{c}*ēzer*) "help." The form /^{c}*iðirtu*/ is probably the reflex of a sound rule involving a vocalic pronunciation of /*r*/, viz. [^{c}iðr̥tu] < *^{c}*iðratu*.[12]

34

p. 383

Sign/Akk.: GIŠ = *iṣu* (or pl. *iṣṣū*) "wood" may be reconstructed on the basis of the other columns.

Hur.: *tali* = "wood, tree"; see Laroche Ug. 5 p. 458-59, GLH 253.

Ugar.: Since incorrect double writings of expected single consonants are rare among the syllabic transcriptions of Ugaritic, and since a sg. form *^{c}*iṣṣu* would be unprecedented in Semitic, read probably pl. *iṣ-ṣú-*[*ma*] (there is room, in the copy, for another sign after the break), i.e., /^{c}*iṣṣūma*/, with double *-ṣṣ-* (as in Akk., with pl. *iṣṣū* vs. sg. *iṣu*). Cf. alphab. ^{c}*ṣ*, pl. ^{c}*ṣm*.

35/36.1

Two possibilities, neither without difficulties, may be suggested for this entry, viz., "star" and "flagon"; see the remarks on the Ugar. column.

Sign/Akk.: For i-ku = GÁN = *kak-ka-bu* "star," see CAD K 46a.

Hur.: Note perhaps *zizzuḫi* "cruche" (Laroche, GLH 306); the form *zu-zu-hé* (ibid. 308) occurs only here. A perusal of Laroche, GLH, indicates that the Hur. term for "star" remains unknown.

Ugar.: Nougayrol read the last sign as *n*[*u* (?)], but the copy permits the beginning of *tu*$_4$. If the Akk. column held *kakkabu* "star," we must take the form in the Ugar. column, *ku-ku-ba-t*[*u*$_4$], to represent sg. /*kōkubatu*/ or pl. /*kōkubātu*/. There are, however, a number of problems with such an interpretation, not the least of which is that alphab. "star(s)" is normally *kbkb(m)*, in which the original *-b-* of the first syllable is retained, vs. a single example of *kkbm* without the *-b-* (KTU 1.10 i 4; scribal

[11]Note also the verb ^{c}*ðr* "to rescue" (UT 454b no. 1831), and the noun *t*^{c}*ðr* in the god-lists KTU 1.47:26, 1.118:26, corresponding to Akk. *tillatu* "military assistance" in the parallel syllabic list Ug. 5 18:25.

[12]See Sivan, Analysis 59, §8.2.1; below, Part III, ch. 2 §C.

error?). The *-u-* of the second syllable is unexpected (cf. Hebrew *kôkāb,* Akk. *kakkabu*), but may perhaps be explained as the result of assimilation of the original unstressed short *a* to the following *m* (see Sivan, Analysis 19-20, for similar NWS examples). Although a fem. derivative (originally **kabkab(a)t-*) is attested in the various languages, it has a restricted meaning ("Venus" in Aramaic; "star-shaped object" in Akk.) that would seem to be out of place in our list. Finally, a pl. form (*/kōkubātu/*; cf. probably alphab. *kbkbt* in KTU 1.13:17 [!; see the photo in CTA pl. 19], 1.92:28) is also unexpected here.

In view of the difficulties of taking the writing in the Ugar. column as "star," Nougayrol, Ug. 5 p. 234 n. 1, suggested a "jeu homophonique" between Akk. *kakkabu* and *kukkubu* "vase," a development that is rather dubious at best. Nevertheless, for Ugar. */kukkubatu/* (a loan from Akk.?; alphab. unattested[13]) elsewhere in Ugarit Akk., cf. probably (pl.) *ku-ku-ba-tu* in PRU 6 158:2,3, an economic text in which several Ugar. words appear (although *ku-ku-ba-tu* may nevertheless be Akk. in that text).

35/36.2

Sign/Akk.: MAL = GÁ = *šakānu* "to place."

Hur.: For *ke-* "to place" (as in imperative *ke=n* corresponding to Akk. *šukun* in the bilingual PRU 3 311f.:1,5), see Wilhelm, Or. 54 492.

Ugar.: */šītu/* = alphab. *št* "to place." The pattern *qīl* for the II-*y* infinitive may be compared with the Hebrew infin. cst. *šît,* and with other *qitl* infinitive/verbal noun forms in these texts: */niǵru/* (no. 159.2), */piṭru/* (194.3), and probably */pirru/* (191.3).

35/36.3

Sign/Akk.: Probably GÁN = IKU = *eqlu* "field" (based on the other columns).

Hur.: *awarre* "(the) field"; see Laroche Ug. 5 450, GLH 65-66. G. Wilhelm, in a private communication, suggests that the double *-rr-* is perhaps caused by stress rather than by the presence of the article.

Ugar.: Restored on the basis of no. 189.2. The writing *ša-du-ú* represents */šadû/* = alphab. *šd* "field"; cf. Hebrew *śāde*. Note the contraction of the final triphthong (< **šadawu*; see Part III, ch. 2 §E 3).

Cf. no. 189.2.

[13]Unless *kknt* "a kind of jar" (KTU 1.6 i 67) is an error for *kkbt*.

35/36.4

Sign/Akk.: MAL = GÁ = *anāku* "I"; restored following the Hur. and Ugar. columns.

Hur.: For *išten* "I," see Laroche Ug. 5 452, GLH 127-28. G. Wilhelm (private communication) notes that *išten* is the absolute form of the pronoun.

Ugar.: /*ʾanākū̆*/ = alphab. *ank* "I."

37.1

Sign/Akk.: EN "lord" = Akk. *šarru* "king" in other lexical texts; see AHw 1189a (*šarru* LL).

Hur.: For *everni* "king" as opposed to *evri* "lord" (see the next entry), with *-ni* as an "individualizing" suffix (not the article; rather, *evrenne* [?] "the king"), see Wilhelm, Or. 54 492.

Ugar.: /*malku*/ = alphab. *mlk* "king."

Cf. no. 188.1.

37.2

Sign/Akk.: EN = *bēlu* "lord."

Hur.: *evri* "lord"; see the Hur. of the preceding entry.

Ugar.: Apparently pl. (of majesty?) /*ba^{c}(a)lūma*/ = alphab. *b^{c}lm*. The writing is ambiguous as to whether /*a*/ followed the /^{c}/; see Part III, ch. 1 §E 4 b (3 a, b ii), ch. 2 §B 1.

Cf. nos. 45.4, 45.5, 63.5, 187.3, 188.2; further, Ug. 5 137 iv b 17 (see the Glossary under B^{c}L).

37.3

Sign/Akk.: Note the following set of correspondences in a lexical text from Ugarit (Diri), RS 22.227B+ i 13ff. (quoted MSL 14 395; reference courtesy P. Steinkeller):

en EN = *e-nu*
en EN = *bé-lu* (cf. the preceding entry [no. 37.2])
ur EN = *SÌ-ir-ru*
ur EN = *a-ra-rù* (cf. no. 37.4 below).

The third of these, despite the unusual incorrect doubling and the use of SUM (*sì*) for *ṣi*$_{x}$, probably represents *ṣīru* "august" (so Civil, MSL 14 395). In our S^{a} Voc.

exemplar here, however, *ṣīru* was, in view of the Hur. and Ugar. columns, apparently misunderstood as *zēru/zīru* "enemy" (cf. also no. 190.5). For the reconstruction [*z*]*é-ru*, which conforms well to the copy, cf. *i-zé-(ʾe-)er* in PRU 3 54ff.:8,12 (legal text).

Hur.: *tor(u)bi* "enemy"; see Laroche, GLH 274; Wilhelm, Or. 54 495.

Ugar.: /*ʾēbu*/ = alphab. *ib* "enemy"; for the form (vs., e.g., Akk. *ayyābu*), we should undoubtedly compare the stative participles of hollow roots in Hebrew, such as *gēr* and *mēt*.[14]

37.4

Sign/Akk.: Cf. the unique equation ur EN = *a-ra-rù* in a Ugarit lexical text, cited above under no. 37.3. The original source of the correspondence is uncertain.[15]

Hur.: *šidarni* "curse" = Akk. *arratu* also in no. 192.2; see Laroche Ug. 5 p. 455, GLH 229.

Ugar.: The writing most likely reflects the root *ṣ-l-y*, probably attested in alphab. in the verb *yṣly* "he curses" (KTU 1.19 i 39), as suggested by Blau-Loewenstamm, Lĕšonénu 35 7-10; Hillers, BASOR 200 18 (others, however, render *yṣly* instead "to entreat pray (for)"; see Dietrich-Loretz-Sanmartín, UF 5 273-74).[16] The text is broken after the PI sign, and so it is not clear whether the word for "curse" here is complete, thus *ṣi-il-yu* = masc. /*ṣilyu*/ or another sign followed, i.e., *ṣi-il-ya-*[*tu*$_4$] = fem. /*ṣilyatu*/. Since *qitl* nouns III-*y* in Ugar. seem generally to lose their *y* (see Part III, ch. 2 §E 2 b), i.e., **qityu* > */*qitû*/, we might expect for a masc. form **ṣilû* rather than /*ṣilyu*/; thus, fem. /*ṣilyatu*/ is the more likely alternative. A possible cognate is Syriac *ᶜelyā* "malice, treachery,"[17] which would point to an original root **ḏ̣-l-y*.

38

Sign/Akk.: IN = *tibnu* "straw."

Hur.: Loan from Akk.; for the Hurrian word for "straw," see Wilhelm, Das Archiv

[14]See Albright, BASOR 89 32 n. 26 (kindly brought to my attention by D. R. Hillers).

[15]Nougayrol, Ug. 5 p. 234 n. 2, suggested EN for ÉN (the latter does not occur in S^a) = *šiptu* "incantation," here transferred to *arāru* "curse."

[16]Note also perhaps *ṣlyh* in a broken context in KTU 1.27:6, for which see Xella, Testi rituali 139-40.

[17]Unless *ᶜelyā* is related to Ethiopic *ᶜalawa* "to pervert, rebel"; but the latter finds a more likely cognate, semantically (though with metathesis of the sonorants), in Syr. *ᶜawlā* and Hebrew *ᶜāwel*/*ᶜawlâ* (once *ᶜalwâ*) "injustice, wrong."

des Šilwa-Teššup 3 93.

Ugar.: */tibnu/* (alphab. unattested); cf. Aramaic *tibnā,* Hebrew *teben.*

39

Sign/Akk.: Undoubtedly URU = *ālu* "town, city," on the basis of the other columns.

Hur.: *arde* "town"; see Laroche Ug. 5 p. 451, GLH 54. As G. Wilhelm points out (private communication), the ending *-na* in the form *ar-de-na* here must, strangely, be the plural article.

Ugar.: */qarītu/* (< **qariytu*) = alphab. *qrt* "town." On the biforms of the word for "town" in NWS, see Part III, ch. 2 §E 1 b.

40.1

Sign/Akk.: Probably EL = SIKIL = *ellu* "pure."

Hur.: *šeḫali* "pure" + adverbial ending *-ae* (vs. no. 174.1 [*ši-ḫ*]*a-al-e*), hence "purely"; see Laroche, Ug. 5 p. 452, 460, GLH 221-23.

Ugar.: Cf. alphab. *sprn ṭhrm* "our documents are 'pure'" (KTU 2.39:33; see Pardee, UF 13 155-56); and *ṭhr* applied to gems (see Blau, IOS 2 77). The form here is probably */ṭuhūru/* < **ṭahūru* (cf. Arabic *ṭahūr,* vs. Hebrew *ṭāhor* < **ṭahur*), with vowel assimilation around the guttural */h/*; see Part III, ch. 2 §A 1 c.

Cf. no. 174.1.

40.2

Sign/Akk.: Perhaps EL = SIKIL = *tēliltu* "purification" or *ebbu* "pure, holy" (see Ugar.); in Ugarit Akk. lexical texts, note NA_4.SIKIL.E.DÈ = *ab-nu ti-lu*(!)*-ti* (var. [*t*]*e-lil-ti*) MSL 10 37ff. A (B) 293 (Ḫḫ XVI); Ú.SIKIL(.E.DÈ) = *te-li*[*l-tu*] MSL 10 107ff. A 89,90 (Ḫḫ XVII).

Ugar.: Nougayrol read : LUGA[L(?)] ? [ ]. The first sign may instead be read RAB, while the second sign conforms to Ú; hence we may propose, with reservation, that the form is */rapʾu/,* a *qatl* noun (or verbal adjective) from the same root as in the *rpum* and Danʾel's epithet *mt rpi* (UT 485 no. 2346), semantically related in some way to Akk. *tēliltu* or *ellu* (cf. also the PN's ^1ÌR-*rap-i* [gen.] PRU 3 145f.:8; ^fDUMU.MÍ-*ra-ap-i* PRU 3 61f.:4,12,14; ^1*rap-a-na* Ug. 5 54:2,18; 5 55:1).

40.3

Sign/Akk.: EL = ?; Nougayrol, Ug. 5 p. 236 n. 1, suggested Sum. EL = IL_5 in the first column, for ÌL = DINGIR = Akk. *ilum*. Alternatively, perhaps the Akk. column had ^{d}[DN].

41.1

Sign/Akk.: IGI = *īnu* "eye"; here perhaps Ass. *ēnu*, or interference from Ugar. /^{c}*ēnu*/ (see under ^{c}YN in the Glossary), although note that the Ugarit Akk. scribes did not distinguish /*i*/ and /*e*/ in Akk. words as consistently as in Ugar. words.

41.2, 41.3

Sign/Akk.: IGI = *pānû* and *maḫrû*, both "former, earlier, first."

41.4

Sign/Akk.: See the Ugar. ☛ p. 383

Ugar.: Although the correspondence IGI = *maḫāru* is not otherwise attested in lexical texts, IGI is occasionally used to write *maḫāru* in other (admittedly late) texts; see CAD M/1 51b. A correspondence Akk. *maḫāru* = Ugar. /*laqāḥu*/ (alphab. *lqḥ*) "to receive" (G infinitive) is at least a possibility.

41.5, 41.6

Sign/Akk.: IGI = *amāru* "to see" in no. 41.5 and, probably, IGI for IGI.GÁL = *dagālu* "to look" in no. 41.6.

43.1

Sign/Akk.: ḪI does not otherwise correspond to *balāṭu* "to live, life," but rather to *balālu* "to mix"; yet Nougayrol's reading *ba-la-ṭu* in Ug. 5 133 i 8' (vs. *ba-la-lu* !) is confirmed by the Ugar. column of UF 11 479:25, which fits most reasonably here. No doubt *ba-la-lu* in some Vorlage was misread *ba-la-ṭu*; the misreading was probably prompted by the close graphic similarity, e.g., in OB script (though not in Ugarit Akk.), of ḪI to DIN, which does correspond to *balāṭu* (P. Steinkeller, oral communication). (As a less likely alternative, we may suggest an equation of the logogram ḪI = TÍ with TI = *balāṭu*; note, however, that ḪI does not have that value, only *ṭí*/*ṭé*, elsewhere in Ugarit Akk.)

Ugar.: For pl. /*ḥiyyūma*/ = alphab. *ḥym* "life"; see Hillers, BASOR 200 18. The form was originally **ḥayyūma* (cf. Hebrew *ḥayyîm,* Aramaic *ḥayyin*); for the raising of **a* to /*i*/ (also pronounced [e]) before /*y*/, see Part III, ch. 2 §A 1 e.

Cf. nos. 50.2, 173.3.

43.2

Sign/Akk.: ḪI = DÙG = *ṭābu* "sweet, fine."

Ugar.: /*ṭābu*/ = alphab. *ṭb* "good, choice, sweet."

44.1

Sign/Akk.: KAM = UDUL$_2$ = *diqāru* "bowl."

Ugar.: The apparent Ugar. relative of Akk. *diqāru* occurs as alphab. (pl.) *dkrt* (KTU 1.4 vi 54) and perhaps *dkrm* (KTU 1.43:19); see Dietrich-Loretz, OLZ 62 538. Thus, despite the use of the QA sign here, we should probably normalize /*dikāru*/ (i.e., *di*-[*k*]*a*$_4$-*ru*).[18] It is not possible to ascertain whether Ugar. /*dikāru*/ reflects a loan of Akk. *diqāru* (with *k* < *q* as partial assimilation to the preceding non-emphatic *d*?), or both the Ugar. and the Akk. reflect early loans from a third, unknown language.[19]

44.2

Sign/Akk.: KAM = *erēšu, erištu*; here, = *mēreltu* "wish, desire" (cf. Amarna ŠU.KAM.MA/MI = *erištu*/*mēreštu*; see Moran, JCS 31 247-48).

Ugar.: /*ʾirištu*/ = alphab. *iršt* "request"; formally a fem. verbal adj. ("thing desired") < **ʾarištu* (like Hebrew *ʾărešet*), with assimilation of the unstressed **a* after initial /*ʾ*/ to the following stressed /*i*/ (see Part III, ch. 2 §A 1 d).

45.1

Sign/Akk.: AN = *šamû* "sky."

[18]For QA with the value *ka*$_4$ in other syllabic transcriptions of Ugar. forms, see Part III, ch. 1 §E 1 b (under /*kă*/).

[19]Hurrian influence as the intermediary of Akk. *diqāru* to Ugar. *dkr,* suggested by Dietrich-Loretz, ibid., is unlikely, for we should then expect alphab. **dgr* (i.e., the voiced velar intervocalically).

Hur.: In view of the long-standing assumption that *ḫavurni* meant "earth" and *eže* "sky" in Hurrian (see GLH 99, 83-84, respectively), Laroche in UF 11 479 naturally expressed surprise at the equation of *ḫavurni* and Ugar. /*šamûma*/ "sky." But G. Wilhelm reports, in a private communication, that according to E. Neu in a forthcoming publication ("Hurriter und Hurritisch"), the equation is correct, i.e., that *ḫavurni* is "sky" and *eže* "earth." Thus, we may also restore [*ḫa-bur*]-*ni* in the Hur. column of no. 198.6 below.

Ugar.: The signs conform only marginally to /*šamûma*/ = alphab. *šmm* "sky"; on the form, < **šamayūma,* see Part III, ch. 2 §E 3. p. 383

Cf. no. 198.6; further, Ug. 5 137 iii 33" (see the Glossary under ŠMY).

45.2 p. 383

Sign/Akk.: Nougayrol suggested that the equation is either AN for EN = *ēnu* (priest), or AN = *e-nu* for *a*!-*nu* (the sky god); cf. other examples of *e* for *a* in the Akk. column of the Ugarit S^a Voc., in nos. 145, 186.1, 193.1, below.

This entry is missing in UF 11 479.

45.3 p. 383

Sign/Akk.: AN = DINGIR = *ilu* "god."

Hur.: *eni* "god"; see Laroche, GLH 80-82.

Ugar.: There are traces of a sign, possibly LU, after I on the photograph in UF 11 480; thus, ⌜*i-lu*⌝ for /*ʾilu*/ = alphab. *il* "god, El."

Cf. no. 198.2; further, Ug. 5 137 iii 35" (see the Glossary under ʾL).

45.4, 45.5 p. 384

Sign/Akk.: For AN = DINGIR = *šarru* "king" in lexical texts, see AHw 1189a (s.v. *šarru,* LL); in no. 45.5, the Akk. column curiously has the pl. *šarrānū* "kings" (cf. LUGAL.E.NE = *šar-ra-nu* in MSL 12 95:74 [Lú], but there the Sum. is also pl.).

Hur.: The meanings of *tani* and *ziyani,* neither of which is expected here, are unclear; see Laroche, UF 11 479.

Ugar.: Laroche reads *ma-a-*[*al-ku*??] in these lines, but an extra vowel sign for a short vowel would be exceptional. More likely, the first sign in each line is BA, and we should read in 45.4 sg. *ba-a-*[*lu*] for /*baʿlu*/, in 45.5 pl. *ba-a-*[*lu-ma*] for /*baʿ(a)lūma*/ = alphab. *bʿl(m)* "lord(s)." (Note, however, that in the photo, UF 11

480, the first sign of no. 45.4 looks more like UR than either MA or BA.)

Cf. nos. 37.2, 63.5, 187.3, 188.2; further, Ug. 5 137 iv b 17 (see the Glossary under BᶜL).

☛ p. 384

46.1

Sign/Akk.: ḪAL = *ḫallu* "crotch."

46.2

Sign/Akk.: See on the Ugar. column.

Hur.: The meaning of *purudani* is unknown; see the commentary on the Ugar. column.

Ugar.: Laroche transliterates only *pu-ru-*[; on the photo, however, there appear to be traces of a sign after *ru,* possibly ZA. Perhaps, therefore, a form of a root *p-r-s* "to divide" is intended, i.e., */pur(r)ŭ̄satu/* or */purussatu/,* meaning "share, division," corresponding to ḪAL = *zâzu* (cf. *zittu* "share"); cf. alphab. *prs,* a fractional measure, and perhaps *šmn prst* in KTU 1.22 ii 15, for which see Caquot-Sznycer-Herdner, Textes ougaritiques 472 n. g; Hebrew *pāras*. Alternatively, perhaps the Ugar. should be reconstructed after the Hur. column.

47.1

Sign/Akk.: See the discussion of the Ugar.

Hur.: *irw/bi* (*irvi*), meaning unknown; see Laroche, GLH 125.

Ugar.: Probably for */kabidu/* = alphab. *kbd* "liver" (cf. Hebrew *kābēd*), corresponding to UR for UR_5 = Akk. *kabattu;* note UR_5 = *ka-bat-tú* in MSL 3 52:12' (S^a Voc.), and that both UR_5 and UR appear in lexical texts for *mitḫāru* (see no. 47.3 below). (A factor against this proposal, it must be admitted, is that Hur. for "liver" is apparently *nibašuri,* not *irvi;* see Laroche, GLH 182.)

Alternatively, UR for UR.SAG = *qar(rā)du* "warrior, hero" = Ugar. */kabidu/* "honored"?

Still another possibility is [UR] = Akk. [*kalbu*] = Ugar. *ka-a*[*l* ?-*bu* ?] "dog"; but the second sign of the Ugar. form seems to be BI, not AL.

47.2

Sign/Akk.: Perhaps UR = TÉŠ = *bâšu* "to come to shame." Note that TÉŠ = *bâšu* in PN's; alternatively, UR for UR$_5$ (as in no. 47.1, preceding entry) = *bâšu* as in the lexical text A v/2:201 (cited CAD B 5b). In Nougayrol's copy, it should be noted, the only sign preserved in the Akk. column resembles KU more than BA; but cf. the copy in UF 11 478.

Ugar.: With some hesitation, we may posit, corresponding to Akk. *bâšu* "to come to shame," /*ḫēbu*/, a *qatl* noun meaning "guilt, shame" (alphab. unattested; cf., e.g., the Aramaic adj. *ḥayyāb*, Arabic *ḫ-w-b*). Note that the Ugar. form is probably not an infinitive, since the Hur. form is not. (A less likely normalization of the Ugar. form is /*ḫību*/, i.e., a *qīl* noun or adj.; see the discussion of /*ĭ*/ and /*ē*/ in Part III, ch. 1 §G 2.)

47.3

p. 384

Sign/Akk.: UR = TÉŠ(.BI) = *mitḫāru* "equal, corresponding" (note also ur UR$_5$ = *mit-ḫa-ru* in MSL 3 51:8'a [S^a Voc.]) and *mitḫāriš* "equally, likewise, to the same extent, everywhere" (note, e.g., both UR$_5^{ur}$.BI and [UR(TÉŠ)]$^{te\text{-}eš}$.BI = *mitḫāriš* in MSL 1 78:62,63 [Ai]).

Ugar.: Probably the preposition /*bi-*/ (corresponding to the Akk. *-iš*) with an unidentified noun /*ru...*/ or /*šub/p...*/,/*θub/p...*/. For /*bi-*/, see also no. 32.6, and in the Glossary under B.

48.1

Sign/Akk.: NE = IZI = *išātu* "fire."

Ugar.: The writing ⌜*i*⌝-*ši-t*[*u*$_4$] apparently reflects alphab. *išt* "fire"; the vowel of the second syllable is difficult to explain in view of Akk. *išātu*, Eblaite ^{d}GIBIL/IZI = *ì-sa-du* (MEE 4 287 no. 783), Ethiopic *ʾesāt*, Syriac *ʾeššātā*. A development from a III-y root, i.e., **ʾišyatu*, seems unlikely, especially if "curse" is /*ṣilyatu*/ (see no. 37.4 above), and the writing *iš-ia-ti-mi* in Ug. 5 84:10 is correctly interpreted as a syllabic spelling of a Ugar. dual form /*ʿišyatēmi*/ "clamps" (see the Glossary under ʿŠY). Further, the PS form of "fire" was almost certainly biradical **ʾiš* (the double *-šš-* of Aramaic and of Hebrew *ʾiššô* being secondary); see Blau, IOS 2 62-65. It might be proposed that an original form **ʾišātu* developed into /*ʾišītu*/ via a sound rule, but no other evidence supports the existence of such a rule. Thus, perhaps the form must be interpreted as /*ʾišītu*/, i.e., the PS base **ʾiš* plus an (abstract?) ending **-īt* (see Barth, Nominalbildung 401-5, §§250-53).

☛ p. 384

48.2

Sign/Akk.: If the assignment of Ug. 5 131 lines 3' and 5' to nos. 47 (UR, see 47.2 above) and 49 (GIBIL, see below) is correct, then presumably line 4' contained no. 48, the NE sign, which has to do with fire, burning, heat, ashes, kilns, boiling, among other values.

Hur.: It is unclear whether a sign preceded *p*]*í-ir-ri*; meaning uncertain.

Ugar.: The reading *ir-KU* seems certain; thus, the form is a *qitl* noun, but none of the possible roots, viz., *ʾ/h/ʿ-r-k/q* (less likely, *-g*), furnishes a meaning corresponding to the presumed NE sign of the first column.

☛ p. 384

49.1

Sign/Akk.: If the interpretation of the Ugar. column is correct, we may reconstruct GIBIL = BÍL, for BÌL (giš + gibil) = Akk. *perʾu* "shoot, sprout, scion, descendant"; see MSL 5 114:266 (and note to 266 [Ḫḫ]); AHw 856a.

Hur.: Apparently unattested otherwise, if the reading is correct; *ḫešši/ḫišši* is not listed by Laroche in GLH.

Ugar.: Nougayrol translated "rejeton?," presumably thinking of alphab. *šp̣ḥ* "scion." This receives confirmation now from the placement of Ug. 5 131 as nos. 46-53/54 of the Sª Voc.; see above on the Sign/Akk.

50.1

Sign/Akk.: KA = ZÚ = *šinnu* "tooth."

☛ p. 385

50.2??

Sign/Akk.: It is difficult to connect any of the values of KA (or of no. 51 SAG) with the meaning "life" of the Hur. and Ugar. columns.

Hur.: *šuḫur(i)-ni* "life"; see Laroche, Ug. 5 p. 456-57, GLH 240.

Ugar.: */ḥiyyūma/*; see no. 43.1 above.

Cf. nos. 43.1, 173.3.

51.1

Sign/Akk.: SAG for SAG.DU = *qaqqadu* "head"; see CAD Q 100 for SAG (as opposed to SAG.DU) = *qaqqadu,* and note that SAG and SAG.DU tend to be used interchangeably in Ugarit Akk.[20]

Hur.: Restore probably *pa-[(a-)ḫi]* = *paḫi* (*paǵi*) "head," with Laroche, GLH 192-93.

51.2?

Sign/Akk.: For SAG = *amīlu,* see CAD A/2 48-49.

Hur., Ugar.: Cf. nos. 24.2, 25.5.

52

Sign/Akk.: ŠÚR = *ezzu* "furious."

This entry is missing in Ug. 5 131, as in the S^a in Ug. 5 113.

53.1

Sign/Akk.: DU (= GIN) = *alāku* "to go."

Hur.: Cf. perhaps the verbal stem *uššu-*, cited in Laroche, GLH 290. A connection between *ušš-* and the stem *un-* "to come" is suggested by Haas-Thiel in Die Beschwörungsrituale 310.

53.2

Sign/Akk.: DU = GUB = *izuzzu* "to stand," here erroneously *izzizu.*

53.3

Sign/Akk.: DU = GIN = *kīnu* (Assyrian *kēnu*) "true, just"; the writing of the Akk. here is curious: either *ken*^{en}*-nu* (although the value *kin/ken* is very rare at Ugarit) or *ke*$_x$*-en-nu* (but KIN for *ki*$_x$ is otherwise unattested in Ugarit Akk.).

Hur.: Note *muš(u)* (*muž-*) "just" in Laroche, GLH 173.

[20]E.g., the town *riš* in alphab. texts appears as ^{uru}SAG.DU (PRU 3 85f.:8; PRU 6 28:4,5; Ug. 7 pl. 13:48; and often), but the genitilic (alphab. *rišy*) is written ^{uru}SAG-*yu* (PRU 6 79:12,14); the month name *riš yn* appears as ITI SAG-GEŠTIN^{meš} (PRU 6 107:11) and ITI SAG.DU-GEŠTIN^{meš} (Ug. 5 99:13).

☛ p. 385

53.4/54

Sign/Akk.: We may posit either no. 53 DU (as a variant of SUḪUŠ) = *išdu* "foundation, base, lower extremities" (cf. CH r. xxvii 24), in which case no. 54 SUḪUŠ would be lacking in Ug. 5 131 (as in Ug. 5 135); or no. 54 SUḪUŠ = *išdu,* in which case no. 53 DU as well as no. 52 ŠÚR would be lacking in Ug. 5 131.

Ugar.: */ʾišdu/* = alphab. *išd* "leg, lower extremities."

55

Sign/Akk.: KAŠ$_4$ = *lasāmu* "to run." For *lasāmu,* cf. also no. 183.2.

56

Sign/Akk.: The I sign is apparently for I$_7$ (ÍD) = *nāru* "river."

56a

Sign/Akk.: IA is equated with Akk. *maṣṣartu* "garrison" only here. On the inclusion of IA in S^a, cf. MSL 3 22:120; Ug. 5 113 ii 10; and see Nougayrol's comments, Ug. 5 p. 238 n. 3.

57.1, 57.2

Sign/Akk.: ŠU = *qātu* "hand" and *gimillu* "favor."

58

Sign/Akk.: ŠÀ (ŠAG$_4$) = *libbu* "heart."

59

Sign/Akk.: ŠA = NA$_5$ = *pitnu* "box, case."

60

Sign/Akk.: Nougayrol read the sign in the first column as ÚḪ, but elsewhere in

Ugarit Akk. ÚḪ is replaced by ÙḪ;[21] the copy permits either reading; = Akk. *ruʾtu* "saliva, splittle."

61.1

Sign/Akk.: AŠ = *it-te-tù,* apparently for the (phonologically curious) MB and peripheral form *ittēltu* "once," found elsewhere at Ugarit in PRU 3 166f.:14; perhaps the form is the result of a scribal error: *it-te<-el>-tù*. The equation is unique (but note AŠ = *ištēn* "one").

Ugar.: /*ʾaḥadu*/ = alphab. *aḥd* "one"; cf. Arabic *ʾaḥad,* Ethiopic *ʾaḥadu,* Aramaic *ḥad* < **ʾaḥad*; a normalization /*ʾaḥḥadu*/ (cf. Hebrew *ʾeḥād* < **ʾaḥḥad-*) is also possible, but orthographically less likely.[22] For the reading, see Borger, RA 63 172, who suggested with equal plausibility that the Ugar. form corresponded with the following entry (Akk. *ēdēnu* "unique").

61.2

Sign/Akk.: AŠ (= DIL) = *ēdēnu* "aloneness, lone person" (cf. AŠ/DIL = *ēdēnû* "single, alone, unique").

(Ugar.: See the preceding entry.)

(**62** ERIN$_2$ follows no. 63, as in the Ugarit S^a texts Ug. 5 112, 113, 114.)

63.1

Sign/Akk.: UD/U$_4$ = *ūmu* "day."

Ugar.: Cf. alphab. *ym* "day." Probably to be read *yu-mu,* for /*yōmu*/ (cf. Hebrew *yôm,* Syriac *yawmā,* Arabic *yawm*). Less likely is *ya-mu* for /*yămu*/ (cf. Hebrew pl. *yāmîm*); see Hillers, BASOR 200 18.

[21] See no. 562 of the signlist in my forthcoming Akkadian of Ugarit.

[22] Although the first sign is broken, there is room only for A, not for AḪ. Double consonants are often written singly in the syllabic transcriptions, as is generally true in Akk. texts (see Part III, ch. 1 §D 1), but an initial *v* sign where *vC* is possible is not common.

63.2

Sign/Akk.: Restore UD = UTU = *šamšu* "sun" or *Šamaš* (the sun god), based on the Ugar. column.

Ugar.: /*šapšu*/ = alphab. *špš* "sun (god)."

63.3

Sign/Akk.: UD = BABBAR = *peṣû* "white," here incorrectly *peṣṣu* (cf., in other Ugarit Akk. lexical texts: *pé-ṣú* MSL 10 107ff.:178 [Ḫḫ XVII]; *pé-SU* MSL 10 37ff. A 152 [Ḫḫ XVI]; but correctly *pé-ṣu-ú* MSL 11 74f.:10 [Ḫḫ XXIII]).

Ugar.: /*labanu*/ = alphab. *lbn* "white" (cf., e.g., Hebrew *lābān*).

☛ p. 385

63.4

Sign/Akk.: See the discussion of the Ugar.

Ugar.: Probably for /*hallinīya*/ = alphab. *hlny* "here, now then," if the Sum. sign is UD, for UD-*ma*; the latter is used to write Akk. *anumma* "now (then), here" in a few texts from Ḫattusas found at Ras Shamra (but not in any texts known to be written at Ugarit; see CAD A/2 148a); note also UD = Akk. *i*/*enūma*, and that *enūma* in Ugarit Akkadian appears to be used adverbially on occasion (e.g., PRU 6 8:7; Ug. 5 28:10), as elsewhere in peripheral Akk. (see CAD I/J 158-59; Moran Or. 29 17 n. 1). On the correspondence of alphab. *hlny* (and *hnny*) to Akk. *anumma*/*enūma* in letters at Ras Shamra, see also Loewenstamm, UF 5 210-11. The vowel of the second syllable of /*hallinīya*/ is apparently short, since the form did not undergo the vowel harmony rule discussed in Part III, ch. 2 §A 1 b.

63.5?

Sign/Akk.: See the Ugar. column.

Ugar.: The reading of the first sign is uncertain; Nougayrol read [*m*]*a*(?)-*a-lu*, but [*b*]*a-a-lu* is also possible. Perhaps, therefore, the line is to be reconstructed as [UD] (= ZALAG) = [*bēlu*] = Ugar. /*ba*^{c}*lu*/ "lord." For the equation, cf. [za-la-ag] [UD] = [*be-lu*] = Hittite EN-*aš*, in a Boğazköy fragment of the S^a Voc., MSL 3 61:4.

Cf. nos. 37.2, 47.4, 47.5, 187.3, 188.2; further, Ug. 5 137 iv b 17 (see the Glossary under B^{c}L).

63.6?

Sign/Akk.: See Ugar. p. 385

Ugar.: Following Nougayrol in reading the first sign as ZU. If the form is read correctly, perhaps it represents a D verb */zuttaru/* = alphab. *ztr* (?) (KTU 1.17 i 28, ii 17), which Aistleitner, Wörterbuch 98 no. 890, glossed "heraus, ausgehen" (though without citing cognates); if that is correct then perhaps the Sum. is UD for ud+du = È = Akk. *(w)aṣû* "to go out." But the meaning of *ztr* is by no means firmly established; see, e.g., Caquot-Sznycer-Herdner, Textes ougaritiques 421 n. n. Further, an intransitive D verb would be somewhat unusual.

62.1

Sign/Akk.: $ERIN_2$ = $ZALAG_2$ = *namru* "bright, shining."

62.2

Sign/Akk.: $ERIN_2$ = *ṣābu* "troop, gang, army."

64

Sign/Akk.: Probably AD = *abu* "father."

142

Sign/Akk.: Probably [LÁL] for LAL = *maṭû* "to diminish, lessen" (so Nougayrol); cf. MSL 3 70:16' (S^a Voc.), and, in a Ugarit lexical text, LAL.LAL = *ma-ṭu-ú* (Nougayrol, AS 16 33ff. C 1 [Silbenvokabular A]).

143

Sign/Akk.: [LÀL] = *dišpu* "honey."

Hur.: See below, on no. 148.

145?

Sign/Akk.: Nougayrol, Ug. 5 p. 238 n. 5, suggested UŠ (S^a no. 147) = a form of *redû*; but no *mapras* form of *redû* is attested, and so in CAD M/2 106b this form is listed as a hapax. Undoubtedly we should understand S^a no.145 ZÉ (ṢI) = *mertu* for *martu* "gall bladder"; the biform *mertu,* likewise written *me-er-tù,* also appears in a lexical text from Boğazköy, KBo 1 51 ii 12 (cited CAD M/1 297a, *martu* lex.). Note *e* for expected *a* in the Akk. column of the Ugarit Sa Voc. exemplars also in *šeḫû* (no. 186.1) and *šeqû* (193.1).

Hur.: The word for "gall bladder" seems not to appear in Laroche, GLH. It is written ZÉ-*ni* in Hurrian omen texts from Boğazköy (e.g., KBo 27 204), as kindly pointed out to me by G. Wilhelm.

147

Sign/Akk.: UŠ = NITA = *zik(a)ru* "male."

Hur.: For *turuḫḫi* "male," see Laroche, GLH 274.

Cf. no. 195.2.

148

Sign/Akk.: $KUŠ_6/KU_7$ = *matqu* "sweet."

Hur.: *ni*?-*šu*?-[; compare *ni*?-[as the beginning of the gloss of LÀL = *dišpu* "honey" in no. 143?

149

Sign/Akk.: SUM = *nadānu* "to give."

Hur.: *ar*- "to give" + *umme* (infinitival ending); see Laroche Ug. 5 p. 448-49, GLH 52-53; further, G. Wilhelm, Or. 54 490.

149a

Sign/Akk.: NAGA (sum + ir) = *uḫūlu* (an alkaline plant); the writing here with -*n*- instead of -*l*- appears to be unique (cf. AHw 1404-5).

Hur.: *uḫḫurri* occurs only here (not listed in Laroche, GLH); apparently a loan from Akk., with *l*/*n* > *r*.

150.1

Sign/Akk.: KID = *kītu* "reed mat."

Hur.: Reading uncertain.

150.2

Sign/Akk.: KID = LÍL = *zīqīqu*/*zāqīqu* "phantom, wind."

151.1

Sign/Akk.: The equation DAG = BARA(G)$_2$ (PÀR) = *šaddu* "extended" is unique, although the sign is equated with the infinitive *šadādu* in MSL 13 142:298 [Izi], from Boğazköy. (See further PSD B 146-47; Steinkeller, ZA 75 44-46.)

151.2

Sign/Akk.: Apparently DAG for ZAG by phonetic confusion (Nougayrol, Ug. 5 p. 241 n. 3) = *pāṭu* "border, boundary" (here with double *-ṭṭ-*, as in *pát-ṭù* MSL 3 85:9 [S^a Voc. from Boğazköy]).

151.3

Sign/Akk.: Probably DAG mistakenly for KISAL by graphic confusion, according to P. Steinkeller (private communication; see his recent comments in ZA 75 44-46). Less likely is Nougayrol's suggestion, Ug. 5 241 n. 3, that DAG is for KIB (also due to graphic confusion). For KISAL and KIB = *puḫru* "assembly," see AHw 876b (*puḫru,* lex.); KISAL probably occurs three lines later in the same text (Ug. 5 137 i 7), as no. 154.

152

Sign/Akk.: E = *iku* "dike."

Hur.: Nougayrol read the first sign as [*r*]*i* (?), but that seems unlikely, unless *tal* is intended, since words do not begin with *r* in Hurrian. Note E = (Hur.) *te-ma-ri* in Syria 12 236ff. iii 17, a lexical text from Ugarit.

153

Sign/Akk.: É = *bītu* "house."

Hur.: Nougayrol read *še*(?)-?-?, but the copy permits ⌜*pu-ur-li*⌝; for *purli* (def. *purulle*) "house," see Laroche, GLH 206-7.

154

Sign/Akk.: KISAL = *kisallu* "courtyard." See also no. 151.3, above, where DAG was misread as KISAL.

☛ p. 385

156

Sign/Akk.: AR is equated with *namāru* "to shine" in only one other text (see CAD N/1 210a).

Hur.: Cf. probably *ḫešmi* "clear, shining," for which see Laroche, GLH 103.

157

Sign/Akk.: MUŠ = *ṣīru* "snake."

Ugar.: */tunnanu/* = alphab. *tnn* "serpent, dragon" (vs. Hebrew, Syriac, Arabic *tannīn*). Formally the word is probably a D verbal adjective in origin, although the etymology remains obscure.

☛ p. 385

158.1

Sign/Akk.: ÚR = *sūnu* "lap, bosom."

Ugar.: */ḥēqu/* < **ḥayqu* (alphab. unattested) "bosom"; cf. Hebrew *ḥêq*. The initial radical is probably *ḥ* rather than *ḫ* in view of Arabic *ḥāqa* "to surround, embrace," Ethiopic *ḥayq*, and OSA *ḥyqn* "cove" (Biella, Dictionary 174-75).

☛ p. 386

158.2

Sign/Akk.: If the Akk. here is indeed *na-ṣa-ru*, then ÚR = URU$_8$ for expected URU$_3$ (ŠEŠ, cf. no. 159.2, below) = *naṣāru* (Nougayrol).

☛ p. 386

158.3

Sign/Akk.: ÚR = *pēm/nu* "foot, leg."

Hur.: Laroche, GLH, lists no lexemes beginning *ib/p/w* or *eb/p/w* with an appropriate meaning. Hur. "foot" is *ugri*; see ibid. 277.

Ugar.: */riglu/* "foot"; cf. Syriac *reglā*, Arabic *rijl*, Babylonian Hebrew *rigl-* (and Hexaplaric *regl-*; vs. Tiberian Hebrew *regel/ragl-*). Alphab. **rgl* is unattested; instead, only *p*ᶜ*n* occurs for "foot" (UT 469b no. 2076; cf. the Akk. column).

159.1

Sign/Akk.: ŠEŠ = *aḫu* "brother."

Hur.: For *šena* (*šēna*) "brother," see, in addition to Laroche, Ug. 5 p. 449, GLH 225-26 (*šeni*), the comments of Wilhelm, Or. 54 487-88, 494.

159.2

Sign/Akk.: ŠEŠ = URU$_3$ = *naṣāru* "to guard."

Ugar.: /*niǵru*/ = alphab. *nǵr*. The *qitl* form here is a G infinitive/verbal noun corresponding to the Akk. infinitive. For similar forms, see also nos. 35/36.2, 191.3, and 194.2.

Cf. no. 158.2.

159.3

Sign/Akk.: ŠEŠ/URU$_3$ = *marāru* "to be bitter."

160.1

p. 386

Sign/Akk.: Perhaps IB = DARA$_2$ = *ulāpu* "bandage," as suggested by von Soden, AHw 1408a. The copy does not conform well to Nougayrol's suggestion that the Akk. here is the sign name *ú-r*[*a-šu*] (see MSL 3 34:296 [S^a]).

160.3?

Sign/Akk.: See Ugar.

Ugar.: A very tentative suggestion, restoring *ḫe*?-*e*[-*ru*] for /*ḥēru*/ < **ḥayru* (alphab. unattested); cf. Arabic *ḥayr* "enclosure"; for the first two columns, we may suggest perhaps IB = *nēbettu* "belt."

160.4

Sign/Akk.: See the Ugar. column discussion.

Ugar.: We may perhaps restore *pí-i-*[*tu* $_4$], for /*piʾtu*/ = alphab. *pit* (pl. *pat*) "corner, edge" (cf. Hebrew *pē*ʾ*â*),[23] corresponding to IB = *tubuqtu* "corner" (see, e.g., MSL 3 144:219 [S^b Voc.]). For the use of the I sign to represent syllable-final /*i*ʾ/, see Part III, ch. 1 §E 4 b (3 b ii).

173.1

Sign/Akk.: Perhaps BAD = BE = *pé*-[*tu-ú*] "to open" (Nougayrol); but see also no. 173.4 below.

173.3

Sign/Akk.: BAD = TIL for TI(.LA) = *balāṭu* "life"; the use of TIL for TI is found elsewhere in Ugarit Akkadian (e.g., PRU 3 93b:11), and in peripheral Akk. generally. In Ug. 5 137 i 20" the writing TIL-*la-ṭu* (or TIL.LA-*ṭu*) is the only example in the Ugarit S^a Voc. exemplars of a logogram used to write (part of) a word in the Akk. column (but cf. DINGIR-*lu*$_4$ in the *Ugar.* column of no. 198.2), unless we are to read *be-la-ṭu* (cf. *e* for *a* in the Akk. of nos. 145, 186.1, 193.1), though that seems unlikely.

Hur., Ugar.: Cf. nos. 43.1, 50.2.

☛ p. 386

173.4

Sign/Akk.: *katāmu* "to cover" (no other reading seems possible) is not equated with BAD elsewhere. Thus, Nougayrol suggested, Ug. 5 p. 240 n. 4, that BAD = TIL was interpreted here as TÍL = DUL = *katāmu*; yet DUL does not appear to have the value *tíl*, only *dul*, in lexical texts, and so we would have to assume TIL for *dul*$_x$. Alternatively, perhaps we should compare BAD = ÚŠ, in [úš] = [BAD] = *pe-ḫu-u ša* DUG "to plug a pot" (Nougayrol, ibid.; see CAD K 219b), transferred here to *katāmu* (?).

Ugar.: Nougayrol suggested [*ku-u*]*s*(?)-*sú*, i.e., a D infinitive /*kussû*/ (< **kussawu*); cf. alphab. *mks* "covering," *kst* "garment," Hebrew D *kissâ* and Syriac D *kassi* (as well as G *ksā*) "to cover." This is difficult, however. While the final triphthong of **kussawu* may well have collapsed, the resulting long vowel would normally be

[23]The sg. also occurs as *pat* = /*pi*ʾ*atu*/ as, e.g., in KTU 4.136:4 (*pat aḥt*), where it probably means "demarcation" (or sim.); see Aistleitner, Wörterbuch 252, no. 2181; Dietrich-Loretz-Sanmartín, UF 5 99.

written with an extra vowel-sign (i.e., **ku-us-sú-ú*; cf. *ša-du-ú* in no. 189.2).[24] A more serious objection is that there is not enough room for [*ku*] at the beginning of the form; on the copy, Nougayrol's *u*]*s* (?) begins immediately below the first sign of the Ugar. column in the preceding line. Thus, we must read either [*I*]*i-ZU* or [*U*]*Z-ZU* for this Ugar. word. Unfortunately, neither reading suggests a Ugar. form with a meaning corresponding to Akk. *katāmu* (or to BAD, for that matter). [*I*]*i-ZU* would reflect a *qitl* infinitive/verbal noun of either a hollow root (*qīl*; cf. /*šītu*/ in no. 35/36.2 above) or a geminate root (*qill*; cf. /*pirru*/ in no. 191.3 below); [*U*]*Z-ZU* would be a *qutl* (*qull*) noun (thus, less likely than [*I*]*i-ZU*, given the infinitive in the Akk. column) of a geminate root, *ʾ/h/ʿ-ð/z/ẓ/s/ṣ*.

173.5

Sign/Akk.: BAD = TIL = *gamāru* "to end, finish."

173.6

Sign/Akk.: Probably BAD = TIL = *labiru, labāru* "(to become) old."

173.7

Sign/Akk.: BAD = ÚŠ/UG$_7$ = *mūtu* "death."

173.8

Sign/Akk.: BAD = ÚŠ = *damu* "blood."

173.9

Sign/Akk.: Perhaps BAD = ÚŠ = *šerʾānu* "ligament"; otherwise unattested, but cf. ÚŠ = *ušultu* "vein" (Nougayrol, Ug. 5 p. 242 n. 1).

173.x?

There is room for this additional line at the bottom of column i in Ug. 5 137.

[24]See Part III, ch. 1 §F 1 a, ch. 2 §E 3.

174.1

Sign/Akk.: KUG/KÙ probably corresponding to *ellu* "pure," in view of the Hur. and Ugar. columns.

Hur., Ugar.: Cf. no. 40.1.

174.2, 174a

Sign/Akk.: KUG/KÙ and KÙ.BABBAR = *kaspu* "silver."

Hur.: For *ušḫuni* "silver," see Laroche, GLH 289.

Ugar.: */kaspu/* = alphab. *ksp* "silver"; note the curious change of spelling from one line to the next in Ug. 5 137 ii: *kàs-pu* in line 2, but *ka-as-pu* in line 3.

174b

Sign/Akk.: kug + gi = GUŠKIN = *ḫurāṣu* "gold."

Ugar.: Quite probably for */ḫurāṣu/* = alphab. *ḫrṣ* "gold" (cf. Akk., vs. Hebrew *ḥārûṣ*).

175

Sign/Akk.: Expected for no. 175 is GIŠIMMAR = *gišimmaru*, which we may restore here.

Ugar.: Perhaps */tamaru/* "date palm" (alphab. unattested), as suggested by Nougayrol; cf. Hebrew *tāmār*, Ethiopic *tamart* (but note also Arabic and Ethiopic *tamr* "dates").

176-178. Nougayrol placed the small fragment of Ug. 5 137 containing the Sumerian of these entries one or two lines too high; see below, at no. 177.2. The first UN (KALAM) sign should be lined up at Ug. 5 137 ii 9' (so in the synopsis of entries above) or 10', rather than at line 8' (Nougayrol).

176.x

Sign/Akk.: Most likely TUR, which has the meanings "small, few; child, infant; servant"; or TUR = DUMU, meaning "child, son, heir."

176.y

p. 386

Sign/Akk.: Cf. no. 176.x, preceding; if the Hur. and Ugar. columns here are interpreted correctly, perhaps here DUMU = *šerru* "child" (but see Hur.) or TUR = *ṣeḫru* "small, young."

Hur.: It is possible to read the signs here *zu-ki*; cf., in a Ugarit lexical text, K[I.LAM.TUR].RA = (Hur.) MIN (= *maḫiri*) *zu-gi,* Syria 12 236ff. ii 19 (= MSL 5 61:131 [Ḫḫ II]: Akk. MIN (= *maḫīru*) *ṣa-aḫ-ri* "low rate of exchange"); see Laroche, GLH 306. As G. Wilhelm notes (private communication), *putki,* not *zugi,* is expected as the Hur. equivalent of DUMU "son."

Ugar.: As a possibility, at least, we may suggest that this column contained */yaldu/* = alphab. *yld* or */waladu/* = alphab. *wld* [25] "child" (cf. in Hebrew both *yeled* and *wālād*; the variation in pattern is also evidenced in Arabic *walad* vs. Ethiopic *wald*). For PI = *yv* at the beginning of a word, cf. *yu-mu* in no. 63.1 above; see further Part III, ch. 1 §E 3 c.

177.1

p. 386

Sign/Akk.: UN (= UKU$_3$) = *nišū* "people" (cf. the Ugar. column).

Hur.: Unclear; the use of the ʾ sign in a Hurrian word is strange.

Ugar.: The traces allow us to restore *na-šu-ma,* for */našūma/* = alphab. *nšm* "men, people" (cf. Akk. *nišū*; vs. Hebrew *nāšîm,* Aramaic *nəšin* "women").

177.2

p. 386

Sign/Akk.: Depending on the placement of the small fragment containing the Sum. signs for this line and the preceding and following one or two lines, the sign corresponding to the Hur. [*u*]-*mi-in*$_4$-*ni* and Ugar. [*ḫ*]*u-wa-tu*$_4$ is either UN (= KALAM) or GÚ, both of which are equated with *mātu* "country"; cf. the S^a Voc. for nos. 177, 178 in MSL 3 p. 77:

line 25'	KALAM.MA	= *ma-a-*[*tu*]
line 26'	gu-u GÚ	= "

Hur.: See Laroche, GLH 281-82, for *omini* (*umini*) "country," *ominne* "the country."

Ugar.: The writing [*ḫ*]*u-wa-tu*$_4$ undoubtedly reflects */ḥuwwatu/* = alphab. *ḥwt* "land,

[25] See, e.g., Gordon, UT 392b no. 803. There is, however, considerable disagreement on the interpretation of *wld*; see Tsumura, UF 11 779-82.

country" (UT 395b no. 850); cf. Caquot, Ug. 7 121-134 passim, especially p. 124 n. 4, where *ḥwt* is compared with this line.[26] That alphab. *ḥwt* is normally singular (vs. the pl. Hebrew cognate *ḥawwôt* "tent-village") is shown by the phrase *ḥwt hyt* "that/said land" in omens (KTU 1.103:55,56), where *hyt* is the fem. sg. oblique of the anaphoric pronoun (cf. *mātu šuāti* in Akk. omens).[27] The form /*ḥuwwatu*/, like Hebrew *ḥawwôt*, is originally a *qatl* (*qall*) form of a geminate root *ḥ-w-w* (cf. also Arabic *ḥawā* "to collect, gather," *ḥiwāʾ* "circle of tents").[28] The /*u*/ of the first syllable is the result of assimilation of the original **a* (cf. the Hebrew) to the following /*w*/; see Part III, ch. 2 §A 1 e. /*ḥuwwatu*/ "land, country" is not to be connected with the Ugar. word that appears in Akk. texts as *ḫa-a-yv, ḫe-e-ia/yu, ḫé-yi-ma, ḫi-i-yi,* probably to be read /*ḫāyu*/, /*ḫīyu*/, for which see under ḪWY in the Glossary.

☛ p. 386

178

Sign/Akk.: See the preceding entry regarding the placement of the fragment containing the Sum. sign; GÚ is more likely than DUR (cf. GÚ = *šu-ub-tù* at Boğazköy, in MSL 13 135:890 [Izi]), although Nougayrol preferred the latter (for which see the next entry).

Hur.: Laroche, GLH, lists many words *Cv-a-ri,* the meanings of most of which are unknown.[29]

Ugar.: Probably for /*ḥudŭru*/ = alphab. *ḥdr* "room," despite the fact that Hebrew *ḥeder*, cst. *ḥădar*, directive *ḥadrâ*, sf. *ḥedrô*, cst. pl. *ḥadrê* all reflect a base **ḥa/idr*- (cf. also, perhaps, ^{é}*ḫi-id-ru* in an unpublished text from Emar).[30]

[26]See also Pardee, AfO 29/30 321-29, for a re-edition of this Ugaritic text, the letter of Queen Puduḫeba (KTU 2.36 + "2.73" + 2.37 + "2.74").

[27]In lines 15,16 of the same text, *hmt* is not a pronoun; read *bhmt ḥwt* "the beasts of the land"; cf. Herdner Ug. 7 pp. 44-60 (her lines 49,50).

[28]Dietrich-Loretz, OLZ 62 539, suggest that *ḥwt* is a loan from Egyptian *ḥ(w)t* "palace, temple"; in view of the probable semantic development in West Semitic from "community of tents" (or sim.; cf. the Hebrew and Arabic) to the larger, political sense "country, realm," however, their suggestion seems unlikely. On alphab. *ḥwt*, see further Dietrich-Loretz-Sanmartín, UF 6 25-26 no. 41.

[29]Note *(a-)a-ri* cultic object; *ḫa-(a-)ri* "route"; *i/e-(y)a-ri*; *ḫeyari* "all"; *ḫiyari* "gold"; *k/ga-(a-)ri* (X of a city/fields); *keri* "long"; *ma-(a-)ri*; *pa-(a-)ri*; *ša-a-ri*; *ta-a-ri*; *tiyari* "spindle"; *wa*$_{a}$*-a-ri* (a weapon); *ziyari* "side" (UŠ).

[30]Cf. Eblaite É.TUR = *ʾà-du-ru*$_{12}$, ŠÀ = *ʾà-du-ru*$_{12}$*/lu-um* = *ḥadru(m)*? (Fronzaroli apud Krebernik, ZA 73 14). Note also the following South Semitic forms, all curiously with initial *ḫ* rather than the *ḥ* of Ugar. alphab. *ḥdr* : Arab. *ḫidr* "chamber," Eth. *ḫadara* "to reside," OSA *ḫdr* "(grave) chamber."

A less likely possibility is to compare alphab. *ḥṭr,* a biform of *ḥẓr* "court," i.e., *ḫu-ṭù-rù* for /*ḥuṭūru*/ cf. JAram. *ḥuṭrā* "enclosure"; but alphab. *ẓ* elsewhere in Ugarit Akk. is represented by Z-signs; see Part III, ch. 1 §E 2.

179

Sign/Akk.: DUR = *rakāsu* "to bind," *riksu* "bond" in lexical texts; it is also used, however, as the logogram for *markasu* "rope, closure, bond (of a wall), link."

Ugar.: If the Akk. column had *markasu,* we may suggest that *ma-a-al-tu*$_4$ represents /*ma*^{cc}*altu*/ < **man*^{c}*altu* (alphab. unattested[31]) "bolt" (cf. Hebrew *min*^{c}*āl*).[32] Note, however, that assimilation of *n* before a guttural is unexpected (cf. the Hebrew); but cf. perhaps the form *yḥ*(?) in KTU 1.12 i 35, possibly from the root *n-ḥ-w* (see Gaster, AcOr 16 46 n. 23; idem, JAOS 70 13b; Marcus, JSS 17 77 n. 3; Caquot-Sznycer-Herdner, Textes ougaritiques 342 n. q).

180.1?

☛ p. 386

Sign/Akk.: See the Ugar. discussion.

Hur.: The word *kalgi* appears only here; see Laroche, GLH 134.

Ugar.: Nougayrol read [*d*]*a-al*!*-lu* "faible"; but in the copy the third sign is KU, while the second does not appear to be AL; further, in no other instance in the Ugarit S^a Voc. exemplars does a single Ugar. word gloss the same sign twice. Thus, a more likely reading is [*d*]*a-aq-qú,* for /*daqqu*/ = alphab. *dq* "small," corresponding perhaps to SIG = *ṣeḫru* "small" in the first and second columns.

180.2?

Sign/Akk.: See Ugar.

Hur.: The reading of the first sign is uncertain, probably either MU or ZI (less likely, ŠE); the word does not appear to be attested elsewhere.

Ugar.: /*dallu*/ = alphab. *dl* "poor," corresponding to SIG, probably equated with Akk. *enšu* "weak, poor," in the first and second columns.

[31] *m*^{c}[*lt*] "stairs, ascent" (KTU 1.41:23, 1.87:25), of course, derives from ^{c}*-l-y*.

[32] One might also think of */*mayyaltu*/, perhaps a loan from Akk. *mayyaltu* "bed," corresponding to the DUR sign understood as DÚR (= *šubtu*). This is ruled out, however, by the fact that a medial glide /*y*/ in Ugar. words is not written with the A sign, i.e., *Ca-a-aC,* in Ugarit Akk. texts; see Part III, ch. 1 §E 3 c (n. 106).

☛ p. 386

180.3?/181?

Sign/Akk.: Either no. 181 SIG$_5$, which in the S^a Voc. text in MSL 3 78:1'-4' is equated with *d*[*a-ma-qu*] "to be good," *a*[*q-ru*] and *a-q*[*a-ru*] "(to be) precious," and *pi-q*[*it-tu*] "administration"; or another entry of no. 180 SIG, in which case no. 181 SIG$_5$ would be missing in this Ugarit exemplar (so Nougayrol).

Hur.: For [*t*]*ap-ša-ḫal-še,* Laroche, Ug. 5 p. 461, suggests a word derived from *tapš-*, meaning perhaps "low" + *aḫal* = *eḫ(e)li* = (class marker) + *-še* (abstract marker); see also idem, GLH 256. The meaning "low" for *tapš-*, however, is based in part on Nougayrol's restorations in the other columns, which are by no means certain (see the Ugar. column). Possibly to be compared with *tapšaḫalše* is *tapšuḫumme* "to be upset, rebel" in no. 184.2 below, q.v.

Ugar.: Nougayrol proposed *ma-aš-k*[*a*(*-i*)*-nu*(??)], corresponding to Akk. *muškēnu* "commoner"; note, however, that SIG does not usually correspond to *muškēnu* (only in SIG = *enšu ša muš-*[*ke-ni*]; see CAD M/2 272-73). The reading of the third sign is not certain; besides Nougayrol's suggested KA, other possibilities are KUM (*qu*), BI, and TUM (*tu*$_4$, *du*$_4$). The form may be *qatl* of a root *m-š/θ-X*, or *maqtvl* of a root with first radical *š/θ*.

182

Sign/Akk.: See the Ugar. commentary.

Hur.: *ḫaḫli* is unattested otherwise.

Ugar.: The final *-n*[*u*(?)] in Nougayrol's transliteration is undoubtedly a typographical error for *-m*[*u*(?)]; cf. the copy, and see Laroche, GLH 89 (s.v. *ḫaḫli*). Thus, the Ugar. word is *la-ḫa-m*[*u*]; the Hur. form *ḫaḫli* indicates that we do not have a verbal infinitive here, but rather a noun or adjective (see below).

Since the line following this entry in Ug. 5 137 clearly contains no. 183 KAR, and since the preceding line has either no. 180 SIG or no. 181 SIG$_5$, this entry must have either no. 181 SIG$_5$ as well or no. 182 TE. Since *la-ḫa-m*[*u*] in the Ugar. suggests no forms corresponding to the former, Nougayrol was undoubtedly correct to restore TE here. Of the several Akk. words with which TE is equated in lexical lists (see, e.g., MSL 13 187:93-110 [Izi]), two in particular suggest themselves as possible counterparts to Ugar. *la-ḫa-m*[*u*], viz., *lētu* "cheek" and *simtu* "that which is seemly, fitting, appropriate."

Nougayrol opted for the former interpretation, translating "joue(s)." But if *la-ḫa-m*[*u*] means "cheeks," the form is unclear. The final consonant *m* cannot be a part of the root, which is clearly *l-ḥ-y* in the cognate languages (cf. Arabic *laḥy*, Hebrew *ləḥî*, sf. *leḥĕyô*, dual *ləḥāyayim*), but would have to reflect the dual ending. Yet other examples of the Ugar. dual nominative in syllabic cuneiform end in /*-āmi*/ or /*-āma*/, not */-āmu/; see Part III, ch. 3 §C 1 d (3). Further, the loss of the third radical *y*, evidenced in the alphabetic dual *lḥm* (KTU 1.5 vi 19, 1.6 i 3), suggests that the base of "cheek" in Ugar. was */liḥy-/ (as in Heb.) rather than */laḥy-/ (as in Arab.), since *qitl* forms of roots III-*y* seem generally to lose the *y*, whereas *qatl* forms retain it; see Part III, ch. 2 §E 2 b. Thus, the interpretation of *la-ḫa-m[u]* as "cheek(s)" is phonologically unlikely.

The second possibility, TE = Akk. *simtu*, recommends itself if we may assume that one of the meanings of the root *l-ḥ-m* [33] in Ugar., thus far unattested in alphab. texts, was "to be fitting, suitable," as in Syriac *lḥem* "to suit, fit with, agree" (especially in the participle *lāḥem*); for the middle radical as *ḥ* (rather than *ḫ*), cf. Arabic *laḥama* "to mend, patch," *laḥima* "to adhere" (further, *luḥma* "woof; kinship").[34] The Ugar. form would thus be /*laḥamu*/, i.e., a *qatal* noun ("that which is suitable," like Akk. *simtu*) or adjective ("suitable"),[35] less likely /*laḥāmu*/, the G infinitive used as a verbal noun (like Sem. *šalāmu*).[36]

183.1

Sign/Akk.: KAR = *eṭēru* "to save."

Hur.: *eǵl-* "to save" + *umme* infinitival ending; see Laroche, Ug. 5 p. 456-57, GLH 75-76 (*eḫ(e)li*).

Ugar.: The form *ḫu-PI-ú* is a D infinitive, the pattern of which in these vocabularies

[33]A lexical association of TE and *l-ḥ-m* may exist in the Eblaite bilingual MEE 4 312 no. 1026, where TE.ME is equation with *ra-ma-núm/nu-um* "person," but in a variant with *a-a-mu-mu*; perhaps the latter represents Eblaite *(l)aḥămum*, although the use of the A sign for *ḥa* would be unusual.

[34]Note also Ḥarsūsi *leḥām* "to touch" (Johnstone, Ḥarsūsi Lexicon 84) and Jibbāli *laḥám* "to jump up and touch" (idem, Jibbāli Lexicon 163). Also exhibiting a root *l-ḥ-m*, of course, are the *qatl* forms meaning "meat" in Arabic and "bread" in Northwest Semitic, i.e., **laḥm-*, with the (probably denominative) verb "to eat" (also in Akk. *lêmu*); a verb meaning "to fight," always in a derived stem (N in Hebrew, Gt in Moabite, Gt and tL in Arabic) and associated noun "fight, battle" (Hebrew *milḥāmâ*, Arabic *malḥama*); and, finally, Ethiopic (Geᶜez) *leḥma* "to be(come) soft, tender, weak, frail" (Dillmann 30-31). In WZKM 62 76-82, Krotkoff argues convincingly that all of these apparently unrelated meanings of *l-ḥ-m* can be traced back to a single original root, which conveyed the idea of "binding, adhering, malleability, softness." It is the notion of "adhering" that would be reflected in Syriac *lāḥem* and, if we are correct, Ugar. *la-ḫa-m[u]* "suitable, fitting."

[35]The Akk. adjective corresponding to the noun *simtu* is *(w)asmu*, which does not appear in lexical lists.

[36]Still a third possibility for this line is to consider TE = Akk. *šišītu* "membrane" (MSL 13 187:107 [Izi]). We might interpret Ugar. *la-ḫa-m[u]* as a noun with similar meaning, in view of Arabic *multaḥama*, which Krotkoff, WZKM 62 81, renders "Bindehaut." But since none of the other languages offers a similar derivative of *l-ḥ-m*, this alternative is less likely.

is *quttalu* (cf. *pu-la-ṭu* "to save" in no. 183.4). It is probably to be read *ḫu-wu-ú,* i.e., */ḥuwwûl* < **ḥuwwayu,* with contraction of the final triphthong; cf. *ša-du-ú* for */šadûl* in no.189.2 (see Part III, ch. 2 §E 3); less likely, but perhaps not to be ruled out, is *ḫu-yu-ú,* for */ḥuyyûl* (likewise with contraction).[37] On the alphab. forms of this verb (*ḥwy*/*ḥyy*), see Marcus, JSS 17 76-82.

☛ p. 387

183.2

Sign/Akk.: KAR = *lasāmu* "to run." Nougayrol, translating "coureur," apparently took the Akk. to be a *parrās* form; but apart from one NA occurrence of the fem. pl. *lassāmātu,* the form *lassāmu* (or *lassamu*) is unattested. Perhaps, therefore, the Akk. should be taken as the infinitive in substantival sense, "running, course"; note that the Hur. is not infinitival in form, however.

Hur.: See Laroche, Ug. 5 p. 461, GLH 130, who also translates "coureur."

Ugar.: */malsamu/*; although the root *l-s-m* "to run" is attested in the participle *lsmm* "runners," no alphab. *mlsm* occurs as yet. The pattern *maqtal* as an agent noun has precedent in Ugar., e.g., in alphab. *mlak* = */*malʾaku*/ "messenger," and perhaps also in another S^a Voc. form, *ma-aš-nu-ú?*, if for */mašnuʾu/* < **mašnaʾu,* in no. 190.5 below; the form in the Akk. column may rule out such an interpretation here, however, and so perhaps a more likely translation is "running, course."

☛ p. 387

183.3

Sign/Akk.: KAR apparently interpreted here as KIR_x, for KIR_4 = *appu* "nose" (Nougayrol); another possible misinterpretation is KAR as KA_x, likewise for KA = KIR_4.

Hur.: The word *puḫḫi* is not listed in Laroche, GLH.

Ugar.: /*ʾappu*/ = alphab. *ap* (root *ʾ-n-p*) "nose."

183.4

Sign/Akk.: KAR = *šūzubu* "to save."

Hur.: For the initial sign as *a-* (*abuškumme*) instead of Nougayrol's *sà-*, see Laroche,

☛ p. 387

[37]Much less likely are the readings *ḫu-wa-ú* (i.e., */ḥuwwa(y)u/*) and *ḫu-ya-ú* (i.e., */ḥuyya(y)u/*), since for final */-yu/* we should expect -PI (or -IA), not -Ú, which is not used otherwise in Ugarit Akk. to indicate the presence of a glide; see Part III, ch. 1 §E 3 c (n. 106).

Ug. 5 461.

Ugar.: D infinitive */pullaṭu/* = alphab. *plṭ* "to save." Cf., e.g., Syr. *plaṭ* "to escape," D *palleṭ* "to save, deliver," Heb. D *pillēṭ* (idem), Akk. *balāṭu* "to live," D *bulluṭu* "to keep alive, revive, etc."

183.5

p. 387

Sign/Akk.: KAR = *kāru* "quay, harbor."

Hur.: *maḫazi* is a loan from Akk. *māḫāzu* (or, less likely, from early Ugar. **maʾḫaðu* [> attested */maʾḫadu/*]).

Ugar.: The alphab. spellings *maḫd* and *miḫd* lead us to expect *ma-aʾ-ḫa-du*. The writing *ma-aḫ-ḫa-[du]* reflects either a scribal error (AḪ for the ʾ sign)[38] or, more likely, the spoken pronunciation of the word, with assimilation of ʾ to the following *ḫ* (i.e., */maʾḫadu /* = [maḫḫadu]); cf. the unique alphab. spelling of the gentilic *mḫdy* in KTU 4.635:17 (vs. more common *maḫdy* and *miḫdy*).[39] On the term in general at Ugarit, see Astour, JESHO 13 113-127.

184.1

Sign/Akk.: BAL = *pilakku* "spindle"; cf. MSL 3 79:16' (Boğazköy S^a Voc. fragment).

Hur.: On *ti/e(y)ari,* see Laroche, Ug. 5 p. 455, GLH 255-56.

Ugar.: */pilakku/* = alphab. *plk* "spindle"; cf., in addition to Akk. *pilakku,* Hebrew *pelek* (also Phoenician *plk*), JAram. *pilkā*.[40] Note the different spellings of the Akk. word (*pí-la-ak-ku*) and the Ugar. (*pí-lak-ku*).

184.2

p. 387

Sign/Akk.: BAL = *nabalkutu* "to jump, rebel."

Hur.: Laroche suggests, Ug. 5 p. 457, GLH 256, that the infinitive *tapšuḫumme* is

[38]Sivan, Analysis 53 n. 8, transliterates the form as *ma-ʾá-ḫa-[du]*, but this would be the sole instance in Ugarit Akk. of AḪ used to write ʾ (in Ugar. or Akk. words); AḪ and the ʾ sign are consistently distinguished in Ugarit Akk.

[39]See further Part III, ch. 2 §A 2 b.

[40]It seems unlikely that the WSem. words are loans from Akk.; rather, all of the Sem. forms probably stem from an early loan of a "Kulturwort" (see Kaufman, Akkadian Influences 82-83).

based on an adjective *tapš-* "low." As noted by G. Wilhelm (private communication), however, the meaning "low" for *tapš-* is based on Laroche's analysis of S^a Voc. no. 180.3/181, which is not secure; "low" in Hur. is *turi* (GLH 273).

Ugar.: Nougayrol suggested *tu-a-bi-*[*ú*], comparing Hebrew *tōhû wā-bōhû* (cf. also alphab. *thw* in KTU 1.5 i 15, probably for */*tuhwu*/ "wasteland"). The Akk. form and the Hur. form in *-umme* indicate, however, that the Ugar. form is probably also an infinitive; thus, we should probably read *tu-a-pí-*[*ku*], for /*tuhappiku*/, i.e., a tD[41] form of alphab. *hpk* "to upset" (cf. Hebrew *hāpak*, Syriac *hpak*; Gordon, UT 392a no. 788, also cites Arabic tD *tahaffaka* "to totter"). For the use of A for Ugar. /*ha*/, cf. *ta-a-ma-tu*$_4$ Ug. 5 137 iii 34"; see Part III, ch. 1 §E 4 b (3 a). A possible difficulty with our proposal is that the form *tuqattil* for the tD infinitive, in view of *quttal* for the D, is rather unexpected.

☛ p. 387

185

Sign/Akk.: ŠUL = *eṭlu* "youth."

Hur.: For *uštanni* "hero," see Laroche, Ug. 5 p. 454-55, GLH 289-90 (*uštay*).

Ugar.: Nougayrol read *ma-aḫ-ḫu-rum*, thinking of alphab. *mhr*, but Ugar. /*h*/ is not written with Ḫ-signs in Ugarit Akkadian.[42] More likely the form is /*baḫḫuru*/ or /*baḥḥuru*/ "youth"; cf. Hebrew *bāḥûr*, pl. *baḥûrîm*; see Blau-Greenfield, BASOR 200 17; Rainey, IEJ 19 107. The etymology of Hebrew *bāḥûr* is suggested by some to be *b-ḥ-r* (with original **ḫ*) "to choose" (see, e.g., BDB 104b). Jirku (apud Caquot-Sznycer-Herdner, Textes ougaritiques 547 n. 1) and Aartun (UF 16 8), however, propose to see the word "youth" in alphab. *bḫr* in KTU 1.15 v 5,22. On the normalization, with short /*u*/ in the second syllable (vs. the Hebrew), see further Part III, ch. 2 §A 1 b.

☛ p. 387

186.1

Sign/Akk.: ŠAḪ = *šaḫû* "pig"; here *šeḫû*, with *e* for *a* (cf. *šeqû* for *šaqû* in no. 193.1, and probably *mertu* for *martu* in no. 145).

Hur.: *uḫi* is attested only here.

Ugar.: /*ḫuzīru*/ "pig," which may be compared with Hebrew *ḥăzîr*, Syriac *ḥzîrā*, Akk. *ḫuzīru* "hog." It is unlikely that alphab. *ḫzr*, which denotes a type of personnel,

[41]On the tD stem in Ugar., see most recently Verreet, UF 16 319-21; Huehnergard, UF 17 402.

[42]See Part III, ch. 1 §E 4 b (1).

reflects the same word (so Gordon, UT 401 no. 948). Dietrich-Loretz-Sanmartín, UF 5 107-8, comparing *ḫušauru/û(tu)* (AHw 361b), consider *ḫzr* to be a Hurrian loanword meaning "prison, captive."

186a

Sign/Akk.: For the sequence ŠAḪ, ŠAḪ.TUR, cf. MSL 8/2 19 (Hh):

159	ŠAḪ	= *šá-ḫu-ú* "pig"
159a	SAL.ŠAḪ	= *šá-ḫi-tu₄* "sow,"
160	ŠAḪ.TUR	= *kur-ki-za-an-nu* "piglet."

Hur.: On the lack of a form in the Hurrian column here, see Nougayrol, Ug. 5 p. 242 n. 4.

Ugar.: Probably /*ḫinnīṣu*/ (alphab. unattested), most likely < **ḫannīṣu*, with vowel assimilation; see Part III, ch. 2 §A 1 b. Blau-Greenfield, BASOR 200 17, compare Arabic *ḫinnawṣ* and Syriac *ḥannuṣā*.

186.2?

p. 387

Sign/Akk.: Uncertain.

Hur.: The word *šuratḫi* is not discussed by Laroche, Ug. 5 458-59 (s.v. *tali* "tree, wood"); in GLH 244, he lists the form only as "plante, de nature inconnue." Note, in a Ugarit lexical text, ŠE.[x?].UD = MIN (= ŠE) *šu-ru-ti-ḫi*, ŠE.[x].E.SUM = MIN (= ŠE) *ša-ri* !(ḪU)-*ti-ḫi a-ḫu-ši*, Syria 12 236ff. ii 4'-5' (see MSL 5 60:114-116 and n. [Hh]; AHw 883a [s.v. *pūṣu*]); further, AHw 1283a: *šuratḫu* (Hur. loan) "ein Baum, ein Farbstoff" (Nuzi, SB).

Ugar.: The writing *qi-i-lu* may reflect a form II-*y*, i.e., /*qīlu*/ (like *ši-i-ru* for /*šīru*/ in no. 197.2 below), or a *qitl* or *qitīl* form of a root II-ʾ, -*h*, or -ᶜ (cf. ⸢*ši-i-ru*⸣ for /*šiʾru*/ in no. 21 above, [*š*]*i?-i-ru* for /*šiᶜīru*/ in no. 199 below). From among these possibilities, we may point to alphab. *qᶜl* in KTU 1.22 i 16 (bis), as proposed by Caquot-Sznycer-Herdner, Textes ougaritiques 475-76 n. f, who suggest "vine blossom" (so also other writers for the alphab.; cf. Arabic *quᶜāl*). Thus, we should normalize either /*qiᶜīlu*/ (< **qaᶜīlu*)[43] or /*qiᶜlu*/. The former seems the more likely if we may compare the Hebrew GN *qəᶜîlâ*.[44]

[43]For vowel assimilation around gutturals, see Part III, ch. 2 §A 1 c.

[44]Note also, perhaps, the Amarna GN ᵘʳᵘ*qí-el-te* (EA 279:12; 280:11; letters of Šuwardata), ⁽ᵘʳᵘ⁾*qí-il-ti* ᵏⁱ (EA 289:28; 290:10,18; Jerusalem).

☛ p. 387

187.1

Sign/Akk.: For LÚ = *šu-ú,* see MSL 12 93:2 (Lú) (where it should probably be understood as "he" rather than as the determinative pronoun, as it is taken in AHw 1254a). This reconstruction conforms better with the Ugar. column than does Nougayrol's LÚ = *nišū* "people."

Hur.: *manni* "he is/exists." Unlike the Ugaritic, the form is not a pronoun; the stem *mann-* means "to be" (*manni* is present form, 3ms; see Laroche, Ug. 5 p. 452-53, GLH 165-66). Note, however, that an independent third person pronoun has not yet been identified in Hurrian. (The demonstrative/relative *man(u)* [Laroche, GLH 167], is not at issue here, since it is never spelled with *-nn-*.)

Ugar.: Nougayrol, following Virolleaud, GLECS 8 66 (reading *ú-wi*), understood *ú-wu* "être," i.e., */huwû/* (< **hawāyu,* with contraction of the final triphthong, as in nos. 173.4, 183.1, and a shift of *a* > *u* before the bilabial, as in no. 32.2, 177.2). As in no. 173.4, however, an extra vowel-sign would be expected at word end if this were the correct interpretation. Thus, read probably *ú-wa* for */huwa/* = alphab. *hw,* the 3ms independent pronoun (which also corresponds more closely to the assumed Sumerogram LÚ than would a verb "to be"; note too that the Hur. is not an infinitive). See Cross, HTR 55 254 n. 124; Rainey, IEJ 19 108; Sivan, Analysis 126.

187.2

Sign/Akk.: Presumably LÚ = *ša,* on the basis of the Ugar. column.

Hur.: See Laroche, Ug. 5 462, on the difficulty of this form, where the relative pronoun *ye-/ya-* is expected; Laroche notes that what most closely resembles the form here is the stem *ai-*, "de valeur nettement conjunctive et subordonnante"; the latter means "if," however (Laroche, GLH 39), and thus does not correspond to the Ugar. */dū/.*

Ugar.: */dū/* = alphab. *d,* the relative pronoun, masc. sg. nominative.

187.3

Hur., Ugar.: See nos. 37.2, 45.4-5, 188.2; further, Ug. 5 137 iv b 17 (see the Glossary under B^{c}L).

☛ p. 388

187.4

Hur., Ugar.: See nos. 22.2, 24.2, 25.5, 51.2.

188.1

Hur., Ugar.: See no. 37.1.

188.2

Ugar.: See nos. 37.2, 45.4-5, 187.3; further, Ug. 5 137 iv b 17 (see the Glossary under BʿL).

189.1 p. 388

Sign/Akk.: We may probably reconstruct MAḪ = *ṣīru* "august, mighty," in view of the Ugar. column (Nougayrol).

Ugar.: */ʾaduru/* = alphab. *adr* "mighty" (vs. Hebrew *ʾaddîr*). Note the lack of assimilation of *a* in the first syllable; see Part III, ch. 2 §A 1 d (end).

189.2

Sign/Akk.: The Hur. and Ugar. indicate that the Akk. here was *ṣēru,* apparently taken as a homophone of *ṣīru* = MAḪ (Nougayrol); *ṣēru* "plain" does not otherwise correspond to MAḪ.

Hur., Ugar.: Cf. no. 35/36.3.

189.3 p. 388

Sign/Akk.: Cf. MAḪ = *ma-a-du* in MSL 3 82:27' (S^{a} Voc.; for other examples, see CAD M/1 20).

Hur.: "Much, many" in Hurrian is *tea, teuni* (see Laroche, GLH 260, 264); the form in this entry is obviously another adjective, which remains unidentified (cf. perhaps *egušši,* ibid. 75?).

Ugar.: The writing *ma-a-du-ma* reflects plural */maʾadūma/* or */maʾdūma/* [45] "many" (not attested in alphab. form as yet, but note sg. *mid* = */maʾdu/* [46]).

p. 388

[45]The writing is ambiguous as to whether /a/ followed the /ʾ/; see Part III, ch. 1 §E 4 b (3 a, b ii), ch. 2 §B 1.

[46]Note also *madtn* in KTU 1.103:1 = Ug. 7 pp. 45-49:35; see Herdner's comments, ibid. p. 59.

p. 388

190.1

Sign/Akk.: Cf. MSL 3 82:37' (Sª Voc.): [ḫu-ul] [ḪU]L = *sa-a-ru* (i.e., *sarru*) "false, wrong."

Hur.: No word glossed "false" (or sim.) appears in Laroche, GLH.

Ugar.: */sarru/* is unattested as yet in alphab. texts. Note perhaps the verb *ystrn* (KTU 1.4 viii 48), possibly a Gt of *s-r-r* (see Caquot-Sznycer-Herdner, Textes ougaritiques 218 n. t).[47] Cf., in addition to Akk. *sar(ā)ru* "(to be) false," Hebrew *sārar,* adj. *sar* "(to be) stubborn, rebellious."

190.2-191.3. The reconstruction of Ug. 5 137 ii 38'-44' presented here is offered as an alternative to that presented by Nougayrol, which suffers from the assumption that in each line the scribe wrote GUL when he intended KUD (see below), and which even so does not account well for the Ugaritic of several of the lines (e.g., 41' and 43').

p. 388

190.2?

Sign/Akk.: See the discussion of the Ugar. column.

Hur.: Note that the form is not an infinitive, which ends in *-umme* (cf., e.g., *abuškumme* in no. 183.4 and *tapšuḫumme* in no. 184.2, above). The word may be a nominal form in *-ubadi,* a formative for abstracts attested elsewhere in Hurrian, as in *nirubadi* "goodness, friendship," from *niri* "good"; *tuppubadi* "strength," from *tuppi* "strong"; for these words and other examples, see Laroche, GLH 185-86, 272; further, Bush, GHK 111 §6.3(7).

Ugar.: Nougayrol suggested GUL (for KUD/TAR) = Akk. *batāqu* (?) = Ugar. *ba-ta-qú*(?) "rompre." The last sign, however, is clearly LU in the copy, not KU; further, the Hur. suggests that the form is to be taken not as an infinitive, but as a *qatal* noun, possibly an abstract of an adjectival root. The root is most likely *b-ṭ-l,* thus far unattested in alphab. texts. The meaning is probably closer to Arabic *baṭala* "to be(come) false, wrong, vain, futile" and Ethiopic *baṭala* "to be vain, empty, invalid" than to Akk. *baṭālu* "to stop, cease" (so also Hebrew *bāṭal* in Eccles. 12:3); note also Syriac *bṭel,* which spans these semantic spheres, meaning "to cease (work), be idle; to fail, come to nought, be void" (cf. also the adjective *baṭṭāl* "idle, vain, empty"). If these suggestions are plausible, Ugar. */baṭalu/* "false(hood), futility,

[47] The form *srr* in KTU 1.123:12, 1.130:9 is probably unrelated, pace Astour JAOS 86 282b; see de Moor, UF 2 315; Xella, Testi rituali 103-4, 220.

idleness(?)," might therefore gloss, in the first two columns of this line, ḪUL = *ṣabru/zapru* "false, malicious" (or perhaps the noun *ṣaburtu/zapurtu* "falsehood, malice").[48]

190.3?, 190.4?, 191.1?

p. 388

Sign/Akk.: See the Ugar. column discussion.

Hur.: The meaning of *šubi* in Ug. 5 137 ii 42' (probably also in line 40') is unknown.

Ugar.: Nougayrol rendered "scindé" in the first instance, "séparé" in the last two; Segert, Basic Grammar 65 (§54.28), follows suit with *ḥarīmu* "separated" vs. *ḫarīmu* "split."

At some point before Ug. 5 137 ii 45', where the ÁŠ section, Sª no. 192, begins, one or more of the lines must comprise the GUL section, Sª no. 191. It is likely, therefore, that two of the instances of *ḫa-ri-mu* represent a single Ugar. word glossing a single Akk. word which corresponds to different Sum. signs, viz., to both no. 190 ḪUL and no 191 GUL. Note too that the Hurrian column may contain the same word in lines 40' and 42'. An Akk. word that fits this criterion, i.e., that is equated with both ḪUL and GUL, is *šulputu* "desescrate(d)," as in MSL 3 82:29',39' (also a Sª Voc. text). We may suggest, therefore, that Ugar. *ḫa-ri-mu* in lines 40' and 42' represents an adjective */ḥarĭmu/* (alphab. unattested), cognate to the Hebrew verb *heḥĕrîm* "to declare sacred, exterminate," Arabic *ḥaruma* "to become sacred, be forbidden."[49]

The remaining instance of *ḫa-ri-mu,* in line 39', will have corresponded to ḪUL if our suggestions concerning line 40', above, and concerning line 41', in the next entry, are correct. Since in no other section of the polyglot vocabularies is one sign glossed more than once by the same Akk. or Ugar. form, it seems likely that *ḫa-ri-mu* in line 39' is distinct from the suggested */ḥarĭmu/* of lines 40',42'.[50] As noted above, the

[48]For ḪUL = *ṣabru/zapru* (*ṣabru* in CAD, *zapru* in AHw), note, e.g., the lexical list Diri II, line 135, a list in which both *sarru* (see the preceding entry) and *zīru* (see no. 190.5 below) are equated with ḪUL (lines 141 and 134, respectively). The noun *ṣaburtu/zapurtu* (really the fem. adjective, substantivized) does not appear in lexical lists; note, however, *za-bur-ta-áš* corresponding to [ḫu]l.a in the bilingual KAR 128:27 (cited CAD Ṣ, 55a).

[49]Cf. also Syriac *ʾaḥrem* "to anathematize." Perhaps, but not certainly, related is Akk. *ḫarimtu* "prostitute"; note also the verb *ḫarāmu* "to separate," which occurs only in late lexical lists; see CAD Ḫ 102a; AHw 325b.

[50]Cf. nos. 198.8 and 198.9, below, where Ugar. *ḫu-ul-ma-tu₄* probably represents */ǵulmatu/* in the first instance and */ḥulmatu/* in the second. It seems entirely possible that these two sets of syllabic homographs in Ug. 5 137 are instances of scribal ingenuity and whimsy. As other examples of this scribe's display of erudition, we may perhaps point to the variant spellings *kàs-pu* and *ka-as-pu* for Ugar. */kaspu/* in ii 2,3, and *pí-la-ak-ku* and *pí-lak-ku* for the Akk. and Ugar., respectively, in ii 22';

root considered by Nougayrol and Segert is *ḫ-r-m* (alphab. unattested), cognate to Arabic *ḫarama* and Hebrew *ḥāram* II, both meaning "to slit, pierce"; these, however, do not correspond to any of the nuances of ḪUL (or, for that matter, of GUL). Thus, I would suggest that the root is *ġ-r-m,* and the form */ġarĭmu/,* cognate to Arabic *ġarīm* "adversary (in litigation)."[51] The first two columns of the entry might then have contained ḪUL = *zāmânu* "foe," as in MSL 3 82:31' (S^{a} Voc.). The word */ġarĭmu/* is not certainly attested in alphab. texts. Note, however, ⸢*ġrm tḫšn*⸣ in KTU 1.4 vii 32, which may be compared with *ib hd«t» lm tḫš* "foe(s) of Haddu, why do you ...?" in ibid.:38; cf. also, perhaps, the difficult *wġrm tθwy* in KTU 1.16 vi (31,)44, which de Moor (QS 2 92 with n. 2), likewise referring to Arab. *ġarīm,* renders "but the *usurer* you allow to stay"; finally, *kqṣm ġrmn* "like a massacre of the enemy(??)" in KTU 1.3 ii 10-11.

☛ p. 389

190.5?

Sign/Akk.: See the Ugar. discussion.

Hur.: No form **tardubarri* or **kuttubarri* (less likely, **ḫaštubarri*) appears in Laroche, GLH.

Ugar.: Nougayrol proposed to take *ma-aš-nu-ú* as "réplique??," corresponding to Akk. *šitūlu* and GUL (for KUD/TAR). This is semantically difficult, since *šitūlu* means not "to repeat, respond," but "to ponder, consider, question (oneself, one another)."

An alternative is to read instead [ḪUL] = [*ziʾru/zīru*] = */mašnŭʾu/* "hated, enemy." For the Sum./Akk., cf. [ḫu-ul] [Ḫ]UL = *zi-i-ru* in MSL 3 82:33' (S^{a} Voc.); cf. also no. 37.3 above. The root *š-n-ʾ* "to hate" (cf. Hebrew *śānēʾ*) occurs in alphab. texts, although a noun *mšnʾ* is not yet attested. The use of Ú for Ugar. */ʾu/* is found, e.g., in $^{\text{lú.meš}}$*mur-ú-ma* = */murʾūma/* (see the Glossary under MRʾ), and elsewhere; see Part III, ch. 1 §E 4 b (3 a). */mašnŭʾu/* may be a *maqtūl* form, "hated" → "enemy"; a major difficulty with this interpretation, of course, is the virtual lack of a passive *maqtūl* form (as in Arabic) in Northwest Semitic in general, and in Ugaritic in particular (see, however, Gordon, UT 78 §9.24; Aartun, UF 17 2-3 on *mṣb*; and note Hebrew *maslûl* "(raised) highway," **maṣpûnîm* "hidden things," *manᶜûl* "bolt"). Another possibility is to take the word as a *maqtal* form with assimilation of the second *a* before the guttural /ʾ/ to the following case-vowel, i.e., **mašnaʾu* >

---

see also the commentary on the Hur. column of no. 191.3 below.

[51]Originally "debtor" or "creditor," the verb *ġarima* meaning "to pay (a fine, etc.)." The root is, to the best of my knowledge, unattested elsewhere in Semitic, with the exception of Ḥarsūsi, where it may be a loan from Arabic.

/*mašnuʾu*/; see Part III, ch. 2 § A 1 c. For *maqtal* as an agent noun, cf. alphab. *mlak* = */*malʾaku*/ "messenger"; see also above, no. 183.2, on /*malsamu*/.

191.1? See no. 190.3.

191.2? p. 389

Sign/Akk.: See the discussion of the Ugar.

Hur.: The meaning of *nakti* is unknown; see Laroche, GLH 177, for other occurrences.

Ugar.: It is not clear to me what Nougayrol had in mind when he rendered *i-pu-ú* with "brisé," except perhaps a comparison with Akk. *ḫepû*. No alphab. forms present themselves as equivalents of this word. If we are still in the GUL section, we may perhaps compare Arabic *ʿafā* "to obliterate, efface" and its verbal noun *ʿafw-* "obliteration," and suggest that *i-b/pu-ú* reflects a *qitl* verbal noun /*ʿipû*/ < **ʿipwu,* with roughly the same nuance. The Akk. column may then have contained *abātu* or *naqāru*.

An alternative interpretation is possible if this line begins the ÁŠ section (Sª no. 192), viz., [ÁŠ] = [*ḫišiḫtu*] = *i-bu-ú* for /*ʾibû*/ < **ʾibyu* "desire, need" (cf. perhaps alphab. *abynt* "wretchedness?"; Hebrew *ʾābâ* "to want, *ʾebyôn* "poor"[52]); cf. no. 192.3 below. But it seems more likely that both this and the next entry continue the GUL section.

191.3? p. 389

Sign/Akk.: See the end of the Ugar. discussion.

Hur.: Given the similarity of Hur. *pí-i-ri* and Ugar. *pí-rù,* it is possible that one of the forms is simply a loan of the other, in which case the word probably refers to an object of some sort. If so, the forms may correspond to Sª no. 192 ÁŠ[53] rather than to no. 191 GUL.

More likely, however, the similarity of the Hur. and Ugar. forms is coincidental, or the result of scribal whimsy.[54] Hur. *pí-i-ri* is probably to be related to the stem

[52]Unless both alphab. *abynt* and Heb. *ʾebyôn* are Egyptian loanwords; see Lambdin, JAOS 73 145-46.

[53]Note, e.g., that ÁŠ occurs in a number of compounds denoting plants.

[54]See the commentary on the Ugar. column of nos. 190.3/190.4/191.1, with n. 50.

**fir-* "to loosen, undo," which in all likelihood also appears in the Nuzi expression *pirankumma epēšu* "to flee" (i.e., "to release, free oneself"; AASOR 16 52:18; see AHw 865b) and the nominal forms *fir=ade* "freeman, noble" and *fir=ad(e)=arde* "nobility (as a social group)" (Laroche, GLH 297; Wilhelm, Or. 54 491), as well as in **pirianni,* probably meaning "freedom"; see Laroche, RHA 28 62; Haas-Thiel, Die Beschwörungsrituale; Wilhelm, Or. 54 491; idem, "Marginalien zu Herodot." See further the Ugar. discussion.

Ugar.: *pí-rù* probably represents */pirru/,* i.e., a *qitl* infinitive/verbal noun[55] of the root *p-r-r,* which seems to have as its basic meaning in Semitic "to separate (intrans.), remove (oneself)," as in Akk. *parāru,* and hence "to flee," as in Arabic *farra*; in transitive forms, the basic notion "to separate" appears in Akk. D *purruru* "to loosen, undo," Arabic (causative) *ʾafarra* "to put to flight," but also "to split," and Hebrew *hēpēr* "to break, annul, violate" (note also the *pōʿēl* form *pôrartā* "you divided" in Psalm 74:13 and the passive *pôr hitpôrərâ* "it is split" in Isaiah 24:19). In the Ugar. alphab. texts, we find intransitive *tpr* "flee" (probably G jussive/volitive, *yaqtvl(a)*; KTU 1.19 iii 14,28) and probably transitive *apr* "I will annul" KTU 1.15 iii 30).[56]

If the Hur. *pirankumma,* noted above, is indeed related to the stem **fir-*, then the latter overlaps in meaning quite broadly with Ugar. *p-r-r,* each denoting both "flee" and "separate, loosen, undo." As to the contents of the first two columns of this entry, several alternatives present themselves, in view of the probable meaning(s) of the Hur. and Ugar. forms, though none is without difficulty: GUL = *nābutu* "to flee," a correspondence not otherwise attested, and thus derived from GUL = *abātu* "to destroy"; GUL = *ḫepû* "to smash, break, annul," the semantic range of which is not precisely that of the Hur. and Ugar.; GUL = SÚN, for SUN_5 (BÚR)[57] = *pašāru* "to loosen" or *(w)uššuru* "to release."

192.1

For this entry, see van Soldt, RA 75 93.

Sign/Akk.: ÁŠ = ZÍZ = *kunāšu* "emmer," in view of the Ugar. column.

Hur.: The form *utte* is not listed in Laroche, GLH.

[55]For similar forms in the Ugarit Sª Voc. texts, see nos. 35/36.2, 159.2, 194.3.

[56]If the semantic developments outlined here are valid, the two alphab. nuances need not be assigned to separate roots, as is done by Gordon in UT 471 nos. 2120-2121.

The *-i-* of the Ugar. form *pí-rù* almost certainly precludes associating it with GUL = SÚN = *rīmtu* "wild cow" and alphab. *pr* (Heb. *par*) "bull."

[57]See n. 3 of the Introduction to Part I above.

Ugar.: */kussumu/* = alphab. *ksm* (pl. *kšmm/kšmn*) "emmer" (cf. Hebrew *kussemet*, late Hebrew *kôsəmîn*).

192.2

Sign/Akk.: ÁŠ = *arratu* "curse."

Hur., Ugar.: Cf. no. 37.4.

192.3

Sign/Akk.: ÁŠ = *ṣibûtu* "desire, wish."

Hur.: Only here.

192.4

Sign/Akk.: ÁŠ does not correspond to *murṣu* "pain, sickness" elsewhere; Nougayrol, Ug. 5 p. 244 n. 3, plausibly suggested that the equivalence may derive from the occurrence of *arratu* two lines earlier, and the common phrase *arratu maruštu* "grievous curse" (see CAD M/1 294).

Hur.: Is *ma-ru-⌜ši ?⌝*, if the last sign is read correctly, a loan from Akk. *murṣu* (or the adj. *marṣu*, fem. *maruštu*), despite the fact that it may also occur (*ma-ru-še-en-ti*) in a text from Boğazköy (KBo 8 155 ii 7; see Laroche, GLH 168-69)?

193.1 p. 389

Sign/Akk.: The Akk. column has KUR-*qu-ú*, which Nougayrol read as *šat-qu-ú* "très haute." Since no *patrvs* form exists in Akk., von Soden, AHw 1200b, suggests that *šat-qu-ú* is a mistake for *šaqû*. Probably we should read *še*!-*qu-ú*, for *šaqû* "high"; cf. *šeḫû* for *šaḫû* in no. 186.1 and probably *mertu* for *martu* in no. 145.

Hur.: *ḫeldi* "high" + *-ae* (adverbial ending); see Laroche, Ug. 5 p. 460, GLH 101.

193.2

Sign/Akk.: Nougayrol understood *ma-aš-šu-ú* as *massû/maššû* "leader"; that word, a Sum. loan, is not equated elsewhere with ÍL, however. Thus, we should read instead *maššû* "(a kind of basket)," as indicated in CAD M/1 390 (s.v. *maššû* A); note there the lexical equations ^{giš}ÍL.LÁ = *maš-šu(-ú)*.

Hur.: The term *pabarra* is not attested otherwise (Laroche, GLH 191-92).

193.3

Sign/Akk.: ÍL here is a graphic variant of NIGIR, = *nāgiru* "herald"; see CAD N/1 115b. As Nougayrol pointed out, Ug. 5 p. 244 n. 5, the NIGIR sign does not appear in the S^a series.

Hur.: Attested only here, *nagiri* is obviously a loan from Akk. (Laroche, GLH 175).

Ugar.: Nougayrol restored *n[a-gi-ru(m)]*, but the word *nāgiru* "herald" is not attested in any Semitic language other than Akk.[58] Further, the initial sign, in Nougayrol's copy, does not look like the beginning of NA (cf. the Akk. column), but rather, perhaps, of MU. The form, therefore, might instead be a derived stem participle, such as */mubašširu/* (cf. alphab. *bšr* "to bring tidings" [UT 377b no. 535]; Hebrew *məbaśśēr* "herald").

193.4

Sign/Akk.: Either ÍL = *zabbilu* "carrier of sheaves" (note ^lú^ŠE.ÍL.ÍL = *za(b)-bi-lu,* cited CAD Z 7a), or = *zābilu* "porter" (although the latter is not written with a logogram elsewhere and does not appear in the lexical lists).

Hur.: None of the various words for professions listed in Laroche, GLH, ends in *-diyaši*. (For a professional term with a similar ending, note, e.g., *ašhiyašši* "sacrificer," ibid., 59-60).

Ugar.: Nougayrol proposed *da-[bi-lu]*, for */dābilu/* (alphab.unattested), i.e., a Ugaritic cognate of Akk. *zābilu,* assuming that the initial consonant was originally *ð* (cf. *da-ka-ru* for original **ðakaru* in no. 195.2 and *da-ab-ḫu* for original *ðabḥu* in no. 197.1, below); this may not be ruled out, be it should be noted that the etymology of this root is complicated, and may involve alphab. *zbl.*[59]

☛ p. 389

194.1

Sign/Akk.: Nougayrol read here the beginning of another ÍL (S^a no. 193), but the copy does not preclude the beginning of GAB (no. 194). Thus, although the Hur. column might indicate otherwise (see below), we may suggest for this line GAB(A)

[58]Alphab. *ngr(t)* in KTU 1.16 iv 3-12 is rendered "herald" by some translators (e.g., Caquot-Sznycer-Herdner, Textes ougaritiques 562-63 n. t); but in the context of building a house, "carpenter" (Sem. *naggār*) is much more likely.

[59]See especially Held, "The Root SBL/ZBL," who showed that Hebrew *z-b-l* is to be associated with Ugar. *zbl,* with the related notions of "to lift up" and "prince(ship)," while Hebrew *s-b-l* and Akk. *zabālu* "to transport, carry a load" go together semantically.

= Akk. [*irtu*]; cf. the Ugar. column.

Hur.: The form *aḫerni,* if correctly read, does not appear in Laroche, GLH. On p. 125 of GLH, Laroche suggests that the word *irti* (*irdi*), which denotes a part of the body, may mean "chest," as a loan from Akk. *irtu.*

Ugar.: If the sign in the first column is GAB, as suggested above, we may read perhaps *i-r*[*a-tu*$_4$], for /*ʾiratu*/ = alphab. *irt* "chest, breast." For the fem. ending *-at,* vs. Akk. *-t* (the latter the result of vowel syncope), cf. Arabic *riʾa* and late Hebrew *rēʾâ* "lung," both < **riʾat-* < **ʾirat-* (metathesis).

194.2

Sign/Akk.: Nougayrol read the Akk. as *ṭ*[*u*]*ḫ*(?)-[*ḫ*]*u*(?)-*ú* "approche(r)"; but GAB/DUḪ is not normally equated with *ṭeḫû* (G or D). Thus, it seems more likely that the equation is: GAB(A) (for GABA.RI) = *gaba*-[*ru*]-*ú,* i.e., *gabarû* "copy"; for the value *gaba* in Ugarit Akk., note ^{kuš}*gaba-bu* ^{meš} in PRU 6 132 r. 5'. A less likely possibility is GAB = DUḪ/ DU$_8$ = *ṭuḫ*-[*du*]-*ú,* i.e., *ṭuḫdu* "abundance," where the extra vowel-sign at word end would be unusual.

Hur.: The meaning of *patpiri* is unknown; note, however, that the form is not an infinitive, another factor militating against Nougayrol's reading of the Akk column.

194.3

☛ p. 390

Sign/Akk.: GAB = DU$_8$ = *paṭāru* "to loosen, separate, leave."

Hur.: On the stem *sul(l)-* (here infinitive *sulludumme*) "to loosen, release," see Laroche, Ug. 5 p. 457, GLH 308 (*zulud-*), and especially Wilhelm, ZA 73 97-99 with nn. 3,11, and idem, "Marginalien zu Herodot," with n. 82.

Ugar.: The form /*piṭru*/ is a *qitl* infinitive/verbal noun (G), corresponding to the Akk. and Hur. infinitives; for similar forms in these texts, see nos. 35/36.2, 159.2, 191.3. Alphab. *pṭr* is not yet attested.[60]

[60]For Virolleaud's *pṭr* in Ug. 5 p. 576:34, read *pẓr,* with KTU 1.107:34; see Freilich-Pardee, Syria 61 29-30. For *bṭr* in KTU 4.382:1,2, Dietrich-Loretz-Sanmartín, UF 5 105, suggest that the term denotes a status, and propose the meaning "befreit, freigelassen," suggesting a biform of *pṭr*; *b* for expected *p* word-initially is unlikely, however (on the voicing and devoicing of stops in Ugar., see Garr, JNES 45 45-52; below, Part III, ch. 2 §A 2 a).

☛ p. 390

194.4

Sign/Akk.: GAB = DUḪ = *tuḫḫu* "bran, residue, scraps," (see Stol, BiOr 28 170-71, AHw 1366b); it does not properly mean "sheath" (Sivan, Analysis 275; Nougayrol: "gaine").

Hur.: The word *šuḫuli* is attested only here.

Ugar.: The form *šu-ḫu-ut-t*[*u*], which has no obvious alphab. parallel,[61] may be analyzed in a variety of ways: *qutull* or *qutul-t* of roots *š/θ-ḥ/ḫ/ǵ-d/ṭ/t, qutul-t* of *š/θ-ḥ/ḫ/ǵ-n,* or a prefixed-*š* form, i.e., *šuqull* of a geminate root, or *šuqūl-t* of a hollow root. A close semantic parallel is afforded by Arabic *ḥatta* "to rub, scrape off," with its derivatives *ḥitta* "piece, morsel" and *ḥutāt* "scraps, morsels, crumbs"; the Ugar. form, if it is cognate to this, would then be */šuḥuttu/*, a *šuqull* form (possibly *šaqull* originally, with vowel harmony around the guttural */ḥ/*; see Part III, ch. 2 §A 1 c).[62]

195.1

Sign/Akk.: ÌR/ARAD = *(w)ardu* "slave, servant"; cf. MSL 3 84:3' (Sª Voc.).

Hur.: *puram(m)i* "slave"; see Laroche, Ug. 5 p. 455, GLH 205 for other occurrences.

Ugar.: */ᶜabdu/* = alphab. *ᶜbd* "slave, servant."

195.2

Sign/Akk.: ÌR/ARAD = NITA$_2$ = *zik(a)ru* "male"; cf. MSL 3 84:2' (Sª Voc.).

Hur.: On *turuḫḫi* "male," see Laroche, Ug. 5 p. 452, GLH 274.

Ugar.: */dakaru/* < **ðakaru,* unattested as yet in alphab. texts;[63] besides Akk. *zik(a)ru,* cf., e.g., Hebrew *zākār* "male," Syriac *dekrā.*

Cf. no. 147, above.

[61]The form *šḥt* in KTU 1.100:65 is probably related to Hebrew *śîaḥ* "shrub"; *bny šḥt* in the letter KTU 2.2:10 is unclear.

[62]*š*- prefix forms are admittedly rare in Ugaritic; note, however, *šbᶜr* "torch" (KTU 1.4 vi 16; see Caquot-Sznycer-Herdner, Textes ougaritiques 203 n. d); *šmrr* (KTU 1.100:4,10,etc.); the epithet *šᶜtqt* (KTU 1.16 vi 1,2, etc.); perhaps also *šlḥmt* (KTU 1.106:25,28; see Herdner, Ug. 7 p. 30); *šnpt* (KTU 1.119:13; see, e.g., Xella, Testi rituali 31); *links šslmt* (KTU 4.46:2,3; 4.144:4; 4.378:11; 4.395:5; see Rainey, Or. 34 16; Dietrich-Loretz, BiOr 23 132b; Dietrich-Loretz-Sanmartín, UF 5 115 no. 65).

[63]Note *ðkr* in PN's, however (UT 388a no. 724).

[**196**]

No. 196, IR_{11} [ìr x še], for which see, e.g., MSL 3 84:3' (S^a Voc.), is missing in Ug. 5 137.

197.1

Sign/Akk.: EZEN = *isinnu* "festival."

Hur.: The word *eli* with the meaning "festival" is not certainly attested elsewhere; see Laroche, GLH 79.

Ugar.: */dabḥu/* < **ðabḥu* = alphab. *dbḥ* "sacrifice." The Ugar. *qatl* form contrasts with the *qitl* form attested in cognates, viz., Aramaic *dibḥā* (Syriac *debḥā*), Hebrew *zebaḥ* (suff. *zibḥô*), Ethiopic *zebḥ*, and Arabic *ðibḥ* (but note the verbal noun *ðabḥ*).

197.2

Sign/Akk.: EZEN = ŠÌR = *zamāru* "song," here incorrectly with double *-mm-* (cf. nos. 63.3, 151.2, above).

Hur.: See Laroche, Ug. 5 p. 455, GLH 90, for other references to *ḫalmi* "song."

Ugar.: */šīru/* "song." Since the Hur. form is a noun rather than an infinitive, we must assume that the Ugar. form is a *qīl* noun, not a G infinitive (cf. Hebrew *šîr*); see Rainey UF 3 166-67 (pace Sivan, Analysis 169,277). The noun is not yet attested in alphab. texts, but note *šr* "to sing," "singer."

198.1

☛ p. 390

Sign/Akk.: IDIM = *naqbu* (*nagbu*) "spring, source," here apparently metathesized to *nabqu*, perhaps under the influence of the Ugar. column (Nougayrol).

Hur.: For the reading of the first sign as *tar* rather than *ḫal* (Nougayrol), see the other attestations of *tarmani* "spring" cited in Laroche, GLH 257.

Ugar.: */nabku/*, probably pronounced [napku] = alphab. *nbk*/*npk* "spring, well." On the devoicing of the middle radical, see Part III, ch. 2 §A 2 a. This word also appears in field designations in Ugarit Akk.; see the Glossary under NBK.

198.2

Sign/Akk.: IDIM = ? Perhaps a DN, in view of the Ugar. column; ^{d}IDIM may correspond to Enlil (Nougayrol) or Enki/Ea.

Ugar.: Presumably for /ʾ*ilu*/ = alphab. *il* "god, El"; the use of a logogram (DINGIR) in the Ugaritic column is paralleled only in the same form in the god-list at the end of Ug. 5 137 (iii 35"; cf. also Ug. 5 18:2; see the Glossary under ʾL). Cf. no. 45.3, above, where *i-lu* is probably written.

198.5ff. For Ug. 5 137 iii 12'-17', Nougayrol's BÁR in the left column is almost certainly a typographical error for IDIM, since he referred to the sign (p. 247) as no. 198; cf. also his n. 2 on p. 247.

198.5

☛ p. 390

Sign/Akk: See the Ugar.

Ugar.: Nougayrol read [*r*]*a-n*[*u* (?) . It is not clear from this or from the copy whether another sign may have followed. If another sign did follow, as seems likely, we may suggest [IDIM] = [*šegû*] (cf., e.g., MSL 13 22: 167d [Proto-Izi]) = [*r*]*a*-[*g*]*a*-[*zu*], for a G infinitive /*ragāzu*/ "to be enraged, agitated" (alphab. unattested; cf. Hebrew *rāgaz*).

198.6, 198.7

Sign/Akk.: On the use of IDIM for *šamû* "sky" and *erṣetu* "earth" in Ugarit Akk., see Nougayrol's comments on Ug. 5 18:11, ibid. p. 49.

Hur.: See no. 45.1 above.

Ugar.: *ša-mu-ma* for pl. /*šamûma*/ = alphab. *šmm* "sky"; *ar-ṣu* for /ʾ*arṣu*/ = alphab. *arṣ* "earth."

Cf. no. 45.1; further, Ug. 5 137 iii 33" (see the Glossary under ŠMY).

198.8?, 198.9?

Sign/Akk.: In view of the two entries following these (i.e., 198.10?, 198.11?), it is likely that both instances of Ugar. *ḫu-ul-ma-tu*$_4$ correspond to IDIM. See further the discussion of the Ugar. column.

Ugar.: Nougayrol proposed Akk. *rūqu* "distant" for the Akk. column of no. 198.8, and refrained from making a proposal for no. 198.9. He suggested for both entries the meaning "future," thinking of alphab. ʿ*lmt* for the writing *ḫu-ul-ma-tu*$_4$. But

Ugar. /^{c}/ is not normally represented by Ḫ-signs in Ugarit Akk.[64] Further, IDIM is not elsewhere equated with Akk. words for "future." The same criticisms apply to Sivan's proposal, Analysis 222, to read */hulmatu/* "hammer": Ugar. */h/* is never represented by Ḫ-signs in Ugarit Akk.;[65] IDIM does not denote "hammer" (or sim.).

Since there are no other examples of the repetition of either an Akk. or a Ugar. word within a section (i.e., glossing one particular sign) of these S^{a} vocabulary texts, it is most likely that we should assume that the two instances of Ugar. *ḫu-ul-ma-tu*$_4$ represent distinct words, and that they have been placed one after the other by the scribe of Ug. 5 137 as a kind of tour de force, as is probably the case with the two examples of *ḫa-ri-mu* in nos. 190.3 and 190.4.[66] And, in fact, two candidates for Ugar. *ḫu-ul-ma-tu*$_4$ corresponding to IDIM suggest themselves.

For no. 198.8, the first two columns can be reconstructed as IDIM = *ekletu* "darkness," as in MSL 13 22:167f (Proto-Izi). Ugar. *ḫu-ul-ma-tu*$_4$ here would then represent */ǵulmatu/*, corresponding to alphab. *ǵlmt*, which probably means "darkness" in KTU 1.4 vii 54 and KTU 1.8 ii 7; for the form, cf. Arabic *ẓulma* and (masc. instead of fem.) Akk. *ṣulmu* "darkness."[67]

Ugar. *ḫu-ul-ma-tu*$_4$ in no. 198.9 may represent */ḥulmatu/*, meaning something like "strength, power, soundness," unattested with fem. *t* in alphab. texts, but corresponding to alphab. *ḥlm* "strength," for which see Dietrich-Loretz-Sanmartín, UF 7 161 (cf. Hebrew and Aramaic *ḥ-l-m* II "to be healthy, strong"). While none of the Akk. words equated with IDIM in lexical texts (see MSL 13 22:167a-f [Proto-Izi]; 14 252:109-24 [Ea II], and pp. 277-29 [A II/3]) signifies "strength" or "soundness," note that IDIM occurs as a logogram for *nakbatu* "military force" (cf. IDIM = *kabtu,*

[64]There is a very small group of exceptions; see Part III, ch. 1 §E 4 b (1).

[65]Ugar. */hulm(at)u/* "hammer" may appear in Ugarit Akk. as (pl.) ^{urudu}*ul-ma-tu* in PRU 6 141: 4,5; see the Glossary under HLM.

[66]See further above, n. 50.

[67]Note further *ǵlm ym* in KTU 1.14 i 19-20, which may mean "darkness of day," and *ǵlm* in KTU 1.16 i 50, meaning perhaps "it got dark." The etymology of these forms is not entirely clear. Note, for instance, that in both KTU 1.4 vii 54-55 and 1.8 ii 7-8, *ǵlmt* occurs in parallel with *ẓlmt*, which is taken by most scholars who would see in *ǵlmt* the word "darkness" simply as the earlier etymon of the former, a linguistically difficult conclusion. There is, in addition, Hebrew ^{c}*-l-m* "to conceal," rarely also connoting "darkness," besides the difficult *ṣlmwt* "darkness." Finally, the precise relationship of Ugar. */ǵ/* to Proto-Semitic **θ* remains less than fully understood. It is possible that part of the confusion of roots **θ̣-l-m*, Ugar. *ẓ-l-m* and *ǵ-l-m*, Hebrew ^{c}*-l-m* is the result of both archaism and interdialectal mixing. In any case, the translation of *ǵlmt* and *ǵlm* as "darkness," "to become dark" does seem the most likely in the passages cited above. A partial bibliography on the problems noted here: Ginsberg, The Legend of King Keret 34,45; Gaster, JQR 37 289-90; Dahood, Biblica 33 206; Driver, Canaanite Myths 100-1,143a; Gray, Krt Text 33; von Soden, "Kleine Beiträge" 291-94; Dietrich-Loretz, WO 4 308,313-14; Scullion, UF 4 115; Caquot-Sznycer-Herdner, Textes ougaritiques 219 n. w, 555 n. x. On archaism, see Blau, JAOS 88 523-26.

as probably in the next entry, no. 198.10). An alternative explanation for the equation of IDIM with Ugar. */ḥulmatu/* would involve assuming that the scribe confused IDIM with BAD (the two are normally written identically in this period), and equated BAD = TIL with Akk. *balāṭu* "life" as in no. 173.3, here with the nuance "vigor, good health."

☛ p. 390

198.10?

Sign/Akk.: Restore perhaps IDIM = *kabtu* "heavy, noble," in view of the Ugar. column (Nougayrol).

Ugar.: *ma*!-*al-ku* "king" is the most likely reading (Nougayrol:]*ma*(?)-*al-ku*), although only Akk. *šarru* is so glossed elsewhere in these lists.

Cf. nos. 37.1, 188.1.

198.11?

Sign/Akk.: See the Ugar.

Ugar.: Nougayrol translated [*ḫ*]*a-ra-š*[*u*] as "labourer??," i.e., as representing alphab. *ḥrθ*, but it is hard to connect that meaning with either S^a no. 198 IDIM or no. 199 ŠE. Thus, it seems more likely that the form represents */ḫar(r)ašu/* "deaf," corresponding to [IDIM] = [*seb/pû*] "deaf," as in MSL 13 22:167c (Proto-Izi); note, however, that *seb/pû* is not attested outside of a few lexical texts (see CAD S 205b). If correctly understood, the *qatal* or *qattal* pattern (less likely, with long *ā* in the second syllable) of the adj. */ḫar(r)ašu/*, which is not attested in alphab. form, contrasts with both the **qatil* form of Aramaic (Syr.) *ḥreš* and the *qittil* form of Hebrew *ḥērēš*. (For the initial radical, cf. Arabic *ḫ-r-s*.)

199?

Sign/Akk.: S^a no. 199 is ŠE, which corresponds to, among other things, Akk. *šeʾu* "barley, grain" (cf. the discussion of the Ugar. column).

Ugar.: Nougayrol suggested "chanteur??" for [*š*]*i*?-*i-ru*, but this does not correspond to any of the meanings of S^a no. 198 IDIM or no. 199 ŠE. If the first sign is correctly read as *ši*, the writing probably represents */šiʿīru/* = alphab. *šʿr* "barley"; the form, from **šaʿīru*, with vowel assimilation around the guttural (see Part III, ch. 2 §A 1 c), would thus go with Arabic *šaʿīr* rather than Hebrew and Aramaic **ši/uʿār-*.

Ug. 5 137 iii 20'

Ugar.: Too little of the form is preserved to permit a reading of the form.

Nougayrol's [*ši*(?)-]*i*(?)-*r*[*u*(?)] "chanteur??," i.e., a repetition of the preceding line, is unlikely.

206-211. Since no reasonable Ugar. forms present themselves as correspondences to Nougayrol's [BARAG] in the second and third last lines before the dividing line after Ug. 5 137 iii 32", an alternative reconstruction of the end of the S^a Voc. seems in order.

206?

If the last two signs are indeed *-na-b/pu,* a possible reconstruction is: 206 [KAB] = [*kappu*] = Ugar. */kanapu/* "wing" (alphab. *knp*; cf., e.g., Hebrew *kānāp*).[68]

207?

The reading of the last two signs of the Ugar. column is by no means certain, and does not in any case suggest a correspondent of the probable sign, S^a no. 207 KIB.

208?

Sign/Akk.: Nougayrol suggested that the sign here was S^a no. 211 BARAG = *parakku* "throne dais, sanctuary." But equally possible is no. 208 TIR = *atmānu* "sanctum, cella," which allows new suggestions to be made for the following lines. See further the discussion of the Ugar. column.

Ugar.: The reading of the last three signs as *qi-id-šu* seems fairly certain. Since */qidšu/* is not an adjectival form, and not genitive, the sign(s) preceding it in the Ugar. column (perhaps, with Nougayrol, simply É) must constitute either an appositive noun (*/bētu qidšu/* "house-sanctuary"?) or a determinative (^{é}*qi-id-šu*); the latter is the more plausible alternative, despite the fact that no other form in the Ugar. column has a determinative. Thus, */qidšu/* is the pronunciation of alphab. *qdš* in the meaning "sanctuary," as in KTU 1.17 i 26,44, ii 16. Note also the equation of ^{d}ŠARA (apparently understood as ^{d}BARAG) = Hur. *ḫamarre* = Ugar. *qi-i*[*d-šu*?] "sanctuary" in the god-list that follows the S^a Voc. in Ug. 5 137, iv a 14; see below in the Glossary under QDŠ b.

[68]The PN *ku-na-pí-li,* PRU 3 142f.:5, which Gröndahl, Personennamen 73, 150, suggests may contain a noun */*kunapu*/ "wing," should perhaps be analyzed instead as */kūna-pī-ʾili/*.

209?

In view of examples in the first column of the Sª Voc. such as ZU = SÚ for SU in no. 21, I for I_7 in no. 56, DAG for ZAG in no. 151.2, etc.,[69] we should probably reconstruct here TUK = DUG_x for DÙG, corresponding to Akk. *birku* "knee" and to Ugar. [*bi*]-*ir-ku* = /*birku*/ (alphab. *brk*) "knee."

210?

Although Sª no. 210 KÍD (TAG_4) does not correspond to Akk. *karṣu* elsewhere, it is equated with the verb *karāṣu* "to pinch, break off." Perhaps, therefore, we may read the Ugar. column as [*q*]*à-ar-ṣú,* for /*qarṣu*/, cognate to Akk. *kar(ā)ṣu*. For the alphab. verb *qrṣ* "to pinch, gnaw" (UT 481a, nos. 2280, 2281), see Caquot-Sznycer-Herdner, Textes ougaritiques 335-36 n. n, 566-67 n. i; the noun /*qarṣu*/ may mean a "pinch" or "piece" (of clay); cf. also, e.g., Syriac *qarṣā* "gnawed morsel," with *ʾekal* "to calumniate," Akk. *karṣa akālu* "to calumniate."

211

Sign/Akk.: For the reconstruction, note, e.g., BARAG = *mu-ša-bu* in the Ugarit lexical text MSL 13 126:5' (Proto-Izi).

Ugar.: The writing *mu-ša-bu* clearly represents /*mōθabu*/ = alphab. *mθb* "dwelling" (cf., e.g., Hebrew *môšāb,* Syriac *mawtbā*), as suggested by Nougayrol.

[69]See n. 3 in the Introduction to Part I above.

PART II

GLOSSARY

Words are listed by root, in the order used by the various Ugaritic lexicons, viz.:

ʾ, b, g, d, ð, h, w, z, ḥ, ḫ, ṭ, ẓ, y, k, l, m, n, s (and *ś*), *ʿ, ǵ, p, ṣ, q, r, š, t, θ.*

Words of uncertain root appear in an Appendix at the end of the Glossary in syllabic transliteration in the order of the Akkadian dictionaries.

The format of the lemmata is as follows:

ROOT
/phonemic normalization/ part of speech, "translation."
text genre: *citation(s) in transliteration* reference(s)
Alphabetic equivalent, if attested, cited with reference to the Glossary in Gordon's UT (ch. 19) or by text according to KTU.
Discussion.

Words attested in the *polyglot S^a Vocabulary exemplars* are marked as such immediately under the citation(s), with the S^a section number. For all discussion of these forms, the reader is referred to the commentary in Part I above.

Cognates are normally cited only for words not attested thus far in alphabetic form. For words that do occur alphabetically, there seems little point in repeating the cognates listed in the Glossary in Gordon's UT (see also Aistleitner, Wörterbuch), except where differing suggestions may be noted.

When two or more derivatives of a root are attested among the syllabic transcriptions, they are listed in succession under the root and designated (a), (b), etc.

ʾ

ʾBD

/naʾbadu/ N v.n./infin. "flight, escape," "to escape, flee."

legal: [lú.m]eš*ú-ru-ba-nu* [*š*]*a* : *na-ba-dì-*⌜*šu-nu*⌝ "the guarantors of (against) their flight" PRU 3 37b:7

Alphabetic: Cf. *ʾbd* Gt "to perish" (KTU 1.14 i 24; also *itdb*, ibid. line 8?); D? "to destroy(?)" (KTU 1.2 iv 3 [?; see Caquot-Sznycer-Herdner, Textes ougaritiques 134 n. e]; 1.100:5,11), etc. (UT 348b no. 13).

The form occurs in the same text as Akk. *i-na-bi-tu₄* (*innabbitū*, line 9), but is marked as non-Akk. by the gloss mark and the *-a-* of the second syllable (vs. Akk. *nābutu*/*naʾbutu*). Use of the N stem probably reflects a technical (legal) calque from Akk., but the form itself (i.e., *naqtal*) must be regarded as Ugar., as suggested by Boyd, Collection 35-37.

?ʾBY: see Sª Voc. no. 191.2, commentary on the Ugar. column.

?ʾBL: see *IB-lu* in the Appendix, below.

☛ p. 390 ʾD: see ʾDN, below.

ʾDM

/ʾadmānu/ n./adj.? "red (soil)"; in field designation.

legal: *i-na* A.ŠÀ : *ad-ma-ni* "in 'redland field'" PRU 3 122f.:8

Alphabetic: Cf. v. *ʾdm* N "to rouge oneself" (UT 352a no. 82).

Identified by Kühne, UF 6 162-63; Boyd, Collection 37-38. Cf., e.g., Heb. *ʾădāmâ* "ground" and *ʾadmônî* "red(dish)."

ʾDN (or ʾD)

/ʾadānu/ n. "father."

lex.: (Sum.) NU = (Akk.) *a-bu* = (Hur.) *at-ta-ni* = (Ugar.) *a-da-nu* Ug. 5 130 ii 9' (polyglot vocab.)

Sª Voc. no. 24.3.

Alphabetic: *adn* (UT 352 no. 86).

On the form, see the Sª Voc. commentary, with n. 2.

ʾDR

/ʾaduru/ ? adj. "mighty, august."

lex.: (Sum.) [MAḪ] = (Akk.) [*ṣīru*] = (Hur.) [ ] = (Ugar.) *a-du-rù* Ug. 5 137 ii 34' (polyglot vocab.)

Sª Voc. no. 189.1.

Alphabetic: *adr* (e.g., KTU 1.12 ii 29; 1.17 v 7 [Caquot-Sznycer-Herdner, Textes ougaritiques 427 n. r], vi 20-23; 4.102:passim; 4.411:7 [vs. *dq* "small"]; see UT 352a no 92).

(In Ug. 5 84:5, read *sà*!(A)-*a*[*p-l*]*u*, with Nougayrol, rather than *a-*⌜*du-ru*⌝, as proposed by Berger, UF 2 355.)

?ʾWṬ: see *ú-ṭu* in the Appendix to the Glossary, below.

?ʾZZ: see *[I]i ?/[U]Z ?-ZU* in the Appendix to the Glossary, below.

?ʾZR

/maʾzaru/ ?, pl. */maʾzarūma/* ?, n. "loincloth(?)."

econon.: 2 $^{túg.meš}$*ma-za-ru-ma* PRU 6 126:4

2 *ma-za-r[u]* PRU 6 168:4

Alphabetic: Cf. dual *mizrtm* "a (doubled) garment(?)" (KTU 1.5 vi 17), *mizrth* (1.17 i 15); note also, probably, *uzr* "clothed, girdled(?)" (i.e., */ʾuzūru/* < **ʾazūru*?; KTU 1.17 i 2-22 passim; see Sanmartín, UF 9 369-70; Dietrich-Loretz, UF 10 65-66; UT 354a nos. 124,125).

See Rainey, IOS 3 46-47; Boyd, Collection 51-54.

Note also, in another list of garments:]-*ú ma-az-ru*, PRU 6 123:2. If the latter is the same word as that represented by *ma-za-ru-ma*, then the latter form cannot reflect */maʾzaru/*, since a change */maʾzaru/* > */mazru/* is most unlikely (pace Sivan, Analysis 242). Rather, the forms would all reflect a *qatl* noun of a root *m-z-r*, viz., */mazarūma/*. With the latter, compare the Akk. verb *mazāru*, which occurs only in lexical texts, but has to do with treating wool (CAD M/1 437b; further, SÍG.AL.ḪI.A = *mazrātum*, ibid. 439a [= MSL 10, p. 128:15]), and which von Soden, AHw 637b, associates with MHeb. *māzar* "to spin (yarn)." It is more likely, however, that *ma-az-ru* in PRU 6 123:2, which may be an Akk. v. adj., is to be separated from the other two forms listed above, as suggested by Boyd, Collection 52, who also rightly concludes that none of these forms should be associated with alphabetic *mḏrn* (a weapon), pace Nougayrol, PRU 6 p. 157.

ʾḤD

/ʾaḥadu/ ? num. "one."

lex.: (Sum.) [AŠ] = (Akk.) *[it-te-tù]* = (Hur.) [ ] = (Ugar.) *[a-ḫ]a-du* Ug. 5 138 1' (polyglot vocab.)

S^{a} Voc. no. 61.1

Alphabetic: *aḥd* (UT 354 no. 126).

See Borger, RA 63 172.

(ʾḪ

/ʾaḫātu/ n. "sister."

legal: in nom. ^{f}*a-ḫa-tu*$_{4}$(-)LUGAL, gen. ^{f}*a-ḫa-ti*(-)LUGAL PRU 3 53b:8,11,18

Alphabetic: *aḫt* (UT 354-55 no. 128); PN *aḫtmlk* (KTU 2.11:4).

The forms cited here may be a title, "king's sister"; see Nougayrol, Ug. 5 p. 261-62. More likely, however, a PN; see most recently Dietrich-Loretz, UF 15 303.)

ʾḪD

/maʾḫadu/ n. "harbor, quay."

lex.: (Sum.) KAR = (Akk.) *ka-a-ru* = (Hur.) *ma-ḫa-[z]i* = (Ugar.) *ma-aḫ-ḫa-[du]* Ug. 5 137 ii 21' (polyglot vocab.)

S^{a} Voc. no. 183.5

Alphabetic: Note the GN *maḫdh* (with directive *-h*?; KTU 4.149:5); gentilic sg. *maḫdy* (4.181:3), pl. *maḫdym* (4.263:5), and *miḫdym* (4.383:1; 4.611 i 1); also, without ʾ, gentilic sg. *mḫdy* (4.635:17).

On the form (a pronunciation [maḫḫadu] < /*maʾḫadu*/ probably reflected), see the S^a Voc. commentary. Cf. Akk. *māḫāzu*.

ʾḪR

/*ʾuḫrāyu*/ n. "end, destiny."

legal: É : *ḫi-ri-ti ù* A.ŠÀ^{meš} *ša uḫ-ra-a-yi* "cemetery and field(s) of destiny" PRU 3 52f.:17-18

Alphabetic: *uḫry(t)* (UT 355b no. 138, to which add *wuḫry ykly* ⌜*ršp*⌝ "and to the hereafter will Resheph destroy (him)" KTU 1.103:39-40 [omens]; differently Herdner in Ug. 7 pp. 48-49, 54-55, lines 15-15bis; Xella, Testi rituali 195).

Gordon, Syria 33 102-3, plausibly suggests that these lines refer to the cemetery of an estate. We should thus translate perhaps "sepulchre and plot(s) of destiny"; the A.ŠÀ^{meš} *ša uḫ-ra-a-yi* would be the parcel of land in which the burial site (/*baytu ḫirīti*/) was located. For the form *uḫ-ra-a-yi*, cf. alphabetic *uḫry(t)* "destiny" in KTU 1.17 vi 35 (Gordon, UT 355b no. 138). The -*āy* ending of the form finds parallels elsewhere in Semitic, e.g., Syriac *(ʾ)ḥrāyā* "latter" (note also the Arabic *al-ʾuḫrā(y)* "the hereafter" [Boyd, Collection 41-42]); whether it is triptotic /*ʾuḫrāyi*/ as rendered here, or diptotic /*ʾuḫrāya*/ cannot be determined because of the polyvalence of the final PI sign (probably not final -*ay*, i.e., *uḫ-ra-a-ay* [so Boyd], however, since the value *vy* is not otherwise attested in Ugarit Akk.).

?ʾṮ(Ṯ): see *ú-ṭu* in the Appendix to the Glossary, below.

?ʾẒẒ: see [*I*]*i* ?/[*U*]Z ?-*ZU* in the Appendix to the Glossary, below.

ʾYB

/*ʾēbu*/ n. "enemy."

lex.: (Sum.) [EN] = (Akk.) [*z*]*é*?-*ru* = (Hur.) *tu-ur-bi* = (Ugar.) *e-bu* Ug. 5 130 iii 15' (polyglot vocab.)

S^a Voc. no. 37.3

Alphabetic: *ib* (UT 356 no. 144, and add KTU 1.103:passim [omens]).

ʾYK

/*ʾayyakku*/ ? n. (Akk. loanword) divine name ("sanctuary").

lex.: (Sum.) [^{d}NIN.SÚN?] = (Hur.) *a-ia-ku-un* = (Ugar.) *a-ia-ku* Ug. 5 137 iv b 15 (polyglot god-list)

Alphabetic: Unattested.

The Hur. and Ugar. apparently represent a hypostatization of Akk. *ayyakku* "sanctuary"; see the comments of Nougayrol, Ug. 5 p. 249 n. 1; Laroche, Ug. 5 p. 460.

?ʾKT

/*ʾiktu*/ ? n. (Hur. loanword?) "mortar."

lex.: (Sum.) NA = (Akk.) *ur-ṣú* = (Hur.) *it-ki* = (Ugar.) *IG-TU*$_4$ Ug. 5 130 ii 10' (polyglot vocab.)

S^a Voc. no. 25.1.

Alphabetic: Unattested.

p. 390

ʾL

/ʾilu/ n. "god"; divine name (El).

lex.: (Sum.) [AN] = (Akk.) [*ilu*] = (Hur.) ⸢*e*⸣-*ni* = (Ugar.) ⸢*i*?-*lu*?⸣ UF 11 479: 30 (polyglot vocab.)

(Sum.) IDIM = (Akk.) [ ] = (Hur.) [ ] = (Ugar.) DINGIR-lu_4 Ug. 5 137 iii 9 (polyglot vocab.)

(Sum.) [ ] = (Hur.) [*k*]*u*-[*m*]*ur*-*wi* = (Ugar.) DINGIR-lu_4 Ug. 5 137 iii 33" (polyglot god-list)

S^a Voc. nos. 45.3; 198.2.

(note also DINGIR-lu_4 in Ug. 5 18:2, corresponding to alphab. *il* in KTU 1.47:3; 1.118:2; either Akk. *ilu* or Ugar. /ʾ*ilu*/ may be intended)

Alphabetic: *il* (UT 357-58 no. 163).

(ʾLḪN

/ʾalaḫḫinu/ ? personal name or n. (Akk. loanword?) "miller"?

econ.: PN DUMU *a-la-ḫi-ni* PRU 6 70:11

Alphabetic: Pl. *alḫnm* (KTU 4.392:4); PN *alḫn* (4.102:25; 4.337:11; see UT 358b no. 179). Cf. Akk. *alaḫḫinu* "miller" (of unknown origin).

It seems more likely that this is a PN, since people are not normally called "son of the X," where X is a profession, in our corpus (the lack of determinative ^{lú} would be unusual, but not unprecedented; cf. under YṢR, MRYN, ǴMR); see Dietrich-Loretz, BiOr 23 128a; Nougayrol, PRU 6 p. 150; Dietrich-Loretz-Sanmartín, UF 6 19 no. 2; Boyd, Collection 28-29. On the term *alḫn* as an intendant, a person in charge of the household, see Del Olmo Lete, UF 10 51; Diakonoff, ArOr 47 40.)

ʾLN

/ʾallānu/ n. "oak"; in field designation.

legal: [*ù* A.ŠÀ$^{meš/ḫi.a}$] *al-la-ni* "and 'oak field(s)'"PRU 3 131f.:9

A.ŠÀ^{meš} ^{1}*al-la-an-še-ri-DA-ni* PRU 3 108f.:5

A.ŠÀ^{meš} *al-la-an* ^{1}*še-er-TA-an-ni* PRU 3 131a:4-6

Alphabetic: Cf. probably *aln* (KTU 1.12 i 20) = Akk. *allānu*, Heb. *ʾallôn*. (*aln* does not correspond to Heb. *ʾēlôn*, as suggested by Caquot-Sznycer-Herdner, Textes ougaritiques 338 n. z, for which we would expect alphab. **iln*.)

For the second and third examples, see Liverani, VT 27 212-16. It is possible that in one or more of the examples, Akk. *allānu* "oak" is intended (Sivan, Analysis 197).

?ʾMM¹

/ʾummatu/ ? n. "clan(?)"; in field designation.

legal: 5 A.ŠÀ *i-na* AN.ZA.GÀR *um-ma-ti* "5 fields in 'clan district(?)'" PRU 3 79ff.:22

Alphabetic: Cf. *umt* "kin, clan(?)" (see UT 360b no. 225; Caquot-Sznycer-Herdner, Textes ougaritiques 264 n. m).

See Sivan, Analysis 201. Although the first two signs of *um-ma-ti* are damaged in the copy, Nougayrol did not indicate any uncertainty about the reading in his transliteration.

?ʾMM²: see *am-ma-ti* in the Appendix to the Glossary, below.

ᵓNK

/ᵓanākŭ/ pronoun 1cs "I."

lex.: (Sum.) [MAL/GÁN] = (Akk.) *a-na-⸢ku⸣* = (Hur.) *iš-te-en*$_6$ = (Ugar.) *a-na-ku* Ug. 5 130 iii 12' (polyglot vocab.)

Sᵃ Voc. no. 35/36.4.

Alphabetic: *ank* (UT 362a no. 249).

ᵓNP

/ᵓappu/ n. "nose."

lex.: (Sum.) KAR = (Akk.) *ap-pu* = (Hur.) *pu-u[ḫ]-ḫi* = (Ugar.) *ap-pu* Ug. 5 137 ii 19' (polyglot vocab.)

Sᵃ Voc. no. 183.3.

Alphabetic: *ap* (UT 362b no. 264).

ᵓNT

/ᵓattă/ pronoun 2ms "you" (ms).

lex.: (Sum.) ZA = (Akk.) *at-ta* = (Hur.) *ši-ni-⸢bi⸣* = (Ugar.) *at-ta* Ug. 5 130 ii 4' (polyglot vocab.)

Sᵃ Voc. no. 22.1.

Alphabetic: *at* (UT 363a no. 272).

☛ p. 390

ᵓNθ

/ᵓunuθθu/ n. (Hur. loanword?) "estate tax."

legal: *ú-nu-uš-ša ša* É *ub-bá-lu* "and they will be responsible for the tax on the estate" PRU 3 53b:20-21

PN [*ù*] PN$_2$ *ú-nu-uš-ša ú-bá-lu* PRU 3 61f.:13-15

ù ú-nu-ša É^{meš} *ub-bal* PRU 3 62f.:17

Alphabetic: *unθ* (UT 363a no. 275).

See Hillers, HTR 64 257-59; Boyd, Collection 47-50. The etymology of this term remains uncertain. It may be Hurrian, as suggested by Speiser, JAOS 75 162; note the existence of a root-complement *-uθθ* (Bush, GHL 187; thus, perhaps roughly "income," from the verbal base *un-* "to come"?). But Speiser's insistence that the word *must* be Hurrian because it may be construed with the Hur. suffix *-uḫli* can no longer be maintained, since that suffix also occurs on words of Semitic origin (Dietrich-Loretz, WO 3 195-96). Further, the word is not certainly attested thus far in Hurrian texts. Thus, it may instead be a Semitic word of a root *ᵓ-n-θ* and the pattern *qutull* (not *qutullā* as suggested by Dietrich-Loretz, ibid., since the writings above do not indicate a final long vowel).

?ᵓSS: see [*I*]*i* ?/[*U*]Z ?*-ZU* in the Appendix to the Glossary, below.

ᵓPY

/ᵓāpiyu/ ? n. (G ptcpl.) "baker."

lex.: (Sum.) [MU] = (Akk.) [*n*]*u-ḫa-ti-mu* = (Hur.) *is-ḫa-⸢ri-ni⸣* = (Ugar.) *:* ⸢*a*⸣-[*p*]*í*?-[*yu*?] Ug. 5 130 iii 4' (polyglot vocab.)

Sᵃ Voc. no. 32.4.

Alphabetic: Sg. *apy* (KTU 4.212:5; 4.362:4,5), pl. *apym* (4.125:10; see UT 364a no. 303).

?ʾPL: see *IB-lu* in the Appendix to the Glossary, below.

?ʾṢṢ: see [*I*]*i* ?/[*U*]*Z* ?-*ZU* in the Appendix to the Glossary, below.

ʾR

/*ʾiratu*/ ? n. "chest(?)."

lex.: (Sum.) G[AB?] = (Akk.) [*irtu*?] = (Hur.) ⌜*a*?⌝-*ḫé-er-ni* = (Ugar.) *i-r*[*a*?-*tu*$_4$?] Ug. 5 137 ii 53' (polyglot vocab.)

Sª Voc. no. 194.1.

Alphabetic: *irt* (UT 365a no. 326; add KTU 1.101:17).

?ʾRG: see [*i*]*r-KU*, Sª Voc. no. 48.2.

ʾRZ

/*ʾarzu*/ (pl. /*ʾarzūma*/ ?) n. "cedar."

econ.: [*ḫ*]*u*?-*ma*^{meš} *ar-zu* PRU 6 114:3 (list of trees/wood)

(note also Ugar. lit.: [*i*]*a*(-)*ab-ṣi-ru ar-zi-ma*["he/I will cut down the cedars(??)" Ug. 5 153:1)

Alphabetic: *arz* (UT 365b no. 346).

The econ. text concerns various types of trees/wood, most of which are probably Ugar. words; see under ʾRN, MSW, θǴR. Thus, despite the lack of determinative ^{giš}, the form here is almost certainly WSem. /*ʾarzu*/, which does not occur in Akk. (But in addition to the cognates listed by Gordon, UT, s.v., add now the fem. Eblaite form ^{giš}NUN.SAL = *ar-za-tum* (MEE 4 252 no. 471).

(The form in Ug. 5 153, if correctly understood, is oblique pl. /*ʾarzīma*/ < *ʾ*arazīma*, with pretonic vowel syncope; see Part III, ch. 2 §B 1.)

ʾRḪ (or **YRḪ**) ☛ p. 390

/*tiʾtarḫu*/ (or /*tittarḫu*/) v., Gt imperfective, 3fs "to hurry(?)" (i.e., "she will hurry(?)").

legal:]*x-i a-na sú-qí ti-ir-ḫu-uṣ : ti-tar-ḫ*[*u*] "she will run quickly into the street" Ug. 5 3 r. 10'

Alphabetic: Unattested.

Nougayrol read *ti-tar-ḫ*[*u-uṣ*], and suggested, p. 6 n. 2, that the scribe wrote pret. *tirḫuṣ* for WS imperfective, then corrected himself with a Gt dur. *tirtaḫ*(*ḫ*)*uṣ* (> *titarḫuṣ* by metathesis); Berger, UF 2 339 n. 1, proposes *tittarḫu*, an N of WSem. *reḫû* (comparing Arabic *rḫw*); Boyd, Collection 169-72, reluctantly follows Berger, noting the morphological difficulty in accounting for the -*t*-, and claiming that the root ʾ-*r*-*ḫ* is impossible, being a later denominative from the primary noun ʾ*urḫu* "way, path"; Rainey, IOS 5 20-21, suggests an Ntn (replacing Gtn) form.

The gloss mark after an Akk. form (preterite for an expected durative form, as frequently happens in Ugarit Akk.) indicates that *ti-tar-ḫ*[*u*] is Ugar. and rules out Nougayrol's and Rainey's suggestions. Berger's proposal is morphologically impossible, unless we wish to posit an Nt or Ntn stem for Ugar. Thus, despite Boyd's caveat, the root is probably either ʾ-*r*-*ḫ* or *y*-*r*-*ḫ*, cognate to Akk. *arāḫu*(*m*)/*warāḫum* "to hurry" (attested from OB on), a root probably unrelated to PS *ʾ*urḫu*; the Akk. and Ugar. verbs are probably in hendiadys: "she will run quickly." The form will be Gt *yaqtulu*, i.e., /*tiʾtarḫu*/ < **tiʾtariḫu* (or /*tittarḫu*/ < **tittariḫu*, if *y*-*r*-*ḫ*; cf. alphabetic *itrθ* for */*ʾittariθ*-/, root *y*-*r*-*θ*, in KTU 1.3 iii 47 [see Gordon, UT 86 §9.48]). For the conjugation, cf. the use of the Gt in Ugar. with *h*-*l*-*k* "to go" and *r*-*q*-*ṣ* "to swoop." For the post-tonic syncope of unaccented *-i-* of the original **ti*ʾ*/tariḫu*, see Part III, ch. 2 §B 2.

?ʾRK: see [*i*]*r-KU*, Sᵃ Voc. no. 48.2.

?ʾRM: see *a-ra-mi-ma* in the Appendix to the Glossary, below.

ʾRN

/ʾ*urnu*/ n. "laurel(?)."

econ.: *15* $^{giš.meš}$*úr-nu* "15 laurel(?) trees/logs" PRU 6 114:1

Alphabetic: Unattested.

See Rainey, IOS 3 46, who cites the Heb. hapax *ʾōren* (Isaiah 44:14). Since ***urnu*** also occurs in Akk., from OAkk. on, we may not be certain the *ur-nu* here is Ugar. (although von Soden, AHw 1431b, suggests that Akk. ***urnu*** may be a WSem. loan). Most of the words for various types of trees/wood in PRU 6 114 are Ugar., however; see ʾRZ, MSW, θǴR.

Note also the form ^{giš}ÚR.NU.UM in a Ugarit lex. text (Syria 12 pl. 46ff. ii 4; see MSL 5 112, notes to lines 237-264) as in the parallel Mesopotamian lex. texts (Ḫḫ III 254, MSL 5 p. 113 notes, p. 114:254).

ʾRṢ

/ʾ*arṣu*/ n. "earth."

lex.: (Sum.) [IDIM] = (Akk.) [*erṣetu*] = (Hur.) [ ] = (Ugar.) *ar-ṣu* Ug. 5 137 iii 14' (polyglot vocab.)

Sᵃ Voc. no. 198.7.

Alphabetic: *arṣ* (UT 366-67 no. 376).

?ʾRQ: see [*i*]*r-KU*, Sᵃ Voc. no. 48.2.

ʾRŠ

/ʾ*irištu*/ ? n. "request, desire."

lex.: (Sum.) [KAM] = (Akk.) [*mēreltu*] = (Hur.) [ ]⌜*x*⌝-*še* = (Ugar.) *i*-[*r*]*i*?-*iš*[-*tu*$_4$?] UF 11 479:28 (polyglot vocab.)

Sᵃ Voc. no. 44.2.

Alphabetic: *iršt* (UT 367a no. 379; add KTU 2.22:4).

On the form, see Part III, ch. 2 §A 1 d. Cf. Heb. *ʾărešet*, Akk. ***erištu*** "request, desire."

ʾRT: see ʾR, above.

ʾŠ

/ʾ*išītu*/ n. "fire."

lex.: (Sum.) IZI = (Akk.) *i-ša-tu* = (Hur.) [ ] = (Ugar.) ⌜*i*⌝-*ši-t*[*u*$_4$] UF 11 479: 37 (polyglot vocab.)

Sᵃ Voc. no. 48.1.

Alphabetic: *išt* (UT 367b no. 391).

On the form, see the Sᵃ Voc. commentary.

In view of the lexical *i-ši-tu*, it is probably best to view *i-ša-ti*, in ⌜URU⌝$^{ḫi.a}$ *i-na* IZI : ⌜*i*-*ša*⌝-*ti* Ug. 5 24:14 (letter), as the Akkadian *išātu*.

ʾŠD

/ʾ*išdu*/ n. "leg, lower extremities."

lex.: (Sum.) [DU/SUḪUŠ] = (Akk.) [*išdu*] = (Hur.) [ ] = (Ugar.) *iš-du*4 Ug. 5 131 8' (polyglot vocab.)

Sª Voc. no. 53.4/54.

Alphabetic: *išd* (KTU 1.1 ii 2, iii 11; 1.3 iii 20, iv 12; 1.101:6; see UT 367-68 no. 394).

ʾŠT: see ʾŠ, above.

ʾT: see ʾNT, above.

(*ʾTT

*/ʾ*it*/ "with."

In Ug. 5 54:6,7,24-26, the inexperienced scribe wrote *it* for expected *it-ti*. It has been suggested by several scholars (see Sivan, Analysis 133 nn. 2-6) that *it* here and in 3 Amarna instances (EA 85:31; 114:46; 130:24) represents a Northwest Semitic ʾ*et* "with." Since the original form of this preposition is presumably **ittV*, it seems unlikely that in a dialect in which final vowels are preserved such a form could be reduced to /ʾ*it*/, and it seems preferable to view these writings as abbreviations (for Akk. *itti* or WSem /ʾ*itta*/). For the Ugarit Akk. examples, furthermore, it should be pointed out that a preposition /ʾ*it(tV)*/ is not attested in alphabetic texts.)

?ʾθB

/ʾ*iθību*/ ? n. month name.

econ.: *i-na* ITI *i*-⌜*ši*?⌝-[*bi*?] PRU 6 152:4 (short list of comestibles)

Alphabetic: *iθb* (KTU 4.219:15; 4.220:6).

Nougayrol transliterated *araḫi-š*[*i(??)-gi*], citing (PRU 6 p. 157 n. 13) other examples of a month written *iš(i)gi* in unpublished lexical texts from Ugarit. The latter writing, however, since it does not correspond to any known alphabetically written month name, is probably logographic. In an economic text, it is more likely that a syllabic transcription of a Ugar. month name would be written (see under ḪLL), and so a form corresponding to alphab. *iθb* is to be preferred. If correctly read, /ʾ*iθību*/ would be a *qitīl* < *qatīl* form; see Part III, ch. 2 §A 1 d. An etymology of the form does not suggest itself.

ʾθR

/ʾ*a*[*θi*]*ratu*/ ?? (also/ʾ*aθratu*/ ?) n. divine name (Asherah, "?").

lex.: (Sum.) [ᵈNIN.LÍL] = (Hur.) [*aš-t*]*e-ku-mur-wi-ni-we* = (Ugar.) ⌜*a*⌝[-*ši*?-*ra*?-*tu*4?] Ug. 5 137 iii 36"

(Sum.) [ ] = (Hur.) [ ] = (Ugar.) [*a*?-*ši*?-*r*]*a-tu*4 Ug. 5 137 iv b 7 (polyglot god-list)

note also ᵈ*aš-ra-tu*4 Ug. 5 18:19 (god-list)

Alphabetic: *aθrt* (UT 370a no. 428).

The first entry is entirely reconstructed apart from the first sign. The second was restored by Nougayrol as *aš*(?)-*r*]*a-tum*, presumably on the basis of the third entry, but the copy indicates more room before *ra* than would be taken up by *aš*. In any case, it is not certain that Asherah occurred at this point in the god-list (see Nougayrol's comments, Ug. 5 p. 248-49, n. 7). The third entry, which corresponds to [*a*]*θrt* in the parallel alphabetic god-list KTU 1.118:19, probably represents the Akk. form of the goddess, Ašratu; it is possible, however, that Ugar.

/ʾaθratu/ is intended, a biform of (reconstructed) /ʾaθiratu/ which has undergone post-tonic syncope (Part III, ch. 2 §B 2).

For ʾθR, see also the next entry.

ʾθRYN

/ʾuθrīyānu/ n. (Hur. loanword?) "crown prince."

econ.: lú.meš*mur-ú uš-r[i-ia]-ni* "the 'commanders' of the crown prince" PRU 3 199ff. iv 21 (list of persons grouped by profession)

Alphabetic: *uθryn* (UT 369b no. 426).

A suggestion by Goetze, RHA 12 (54) 4, that this term is Hurrian in origin has been questioned by Dietrich-Loretz, WO 3 239. (As an alternative possibility, perhaps the form is instead Semitic in origin, from the root *ʾ-θ-r*, as in **ʾaθru* "place"; i.e., */ʾuθr+īy+ān-u/* [cf. "lieutenant"]; see Segert, Basic Grammar 43 §43.29. A difficulty with this suggestion is that the order of the morphemes *-ī(y)* and *-ān*, when both occur on forms elsewhere in Semitic, is reversed.)

B

B

/bi(-)/ prep. "in."

lex.: (Sum.) [MU] = (Akk.) ⸢*i*?⸣-[*n*]*a* = (Hur.) *i-gi-da* = (Ugar.) ⸢*bi*⸣-*i*[Ug. 5 130 iii 6′ (polyglot vocab.)

(Sum.) UR = (Akk.) *mi-it-*[*ḫ*]*a-ri-i*[*š*] = (Hur.) [ ] = (Ugar.) *bi-ru/šub/p*[UF 11 479:36 (polyglot vocab.)

Sª Voc. nos. 32.6, 47.3.

(note also perhaps Ugar. lit.: the *BI* sign in Ug. 5 153 r.6′,7′)

Alphabetic: *b* (*by* in KTU 2.38:13,25; see UT 370 no. 435).

For the writing *bi-i* in the first example above, see the Sª Voc. commentary.

☛ p. 390

BDL

**/bidălu/*, pl. */bidălūma/na/*, n. "merchant."

econ.: lú.mešDAM.GÀRmeš : *bi-da-lu-ma* PRU 3 199ff. ii 12 (list of persons grouped by profession)

[lú.m]eš*bi-da-lu-na* PRU 3 204f.:14

Alphabetic: *bdl* (UT 371a no. 448). In addition to the Arabic *bad(d)ala* "to exchange," note also now Eblaite *ba-da-lum* "merchant" (see Fronzaroli, QS 13 137).

See Kühne, UF 6 158 n. 9; Astour, ABAW NF 75 11-12. On the function of the gloss mark separating *tamkārū* and Ugar. */bidălūma/*, see Part III, ch. 1 §C 3 b. For the final *-na* of the second example, see Part III, ch. 3 §C 1 d (1).

BḤR[1]

**/biḥīru/* ?, pl. bound */biḥīrū/*, n. "elite (troop)(?)."

econ.: lú.mešb[i]-ḫi-ru uruu-g[a-ri-it] "the 'elite troops' of Ugarit" PRU 6 71:5'

Alphabetic: Unattested.

A pl. bound form */biḥīrū/*, from **b-ḥ-r* "to choose" (cf. Heb. *bāḥar*, Syr. *bḥar*, Akk. *bêru*). Probably a *qatīl* form, > *qitīl* with vowel assimilation around the guttural (see Part III, ch. 2 §A 1 c). Boyd, Collection 76-77, notes similar terms in Amorite and at Mari; see CAD B 211-12 for Mari *biḫrum*/ *biᵓrum*; Gelb, AS 21 pp. 16a, 571 (no. 1209) for Amorite *bi-ḫi-rum*.

See also the following entry.

?BḪR (or ?BḤR²)

/baḫḫuru/ or */baḥḥuru/* n. "youth."

lex.: (Sum.) ŠUL = (Akk.) *eṭ-lu* = (Hur.) *uš-ta-an-ni* = (Ugar.) ⸢*ba*⸣*-aḫ-ḫu-rù* Ug. 5 137 ii 24' (polyglot vocab.)

Sª Voc. no. 185.

Alphabetic: Cf. *bḫr* (KTU 1.15 v 5,22)?; see the Sª Voc. commentary.

?BṬL

/baṭalu/ ? adj./n.? "false(hood)(?)."

lex.: (Sum.) [ḪUL?] = (Akk.) [*zapru*/*ṣabru*?] = (Hur.) [ ]-*ba-di* = (Ugar.) *ba-TA-lu* Ug. 5 137 ii 38' (polyglot vocab.)

Sª Voc. no. 190.2.

Alphabetic: Unattested.

??BLM

/šablimu/ ?? n. (Š v.n./infin.?) "retaining wall(??)." p. 391

legal:]⸢*x*⸣-[*r*]*a*? *qa-du* éIM.D[Ù?.A?-*š*]*u*? : *šab*-⸢*li*?-*mi*?⸣ "... with its retaining wall(?)" PRU 6 56:4'

Alphabetic: Unattested.

This line is extremely obscure. Nougayrol read é*em-q*[*a*(?)-*š*]*u šap-l*[*i*]-*m*[*i*] and translated "ainsi que sa(?) maison-basse(?)," referring, PRU 3 p. 58 n. 2, to *a*/*emqu* in PRU 3 118:12 (see ᶜMQ¹ below). (The gloss mark before ŠAB, omitted by Nougayrol, was noted by Kühne, UF 5 188.) Boyd, Collection 57-59, read instead É *im-q*[*í-š*]*u* : *šap-l*[*i*]-*m*[*i*](?) (*q*[*í*] would conform better to the copy than *q*[*i*]), and translated "[hi]s vall[ey] house," suggesting, p. 215-16, that : *šap-l*[*i*]-*m*[*i*](?) was added as a Ugar. gloss (*/*šaplu*/ "low place") to indicate that *im-q*[*í-š*]*u* denoted Ugar. /ᶜ*imqu*/ "valley" rather than Akk. *emqu* "wise." But this would be the only instance in these texts of a Ugar. word glossing another Ugar. word. It is more likely, therefore, that the form before the gloss mark is a logogram. (For the sequence {logogram+pron. suff. :Ugar. word}, cf. *qa-du* éAN.ZA.GÀR-*šu* : *ha-a-yi* in PRU 3 95f.:6; see under ḪWY, below; see further Part III, ch. 1 §C 3.) A possible candidate is IM.DÙ.A (Akk. *pitiqtu*), perhaps here in the sense "retaining wall," although a determinative é would admittedly be unusual in that case. As for the Ugar. gloss, the damaged middle sign prevents any certain analysis; despite the apparent third vertical in the copy, Nougayrol's ⸢*li*⸣ seems the most likely reading. Since a dual form (/*šaplēmi*/ "two low places"??) has little to recommend it, perhaps we may suggest, with considerable reservation, a *šaqtil* form (or Š verbal noun) of the NWS root *b-l-m* "to curb, restrain," in keeping with our proposal above concerning the logogram. Forms with prefix *š* are of course rare in Ugaritic; see, however, the forms cited above in Part I, Sª Voc. no. 194.4, with n. 60.

BNŠ

/bunūšu/ n. "man."

lex.: (Sum.) ZA = (Akk.) *a-mi-lu* = (Hur.) *tar-⸢šu-wa-an⸣-ni* = (Ugar.) *: bu-nu-⸢šu⸣* Ug. 5 130 ii 5' (polyglot vocab.)

(Sum.) NU = (Akk.) *a-mi-lu* = (Hur.) *tar-šu-wa-an-ni* = (Ugar.) *[b]u-nu-šu* Ug. 5 130 ii 8' (polyglot vocab.)

(Sum.) [SAG?] = (Akk.) *[amīlu?]* = (Hur.) *[tar]-š[u-w]a-an-ni* = (Ugar.) *: bu-nu-šu* Ug. 5 131:7' (polyglot vocab.)

(Sum.) [LÚ] = (Akk.) *[amīlu]* = (Hur.) *[tar-š]u-wa-ni* = (Ugar.) *bu-nu-šu* Ug. 5 137 ii 31' (polyglot vocab.)

S^a Voc. nos. 22.2; 24.2; 51.2; 187.4.

Alphabetic: *bnš* (UT 373-74 no. 486). On the derivation of the form, see S^a Voc. no. 22.2, Ugar. commentary.

☛ p. 391

B^{c}L

/ba^{c}lu/, pl. */ba^c(a)lūma/*, n. "lord"; divine name (Baal).

lex.: (Sum.) [EN] = (Akk.) *[be]-lu* = (Hur.) *e-wi-ri* = (Ugar.) *ba-a-lu-ma* Ug. 5 130 iii 14' (polyglot vocab.)

(Sum.) [AN?] = (Akk.) *[šarru?]* = (Hur.) *ta-ni* = (Ugar.) *ba!?-a-[lu?]*(?) UF 11 479:31 (polyglot vocab.)

(Sum.) [AN?] = (Akk.) *[šarrānū?]* = (Hur.) *zi-ia-ni* = (Ugar.) *[b]a?-a-[lu-ma(?)]* UF 11 479:32 (polyglot vocab.)

(Sum.) [UD?] = (Akk.) *[bēlu?]* = (Hur.) [ ] = (Ugar.) *[b]a?-a-lu* Ug. 5 138 6' (polyglot vocab.)

(Sum.) [LÚ] = (Akk.) *[bēlu]* = (Hur.) *⸢e?⸣-wi-ri* = (Ugar.) *ba-a-lu-ma* Ug. 5 137 ii 30' (polyglot vocab.)

(Sum.) [LUGAL] = (Akk.) *[bēlu]* = (Hur.) *[ewiri]* = (Ugar.) *[b]a-⸢a-lu-ma⸣* Ug. 5 137 ii 33' (polyglot vocab.)

(Sum.) ^{d}IM.ZU.AN.NA = (Hur.) *te-eš-ša-a[b]* = (Ugar.) *ba-a-lu* Ug. 5 137 iv b 17 (polyglot god-list)

S^a Voc. nos. 37.2; 45.4; 45.5; 63.5; 187.3; 188.2.

Alphabetic: *b^{c}l(m)* (UT 374-75 no. 493).

(?BṢR

/yabṣiru/ ? or */ʾabṣiru/* ? v., G imperfective, 3ms or 1cs "to cut down(?)."

Ugar. lit: [*i]a(-)ab-ṣi-ru ar-zi-ma*["he/I will cut down the cedars(??)" Ug. 5 153:1

Alphabetic: Unattested; *bṣr* in Aqht (UT 375b no. 500) is probably unrelated (see Caquot-Sznycer-Herdner, Textes ougaritiques 439 n. a).

If the word at the end of the line is correctly understood as */ʾarzīma/* "cedars," it is likely that this form is cognate with Hebrew *bāṣar* "to gather (grapes)," JAram. D *baṣṣar* "to cut off." Whether *IA* before *ab-ṣi-ru* is part of the verb (thus, 3ms/*yabṣiru/*) or is a 1cs suffix on the preceding form (thus, 1cs */ʾabṣiru/*) is unclear.)

BRḤ

barḫu (Akk. form, for Ugar.*/*bariḫu*/ ?), fem. */bariḫtu/*, adj./n. "fugitive, rustic(?)."

lex.: PA.GÁ = *nu-ʾu-ú* lú*ba-ar-ḫu* RA 63 83f. iv 8' (Silbenvokabular A)
PA.PA.GÁ = *nu-ʾu-ú* mí*ba-ri-iḫ-tu*$_4$ ibid. iv 9'

Alphabetic: Cf. v. *brḥ* "to flee"; see discussion.

These forms are probably Ugar. equivalents of the Akk. *nuʾû (nu(w)āʾum)* "rustic" (← "displaced" ← "fugitive"); see Nougayrol's comments, RA 63 p. 84; AHw 1547a, s.v. *barḫu*. On the unnecessary separation of alphabetic *brḥ* I and II (Gordon, UT 376 nos. 515, 516), both "to flee," see Dietrich-Loretz, OLZ 62 537. The masc. form *barḫu*, for expected **bariḫu*, is apparently in imitation of the Akk. v. adj. form (see Part III, ch. 3 §G 2); the fem. */bariḥtu/* may represent either Akk. or Ugar.

BRK

/birku/ ? n. "knee."

lex.: (Sum.) [TUK??] = (Akk.) [*birku*??] = (Hur.) [ ] = (Ugar.) [*bi*?]-*ir*?-*ku* Ug. 5 137 iii 30" (polyglot vocab.)
S^a Voc. no. 209.

Alphabetic: *brk* (UT 376b no. 518).

?BRR

/burru/ ? n. "(a bright metal?)" or "lye(?)."

econ.: ⌈*1*⌉ GÚN *bu-ri* GAL "1 large talent of *b.* " PRU 6 158:14 (list of various items)

Alphabetic: See discussion.

The word may be compared with alphab. *br* in KTU 1.4 i 35, which Caquot-Sznycer-Herdner, Textes ougaritiques 196 n. n, translate "(métal) brillant," plausibly suggesting a connection with alphab. *brr*, a metal which occurs in economic texts (UT 377a no. 526). (The latter term, the form of which may be compared with Hebrew *bārûr* "pure" and Ethiopic *berur* "silver," probably means "tin" [Zaccagnini, OA 9 317-24].) Alternatively, note Hebrew *bōr* "lye." In either case, the word will be an abstract *qutl* (*qull*) form of *b-r-r* "to be pure." (The use of the genitive, */burri/*, after the unit of measure, GÚN = *biltu* or Ugar. */kakkaru/*, is normative in Ugarit Akk.; see JCS 33 205.)

??BŠR: see S^a Voc. no. 193.3.

G

?GBN

/gabīnu/ ? n. "hillock(?)"; in field designation.

legal: [*ù* A.ŠÀ]ḫi.a *: ga-BI-ni* [*qa-du* é]AN.ZA.GÀR-*šu* "'hillock(?) field' with its tower" PRU 3 119f.:12

Alphabetic: Unattested.

For the etymology, see Kühne, UF 6 164-65, who cites Syriac *gbinā* "brow, ridge," JAram. *gəbinā* and Hebrew *gibbēn* "humpbacked," Hebrew *gabnunnîm* "peaks," Arabic *jabīn* "brow, forehead"; Kühne nevertheless prefers to read */gapinu/* < **gapnu* "vine" (so also Boyd,

Collection 81; Sivan, Analysis 218). The latter is unlikely, however, since we have no other examples of anaptyxis in Ugar. *qatl* forms.

??GBR

/tagabbiru/ ?? n. (tD v.n./infin.?) "?"; in field designation.

econ.: ^{é}AN.ZA.GÀR *ta-ga-bi-ra* Ug. 5 96:4,22, *-yv* line 15; perhaps also *ta$_5$-ga$_{14}$-bar!-yv!*(??) in line 2

Alphabetic: *g*⌜*t*⌝ [*tg*]⌜*br*⌝*y* and [*gt*?] *tgbry* (KTU 4.271:7,9), [*gt*?] *tgbry* (KTU 4.296:13).

KTU 4.296:13 reads *g*]*t gbry*, but since *gt* is followed by a word-divider elsewhere in this text, *tgbry* should be read together; cf. also under SKN b, ᶜBR. The form */tagabbir-/* may be a tD verbal noun originally (here as a gentilic?). Note that the root *g-b-r* occurs in the tD in Hebrew, Aramaic, Arabic meaning "to act mightily, proudly," and in Ethiopic (Geᶜez) meaning "to work (esp. land)."

GWL

/guw(w)ălu/ n. "circuit(?)"; in field designation.

legal: *ù* A.ŠÀ^{meš} *ša* LUGAL *ša* A.ŠÀ^{meš} *gu-wa-*⌜*li*⌝ "and the royal fields in 'circuit(?) field(s)'" PRU 3 151f.:11-12

Alphabetic: *gt gwl*; note also the GN *gwl* (UT 379a no. 566).

Since the form *gu-wa-*⌜*li*⌝ does not have the determinative ^{uru}, it probably denotes a common noun here (see the Introduction, pp. 10-11, with n. 51). For the root, cf. Arabic *jawl(at)* "circuit, round" and the Hebrew GN *gôlān*. The form may be *qut(t)ăl* or, originally, *qat(t)āl* (with **a* > */u/* before */w/*; see Part III, ch. 2 §A 1 e).

?GL(GL): see QLQL, below.

?GLB

/gallăbu/ n. (Akk. loanword?) "barber."

econ.: ^{lú}*ga$_5$*(QA)*-la-b*[*u*?] PRU 6 136:10 (list of professions)

Alphabetic: See below.

The word may be Akk. (*gallābu* "barber") rather than Ugar.; note, however, that all other syllabic spellings in this text reflect Ugar., not Akk., terms for professions. Cf. Heb. *gallāb*, Phoenician *glb*, Syriac *gallābā*; it is possible, but by no means certain, that all of these are borrowed from Akk. (see, e.g., AHw 274b; Kaufman, Akkadian Influences 51).

The alphabetic *glb* in *prš glbm* (KTU 4.269:29; 4.275:26) is probably unrelated; see Dietrich-Loretz-Sanmartín, UF 5 106.

?GL(L), ?GLGL: see QLQL, below.

GMR

/magmaru/ n. month name.

lex.: *ina* ITI *ma-ag-ma-r*[*i*] RS 25.455 ii 2

Alphabetic: *yrḫ mgmr* (UT 430b no. 1418).

For the reference, see AHw 577a, CAD M/1 46a.

?GPN: see GBN, above.

(GRBZ

/gurbizu/ n. (loanword) "hauberk."

econ.: *3 gur-BI-ZU*^meš PRU 6 132 r. 5'

Alphabetic: *grbz*; see discussion.

Nougayrol's *-su* is a typographical error for *-sú* (ZU); cf. the copy. Since the form is probably pl., it is more likely that Akk. *gurpisū* is intended here than Ugar. */gurbizu/*, which would be sg. (For the final *z* of alphabetic *grbz* in KTU 4.363:2, see Dietrich-Loretz-Sanmartín, UF 5 86; the */z/* may reflect intervocalic voicing; see Part III, ch 2 §A 2 a.) The origin of Akk. *g/qurpisu* (CAD G 139-40; AHw 929b), Hur. *kurbiži* (*gurpiši*; Laroche, GLH 155), and Ugar. */gurbizu/* is unknown.

Note also, in another econ. text, *21* URUDU^meš *gu*!-*ur*!-*BI-su*, PRU 6 140:1 (Kühne, UF 5 189).)

?GRLN: see *KI-ra-li-nu* in the Appendix to the Glossary, below.

GθR

/gaθaru/ n. divine name ("strong").

lex.: (Sum.) ^dTIŠPAK = (Hur.) *mi-il-ku-un̩-ni* = (Ugar.) *ga-š[a-ru]* Ug. 5 137 iv a 15 (polyglot god-list)

(Sum.) [ ] = (Hur.) *mi-il-ku-u[n-ni?]* = (Ugar.) *g[a]-ša-ru* ibid. iv b 13.

Alphabetic: *gθr* (UT 382b no. 631; KTU 1.108:2,6; 1.112:18-20).

D

D

/dū/ determinative/relative pronoun.

lex.: (Sum.) [LÚ] = (Akk.) [*ša*?] = (Hur.) *a-wV* = (Ugar.) *du-ú* Ug. 5 137 ii 29' (polyglot vocab.)

S^a Voc. no. 187.2.

Alphabetic: *d, dt* (see UT 39-40 §§6.23-27; 382-83 no. 632).

DBḤ

/dabḥu/ n. "sacrifice."

lex.: (Sum.) EZEN = (Akk.) *i-sí-nu* = (Hur.) *e-⌜li?⌝* = (Ugar.) *da-ab-ḫu* Ug. 5 137 iii 6 (polyglot vocab.)

S^a Voc. no. 197.1.

Alphabetic: *dbḥ* (UT 383b no. 637).

??DBL: see S^a Voc. no. 193.4, above.

DBQ

Akkadianized *udabbiq(annī)* v., D, preterite, "to join together."

lit.: *ú-par-ri-ra-an-ni ú-dáb-bi-qa-an-ni* "he took me apart and put me together" Ug. 5 162:37'

Alphabetic: Unattested.

See von Soden, UF 1 191, who translates "er 'löste mich auf' und fügte mich zusammen." Noting that Nougayrol's *tabāku*, D, does not provide the needed semantic opposite of *purruru*, von Soden compares WSem. *dbq* D, "zusammenkleben, -fügen." This seems the most likely reading, despite the nonoccurrence of TAB with the value *dáb* elsewhere in the corpus of Ugarit Akk. Note that the morphology of the form is Akk., as is true of the few other Ugar. verbal roots in the literary texts (see PḤ/ḪD, RðY below; and Part III, ch. 3 §G 3).

(DGN

lex.: ᵈ*da-gan* Ug. 5 18:3, 5 170:17' (god-lists)

These examples correspond to *dgn* in the parallel alphab. god-lists KTU 1.47:4; 1.118:3. Since the name in the syllabic texts is written without a case-ending, it is likely that Akk. *dagan* is intended, rather than Ugar. */*dagan(u)*/.)

?DWR: see DYR, below.

(?**DYR**

/*dīru*/ ? adj. "hateful(?); foul(?)."

Ugar. lit.: [*d*]*a-mu TI-ru da-mu la TI-r*[*u* "foul blood, not foul blood(??)" Ug. 5 153:r.3'

Alphabetic: Unattested.

Note that it is not certain that Ug. 5 153 is a Ugaritic text. Line r.3' is one of the few in which the word division is relatively secure, and *TI-ru* would seem to be an adjective modifying *dm* "blood": "X blood, un-X blood." Of the possible roots, *d*/*ṭ*/*t-w*/*y-r*, only *d-y-r*, originally **ð-y-r*, presents a plausible meaning; cf. Arabic *ðāra* (*ð-y-r*) "to hate; to stink"; Hebrew *z-w*/*y-r* "to stink" (only *rûḥî zárâ lə-ʾištî* Job 19:31); note also Akk. *zêru* "to hate" (originally probably II-*y*, i.e., *ziārum*).)

DKR¹

/*dakaru*/ n. "male."

lex.: (Sum.) NITA$_2$ = (Akk.) *zi-ka-rù* = (Hur.) *tu-ru-ḫi* = (Ugar.) *da-ka-rù* Ug. 5 137 iii 5 (polyglot vocab.)

Sᵃ Voc. no. 195.2.

Alphabetic: Unattested.

DKR²

/*dikāru*/ n. (loanword?) "bowl."

lex.: (Sum.) [KAM] = (Akk.) [*diqāru*] = (Hur.) [ ] =(Ugar.) *di-*[*k*]*a*$_4$(QA)*-ru* UF 11 79:27 (polyglot vocab.)

Sᵃ Voc. no. 44.1.

Alphabetic: Pl. *dkrt*, also *dkrm* (?); see the Sᵃ Voc. commentary.

DLL

/*dallu*/ adj. "poor."

lex.: (Sum.) [SIG] = (Akk.) [*enšu*] = (Hur.) [*z*]*i*/[*m*]*u-na-ar-ḫi* = (Ugar.) *da-al*!?-⌜*lu*⌝ Ug. 5 137 ii 14' (polyglot vocab.)

Sᵃ Voc. no. 180.2.

Alphabetic: *dl* (UT 385a no. 664; perhaps also KTU 1.107:20).

(?DM

/damu/ ? n. "blood."

Ugar. lit.: [*d*]*a-mu TI-ru da-mu la TI-r*[*u* "foul blood, not foul blood(??)" Ug. 5 153:r.3'

note also]*da-m*[*i* ibid.:r.7'

Alphabetic: *dm* (UT 385b no. 669).

Note that it is not certain that Ug. 5 153 is a Ugaritic text. Line r.3' is one of the few in which the word division is relatively secure. For *TI-ru*, see under DYR, above.)

?DMG, ?DMK, ?DMQ: see TMK, below.

DPR

**/diprānu/*, pl. */diprānūma/*, n. "juniper."

legal: A.ŠÀ$^{hi.a}$: *dì-ip-ra-ni-ma* "juniper field(s)" PRU 3 64a:4

Alphabetic: *dprn*; cf. esp. *gt dprnm* (UT 386b no. 693).

The form here is oblique pl. */diprānīma/*. See Kühne, UF 6 163.

DQQ

/daqqu/ ? adj. "small(?)."

lex.: (Sum.) [SIG] = (Akk.) [*ṣeḫru*] = (Hur.) ⌜*ga*?⌝-*al-gi* = (Ugar.) *d*[*a*]-*aq*!?-*qú* Ug. 5 137 ii 13' (polyglot vocab.)

S^a Voc. no. 180.1.

Alphabetic: *dq* (UT 386b no. 695; KTU 1.106:20,31; 1.112:27); see Caquot-Sznycer-Herdner, Textes ougaritiques 256 n. i.

DQR: see DKR², above.

DRK: see DRQ, below.

DR^c

/midar^{c}u/ ? (< **miðra^{c}u* ?) n. "seed-land"; in field designation.

legal: A.ŠÀ$^{hi.a}$: *mi-TA-ar-ú*(!) "seed-land field(s)" PRU 3 47a:12

Alphabetic: *mdr^c*; cf. also v. *dr^c* "to sow" (UT 387 no. 705; perhaps also KTU 1.146; see Xella, Testi rituali 149).

See Kühne, UF 7 257-58, whose reading *mi-dá-ar-ú*, with final *-ú*, is preferable to Nougayrol's *mi-ṭá-ar* É. In CAD M/2 144b the reading *mi-ṭá-ar-ú* "field irrigated by rain" (WSem. *miṭru*) is suggested, but broken writings in these texts nearly always indicate the presence of a guttural see Part III, ch. 1 §E 4 b (3). For the development **midra^{c}u* > */midar^{c}u/*, see Part III, ch. 2 §C.

?DRQ

/darqu/ ? n. "path."

lex.: KI.UŠ = *TAR-QU* Syria 12 231ff. (MSL 5 p. 71:281; Ḫḫ II)

Alphabetic: Cf. *tdrq* "tread, gait"? See discussion.

This entry in Ḫḫ II 281 corresponds to *da-rag-gu* in the canonical SB version. The Akk. word *daraggu* "path" is late (SB) and with one exception found only in lexical texts. A connection of the latter with Hebrew *derek* is possible (AHw 163a), and it may be a loan from a WSem. dialect. The alphabetic form *tdrq* "tread, gait" may also be related to Hebrew *d-r-k* (Dietrich-Loretz, OLZ 62 538), although Gordon, UT 387b no. 708, plausibly compares instead Arabic *daraqa* "to walk hastily" (see further Dietrich-Loretz-Sanmartín, UF 6 24-25 nos. 34, 110). It is possible, at least, that *TAR-QU* is to be read dar_6*-qu* = Ugar. /*darqu*/ "path," related to the alphabetic *tdrq*, although TAR = dar_6 is otherwise attested in Ugarit Akk. only in the Hurrian loanword *pa-ḫa-*dar_6*-ru* in PRU 3 206f.:9 (see PǴ(N)DR, below). (A reading dar_6-ku_{13} = Ugar. /*darku*/ [cf. alphab. *drkm* "marchers(?)" KTU 4.688:5] cannot be ruled out entirely, but note that QU = ku_{13} is not otherwise certainly attested in Ugarit Akk.) It is equally possible, however, that a simple biform of later Akk. *daraggu* is intended, rather than a Ugar. word.

(As still another possibility, we might read *ṭar-qu*, and suggest a Ugar. word /*ṭarqu*/ "path" [alphabetic unattested]; cf. Arabic *ṭurqa* and *ṭarīq* "way, road.")

ð

ðKR: see DKR[1], above.

*ðQN: see /*sikānu*/, under SKN b, below.

H

-H

/*-hŭ*/ pron. suff. 3ms "his."

econ.: PN [l]lú*ḫa-ma-ru-ú*[PRU 6 79:11
PN lú*ḫa-*[*a*]*m-*[*r*]*u-ú* ibid.:13

Alphabetic: *-h* (UT 36,38 §§6.7,17).

In both, the meaning is "PN his apprentice," i.e., /*ǵam(a)ru-hu*/; see Rainey, IOS 3 43.

?HBL: see *IB-lu* in the Appendix to the Glossary, below.

HW[1]

/*huwa*/ pronoun 3ms "he."

lex.: (Sum.) [LÚ] = (Akk.) [*šū?*] = (Hur.) *ma-an-ni* = (Ugar.) *ú-wa* Ug. 5 137 ii 28' (polyglot vocab.)
Sa Voc. no. 187.1.

Alphabetic: *hw* (UT 389b no. 753).

HW[2]

/*huwătu*/ n. "word."

lex.: (Sum.) [MU] = (Akk.) [*zikru*] = (Hur.) [ ] = (Ugar.) *ú-*[*P*]*I*!?-[*t*]u_4 UF 11 479:12 (polyglot vocab.)

S^{a} Voc. no. 32.2.

Alphabetic: *hwt* (UT 389b no. 756).

On the form, see Part III, ch. 3 §C 2 a (*qul*).

?HWṬ: see *ú-ṭu* in the Appendix to the Glossary, below.

?HZZ, ?HẒẒ: see [*I*]*i* ?/[*U*]Z ?-*ZU* in the Appendix to the Glossary, below.

?HLM

**/hulm(at)u/*, pl. */hulmātu/* ?, n. "hammer(?)."

econ.: *4* ^{urudu}*ul-ma-tu* GAL^{meš} *šá* ^{giš}MÁ "4 large ship's hammers(?)" PRU 6 141:4 (list of implements)

20 ^{urudu}*ul-ma-tu* TUR^{meš} "20 small hammers(?)" ibid.:5

Alphabetic: Cf. v. *hlm* "to strike" (UT 390b no. 770)?

Since some of the items in this text are Ugar. (*/mamṣar/*, */ḫarmiθātu/*) and others probably Akk. (*abšānu*, *qû*), it is difficult to decide whether *ul-ma-tu* denotes Ugar. */hulm(at)u/*, probably in the pl. */hulmātu/* (< **hulamātu*, with syncope) "hammers" (cf. Heb. *halmût*), as suggested by Nougayrol (PRU 6 p. 157 n. 11), or a pl. of Akk. *ulmu* "axe" (see AHw 1410b).

(The lex. forms written *ḫu-ul-ma-tu*$_4$, Ug. 5 137 iii 15',16', do not belong here, since Ugar. */h/* is never represented with Ḫ-signs in our corpus [pace Sivan, Analysis 222]; see below, under ḤLM and ǴLM.)

HLNY

/hallinīya/ ? adv. "here, now then."

lex.: (Sum.) [UD?] = (Akk.) [*anumma*?] = (Hur.) [ ] = (Ugar.) *al-li-ni-ya* Ug. 5 138 5' (polyglot vocab.)

S^{a} Voc. no. 63.4.

Alphabetic: *hlny* (e.g., KTU 2.1:3; 2.13:9; 2.21:7; 2.24:8; 2.30:8,12; 2.70:11).

?HMM: see *am-ma-ti* in the Appendix to the Glossary, below.

?HSS: see [*I*]*i* ?/[*U*]Z ?-*ZU* in the Appendix to the Glossary, below.

?HPK

/tuhappiku/ ? tD v.n./infin. "to be upset(?)."

lex.: (Sum.) BAL = (Akk.) *na-bal-ku-tu*$_4$ = (Hur.) *tap-šu-ḫu-um-me* = (Ugar.) *tu-a-pí-*[*ku*(?)] Ug. 5 137 ii 23' (polyglot vocab.)

S^{a} Voc. no. 184.2.

Alphabetic: Cf. G v. *hpk* "to upset, overthrow" (UT 392a no. 788; KTU 1.103:52).

?HPL: see *IB-lu* in the Appendix to the Glossary, below.

?HṢṢ: see [*I*]*i* ?/[*U*]Z ?-*ZU* in the Appendix to the Glossary, below.

HR: see HRT, below.

?HRG, ?HRK: see [*i*]*r-KU*, S^{a} Voc. no. 48.2.

?HRM: see *a-ra-mi-ma* in the Appendix to the Glossary, below.

?HRQ: see [*i*]*r-KU*, S^a Voc. no. 48.2.

(HRT

/*harītu*/ n. (Akk. loanword?) "shield."

legal: PN DUMU LÚ A.RIT PRU 3 68f.:6

lex.: A.PAB = *a-ri-*tu_4 AS 16 33ff. C 27 (Silbenvokabular A)

Alphabetic: *hrt* (UT 392a no. 791); see discussion.

It is likely that Akk. *arītu* "shield" is intended in both instances. The pseudo-logogram A.RIT is also attested in Neo-Assyrian texts (CAD A/2 270); the Ugarit exemplars of the Silbenvokabular exhibit little, if any, WSem. influence. Nevertheless, it is possible that one or both examples may reflect Ugar. /*harītu*/, itself possibly an Akk. loan; for the association of alphabetic *hrt* and Akk. *arītu*, see Dietrich-Loretz-Sanmartín, UF 5 87.)

W

(?W

/*wa-*/ ? conjunction "and."

Ugar. lit.: the *PI* sign in Ug. 5 153 r.5',6',7'

It is possible that the *PI* sign in these lines of Ug. 5 153, if the text is Ugaritic, represents the conjunction /*wa-*/, the vocalization of which must be based on comparative evidence, since the vowel of the *PI* sign is ambiguous.)

?WLD: see YLD, below.

Z

?Z-Z-Ḥ/Ḫ/Ǵ-L: see *ZI-ZA-ḫal-li-ma* in the Appendix to the Glossary, below.

☛ p. 391

?ZTR

/*zuttaru*/ D v.n./infin. "to go out(?)."

lex.: (Sum.) [UD?] = (Akk.) [*(w)aṣû*??] = (Hur.) [ ] = (Ugar.) [*z*]*u-ut-ta-ru* Ug. 5 138 7' (polyglot vocab.)

S^a Voc. no. 63.6.

Alphabetic: Cf. *ztr* (UT 393b no. 830)? See the S^a Voc. commentary.

Ḥ

?ḤBB: see *ḫa-AB-BI/BU* in the Appendix to the Glossary, below.

☛ p. 391

?ḤBṬ: see *ha-ba-ṭu* in the Appendix to the Glossary, below.

?ḤBL

*/*ḥablu*/ ?, pl. /*ḥabalūma*/, n., "rope, portion, lot(?)"; in field designation.

legal: *iš-ši-ma*(!) PN *4 me-at* KÙ.BABBAR *ù* A.ŠÀ[meš] *ḫa-ba-li-ma ša* DUMU.MÍ PN_2 *ù id-din-šu a-na* PN_3 "PN took and gave 400 silver and 'lot(?) field(s),' belonging to PN_2's daughter, to PN_3" PRU 3 45f.:7-9

Alphabetic: *ḥbl* (UT 394a no. 832).

Nougayrol translated "les terres de gages." Boyd, Collection 98-99, notes that the form is Ugar., oblique pl., and proposes the translation "encumbered (field)," i.e., presumably, a *qat(a)l* noun (a *qatal* adjective, passive, is unlikely).

A more likely alternative is /*ḥabalīma*/, pl. of */*ḥablu*/, originally meaning "rope," but extended in meaning to "measurement, portion, lot, region," as in Hebrew and Aramaic (note also Akk. *eblu* "rope," a surface measure).

ḤDR

/*ḥudŭru*/ n. "room(?)."

lex.: (Sum.) G[Ú] = (Akk.) [*šubtu*?] = (Hur.) [*x-x*]*-a-ri* = (Ugar.) ⌜*ḫu*⌝*-du-rù* Ug. 5 137 ii 11' (polyglot vocab.)

S[a] Voc. no. 178.

Alphabetic: *ḥdr* (UT 394-95 no. 394)? See the S[a] Voc. commentary.

ḤWW

/*ḥuwwatu*/ n. "country."

legal: *ša i-na* A.ŠÀ[meš] *ḫu-wa-*⌜*ti*⌝ Syria 18 251ff.:5

lex.: (Sum.) U[N] = (Akk.) [*mātu*] = (Hur.) [*u*]*-mi-in*$_4$*-n*[*i*] = (Ugar.) [*ḫ*]*u-wa-tu*$_4$ Ug. 5 137 ii 10' (polyglot vocab.)

S[a] Voc. no. 177.2.

Alphabetic: *ḥwt* (UT 395b no. 850); see the S[a] Voc. commentary.

It is not clear whether the legal example (a field designation) belongs here; "fields of the land/country" is difficult.

ḤWY[1]: see ḤYY[1], below.

?ḤWY[2]: see ḪWY, below.

?ḤWL: see ǴWL in the Appendix to the Glossary, below.

?ḤṬR: see ḤDR, above.

?ḤY: see ḪWY, below.

ḤYY[1]/ḤWY[1]

(a) /*ḥuwwû*/ D v.n./infin. "to save."

lex.: (Sum.) KA[R] = (Akk.) [*eṭēru*?]= (Hur.) *eḫ-lu-um-me* = (Ugar.) *ḫu-PI-ú* Ug. 5 137 ii 17' (polyglot vocab.)

S[a] Voc. no. 183.1.

Alphabetic: *ḥwy* (UT 396a no. 856); see Marcus, JSS 17 76-82.

For the normalization, see the S[a] Voc. commentary, and Part III, ch. 2 §E 3 with n. 107.

(b) */ḥiyyūma/* (< **ḥayyūma*) n. pl. "life."

lex.: (Sum.) [ḪI] = (Akk.) [*balāṭu*] = (Hur.) [ ] = (Ugar.) *ḫi-*[*i*]*u?-ma* UF 11 479:25 (polyglot vocab.)

(Sum.) [KA??] = (Akk.) [??] = (Hur.) [*š*]*u-ḫu-ur-ni* = (Ugar.) *ḫé-yu-ma* Ug. 5 131 6' (polyglot vocab.)

(Sum.) TIL = (Akk.) TIL-*la-ṭu* = (Hur.) *šu-ḫ*[*u-ur-ni*] = (Ugar.) [*ḫ*]*é-*⌜*yu*⌝-[*m*]*a* Ug. 5 137 i 20" (polyglot vocab.)

Sᵃ Voc. nos. 43.1; 50.21; 173.3.

Alphabetic: *ḥym* (KTU 1.17 vi 27; with suff., *ḥyk*, KTU 1.16 i 14); cf. Heb. *ḥayyîm*, Aram. *ḥayyin* (Syr. *ḥayye*).

?ḤYY²: see ḪWY, below.

ḤYQ

/ḥēqu/ n. "lap."

lex.: (Sum.) [ÚR] = (Akk.) [*sūnu*] = (Hur.) [*ḫuzi*...] = (Ugar.) *ḫé-qu* Ug. 5 137 i 9' (polyglot vocab.)

Sᵃ Voc. no. 158.1.

Alphabetic: Unattested.

For the initial radical */ḥ/*, see the Sᵃ Voc. commentary.

?ḤYR

/ḥēru/ ? n. "enclosure(?)."

lex.: (Sum.) [IB] = (Akk.) [ ] = (Hur.) [ ] = (Ugar.) *ḫe?-e*[*-ru?*] Ug. 5 137 i 12' (polyglot vocab.)

Sᵃ Voc. no. 160.3.

Alphabetic: Unattested.

?ḤL: see ǴWL, below.

(ḤLB

(NA₄.)*ḫi-li-ba* n. "(a kind of stone)."

econ.: *2 me-at* NA₄ *ḪI-LI-BA* ⌜ZA?⌝[.GÌN(?)] PRU 6 149 ii 9

It is possible that this form is to be read phonetically as ⁿᵃ⁴*ḫi-li-ba*, and corresponds to alphab. *ḥlb* in KTU 4.272:4,5 (see Gordon, UT 396b no. 862), and that both denote the word "milk" in an extended sense referring to a type of stone of milky appearance; if so, the syllabic writing would suggest Ugar. */ḥilību/* (< **ḥalību* [cf. Arabic *ḥalīb* "milk"], with irregular vowel assimilation). (For Nougayrol's NA₄ GA = *aban šizbi* "pierre de lait" in Ug. 5 12:10,13,35, to which he referred in PRU 6 p. 157 n. 14, read instead NA₄ [= *aban*] *ga-b*[*é-e*]; see AHw 1254a, 1555a.)

It is much more likely, however, that the writing is logographic, NA₄.ḪI.LI.BA, as in the Ugarit lexical text MSL 10 37ff. A,D lines 301,304,305, and elsewhere. The term was borrowed into Akk. both as *ḫilibû* (see CAD Ḫ 186a, AHw 345) and, in the West, with the determinative pronounced (as *ia₄*), as *e/iḫlib/pakku* (< **iaḫiliba(k)*); see MSL 10 p. 28 ad lines 369-373. (Add to the occurrences of *e/iḫlib/pakku* listed in the dictionaries the following, from a letter of uncertain provenance: ⁿᵃ⁴·ᵐᵉˢ*me-e-ku* : *iḫ-li-pá-ak-ku*, PRU 6 6:40.))

ḪLL

p. 391

/ḫallatu/ n. month name.

econ.: *i-na* ITI *ḫal-⌜la⌝-t[u?]* (gen.!) PRU 6 101:5'

lex.: ITI *ḫal-la-ti* MSL 10 37ff. A colophon (p. 37 n. 1, line 5; Ḫḫ XVI)

Alphabetic: *ḫlt* (KTU 4.219:13; 4.220:4).

One wonders whether this MN is to be associated with the Akk. MN *Elūlu/Ulūlu* (although early writings such as *e/é-lu-nu-um* [Gelb, MAD 3 41] may indicate that the root of the Akk. MN was originally *ʾ$_x$-l-n*; alternatively, *Elūnum* may reflect an early, dialectal dissimilation). Both forms might be connected with a root *ḫ-l-l* as in Syriac *ḫallel* "to purify" and Akk. *elēlu* "to be(come) pure." For the root in Ugar., note, perhaps, *š ḫll ydm* (KTU 1.115:6); *mḫllm* (1.119:23), and the phrase *ḫl mlk* (common in rituals; see Xella, Testi rituali 367); see Herdner, Ug. 7 pp. 24-25,35; Xella, op. cit. 28-29,32-33,107-8.

?ḪLM

/ḫulmatu/ n. "strength, potency, soundness(?)."

lex.: (Sum.) [IDIM?] = (Akk.) [*nakbatu?/balāṭu?*] = (Hur.) [ ] = (Ugar.) [*ḫ*]*u-ul-ma-tu*$_4$ Ug. 5 137 iii 16' (polyglot vocab.)

S^a Voc. no. 198.9.

Alphabetic: Cf. *ḫlm* II "strength(?)"; see the S^a Voc. commentary.

ḪMY

/ḫāmītu/ n. (G ptcpl. fem.) "wall."

legal: [*qa-du*(??)]⌜*x*⌝ : *ḫa-me-ti* PRU 3 137f.:4

Alphabetic: *ḫmt*, pl. *ḫmyt* (UT 397b no. 876; KTU 1.119:27,29,36 [pl.]).

Nougayrol's restoration of Akk. [... *du-r*]*i* (?) before the gloss is quite uncertain; see Part III, ch. 1 §C 3. On the form of */ḫāmītu/*, originally **ḫāmiytu* and probably pronounced [ḫāmētu], see Part III, ch. 1 §G 2 with n. 204.

?ḪML

/ḫumălu/ ? n. "pity(?)."

lit.: [*x*]-⌜*x*⌝-*en-tu ḫu-ma?-lu? ul il-ta-si-ma-ku* (translation see discussion) Ug. 5 162:27'

Alphabetic: Unattested.

The reading presented here is von Soden's, UF 1 191, who suggests that *ḫu-ma?-lu?* may be "kanaanäisch," and translates this line, "hätte die ... 'Mitleid!' nicht gerufen!" Cf. Hebrew *ḥāmal* (v.n. *ḥumlâ*) "to spare."

?ḪNW

/ḫinōtu/ ? n., and */ʾvḫnōtu/* ? n., "(an implement)."

econ.: 2 *ḫi-nu-ta-me* URUDU^{meš} "2 copper *ḫ*.'s" PRU 6 163 r. 5' (list of items)

1 ⌜*vḫ?*⌝*-nu-tu*$_4$ *1 me* "1 *ḫ*., 100(-weight)" Ug. 5 84:8 (list of items)

Alphabetic: Unattested.

The first example is dual nom. */ḫinōtāmi/*.

It is by no means certain either that the first sign of the second example is AḪ (see the copy), or, even if it is, that these forms represent the same word, as Nougayrol astutely suggested (Ug. 5 p. 178 n. 4). If they do, the second form exhibits the sole example of prothetic /ʾ/ among the syllabic transcriptions; for the phenomenon in alphabetic forms, see Part III, ch. 2 §D.

Of the possible roots reflected by these writings (viz., *ḥ/ḫ/ǵ-n-w/y*), the only one likely to have a derivative denoting an implement is *ḥ-n-w* "to incline, bend, curve," i.e., a curved or bent device (cf. Arabic *ḥinw* "bend, bow, curve"). The forms apparently have the pattern *qital-t*, i.e., **ḥinawtu* > /*ḥinōtu*/ (> /ʾ*vḥnōtu*/); for another possible *qital* form denoting an implement, see under ŠHR below.

?ḤPP: see *ḫa-AB-BI/BU* in the Appendix to the Glossary, below.

☛ p. 392 ?ḤRḏ, ?ḤRZ, ?ḤRẒ: see *ḫa-ar-ZA-ti* in the Appendix to the Glossary, below.

☛ p. 392

ḤRḤR

/*ḥurḥur(r)atu*/ n. "(a plant)."

letter: *e-nu-ma* NUMUN <*ḫur-*>*ḫu-ra-ti ṣa-bu-tu*$_4$*-ia* NUMUN *ḫur-ḫu-ra-ti šu-bi-la-an-ni* "now then, my request is *ḥ*.-seed; send me *ḥ*.-seed" PRU 6 8:6-10

Alphabetic: Cf. dual(?) *ḥrḥrtm* (KTU 1.2 iii 13)?

The emendation to <*ḫur-*>*ḫu-ra-ti* is suggested by Boyd, Collection 89-90. The context in which alphabetic *ḥrḥrtm* (dual?) appears is broken. The same word occurs in Akk., viz., *ḫurḫuratu* (a red dye; CAD Ḫ 250-51); note also *ḫūratu* (a plant, a dye from the plant; ibid. 247-48).

?ḤRẒ: see *ḫa-ar-ZA-ti* in the Appendix to the Glossary, below.

ḤRM

(a) /*ḥarīmu*/ adj. "desecrated(?)."

lex.: (Sum.) [ḪUL?] = (Akk.) [*šulputu*?] = (Hur.) [*šu*?]*-bi* = (Ugar.) *ḫa-ri-mu* Ug. 5 137 ii 39' (polyglot vocab.)

(Sum.) [GUL?] = (Akk.) [*šulputu*?] = (Hur.) *šu-bi* = (Ugar.) *ḫa-ri-mu* Ug. 5 137 ii 42' (polyglot vocab.)

S^{a} Voc. nos. 190.4, 191.1.

Alphabetic: Unattested.

(b) /*ḥarmānu*/ n. "sacred place(?)."

legal: KI^{meš} *ḫa-ar-ma-ni* "area of the sacred place(?)" PRU 3 75b:5

Alphabetic: Unattested.

Note the lack of a determinative, unless KI^{meš} functions as such. Cf. the Hebrew GN *ḥermôn*.

?ḤRS, ?ḤRṢ: see *ḫa-ar-ZA-ti* in the Appendix to the Glossary, below.

ḤRR: see ḤRḤR, above.

ḤRŠ

/*ḥarrāšu*/ n. "artisan."

lex.: (Sum.) [GIM?] = (Akk.) [*bānû/itinnu*?] = (Hur.) *i-x-*[*x*]*-e* = (Ugar.) *ḫa-ra-*⸢*šu*?⸣ UF 11 479:7 (polyglot vocab.)

S^{a} Voc. no. 30.1.

Alphabetic: *ḥrš* (UT 399a no. 903).

?ḤTT

/šuḥuttu/ ? n. "bran, residue(?)."

lex.: (Sum.) DUḪ = (Akk.) *tu-uḫ-ḫu* = (Hur.) *šu-ḫu-li* = (Ugar.) *šu-ḫu-ut-t*[*u*?] Ug. 5 137 iii 3 (polyglot vocab.)

S^{a} Voc. no. 194.4.

Alphabetic: Unattested.

Ḫ

?ḪBB: see *ḫa-AB-BI/BU* in the Appendix to the Glossary, below.

?ḪBṬ: see *ḫa-ba-ṭu* in the Appendix to the Glossary, below.

ḪBL: see ḤBL, above.

?ḪWY

p. 392

/ḫāyu/, also [ḫēyu], */ḫīyu/*, pl. m. [ḫīyūma], adj. "vacant, unoccupied, unused(?)."

legal: PN ... *it-ta-din 3* IKU A.ŠÀ^{meš}-*šu qa-du* ^{é}AN.ZA.GÀR-*šu : ḫa-a-yi a-na* PN$_2$ "PN gave PN$_2$ his 3-*ikû* field with its unused(?) tower" PRU 3 95f.:4-7

PN *il-te-qè* É *ḫe-e-ia iš-tu* PN$_2$ ... *i-na 20* KÙ.BABBAR É *ḫe-e-yu ṣa-ma-at i-na* ^{d}UTU UD-*mi* "PN received an unoccupied(?) estate from PN$_2$ for 20 silver; the unoccupied(?) estate is transferred to 'in the light of day'" PRU 3 86ff. r. 6'-9'

É$^{\text{ḫi.a}}$ KISLAḪ^{meš} *: ḫé-yi-ma* (acc.) "unused(?) dwellings(?)" PRU 3 102ff.:15

4 IKU A.ŠÀ$^{\text{ḫi.a}}$ *ù 1/3* IKU A.ŠÀ *ù 5/6* IKU ^{giš}GEŠTIN *qa-du* ^{giš}GI.DÌM^{meš}-*šu qa-du : ḫi-i-yi-šu ša* PN ... *i-na* A.ŠÀ *: ad-ma-ni ù 5*(?) IKU A.ŠÀ$^{\text{ḫi.a}}$ *ù 1/2* IKU ^{giš}GEŠTIN *qa-du* ^{giš}GI.DÌM^{meš}-*šu* [*qa-du*] *: ḫi-i-yi-šu ša* PN$_2$ ... *i-na* A.ŠÀ *: ad-ma-ni* "a 4-*ikû* field, a 1/3-*ikû* field, a 5/6-*ikû* field with its olive orchard and its unused area(s)(?), belonging to PN ... in 'redland field'; a 5-*ikû* field and a 1/2-*ikû* vineyard with its olive orchard [and] its unused area(s)(?), belonging to PN$_2$ in 'redland field'" PRU 3 122f.:4-12

Alphabetic: Unattested.

A review of the proposals for this difficult term is offered by Boyd, Collection 91-94; see also Rainey, "The Scribe" 135 n. 51; Artzi, Bar-Ilan 1 44.

As to the form, it should be noted that the writing *ḫe-e-ia* clearly indicates final radical */y/*, so that PI in the other examples must be read *-yv*, not *-wv*. That in five out of six instances an extra vowel-sign appears almost certainly indicates the presence of a medial long vowel, originally *ā* as in *: ḫa-a-yi*, but also pronounced [ē] and [ī] by assimilation to the following */y/* (see Part III, ch. 2 §A 1 e). Since the sequence *-v̄y-* is not an expected resolution of **-ayy-* in Semitic, it is unlikely that these forms should be related to the adjective **ḥayyu* "alive" (pace Boyd); note that in the lex. writings of "life," viz., *ḫé/ḫe-yu/iu-ma* for */ḥiyyūma/* < **ḥayyūma* (see under ḤYY^1/ḤWY^2 above), an extra vowel-sign does not appear. A connection with the root *ḥ-w-w/y* (Hebrew *ḥawwôt* "tent-village" and Arabic *ḥiwāʾ* "circle of tents") is also ruled out by the occurrence in the Ugar. lexicon of */ḥuwwatu/* (< **ḥawwatu*) from that root (see ḤWW). (D. Marcus, JSS 17 77 n. 3, would also divorce the word under discussion from both *ḥ-y-y* "to live" and *ḥ-w-w/y*.) The word would seem, rather, to be a *qāl* form (like PNWS **ḥāl-*

"sand," *$q\bar{a}l$*- "voice," or *$\d{t}\bar{a}b$*- "good"), thus, /*ḥāyu*/, /*ḫāyu*/, or /*ǵāyu*/.

In view of the above considerations, a new suggestion is in order. It is possible that the word under discussion does not gloss either éAN.ZA.GÀR (Akk. *dimtu*; PRU 3 95f.:4-7) or É$^{hi.a}$ KISLAH^{meš} (Akk. *maškanu*; PRU 3 102ff.:15), but rather modifies both these terms and É (PRU 3 86ff. r. 6'-9', bis), as an adjective. The root *ḫ-w-y*, though admittedly attested only in South Semitic, suggests the form /*ḫāyu*/ (cf. /*ṭābu*/), and a meaning which fits all attested occurrences, viz., "vacant, unoccupied, unused"; cf. Arabic *ḫawā* "to become empty, vacant, unoccupied" (of a house), *ḫawā*ʾ "wide tract" (without herbage or habitations), *ʾarḍ ḫāwiya* "a land devoid of its inhabitants" (Lane, Lexicon 827-28); Sabaean *ḫ-w-y* in the form *hḫw*- "to make void, unnecessary" (Beeston, et al., Dictionary 64); Jibbāli *ḫē* "to be empty" (of a house; Johnstone, Jibbāli Lexicon 31). In PRU 3 122f.:4-12 (bis), the term (here /*ḫīyu*/) must be understood to be substantivized: "unused area." If this interpretation is correct, the use of a Ugar. rather than an Akk. term in these examples (e.g., *nadû*) might indicate that the Ugar. word had a specific technical or legal sense.

The lack of agreement exhibited by the adj. in PRU 3 95f.:4-7 is only apparent, since éAN.ZA.GÀR probably represents not fem. *dimtu*, which never appears syllabically in Ugarit Akk. texts, but rather masc. *dunnu*, as in PRU 3 52f.:15, or, more likely, an underlying Ugar. word, probably *mgdl* (although AN.ZA.GÀR also corresponds to alphab. fem. *gt* in a few instances; see Introduction, n. 51). Note also that pronominal reference to AN.ZA.GÀR is masc., e.g., in éAN.ZA.GÀR *qa-du* A.ŠÀ^{meš}-*šu* PRU 3 66b:4.

?ḪWL: see ǴWL, below.

ḪZR

/*ḫuzīru*/ n. "pig."

lex.: (Sum.) [ŠA]Ḫ = (Akk.) *še-ḫu-ú* = (Hur.) *ú-ḫi* = (Ugar.) *ḫu-zi-rù* Ug. 5 137 ii 25' (polyglot vocab.)

S^{a} Voc. no. 186.1.

Alphabetic: *ḫzr* "(a profession)" (UT 401a no. 948) is probably unrelated; see the S^{a} Voc. commentary.

ḪY: see ḪWY, above.

?ḪYB

/*ḫēbu*/ ? n.? "shame(?)."

lex.: (Sum.) TÉŠ = (Akk.) ⸢*ba*?⸣[-*a-šu*??] = (Hur.) [ ] = (Ugar.) *ḫe-bu* UF 11 479:35 (polyglot vocab.)

(Sum.) [ ] = (Akk.) [ ] = (Hur.) [*i*]*n-ni* = (Ugar.) *ḫé-bu* Ug. 5 131:3' (polyglot vocab.)

S^{a} Voc. no. 47.2.

Alphabetic: Unattested.

ḪYY: see ḪWY, above.

☛ p. 392 **ḪYR**

/*ḫiyyāru*/ n. month name.

econ.: *i-na* ITI *ḫi-ia-*⸢*ri*? *x*⸣[Ug. 7 pl. 50 r. 1'

lex.: *ḫi-ya-ri* RS 25.455+ (transliteration only, cited by Gordon, UT 401b no. 959)

Alphabetic: *ḫyr* (UT 401b no. 959).

Note also ITI *ḫi-a/ia-ri(-i/e)* in texts from Alalaḫ and Nuzi (AHw 342b), and *ḥyr* in Phoenician. These forms are probably related to the Akk. month name *ayyāru*, which was borrowed into Hebrew and Syriac as *ʾiyyār*, and into Arabic as *ʾayyār*. See Gordon-Lacheman, ArOr 10 56-58.

?ḪL: see ǴWL, below.

ḪLM(T): see ḤLM above, and ǴLM below.

ḪNṢ

p. 392

/ḫinnīṣu/ ? n. "piglet."

lex.: (Sum.) [ŠAḪṬU]R? = (Akk.) *kur-ku-za-nu* = (Hur.) — = (Ugar.) *ḫe-en-ni-ṣu* Ug. 5 137 ii 26' (polyglot vocab.)

S[a] Voc. no. 186a.

Alphabetic: Unattested.

?ḪPP[1]

/ḫupp(at)u/ ?, pl. */ḫuppātu/* ?, n. "shore(?)."

legal: *qa-du* A.ŠÀ[meš] *a-ra-mi-ma ša i-na ḫu-up-pa-ti* "with the *a.*-field(s) at the shore(?)" PRU 3 148a:10-11

Alphabetic: Cf. *ḫp y[m]* "seashore?" (KTU 1.3 ii 7; also *ḫph* 1.107:7?).

The form may be fem. sg. */ḫuppatu/* (cf. Heb. *ḥuppâ* "covering, canopy"?), or the pl. of the same or of */ḫuppu/*, which may be compared with alphabetic *ḫp* "shore" (cf. Heb. *ḥôp*; note, however, that Arabic has *ḥāffa*, *ḥawf*, and *ḥāfa* "edge, etc.," all with *ḥ*). Alternatively, it may be a pl. of Akk. *ḫuppu/uppu* "depression, hole."

?ḪPP[2]: see *ḫa-AB-BI/BU* in the Appendix to the Glossary, below.

?ḪṢṢ

/maḫṣīṣu/ ? n. "divide, separation(?)"; in field designation.

legal: *it-ta-aš-ši* ... A.ŠÀ[ḫi.a] [*ša*(?)] *i-na* SAG.DU *: ma-aḫ-ZI-ZI* "took ... the field at the head of the 'divide(?)'" PRU 3 148f.:15-17

Alphabetic: Unattested.

Nougayrol took *: ma-aḫ-ZI-ZI* to be a gloss of SAG.DU (see PRU 3 p. 266b). More likely, *i-na* SAG.DU *: m.* is to be understood as "at the head of *m.*" (see Kühne, UF 7 256-57; further, Astour, JESHO 13 115 n. 4). Boyd, Collection 72-73, suggests that the term is from the root *ʿ-z-z* "to be strong," thus, "strong place." But since Ugar. */ʿ/* is not normally written with the AḪ sign in these texts (see Part III, ch. 1 §E 4 b), the root is probably *ḫ-ṣ-ṣ*, which may be compared with Heb. *ḥāṣaṣ* "to divide" and Akk. *ḫaṣāṣu* "to break, cut"; thus, perhaps */maḫṣīṣu/* "(geographical) divide." (For another possible root, cf. the GN "Gaza," Arabic *ǵazza*.)

?ḪRḏ, ?ḪRZ, ?ḪRẒ: see *ḫa-ar-ZA-ti* in the Appendix to the Glossary, below.

*ḪRY

/ḫirītu/ n. (Akk. loanword) "cemetery, grave."

legal: É *: ḫi-ri-ti* PRU 3 52f.:17

Alphabetic: *ḫrt* (UT 404b no. 1006).

Gordon, Syria 33 102-3, plausibly associates this word with Akk. *ḫirītu* "ditch, canal." Since the form is preceded by a gloss mark, we must consider it to represent a Ugar. word, a conclusion confirmed by alphab. *ḫrt*. The root is undoubtedly *ḫ-r-*weak; note, however, that only Akk. exhibits such a root with the meaning "to dig," viz., *ḫerû* (Old Akk. *ḫarā*ʾ*um*), which is probably cognate, via a rare but well-attested spirantization process in Akk. (see Knudsen, AOAT 1 147-55), to the root *k-r-y* elsewhere in Semitic (Eth. *karaya*, Arab. *karā*, Heb. *kārâ*, JAram. *kərā*), including Ugaritic (KTU 1.12 i 23; see Caquot-Sznycer-Herdner, Textes ougaritiques 339 and n. d). (The geminate Arabic *ḫa/urr* and Hebrew *ḥōr*, as well as Geᶜez *ḫarawa*, noted by Leslau, Or. 37 355, all reflect roots meaning properly "to bore, pierce, incise," rather than "to dig.") Thus, Ugar. */ḫirītu/* should be considered a loanword from Akk. (The vowel pattern of */ḫirītu/*, too, suggests the possibility of a loan: none of our sound rules, Part III, ch. 2 §A 1, would derive */ḫirītu/* from an original *qatil-t* form [though the Akk. form may be *ḫerītu* < **ḫariy-t*], and so we would need to posit an original *qitil-t* form; the latter is rare in NWS, common in Akk.)

ḪRM: see ḤRM, above.

ḪRMθ

**/ḫarmiθ(a)tu/*, pl. */ḫarmiθātu/*, n. (loanword?) "sickle(?)."

econ.: 2 ^{urudu}*ḫa-ar-me-ša-tu* ^{giš}MÁ^{meš} "2 ship's *ḫ*.'s" PRU 6 141:3 (list of implements)

Alphabetic: *ḫrmθt* (UT 405a no. 1009).

Cf. Heb. *ḥarmēš* "sickle"; whether these forms are true Semitic quadriradicals, or borrowed from an unknown language, is uncertain. As a marine implement in the example above, the term may mean "grapple" (W.M. Thackston, private communication).

?ḪRS: see *ḫa-ar-ZA-ti* in the Appendix to the Glossary, below.

ḪRṢ[1]

/ḫurāṣu/ n. "gold."

lex.: (Sum.) [GUŠKIN] = (Akk.) [*ḫurāṣu*] = (Hur.) [ ] = (Ugar.) *ḫu-r*[*a-ṣu*] Ug. 5 137 ii 4 (polyglot vocab.)

S^a Voc. no. 174b.

Alphabetic: *ḫrṣ* (UT 405a no. 1014).

?ḪRṢ[2]: see *ḫa-ar-ZA-ti* in the Appendix to the Glossary, below.

?ḪRŠ

/ḫar(r)ašu/ adj. "deaf(?)."

lex.: (Sum.) [IDIM?] = (Akk.) [*sebû*?] = (Hur.) [ ] = (Ugar.) [*ḫ*]*a-ra-š*[*u*] Ug. 5 137 iii 18' (polyglot vocab.)

S^a Voc. no. 198.11.

Alphabetic: Unattested.

ḪTN

/ḫatnu/ (or Akk. form, for Ugar. **/ḫatanu/* ?) n. "son-in-law."

legal: PN : *ḫa-at-ni* PN$_2$ "PN the son-in-law of PN$_2$" PRU 3 142b:5

Alphabetic: *ḫtn* (UT 405b no. 1025).

The gloss mark indicates that the form is non-Akkadian, as noted by Nougayrol, PRU 3 p. 233; Boyd, Collection 97-98. The syllabic transcription may exhibit Akk. morphology (cf. Akk. *ḫatnu* alongside *ḫatanu*; see Part III, ch. 3 §G); otherwise, it reflects a *qatl* form, as opposed to the *qatal* of Heb. *ḥātān*, Arab. *ḫatan*.

Ṭ

ṬB: see ṬW/YB, below.

ṬHR

/ṭuhūru/ adj. "pure."

lex.: (Sum.) [SIKIL] = (Akk.) [*ellu*] = (Hur.) *ši-ḫa-la-e* = (Ugar.) *ṭu-ú-ru* Ug. 5 130 iii 19' (polyglot vocab.)

(Sum.) [KÙ] = (Akk.) [*ellu*?] = (Hur.) [*ši-ḫ*]*a-al-e* = (Ugar.) *ṭu-ú-ru* Ug. 5 137 ii 1 (polyglot vocab.)

Sª Voc. nos. 40.1; 174.1.

Alphabetic: *ṭhr* (UT 406a no. 1032); see the Sª Voc. commentary.

ṬW/YB

(a) */ṭābu/* adj. "sweet, pleasant."

lex.: (Sum.) [DÙG] = (Akk.) [*ṭābu*] = (Hur.) [ ] = (Ugar.) *ṭa-bu* UF 11 479:26 (polyglot vocab.)

Sª Voc. no. 43.2

Alphabetic: *ṭb* (UT 406a no. 1028).

(b) See Sª Voc. no. 32.1, commentary on the Ugaritic column.

?ṬW/YR: see DYR, above.

?ṬRQ: see DRQ, above.

Ẓ

?ẒRW

/ẓurwu/ ? (or */ṣurwu/* ?) n. "(aromatic) resin." p. 392

letter:] *karpatu* (DUG) *riq-qú* : *ZU-ur-wu* "jar of aromatic substance: resin" EA 48:8

Alphabetic: *ẓrw* (KTU 1.148:22; 4.402:11); see discussion.

Note that the Ugaritic provenance of EA 48 is likely, but not certain. It is likely that : *ZU-ur-wu* does not actually gloss Akk. *riqqu*, but rather qualifies it, specifying the precise substance.

The form : *ZU-ur-wu* is listed here as */ẓurwu/*, with initial */ẓ/*, because of the two alphabetic writings *ẓrw*. Yet cognates in Arabic (*ḍa/irw*) and Sabaean (*ḍrw*) indicate that the initial consonant was originally *ḏ̣* (Syriac *ṣarwā* is presumably a loanword), which should yield Ugar. */ṣurwu/*, an equally possible normalization of the syllabic writing. It is possible, if rather unlikely, that /*ṣurwu*/ is in fact the underlying Ugar. form, and that *ẓ* in alphab. *ẓrw* is in both instances the result of intervocalic voicing (in sandhi; for other examples of the voicing of *ṣ* to *ẓ*, including a word-initial *ẓ* < *ṣ* in sandhi, see Garr, JNES 45 48; see also Part III, ch. 2 §A 2 a).

For the *qutl* pattern (vs. Arabic *ḍalirw*, Syriac *ṣarwā*), cf. Hebrew *ṣŏrî*, pausal *ṣṓrî*.

Y

-Y1

/*-īyu*/ (rarely /*-āyu*/, /*-ūyu*/) ending for relative/gentilic adjectives.

For examples, see Part III, ch. 1 §E 3 c (/*y*/).

Alphabetic: *-y* (see UT 61-62 §8.52).

(?Y2

/*-ya*/ ? pron. suff. 1cs "my."

Ugar. lit.: [*l*]*a-ša-na-ia* "my tongue(?)" Ug. 5 153 r.4'

Alphabetic: *-y* passim; see discussion.

If Ug. 5 153 is a Ugaritic text, it is likely that the writing cited here reflects accusative /*lašāna-ya*/ "my tongue"; the 1cs possessive suffix has the allomorph *-y* = */*-ya*/ on acc. sg. nouns (see UT 36 §6.6).)

YBL

(a) v., G suffix-conj., 3ms? "to bring, bear."

econ.: GN *X* ŠEN^{meš}(*ruqqī*) *i-bi-la* "GN brought X kettles" PRU 6 134:3,5,7

X NA^{meš} *šá i-bi-la* PN "X NA, which PN brought" PRU 6 145:1-2

Alphabetic: *ybl* (UT 408a no. 1064); cf. especially the following: "(commodities)" *d ybl blym* (KTU 4.272:7); *rṯ l ql d ybl* PN (KTU 4.337:12).

For discussion of the form, see under YṢʾ, below.

(b) /*mōbalu*/ ? n. "produce(?), load(?)"; in field designation.

legal: *qa-du* A.ŠÀ^{meš} *mu-ba-li* "with 'produce(?) field'"PRU 3 148a:8

Alphabetic: Unattested; for the root, see under a.

A *maqtal* form, identified by Boyd, Collection 223-24; cf. Syriac *mawblā* "burden, load, cargo."

((c) /*yvšōbilu*/ ? or /*šōbilū*/? v., Š imperfective 3ms or imperative mp, respectively, "to have brought(?)."

Ugar. lit.: [*i*]*a*(-)*šu-bi-lu ša-*⌜*BI*⌝*-x*[Ug. 5 153:2

Alphabetic: See discussion.

Assuming that Ug. 5 153 is a Ugaritic text, the most likely interpretation of *ia*(-)*šu-bi-lu* is as a Š verb, either /*yvšōbilu*/ < **yvšawbilu*, i.e., *yaqtulu* 3ms "he will have brought," or /*šōbilū*/ < **šawbilū*, i.e., imperative mp "have brought." It should be noted, however, that the Š stem of *ybl* is unattested in alphab. texts.)

YDᶜ: see MD, below.

YWM

/yōmu/ (less likely, */yămu/*) n. "day."

lex.: (Sum.) [UD] = (Akk.) [*ūmu*] = (Hur.) [ ] = (Ugar.) *yv-mu* Ug. 5 138 2' (polyglot vocab.)

(Sum) ᵈ[U]D = (Hur.) *tu-en-ni* = (Ugar.) *yv-m*[*u*] Ug. 5 137 iv a 17 (polyglot god-list)

Sª Voc. no. 63.1.

Alphabetic: *ym* (UT 411a no. 1100).

?YLD or ?WLD

/yaldu/ ?? or */waladu/* ?? n. "child."

lex.: (Sum.) [TUR] = (Akk.) [*šerru*?] = (Hur.) [*z*]*u*?-[*k*]*i*!? = (Ugar.) *P*[*I*?-*al*/*la*?-*d*]*u*? Ug. 5 137 ii 8' (polyglot vocab.)

Sª Voc. no. 176.y.

Alphabetic: *yld* "child" (KTU 1.124:3?; *yldy* 1.23:53); *wld* "child" (KTU 1.14 iii 48, vi 33), unless we are to read *w ld* (cf. Akk. *lidu* "child"), or *k*!*t*!*ld* (McBride apud Cross, Canaanite Myth 181 n. 152; see also Tsumura, UF 11 779-82).

YM "day": see YWM, above.

YṢʾ

☛ p. 392

v., G suffix-conj., 3ms? "to go out."

econ.: ŠU.NIGIN$_2$ *50* GUR 2-BÁN ZÍZ.AN.NA *ša i-ṣa-ʾv i-na* ITI *ḫal-*⌜*la*⌝*-t*[*u*?] "total 50 *kurru* 2 *sūtu* emmer, which went out in the month of Ḥallatu" PRU 6 101:3'-5'

Alphabetic: *yṣʾ* (UT 413b no. 1138); cf. especially the following: *θlθ d yṣa bd* PN (KTU 4.43:1-2); *spr npṣm d yṣ* «.»*a b mid*!(*l*)*ḫ* (KTU 4.166:1); *byrḫ pgrm yṣa lbš* (KTU 4.193:6-9, cf. 1-3);*w šbᶜ ᶜšr šmn d l yṣa bt mlk* (KTU 4.341:20-21).

Both Kühne, UF 5 188-89, and Rainey, IOS 3 45-47, have noted the irregularity of past-tense *i-ṣa-ʾv* here and *i-bi-la* (cited above, under YBL), for the expected Akk. preterite forms *uṣi* and *ubil*. It seems likely that the final vowel of *i-bi-la* reflects an underlying Ugar. suffix-conjugation 3ms marker */-a/*, rather than the Akk. ventive, which was not well understood by the scribes of Ugarit Akk. The consensus vocalization of alphabetic *ybl* in the suffix-conjugation is */yabala/*, i.e., *qatala*, but it should be noted that there is little internal or comparative evidence for this (other than that most active roots are *qatala*); perhaps, therefore, *i-bi-la* reflects suffix-conjugation */yabila/*, i.e., a *qatila* form. (For another active *i - a* [*qatila - yiqtal*] root in early NWS that is not II- or III-Guttural, cf. perhaps *g-m-r* "to finish"; see the PN's discussed in Sivan, Analysis, 142, 152, 220.) Alternatively, of course, the theme-vowel *i* may reflect Akk. *ubil*. In any event, the prefix *i-* of both *i-bi-la* and *i-ṣa-ʾa* is very strange, since it represents neither Akk. *u-* nor Ugar. */ya-/*. (It is unlikely that we should assume the existence of a vowel reduction rule affecting the first syllable, i.e., */yaṣaʾa/* > [yəṣaʾa] > [īṣaʾa] [cf. Aramaic *īteb* "he sat"]; other evidence, especially the syncope of *medial* short vowels in some forms, suggests that the initial syllable of forms like */yaṣaʾa/* was stressed; see Part III, ch. 2 §B 2). Kühne suggests that the initial *i-* results from an analogy in the scribes' minds by which syllabic *i-* of Akk. *iparras* was equated with the Ugar. morph */ya-/* of */yaqtul-/*, then generalized so that, e.g., *i-ṣa-ʾa* is a kind of morphographemic expression of */yaṣaʾa/*. While this seems forced, perhaps it is the best explanation of the curious prefix.

?YṢḤ: see YṢR, below.

YṢR

/yāṣiru/, pl. */yāṣirūma/*, n. (G ptcpl.) "potter."

econ.: [lú]*ia-ṣí-[ru*] PRU 6 136:11 (list of professions)

ia-ṣí-ru-ma PRU 3 195b B i 12 (list of PN's)

Alphabetic: *yṣr*, pl. *yṣrm* (UT 414a no. 1142).

See Alt, ZA 52 330. In addition to Hebrew *yōṣēr* (and the rare Akk. *ēṣiru* "carver"), cf. Eblaite BAḪAR (→ Akk. *paḫāru* "potter") = *wa-zi-lu-um* = */wāṣirum/*; see Krebernik, ZA 73 36.

In the first example, [lú]*ia-ṣí-[ḫu]* for */yāṣiḫu/* (alphabetic *yṣḥ*, member of a certain guild), is also possible; cf., e.g., KTU 4.99:19 (and 11). (Dietrich-Loretz, BiOr 23 130a, suggest the meaning "crier, herald" for *yṣḥ*; the form cannot, however, be derived directly from the root *ṣyḥ* "to call out," as is also proposed, ibid.)

YQŠ

/yāqišu/ n. (G ptcpl.) "fowler."

econ.: [lú]*ia-qí-š[u*] PRU 6 136:12 (list of professions)

Alphabetic: Pl. *yqšm* (UT 414a no. 1145).

?YRʾ

*/*mōruʾu*/, pl. /*mōruʾūma*/ ?, n. "(a garment)."

econ.: 2 [túg.meš]*mu-ru-ú-ma* [meš] PRU 6 126:3 (list of garments)

Alphabetic: Unattested.

The ending */-ūma/* marks the form as Ugar. pl. Nougayrol, PRU 6 p. 159 n. 2, suggested a connection with Akk. *mu-ur-ḫu*. While such a connection cannot be ruled out completely, *mu-ur-ḫu*, with variant forms *mu-ur-ri, mu-ri-a, mu-ri-ku-ú-a*, appears only in lexical texts, where it is glossed as "Subarean garment" (CAD M/2 219b). The form of *mu-ru-ú-ma*, too, is sufficiently different to suggest an alternative derivation.

The spelling *mu-ru-ú-ma* suggests a form III-ʾ, *-h*, or-ᶜ. If the word is Semitic, it may be *qutul, qutūl*, or *qutal* (with vowel harmony around the guttural; see Part III, ch. 2 §A 1 c) of a root *m-r-ʾ/h/ᶜ*, or, perhaps more likely, *maqtal* (again, with vowel harmony; less probably *maqtul* or *maqtūl*) of a root originally **w-r-ʾ/h/ᶜ*. Thus, perhaps we may compare Ethiopic (Geᶜez) *morāʾ/ moreʾ* "(short) apron" (as in Genesis 3:7; Jeremiah 13:1,2; see Dillmann, Lexicon 899). If the Ugar. and the Ethiopic words are cognate, the Ugar. form will be pl. */mōruʾūma/* (< **mawraʾūma*; less likely, */mōrūʾūma/*). For the root **w-r-ʾ*, compare perhaps Akk. *(w)arû(m)/(w)urrû(m)* "to cut" (AHw 1497a, CAD A/2 317 [*arû* C]; vs. Hebrew and Ugar. *y-r-ʾ* < **w-r-ʾ* "to fear," Arabic *waraʾa* "to repel; to become full").

?YRḪ: see ʾRḪ, above.

YRQ

/yarqānu/ adj./n. "yellow/green"; in field designation.

legal: *qa-du* A.ŠÀ[meš] *ia-ar-qa-ni* PRU 3 148a:9

Alphabetic: Unattested; cf. *yrq* "gold" (UT 415b no. 1160).

As noted by Boyd, Collection 227-28, the initial *ia-* of this form marks it clearly as non-Akkadian. Boyd suggests a comparsion with the Hebrew river name *mê hay-yarqôn* (Joshua 19:46).

YθB

(a) /*ʾaθib*/ v. G jussive, 1cs? "to sit, dwell" ("I will not dwell").

legal: *ù šum-ma* PN *i-z[e-er]* PN$_2$ NIN-*šu ù [iqabbi mā] it-ti-ki la-a a-ši-ib* "if PN det[ests] his sister PN$_2$, [he will say,] 'I will not dwell with you'" Ug. 5 81:24-26

Alphabetic: *yθb* (UT 416 no. 1177; for 1cs *aθb*, cf., e.g., KTU 1.16 vi 38,53).

la-a a-ši-ib, for expected Akk. prohibitive *lā uššab* (less likely, *lā ašbāku*), apparently reflects Ugar. /*lā ʾaθib*/, jussive (*yaqtul*) 1cs.

(b) /*mōθabu*/ n. "seat."

lex.: (Sum.) [BARAG] = (Akk.) [*mūšabu*] = (Hur.) [ ] = (Ugar.) *mu-ša-bu* Ug. 5 137 iii 32" (polyglot vocab.)

S^a Voc. no. 211.

Alphabetic: *mθb* (UT 416 no. 1177).

K

KBB: see KKB, below.

?KBD

p. 392

(a) /*kabidu*/ ? n. "liver(?)."

lex.: (Sum.) [UR?] = (Akk.) [*kabattu*?] = (Hur.) *ir-bi* = (Ugar.) *ka-bi-[du*(?)] UF 11 479:34 (polyglot vocab.)

S^a Voc. no. 47.1.

Alphabetic: *kbd* ("liver" in KTU 1.12 i 13; 1.19 i 35; see UT 417a no. 1187).

(b) */*kubuddatu*/ ?, pl. /*kubuddātu*/, n. "honoring gift."

legal: *ù* PN *i-ta-din 1 me-at 50* GUŠKIN *ku-bu-da-ti* LUGAL EN-*li-šu* "and PN gave 150 gold as honoring gift(s) for (of) his lord the king" PRU 3 98f.:6-8

Alphabetic: Unattested.

The form here is fem. pl. Boyd, Collection 109-11, is probably correct in taking this form as Ugar. rather than as a rare Akk. term (possibly also in EA 26:57, from Mittanni), *pace* the dictionaries (s.v. *kubbuttu*). Cf. also, perhaps, the Heb. hapax *kəbu(w)ddâ* "riches, valuables" (Judges 18:21).

KBKB: see KKB, below.

KBS

(a) /*kābisu*/ n. (G ptcpl.) "launderer."

econ.: ^{lú}*ka*$_4$-*bi-s[ú*] PRU 6 136:8 (list of professions)

Alphabetic: *kbs/š*, pl. *kbs/šm* (UT 417b no. 1193).

The syllabically spelled words in this list are all Ugar. For *kbs/š* in a similar alphabetic list, cf. KTU 4.99:7.

(b) */kubsatu/* ? n. "laundering(?)."

legal: A^{meš} *ku-ub-ZA-ti-ša qa-du* ZAG*: pa-ṭì-: šu ù* ^{giš}GEŠTIN *ù* $^{\text{kiri}_6}$GEŠTIN*: kí-[ru-ú] ša* PN *ù* A.ŠÀ PN$_2$ *am-ma-:*⌜*ka-ma*⌝ "its (scil.: a town) water for laundering with its (the water's) bank, and the vineyard and orchard of PN, and the field of PN$_2$ there" PRU 3 47f.:10-16

Alphabetic: Unattested.

See Gordon, RA 50 129; Cazelles, VT 6 220.

?KBR: see KPR, below.

KDD

/kaddu/, pl. */kaddūma/*, n. "jar."

econ.: *x* ^{dug}*ka-du-ma* ^{meš} PRU 6 147:4,6,14 (inventory of */kaddu/* 's);

cf. ^{dug}*ka-du<-ma?>*^{meš} ibid.:1,16

perhaps *1* ⌜*ka?*⌝*-dú* PRU 6 163:2 (list of various items)

Alphabetic: *kd*, pl. *kdm* (UT 417b no. 1195).

KDN: see QṬN, below.

KDR: see QDR, below.

KKB

/kukkubatu/ ?, pl. */kukkubātu/* ?, n. (Akk. loanword?) "vase(?)."

econ.: *2 ku-ku-ba-tu*[ ]*-tu* PRU 6 158:2

2? [*k*]*u*-[*k*]*u-ba-tu*[ ] ZÍZ.AN.NA ibid.:3

lex.: (Sum.) [MAL/GÁN?] = (Akk.) [*kukkubu*??] = (Hur.) *zu-zu-ḫé* = (Ugar.) *ku-ku-bá-t*[*u* $_4$?] Ug. 5 130 iii 9' (polyglot vocab.)

S^a Voc. no. 35/36.1.

Alphabetic: Unattested, unless *kknt*, a kind of jar (KTU 1.6 i 67), is an error for *kkbt*.

The word must be compared with Akk. *kukkubu* "small jar, vase," which may be what is actually intended (pl.) in the econ. examples. The Ugar. form, for which see the S^a Voc. commentary, may be a loan of the Akk.

KKR

/kakkaru/ n. "talent."

legal: *1 QA-QA-ra* GUŠKIN ... *ù 5 QA-QA-ra* K[Ù.BABBAR] "1 talent of gold ... and 5 talents of silver (acc.)" PRU 3 153f.:20,22

2 QA-QA-⌜*ra*⌝ KÙ.BABBAR*-pí* "2 talents of silver (acc.)" PRU 3 51f.:23

Alphabetic: *kkr* (UT 419a no. 1229).

Though neither dictionary lists Akk. *kakkaru* as a WSem. loanword, its presence only in Western texts (Mari ["loaf"], Amarna [Ḫattusas, Qatna], Ras Shamra; Akk. loanword in Hittite) and the existence of alphabetic *kkr*, Heb. *kikkār*, argue that the word is WSem. in origin (so also Nougayrol, PRU 3 p. 224). For the reading of the second example, see Boyd, Collection 107-8; Huehnergard, UF forthcoming.

☛ p. 393 ?KLB: see S^a Voc. no. 47.1, end of the Ugar. discussion.

?KMʾ

*/kamʾ(at)u/, pl. /kamaʾātu/ ?, n. "truffle."

econ.: [*k*]*a*?-*ma*-ʾ*a*-⌜*tu*⌝ *4* [PRU 6 159:3' (list of foodstuffs)

Alphabetic: Unattested.

Nougayrol did not read the first sign, tranliterating simply *? ma*-ʾ*a*-[*t*]*u 4*[(?) , and leaving the line untranslated. The preserved fragment of this tablet appears to be a list of foodstuffs; note *šu-uq-du(-)ma* "almonds" (see θQD, below) and LÀL "honey" in the following lines. What remains of the first sign of line 3', which like that of line 2' appears to be farther left than the beginnings of lines 4'f., conforms reasonably well to the end of KA (see the KA in line 2'). Thus, it is at least possible, faute de mieux, to suggest a reading [*k*]*a-ma*-ʾ*a*-⌜*tu*⌝, and to compare the Mari pl. form *kamʾātum*, which may likewise be West Semitic, since the only other Akk. occurrence, ᵘ*kaʾmatu* (with metathesis) appears in a SB lexical list (CAD K 120b). For the meaning, cf. Arabic *kamʾ(a)* truffle(s)." The Ugar. form above, if correctly interpreted, would be a *qatal-āt* pl. of a *qatl(-at)* noun.

?KMR

/*kumru*/ ? n. "(a priest)."

legal: É-*tu*₄ ᵈIM ḪUR.SAG [*ḫa-zi*] *ù* ˡᵘ́·ᵐᵉˢ*GU-um*-[*ru-šu*??] *a-na* PN *la-a ú-te-bu-ú* "the temple of *bʿl ṣpn* and [its?] *k.*-personnel will not raise a claim against PN" PRU 3 69f.:21-24

Alphabetic: See discussion.

Nougayrol read *ku*₈-*um*-[*ra-šu* (??)], and translated "ses des[servants(??)]." Boyd, Collection 113-14, noting that Akk. *kumru* is attested only in OA, MA, and Mari (CAD K 534-35; the fem. *kumirtu* in SB may be an Aram. loanword; see ibid. 532-33), suggested that the word here may be Ugar.; cf. Hebrew *kōmer* (see most recently M. Görg, BN 30 7-14), Aramaic *kumrā*. While admittedly no other reading of ˡᵘ́·ᵐᵉˢ*GU-um*[in this context suggests itself, it should be noted that the value *ku*₈ for GU is attested in only one other instance in Ugarit Akk., in a lexical text (MSL 11 43ff. iv 49). Further, it is surprising, if /*kumru*/ is a Ugar. word, that it has not appeared in any alphabetic texts, unless the reduplicated *kmr kmrm* in KTU 1.19 i 12 is to be so interpreted (so Caquot-Sznycer-Herdner, Textes ougaritiques 442 n. o; but see Gordon, UT 420b no. 1260).

?KND

/*kan(n)ădu*/ n. "(type of garment)."

econ.: *1* ᵗᵘ́ᵍ?*ka-na-dú* PRU 6 163 r. 4' (list of various items)

Alphabetic: Cf. pl.(?) *kndwm*; see discussion.

Note alphabetic *θn kndwm adrm* "two fine(?) *k.*'s" (KTU 4.4:2, a list of garments: note *pldm* in lines 4,5; for line 1, see PǴ(N)DR, below). (For *kndpnθ* in ibid.:3, Dietrich-Loretz, UF 9 340, plausibly compare Akk. [M/NA] *kindabašše*.) Gordon, UT 421 no. 1266, notes that alphabetic *kndwm*, following *θn* "two," should be dual, and that "the sg. apparently ends in *-ū*, whence *-wm* in the du." Dietrich-Loretz, UF 9 340, however, take *kndwm* to be pl. and {*w*} in {*wm*} as a vowel letter (i.e., for /*-ūma*/). (For the use of the pl. rather than the dual after "2," see Sivan, Analysis 112-13; further, below, Part III, ch. 3 §C 1 d [3].) Dietrich-Loretz's proposal seems the more likely in view of the syllabic writing cited above. They further suggest a connection of alphabetic *knd* with Akk. *kamdu*/*kandu* (and with the Ugarit Akk. ᵗᵘ́ᵍ*ki-im-da* [PRU 3 206f.:13]; but there the medial *-m-* rules out a connection with alphabetic *knd*, since Ugar. does not otherwise attest an *m* - *n* alternation). If alphabetic *knd* were related to Akk. *kam*/*ndu*, it could only be as a loan into Ugar. of the later form *kandu*, in which the original *m* has become *n* before the dental (an Akk. sound rule); the syllabic transcription ^{túg}*ka-na-dú* cited here militates against this.

?KNP

(a) /*kanapu*/ ? n. "wing(?)."

lex.: (Sum.) [KAB?] = (Akk.) [*kappu*?] = (Hur.) [ ] = (Ugar.) [*ka-n*]*a-pu* (?) Ug. 5 137 iii 27" (polyglot vocab.)

S^a Voc. no. 206.

Alphabetic: *knp* (UT 421 no. 1273).

(b) /*kannăpīyu*/ ? "?"; in field designation.

legal: *ù* A.ŠÀ *: ka-na-pí-yv* PRU 3 85f.:11

A.ŠÀ *: ka-an-na-pí-yv* PRU 3 79ff.:7

Alphabetic: *gt knpy* (KTU 4.243:18; 4.271:1; 4.296:10).

Boyd, Collection 20, lists these, transliterated *: ka-(an-)na-bi-we*, as the sole examples of the use of the gloss mark to indicate a non-Semitic Flurname. Sivan, Analysis 261, normalizes *qannābu* and translates "type of field (reaped field)" (presumably on the basis of MHeb. and JAram. *q-n-b* "to trim"). It is difficult, however, to separate these entries from the alphabetic *gt knpy* cited above, as noted by Kühne, UF 7 253-56. Kühne takes the form as a nisba of Ugar. /*kanapu*/ "wing, extremity" (see under a above), and prefers to see it as a toponym, less likely a PN or a gentilic. A derivation from /*kanapu*/ seems unlikely, however, in view of the double *-nn-* written in PRU 3 79ff.:7 (also noted by Kühne; see Part III, ch. 1 §D 2). Thus, the meaning of /*kannăpīyu*/ remains uncertain; cf. perhaps Arabic *kanaf* with the meaning "neighborhood, region" (Kraemer-Gätje-Ullmann, Wörterbuch 1 391)?

KNR

/*kinnāru*/ n. divine name ("lyre").

lex.: $^{\text{d.giš}}$*ki-na-rù* Ug. 5 18:31 (god-list)

Alphabetic: Corresponds to *knr* in the parallel alphabetic god-list KTU 1.118:31; note also *knr* as a common noun "lyre" (KTU 1.19 i 8; 1.101:16; 1.108:4; see UT 421b no. 1274). Since *kinnāru* is attested in Akk. only in a text from Mari (ARM 13 30), and at Alalaḫ in the profession *kinnāruḫuli* (Dietrich-Loretz, WO 3 192), we may assume that the form represented here is Ugar.

?KSW: see [*l*]*i* ?/[*U*]Z ?-*ZU* in the Appendix to the Glossary, below.

?KSL

/*kussŭlu*/ ? n. "(a kind of stone)."

econ.: *70* GÍN KÙ.BABBAR^{meš} $^{\text{na4}}$*ku-s*[*ú*?-*li*?-*ma*?]^{meš} "70 shekels silver, *k.*-stones" PRU 6 155:5 (list of various items)

Alphabetic: See discussion.

The suggestion to compare this entry with alphabetic *ksl(m)* in KTU 4.182:9,26 is Nougayrol's, PRU 6 p. 157. KTU 4.182 is a list which includes, in addition to terms for clothing, *iqni* "lapis-lazuli" and *abn ṣrp* "*ṣ* -stone." For the root *k-s-l* here, compare perhaps Syriac *ksālā* "plaster."

KSM

/kussumu/ n. "emmer."

lex.: (Sum.) [ÁŠ] = (Akk.) [*ku-na*]-*šu* = (Hur.) *ut-te* = (Ugar.) ⌜*ku*⌝-*sú-m*[*u*] Ug. 5 137 ii 45' (polyglot vocab.)

S^a Voc. no. 192.1

Alphabetic: *ks/šm(m/n)* (UT 422a no. 1283).

See Van Soldt, RA 75 93.

KSP

/kaspu/ n. "silver."

lex.: (Sum.) [KÙ] = (Akk.) [*kaspu*?] = (Hur.) [*uš-ḫ*]*u*?-*ni* = (Ugar.) *kàs-pu* Ug. 5 137 ii 2 (polyglot vocab.)

(Sum.) [KÙ.BABBAR] = (Akk.) [*kaspu*] = (Hur.) [ ] = (Ugar.) *ka-as-p*[*u*] ibid. ii 3 (polyglot vocab.)

S^a Voc. nos. 174.2; 174a.

Alphabetic: *ksp* (UT 422a no. 1284).

?KPR

**/kupāru/*, pl. */kupārātu/* ?, n. "(a bowl?)."

econ.: [*x* ^{d}]$^{\text{ug!?}}$*ku*?-*BA-ra-tu*^{meš} PRU 6 158:13 (list of items, mostly jars)

Alphabetic: Unattested, unless so understand *kbrt* in KTU 1.6 v 16 (i.e., [kubārātu]; see discussion). (*kpr* in KTU 1.3 ii 2; 1.7:15,35 is probably unrelated; see Caquot-Sznycer-Herdner, Textes ougaritiques 157 n. b.)

Nougayrol read [*š*]*a* (?) *di-ba-ra-tu*^{meš}, and did not translate. Boyd, Collection 158-59, suggests that lines 12-13 be read as *2 qà-da-ru-ma*^{meš} *ša*! *di-pá-ra-tu*^{meš} "two containers for torches" (Akk. *dipāru*); see also QDR, below. This is difficult both semantically and because the form in question is nominative, not genitive as one would expect after *ša*. The alternative reading proposed here, while it conforms only marginally to the copy, has the advantage of eliminating the difficult *ša*. Ugar. */kupāru/*, if the reading is correct, would be identical with Hebrew *kəpôr* "bowl" (loaned into Targumic Aramaic as *kəporā*; cf. also Ethiopic *kafar* "bushel (basket)"). A difficulty with this interpretation, even if the reading is correct, is that BA is not used with the value *pá* in any other syllabic transcription in our corpus; but perhaps the writing reflects the pronunciation [kubārātu], with intervocalic [b] for */p/*; see Part III, ch. 1 §A 1, ch. 2 §A 2 a.

An alternative possibility is to understand */kubarātu/*, pl. of **/kubar(a)tu/* "sieve," the likely meaning of alphab. *kbrt* (KTU 1.6 v 16), cognate with Hebrew *kəbārâ*. But "sieve" would probably not be preceded by the determinative ^{dug} (for jars, pots, etc.; though note dug.sig$_5$.ga.šu.tag.ga, etc. = *mašḫalu* "sieve" [see CAD M/1 365a]). Further, the bisyllabic pattern *qutal*, suggested by the Hebrew cognate, is at best very rare in Semitic in sg. forms outside of Arabic (but perhaps the Ugar. and Heb. forms reflect different bases, Ugar. **/kubr(at)u/*, pl. */kubarātu/*, Heb. **kabarat-*).

?KPθ

/kupθu/ ? n. "(a headdress)."

econ.: *10* $^{\text{túg.meš}}$*ku-up-šu* KTU 4.165:20 (= PRU 6 p. 99c:5; list of garments)

Alphabetic: *kpθ* (KTU 1.108:8; 4.689:6); see discussion.

KTU 4.165 is a rare example of a tablet with alphab. writing on one side (names and amounts) and syllabic on the other. The five-line syllabic text is a list of garments, all written with logograms except for the line under discussion here.

It seems likely that alphab. *kpθ* is the same word as Akk. *kupšu* (see below) "headdress, cap." In KTU 1.108:8, ᶜAnat is [*b*ᶜ]*lt kpθ*, in which *kpθ* probably denotes a divine headdress; cf. the Akk. divine epithets *bēl kupši* (CAD K 485-86, *kubšu* 1c; AHw 498a, *kubšu* 3) and *bēl agê* (*agû* "crown"; CAD A/1 154-55, *agû* A 1a; AHw 16b, *agû* 1). In KTU 4.689, a list of "ship's gear" (*spr npṣ any*), *kpθ* may denote the top part of a mast (cf. *trn* [= Heb. *tōren*] "mast" in the preceding line). Note that although in both CAD (K 485-86) and AHw (497-98) the normalization is *kubšu*, it is equally possible orthographically that the Akk. word is *kupšu*; cf. further MHeb. *kōpeš* "(a broad-rimmed vessel)," (Levy, Wörterbuch 2 390b) and Syr. *kuptā* "calyx (of a flower)," which suggest that **kupθu* was widespread in Semitic, and that Ugar. /*kupθu*/ is therefore not necessarily an Akk. loanword, as suggested by Dietrich-Loretz, OLZ 62 541a.

In the example above, either Ugar. /*kupθu*/ or Akk. *kupšu* may be intended. In another Ugarit Akk. text, also a list of garments, note 2 ^{túg}ŠAGŠU^{meš} (ŠAGŠU = Akk. *kupšu*) PRU 6 128:4.

?KRB

*/*karvbu*/, pl. fem. /*karbātu*/ ?, adj. "twisted(?)."

econ.: *X* UDU$^{\text{ḫi.a}}$ *: KA-ar-ba-DU*["X *k*.- sheep" PRU 6 121:4

Alphabetic: See discussion, end.

Nougayrol read *ka-ar-ba-du*[*-ma*](?). In PRU 6 p. 155, noting UDU.KI ^{d}IŠKUR.RA = *immer ēqi* in MSL 8/1 22 i 163, he suggested *kar(i)b-^{d}adu* (followed by Sivan, Analysis 143,261: *qarbaddu* [< **qarib+addu*]). Boyd, Collection 237-38, notes that the gloss sign marks the form as non-Akk., and suggests that a quadriliteral root may underlie the form.

It is unlikely that a MA sign appeared at the end of the form, as suggested by Nougayrol, since at least the lower of the horizontals should appear (cf. the copy). The short vertical seen by Nougayrol is more likely a scratch on the tablet (no photo). If so, the form is probably a fem. pl. adjective (**qatvl-ātu* > *qatlātu*, with pretonic syncope; see Part III, ch. 2 §B 1), modifying UDU$^{\text{ḫi.a}}$ (cf. alphabetic *ṣin mrat* "fat sheep" KTU 4.128:2). The term presumably refers to a particular characteristic of the sheep or, more likely, of their wool. A meaning "twisted, curly" or "matted" is suggested by cognates such as Arabic *karaba* "to twist (rope)" (Lane, Lexicon 2602b), Syriac *ʾetkreb* "to be twisted, plaited" (Brockelmann, Lexicon 343a), Ethiopic *karabā* "plaited (wicker) basket" (Dillmann, Lexicon 837); though the connection is admittedly distant, note also the Ḥarsūsi noun *kerrōb* "tuft (on the end of the tail)" from *kerōb* "to screw" (Johnstone, Ḥarsūsi Lexicon 69); and finally, perhaps also the Hebrew root *k-b-r* II (metathesis?), as in *mikbār* "lattice-work." A meaning "twist, curl, bend" might also fit alphabetic *tkrb* in KTU 1.19 i 2 (parallel to *tql* "she falls, stoops"?).

☛ p. 393

KRK

/*kurēku*/ ?, pl. /*kurēkātu*/ ?, n. "(type of implement)."

econ.: *1 ku-re-ku* PRU 6 157:12 (list of implements)

2 ku-re-ka-m[*a*? ibid.:2

4 ku-re-ka-a[*t*?] ⌜*x*⌝*-ṣi?*[ibid.:3

2 ku-r[*e*]*-k*[*a-ma*?] *1 x x* ibid.:6

2 ku-re-[PRU 6 168:5 (list of implements)

Alphabetic: *krk*, fem. (Gordon, UT 423a, no. 1030; note also du. *θt krkm* KTU 4.184:3).

Some of the readings cited above differ from Nougayrol's. In PRU 6 157:3, he read *4 ku-ri-ka-at*[ ] *er*[*û* ^{M}]$^{(?)}$; in the copy, however, before the break at the end of the line, *x-ṣi* (cf. *ṣi* in line 11) appears more likely than URUDU (*erû*; cf. URUDU in line 4), and so the line is probably a genitive chain: "4 *k.*'s of *x*." In line 2, rather than Nougayrol's *2(?) ku-ri-ka-a[t*, dual *2 ku-re-ka-m[a* is preferable; so also in line 6.

For a cognate, Greenfield, JCS 21 92-93, plausibly points to Akk. *karāku* "to dam (a canal or waterway)"; less likely is his comparison of MHeb. *kərîkâ* "a small 'sheaf' of grain" and Aramaic *məkārəkîn kərîkān* "binding bundles" (ibid.). Greenfield also convincingly refutes earlier proposals by Gordon, UT 423a no. 1030; and by Dietrich-Loretz, BiOr 23 131b. The form is normalized here as *qutēl* < **qutayl* (diminutive), as suggested by Boyd, Collection 111-13.

KRKR: see KKR, above.

?KRLN: see *KI-ra-li-nu* in the Appendix to the Glossary, below.

KRR: see KKR, above.

KθR

/kōθaru/ n. divine name (Kothar, "?").

lex.: (Sum.) ^{d}A.A = (Hur.) *e-ia-an* = (Ugar.) *ku-šar-ru* Ug. 5 137 iv a 19 (polyglot god-list)

Alphabetic: *kθr* (UT 424-25 no. 1335).

For the doubled *-rr-* in the writing here, see Part III, ch. 1 §D 2. The syllabic transcription (note also PN's such as *ku-šar-a-bu/bi*, PRU 3 154f.:5; Ug. 5 96:27) must reflect either */kōθaru/* or */kŭθaru/*. The evidence of the cognate languages is ambiguous here; Arabic *kawθar* "abundance" clearly suggests a vocalization */kōθaru/*, which has been adopted throughout this study, but the relatedness of the Arabic form and the Ugar. DN is by no means certain. The relatedness of the DN and Hebrew *kôšārôt* (Psalm 68:7) is disputed (see, e.g., Margulis, JANES 4 53-61, 113-17; Lichtenstein, JANES 4 97-112), and in any case, the Hebrew form could conceivably derive either from **kawθar* as in the Arab. form or, with some difficulty, from **kuθar* (cf. *šorāšā(y)w* < **šuraš-* "its roots"). Van Selms, UF 11 741, concludes that the vocalization of the Ugar. DN was */kuθaru/*, but his evidence—other Ugar. DN's of equally uncertain vocalization, place names, and the rare Arabic *qutal* pattern—is not persuasive without additional support.

L

L¹

/lā/ adv. "not."

lex.: (Sum.) NU = (Akk.) *la-a* = (Hur.) *ma-nu-ku* = (Ugar.) *[l]a-a* Ug. 5 130 ii 7' (polyglot vocab.)

(Sum.) [NA] = (Akk.) *[l]a-a* = (Hur.) *ma-nu-ku* = (Ugar.) *l[a]-a* Ug. 5 130 ii 12' (polyglot vocab.)

S^{a} Voc. nos. 24.1, 25.3.

(note also Ugar. lit.: *la* Ug. 5 153 r.2'[bis],3',5'; *la-a* ibid. r.7')

Alphabetic: *l* (passim; see UT 108 §12.4, 425b no. 1338).

L²

/li(-)/ prep. "to, for."

lex.: (Sum.) [MU] = (Akk.) *a-na* = (Hur.) *i-di-da* = (Ugar.) *le-⌜e⌝* Ug. 5 130 iii 5' (polyglot vocab.)

Sᵃ Voc. no. 32.5.

Alphabetic: *l* (passim; see UT 92-93 §10.1, 425a no. 1337).

For the vocalization, see the Sᵃ Voc. commentary, and Part III, ch. 1 §G 2.

LBN¹

/labanu/ adj. "white."

lex.: (Sum.) [BABBAR] = (Akk.) [*peṣû*] = (Hur.) [ ] = (Ugar.) *la-ba-nu* Ug. 5 138 4' (polyglot vocab.)

Sᵃ Voc. no. 63.3.

Alphabetic: Pl. *lbnm* (KTU 4.182:4; cf. Heb. *lābān* "white," Arab. *laban* "milk").

LBN²

/labbǎnu/ n. "brickmaker."

econ.: PN DUMU PN_2 ˡᵘ́*la-⌜ba?⌝-nu* PRU 3 199ff. iii 55 (list of persons grouped by profession)

Alphabetic: Unattested; cf. *lbnt* "brickwork" and denominative v. *lbn* "to make bricks" (UT 426b no. 1350).

Noted by Boyd, Collection 114, who compares Arabic *labbān*.

?LGM: see *ri/tal-GI-⌜mu ?⌝* in the Appendix to the Glossary, below.

?LWZ: see [*l*]*i* ?/[*U*]Z ?-*ZU* in the Appendix to the Glossary, below.

?LWḤ, ?LWḪ: see *lu-ḫu-ma* in the Appendix to the Glossary, below.

?LWẒ, ?LWS: see [*l*]*i* ?/[*U*]Z ?-*ZU* in the Appendix to the Glossary, below.

?LWǴ: see *lu-ḫu-ma* in the Appendix to the Glossary, below.

?LWṢ: see [*l*]*i* ?/[*U*]Z ?-*ZU* in the Appendix to the Glossary, below.

?LḤ(Ḥ): see *lu-ḫu-ma* in the Appendix to the Glossary, below.

?LḤM

/laḥǎmu/ ? n.?/adj.? "what is suitable, fitting(?)."

lex.: (Sum.) [TE?] = (Akk.) [*simtu*?] = (Hur.) *ḫa-*[*a*]*ḫ-li* = (Ugar.) *la-ḫa-m*[*u*?] Ug. 5 137 ii 16' (polyglot vocab.)

Sᵃ Voc. no. 182.

Alphabetic: Unattested; see the Sᵃ Voc. commentary.

?LḪ(Ḫ): see *lu-ḫu-ma* in the Appendix to the Glossary, below.

?LYZ, ?LYẒ: see [*l*]*i* ?/[*U*]Z ?-*ZU* in the Appendix to the Glossary, below.

?LYL: see *li-x*[in the Appendix to the Glossary, below.

?LYS, ?LYṢ: see [*l*]*i* ?/[*U*]Z ?-*ZU* in the Appendix to the Glossary, below.

?LKM: see *ri*/*tal*-*GI*-⌜*mu* ?⌝ in the Appendix to the Glossary, below.

?LL: see *li*-*x*[and *lu*-*l*[*a* in the Appendix to the Glossary, below.

LSM

/*malsamu*/ n. "course(?)/courier(?)."

lex.: (Sum.) KAR = (Akk.) *la*-*sà*-*mu* = (Hur.) *i*-*z*[*u*]-*ri* = (Ugar.) ⌜*ma*⌝-*al*-*sà*-*mu* Ug. 5 137 ii 18' (polyglot vocab.)

S^{a} Voc. no. 183.2

Alphabetic: Unattested; cf. v. *lsm* "to run," pl. n. *lsmm* "runners," perhaps *lsmt* "course?" or "speed?" (UT 429a no. 1389).

?LǴ(Ǵ): see *lu*-*ḫu*-*ma* in the Appendix to the Glossary, below.

?LQḤ

p. 393

(a) /*laqāḥu*/ ? G v.n./infin. "to receive(?)."

lex.: (Sum.) [IGI?] = (Akk.) [*maḫāru*?] = (Hur.) [ ] = (Ugar.) [*la*?-*q*]*a*?-*ḫu* UF 11 479: 24 (polyglot vocab.)

S^{a} Voc. no. 41.4.

Alphabetic: *lqḥ* (UT 429 no. 1396).

(b) /*maqqaḥu*/ n. "(pair of) tongs(?)."

econ.: *1 ma*-*qa*-*ḫa* IZI^{meš} *1 ma*-*qa*-*ḫa me*-*e* PRU 6 157:13,14 (list of implements)

Alphabetic: *mqḥ*, dual *mqḥm* (UT 429 no. 1396).

The forms above represent /*maqqaḥā*/, dual nom. bound form, the number "1" indicating probably "one pair/set (of tongs)." Cf. Heb. *ma*/*elqāḥayim*.

?LQM: see *ri*/*tal*-*GI*-⌜*mu* ?⌝ in the Appendix to the Glossary, below.

LŠN

/*lašānu*/ n. "tongue."

lex.: ^{ú}EME.UR.GI$_7$ = *la*-*ša*-*nu* UR.GI$_7$^{meš} MSL 10 107ff. A 110 (Ḫḫ XVI)

(note also Ugar. lit.: [*l*]*a*-*ša*-*na*-*ia* Ug. 5 153 r.4')

Alphabetic: *lšn* (KTU 1.103:31,53; dual *lšnm* 1.83:5; v. *lšn* "to malign" 1.17 vi 51).

The lexical writing is for expected Akk. *lišān kalbi*, lit. "hound's-tongue," a medicinal plant; see CAD L 209a. Since Akk. for "tongue" is *lišānu*, with -*i*- in the first syllable, as in Arabic (and cf. Ethiopic *lesān*, Aram. *leššānā*, Eblaite *li*-*sa*-*nu* [MEE 4 218 no. 180], also < **lišān*-), it is likely that the form here reflects instead the Ugar. pronunciation, with -*a*-, as in Heb. *lāšôn*. (The form in Ug. 5 153, if it is correctly interpreted as Ugar., is apparently the same word, accusative, with 1cs suffix, i.e, /*lašāna*-*ya*/.)

M

M^{ɔ}

/*mi*^{ɔ}*tu*/ num. "hundred."

legal: *i-na 2 me-te* KÙ.BABBAR *ṣár-pu i-na* ŠÀM.TIL.LA "for 200 (shekels) of fine silver, full price" PRU 3 169a:14-15

Alphabetic: *mit*, pl. *mat* (UT 430a no. 1404).

The writing represents the dual oblique bound form /*mi*^{ɔ}*tē*/.

M^{ɔ}D

*/*ma*^{ɔ}*du*/ ?, pl. /*ma*^{ɔ}*(a)dūma*/, adj. "much, many."

lex.: (Sum.) [MAḪ] = (Akk.) [*mādu*/*ma*^{ɔ}*du*] = (Hur.) [ ]-*ši* = (Ugar.) *ma-a-du-ma* Ug. 5 137 ii 36' (polyglot vocab.)

S^{a} Voc. no. 189.3.

Alphabetic: *mid* (UT 430a no. 1406; cf. *madtn* KTU 1.103:1).

?M^{ɔ}ZR: see ^{ɔ}ZR, above.

M^{ɔ}ḪD: see ^{ɔ}ḪD, above.

?M^{ɔ}R: see *ma-ar-*⌜*tu* ?⌝ in the Appendix to the Glossary, below.

M^{ɔ}T: see M^{ɔ}, above.

MGMR: see GMR, above.

MD (original root YD^{c})

/*mūdû*/, pl. /*mūdûma*/, n. (Akk. loanward) "(an official)" ("courtier"?).

legal: PN *mar-ia-nu* LUGAL *ù mu-du* LUG[AL] "PN is a king's charioteer and king's courtier" PRU 3 79ff.:17-18

ù šu-ú ú-ra še-ra ^{lú}*mu-du* LUGAL "and in future he is a king's courtier" PRU 3 81ff.:20-21; 3 85f.:15-16

ù PN ^{lú}*mu-du-ú* LUGAL "PN is a king's courtier" PRU 3 83f.:20

ù PN *ù* DUMU^{meš}-*šu* ^{lú}*mu-du-ú* MÍ.LUGAL "PN and his sons are queen's courtiers" PRU 3 113ff.:30-31

[P]N ^{lú}⌜*mu*?⌝-*d*[*u* PRU 3 115f. r. 3'

ù iš-ku-un-šu i-na mu-de$_4$ MÍ.LUGAL-*ti* "and installed him among the queen's courtiers" PRU 3 162f.:6

ù il-ta-kán^{an}-*šu i-na* $^{lú.meš}$*mu-de*$_4$ LUGAL "and installed him among the king's courtiers" PRU 3 134f.:11-12

econ.: ^{lú}*mu-du-ma* PRU 6 93:10 (list of professions)

lex.: NU.NU = *mu-du-ú, kab-zu-zu, ṣi-ib-ba-ru* AS 16 33ff. D 15'-17' (Silbenvokabular A)

Alphabetic: pl. *mdm* (UT 430-31 no. 1427); see discussion.

These entries have generated a considerable amount of discussion; see most recently Thiel, UF 12 349-56; Vargyas, UF 13 165-79. It seems certain that the Ugar. pl. ^{lú}*mu-du-ma* in the econ.

text PRU 6 93:10 must correspond to alphabetic *mdm* in, e.g., KTU 4.99:4, in view of the similarity of the texts (see, e.g., Heltzer apud Nougayrol, PRU 6 151 n. 1; Dietrich-Loretz-Sanmartín, UF 5 92; Vargyas, UF 13 169). Further, there is no compelling reason to divorce ^{lú}*mu-du-ma* from the examples of $^{(lú)}$*mu-du(-ú) šarr(at)i* and $^{(lú.meš)}$*mu-de*$_4$ *šarr(at)i* in the legal texts (Vargyas, ibid. 170). The spellings in the legal texts, with extra final vowel signs in some and no indication of a double *d* in any, leave little doubt that the term is to be associated with Akk. *mūdû*, the participle of *idû* "to know," rather than the Ugar. root *m-d-d* "to measure" (see CAD M/2 167b; pace Gordon, UT 430-31, no. 1427; AHw 666a). Finally, both the syllabic spellings $^{(lú)}$*mu-du* and ^{lú}*mu-du-ma* as well as the alphabetic spelling *mdm* indicate that the term is not native to Ugar. (where we should expect the original ᶜ of the root *y-d-*ᶜ to appear), but rather a loanword into Ugar. of Akk. *mūdû* (so also Boyd, Collection 224-27).

?MDD

/maddatu/ ? n. "measurement."

legal: *5 pu-ri-du*$_4$ A.ŠÀ GÍD.DA *ù 3 pu-ri-du*$_4$ A.ŠÀ *ra-pí-iš : ma-ad-da-tù* É *: ku-na-ḫi* (translation given below) Ug. 5 5:6-10

Alphabetic: Unattested; cf. perhaps v.(?) *ymd* (KTU 4.609:31).

Nougayrol rendered *: ma-ad-da-du* "c'est mesuré," apparently taking the form as an aberrant Akk. predicative adj. (for G *madid* or D *muddud*, Ass. *maddud*). Since the form does not follow (i.e., gloss) a logogram, however, the gloss mark indicates that it should be considered non-Akk. (see Part III, ch. 1 §C 4). Boyd, Collection 123-26, suggests that *: ma-ad-da-du* reflects a Ugar. D suffix-conj. form */maddadū/* "they have measured." This seems forced, however (for a more likely D suffix-conj. form, see below under ŠLM b). More likely, the form is *: ma-ad-da-tù*, i.e., a *qall-at* noun */maddatu/* "measurement" (vs. Akk. *middatu* and Heb. *middâ* with *-i-* [cf. Ugar. */dabḥu/*, above, vs. **ðibḥ-* elsewhere]; note also Heb. *maddîm* "measures" Arab. *madd* "extension,"*mudda* "interval"), in construct to the following *bīt kunaḫi*. Lines 9-10 probably constitute an explanatory parenthesis, in apposition to lines 6-8 (cf. the following in a letter from Carchemish: *anumma middata—mūrak u rupša—ultēbilakku* "I herewith send you the measurement—length and width" PRU 4 194:6-8). The entire text (except witnesses) may be translated as follows:

> From this day, in the presence of witnesses, PN and his wife PN$_2$ have sold a plot 5 *purīdu* in length and 3 *purīdu* in width—the measurement of a/the *kunaḫi*-house—to PN$_3$ for 30 silver. The 5-*purīdu* p[lot] is transferred "i[n the light of day]" to PN$_3$ and his children. And PN$_3$ bought the 5-*pu[rīdu* plot] to build and m[aintain?] (*r[a-ṣa-pí]*?) a/the *kunaḫi* -house of Ištar. And it is (to be?) sacred t[o Ištar] and transferred [to] Ištar(?).

MDRᶜ: see DRᶜ, above.

MDT: see MDD, above.

?MHR: see *ma-ar-*⸢*tu* ?⸣ in the Appendix to the Glossary, below.

?MW/YR

/mār/ (for */māra/*) v., G suffix-conjugation, 3ms?, "to (be) exchange(d)(?)." p. 393

legal: É-*tu*$_4$ *: qú-bu-ri ša-a* PN *a-na* PN$_2$ *ma-a-*⸢*ar*?⸣ "the burial ground of PN is exchanged to PN$_2$" PRU 3 51f.:8-9

Alphabetic: Unattested.

For the reading and interpretation here, see Huehnergard, UF forthcoming. Cf. Hebrew *m-w/y-r* "to (be) change(d), exchange" (N and Hiphil), Syriac *mār* "to supply," Aphel "to sell, barter (grain)." The form here is partly Akkadianized, in that it lacks the expected 3ms marker */-a/*; see Part III, ch. 3 §G 3.

(MWT

/mītu/ ?? G v.n./infin. cst.? "to die."

legal:]*i-šak-kán-šu-nu a-di : mi-ti-šu-nu* "will put them to death" PRU 3 96ff.:35-36

letter: [... *a-di* (?)] *mi-ti al-ta-kán* PRU 3 4b:13

Alphabetic: Cf. v. *mt* (UT 431a no. 1443).

In the first example, the "gloss mark" does not indicate a gloss, but rather that *mi-ti-šu-nu* goes with the preceding line, after *a-di* (see Part III, ch. 1 §C 2 a). If the form is taken as Akk., the meaning is literally "until their dead (one)." Thus, in CAD M/2 144a, an emendation is proposed: *a-di mi* <*-tu* >*-ti-šu-nu* "until their death/dying." But a scribal error seems unlikely in view of the analogous clause in the second example (unless *mi-ti* there is the end of a different word). Given the several G verbal nouns of the pattern *qitl* (see Part III, ch. 3 §D 2 a), perhaps these forms should be considered WSem. infinitives, */mītu/*. But militating against such a proposal, of course, is that the expected infinitive of this II-*w* root is */mūtu/* (cf. Heb. *mût*).)

MZR: see ᵓZR, above.

☛ p. 393

MḪṢ

(a) */māḫiṣu/* n. (G ptcpl.) "(member of a certain guild)."

econ.: [*1 m*]*e* (??) ⌜lú⌝*ma-ḫi-ṣu ub-x*[PRU 6 166 inner margin 4

lú*ma-ḫ*[*i?-ṣú?*] PRU 6 136:7 (list of professions)

Alphabetic: *mḫṣ*, pl. *mḫṣm* (UT 432 no. 1456).

It is probable that the term in these examples is Ugar. rather than Akk. *māḫiṣu*; in PRU 6 136, all syllabically spelled words are Ugar. (cf. *mḫṣm* in KTU 4.99:15, a similar alphabetic list). Whether Ugar. */māḫiṣu/* has some or all of the same meanings as Akk. *māḫiṣu* —"weaver, plowman; hunter"—is uncertain.

(b) */*miḫīṣu*/, pl. */miḫīṣūma/*, n. "(type of tool or weapon)."

econ.: [*x* urudu.meš]*me-ḫi-*[*ṣ*]*u-*⌜*ma*⌝meš PRU 6 142:4 (list of implements)

Alphabetic: Cf. *mḫṣ* in KTU 1.2 i 39, probably a noun denoting a weapon (parallel to *mšḫt*, ibid.), rather than a verb (so Gordon, UT 432b no. 1456).

From **maḫīṣu*, with vowel assimilation around the guttural; see Part III, ch. 2 §A 1 c.

MṬR: see under DRᶜ, above.

MYR: see MWR, above.

?MKR

/makāru/ ? G v.n./infin. "to trade, sell."

econ.: (various items) *qāt* (ŠU) PN *na-din a-na ma-ka-ri* "(various items) given to PN for trading/selling" PRU 6 156(:6)

Alphabetic: Verb(?) *tmkrn* "they may trade/sell" (KTU 3.8:16; see Dietrich-Loretz-Sanmartín, UF 6 446-47); agent noun *mkr(m)* "merchant(s)" (UT 433 no. 1477).

Although it has several common derivatives, the verb *makāru* seems to have fallen out of general use in Akkadian, since it is extremely rare (see the dictionaries, s.v.). Thus, it is likely that the Ugar. verb rather than the Akk. is intended here. (*m-k-r* "to trade, sell" is a genuine Semitic root, Sumerian dam.gàr being a loan of Akk. *tamkāru*, not vice-versa; so also, e.g., von Soden, AHw 1314b.)

MLK

(a) Akkadianized *imallik* v., G, "to have authority."

legal: *ù* ^{lú}*ḫa-za-nu* URU^{ki} *ù* ^{lú}UGULA A.ŠÀ^{meš} *la-a i-ma-li-ik* UGU-*šu* "the mayor and the overseer of the fields will have no authority over him" PRU 3 134f.:15-16

Alphabetic: V. *mlk* (UT 433-34 no. 1483).

See AHw 594a (*malāku* III); Boyd, Collection 128-29; CAD M/1 158a; Sivan, Analysis 179-80. Akk. *malāku* means "to counsel"; since the term here denotes "to have authority," it must reflect WSem. *m-l-k*. The form is Akkadian in its morphology, however. Cf. the similar use, in a Ugarit Akk. text, of *(m)uʾʾuru*, also with *eli*: ^{lú}UGULA ^{giš}GIGIR *la ú-ma-ʾe-er* UGU PN *ù* UGU DUMU^{meš}-*š*[*u*] "the overseer of the chariots will have no authority over PN or over his sons" PRU 3 79ff.:31-33.

(b) */malku/* n. "king."

lex.: (Sum.) [EN] = (Akk.) [*ša*]*r-ru* = (Hur.) *i-wi-ir-ni* = (Ugar.) *ma-al-ku* Ug. 5 130 iii 13' (polyglot vocab.)

(Sum.) [LUGAL] = (Akk.) [*šarru*] = (Hur.) [*e-wi-i*]*r-ni* = (Ugar.) *ma-al-ku* Ug. 5 137 ii 32' (polyglot vocab.)

(Sum.) [IDIM?] = (Akk.) [*kabtu*??] = (Hur.) [ ] = (Ugar.) *ma*!?-*al-ku*[Ug. 5 137 iii 17' (polyglot vocab.)

S^{a} Voc. nos. 37.1, 188.1, 198.10.

Alphabetic: *mlk* (UT 434a no. 1484).

(c) note also

lex.: ^{d}*ma-lik* ^{meš} Ug. 5 18:32 (god-list)

Alphabetic: See discussion.

The curious writing of the form here may be intended to represent */mālikūma/*, i.e., the determinative ^{meš} for */-ūma/*, since the entry corresponds to *mlkm* in the parallel alphabetic god-lists KTU 1.47:33; 1.118:32; thus, a G ptcpl. "counsellors" or "rulers." There are, however, no parallels of such a graphic device elsewhere in our syllabic transcriptions, and it seems equally possible that the syllabic *ma-lik* reflects a traditional writing of the Mesopotamian god Malik (see Nougayrol's comments, Ug. 5 p. 60). In any case, the transcription militates against a formal association of alphab. *mlkm* with the Ammonite divine name *milkôm* (as suggested by Gordon, UT 434a no. 1484; *mlkm* in KTU 1.22 i 17, also cited by Gordon in this connection, is probably "kings").

MLSM: see LSM, above.

MSW

p. 393

**/maswatu/* ?, pl. */mas(a)wātu/*, n. "cypress(?)."

econ.: *220* $^{\text{giš.meš}}$*ma-á*[*s-w*]*a-tu a-na* L[Ú]^{meš} GN *230* $^{\text{giš.meš}}$*ma-sa-wa-tu a-na* ^{uru}*ib*?-*na-li-yi-*[*m*]*a* (!) "220 cypress(?) logs for the people of GN, 230 cypress(?) logs for the Ibnalites" PRU 6 113

20 ^{giš}*ma-ás-wa-tu* "20 cypress(?) logs" PRU 6 114:7 (list of trees/wood)

Alphabetic: Unattested; for *mswn*, see the discussion.

In Nougayrol's transliteration of PRU 6 113, the final -*[m]a* appears at the end of the preceding line, after *ma-sa-wa-tu*. In the copy, however, it appears to follow the PI sign in line 6 (slanting somewhat, as does PI itself, probably at the edge of the tablet), and this is more likely the correct reading: an ending -*ma* on the Ugar. fem. pl. */masawātu/* (see below) is unexpected; further, a plural gentilic in line 6 parallels the expression ⸢LÚ⸣^{meš} $^{[ur]u}$GN in line 3.

PRU 6 114 contains several other Ugar. words for types of trees/wood; see under ʾRZ, ʾRN, θǴR. Boyd, Collection 120-22, very plausibly points to Syriac *msutā* "cypress" as a cognate of the forms cited above. All three examples above are probably plural (so also Boyd, ibid.), properly */masawātu/* as in 6 113:5, with the two forms */maswātu/* reflecting the sporadic pretonic syncope attested in other syllabic writings of Ugar. words (see Part III, ch. 2 §B 1; see under ǴMR for another example of the same form both with and without syncope in a single text). (An alternation of sg. */maswatu/* and pl. */masawātu/*, as suggested by Rainey, IOS 3 46, and Sivan, Analysis 81, is unlikely, especially after the numbers "220" and "230," respectively, in 6 113.) Jirku, JNSL 3 34, associated */maswatu/* with the alphabetic *mswn* (KTU 1.14 iii 21; 1.15 i 4), suggesting that the latter may denote "a building constructed of this kind of timber" (i.e., of */maswatu/*). If the words are related, alphabetic *mswn* would be a noun bearing the affix */-ān/*, i.e., **/maswānu/* (for */-ān/*, see Part III, ch. 3 §C 1 n).

?MSḤṬ, ?MSḪṬ, ?MSǴṬ: see θḪṬ, below.

MᶜL(T): see NᶜL, below.

MᶜṢD: see ᶜṢD, below.

?MᶜR: see *ma-ar-*⸢*tu* ?⸣ in the Appendix to the Glossary, below.

MᶜŠR: see ᶜŠR^{2}, below.

MṢL: see ṢLL, below.

MṢR

/mamṣar(u)/ n. "knife(?)."

econ.: 2 ^{urudu}*ma-am-ṣa-ar bu-li* "2 animal knives(?)" PRU 6 141:2 (list of implements)

Alphabetic: Unattested.

Cf. Akk. *namṣaru*; the preformative */ma-/*, vs. Akk. *na-*, marks the form as WSem. Note the rare lack of a case-ending in the bound form here (see Part III, ch. 3 §C 1 f). One wonders whether the scribe mistakenly wrote *ar* for *ra* (i.e., dual nom. bound */mamṣarā/*).

MQB: see NQB, below.

MQD: see NQD, below.

MR: see MW/YR, above.

MRʾ^{1}

/murʾu/ n. "commander(?)."

legal: $^{\text{lú.meš}}$*mur-ú* ^{lú}MAŠKIM (gen.!) "prefect's commanders" PRU 3 145f.14

$^{\text{lú.meš}}$*mur-i* RN "royal commanders" PRU 3 162f.:5

econ.: *ina* ŠU PN DUMU PN_2 ^{lú}*mur-u* (gen.!) "in the possession of PN son of PN_2 the commander" PRU 3 194f.:22

^{l}[^{ú}*mu*]*r-ú* (pl.) LUGAL, ^{lú}*mur-ú* (pl.) ^{lú}*sà-ki-ni*, ^{lú}*mur-ú* (sg.) ^{I}*i-bi-ra-na* "royal commander, prefect's commander, ʾIbīrānu's commander" PRU 6 93: 2,9,16 (list of professions)

KÙ.BABBAR *ša* ^{lú}*mur-ú-ma* "silver which the commanders (gave)" PRU 6 116:5

$^{\text{lú.meš}}$*mur-ú-ma* PRU 6 131:5 (list of professions)

^{lú}*mur-ú*[ ] PRU 6 136:14 (list of professions)

$^{\text{lú.meš}}$*mur-ú uš-r*[*i-ia*]*-ni* "commanders of the crown-prince" PRU 3 199ff. iv 21 (list of persons grouped by profession)

Alphabetic: *mru*, pl. *mrum*, obl. *mrim* (UT 437 no. 1543; cf. v. *mrʾ* "to command," in *ymru* "he commands" KTU 1.4 vii 50, parallel to *ymlk* "he rules" ibid. 49).

As noted by Boyd, Collection 129-33, the reading *mur* for ḪAR in these examples is assured by the correspondence of ^{lú}*mur-ú* ^{lú}*sà-ki-ni* and ^{lú}*mur-ú* ^{I}*i-bi-ra-na* in PRU 6 93:9,16 to alphabetic *mru skn* and *mru ibrn* in KTU 4.99:13,12 (and elsewhere). Boyd is also correct in disassociating /*murʾu*/ from Akk. *(w)arû(m)* "to lead" (compared by Rainey, JNES 24 18; *(w)arû(m)* is originally III-*w*, not III-ʾ), from OAkk. and Mari *merḫu* (a connection proposed by Dietrich-Loretz, OLZ 62 543), and from Ethiopic *marḥa* "to lead."

?MRʾ^{2}, ?MRH: see YRʾ, above.

MRDMT: see RDM, below.

MRDT: see RDY, below.

MRZḤ/MRZᶜ: see RZḤ/RZᶜ, below.

MRḪŠ: see RḪŠ, below.

MRYN

/*maryannu*/, pl. /*maryannūma*/, n. (loanword) "charioteer."

legal: PN *mar-ia-nu* LUGAL "PN, royal charioteer" PRU 3 79ff.:17

⸢*i*⸣*-na* $^{\text{lú.meš}}$*mar-ia-an-ni* [LUGAL?] "among the [royal(?)] charioteers" PRU 3 140f.:6

econ.: ^{lú}*mar-ia-nu-ma* PRU 6 93:1 (list of professions)

x ^{lú}*mar-ia-nu* GN "x charioteers of GN" PRU 3 192f.:24,30

$^{\text{lú.meš}}$*mar-ia-nu* GN Ug. 7 pl. 50:15', r. 11'

Alphabetic: *mryn*, pl. *mrynm* (UT 438a no. 1551).

A loanword from Indo-European via Hurrian; see Gordon, UT 438a no. 1551; Rainey, JNES 24 19-22; Boyd, Collection 117-20; Laroche, GLH 168. (Note also the Akk. pl. form $^{\text{lú.meš}}$*mar-ia-nu-ti*, PRU 6 31:23.)

?MRᶜ: see YRʾ, above.

MRR: see MW/YR, above.

MŠʾL: see ŠᶜL, below.

?MŠḤṬ, ?MŠḪṬ: see θḪṬ, below.

?MŠLḤ, ?MŠLḪ, ?MŠLĠ: see ŠLḤ, below.

MŠN$^{\supset}$: see ŠN$^{\supset}$, below.

MŠ^{c}L: see Š^{c}L, below.

?MŠǴṬ: see θḪṬ, below.

MT: see MWT, above.

MθB: see YθB, above.

?MθḤṬ: see θḪṬ, below.

MθḪṬ: see θḪṬ, below.

?MθLḤ, ?MθLḪ, ?MθLǴ: see ŠLḤ, below.

MθN: see θNY, below.

?MθǴṬ: see θḪṬ, below.

N

☛ p. 393
☛ p. 394

N$^{\supset}$

/ni$^{\supset}$tu/, pl. */ni$^{\supset}$ātu/*, n. "(type of tool)."

econ.: *1 ni-i$^{\supset}$-tu ša* ŠU[^{meš}] "1 hand *n*." PRU 6 168:11

7 ni-$^{\supset}$a-[tu] ibid.:2

5 $^{urudu.meš}$*ni-$^{\supset}$a-tu* ŠU^{meš} "5 (bronze) hand *n*.'s PRU 6 142:2 (list of implements)

1 ni-i$^{\supset}$-⌜tu ŠU⌝^{meš} PRU 6 157:5

6 ni-$^{\supset}$a-t[u ŠU^{meš}(?)] ibid.:1

1 ni-it 1 me "1 *n*., 100(-weight)" Ug. 5 84:13

Alphabetic: *nit*, dual *nitm* (UT 440 no. 1590); see discussion.

As noted by Gordon, UT s.v., the alphabetic phrase *θt nitm* in KTU 4.625:5 indicates that *nit* is fem., and thus that the *-t* of */ni$^{\supset}$tu/* is the fem. marker. Accordingly, Kühne, UF 5 187, is undoubtedly correct to suggest that the pl. forms in syllabic spelling be transliterated *ni-$^{\supset}$a-tu*, for */ni$^{\supset}$ātu/*. (Note that other Ugar. terms that follow numbers higher than "1" in PRU 6 142 and 6 157 are marked as plural with */-ūma/*.)

The etymology of the word is uncertain. The suggestion of Dietrich-Loretz, BiOr 23 131a, to connect it with Hebrew *$^{\supset}$ēt* "plowshare" is, as pointed out by Greenfield, JCS 21 93, implausible, since it requires positing a preformative *n-* (not associated with the N stem). Greenfield's own suggestion, ibid., is to compare the Arabic root *n-$^{\supset}$-y*, which in the causative denotes "to remove an object," hence "to dig a trench" (if correct, Greenfield's etymology would require that all of the forms above be read as sg. *ni-$^{\supset}$i-tu* = */ni$^{\supset}$ītu/* < **na$^{\supset}$iy-tu*, with assimilation of **a* > */i/* around the guttural; see Part III, ch. 2 §A 1 c). More likely, however, is Boyd's comparison, Vocabulary 143-44, of Old Akk. *nātum* "handle (of a knife)," for which see CAD N/2 121a.

Alphab. *nat* in the difficult phrase *dt nat* (KTU 1.127:4,10) is probably a different word; for a review of proposals, see Xella, Testi rituali 181-82.

?NʾG: see NGD, below.

*NʾD: see ND, below.

?NʾK, ?NʾQ: see NGD, below.

NʾT: see Nʾ, above.

NBK

/nabku/ (pronounced [napku]), pl. */nab(a)kūma/,* n. "well, spring"; in field designation.

legal: *i-na* A.ŠÀ : *na-AB-ki-ma* "in 'spring field'" PRU 3 49b:5

u $KIRI_6$ *i-na* :*na-AB-ki-ma* "and the orchard in 'spring field'" PRU 3 83f.:9

[*ša i-na* : (?)*na*]-*AB-ki-ma* PRU 3 115f.:6'

ša i-na A.ŠÀ$^{(meš)}$: *NAB*/*na-AB-ki-ma* "which is in 'springs field'" PRU 6 56 r. 5',7',9' (note: the gloss mark is broken in r. 5' [from obv. 7'] and 9')

u $KIRI_6$: *kí-ru-ú i-na* : *na-bá-ki-ma* PRU 3 47a:16

u $^{a.šà}KIRI_6^{ki}$ *i-na na-ba-ki-mi* PRU 3 79ff.:8

econ.: (cf. ^{uru}*na-ba-ki* Ug. 5 12:35)

lex.: (Sum.) IDIM = (Akk.) *na*[*b-qu*?] = (Hur.) ⌜*tar*⌝-*m*[*a*?-*n*]*i* = (Ugar.) *NAB-ku* Ug. 5 137 iii 8 (polyglot vocab.)

S^a Voc. no. 198.1.

Alphabetic: *nb*/*pk*; the legal examples = *gt nb*/*pk* (UT 441a no. 1597).

In four of the pl. examples, the stem */nab/pk-/* for expected */nabak-/* reflects the sporadic pretonic syncope of unstressed vowels in Ugar. (see Part III, ch. 2 §B 1). The form *na-ba-ki-mi* is probably a scribal error (*-mi* for *-ma*; hardly the result of assimilation of *-īma* > *-īmi*, pace Kühne, UF 6 260); less likely, a dual formed on the pl. base */nabak-/* (i.e., */nabakēmi/*). On the alternation of */b/* and */p/* in this word, see Kühne, UF 6 259-60; Garr, JNES 45 45-52; and below, Part III, ch. 1 A 1, ch. 2 A 2 a. Our transliterations *na-ba-ki-mi* and *na-bá-ki-ma* above also reflect the fact that PA is often used for *bá*, but BA only rarely for *pa* in these texts.

?NGD

/nagdu/ ? n. "(a linen garment)."

econ.: [*x n*]*a*?-*x*-TU_4 GADA 2 *x*["[x] linen *n.*'s" PRU 3 206f.:6 (list of garments)

12 ^{túg}*X 1* $^{túg?}$*na-AG*?[ibid.:11

10 na-x-TU GADA *3* ^{túg}[ibid.:14

⌜*3*?⌝ *na-AG*?-TU_4 ŠU GADA["3(?) linen hand-*n.*'s" ibid.:15

Alphabetic: Unattested.

It is quite uncertain whether the same word is written in all four lines. Nougayrol read *na-ak* (?)-*tu(m)* in lines 6 and 14, but on the copy the second-last sign in both of these looks more like LAGAB than AG. In line 15, rather than Nougayrol's $^{subat(?)}$*na-ak-tum-šu* "its *n.*," read probably ⌜*3*?⌝(see copy) *na-AG*?-TU_4 ŠU "3 *n.*'s for the hand." Whether this word (or these words) is Semitic, and if so the composition of the root, remain uncertain. Possible Semitic etymologies are *qatl* of *n-g/k/q-d/t/ṭ,* and *qatal-t* of middle-guttural *n-ʾ/h/ʿ-g/k/q*?. The examples are listed here as */nagdu/* on the basis of comparison with a possible Arabic cognate, *najd,* in the plurals *nujūd, ʾanjād,* which denote household furnishings such as carpets, spreads, curtains, cloths (Lane, Lexicon 2767c).

?NGṬ, ?NGT: see NGD, above.

ND

/nādu/ ? n. (Akk. ← Sum. loanword) "stela(?)."

lex.: (Sum.) [N]A = (Akk.) *na-a-du* = (Hur.) *na-di* = (Ugar.) *na-du* Ug. 5 130 ii 11' (polyglot vocab.)

S[a] Voc. no. 25.2.

Alphabetic: Unattested.

?NHG, ?NHK, ?NHQ: see NGD, above.

(*NHR

Note [íd]*na-aḫ-ra(-yv)* (PRU 3 127f.:7,17,22; 3 83f.:6); *na-[a]ḫ-ra-yv* (PRU 3 129a:11-13; 3 115f.: 9'?); [íd]*na-ḫa-ra* PRU 3 89f.:4. Since Ugar. /h/ is not otherwise represented by Ḫ-signs in Ugarit Akk. (see Part III, ch. 1 §E 4 b [1]), it is more likely that these writings correspond to alphab. *nḫr(y)* (so also Nougayrol, PRU 3 p. 266b; Hillers, JNES 29 299-300) than to *nhr* "river" (so Sivan, Analysis 251).)

*NWD: see ND, above.

?NW/YR

/nēru/ ? or */nīru/* ? n. "lamp(?)."

econ.: *15 ni-r[u]* PRU 6 168:1 (list of implements and vessels)

Alphabetic: *nr* (KTU 4.284:6).

This form is interpreted as a Ugar. word, rather than as Akk. *nīru* "yoke" (so Nougayrol) because all other syllabically written forms in PRU 6 168 are (or may be taken as) Ugar. The phonemic quality of the vowel is uncertain (cf. Hebrew *nēr* and *nîr*). Also unclear is whether a sg. form *ni-r[u]* or pl. *ni-r[u-ma* [(meš)]] is written; in favor of the sg., perhaps, is the fact that the pl. of Heb. *nēr* is *nērōt*.

See also *ni-ru?/ú?-[* , in the Appendix to the Glossary, below.

*NḪL: see NḪL, below.

?NḪL

/naḫal(l)u/ ? n. "wadi, ravine(?)"; in field designation.

legal: *u* A.ŠÀ[meš] *na-ḫa-li* "and 'wadi field'" PRU 3 108f.:7

Alphabetic: *nḫl*, esp. in *gt nḫl* (UT 443a no. 1636; add KTU 1.100:68).

This term is usually taken to be */naḥalu/* "inheritance" (for expected */naḥlatu/*; cf. alphab. *nḥlt*, Heb. *naḥalâ*); see Nougayrol, ad loc. ("(son) patrimoine"); Boyd, Collection 140-41; Sivan, Analysis 251. More likely, however, the term refers to a geographical feature (as is usually true in such field names/descriptions), and corresponds to alphab. *gt nḫl* in KTU 4.296:9. Thus, */naḫal(l)u/* "wadi, ravine" seems preferable; cf. Heb. *naḥal* (which, however, reflects **naḫl-*), Aram. *naḥlā*. It is also possible that the term is simply Akk. *naḫallu*; see CAD N/1 124-25.

?NYR: see NW/YR, above.

?NKD, ?NKṬ, ?NKT: see NGD, above.

*NKY: see θNQ, below.

NSK

p. 394

/nāsiku/ n. (G ptcpl.) "metalsmith."

econ.: lú*na-s[í-ku]* PRU 6 136:15 (list of professions)

Alphabetic: *nsk* (UT 444b no. 1662).

(NSS

/nissatu/ ? n. "old age(?), debility(?)."

legal: *i-na ni-is-sà-at* ŠÀ-*ša* É *a-bi-ša tù-šab* (translation see below) PRU 3 54ff.:24-25

Alphabetic: See discussion.

See CAD N/2 275b, where this clause is cited along with ARM 14 1:26 under *nissatu* B, possibly a WSem. word meaning "old age(?), debility," following Birot, ARMT 14 p. 261, sub a; cf. Syriac *nassis* "weak, infirm, sickly," and the Hebrew hapax *nōsēs* "sick man" (Isaiah 10:18). (The meaning of alphab. *al yns* in the broken context of KTU 1.4 iii 5 is unknown.) It is difficult to construe *nissatu* "old age" with the genitive *libbīša* "of her heart," however; Nougayrol's "dans la tristesse de son coeur," with the normal meaning of Akk. *nissatu,* is preferable.)

?NᶜG, ?NᶜK: see NGD, above.

?NᶜL

/maᶜᶜaltu/ ? n. "bolt(?)."

lex.: (Sum.) D[UR] = (Akk.) [*markasu*??] = (Hur.) [ ]-*a*? = (Ugar.) *ma-a-al-tu*$_4$ Ug. 5 137 ii 12' (polyglot vocab.)

Sᵃ Voc. no. 179.

Alphabetic: Unattested.

?NᶜQ: see NGD, above.

NǴR

(a) */nāǵiru/* n. (G ptcpl.) "guard."

econ.: lú*na-ḫi-ru*[PRU 6 136:9 (list of professions)

Alphabetic: *nǵr* (UT 445b no. 1670).

(b) */niǵru/* G v.n./infin. "to guard"

lex.: (Sum.) [ŠEŠ] = (Akk.) [*naṣāru*] = (Hur.) [ ] = (Ugar.) *ni-iḫ-rù* Ug. 5 137 i 11' (polyglot vocab.)

Sᵃ Voc. no. 159.2.

Alphabetic: Cf. *tǵr* = */*taǵǵurū*/ "may they guard" (UT 445b no. 1670). On *nǵr* < **nθ̣r* as the root of this alphab. form, see Rainey, Lĕšonénu 35 11-15; Loewenstamm's arguments for deriving *tǵr* from a root *ǵyr* (Comparative Studies 362-65, 433-39) are not convincing.

NPK: see NBK, above.

NQB

p. 394

/maqqabu/, pl. */maqqabūma/*, n. "hammer."

econ.: [*x* urudu.meš]*ma-qa-bu-ma* meš PRU 6 142:5 (list of implements)

3 ma-qa-bu-ma URUDU^{meš} PRU 6 157:4 (list of implements)

... *2 ma-qa-bu-ma* ibid.:12

4 ma-qa-[bu-ma] PRU 6 168:3 (list of implements)

1 ma-qá!?-bu 1 [ ] ibid.:9

Alphabetic: *mqb* (UT 437a no. 1533); perhaps also *mqp* (437a no. 1537, *mqpm* KTU 3.6:5?; see Dietrich-Loretz, OLZ 62 543).

In the last example cited, Nougayrol transliterated *ma-qáb-bu*, which, if correct, would exhibit incorrectly double *-bb-* for expected /*maqqabu*/ "hammer." In the copy, however, the second sign does not resemble KAB as it is written elsewhere in Ugarit Akk. texts (e.g., PRU 3 119f.[RS 16.204]:8,11,r.2'; 3 188f.[RS 10.044]:6'; 3 189b[RS 11.790]:2'; 3 190a[RS 11.800]:6'; PRU 6 38:19). Rather, it appears to be a conflation of KAB, which the scribe may have begun to write, and GA, with which the scribe apparently tried to correct himself. Thus, it is likely that *ma-qá!-bu* is intended, as opposed to *ma-qa-[bu-ma]* in line 3 of the same text; cf. the variants ^{uru}*ma-qa-bi* and ^{uru}*ma-*⸢*qá*⸣*-bi* in PRU 3 40b:2,3.

Greenfield, JCS 21 92, suggests that alphab. *mqb* and *mqp* represent the same word (with *b*/*p* alternation; see also Garr, JNES 45 46), derived from a root *n-q-p*, and denote an agricultural implement "trimmer, hedge cutter" (comparing Hebrew *nāqap* "to trim" Isaiah 10:34). While his interpretation may not be ruled out, Boyd, Collection 144-48, is correct to point out that the contexts in which alphab. *mqb* and the syllabic writings listed above occur do not require that the implement be agricultural in nature. Thus, /*maqqabu*/ "hammer" seems preferable. As cognates, note Heb. *maqqebet* (pl. *maqqābôt*) "hammer" and the *maqtil* form *ma-qí-bu* in EA 120:11 (from Byblos); cf. also *na-aq-qa-bi* in ARMT 21 270:1, with Durand's comments ibid. pp. 308-9 n. 11.

NQD^1

/*maqqadu*/ and /*muqqādu*/ ? n. "grazing rights(?)."

legal: ŠE^{meš}*-šu* KAŠ^{meš}*-šu ša : ma-aʾ-ša-ri-ša u* UDU^{meš} *: ma-aq-qa-du a-na* PN*-ma* "the grain and beer of its (scil.: a GN) tithe and the sheep—the grazing rights(?)—likewise belong to PN" PRU 3 146f.:10-13

econ.: DUB*-pu* KÙ.BABBAR *ša* MA.KAD *6* KÙ.BABBAR *ša it-ta-din* LÚ^{meš} GN *3* KÙ.BABBAR *ša* ^{lú}*a-ši-ru-ma 3* KÙ.BABBAR *ša* ^{lú}*mur-ú-ma* KÙ.BABBAR *an-nu-ú ša mu-qa-dì-IM ša ir-te-e[ḫ?]* "tablet of the silver for grazing rights(?): 6 silver which the people of GN gave, (viz.,) 3 silver which the *ʿāširu*'s (gave), 3 silver which the 'commanders(?)' (gave). This silver is (that) for grazing-rights(?) that remained (to be paid)" PRU 6 116 (complete text)

Alphabetic: The meaning of *mqdm* KTU 4.158:19, and thus a possible connection with the examples cited above, remain uncertain. (Dietrich-Loretz, OLZ 62 543, compare alphab. *mqd* with Akk. *mak*/*qaddu* "(a large vessel or implement)," which occurs only in a lexical text and at Alalakh.) Otherwise, note *nqd* "shepherd" (UT 447a no. 1694).

It is difficult to reconcile the expected form /*maqqadu*/ of PRU 3 146f.:12 with the curious *mu-qa-dì-im* in PRU 6 116:7. The latter, occurring in the same text as the pseudo-logogram MA.KAD (which reflects /*maqqadu*/), is apparently a *muqtāl* form, for which we have little evidence in Ugar. otherwise. The indication of mimation, rare on Akkadian words in our corpus, is unprecedented on a Ugar. word; read $^{ḫi.a!}$ instead of IM? Von Soden's suggestion, AHw 674b, to read /*mūqadu*/ "burning" (cf. Heb. *môqēd*), is unlikely, as also noted by Boyd, Collection 148-50.

?NQD^2, ?NQṬ, ?NQT: see NGD, above.

?NR: see NW/YR, above.

NŠ

pl. */našūma/* n. "people, men."

lex.: (Sum.) U[N] = (Akk.) [*nišū*] = (Hur.) [*x*]-*lu*-ʾ- [*x*] = (Ugar.) ˹*na*˺-[*š*]*u*-˹*ma*˺ Ug. 5 137 ii 9' (polyglot vocab.)

Sª Voc. no. 177.1.

Alphabetic: *nšm* (UT 447b no. 1708).

p. 394

S

?Sʾ N

/suʾnu/ ? n. "trim(ming), hem."

econ.: *1* ᵗᵘ́ᵍTÙN!? :!?*su-nu* PRU 6 126:2 (list of garments)

Alphabetic: *sin* (KTU 1.6 ii 10); see discussion.

Nougayrol read *1* ˢᵘᵇᵃᵗ*a-ga-su-nu*, a form that is otherwise unknown. For the reading proposed here, note that ᵗᵘ́ᵍTÙN = *sūnu*, the Akk. cognate of alphab. *sin* (with *i* for syllable-closing aleph, i.e., */suʾnu/*) and Hebrew *səʾôn* (< [sōn] < **suʾn*); see Dietrich-Loretz, OLZ 62 544; Moran, RA 77 93-94. Although the reading TÙN is not certain, and does not resemble precisely the *ṭu* (= TÙN) in the preceding line, it seems no less likely than Nougayrol's *a-ga* (see the photo in Ug. 4 p. 128 fig. 107). Since the gloss mark before *su-nu* follows the logogram denoting the same item, it does not necessarily mark *su-nu* as Ugaritic rather than Akk. *sūnu* (see Part III, ch. 1 §C 3). Nevertheless, all other syllabically written forms in PRU 6 126 are probably Ugar., and so it is likely that Ugar. */suʾnu/* is intended in line 2 as well. Though the Akk. term properly means "trim, hem (of a garment)" (Moran), note that *sūnu*'s also appear as separate items in, e.g., MB econ. texts (see CAD S 389a).

SGR/SKR

(a) */suguru/* ? or */sukuru/* ? n. "bolt, bar."

legal: *u* ᵗᵘ́ᵍG[Ú.È(*naḫlapta*)-*šu i-n*]*a* ᵍⁱˢ*sú-KU*!(QI)-*ri i-šak-kán* [*ù*] *it-te-ṣi a-na sú-qi* "and he will place [his] c[loak o]n the bolt [and] go out into the street" Ug. 5 83:8-10

lex.: note the following forms in RS 17.98 (Ḫḫ V), cited in MSL 6 p. 28, notes to lines 271ff.:

line	Sumerian	canonical Ḫḫ V	RS 17.98
271	GIŠ.SAG.GÚL	*si-ik-ku-ru*	*sú-KU-ru*
274	GIŠ.SAG.GÚL.ŠU.LÁL (RS: GÚL.LÁ.LÁ)	*sik-kur šá-qí-li*	*ŠU-KU-ru sà-GI-ru*
275	GIŠ.ÉŠ.SAG.GÚL	*e-bi-il si-ku-ri*	*eb-lu sú-KU-ri*
276	GIŠ.MUD.SAG.GÚL	*šul-bu-ú*	*up-pu sú-KU-ri*

Alphabetic: Cf. *sgr* in the phrase *lpš (d)sgr*, perhaps "garment with fastener"; further, the v. *sgr* (see UT 449a no. 1738; add *sgrt* in KTU 1.100:70). Note also *il sk*[*r*] in KTU 1.148:42, parallel to syllabic ˹DINGIRᵐᵉˢ ᵍⁱˢSAG.GÚL˺ (*ilānū sikkūri*) in Ug. 5 170:2' (see Xella, Testi rituali 100).

For the legal example, cf., in another Ugarit Akk. text, *ù* ^{túg}GÚ.È(*naḫlapta*)-*šu i-šak-kán-ma a-na* ^{giš}SAG.GÚL (*sikkūri*) *ù i-pát-ṭar a-na* SILA$_3$ (*sūqi*) "and he will place his cloak on the bolt and depart into the street" Syria 18 249f.:22-23.

Berger, UF 2 339-40, suggests that *sú-QI-ri* is a WSem. noun of the pattern *qūtil*, for expected Akk. *sikkūru* "bar, bolt." Boyd, Collection 176-77, while concurring that the form is probably WSem., rightly notes that a pattern *qūtil* is unknown is Semitic, and that *qutil* and *qutayl* would be "equally strange"; thus, he wonders whether the scribe intended *sú-uk*!-*ri* or *sú-ku*!-*ri*, a plausible suggestion, since QI for ki_x or gi_x is otherwise unattested in Ugarit Akk. (with the possible exception of *QI-en-nu* for *kīnu* in Ug. 5 135:7').

Boyd's suggestion of a scribal error (due in part, perhaps, to *sú-qi* in the following line) is confirmed by the forms *sú/ŠU-KU-ru/ri* in the lexical text RS 17.98, which undoubtedly give the Ugar. correspondent of Akk. *sikkūru* (cf., e.g., Ugar. *la-ša-nu* for Akk. *lišānu*, under LŠN, above; see the Introduction, with n. 28). (The use of ŠU for /*su*/ in line 274 [if it is not simply a scribal error, since it occurs between forms written with ZU], is strange, but not unique in Ugarit Akk.; note *ŠU-um-mu-*[*uḫ*] for *summuḫ* in PRU 3 58a:8; see Part III, ch. 1 §A 2.) Whether the form is medial *-g-* or *-k-* cannot be determined, since alphab. texts (see above) exhibit both *sgr* and, once, *sk*[*r*] (unless the latter is a loan of Akk. *sikkūru*); further, the phenomenon of intervocalic voicing may also be involved (see Part III, ch. 1 §A 1). The consistent use of KU, however, argues for medial *-k-*, since KU for gu_5 is rare in Ugarit Akk. (Note also that Heb. and Aram. have both *s-g-r* and *s-k-r*.) The pattern of the form is also uncertain, although Syr. *sukrā* "bolt, bar, lock" and Heb. *səgôr* "enclosure" both suggest *qutul*.

(b) /*sāgiru*/ or /*sākiru*/ n./adj. (G ptcpl.) "closing(?)."

lex.: *ŠU-KU-ru sà-GI-ru* RS 17.98 (Ḫḫ V), cited MSL 6 28, note to line 274

Alphabetic: See under (a).

For the text, see above under (a). The phrase apparently reflects a mishearing and/or misunderstanding of canonical *sikkūr šāqili*, a phrase of uncertain meaning (see CAD S 258b, *sikkūru* 1f). The form *sà-GI-ru* is probably a Ugar. G participle. As with the form discussed above under (a), whether medial *-g-* (*sà-gi-ru*) or *-k-* (*sà-kí-ru*) is intended is unclear.

?SWK: see SKN b, below.

?SḤṬ, ?SḪṬ: see θḪṬ, below.

?SYK: see SKN b, above.

SK: see SKK, below.

☛ p. 395

?SKK

*/*sukku*/ ?, pl. /*sukkūma*/ ?, n. "(a garment)."

econ.: ^{túg}⌜*ZU/SU?-ku?-ma* ^{meš}⌝ PRU 6 127:6 (list of garments)

Alphabetic: Pl. *skm* (KTU 4.270:6 [garments]), dual *skm* (KTU 1.148:19).

Aistleitner, Wörterbuch 219 no. 1905, compares alphab. *skm* with Hebrew *śaq*, but this is etymologically difficult, as pointed out by Dietrich-Loretz, BiOr 25 101b; the latter compare instead the OA word *sikkum* "seam" (= Old Babylonian *sissiktum*; see AHw 1042). A closer cognate, however, is the Hebrew root (or roots) *s-k-k* "to cover, screen" and "to weave," especially in the derivatives *sōk* and *sukkâ* "covering, thicket, shelter," *māsāk* "covering, large cloth"; note also the Mari OB term *sakkum*, which Durand, ARMT 21 411-12, describes as "une ample pièce d'étoffe épaisse."

SKN

☛ p. 395

(a) /*sākinu*/ n. (G ptcpl.) "prefect."

letter: [l]lú*sà-ki-in-ni* PRU 6 3:3

l*sà-ki-in-ni* PRU 6 8:1

l*sà-ki-in<-ni>* Ug. 5 54:1

legal: lú*sà-ki-in-ni* PRU 3 35f.:10 (cf. lúGAR-*kín* KUR-*ti*, ibid.:6)

l*sà-ki-ni* PRU 3 38b:4

econ.: lú*mur-u* lú*sà-ki-ni* PRU 6 93:9 (list of professions)

Alphabetic: *skn* (UT 449-50 no. 1754).

For discussion of this term, formally a G participle, see Buccellati, OA 2 224-28; Rainey, Or. 35 426-28; Lipiński, UF 5 195-99; CAD S 76-77. The spellings with *-nn-* are discussed in Part III, ch. 1 §D 2, the determinative l in Part III, ch. 1 §B

(b)*/*sikānu*/ ?, pl. /*sikānūma*/ ? n. "statue(??)."

econ.: éAN.ZA.GÀR *ZI-GA/QA-ni-ma* "statues(?) district" Ug. 5 96:0,17

Alphabetic: *gt sknm* (UT 450a no. 1754).

Since éAN.ZA.GÀR corresponds to alphab. *gt* in other terms in Ug. 5 96 (see under GBR, cBR and in the Introduction, n. 51), the equation of this phrase with alphab. *gt sknm* seems relatively secure. For alphab. *skn* as "substitute, image," and a possible Phoenician vocalization **s(i)kōn* < **sikān-*, see Lipiński, UF 5 200-2, 207. But whether the word in question derives in fact from the root *s-k-n*, or is instead a *qīl* form of a II-weak root *s-w/y-k* with suffix /*-ān*/, cannot be determined with certainty.

SKR: see SGR, above.

SLc

/*silcu*/ n. "cliff(?)"; in field designation.

legal: A.ŠÀmeš KAR A.ŠÀ *sí-il-a* "'harbor field(s),' 'cliff field'" PRU 3 96ff.:5

i-na A.ŠÀ *: sí-il-a* "in 'cliff field'" PRU 3 119f.:5,9

] A.ŠÀ *: sí-il-a* [PRU 3 163f.:4, cf. [*sí-i*]l-*a* ibid.:8

Alphabetic: Unattested.

Cf. Heb. *selac* (*salc-*) "cliff," Arabic *silc* (Lane, Lexicon 1406) and *salc* (Wehr, Dictionary 422b) "cleft." Note the diptotic genitive in *-a* (Boyd, Collection 178).

?S-S-Ḥ/Ḫ/Ǵ-L: see *ZI-ZA-ḫal-li-ma* in the Appendix to the Glossary, below.

?SǴṬ: see θḪṬ, below.

SPL

/*saplu*/ n. "cauldron."

legal: [*1*] *sà-ap-lu* URUDU GAL "[1] large copper cauldron" PRU 3 156f. r. 9'

1(*-en*) *sà-ap-lu* ZABAR "1 bronze cauldron" PRU 3 79ff.:24; PRU 6 49:12'

sà-ap-lu ZABARmeš Syria 18 249f.:9

econ.: *1 sa-ap-lu* PRU 6 168:8

3 sà!(A)-*a*[*p-l*]*u* Ug. 5 84:5 (with Nougayrol; not *a-*⌜*du-ru*⌝ [Berger, UF 2 355])

Alphabetic: *spl* (UT 451 no. 1791; add KTU 1.104:8).

The alphab. occurrences of *spl* show that Ugar. had a word corresponding to Akk. *saplu* "(a bowl)," and Hebrew and Aramaic **sipl* (Heb. *sēpel*, Aram. *siplā* [> Arabic *sifl*]). It is unclear whether the *qatl* form reflected by the syllabic spellings cited above represent the Ugar. word (thus at variance with the *qitl* form elsewhere in NWS; cf. Ugar. /*dabḥu*/, vs. **ðibḥ-* elsewhere) or simply the Akk. *saplu*. The probable plural form *sà-ap-lu* ZABAR^{meš} in Syria 18 249f.:9, without Ugar. /*-ma*/ (i.e., *saplū* rather than **saplūma*) may suggest that the Akk. is more likely there. In PRU 6 168, however, all other identifiable syllabically written words are Ugar. (see the Introduction, p. 7 with n. 37). (Note also the possibility that Akk. *saplu*, attested only beginning with MB and MA [AHw 1027a, CAD S 165], may itself be a WSem. loan.)

☛ p. 395

SRR

/*sarru*/ adj. "false."

lex.: (Sum.) [ḪUL] = (Akk.) [*sarru*] = (Hur.) [ ]-*ri* = (Ugar.) *sar-ru* Ug. 5 137 ii 37' (polyglot vocab.)

S^{a} Voc. no. 190.1.

Alphabetic: Unattested; note perhaps the v. *ystrn* (KTU 1.4 viii 48), possibly a Gt of *s-r-r*. See the S^{a} Voc. commentary.

^{c}

^{c}BD

/^{c}*abdu*/ n. "slave, servant."

lex.: (Sum.) ÌR = (Akk.) *ar-du* = (Hur.) *pu-ra-me* = (Ugar.) *ab-du* Ug. 5 137 iii 4 (polyglot vocab.)

S^{a} Voc. no. 195.1.

Alphabetic: ^{c}*bd* (UT 452-53 no. 1801).

?^{c}BL: see *IB-lu* in the Appendix to the Glossary, below.

^{c}BR

/*ma*^{c}*baru*/ n. "ford, pass."

econ.: ^{é}AN.ZA.GÀR *ma-ba-ri* GN "district of the ford of GN" Ug. 5 96:6-7,19-20

Alphabetic: *gt m*^{c}*br* (KTU 4.243:12).

The interpretation of this form as a Ugar. noun, proposed by Boyd, Collection 56-57, is eminently plausible; for ^{é}AN.ZA.GÀR corresponding to alphab. *gt* in instances in Ug. 5 96, see under GBR and SKN b (see the Introduction, n. 51). (Gröndahl's suggestion, Personennamen 306, to take the form as a PN, is considerably less likely, both semantically and in view of the lack of a PN determinative [1].) Cf. Heb. *ma*^{c}*ăbār*, Syr. *ma*^{c}*brā*, Arab. *ma*^{c}*bar*, all "ford, pass, etc."

^{c}ðR

/^{c}*iðirtu*/ n. "help."

lex.: (Sum.) [DAḪ] = (Akk.) [*re*]-⌜*e*?⌝-[*s*]*ú*? = (Hur.) *ma-zi-ri* = (Ugar.) *i-zi-ir-*[*tu*$_4$?] Ug. 5 130 iii 7' (polyglot vocab.)

S^{a} Voc. no. 33.

Alphabetic: *ᶜðrt* (KTU 1.140:8); see the S^{a} Voc. commentary.

?ᶜWṬ: see *ú-ṭu* in the Appendix to the Glossary, below.

?ᶜWL

/*ᶜūlu*/ ? n. "young (child or animal) (?)."

econ.: ^{m}]^{eš} *30* ^{udu}ÙZ(.)X *ú-lu* PRU 6 117:2; cf. also line 3?

$^{\text{udu?}}$]$^{\text{.mí}}$EŠGAR^{meš} *ú-lu* ibid.:5

42 ÙZ.MÁŠ^{meš} *ú-lu 44* ^{mí}EŠGAR^{meš} PRU 6 120:3

Alphabetic: *ᶜl* KTU 1.6 iv 19; 1.17 v 36; 4.749:1,2? See discussion.

There are several difficulties with the identification proposed here. First, it is not certain that *ᶜl* in the alphab. texts cited above denotes "young (child or animal)," cognate with Heb. and Aram. *ᶜūl*, especially since Arabic *ǵ-y-l* is also usually cited as cognate with the latter; see, however Caquot-Sznycer-Herdner, Textes ougaritiques 264 n. m, 429 n. d; Xella, Testi rituali 38-39. Second, the relationship of *ú-lu* to the nouns ÙZ = (Akk.) *enzu* "she-goat," EŠGAR (ÁŠ.GAR) = (Akk.) *unīqu* "female kid," and ÙZ.MÁŠ (= ?) is not clear; *ú-lu* cannot be an adjective, since these nouns are probably plural (or sg. after numerals?), and two are fem. Further, since various words for young sheep and goats existed, it would be odd to find the qualification "young" with these nouns. Finally, the possibility that Ú.LU is a hitherto unidentified logogram should not be ruled out. Nevertheless, despite these problems, the form is listed here, faute de mieux, to call attention to it.

ᶜWR

/*ᶜōru*/ ?, pl. /*ᶜōrātu*/, n. "skin, hide."

lex.: (Sum.) SU = (Akk.) *ma-aš-ku* = (Hur.) *aš-ḫé* = (Ugar.) [*ú*?]-*ru* Ug. 5 130 ii 6' (polyglot vocab.)

S^{a} Voc. no. 23.

econ.: *2* ^{túg}*ú-ra-tu* PRU 6 126:6 (list of garments)

Alphabetic: Unattested; see the Ugar. commentary on S^{a} Voc. no. 23, with n. 1.

For discussion of the root of these forms, see the S^{a} Voc. commentary on no. 23.

Sivan, Analysis 207, identified the econ. example as sg. form related to /*ᶜōru*/ "skin," denoting a garment made of leather. It is more likely, however, that ^{túg}*ú-ra-tu*, despite the determinative (^{kuš} is expected), is simply the plural of the latter, i.e., /*ᶜōrātu*/ (cf. Hebrew *ᶜôr*, pl. *ᶜôrōt*); for plural forms for expected duals (after "2"), see, e.g., under ᵓZR, YRᵓ, ḪRMθ, ṢWᶜ.

ᶜZZ: see ḪṢṢ above, and [*l*]*i* ?/[*U*]Z ?-*ZU* in the Appendix to the Glossary, below. p. 395

?ᶜṬ(Ṭ): see *ú-ṭu* in the Appendix to the Glossary, below.

?ᶜẒẒ: see [*l*]*i* ?/[*U*]Z ?-*ZU* in the Appendix to the Glossary, below.

(?ᶜYN

/*ᶜēnu*/ ? n. "eye."

Ugar. lit.: [ ]⌜*x*⌝-*ni e*-⌜*nu*? *x*⌝[Ug. 5 153:3

Alphabetic: *ᶜn* (UT 455b no. 1846).

It is not entirely certain that Ug. 5 153 is a Ugaritic text. The reading and interpretation suggested here are also quite uncertain.)

?^{c}L: see ^{c}WL, above.

^{c}LY

(a) */^{c}alīyu/* or */^{c}āliyu/* adj. "ascendant" (divine epithet); in field designation.

legal: *8* $^{\text{a.šà}}$MAŠ.GÁN$^{\text{ḫi.a}}$ *ša* ^{1}[PN] DUMU ^{1}PN$_2$ *ša i-na* A.Š[À$^{\text{ḫi.a}}$] ⌜^{d}*?a?*⌝*-li-yi* "8 habitations(?) of [PN] son of PN$_2$ that are in the 'fiel[d(s)] of the Ascendant(?)'" PRU 6 55:3'-4'

Alphabetic: ^{c}*ly* (UT 456 no. 1855); see discussion.

Since we find "the fields of Ištar" (A.ŠÀ$^{\text{ḫi.a}}$ ^{d}IŠTAR) elsewhere in the same text (lines 6', 8',9',11'), it is entirely possible that here too we have a divine name or epithet, as proposed by Nougayrol, PRU 6 p. 55 n. 1. His comparison with alphab. ^{c}*ly*, which occurs in parallel with the DN *b*^{c}*l* in KTU 1.16 iii 5-9, is also apt. (Nougayrol's alternative proposal, loc. cit., to connect the form with alphab. *aliy* is much less felicitous, since the second aleph of the latter would have been indicated in syllabic transcription by a broken writing [i.e., * ^{d}*al-i-yi*].)

If the sign before *-li-yi* is indeed *a*, as seems most likely (see the copy), then the form reflects either a *qatil* or *qatīl* adjective, */^{c}alīyu/* "ascendant (one)" (cf. Arab.^{c}*alīy*), or a participle, */^{c}āliyu/* "rising (one)."

(b) */^{c}ilāyu/* ? n. "upper (part)(?)"; in field designation.

legal: [*ša i*]*-n*[*a?*] ⌜A.ŠÀ^{meš}⌝(??) ⌜*e?*⌝*-la-yi* "[which are i]n 'upper(?) field'" PRU 6 29:5

Alphabetic: ^{c}*ly-h* (KTU 1.106:14; cf. Herdner, Ug. 7 p. 28-29 and n. 90: "sa partie élevée").

The form is analyzed here as a *qitāl* noun; cf. Syr. adj. ^{c}*el(l)āy* "upper, supreme; upper (chamber)"

?^{c}MM: see *am-ma-ti* in the Appendix to the Glossary, below.

^{c}MQ^{1}

/^{c}amqu/ n. "stronghold, fort(?)."

legal: [*u* AN.ZA].GÀR *: am-qa* [*š*]*a* PN *qa-du gab-bi mim-mu-šu* "[and] the fort [distr]ict [o]f PN with everything" PRU 3 118:12

☛ p. 395 RN ... *it-ta-ši* ^{uru}*ku-um-ba : [x]-KA ù it-ta- din-šu* ... "RN ... took and gave K. the [fo]rt(?) ... " PRU 3 152f.:3-4

Alphabetic: ^{c}*mq* "strong" (UT 457b no. 1874); note especially *gt* ^{c}*mq* (UT 457b no. 1873); see discussion.

On alphab. ^{c}*mq* "strong" (cf. Akk. *emūqu* "strength"), see Greenfield, JCS 21 89. Boyd, Collection 59-60 (cf. Nougayrol, PRU 3 p. 217-18), suggests that */^{c}amqu/* is the Ugar. gloss of the logogram AN.ZA.GÀR. But in view of alphab. *gt* ^{c}*mq*, it is more likely that AN.ZA.GÀR here corresponds to *gt* (see the Introduction, n. 51). In the second example above, read perhaps ^{uru}*ku-um-ba :[am]-qà* "Kumba the fort."

See also ^{c}MQ^{2}.

^{c}MQ^{2}

/^{c}amuqu/ adj./n. "deep (place), valley."

lex.: ^{d}ḪUR.SAG^{meš} *u a-mu-q*[*u- (ma?)*] "Mountains and Valleys" Ug. 5 18:18 (god-list)

Alphabetic: Cf. *ᶜmq* "valley, plain" (UT 457b no. 1873).

The reading *a-mu-q*[*u*] (vs. Nougayrol's *a-mu-tu*[*m*]) is proposed by Borger, RA 63 171-72. Rainey, IOS 5 22, compares the alphab. text Ug. 5 V 9 = KTU 1.148, line 6, where KTU now reads *ǵrm* . ⸢*wᶜm*⸣[*q*]*t*; if the latter reading is correct, perhaps the form above should instead be read *a-mu*<*-qa*>*-t*[*u* $_4$]. Whether we read masc. sg. */ᶜamuqu/*, masc. pl. */ᶜamuqūma/*, or fem. pl. */ᶜamuqātu/*, the form is undoubtedly a substantivized *qatul* adjective; cf. Heb. *ᶜāmōq*, Akk. *emuq-*.

For É IM⸢*x*[ ]*x*⸣ : *ŠAB-*⸢*li*?*-mi*?⸣ in PRU 6 56:4', at the beginning of which Boyd, Collection 57-59, suggests a Ugar. form */*ᶜimqu*/, see under BLM, above.

?ᶜN: see ᶜYN, above.

ᶜNT

/*ᶜanatu*/ n. divine name (ᶜAnat, "?").

lex.: ^{d}*a-na-tu*$_4$ Ug. 5 18:20 (god-list)

(Sum.) [ ] = (Hur.) [*a-n*]*a-tu*$_4$ = (Ugar.) [*a*]*-na-tu*$_4$ Ug. 5 137 iv b 12 (polyglot god-list)

Alphabetic: *ᶜnt* (UT 458-59, no. 1889).

The first entry corresponds to *ᶜnt* in the parallel alphab. god-list KTU 1.118:20; see Nougayrol's comments, Ug. 5 p. 55.

?ᶜSS: see [*I*]*i* ?/[*U*]Z ?*-ZU* in the Appendix to the Glossary, below.

?ᶜPW

/*ᶜipû*/ ? n. "destruction(?)."

lex.: (Sum.) [GUL??] = (Akk.) [*abātu*/*naqāru*??] = (Hur.) *na-ak-di* = (Ugar.) *i-pu-u* Ug. 5 137 ii 43' (polyglot vocab.)

S^a Voc. no. 191.2.

Alphabetic: Unattested.

?ᶜPL: see *IB-lu* in the Appendix to the Glossary, below.

ᶜPR

/*ᶜapīru*/ n. "(a social class)."

econ.: *3* DUG Ì.GIŠ MIN (= UGU) PN DUMU PN$_2$ *ḫa-pí-ri* "3 jars of oil: ditto (= charged to) PN son of PN$_2$ the *ᶜapīru*" PRU 6 112:5

Alphabetic: *ᶜpr* (UT 459-60 no. 1899).

The rare writing of Ugar /ᶜ/ with ḪA probably indicates a learned spelling of the Akkadianized form of the word (*ḫapiru*); see Part III, ch. 1 §E 4 b (1).

ᶜṢ

*/*ᶜiṣu*/ ?, pl. /*ᶜiṣṣūma*/ ?, n. "tree(s), wood." p. 395

lex.: (Sum.) [GIŠ] = (Akk.) [*iṣṣū*?] = (Hur.) *ta-li* = (Ugar.) *iṣ-ṣú-*[*ma*?] Ug. 5 130 iii 8' (polyglot vocab.)

S^a Voc. no. 34.

Alphabetic: *ᶜṣ*, pl. *ᶜṣm* (UT 460a no. 1903).

^{c}ṢD

/ma^{c}ṣadu/, pl. */ma^{c}ṣadūma/*, n. "adze, axe(?)."

econ.: *1 ma-ṣa-du* PRU 6 157:15 (list of implements)

[x] $^{urudu.meš}$*ma-ṣa-du-ma* ^{meš} PRU 6 142:3 (list of implements)

Alphabetic: *m^{c}ṣd* (UT 460a no. 1904).

The ending */-ūma/* in PRU 6 142:3 marks this form as Ugar., and so Nougayrol, PRU 6 p. 157 n. 5, was correct to equate it with alphab. *m^{c}ṣd* rather than Akk. *maṣādu* (so AHw 619b), despite the lack of overt writing of */^{c}/* in both examples. On the meaning of the term, see Greenfield, JCS 21 92.

?^{c}SṢ: see *[l]i* ?/*[U]*Z ?-*ZU* in the Appendix to the Glossary, below.

☛ p. 395

^{c}ṢR

/^{c}uṣṣūru/ n. "bird."

lex.: ^{íd}MUŠEN = *u-ṣú-ru* MSL 11 43ff. A iii 42 (Ḫḫ XX-XXII)

^{na_4}NÍR.PA.MUŠEN.NA = *[ša] kap-pa ú-ṣú-ri* MSL 10 37ff. A 110 (C: *ša kap-pi* MUŠEN; Ḫḫ XVI)

Alphabetic: *^{c}ṣr* (UT 460a no. 1905).

For the second example, cf. canonical *šá kap-pi iṣ-ṣu-ri* (MSL 10 p. 8:146). Unless some kind of vowel harmony is at work (unlikely), we should probably take these forms as reflecting the pronunciation of alphab. Ugar. *^{c}ṣr*. (Note that neither AHw nor CAD lists an Akk. variant with initial *u-* for *iṣṣūru*.) The Ugar. form thus corresponds to Arabic *^{c}uṣfūr* in vocalization (albeit, of course, with assimilation of **-ṣp-* to *-ṣṣ-* as in Akk.; see Leslau, Or. 37 361).

^{c}RB

/^{c}ur(r)ŭb(b)ānu/ n. "guarantor."

legal: *u* PN ... *[u* P]N$_2$ ... $^{[lú].meš}$*ú-ru-ba-nu [š]a* (?) *: na-ba-dì-⌜šu-nu⌝* "and PN ... [and P[N$_2$ are the guarantors [o]f (against) their flight" PRU 3 37b:5-8

Alphabetic: Pl. *^{c}rbnm* (KTU 3.3:1,7).

Since the form lacks the Ugar. pl. ending */-ūma/*, it must be considered either a collective singular (despite the determinative), as suggested by Boyd, Collection 64, or an Akk. pl. in *-ū* (unless the scribe intended the bound form in */-ū/* and then incorrectly wrote *ša*). Nougayrol, PRU 6 p. 64 n. 2, very plausibly suggested that the same word is indicated by the logogram $^{lú.meš}$ŠU.DUG$_8$.⌜A⌝ in PRU 6 69:8' (= OB and OA *ša qātātim*; see CAD Q 172). The pattern of this word is uncertain: suffix */-ān/* on *qutul, qutūl, quttul, quttūl* (< **qattūl*?), or even *qutull* (cf. Heb. *^{c}ărubbâ* "pledge"; note aslo *^{c}ērābôn* "pledge" < **^{c}irrab-ān*).

For the form *e-ru-ub* in the phrase A.ŠÀ^{meš} PN ... *e-ru-ub a-na* PN$_2$ "PN's field ... entered (as pledge) for PN$_2$" (PRU 3 138f.:15-17,18-20), Boyd, Collection 231-32, is probably correct in seeing an Akk. preterite verb *ērub* serving as a loan translation of Ugar. *^{c}rb b* "to enter (as pledge) for," rather than a Ugar. noun *^{c}erub*, as suggested by Nougayrol, PRU 3 p. 46 n. 1 and p. 219 (followed by Sivan, Analysis 206). Both the form (noun pattern *qitul*?) and the lack of a case-ending militate against Nougayrol's proposal.

☛ p. 395 ?^{c}RG, ?^{c}RK: see *[i]r-KU*, S^{a} Voc. no. 48.2.

☛ p. 396 ?^{c}RM: see *a-ra-mi-ma* in the Appendix to the Glossary, below.

?^{c}RQ: see *[i]r-KU*, S^{a} Voc. no. 48.2.

?^{c}RR: see ^{c}WR, above.

?^{c}ŠY

/^{c}*išyatu*/ ? n. "pressing(?); clamp(?)."

econ.: *1 mar-ḫi-iš iš-ia-ti-mi 1*? ME "1 pan(?) with clamps(?), 100(-weight)" Ug. 5 84:10 (list of utensils and other items)

Alphabetic: See discussion, second paragraph.

The meaning of this phrase is quite uncertain. That it is WSem. rather than Akk. (despite the lack of a case-ending on the first item; note also *ni-it* for expected /*ni*ʾ*tu*/ in line 13 [see Part III, ch. 3 §C 1 f]) seems assured by the shape of the second term, with post-consonantal /*y*/. Most of the objects listed in Ug. 5 84 are utensils (*ruqqu, saplu, nam*[*sītu*]) and other household items (beds, chairs, table). Thus, perhaps we should compare *mar-ḫi-iš* with Hebrew *marḥešet* "sauce-pan" (Lev. 2:7, 7:9; in MHeb., "a deep, lidded pan" Menahot 63a; see Kennedy, "Cooking and Cooking Utensils" 891), the root of which is apparently *r-ḥ-š* "to move, creep, seethe" (cf. Aramaic *rḥeš*, Akk. *raḫāšu*?). The same or a similar word probably occurs in Mari OB as *marḫališum* denoting a container or utensil (see Nougayrol, Ug. 5 p. 178 n. 6; CAD M/1 280b; and especially Durand, ARMT 21 pp. 32-33 n. 3).

For the root and meaning of *iš-ia-ti-mi*, evidently a *qitl-at* form I-guttural and III-*y*, compare the alphab. *yn* ^{c}*šy lḥbš* in KTU 1.17 vi 8, which Caquot-Sznycer-Herdner, Textes ougaritiques 430, render "du vin exprimé du pressoir," comparing ^{c}*šy* with Hebrew ^{c}*iśśâ* "to press" (ibid. n. i); note also perhaps Arabic ^{c}*ašiya* ^{c}*ilay* "to wrong, treat unjustly" (Lane, Lexicon 2055a), which suggests that the verb ^{c}*šy* which appears elsewhere in KTU 1.17 (i 29,47, ii 19) reflects the same root. The form here is apparently dual oblique, /^{c}*išyatēmi*/. Thus, /*marḫiš(u)* ^{c}*išyatēmi*/ may denote a cooking utensil with parts that were pressed or squeezed together, perhaps clamps.

^{c}ŠR^{1}

p. 396

/^{c}*ašīru*/ or /^{c}*āširu*/, pl. /^{c}*ašīrūma*/ or /^{c}*āširūma*/, n. "(a royal official)."

legal: *iš-tu píl-k*[*i*] $^{lú.meš}$*a-ši-ri-ma* "from the obligations of the ^{c}.'s" PRU 3 134f.:9

econ.: ^{lú}*a-ši-ru-ma* PRU 6 93:4 (list of professions)

$^{lú.meš}$*a-ši-ru-ma* PRU 6 131:3 (list of professions)

KÙ.BABBAR *ša* ^{lú} *a-ši-ru-ma* "silver which the ^{c}.'s (gave)" PRU 6 116:4

$^{[l]ú.meš}$*a-ši-ru-ma* PRU 3 199ff. iii 1 (list of persons grouped by profession)

[$^{lú.meš}$*muš-ke-nu*]-*tu*$_4$ $^{lú.meš}$*a-ši-ru-ma* ibid. iii 30

Alphabetic: pl. ^{c}*šrm* (UT 462 no. 1932).

That the syllabic spellings above reflect alphab. ^{c}*šrm* seems assured by the fact that both occur in lists of professions which share many terms in common (e.g., syllabic PRU 3 199f.; PRU 6 93; alphab. KTU 4.68:60ff.; 4.99; 4.126). Rainey's objection, JNES 26 297, that the initial /^{c}/ should be written with *ḫa* is unfounded, as Boyd, Collection 70-71, has pointed out (see also Part III, ch. 1 §E 4 b).

Both the etymology and the precise form of this word remain uncertain. It may derive either from a root ^{c}-*š*-*r* "to serve, pour (drinks)" (also much discussed; see UT s.v.; Caquot-Sznycer-Herdner, Textes ougaritiques 154 n. j) or from ^{c}*šr* "ten" (see ^{c}ŠR^{2}, below). One expects the form to be *qātil* (i.e., G participle /^{c}*āširu*/), but as Boyd, Collection 71-72, has noted, the form *a-ši-ru-ma* in EA 268:19 (from Gezer)—if it denotes the same word—should instead be /^{c}*ōširūma*/, written with initial *ú*-; thus, /^{c}*aširu*/ or /^{c}*ašīru*/ may be more likely.

For further discussion, see also Astour, ABAW 75 NF 15-26.

ᶜŠR²

/maᶜšaru/ n. "tithe."

legal: *ù ma-ša-ra ša* GN "and the tithe of GN" PRU 3 93b:7

ŠE^meš^-*šu* KAŠ^meš^-*šu ša : ma-a*ʾ*-ša-ri-ša* (scil.: a GN) *u* UDU^meš^ *: ma-aq-qa-du a-na* PN-*ma* "the grain and beer of its (scil.: a GN) tithe and the sheep—the grazing rights(?)—likewise belong to PN" PRU 3 146f.:10-13

Alphabetic: Unattested; cf. *ᶜšr* "ten" (UT 462a no. 1931).

The same word may be represented by the logogram ZAG (for ZAG.10) in PRU 3 69f.:8 (= Akk. *ešrētu*, unattested in syllabic spelling in the Ugarit Akk. corpus). The *maqtal* pattern of the Ugar. form contrasts with both Heb. *maᶜăśēr* and Arabic *miᶜšār* "tenth, tithe."

☛ p. 396 **ᶜθTR**

/ᶜaθtaru/ n. divine name (Athtar, "?").

lex.: (Sum.) ᵈL[UGAR.MÁ]R?.D[A?] = (Hur.) *aš-ta-bi-[n]i*? = (Ugar.) *aš-ta-ru* Ug. 5 137 iv b 16 (polyglot god-list)

Alphabetic: *ᶜθtr* (UT 463-63 no. 1941).

Ǵ

?ǴBB: see *ḫa-AB-BI/BU* in the Appendix to the Glossary, below.

?ǴBṬ: see *ḫa-ba-ṭu* in the Appendix to the Glossary, below.

?ǴWY: see ḪWY, above.

?ǴWL

/ǵōlu/ ? n. "low ground(?)"; in field designation.

legal: A.ŠÀ^ḫi.a^ *: ḫu-li* PRU 3 143ff.:3

Alphabetic: *gt ǵl* (UT 464a no. 1962; add KTU 4.200:8; also in *ǵl il*, UT 464a no. 1963).

Kühne, UF 6 166-67, plausibly compares the alphab. GN *gt ǵl*, and Arabic *ǵawl* "viel Erde, tiefgelegener Landstrich, Senke." His alternative proposal, that the form represents */ḥōlu/* < **ḥawlu* "sand" is less felicitous, since comparative evidence, as noted by Boyd, Collection 102-4, indicates that the PNWS of "sand" was **ḥāl*, not **ḥawl*. (On alphab. *ḥl*, see Berger, UF 2 340-46; as pointed out by Boyd, loc. cit., it is unlikely that *: ḫu-li* is to be connected with alphab. *ḥl*,, which is never associated with fields.)

?ǴZZ: see ḪṢṢ, above.

?ǴY(Y): see ḪWY, above.

?ǴLM

/ǵulmatu/ n. "darkness, blackness(?)."

lex.: (Sum.) [IDIM?] = (Akk.) [*ekletu*?] = (Hur.) [ ] = (Ugar.) *ḫu-ul-ma-tu*$_4$ Ug. 5 137 iii 15' (polyglot vocab.)

S^a^ Voc. no. 198.8.

Alphabetic: *ǵlm(t)* "dark(ness)(?)"; see the Sᵃ Voc. commentary.

See also ḪLM, above.

ǴMR

/ǵamaru/, pl. */ǵam(a)rūma/*, n. "apprentice."

econ.: PN [lú]*ḫa-am-ru<-šu>-nu* "PN their(!) apprentice" PRU 6 79:9 (list of persons)

PN [[l]ú]*ḫa-ma-ru-ú*["PN his apprentice" ibid.:11

PN [lú]*ḫa-*[*a*]*m-*[*r*]*u-u* ibid.:13

[lú.meš]*ḫa-am-ru-ma* [meš] "apprentices" RS 25.428:6 (PRU 6 p. 150 n. 3)

[*ḫ*]*a-ma-ru-m*[*a*[(meš)]] PRU 3 196 i 1 (list of persons)

Alphabetic: *ǵmr*, pl. *ǵmrm* (UT 464-65 no. 1974).

The reading in the last example is new; the first sign is broken but ends in a Winckelhaken; there is no room for [lú.meš] before the form. For professions heading lists of persons, cf. PRU 3 195 i 12 (*ia-ṣí-ru-ma*, also without [lú.meš]) and PRU 3 199ff. passim.

In the second and third examples, the final *-u* represents Ugar. */-hū̆/* "his"; see Rainey, IOS 3 43.

The sg. *ḫa-ma-ru-u* in the second example indicates clearly that the underlying form is *qatal*; a base *qatal*, which may be pl. of either *qatl* or *qatal*, also appears in the plural */ǵamarūma/* of the last example. The other three forms show the effect of the sporadic syncope of unstressed short vowels, pretonic in pl. */ǵamrūma/*, post-tonic in sg. */ǵamru-hū̆/*; see Part III, ch. 2 §B. An Arabic cognate of this word, *ǵum(u)r*, was pointed out by Bravmann, JCS 7 27.

?ǴPP: see *ḫa-AB-BI/BU* in the Appendix to the Glossary, below.

?ǴRꝺ, ?ǴRZ, ?ǴRẒ: see *ḫa-ar-ZA-ti* in the Appendix to the Glossary, below.

?ǴRM

/ǵarĭmu/ ? adj./n. "foe, adversary(?)."

lex.: (Sum.) [ḪUL?] = (Akk.) [*zāmânu*?] = (Hur.) [ ] = (Ugar.) *ḫa-ri-mu* Ug. 5 137 ii 39' (polyglot vocab.)

Sᵃ Voc. no. 190.3.

Alphabetic: Perhaps *ǵrm* in KTU 1.4 vii 32; 1.16 vi (31,)44; cf. *ǵrmn* (KTU 1.3 ii 11); see the Sᵃ Voc. commentary.

?ǴRS, ?ǴRṢ: see *ḫa-ar-ZA-ti* in the Appendix to the Glossary, below.

☛ p. 396

P

Pᵓ

/piᵓtu/ ? n. "corner(?)."

lex.: (Sum.) [IB] = (Akk.) [*tubuqtu*] = (Hur.) [ ] = (Ugar.) *pí- i*?-[*tu* $_4$?] Ug. 5 137 i 13' (polyglot vocab.)

Sᵃ Voc. no. 160.4.

Alphabetic: *pit* and *pat*, pl. *pat* (UT 465-66 no. 1994; KTU 1.103:54).

p. 396

PDY

/tapdētu/ n. (Gt v.n./infin.?) "exchange."

legal: PN *it-ta-din 3* IKU A.ŠÀ^{meš} *i-na* A.ŠÀ^{meš} *: ḫa-ar-ZA-ti ù 5 me-at* KÙ.BAB-BAR *a-na* PN_2 *tap-de$_4$-ti* A.ŠÀ^{meš}*-šu* "PN gave PN_2 a 3-*iku* field in '*ḫ.*-field' and 500 silver (as) exchange for his field" PRU 3 95f.:8-14

PN *ti-it-ta-aš-ši* A.ŠÀ ... *ù ti-it-ta-din-šu-nu a-na* PN_2 ... *: ta-ap-de$_4$-ti* A.ŠÀ$^{hi.a}$-*šu* "PN took and gave PN_2 a field ... (as) exchange for his field(s)" PRU 3 129a:4-9

u A.ŠÀ^{meš} PN *i-na* A.ŠÀ^{meš} *qú-ul-qú-li tap-de$_4$-tu$_4$* A.ŠÀ^{meš} PN_2 *e-ru-ub a-na* PN_3 "and PN's fields in 'cassia(?) field,' the exchange for PN_2's field, entered (as pledge) for PN_3" PRU 3 138f.:18-20

Alphabetic: Unattested; cf. v. *pdy* "to ransom" (KTU 3.4:2,12)

In view of the contexts in which it occurs, this word must be seen as a derivative of Ugar. *p-d-y* "to ransom, release" (Nougayrol, PRU 3 p. 219, 229; Boyd, Collection 151-53), rather than as the Akk. noun *teptītu* (from *petû* "to open"; so von Soden, AHw 1347-48). The consistent writing with TE = *de$_4$* when no conditioning sonorant precedes or follows suggests that the vowel of the second syllable is */ē/* rather than */ī/* (see Part III, ch. 1 §G 2). Thus, the form is probably */tapdētu/* < **tapdaytu*, i.e., a Gt verbal noun (*taqtal*), as the meaning might suggest, rather than */tapdītu/*, a D verbal noun. Since the examples are probably all singular (for plural, we would expect **tapdayātu*), the final *-i* of the first two examples, where acc. */tapdēta/* is expected, is apparently due to sandhi with the following *eqli*.

PWT

/puwwatu/i/ ? n. "madder(?)."

econ.: ⌜*1 li-im* KID??⌝ *: pu-wa-ti* PRU 3 208b:3,6,10

Alphabetic: *pwt* (KTU 4.182:10; 4.626:6).

For alphab. *pwt* as "madder (root)" or "red dye," see Astour, JNES 24 348-49, and Hoffner, JAOS 87 300-3, who compare Arabic *fuwwat* and Syriac *putā* (both "madder") and the Hebrew PN *puwwâ/pûʾâ*; Hoffner also notes Hittite *puwattiš*. As pointed out by Boyd, Collection 156-58, it seems likely that *: pu-wa-ti* should be associated with alphab. *pwt*, rather than with the Egyptian word *b/puati* "bracelet," which appears in EA 14 (see Lambdin, Or. 22 364).

PḤ/ḪD

Akkadianized *lipḥ/ḫudū* v., G, precative, "to dread, fear."

lit.: *lip-ḫu-dú-ma* Ug. 5 17 r. 7'

Alphabetic: Unattested.

Von Soden, UF 1 190, translates "sie mögen erschrecken," and notes that the root must be "ka-naan. *pḫd*" (so also in AHw 810a, s.v. *paḫādu*). Cf. Hebrew *pāḥad*, Targumic Aramaic *paḥdā*; without alphab. examples or additional cognates, it cannot be determined whether the middle radical is *ḥ* or *ḫ*. Note that the form exhibits Akk. morphology (see Part III, ch. 3 §G 3).

(PḪR

lex.: ^{d}*pu-ḫur* DINGIR^{meš} Ug. 5 18:28 (god-list)

This entry corresponds to *pḫr ilm* in the parallel alphab. god-lists KTU 1.47:29; 1.118:28. Since it lacks a case-ending (see Part III, ch. 3 §C 1 f), *pu-ḫur* is probably the bound form of Akk. *puḫru* rather than a Ugar. word */*puḫŭru*/.)

PṬR

p. 397

(a) */piṭru/* G v.n./infin. "to loosen."

lex.: (Sum.) DU$_8$ = (Akk.) *pa-ṭá-[r]u* = (Hur.) *zu-lu-du-me* = (Ugar.) *pí-iṭ-r[ù?]* Ug. 5 137 iii 2 (polyglot vocab.)

S^{a} Voc. no. 194.3.

Alphabetic: Unattested (see the S^{a} Voc. commentary, with n. 60).

(b) */napṭarū/* v., N, suffix-conj., 3mp(?) "to exchange" (lit., "to release to one another"?).

legal: PN *u* PN$_2$ ... *na-ap-ṭa-ru* A.ŠÀ$^{\text{ḫi.a}}$ *i-na* A.ŠÀ$^{\text{ḫi.a}}$ (translation given in discussion, end) PRU 3 89a:4-5

Alphabetic: See under (a).

Nougayrol, PRU 3 p. 219, suggested that *na-ap-ṭa-ru* was "un nom employé au statif avec un sens transitif: 'sont échangeurs de, troquent.'" His semantic analysis seems entirely justified: in the following lines, we find: *eqelšu ša* PN *ana* PN$_2$ *ṣamit ana dārīti u eqelšu ša* PN$_2$ *[an]a* P[N] *ṣamit [ana dārīti]* "PN's field is transferred to PN$_2$ forever, and PN$_2$'s field is transferred t[o] PN [forever]" (lines 6-10). It seems clear, therefore, that *na-ap-ṭa-ru* has nothing to do with the OB (later, lexical only) noun *napṭaru(m),* for which see Kraus, RA 70 165-72. (The inclusion of this clause s.v. *napṭaru* in CAD N/1 324a ["PN and PN2 ... are *n.*'s before Niqmepa, king of Ugarit"] is somewhat misleading, since the phrase A.ŠÀ$^{\text{ḫi.a}}$ *i-na* A.ŠÀ$^{\text{ḫi.a}}$ in line 5 cannot be separated from the *napṭaru* clause.) Nougayrol's morphological analysis must be reconsidered, however. First, since *na-ap-ṭa-ru* is, as noted above, distinct from the OB noun *napṭaru,* his "nom employé au statif" would have to be a different noun, for which there is no evidence otherwise. Further, we have no other examples of nouns in the Akk. predicative form in Ugarit Akk. (or elsewhere in WPA; see Huehnergard, ZA 76 218-49 §6). Thus, we may consider the possibility that *na-ap-ṭa-ru* is a Ugaritic form. Since nouns with prefix *n-* are at best extremely rare in Ugar., the form should be seen as N stem, either a participle, masc. pl. construct, which would be very difficult syntactically (*/napṭarū/ eqli ina eqli* "exchangers of field for field"), or, much more likely, suffix-conjugation 3mp */napṭarū/*. The form would be both reciprocal (cf. N *ynθkn* = */yinnaθikāni/* "they (dual) bite each other" KTU 1.6 vi 19) and transitive, with A.ŠÀ$^{\text{ḫi.a}}$ as direct object (no clear alphab. analogues; in Hebrew, cf., e.g., *mah-nidbarnû ʿāle(y)kā* "what have we spoken among ourselves against you," Malachi 3:13). Thus, the clause may be rendered, "PN and PN$_2$ ... released to one another (i.e., exchanged) field for field."

(c) */napṭaru/* ?, N v.n./infin.(?) "exchange, ransom(?)."

legal: *u* PN *[a]-na re-ṣú-ti la i-la[k] ù na-ap-ṭá-:ra la ú-bal* "and PN (need) not co[me] to 'aid' and is not responsible for ransom" PRU 3 79ff.:14-16.

Alphabetic: See under (a).

Nougayrol, PRU 3 p. 223, reasonably proposed that *na-ap-ṭá-:ra* here, in contradistinction to PRU 3 89a:5 above, is "plutôt un doublet ... de *ipṭeru,* 'rançon, prix de rachat.'" Since, again, no connection with Akk. *napṭaru* is evident, perhaps here too we must see a Ugar. form, an N verbal noun/infinitive */napṭaru/* (cf. */naʾbadu/* above, under ʾBD) "exchange (of captives)."

PLD

/palīdu/, pl. */palīdūma/*, n. "(type of garment or other article of fabric)."

econ.: *3* ^{túg}*pa-[l]i?-du-ma* PRU 6 127:4

5 ^{túg}*pa-li-du-m*[*a*] PRU 6 128:3

^{túg}*pa-l*[*i-du*] PRU 6 129:5'

Alphabetic: *pld*, pl. *pldm* (UT 468a no. 2045).

Probably related to Hebrew *pəlādôt* "blankets(?)" in Nahum 2:4 (Dietrich-Loretz, BiOr 25 100-1 [not a garment]; Dahood, Biblica 51 396-97), although the ultimate etymology of the term remains obscure. See also Boyd, Collection 153-56; Sivan, Analysis 257.

PLṬ

/pullaṭu/ D v.n./infin. "to save."

lex.: (Sum.) KAR = (Akk.) *šu-zu-bu* = (Hur.) ⸢*a*⸣*-bu-uš-ku-me* = (Ugar.) *pu-la-ṭu* Ug. 5 137 ii 20' (polyglot vocab.)

S^a Voc. no. 183.4.

Alphabetic: *plṭ* (UT 468b no. 2048).

PLK[1]

/pilakku/ n. (loanword) "spindle."

lex.: (Sum.) BAL = (Akk.) *pí-la-ak-ku* = (Hur.) *te-a-ri* = (Ugar.) *pí-lak-ku* Ug. 5 137 ii 22' (polyglot vocab.)

S^a Voc. no. 184.1.

Alphabetic: *plk* (UT 468b no. 2050).

(PLK[2]

Akk. *pilku* "feudal service."

The word *pilku* occurs in some 40 Akk. texts at Ugarit, where it has generally replaced normative Akk. *ilku*; the latter occurs only in PRU 3 117 r. 10; 3 118:26; 3 135f.:22; PRU 6 77:4,9 (see Boyd, Collection 245-54). Further, *pilku* normally means "demarcation, district" in Akk. rather than "service, tax." Dietrich-Loretz's suggestion, UF 4 165-66, that Ugarit Akk. *pilku* is in fact to be read *(y)ilku* (i.e., *pîl-ku* as *yil/il$_x$-ku*, *pí-il-ku* as *(y)i$_4$-il-ku*), is not possible, since the requisite values of BÍL and BI would exist only in Ugarit Akk., and only for these forms (so also Boyd, Collection 255-56). The suggestion of von Soden, AHw 863b (*pilku* II), that Ugarit Akk. *pilku* is from (Ugar.) */pa-/* + (Akk.) *ilku* is, as Boyd notes (p. 255), likewise most unlikely. Boyd also points out (ibid.) that *pilku* in the meaning at Ugarit does in fact occur also in OB texts from Susa (cited AHw 863a, s.v. *pilku* I 6). Thus, we must agree with Boyd (p. 256) and with Speiser, JAOS 75 162, that *pilku* is not Ugaritic, but simply an Akk. term, curiously used by the Ugarit scribes instead of *ilku*. The corresponding Ugar. term, in alphab. texts and in a few Akk. texts, is */ʾunuθθu/*; see ʾNθ, above.)

?PSL

/pasīlānu/ ? n./adj.(?) "?"

econ.: *1* DUG.SAG *pa-*⸢*si*?⸣*-la-nu re-*⸢*qu*⸣ "1 empty high-quality(?) pot, *p.* style(?)" PRU 6 158:6 (list of items, mostly jars)

Alphabetic: Unattested; cf. *psl* "sculptor" (UT 469a no. 2073)?

Nougayrol read the line as follows: *1* ^{karpat}*kap(?)-pa-al(?)-la-nu re-qu*. The sign following DUG, however, is clearly SAG in the copy, and the sign between *pa* and *la* appears to be *si* (see also the photo in Ug. 4 p. 118 fig. 95). The vessel called DUG.SAG ("pot of superior quality"?) while admittedly rare, does occur in a few MB texts (BE 14 80a:3, PBS 1/2 31:4; see Waschow, MAOG 10/1 16), including a ritual text from Boğazköy (ZA 45 204 ii 34; see

Meier's brief note, ibid. 213). (For dug.sag(.gá) in Ur III texts, see A. Salonen, Hausgeräte 2 60 no. 25.) That *pa-⌜si?⌝-la-nu* is a Ugar. word seems likely, in view of alphab. *psl* "sculptor" and the fact that most, if not all, of the syllabically written items in PRU 6 158 are probably also Ugar.; whether it functions here as a noun glossing DUG.SAG, or as an adjective qualifying the latter is unclear. Presumably the term has to do with sculpture.

PǴ(N)DR

/pağan/ddarru/ n. (Hur. loanword) "(type of garment)."

econ.: *3* ^{túg}*pa-ḫa-*dar_6(TAR)*-ru* GADA "3 linen *p.*'s" PRU 3 206f.:9 (list of garments)

Alphabetic: dual/pl. *pǵ(n)drm*; see discussion.

A Hurrian word, *pağandarri* (see Laroche, GLH 192), which also appears in Akk. texts from Alalaḫ and Nuzi (AHw 810a, s.v. *paḫantar(r)u*). Borrowed into Ugar., the word appears in alphab. texts both as *pǵndr* (dual/pl. *pǵn* «.»*drm*[!] KTU 4.4:1-2; also noted by Dietrich-Loretz, UF 9 340) and, with *n* assimilated as in the syllabic transcription above, as *pǵdr* (pl. *pǵdrm* KTU 4.270:10).

PR: see PRR, below.

?PRS

p. 397

/pur(r)ŭs(s)atu/ ? n. "division(?)."

lex.: (Sum.) [ḪAL?] = (Akk.) [*zittu*??] = (Hur.) *pu-ru?-da-ni* = (Ugar.) *pu-ru-s*[*à?-*tu_4?] UF 11 479:33 (polyglot vocab.)

S^a Voc. no. 46.2.

Alphabetic: Cf. *prst* (KTU 1.22 ii 15), *prs* "(a fractional measure)" (UT 470b no. 2110)? See the S^a Voc. commentary.

?PRR

p. 397

/pirru/ ? v.n./infin. "flight(?)/separation(?)."

lex.: (Sum.) [GUL??] = (Akk.) [*nābutu/ḫepû/pašāru*?] = (Hur.) *pí-i-ri* = (Ugar.) *pí-ru* Ug. 5 137 ii 44' (polyglot vocab.)

S^a Voc. no. 191.3.

Alphabetic: Cf. *tpr* "flee" (1.19 iii 14,28), *apr* "I will annul" (KTU 1.15 iii 30); see the S^a Voc. commentary.

Ṣ

ṢBR

/ṣibbīru/ n. "collective/public land(?)"; in field designation.

legal: *u* A.ŠÀ^{meš} *: ṣí-ib-bi-ri* "and 'public(?) field(s)'"PRU 3 83f.:7

A.ŠÀ *: ṣí-ib-bi-ri* PRU 3 79ff.:6

x A.ŠÀ$^{\text{ḫi.a}}$ DUMU PN LÚ GN *ša i-na* A.ŠÀ$^{\text{ḫi.a}}$ *ṣí(-ib)-bi-ri* "x fields of PN's son, citizen of GN, which are in 'public(?) field(s)'" PRU 6 55:19',21',23',25',27',29',31'

Alphabetic: Note perhaps *gt ṣb⌜r?⌝* (KTU 4.400:2); cf. *ṣbr* "team, group" (UT 472b no. 2142).

See Nougayrol, PRU 6 p. 146b; Rainey, IOS 3 40; Heltzer, OLP 8 47-55; Sivan, Analysis 269.

ṢWᶜ

/ṣāᶜu/, pl. */ṣāᶜātu/* n. "bowl, basin"; sg. only in field designation.

legal: A.ŠÀ PN *i-na : ṣa-i* "PN's field in 'the basin'" PRU 3 47a:11

i-na A.ŠÀ *ṣa-a-i* "in 'basin field'" PRU 3 50f.:6; 3 118:5; 3 135f.:5

ša i-⌜*na*⌝ A.⌜ŠÀ⌝$^{\text{ḫi.a}}$ *ṣa-i* PRU 3 35f.:5

ša i-na A.ŠÀ^{meš} *ṣa-i* PRU 3 136b:6,12; PRU 6 34:7'; Ug. 5 159:7

i-na A.ŠÀ^{meš} *ṣa-a-i* PRU 3 138f.:6; Ug. 5 6:7

econ.: 2 $^{\text{giš.meš}}$*ṣa-ʾa-tu* É "2 (wooden) bowls for the house" PRU 6 163 r. 4'

Alphabetic: *ṣᶜ* (UT 475a no. 2178; KTU 1.101:14; 1.13311).

Alphabetic *ṣᶜ* means "bowl"; in the legal texts above, */ṣāᶜu/* undoubtedly denotes a geographical feature (note Arabic *ṣāᶜ*, both a vessel and measure, and "a narrow, depressed piece of ground; a piece of arable land" [Lane, Lexicon 1746a-b]; cf. e.g., English "basin"). Note that the term is also the name of a town, alphab. *ṣᶜ* (see Gordon, s.v.), syllabic ^{uru}*ṣa-i* (note the determinative) PRU 6 78:13.

The econ. example cited above represents the pl. of */ṣāᶜu/*, viz., */ṣāᶜātu/* "2 (wooden) bowls for the house." Use of the plural after the numeral "2" is attested in other texts, e.g., 2 *qà-da-ru-ma* ^{meš} PRU 6 158:12; see Part III, ch. 3 §C 1 d (3). For the determinative $^{\text{giš.meš}}$, cf., e.g., $^{\text{giš.meš}}$NÁ "beds" ibid.:9.

ṢYṢ

**/ṣēṣu/* or **/ṣīṣu/*, pl. */ṣēṣūma/* or */ṣīṣūma/*, n. "salt(-producing) field."

legal: [*ù*] *píl-ka ia-nu* [*i-na* (??)] *: ZI-ṣú-ma an-nu-tu*₄ "[and] there is no service [for?] these salt fields" PRU 3 125 r. 3'-4'

] *u* A.ŠÀ MUN^{meš} *: ZI-ṣú-ma* (acc.?) PRU 3 124:12

A.ŠÀ MUN *:* ⌜*ZI-ṣú-ú-ma*⌝ (acc.??) PRU 6 28 r. 2'

Alphabetic: *ṣṣ* (UT 475b no. 2187).

The gloss in the last two examples probably refers to the entire logographic complex A.ŠÀ MUN$^{(\text{ḫi.a/meš})}$, i.e., *eqel ṭābti* "salt field," and not simply to MUN = *ṭābtu* "salt(s)," as was suggested by Moran, Bibilica 39 69-71. See Dietrich-Loretz, WO 3 221 n. 61; Heltzer, AION 18 355-61. Whether the word is */ṣīṣu/* as in Hebrew *ṣîṣ* (Jeremiah 48:9; cf. Sirach 43:19) or */ṣēṣu/* < **ṣayṣu* (Moran, Biblica 39 70), is uncertain. (The form *ṣe-e-ṣi-ma* in PRU 4 108b:9, a text from Ḫattusas or Carchemish, may argue for the latter.) Also unclear is why the form invariably appears in the nominative (pl.) in the Ugarit Akk. corpus.

ṢLY

/ṣilyatu/ ? (or */ṣilyu/* ?) n. "curse."

lex.: (Sum.) [EN] = (Akk.) [*a-r*]*a-ru* = (Hur.) *ši-da-ar-ni* = (Ugar.) *: ṣi-il-yv*[ ] Ug. 5 130 iii 16' (polyglot vocab.)

Cf. (Sum.) [ÁŠ] = (Akk.) [*a*]*r-ra-tu* = (Hur.) *ši-da-ar-ni* = (Ugar.) *ṣ*[*i-il-yv* (?)] Ug. 5 137 ii 46' (polyglot vocab.)

S^{a} Voc. nos. 37.4, 192.2.

Alphabetic: Unattested; cf. perhaps v. *yṣly* "he curses(?)" (KTU 1.19 i 39), n. *ṣlyh* (1.27:6); see the S^{a} Voc commentary on no. 37.4. On the form, see Part III, ch. 2 §E 2 b.

ṢLL

/maṣillu/ n. "cymbalist."

econ.: lú*ma-ṣi-lu* PRU 6 93:25 (list of professions)

Alphabetic: pl. *mṣlm* KTU 4.126:30 (see UT 474a no. 2164); note that KTU 4.126 is a list of professions closely parallel to PRU 6 93.

A *maqtil* (> *maqill*) form of the geminate root *ṣ-l-l* (also reduplicated *ṣ-l-ṣ-l*) "to ring, tinkle."

ṢMT

p. 397

/ṣamata/ and */ṣamatū/* v., G suffix-conj., 3ms and 3mp; also Akk. forms *ṣamat, ṣamit,* D *ṣummuta*; "to transfer."

the following all occur in legal texts:

(a) *u* É-*tu*4 PN *a-na* 1MÍ.⌜LUGAL⌝-*ti* : *ṣa-ma-ta* "and PN's estate is transferred to the queen" PRU 3 51f.:15-16;

annûtu ana pānī šarri ŠÀM.TIL.LA.BI.ŠÈ : *ṣa-ma-tu* "these are transferred for full value in the presence of the king" PRU 3 90b:12-13

(b) *x* IKU *ṣa-ma-at a-na* lú*sà-ki-in-ni* "x *iku* is transferred to the prefect" PRU 3 35f.:9; *ṣa-ma-at* also in PRU 3 86ff. r. 9'; 3 113ff.:7; 3 124:17; PRU 6 66:4'; Ug. 5 6:11; 5 85:6

(c) A.ŠÀmeš PN *ṣa-mi-it a-na* PN2 ... *a-na da-ri-ti* "PN's fields are transferred to PN2 ... in perpetuity" PRU 3 95f.:18-19, cf. 20-23; *ṣa-mi-it* also in PRU 3 35a:8; 3 99b:9; 3 121f.:10; 3 126:14; 3 127f.:10,25; 3 129a:16; 3 130a:8,10; 3 138f.:9,22,26; 3 141f.:10; 3 143a:8; 3 145f.:10; 3 154f.:8; 3 159f.:17; 3 161b:12; 3 163f. r. 2'; 3 173c:4'; PRU 6 27:20,«16»; Ug. 5 5:14,23; 5 159: 11; 5 161:12(?)

(d) *i-na* ŠÀM.TIL.LA<.BI>.ŠÈ : *ṣú-um-mu-ta* "transferred for full value" PRU 3 63b:12

Alphabetic: See discussion.

That at least the examples under (a) and (d) represent Ugar. words is assured by the gloss mark that precedes them. The gloss mark in these examples indicates only that a non-Akk. word follows; this is obvious in PRU 3 51f.:15-16 (under a), of course, but it is also true in PRU 3 90b:12-13 (a) and PRU 3 63b:12 (d). In the latter two instances, the forms do not gloss ŠÀM. TIL.LA.BI.ŠÈ (pace Kühne, UF 6 158 n. 9) which, as always in texts written at Ugarit, has its expected meaning, viz., *ina/ana šīmi gamri* "for (the) full value"; with PRU 3 90b:12-13 (a), e.g., compare the following clause in the same text, lines 4-8: [PN] ...⌜*il-te-qè*⌝ A.ŠÀmeš PN2 ... *i-na 2 me-at* KÙ.BABBAR ŠÀM.TIL.LA.BI.ŠÈ "PN ... received PN2's ... field(s) for 200 silver, for full value." It is only the logographic compound ŠÀM/ŠÁM.TIL.LA that has the value *ṣami/at*, a value unique to texts written at Ugarit: ŠÀM.TIL.LA, with ŠÀM, always = *ṣami/at* (PRU 3 89a:7,9,14; PRU 3 109b:9; Ug. 5 9:9); ŠÁM.TIL.LA, with ŠÁM written ninda x še + an, also = *ṣami/at* in PRU 3 71f.:19 (but *i-na* ŠÁM.TIL.LA, with ŠÁM written ninda x še + a + an, PRU 3 169a:15, represents *ina šīmi gamri*; so also ŠÁM-šu TIL.LA = [acc.] *šīmšu gamra* in PRU 3 102ff.:17).

The root of these forms is not clear from the syllabic writings. Nougayrol consistently transliterated them as *ṣ-m-d*, and noted in PRU 6 p. 154 n. 2, "il ne me paraît pas indispensible d'admettre un verbe *ṣamâtu* particulier à Ugarit." The Akk. verb *ṣamādu*, however, is not used elsewhere of transactions involving property. More likely, these forms are to be compared with Hebrew *ṣəmītūt*, roughly "permanent transfer," as first suggested by Rabinowitz, VT 8 95, and elaborated by Loretz, BZ 6 269-79. Whether the forms, and Hebrew *ṣəmītūt*, are to be associated with the root *ṣ-m-t* "to destroy" in Hebrew and Ugar. (UT 475a no. 2176; also Syriac *ṣmat*, Arabic *ṣamata* "to be silent") remains unclear, although a strong case for a connection is made by Loretz, pp. 273-75, and by Boyd, Collection 204-5. Note also alphab. *ṣmt* perhaps in the sense "grasp, hold on" in KTU 1.12 ii 34; see Caquot-Sznycer-Herdner, Textes ougaritiques 346 n. h.

Four distinct forms appear in the examples listed above:

(a) The Ugar. suffix-conjugation, 3ms */ṣamata/* and 3mp */ṣamatū/*; these apparently display the actual theme-vowel of the Ugar. form, *-a-* (*qatala*), rather surprising in view of the intransitive, indeed passive, meaning of the form ("is transferred"), as noted by Sivan, Analysis 137.

(b) The forms written *ṣa-ma-at* reflect the Ugar. theme-vowel, but are partially adapted to the Akk. predicative form, which lacks the final */-a/* (see Part III, ch. 3 §G 3).

(c) The forms *ṣa-mi-it*, which comprise the largest group of examples, display a completely Akkadianized morphology, the predicative *paris* (see ibid.)

(d) The form *: ṣú-um-mu-ta* is most peculiar. In view of the D infinitive pattern *quttalu* found in the polyglot vocabulary texts (*pu-la-ṭu*, Ug. 5 137 ii 22'; see above, under PLṬ), which probably reflects the Proto-NWS passive D verbal noun (cf. Hebrew *puᶜᶜal*), it is unlikely that the vocalism of *: ṣú-um-mu-ta* reflects Ugar. morphology. Rather, the form must apparently be taken as an Akk. D verbal adjective (i.e., "stative") base *purrus*, with the Ugar. 3ms suffix-conjugation ending */-a/*. Why a D stem appears uniquely in PRU 3 63b:12 is not clear. (The form *mṣmt* in KTU 4.126:1, listed as a [D] participle of *ṣ-m-t* in Gordon, UT 475a no. 2176, should instead probably be connected with the root *ṣ-m-d*, i.e., a *maqtvl-t* noun, **/maṣmvtt/* < **maṣmvd-t*; see Dietrich-Loretz-Sanmartín, UF 5 100 and n. 22, who translate "treaty," citing Weippert. Since the text is a label, *mṣmt* could also conceivably mean something like "tag, label," likewise from *ṣ-m-d* "to join, tie.")

Ṣᶜ: see ṢWᶜ, above.

ṢṢ: see ṢYṢ, above.

Q

QBR

/qubūru/ n. "burial, grave."

legal: É-*tu*4 *: qú-bu-ri* "burial ground" PRU 3 51f.:8,18

Alphabetic: *qbr* (KTU 1.19 iii 44).

For the transliteration and translation, which is preferable to Nougayrol's É-*tu*4 *: gu*5*-bu-ri* "maison-forte(?)," see Gordon, Syria 33 102. The form *qubūru* "grave" is also found in Akk.; the gloss mark, however, indicates that the form here is non-Akk. For an extensive discussion of Akk. and NWS *qubūru* as "funeral, burial" (and **baytu qubūri* as "burial place," cf. Syriac *bet qburā*), as opposed to **qabru* "grave," see Boyd, Collection 160-63.

QDR

**/qad(da)r(at)u/*, pl. */qad(d)arūma/*, n. "(a container)."

econ.: *2 qà-da-ru-ma*^{meš} PRU 6 158:12 (list of items, mostly jars)

Alphabetic: Unattested.

As cognates, Boyd, Collection 158-59, cites, inter alia, Arab. *qadara* "small bottle, flask,"

Syr. *qdur(t)ā* "small pot, vase," MHeb. *qādēr, qədērâ* "pot." Because of the variation these exhibit, the pattern of the Ugar. form above is uncertain: it may be a *qatal-* base pl. of a *qatl* sg., /*qadru*/; the Arab. cognate suggests that the sg. may be /*qadar(at)u*/; finally, the several Heb. words for vessels with the pattern *qattalat* < **qattalt* (see Cathcart, RSO 47 55-58), though not including the root under consideration, suggest /*qaddar(at)u*/.

QDŠ

(a) v., G suffix-conj. (Ugar. /*qadiš(a)*/ or Akk. form *qadiš*), "to be sacred."

legal: É : *ku-na-ḫi* ... *ù qa-dì-iš a-n*[*a* DN(?)] "the *k.*-house ...; and it is (to be?) sacred t[o Ištar?]" Ug. 5 5 20-22

Alphabetic: Cf. adj. *qdš* "sacred" (e.g., KTU 1.3 i 13; see UT 477a no. 2210).

A translation of Ug. 5 5 appears above, under MDD.

Since the G of Akk. *qadāšu* occurs otherwise only in one lexical text (see CAD Q 46a), it is likely that *qa-dì-iš* reflects Ugar. suffix-conjugation /*qadiša*/ (*qatila* pattern; cf. Hebrew pausal *qādēšu* Numbers 17:2). (The verb probably also occurs in an Amarna letter from Byblos: *i-nu-ma* DINGIR^{meš} ^{uru}*gub-la qa-di-šu* "that the gods of Byblos are holy" EA 137:31-32.) The form exhibits Akk. morphology (*paris*), however, without the 3ms marker /*-a*/ (see Part III, ch. 3 §G 3).

(b) /*qidšu*/ n. "sanctuary, shrine."

lex.: (Sum.) [TIR?] = (Akk.) [*atmānu*?] = (Hur.) [ ] = (Ugar.) [^{é}?]⌜*qi*?-*id*?-*šu*?⌝ Ug. 5 137 iii 29" (polyglot vocab.)

S^{a} Voc. no. 208.

(Sum.) ^{d}ŠARA/BARAG = (Hur.) *ḫa-ma-ar-re* = (Ugar.) *qi-i*[*d-šu* (?)] Ug. 5 137 iv a 14 (polyglot god-list)

Alphabetic: *qdš* "shrine" (UT 477a no. 2210).

In the second example, the sign for the god Šara, who normally appears at this point in the god-list An (also in other Ugarit Akk. texts—see Ug. 5 texts 121-123, no. 26 [pp. 212-13]), was apparently understood by the scribe as BARAG = *parakku* "throne dais, sanctuary," in view of the Hurrian column, where *ḫa-ma-ar-re* must surely denote the definite form, *ḫamarre*, of the Hurrian noun *ḫamri* "sanctuary" (pace Laroche, GLH 91, who lists this reference separately from *ḫamri*/*ḫamarre*, p. 91-92). (For the loanword *ḫamru* in Akk. texts, see CAD Ḫ 70, AHw 318a, 1558-59.) Thus, Nougayrol was undoubtedly correct in restoring *qi-i*[*d-šu*] in the Ugar. column.

In view of these two syllabic examples, alphab. *qdš*, when it means "shrine" (e.g., KTU 1.14 iv 34), should be vocalized /*qidšu*/; cf. the GN *Qidšu* in EA 151:6, 189:11, and the Heb. GN *Qedeš*.

(c) note also

legal: RN ... *ú-za-ak-ki* PN ... ⌜*ù*⌝ *il-ták-na-aš-šu* ⌜*i*⌝*-na* $^{lú.meš}$*mar-ia-an-ni i-na qa-ad-šu-ut-ti iš-ši-šu*!(*ma*) "RN ... freed PN ... and installed him among the *maryannu*'s; he elevated him(!) from the status of a *qdš*" PRU 3 140f.:2-8

For the reading and meaning of *qa-ad-šu-ut-ti*, see von Soden, UF 2 329-30. Since a masc. form *qad(i)šu* is unattested in Akk. otherwise (see CAD Q 50; rather, *qašdu*, and abstract *qašdūtu*, with metathesis [ibid. 146-47], although the fem. remains *qadištu* [ibid. 48-50]), the base of this word must be Ugar. */*qad(i)šu*/ (a type of priest). Whether the word reflects a Ugar. abstract /*qadšūtu*/ (with incorrectly doubled *-tt-*, and with vowel syncope), or an Akkadianized (Assyrian) form *qadšuttu*, must remain uncertain.

☛ p. 398

?QṬN

/qaṭinnu/ ?, pl. */qaṭinnūma/* ?, n. (Hur. loanword?) "(an implement)."

econ.: *2 qà?-ṭi-nu-[ma?*^{me}]$^{š?}$ PRU 6 157:11 (list of implements)

Alphabetic: *qṭn* (UT 477b no. 2219); see discussion.

Nougayrol read line 11 as follows: *2 ka(?)-di-nu [2]0(?) ḫa-ṣi-nu*. Note, however, that the total given in line 16 for the number of items in lines 11-15 is *10*. There are ten items in lines 11-15 only if only one "axe" (*ḫaṣṣinu*) is listed. Thus, it is more likely that the ends of the Winckelhakens visible before the *ḫa* of *ḫa-ṣi-nu* are the end of a MEŠ sign; admittedly this MEŠ, composed of [diš+e]š, would differ from MEŠ elsewhere in this text, viz., me+ḫal in lines 4,5,13, but variant forms of MEŠ appear in other individual Ugarit Akk. texts (e.g., PRU 3 135f.: diš+eš in lines 6,7,14,21, but me+ḫal in lines 10,18). There is room between MEŠ and the *nu* of *qà?-ṭi-nu* for *ma*, and so we propose that the entire line reads *2 qà?-ṭi-nu-[ma?*^{me}]^{š} *ḫa-ṣi-nu* "2 *q.*'s; (1) axe"; for the complex {2 + pl. + ^{meš}}, compare *2 qà-da-ru-ma*^{meš}, under QDR, above.

Dietrich-Loretz, BiOr 23 132a, compare alphab. *qṭn* (in *ḥrš qṭn* "makers of *q.*" KTU 4.98:9, 4.609:23) with the word *KA/GA-ti(n)-ni* attested in texts from Nuzi, Alalaḫ, and Amarna (Mittanni) (AHw 466a, CAD K 307a), to which we may now add the example above from a Ugarit Akk. text. The word may be Hurrian (*kadinni*?) in origin. (It is likely that Hebrew *(kəlê) hqṭn* in Isaiah 22:24 is to be compared with the Ugar. */qaṭinnu/*; see Loewenstamm, Comparative Studies 223-29, who also cites N. H. Tur-Sinai in this regard.)

*Q(Y)L: see QᶜL, below.

QLL

/qallu/ adj. "small; inferior (quality)."

legal: RN ... *it-ta-ši*! ... A.ŠÀ^{meš} *qá-al-lu* (acc.!) *ša* PN "RN ... took ... the small field(s) of PN" PRU 3 112a:2-5

econ.: *12* TÚG *qal-lu* "12 small garment(s)" PRU 3 206f.:1 (list of garments)

Alphabetic: For alphab. *ql* "schlecht, minderwertig" in KTU 3.1:5, see Dietrich-Loretz-Sanmartín, UF 7 166 no. 64.

It is possible that either or both of these examples may reflect Akk. *qallu* (same meanings), rather than a Ugar. word. In the field designation *qá-al-lu* in PRU 3 112a:5, another possibility is the rare Akk. word *qallu* "forest" (equated with *qištu*), of unknown origin, attested in a lexical text and in the literary EA 359 r. 5,18 (King of Battle); see AHw 894b (*qallu* II), CAD Q 66 (*qallu* B).

QLQL

/qulqullu/ ? n. (Akk. loanword?) "cassia"; in field designation.

legal: *i-na* A.ŠÀ^{meš} *KU-ul-KU-li* "in 'cassia field(s)'" PRU 3 138f.:18,25

Alphabetic: *qlql*; see discussion.

For alphab. *qlql* (KTU 1.71:8) as "cassia (pulp)," related to Akk. *qulqullânu* (CAD Q 301), see Aistleitner, Wörterbuch 277 no. 2415; Cohen-Sivan, Ugaritic Hippiatric Texts 24-25. It seems more likely that the form *qú-ul-qú-li* above represents the Ugar. equivalent of Akk. *qulqullânu* (viz., *qlql*) than that it represents Akk. *qulqullu*, which has to do with textiles (CAD Q 301-2). For other designations of fields by their predominant vegetation, see under ᵓLN, YRQ.

An alternative possibility that should be mentioned is a connection with the root *g-l-l*, or *g-l-g-l*; cf., e.g., the Hebrew GN *gilgāl*.

?QNB: see KNP b, above.

?QNN

/qunnanu/ ? adj.(?) (Akk. loanword?) "coiled(?)."

lex.: (Sum.) LUM = (Akk.) *qa-an-nu-nu* = (Hur.) *ḫí-iš-la-e* = (Ugar.) *qu-u*[*n*?]-*n*[*a*?-*nu*?] Ug. 5 130 ii 2' (polyglot vocab.)

S^a Voc. no. 20.2.

Alphabetic: Unattested.

?QNP: see KNP b, above.

?Q^{c}L

/qi^{c}īlu/ ? (less likely, */qi^{c}lu/* ?) n. "(type of plant, flower, tree)" ("vine-blossom?"). p. 398

lex.: (Sum.) [ŠAḪ??] = (Akk.) [ ]-*ru* = (Hur.) *šu-ra-at-ḫi* = (Ugar.) *qi-i-lu* Ug. 5 137 ii 27' (polyglot vocab.)

S^a Voc. no. 186.2.

Alphabetic: *q^{c}l* (KTU 1.22 i 16 bis); see the S^a Voc. commentary.

QRB: see KRB, above.

QRY

/qarītu/ n. "town."

lex.: (Sum.) [URU] = (Akk.) [*ālu*] = (Hur.) *ar-de-na* = (Ugar.) *qa-ri-t*[u_4] Ug. 5 130 iii 18' (polyglot vocab.)

S^a Voc. no. 39.

Alphabetic: *qrt*.

?QRLN: see *KI-ra-li-nu* in the Appendix to the Glossary, below.

QRṢ

/qarṣu/ ? n. "piece; calumny(?)."

lex.: (Sum.) [KÍD??] = (Akk.) [*karṣu*??] = (Hur.) [ ] = (Ugar.) [*q*]*à*?-*ar-ṣu* Ug. 5 137 iii 31" (polyglot vocab.)

S^a Voc. no. 210.

Alphabetic: Cf. v. *qrṣ* "to pinch, gnaw"; see the S^a Voc. commentary.

QRT: see QRY, above.

QŠ

/qaštu/ n. "bow."

lex.: (Sum.) [BAN] = (Akk.) [*qaštu*?] = (Hur.) [ ] = (Ugar.) ⌜*qa*⌝-*aš*-tu_4 UF 11 479:9 (polyglot vocab.)

S^a Voc. no. 30a.y.

Alphabetic: *qšt* (UT 481 no. 2287).

QŠT: see QŠ, above.

R

?R'B, ?R'P, ?RHB, ?RHP: see *ra-⸢PA⸣-ni* in the Appendix to the Glossary, below.

RBB

(a) */rabbu/* ?, fem. */rabbatu/*, adj. "large, great."

legal: $^{\text{na}_4}$KUNUK LUGAL-*ri* GAL-*bu* "the great royal seal" PRU 3 49b:25

]*ra-bu* PRU 3 56f.:7

i-na A.ŠÀ *ra-ba-ti* (see discussion) Ug. 5 7:4

Alphabetic: *rb(t)* "great" (UT 482a no. 2297); for the last example, cf. especially *gt rb⸢t⸣* (KTU 4.125:16).

In the first example, the lack of a final *-ú* for Akk. *rabû* may indicate that the scribe intended, no doubt inadvertently, Ugar. */rabbu/*. The phrase A.ŠÀ *ra-ba-ti* in Ug. 5 7:4 and *gt rbt* in KTU 4.125:16 may mean either "the field of the Lady," perhaps a reference to the goddess ʾAθ(i)ratu (Boyd, Collection 164-65), or "the great field" (*gt* is fem.). Note also lit. DINGIR^{meš} *ra-ab-bu-ti* Ug. 5 167:9, in which the doubly-written *-bb-* may reflect the Ugar. base */rabb-/*; the m. pl. ending, however, is Akk.; further, another incorrectly doubled consonant appears in line 1 of the same text, in *im-lik-ku* for *imlikū*.

(b) ?: see *ra-⸢PA⸣-ni* in the Appendix to the Glossary, below.

?RBN: see *ra-⸢PA⸣-ni* in the Appendix to the Glossary, below.

RBṢ

/tarbaṣu/ n. (Akk. loanword?) "stable, sheepfold."

legal: É-tu_4 : *ta-ar-bá-ṣí u* É-tu_4 GUD^{meš} *a-na ša-šu-ma* "the stable and the cattle-pen are likewise his" PRU 3 91f.:17

Alphabetic: *trbṣ* (UT 482b no. 2304).

Since the gloss mark serves no other obvious function here, it must mark the following word as non-Akk., i.e., as Ugar. (see Kühne, UF 6 159 n. 14 end; below, Part III, ch. 1 §C 4). Whether Ugar. */tarbaṣu/* is native to the language, or a loan from Akk., cannot be determined, as noted by Boyd, Collection 165-66. (Note, e.g., that Aramaic *tarbāṣā* is probably an Akk. loan; see Kaufman, Akkadian Influences 107 and n. 381.)

☛ p. 398

?RGZ

/ragāzu/ ? G v.n./infin. "to be enraged(?)."

lex.: (Sum.) [IDIM] = (Akk.) [*šegû*??] = (Hur.) [ ] = (Ugar.) [*r*]*a*-[*g*]*a*?-[*zu*?] Ug. 5 137 iii 12' (polyglot vocab.)

S^a Voc. no. 198.5.

Alphabetic: Unattested.

RGL

/riglu/ n. "foot."

lex.: (Sum.) [ÚR] = (Akk.) [*pēnu*] = (Hur.) [*ip*...] = (Ugar.) *ri-i*[*g*]*-lu* Ug. 5 137 i 10' (polyglot vocab.)

S^a Voc. no. 158.3.

Alphabetic: Unattested.

?RGM

p. 398

/ragāmu/ ? G v.n./infin. "to speak."

lex.: (Sum.) [MU] = (Akk.) [*z*]*a-ka*$_4$*-ru* = (Hur.) [ ] = (Ugar.) *ra-g*[*a?-mu?*] Ug. 5 130 iii 3' (polyglot vocab.)

S^a Voc. no. 32.3.

Alphabetic: *rgm* (UT 482-83 no. 2307).

See also *ri/tal-GI-*⌜*mu?*⌝ in the Appendix to the Glossary, below.

?RDY

/mardētu/ ? n. "(type of garment or fabric?)."

econ.: [*x* ^{túg}*m*]*ar-de*$_4$*-tu* GADA "[x] linen *m.*'s" PRU 3 206f.:5 (list of garments)

Alphabetic: Cf. *mrdt* in KTU 2.72:25 (*mrdtt*) and 4.205:4,6? See discussion.

Although a connection with the Akk. word *mardatu*, which denotes a fabric of Western origin (CAD M/1 277-78), seems inescapable, the spelling here indicates a pronunciation */mardētu/*, which in turn suggests a *maqtal-t* form of a root III-*y*, viz., unattested *r-d-y*; cf. perhaps Arabic *r-d-y* Gt and tD "to put on a garment," *ridā*ʾ "cloak, robe." (On alphab. *mrdt* and Akk. *mardatu* "rug," see Dietrich-Loretz, OLZ 62 543; WO 3 192; Mayer, UF 9 173-89.)

See also *ma-ar-*⌜*tu?*⌝ in the Appendix to the Glossary, below.

?RDM

/mardimtu/ ? n. "path(??)."

lex.: GUD.DA.KALAM.MA = *mar-de*$_4$*-em-tu* Syria 12 231ff.:6 (Ḫḫ II forerunner)

Alphabetic: Unattested.

The canonical text here has KI.UŠ.KALAM.MA = *nàr-da-mu* MSL 5 p. 71:278 (Ḫḫ II). (In the Ugarit text, the Sumerian column repeats that of the preceding line, viz., GUD.DA. KALAM.MA = *<pa->da-nu*.) The rare Akk. noun *nardamu* (also *nardamtu*) occurs only in lexical texts, and, from its proximity there to *padānu* and *ṭūdu*, apparently means "path" or the like. The form *mar-de*$_4$*-em-tu* here appears to be a *maqtil-t* noun from the same root as *nardam(t)u*, and, since it does not exhibit initial *m* > *n*, is presumably Ugaritic. Whether it too means "path" cannot be determined. A root *r-d-m* is thus far unattested otherwise in Ugar. In Hebrew, the N *nirdam* means "to fall sound asleep" (cf. Eblaite MA.MU "dream" = *ra/la-da-mu(-mu)* MEE 4 292 no. 820; see Krebernik, ZA 73 32), while Arabic *radama* denotes "to fill up, mend; to be worn out"; Akk. *radāmu* is rare and of uncertain meaning (AHw 941a).

RðY

Akkadianized *arraððu* v., N, durative, "to grow thin, weak."

lit.: [*i-na mu*]*-ur-ṣa-am-ra-ṣu a-na-ku ar-ra-*⌜*zu*⌝ Ug. 5 162:22'

Alphabetic: Unattested.

Von Soden, UF 1 191, translates "[Bei der] Krankheit, an der ich erkrankt war, schwand ich dahin," and notes that since there is no Akk. verb *razû*, here "liegt ein Kanaanismus vor" (comparing Hebrew *mišman bəśārô yērāze* "the 'fat' of his flesh grows lean" Isaiah 17:4; cf. also Arabic *raðiya* "grow thin and weak"). Ugar. */ð/* has not shifted to */d/* in this root, perhaps because of the presence of */r/* (see Gordon, UT 26-27 §5.3); as in *i-zi-ir-*[*tu*$_4$] (under ᶜðR, above), */ð/* is written with a Z sign; see Part III, ch. 1 §E 2. As with other Ugar. verbs in Akk. literary texts, the morphology of this form is Akk.; see Part III, ch. 3 §G 3.

p. 398

RZḤ/^{c}

*****/*marzaḥu*/ (genitive phonetically [marza^{c}i], [marziḥi], [marzi^{c}i]) n. "symposium."

legal: (É) LÚ^{meš} *mar-za-i(-ma)* "(house of) the men of the symposium" PRU 3 88b:4,6

LÚ^{meš} *mar-zi-i ša ša-at-ra-na* "men of the symposium of Šatrana" PRU 3 130a: 4,7,10,15

] LÚ^{meš} *ma-ar-zi-ḫi* Syria 28 173f.:3

(cf. also [L]Ú$^{\text{me[š]}}$ *ma-*[Ug. 5 87:9'??)

Alphabetic: *mrzḥ*, [*m*]*rz^{c}y* (KTU 1.21 ii 1,5; 1.114:15; 3.9:1,13; 4.642:2,4-7; cf. UT 483 nos. 2312,2313); see discussion.

Note, in addition, LÚ^{meš} *mar-zi-i* in PRU 4 230a:7,10, a text from Siyannu.

Nougayrol consistenly took LÚ^{meš} to be a determinative, and *mar-za-i*, etc., thus as a pl. noun referring to people. But since the word is certainly Ugar. rather than Akk., and does not have the pl. marker /*-ūma, -īma*/, we must take LÚ^{meš} as a logogram, thus *amīlê m.* "men of the *m.*"; cf. alphab. *mt mrzḥ* KTU 3.9:13 (also, Palmyrene *bny mrzḥ*, noted by Boyd, Collection 175). (In PRU 3 88b:6, *a-na* LÚ^{meš} *mar-za-i-ma* means "to those very men of the *m.*"; the *-ma* serves as an emphasizing particle [cf. PRU 3 91a r. 8'-11'], pace Sivan, Analysis 245.) On the *m.* institution at Ugarit, see, inter alia, Eissfeldt, Ug. 6 pp. 187-95; Miller, AnOr 48 37-48; Greenfield, AcAntHung 22 451-55.

The consistent indication of the Ugar. guttural consonants in the syllabic transcriptions indicates that only the spelling *ma-ar-zi-ḫi* represents the phonetic realization [marziḥi] expected on the basis of alphab. *mrzḥ*. The writings *mar-za-i* and *mar-zi-i*, on the other hand, reflect [marza/i^{c}i], with the intervocalic voicing of /*ḥ*/ to [^{c}] that is also evident in the alphab. spelling [*m*]*rz^{c}y* (see Eissfeldt, Ug. 6 p. 195; L'Heureux, Rank among the Canaanite Gods 142; Garr, JNES 45 49; and below, Part III, ch. 2 §A 2 a).

The alternation of the second vowel in these forms is difficult if we assume the underlying form to have been *maqtil* as in Hebrew *marzēaḥ* (Jer. 16:5), since there is no other evidence for the operation of a sound rule in Ugar. which lowers /*i*/ to [a] before a guttural, by which we might account for [marza^{c}i] from a base form */*marziḥi*/ (as perhaps in the Heb. construct *mirzaḥ* in Amos 6:7, which may reflect either *maqtal* or *maqtil* [i.e., *mirzaḥ* < **marzaḥ* < **marziḥ*, with unstressed **i* > *a* before the guttural]). Thus, despite Heb. *marzēaḥ*, the Ugar. form was probably *maqtal*, i.e., /*marzaḥu*/; the writings *ma-ar-zi-ḫi* and *mar-zi-i* probably represent phonetic [marziḥ/^{c}i], and show the effect of vowel harmony around the guttural (see Part III, ch. 2 §A 1 c).

RḤB

/*raḥbānu*/ n. "wide place"; in river/canal designation.

legal: *i-*[*n*]*a* A.ŠÀ ^{íd}*ra-aḫ-ba-ni* "in 'wide(-river) field'" PRU 3 66b:5

i-na A.ŠÀ *: ra-aḫ-ba!-na* PRU 3 91f.:6

A.ŠÀ$^{\text{ḫi.a}}$ ^{íd}*ra-aḫ-ba-ni* PRU 3 126:5, but A.ŠÀ$^{\text{ḫi.a}}$ *ra-aḫ-ba-na* ibid.:12

[*qa-du* (?)] A.ŠÀ^{meš} ^{íd}*:ra-aḫ-ba-n*[*a*] PRU 6 56 r. 2'

$^{\text{[í]d}}$*ra-aḫ-bá-ni*/*na* PRU 3 72f.:8,11

also: PRU 3 59f.:7,9; 3 73f.:7; 3 83f.:8; 3 138f.:16,21; 3 140f.:9; 3 143ff.:8; 3 173b:2'; PRU 6 27:6; Syria 18 249f.:12

Alphabetic: Note *rḥbn* (KTU 4.143:1); cf. *rḥb* "wide(?)" (1.16 i 9, ii 47; see Caquot-Sznycer-Herdner, Textes ougaritiques 550-51 n. h).

Note that the word occurs in the genitive with both triptotic */-i/* and diptotic */-a/*. For cognates, cf. Heb. *rāḥāl/ăb* "(to be) wide" (and the GN *rəḥōbôt*); Arab. *raḥi/uba,* Eth. *reḥba* "to be wide." (For *: ra-⌜PA⌝-ni* in PRU 3 140:26, see the Appendix to the Glossary, below.)

?RḪŠ

/marḫiš(u)/ n. "(a household utensil)."

econ.: *1 mar-ḫi-iš iš-ia-ti-mi 1* ME Ug. 5 84:10.

Alphabetic: Unattested.

For an interpretation of this phrase, see the discussion under ᶜŠY, above.

?RKB

/markabtu/ ? n. "chariot."

legal: *a-nu-ma* É PN *: a-QA?-[ ] a-na mar-kab-te[ ]da[ ]* ḪA.LA^{meš} PN_2 (translation given in discussion) PRU 3 96ff.:27-29

Alphabetic: *mrkbt* (UT 484b no. 2331)? See discussion.

Although it is generally accepted that *mar-kab-te* is a syllabic writing of alphab. *mrkbt* "chariot" (e.g., Nougayrol, PRU 3 p. 98 n. 1; AHw 612a; Boyd, Collection 172; CAD M/1 282b; Sivan, Analysis 244), it should be noted that "chariot" makes little, if any, sense in the context, which is as follows:

> PN and PN_2 made a copy of the great royal seal; they were caught, the king did not kill them; but, they are "false," their sons [are "false"?], they may not enter the palace, they may not enter the A.ŠÀ of the city; now then the estate of Kizana *: a-qa[ ] / a-na mar kab te[ ]da[ ]* / the shares of Ṭābīyānu and [ ] from Kalb[īyu and?] from his sons[ ]; if in future Ṭābīyānu and his sons [raise?] any? case? against Kalbīyu and his sons, they will cut off their to[ngues?]; [ ]they will put them to death.

What is expected here, rather, is a PN. Further, the spelling *mar-kab-te* would represent one of the few exceptions to the writing of the allophone [i] of Ugar. */i/* with an *e* -sign (TE), unless dual */markabtē/* is intended. Yet *mar-kab-te[* does not appear to be analyzable as a PN; nor should *mar* be taken to represent Akk. *mār* "son" (e.g., *mar kab-te-[ya]* "son of K.," or similar; PN's normally lack the personal determinative ^{1} after "son of"), since a syllabic writing of *māru* would be unprecedented in this corpus. Thus, "chariot," though difficult, remains the most likely interpretation.

?RKM: see *ri/tal-GI-⌜mu ?⌝* in the Appendix to the Glossary, below.

?RᶜB, ?RᶜP: see *ra-⌜PA⌝-ni* in the Appendix to the Glossary, below. p. 398

?RPᵓ

/rapᵓu/ ? n. (adj.?) "purification(?)" ("holy"??).

lex.: (Sum.) [SIKIL?] = (Akk.) *[tēliltu?/ebbu??]* = (Hur.) *⌜x-x-x-ni⌝-ḫi* = (Ugar.) *: rap-⌜ú?⌝[* Ug. 5 130 iii 20' (polyglot vocab.)

Sᵃ Voc. no. 40.2.

Alphabetic: Cf. *rpu/im* "shades," epithet *mt rpi* (UT 485 no. 2346); see the Sᵃ Voc. commentary.

?RPN, ?RPP: see *ra-⌜PA⌝-ni* in the Appendix to the Glossary, below.

?RQM: see *ri/tal-GI-⌜mu ?⌝* in the Appendix to the Glossary, below.

Š

Š'L

/*maš'alu*/ ? n. "oracle(?)"; in field designation.

legal:]*x* (-)*a-di* (?) A.ŠÀ^{meš} *ma-aš-a-li* "... 'oracle(?) field'" PRU 3 54ff.:24-25

☛ p. 398

Alphabetic: Unattested.

The reading adopted here is that suggested in AHw 623b and by Boyd, Collection 211-12; the latter compares the Hebrew GN *miš'āl* (Joshua 19:26, 21:30). An alternative possibility is /*maš*ᶜ*ālu*/, which may be compared with Hebrew *miš*ᶜ*ôl* ("bordered/narrow path?" Num. 22:24); but since the pattern *maqtāl* is very rare in Semitic, the latter probably derives from P(NW)S **miš*ᶜ*ālu*.

Š'R

/*ši'ru*/ n. "flesh."

lex.: (Sum.) [Z]U = (Akk.) *ši-i-ru* = (Hur.) *ú-zi* = (Ugar.) ⌜*ši-i-ru*⌝ Ug. 5 130 ii 3' (polyglot vocab.)

S^{a} Voc. no. 21.

Alphabetic: *šir* (KTU 1.96:3; 1.103:1; see UT 487a no. 2372).

See also below, under ŠYR and ŠᶜR.

ŠDW

/*šadû*/ n. "field."

lex.: (Sum.) [MAL/GÁN] = (Akk.) [*e*]*q*?-[*lu*?] = (Hur.) *a-wa-ar-re* = (Ugar.) : *ša-d*[*u-ú*?] Ug. 5 130 iii 11' (polyglot vocab.)

(Sum.) [MAḪ] = (Akk.) [*ṣēru*] = (Hur.) [*a-wa-a*]*r-re* = (Ugar.) : *ša-du-u* Ug. 5 137 ii 35' (polyglot vocab.)

S^{a} Voc. nos. 35/36.3, 189.2.

(note also perhaps Ugar. lex.: *ša-TI-i* Ug. 5 153 r.6')

Alphabetic: *šd* (UT 488a no. 2385).

(The reading and interpretation of the example in Ug. 5 153, gen. /*šadî*/?, are extremely uncertain.)

?ŠHR

/*šiharu*/ ? n. "crescent-shaped sickle(?)."

econ.: *1 ši-a-ru*?[PRU 6 168:6 (list of metal objects, mostly Ugar.)

Alphabetic: Unattested.

Boyd, Collection 213-14, notes that most of the items in this list are agricultural implements; he compares Hebrew *śahărōnîm* and Syriac *sahrāne* "crescent-shaped ornaments" (cf. Syriac *sahrā*, Arabic *šahr*, Ethiopic *šāhr*, Eblaite *sa-'à-lum/a-um* = *śah(r)um*, all "(new) moon"). For another *qital* form denoting an implement, see under ḤNW above.

?ŠḤṬ: see θḪṬ, below.

ŠḤT: see ḤTT, above.

?ŠḪṬ: see θḪṬ, below.

ŠYR

/šīru/ n. "song."

lex.: (Sum.) EZEN = (Akk.) *za-am-ma-ru* = (Hur.) *ḫal-mi* = (Ugar.) *ši-i-ru* Ug. 5 137 iii 7 (polyglot vocab.)

Sª Voc. no. 197.2.

Alphabetic: Cf. v. *šr* "to sing" (UT 489b no. 2409).

See also Šʾ R above, and Šʿ R below.

ŠYT

/šītu/ G v.n./infin. "to place."

lex.: (Sum.) [MAL/GÁN] = (Akk.) ⌜*ša?*⌝-[*ka-nu?*] = (Hur.) *ke-um-mi* = (Ugar.) *ši-tu* Ug. 5 130 iii 10' (polyglot vocab.)

Sª Voc. no. 35/36.2.

Alphabetic: *št* (UT 489b no. 2410).

?ŠKN

/maškanu/ ? n. "habitation(?)"; in field designation.

legal: [*i-n*]*a* A.ŠÀ.GÁN$^{hi.a}$ *maš-ka-ni*["[i]n 'habitation(?) field'" PRU 6 47:5

Alphabetic: Cf. pl. *mšknt* (UT 490a no. 2414).

It is unclear whether Ugar. */maškanu/* (cf. Hebrew *miškān*) or Akk. *maškanu* "threshing floor; emplacement, location" is intended here.

ŠLḤ

/mašlaḥu/ n. "(a garment)" ("throw"?).

econ.:]-*ú ma-aš-la-ḫa-ma* PRU 6 123:3 (list of garments)

Alphabetic: *mšlḥ*, in *spr npṣ any* / *tšʿ mθ<ḫ>ṭm* / *mšlḥ ḥdθ* "account of ship's gear: nine */maθḫaṭu/*'s (? see θḪṬ, below); a new */mašlaḥu/*" (KTU 4.689:1-3).

The form here is apparently dual, nom. */mašlaḥāma/* (see Sivan, Analysis 111-12; below, Part III, ch. 3 §C 1 d [3]); the only other formal possibility is sg. acc. with enclitic *-ma*, and both the acc. case and the enclitic would be quite unexpected in a list. It is uncertain whether the word is to be connected with the v. *šlḥ* "to send." Alternatively, cf. perhaps Arabic *mašlaḥ* "long, flowing cloak of wool or camel's hair" (Wehr, Dictionary 484b), which, unless the root is a loan in Arab., points to an original PS root **ś-l-ḥ*.

?ŠLḪ: see ŠLḤ, above.

ŠLM

(a) */šalimu/* adj. (G v. adj.) divine name (Šalim, "whole, sound").

lex.: ᵈ*SA-li-mu* Ug. 5 18:33 (god-list)

Alphabetic: DN *šlm* (UT 490b no. 2424).

The entry corresponds to *šlm* in the parallel alphabetic god-lists KTU 1.47:34; 1.118:33. Since the form bears a case-ending, the writing may be taken to represent Ugar. */šalimu/* rather than the Akk. DN *šalim*. The curious use of SA (for *ša* $_{10}$?) rather than expected ŠA is discussed in Part III, ch. 1 §A 2.

(b) */šallima/* v., D suffix-conj., 3ms, "to pay, deliver."

econ.: ᵉAN.ZA.GÀR GN *n* ⁽ˡᵘ́⁾ÌR⁽ᵐᵉˢ̌⁾ *(la) šal/ša-li-ma* (translation see discussion) Ug. 5 96 passim

Alphabetic: v. *šlm* D "to pay"; see discussion.

Nougayrol rendered these clauses as follows: "Ferme de [GN]: [n] valets. Inachevé/Achevé." Thus, he understood the forms *šal/ša-li-ma* to be the stative G stem, presumably Ugar. */šalima/*. Since, however, the incorrect double writing of single consonants is rare in Ugarit Akk. texts, especially in Ugar. forms (see Part III, ch. 1 §D 2), the spelling *šal-li-ma* in lines 1 (*šal-li* <*-ma* >),16,18,21,23 must represent the D suffix-conjugation, 3ms */šallima/* (so also, therefore, *ša-li-ma* in lines 3,5,8). The meaning of the clauses, accordingly, is: "the manor of GN has (not) delivered *n* /*ᶜabdu*/'s (slaves/workers)." The D of *š-l-m* in the sense "to restore, pay (in full), deliver" is found in several Semitic languages. For Ugar., note probably the following alphab. examples: PN *ᶜšrm kk[r]* PN_2 *θlθ ᶜšr [kkr]* (etc. ...) *bd* PN_5 *l šlm* "PN 20 talents, PN_2 13 talents ... to PN_5 have not paid (**/šallimū/*)" KTU 4.342; *ksp d šlm* PN *ᶜl bt* "silver which PN paid to 'the house'" 4.755:1-2; cf. also 4.398:6,7; and perhaps 1.14 iii 26 (see Caquot-Sznycer-Herdner, Textes ougaritiques 523-24 n. y). (For ᵉAN.ZA.GÀR construed as masc. [vs. Akk. *dimtu*] in Ugarit Akk. texts, see above under ḪWY, end. For a discussion of *qattila* as the vocalization of the Ugar. D suffix-conj., see Part III, ch. 3 §D 2 d.

?ŠLǴ: see ŠLḤ, above.

?ŠLR: see θǴR, below.

ŠMY

pl. */šamûma/* n. "sky."

lex.: (Sum.) [AN] = (Akk.) [*šamû*] = (Hur.) [*ḫa-b*]*ur-ni* = (Ugar.) [*š*]*a*!?-[*m*]*u*?-*ma*? UF 11 479:29 (polyglot vocab.)

(Sum.) [IDIM] = (Akk.) [*šamû*] = (Hur.) [*ḫa-bur*]-*ni* = (Ugar.) *ša-mu-ma* Ug. 5 137 iii 13' (polyglot vocab.)

Sᵃ Voc. nos. 45.1, 198.6.

(Sum.) [AN] = (Hur.) [*a-n*]*i* = (Ugar.) *ša-mu-ma* Ug. 5 137 iii 33" (polyglot god-list)

Alphabetic: *šmm* (UT 491 no. 2427).

☛ p. 398

ŠN

/šanatu/ ? n. "year."

lex.: (Sum.) [MU] = (Akk.) [*šattu*] = (Hur.) [ ] = (Ugar.) *ša*?-*na*!?-[*t*]u_4 UF 11 479:11 (polyglot vocab.)

Sᵃ Voc. no. 32.1.

Alphabetic: *šnt* (UT 492b no. 2447).

ŠNᵓ

/mašnŭ̄ᵓu/ ? adj./n. "enemy(?)."

lex.: (Sum.) [ḪUL?] = (Akk.) [*zīru*?] = (Hur.) [TA]R?-*du-bar-ri* = (Ugar.) *ma-aš-nu-ú*? Ug. 5 137 ii 41' (polyglot vocab.)

Sᵃ Voc. no. 190.5.

Alphabetic: Cf. v. *šnᵓ* "to hate" (UT 492b no. 2449).

The form may be *maqtul* < *maqtal* or passive *maqtūl*; see the S^a Voc. commentary.

ŠNT: see ŠN, above.

?Š^{c}L: see Š'L, above.

Š^{c}R

(a) */ši^{c}īru/* ? n. "barley(?)."

lex.: (Sum.) [ŠE?] = (Akk.) [*še'u?*] = (Hur.) [ ] = (Ugar.) [*š*]*i?-i-ru*[Ug. 5 137 iii 19' (polyglot vocab.)

S^a Voc. no. 199.

Alphabetic: *š^{c}r* (UT 493a no. 2459).

(b) */ša^{c}artu/* n. "wool."

econ.: *1* ^{túg}*šá-ḫar-tu* "1 wool(en garment)" PRU 6 128:5 (list of garments)

Alphabetic: *š^{c}rt* (UT 493a no. 2460; also, e.g., KTU 4.705:1,6!; 4.707:16,18; 4.709:1).

If the reading is correct (see below), this is one of the few Ugar. words in which /^{c}/ is written with a Ḫ-sign; see Part III, ch. 1 §E 4 b (1). (The readings ^{túg}*šá-àr-tu* and ^{túg}*šá-ur$_5$-tu* are ruled out, since in Ugarit Akk. ḪAR = *àr* is otherwise unattested and ḪAR = *ur$_5$* occurs only in the adverb *ur$_5$-ra* [in *urra šēra* "in future"; PRU 3 99b:12; 3 109b:12, and often]; ^{túg}*šá-ḫur-tu* is orthographically possible, but less felicitous etymologically.) For the form, cf. common Semitic **śa^{c}rat* "hair." As with /*^{c}iðirtu*/ (see ^{c}ðR), a Semitic *qv$_1$tlat* pattern here appears as *qv$_1$tv$_1$lt*; see Sivan, Analysis 58-59; Part III, ch. 2 §C. That the meaning of this word is "wool" rather than "hair" is argued by Boyd, Collection 209-10; note also that the alphab. GN *š^{c}rt* appears in syllabic texts as the logogram ^{uru}SÍG (= Akk. *šīpātu*) "wool," e.g., PRU 3 189b:1'; Ug. 7 pl. 13:28.

Other, less likely readings, without semantically related alphabetic equivalents, are ^{túg}*šá-mur-tu* = /*šamurtu*/ or /*θamurtu*/; ^{túg}*šá-kin-tu* = /*šakintu*/ or /*θakintu*/ (though we would expect */*š*/*θakittu*/).

?ŠĠṬ: see θḪṬ, below.

ŠP(T): see the commentary on S^a Voc. no. 32.1.

ŠPḤ

/šapḥu/ n. "sprout, scion."

lex.: (Sum.) [GIBIL] = (Akk.) [*per'u?*] = (Hur.) [*ḫ*]*i?-iš-ši* = (Ugar.) *šap-ḫu* Ug. 5 131 5' (polyglot vocab.)

S^a Voc. no. 49.

Alphabetic: *špḥ* (UT 493b no. 2462), and, apparently with voicing, *šbḥ* (KTU 1.17 vi 25; see Garr, JNES 45 51).

?ŠPL: see BLM, above.

p. 398

ŠPŠ

/šapšu/ n. "sun (god)."

lex.: (Sum.) [UTU] = (Akk.) [*šamšu*/*Šamaš*] = (Hur.) [ ] = (Ugar.) *ša-ap-šu* Ug. 5 138 3' (polyglot vocab.)

S^a Voc. no. 63.2.

(Sum.) ^{d}[UT]U = (Hur.) *ši-mi-gi* = (Ugar.) *ša-ap-šu* Ug. 5 137 iv a 18 (polyglot god-list)

(Sum.) [^{d}] = (Hur.) *ši-mi-gi* = (Ugar.) *š[a]-ap-šu* Ug. 5 137 iv b 14 (polyglot god-list)

Alphabetic: *špš* (UT 493-94 no. 2468).

☛ p. 398

(*Š/θQL

**šu-qa-al*

In Syria 18 251ff.:6-7, read not *qa-du* A.ŠÀ^{meš} *šu-qa-al* ^{giš}*sé-er-di-sa* (Thureau-Dangin), but *qa-du* A.ŠÀ^{meš}-*šu qa-du*! ^{giš}*sé-er-di-sa*.)

ŠR: see ŠYR, above, and θRR, below.

?ŠRL: see θǴR, below.

☛ p. 399

ŠRR: see θRR, below.

ŠT: see ŠYT, above.

T

Tʾ N

/tiʾnatu/ n. "fig."

lex.: (Sum.) [PÈŠ] = (Akk.) [*tittu*] = (Hur.) [ ] = (Ugar.) *ti-*[*n*]*a*?-[*t*]*u*$_4$ UF 11 479:10 (polyglot vocab.)

S^{a} Voc. no. 31.

Alphabetic: Unattested.

TBN

/tibnu/ n. "straw."

lex.: (Sum.) [IN] = (Akk.) [*ti-i*]*b-nu* = (Hur.) *ti-ib-ni* = (Ugar.) *ti-ib-nu* Ug. 5 130 iii 17' (polyglot vocab.)

S^{a} Voc. no. 38.

Alphabetic: Unattested.

TB^{c}

/taba^{c}a/ v., G suffix-conj., 3ms, "to depart."

econ.: PN *ša ta-ba-ʾa* GN "PN who departed (from) GN" PRU 6 77:1-2

Alphabetic: *tb^{c}* (UT 496 no. 2517); see discussion.

Nougayrol translated *ša ta-ba-ʾa* as "que tu recherches." As Rainey, IOS 3 40, points out, however, a second person form is not expected in an economic list. Rather, as Rainey suggests, the form should be taken as Ugar. */taba^{c}a/* "PN, who left GN." For a parallel in an alphab. econ. text, note perhaps [ ]*rm d tb^{c}* / [ ]⌜*θ*⌝^{c}*r* KTU 4.210:1-2; cf. also 4.213:27.

THM

/tahāmatu/ n. "the deep."

lex.: (Sum.) [AN-tu_4] = (Hur.) *[a]š-[t]e-a-ni-wi* = (Ugar.) *ta-a-ma-tu_4* Ug. 5 137 iii 34" (polyglot god-list)

Alphabetic: *thm(t)*; dual *thmtm* (UT 497a no. 2537); see discussion.

The form is probably singular; the existence of a sg. form with fem. *-t*, alongside one without (*thm* in KTU 1.23:30; 1.100:1), is assured by the alphab. dual form *thmtm* (i.e., */tahāmatāmi/*, e.g., KTU 1.4 iv 22; 1.6 i 34; 1.17 vi 48; 1.19 i 45; 1.100:3). (It is not possible to determine whether the form *thmt* [e.g., KTU1.3 iii 25, iv 17; 1.17 vi 12; 1.92:5] is sg., or pl. */tahāmātu/*.) The vowel of the first syllable, for expected **tihāmatu* (Akk. *tiāmtum*, Eblaite AB.A = *ti-ʾà-ma-tum* [MEE 4 336 no. 1343'], [Arab. *tihāma*, loan?]), is the result of vowel harmony around the guttural; see Part III, ch. 2 §A 1 c.

TWK

/tōkīyu/ adj. "inner."

econ.: *i-na* ^{uru}*ga-li-li tu-ki-ii* "in Inner Galīlu" PRU 6 78:9

Alphabetic: *gll (.) tky*; cf. *tk* "midst" (UT 497 nos. 2538,2550).

The form */tōkīyu/* is a nisba adjective formed from the noun **/tōku/* (alphab. *tk*) "midst" (cf. Hebrew *tāwek*); see Kühne, UF 7 255 n. 8; Sivan, Analysis 13, 279.

?TW/YR: see DYR, above.

TK(Y): see TWK, above.

TKN: see under θNQ, below.

?TMK

/tamku/ ? n. "?"

legal: RN ... É KISLAḪ *: TA-am-GI ša* PN ... *a-na* PN_2 ... *it-ta-din-šu* "RN ... gave PN_2 ... the *t.* habitation of PN ..." PRU 3 169a:2-6

Alphabetic: Unattested.

Nougayrol's suggested association of *: TA-am-GI* with the gloss *: am-qa* of PRU 3 118:12 (PRU 3 p. 218; see also Artzi, Bar-Ilan 1 45) is unlikely, as Boyd, Collection 217, has pointed out. Since the etymology of *: TA-am-GI* is unclear, it is uncertain whether the form glosses É KISLAḪ (Boyd, ibid.) or qualifies it; since the form is genitive, the latter is the more likely alternative (unless it glosses only KISLAḪ, genitive after É). Sivan, Analysis 278, reads */tamku/* "place of dwelling" and plausibly compares the root *t-m-k* "to support."

TMR

☛ p. 399

/ta[maru]/ ? n. "date palm(?)."

lex.: (Sum.) [GIŠIMMAR] = (Akk.) [*gišimmaru*?] = (Hur.) [ ] = (Ugar.) *ta-[ma?-ru?]* Ug. 5 137 ii 5 (polyglot vocab.)

S^a Voc. no. 175.

Alphabetic: Unattested.

TNN

/tunnanu/ n. "serpent."

lex.: (Sum.) [MUŠ] = (Akk.) [*ṣīru*] = (Hur.) [*apši*...] = (Ugar.) *tu-un-na-nu* Ug. 5 137 i 8' (polyglot vocab.)

S^a Voc. no. 157.

Alphabetic: *tnn* (UT 498b no. 2575).

On the form, see the Sª Voc. commentary.

p. 399

TRR

/tāriru/ or */tarīru/* n. "(member of a profession)."

econ.: ^lú^*ta-ri-ru-ma* PRU 6 93:5 (list of professions)

Alphabetic: Pl. *trrm* (UT 499b no. 2612; add KTU 4.7:1).

The meaning of the root *t-r-r* is unknown, and so we are unable to determine whether the pattern of this word is *qātil* or *qatīl*.

θ

?θ'R: see Š'R, above.

?θḤṬ: see θḪṬ, below.

p. 399

?θḪṬ

**/maθḫaṭu/* ?, pl. */maθḫaṭūma/* ?, n. "(a cloth item)."

econ.: *7* TÚG^meš^ ^giš^MÁ^meš^ *ma-áš-ḫa-ṭu-ma* "7 ship's cloths: *m.*'s" PRU 6 126:1 (list of garments bound for Byblos)

Alphabetic: See discussion.

Nougayrol, PRU 6 p. 159, suggested (apparently from the context) "couvre-bateau amovible(??)." Boyd, Collection 212-13, compares alphab. *mšḫṭ*, but notes that the latter is probably a weapon. (Boyd also points out that Akk. *mašḫaṭu* "small staircase," suggested by von Soden, AHw 625b, is unlikely in this context.)

Compare the following in an alphab. economic text: *spr npṣ any / tšᶜ mθṭm / mšlḥ ḥdθ* "account of ship's gear: nine *m.*'s; a new */mašlaḥu/* (see ŠLḤ, above)" (KTU 4.689:1-3); in line 2, perhaps we should read *mθ<ḫ>ṭm*, the same word as in the syllabic transcription, especially since the latter are specifically labeled "ships' cloths" (TÚG^meš^ ^giš^MÁ^meš^). As a cognate, note Akkadian *šeḫṭu*, a type of sack (a derivation of which from *šaḫāṭu* I "to jump; to seize, receive," for which no cognates are listed in AHw [1130a], seems more likely than the one from *šaḫāṭu* II "to tear, rip" suggested by von Soden, AHw 1209b). (Note also perhaps Middle Ass. ^túg^*ma-áš-ḫu* [, cited AHw 625b: read ^túg^*ma-áš-ḫu-*[*ṭu*], i.e., *mašḫuṭu*, Ass. for *mašḫaṭu*??)

?θLḤ, ?θLḪ, ?θLǴ: see ŠLḤ, above.

?θLR: see θǴR, below.

θLθ

/θalθu/ ? n. "copper(?)."

econ.: *1 ša-al-šu-ma* Ug. 5 84:11

Alphabetic: *θlθ* (UT 503a no. 2691).

Zaccagnini, OA 9 317-19, concludes that alphab. *θlθ* denotes both copper and bronze. The reason for the pl. */θalθūma/* after the numeral "1" in the syllabic transcription above is quite unclear; perhaps "1 (lot of) copper(-ingot)s" is intended; Zaccagnini, OA 9 318 n. 26, suggests "(oggetti di) rame."

?θNY

/maθna/â/ ? adv.(?) "second(ly)(?)."

legal: PN ... *it-ta-ši* É-*šu* [?] / *ma-aš-na* É-*šu* [?] / *ù it-ta-din*[-*šu*?] / *a-na* P[N_2] (... LÚ *ma-am-ma-an la-a i-la-qé-šu*) (translation see discussion) PRU 3 109b:2-6(,13-14)

Alphabetic: Cf. n. *mθn* "repetition" (see UT 504 no. 2705)?

Nougayrol, PRU 3 p. 218 (infra), compared *ma-aš-na* with Akk. *šanâm-ma* and *ina šanîšu* in other legal texts, and rendered the form "deuxièmement" (on p. 109, "secondement"); cf. AHw 628b ("zum 2. Mal"), CAD M/1 381b ("secondly, for the second time," comparing alphab. *mθn*). If this interpretation is correct, the form would be */maθnâ/*, i.e., a noun "repetition" used adverbially in the acc. Note that there are difficulties with such an interpretation, however. The first is that the final vowel of the form ought to be long (< **maθnaya*), and indicated as such in the orthography with an extra vowel-sign (see Part III, ch. 1 §F 1 b; scribal error: *ma-aš-na*<*-a*>?). More serious is the fact that a meaning "secondly" does not fit the context as it is preserved, since *ittaši* and *ittadin*, as in many other texts, are co-ordinated verbs, not parts of separate sentences (see Greenfield, "*našû-nadānu* and its Congeners"): "PN ... took and gave his house [ ] *ma-aš-na* his house to PN_2 (... no one may take it)." An alternative interpretation of *ma-aš-na* É-*šu* does not present itself, however.

For S^a Voc. no. 190.5 *ma-aš-nu-ú* (Ug. 5 137 ii 41'), see under ŠNʾ, above.

θNN

/θannănu/ n. "archer(?)."

econ.: [lú]*ša-na-nu-ma* PRU 6 93:6 (list of professions)

i-na ŠU PN [lú]*ša-na-ni* PRU 3 194f.:5,6,20

Alphabetic: *θnn*, pl. *θnnm* (UT 504b no. 2708).

For an etymology connecting this word with Akk. *šanānu*, Ethiopic *tasannana* "to contest, strive," see Albright apud Wiseman, Alalakh 11 n. 4. See AHw 1161a (s.v. *šanannu*) for occurrences of this term in texts from Alalaḫ. As Boyd, Collection 220-22, suggests, the form is probably *qattăl*, despite the unusual Alalakh spellings.

(θNQ

/θanăqv/ n. GN

econ.: LÚ [uru]*ša-na-qi* [uru]*ta* (!)-*ku-ni* PRU 6 93:15 (list of professions)

LÚ[meš] *ša-na-qi* PRU 3 199ff. iii 56 (list of persons grouped by profession)

cf. LÚ[meš] *ta*!-*ku*-[*ni*] ibid. iv 40

Alphabetic: GN *θnq*, gentilic pl. *θnqym* (UT 505a no. 2712); see discussion.

This entry is presented here, even though it is a GN, to call attention to the new readings.

In PRU 6 93:15, Nougayrol read LÚ URU *ša na-qi* URU *ša* (?)-*ku-ni* "X de(s) offrande(s), X de(s) dépôt(s)(??)"; in PRU 3 199 iii 56, he read [lú.meš]*ša na-qi* "libateur" (ibid. p. 236) and in ibid. iv 40 [lú.meš]*ša K*[*U* . These texts, which list guilds and amounts (6 93) or members of guilds (3 199ff.), have close analogues in the alphabetic text KTU 4.126, in which many of the same guilds appear. There we find *θnqym* "Thanaqians" in line 21, and *tkn*⌜*m*?⌝ "(men of?) Takunu" in line 31. (Note also KTU 4.355, in which both towns also appear, *θnq* in line 29, *tkn* in line 27.) Gordon, UT 505 no. 2712, is thus probably correct in suggesting that *θnqym* are "members of a certain guild named after their town." (The same conclusions regarding these forms have also been reached by Wesselius, UF 15 315.))

?θᶜD or **?θᶜY**

/θāᶜittu/ ? or */θāᶜītu/* ? n. (G ptcpl. fem.) "(a container)."

econ.: *3* ^{mí}*4 1 ša-i-tu₄ a-na* $^{lú.meš}$ḪUN.GÁ "3 'quarts,' 1 *θ*. for the hirelings" Ug. 5 99:10

Alphabetic: *θᶜt* (KTU 4.751:6); see discussion.

Nougayrol's interpretation of this line is "3 quarts(?) (et) 1 *šaitum* (d'huile) pour les journaliers," plausibly taking ^{mí}*4* as "quart (de jarre)" and *ša-i-tu₄* as "un type de récipient subdivision de la jarre" (see Ug. 5 p. 193 nn. 1,2). (Nougayrol's comparison of *ša-i-tu₄* with vessel called *šaḫītu* in MSL 7 81:96 is less felicitous; the latter term probably denotes "sow," since it occurs in a sequence of several terms for animal-shaped drinking vessels; see AHw 1132a, CAD M/1 384a [*mašqu* lex.]). As noted by Dietrich-Loretz-Sanmartín, UF 6 37 no. 115, alphab. *θᶜt nbt* in KTU 4.751:6 must denote "a container/pot/jar of honey." Thus, it seems reasonable to associate syllabic *ša-i-tu₄* and alphab. *θᶜt*.

The etymology of the word is quite uncertain. None of the other Semitic languages has a similar term denoting a type of container. It is possible that the root is Ugar. *θ-ᶜ-y*, "to offer" (KTU 1.40:24), with its derived noun *θᶜ* "offering" (ibid.; see Aistleitner, Wörterbuch 340 no. 2907; cf. OSA *mθᶜy* "incense offering" [Biella, Dictionary 548]; on the various alphab. Ugar. forms written *θᶜ(y)*, see also Dietrich-Loretz-Sanmartín, UF 5 116-17). Since the *a*-vowel of the first syllable has not assimilated to the following */ī/*, even though a guttural intervenes (see Part III, ch. 2 §A 1 c), it is probably long */ā/*, and so the form would be participial, i.e., */θāᶜītu/*.

Also a possible root is *θ-ᶜ-d*, which means "to irrigate" in a derived form in OSA (Biella, Dictionary 548); cf. also Arabic *θaᶜd* "moist, fresh" (usually of dates), which may also occur in alphab. Ugar. *ḫmš θᶜdt* (KTU 4.150:5). Again the form would be participial, */θāᶜittu/*, since the *a*-vowel has not become */i/*. (For the assimilation of */d/* to a following */t/*, see Gordon, UT 34 §5.35.)

?θǴṬ: see θḪṬ, above.

?θǴR

**/θaǵru/* ?, pl. */θaǵarūma/* ? n. "gate, door-leaf(?)."

econ.: *u* ^{giš}*šá-[ḫ]a!?-⌜ru?⌝-ma* PRU 6 114:5 (lists of types and items of wood)

Alphabetic: *θǵr* "gate" (UT 505b no. 2721).

The reading and interpretation proposed here are extremely uncertain: the sign after *ša* is quite damaged, and appears to be the end of *li*, but no root *š/θ-l-r* with an appropriate meaning is known; the meaning of */θaǵru/* (if the reading is correct), preceded with the determinative ^{giš} and occurring in a list of items of wood, would have to be "door-leaf," whereas alphab. *θǵr* in its few attestations seems only to mean "gateway"; finally, the alphab. pl. of *θǵr* is *θǵrt*, not **θǵrm*, in KTU 1.3 ii 3 (note, however, the Hebrew pl. *šəᶜārîm*). Nevertheless, no other interpretation presents itself.

θQD

/θuqdu/ ? n. "almond."

econ.: BÁN (or *1/2*) ^{giš}*šu-uq-du(-)ma[* (see discussion) PRU 6 159:4' (list of foodstuffs)

Alphabetic: *θqd* (UT 506a no. 2734).

It is not clear whether the initial BAR sign denotes "1/2 (measure)" (Nougayrol) or BÁN (= Akk. *sūtu*) "seah" (AHw 1247b), nor whether the MA sign before the break is part of the Ugar. pl. marker (thus, */θuqdūma/* "seah/half-measure (of) almonds") or the beginning of a following (qualifying?) word (cf. alphab. *θqd . mr* = */θuqdu marru/* "bitter almond(s)" in KTU 1.85:7; see Cohen-Sivan, Ugaritic Hippiatric Texts 23). If the form is simply *giššu-uq-du*, it may be Akk. *šuqdu* (so AHw) rather than the Ugar. word for "almond," although another word in the same list is also probably Ugar.; see under KMʾ.

*θQL: see *ŠQL above, and *mi(-)iš(-)KU(-)la(-)t[i]* in the Appendix to the Glossary, below.

?θRL: see θǴR, above.

?θRR

/θarru/ ? adj. "small(?)"; in field designation.

legal: *qa-du* A.ŠÀ^{meš} *ša-ri-ma* "with 'small field(s)'" PRU 3 148a:7

Alphabetic: Cf. *θrr* "small" (UT 507 no. 2754)? See discussion.

Cf. perhaps alphab. *θrr* (*/θurēru/*?) "small." Alternatively, the form may reflect the alphab. GN *θrm* (if. sg., diptotic here), although without the determinative ^{uru} that is unlikely; or the pl. of one of several alphab. words *šr* (see Gordon, UT 494).

Appendix

Ugaritic Words of Uncertain Root

**a-ga-su-nu* (PRU 6 126:2): see SʾN, above.

am-ma-ti n. "?"

p. 399

legal: *i-na* DUMU *am-ma-ti* Ug. 5 2:4
DUMU^{meš} *am-ma-ti* Ug. 5 81:4
DUMU^{meš}-*šu* [*ša*?] ⌜*am*⌝-*ma-ti* Ug. 5 82:5-6

DUMU$^{(meš)}$ *am-ma-ti* evidently denotes a particular kind of adoption. Since the expression occurs only in these texts, *am-ma-ti* may well reflect a Ugar. word, as suggested in CAD A/2 75b; the root may be *ʾ-m-m, h-m-m*, or *ʿ-m-m*. (See Rainey, Or. 34 15, IOS 5 20, for surveys of possible interpretations.)

a-QA?-[

legal: *a-nu-ma* É PN : *a-QA*?-[ ] *a-na mar-kab-te*[ ] *da*[ ] ḪA.LA^{meš} PN$_2$ PRU 3 96ff.:27-29

For a translation, see under RKB, above.

a-ra-mi-ma n.?/adj.? (m. pl.) "?"; in field designation.

legal: *qa-du* A.ŠÀ^{meš} *a-ra-mi-ma* "with '*a.* fields'" PRU 3 148a:10

Plural of a *qatl* or *qatal* form, root *ʾ-r-m, h-r-m* (cf. v. *hrm* KTU 1.107:9,19?), or *ʿ-r-m*. Some scholars have seen here a reference to the Arameans (see Boyd, Collection 33-34; Sivan, Analysis 197), otherwise unattested at Ugarit. For other alternatives, note the alphab. GN *ʿrm* (with genitilic *ʿrmy*), and Heb. *ʿarmôn* "plane-tree" (cf., e.g., [A.ŠÀ^{meš}] *al-la-ni* "fields of the oaks" PRU 3 131f.:9, for which see above, under ʾLN; see also under QLQL).

**di-ba-ra-tu* ^{meš} (PRU 6 158:13): see KPR, above.

e-la-mu n. "(type of tree/wood)."

econ.: ⸢^{giš}*e?-la-mu*⸣ PRU 6 158:10.

If Semitic, a *qitāl* form of *ʾ/h/ʿ-l-m*.

☛ p. 399

ḫa-AB-BI/BU n. "?"; in field designation.

legal: PN *il-te-qè* [*x* IKU] A.ŠÀ$^{\text{ḫi.a}}$ ... *ù qa-aq-qa-ru* [*ù*] *ḫa-AB-BU* [*q*]*a?-dú* GIŠ^{meš}-*šu* [*ša* (?)] *i-na* ŠÀ-*šu* [*ina*] *2 me-at* KÙ.BABBAR [ŠÁM.TIL.LA?] *ṣa-mi-it* [*a-na*] PN "PN received [x *ikû*] field(s) ...; and the ground [and] the *ḫ*. [w]ith its trees [that?] are therein are transferred [to] PN [for] 200 silver, [full value]" PRU 3 161b:4-10

ù A.ŠÀ$^{\text{ḫi.a}}$ PN *ša i-na : ḫa-A*[*B-B*]*I* "and PN's field that is in *ḫ*." PRU 3 148f.:6

In the first example, Nougayrol read [*š*]*a*(??) before *ha-AB-BU*, but the copy indicates that *ù* is equally possible.

Since incorrectly doubled writings of single consonants are rare in our corpus (see Part III, ch. 1 §D 2), we are almost certainly dealing with a geminate root here, *ḥ-b/p-b/p*, *ḫ-b/p-b/p*, or *ǵ-b/p-b/p*. Thus, Kühne's proposals in UF 6 165, viz., */ḥāpu/* "shore" (cf. Heb. *ḥōp*) or */ǵābu/* "thicket" (cf. Syriac *ʿābā*, Arabic *ǵāba*) must be ruled out on formal grounds. Other possible cognates mentioned by Kühne, such as Akk. *ababu* "forest" (lex. only) and Mari Akk. *ḫibbu* "?" (hapax), also differ formally from the word under consideration, and are in any event too rare for analysis. Finally, a connection with alphab. *ǵb* (KTU 1.101:8; 1.105: 7,14,16; for *gt ǵ*⸢*b*⸣ in PRU 5 13:15, KTU 4.636:15 reads *gt ǵl*), suggested by de Moor, UF 2 320 and n. 97, remains at best only a possibility.

☛ p. 399

ḫa-ba-ṭu v., G suffix-conj., 3mp?, "?"

econ.: garments ... ŠU PN *ki ḫa-ba-ṭu*[ ] (end) PRU 6 128:6-7

Nougayrol rendered *ki ḫa-ba-ṭu* "quand(?) ils ont disparu(??) [," without comment. Since, with rare exception, ṬU in Ugarit Akk. only has the value *ṭu* (*tu*$_{\text{x}}$ in a few words in lexical texts), however, it is unlikely that any of the several Akk. verbs *ḫabātu* (see Kraus, RA 69 31-40) is intended. Further, *ḫa-ba-ṭu* has the appearance of a Ugar. suffix-conjugation form, 3mp (i.e., *qatalū*; a *qattāl* noun is unlikely). The root may be *ḥ-b-ṭ* (cf. the obscure *tḥbṭ* in KTU 1.82:25), *ḫ-b-ṭ*, or *ǵ-b-ṭ*, none of which has a meaning in the cognate languages that clarifies this difficult phrase.

ḫa-ar-ZA-ti n.?/adj.? "?"; in field designation.

legal: *i-na* (A.ŠÀ^{meš}) *: ḫa-ar-ZA-ti* PRU 3 95f.:11,20

See Kühne, UF 6 165-66. Of the many possible roots (*ḥ/ḫ/ǵ-r-ð/z/ẓ/s/ṣ*), perhaps the most likely is *ḥrṣ*, and the meaning "furrowed area" or "ditch" (so Boyd, Collection 90-91; on alphab. *ḥrṣ*, see Dietrich-Loretz, UF 11 193-97). Alternatively, note Arabic *ǵars* "plant," *ǵirās* "cultivation" (cf. MHeb. *ʿārîs* "arbor"?).

IB-lu n. "(a garment)."

econ.: ^{túg}*IB-lu* GAL^{meš} "large(?) *i*.- garments" PRU 6 123:1 (list of clothing)

Conceivably we might read instead ^{túg}*IB-lu-ma*!^{meš}, i.e., a pl. in */-ūma/*, but GAL is indicated both in Nougayrol's copy and transliteration and in the photo in Ug. 5 p. 635 fig. 20 lower. Nougayrol, PRU 6 p. 158 n. 3, suggested that *ib-lu* may reflect a Ugar. reading of Sumerian ^{túg}ÍB.LÁ (= Akk. *nēbeḫu* "sash"), but this seems unlikely. More likely the form is Semitic, possibly Ugaritic, although none of the possible roots—*ʾ/h/ʿ-b/p-l* —suggests a cognate.

il-[n. divine name.

lex.: (Sum.) dNIN.A.ZU = (Hur.) *ši-ru-ḫi* = (Ugar.) *il*-[Ug. 5 137 iv a 16 (polyglot god-list)

ir?-KU n. "?" p. 399

lex.: (Sum.) [UR/NE?] = (Akk.) [ ] = (Hur.) [*x-p*]*í-ir-ri* = (Ugar.) *i*[*r*]*?-KU* Ug. 5 131 4' (polyglot vocab.)

Sa Voc. no. 48.2.

iš-ši-KI, iš-<ši->GI n. "?"; in field designation.

legal: *ša i-na iš-ši-KI* "which is in *i*." PRU 3 129a:6

A.ŠÀmeš PN ... *ša i-na* A.ŠÀmeš *iš-<ši->GI* "field(s) of PN ... that are in '*i*. field'" PRU 3 148a:4

Apparently a *qittīl* (< **qattīl*; see Part III, ch. 2 §A 1 b) form, root (ʾ/*h*/ʿ-*š*/*θ*-*g*/*k*) and meaning unknown; "oppression" (so Sivan, Analysis 207) seems unlikely as a field designation; Nougayrol, PRU 6 p. 157 n. 13, with reference to a month name *iš(i)gi*, considered a connection with spirits of the dead ("manes").

* dug*kap* (?)-*pa-al* (?)-*la-nu* (PRU 6 158:6): see PSL, above.

KI-ra-li-nu n. (loanword?) "(a type of jar)."

econ.: *1* dug*KI-ra-li-nu x-ṣi* PRU 6 158:6 (list of items, mostly jars)

The form appears to be non-Semitic in origin.

KI-ša/*TA?-b*[*a-tu*] or *KI-TA?-Z*[*U-ma*] n. (pl.) "(a garment)."

econ.: *6* túg*KI-ša*/*TA?-b*[*a-tu*] (or: *6* túg*KI-TA?-Z*[*U-ma*]) PRU 6 128:2 (list of garments)

Nougayrol read *6* *ṣubat**KI.ŠA.B*[*A* (?) . On the copy, it appears that the sign after KI may be ŠA or TA, and the last sign the beginning of BA or ZU. If the word is Ugar., it is apparently a pl. (in /*-ātu*/ or /*-ūma*/) of *qitl(at)* or *qitāl(at)*.. Possible roots: *k*/*q-š*/*θ-b*, *k*/*q-d*/*ṭ*/*t-b*, *k*/*q-d*/*ṭ*/*t-s*/*ṣ*.

**ku-ni* (PRU 6 93:15): see under θNQ, above.

li-x-[n. divine name.

lex.: (Sum.) dKA.NI.SUR.RA = (Hur.) *ka-ni-z*[*u-r*]*a?-an?* = (Ugar.) *li-x*[Ug. 5 137 iv a 11 (polyglot god list)

The goddess Kanisurra remains poorly understood; see Edzard, RlA 5 389. One wonders whether the Ugar. column is to be read *le-l*[*u*] = /*lēlu*/, i.e., a divine name "Night"; see UT 428 no. 1379 and Xella, Testi rituali 372, for other references for alphab. *ll*.

[*l*]*i?*/[*U*]*Z?-ZU* "to cover(?)," "covering(?)." p. 399

lex.: (Sum.) BAD = (Akk.) *ka-ta-mu* = (Hur.) *ḫu-x*[ ] = (Ugar.) [*l*]*i?*/[*U*]*Z?-ZU* Ug. 5 137 i 21" (polyglot vocab.)

Sa Voc. no. 173.4.

lu-ḫu-ma n.?/adj.? (m. pl.) "(type of garment)."

econ.: *6* túgLAmeš *lu-ḫu-ma* meš PRU 6 126:5 (list of garments)

Neither the logogram nor the syllabic spelling is understood. The root of (pl.) *lu-ḫu-ma* may be hollow *l-w-ḥ*/*ḫ*/*ǵ* or geminate *l-ḥ-ḥ*/*ḫ-ḫ*/*ǵ-ǵ* (or, conceivably, III-weak *l-ḥ*/*ḫ*/*ǵ-w*/*y*, i.e., */*luXûma*/ < **luXayūma*).

lu-l[*a*] n. divine name.

lex.: (Sum.) ^{d}LÚ.LÀL = (Hur.) *lu-la-a*[*ḫ-ḫ*]*é* = (Ugar.) *lu-l*[*a*] Ug. 5 137 iv a 12 (polyglot god-list)

The form represents a Ugariticized version of either the Sum. or the Hur. form of the DN (alphab. unattested).

ma-ʾ-⸢*tu*⸣ (PRU 6 159:3'): see KMʾ, above.

ma-KI!?/*DI*?-*ZU* n. "(a garment)."

econ.: *x* ^{túg}*ma-KI*!?/*DI*?-*ZU 10 x*[PRU 3 206f.:4 (list of garments)

Although the copy suggests that the second-last sign is DI, Nougayrol was probably correct to read KI, since the following radical of the form is a dental. Even so, the pattern of the form militates against deriving it from *k-s-w* "to cover, clothe" (the form would have to be */*makis(s)û*/, i.e., an otherwise unknown pattern *maqit(t)vl*, and written without indication of the final long vowel), and thus we may not, with any confidence, connect it with alphab. *mks* "garment, covering." More likely possibilities: *qặtīl* of *m-g/k/q-ð/z/ẓ/s/ṣ*, or *maqīl* or *maqill* of a hollow or geminate root with first radical *g/k/q* and final radical *ð/z/ẓ/s/ṣ*, or *maqtil* of a root I-*ʾ/h/ʿ*.

ma-am-[n. "?"

econ.: *2* $^{giš.meš}$*ma-am-*[PRU 6 151:4' (list of types/items of wood)

Since none of the few words beginning *mam-* in Akkadian denotes an item or type of wood, this form is probably Ugar., perhaps a *maqtvl* form of a root I-*m*.

ma-ar-TU(?) n. "(type of garment)."

econ.: *3* TÚG^{meš} *ma-ar-*⸢*TU*?⸣ PRU 6 126:8 (list of garments)

2 TÚG *ma-a*[*r*?-*TU* (?)] PRU 6 129:11' (list of garments)

Several possibilities may be noted for this term for a garment: (1) a reading *ma-ar-*⸢*dú*⸣-[*ú*], connected with the root RDY, for which see above; (2) a scribal error, perhaps *ma-ar-*<*da-*>⸢*tu*⸣ or *ma-ar-*<*de*$_4$->⸢*tu*⸣, for both of which see under RDY, above; (3) in view of the writing *ma-ar* rather than the much more common MAR sign for words beginning /*mar-*/ (see Part III, ch. 1 §A 4), perhaps the root is instead II-guttural, viz., *m-ʾ-r*, *m-h-r*, or *m-ʿ-r*, and the form /*maXartu*/ (with *X* representing *ʾ/h/ʿ*), i.e., *qatal-t* (possibly from *qatl-at*, like /*šaʿartu*/ < **śaʿratu*; see ŠʿR b, above); but no cognates suggest a meaning for such a form.

☛ p. 400

ma-aš-⸢*x*⸣[n.? "?"

lex.: (Sum.) [SIG/SIG$_5$?] = (Akk.) [?] = Hur. [*t*]*ap-ša-ḫal-še* = (Ugar.) *ma-aš-*⸢*x*⸣[Ug. 5 137 ii 15" (polyglot vocab.)

S^{a} Voc. no. 180.3?/181?

(**mi*(-)*iš*(-)*KU*(-)*la*(-)*t*[*i*]

lit.: *ni-is-sà-ti mi iš KU la t*[*i*] Ug. 5 165:7' (bilingual, precepts)

For the Sumerian of this line, lu.ul.bi ù.[ ], see Krecher, UF 1 152. Nougayrol rendered the line "soucis (et) ...," leaving *mi iš KU la t*[*i*] untranslated. Von Soden, UF 1 194-95, proposed reading *mi-iš-qú-la-t*[*i*] and taking the form as a Ugar. passive participle of *θ-q-l* "to weigh," with pattern *miqtūl* rather than expected *maqtūl*. But since, as von Soden admits, the use of *θ-q-l* in the transferred meaning that would be required here is otherwise unattested in Ugar. (likewise of *šaqālu* in Akk.), and further, the significance of "(ab)gewogen Klagen" is unclear, it seems unlikely that his proposal is correct. The editors of CAD, more plausibly, read the Akk. of this line *nissatī miš qūla t*[*i*] (CAD N/2 275a, Q 304a; cf. *ina ... qūli ku-ú-ri nissati* ZA 65 58:83, cited ibid.), though still the meaning remains obscure.)

**na-qi/qí* (PRU 3 199ff. iii 56; PRU 6 93:15): see θNQ, above.

ni-d[a] n. divine name.

lex.: (Sum.) dLA.TA.RA.AK = (Hur.) *ša-ar-ra-[a?]-ni* = (Ugar.) *ni-d[a]* Ug. 5 137 iv a 13 (polyglot god-list)

Alphab. unattested.

ni-ru?/ú?-[n. "?"

econ.: *3* giš.meš*ni-ru/ú-[* PRU 6 151:3' (list of types/items of wood)

Nougayrol transliterated *3* iṣM*ni-ru(?)[* , but his copy clearly has *ú*, not *ru*, after *ni*. If giš.meš*ni-ru* is correct, it is likely that Akk. *nīrū* "yoke(s)" is intended. The form is listed here because at least one other word in this list, in the following line, is probably Ugar. (see *ma-am-[*, above).

See also NW/YR, above.

ra-⌜PA⌝-ni n.?/adj.? "?"; in field designation. p. 400

legal: Éḫi.a DUMU PN *š[a? i?-n]a? : ra-⌜PA⌝-ni* lú.mešDI.KUDmeš PRU 3 140f.: 25-26

The above may be translated: "The estate of the son of PN in (the area called) 'the Judges' ...'" The gloss mark denotes a non-Akk. word. Nougayrol suggested "sise dans le Raḫbanu(?) des Juges," thus associating the form with the river/canal designation */raḥbānu/*, which appears frequently in these texts (see RḤB, above); so also Boyd, Collection 168, 275. But */raḥbānu/*, in all well-preserved contexts, seems always to be associated with fields, while *: ra-⌜PA⌝-ni* is not. Further, */raḥbānu/* is never qualified by "of the judges," as *: ra-⌜PA⌝-ni* is here. Finally, it would be unusual for Ugar. */ḥ/* not to be reflected in the writing (see Part III, ch. 1 §E 4 a). Thus, despite the probable occurrence of */raḥbānu/* in line 9 of the same text, it seems likely that *ra-⌜PA⌝-ni* denotes a different term. It is uncertain whether the root is *r-b-n*, *r-p-n*, or, if the form exhibits an afformative */-ān/*, geminate *r-b-b*, *r-p-p*, or II-guttural *r-ʾ/h/ᶜ-b/p*.

ri/tal-GI-mu? n.? "?" p. 400

lex.: (Sum.) [GIM/BAN?] = (Akk.) [?] = (Hur.) x-x[ ] = (Ugar.) *ri/tal-GI-⌜mu ?⌝* UF 11 479:8 (polyglot vocab.)

Sa Voc. no. 30.x/30a.x.

TA-a[l-] "?"; in field designation.

legal: A.ŠÀḫi.a PN DUMU [PN2] *i-na : TA-a[l-]* PRU 3 155f.:5-6

TA-r[a-] "?"; in field designation.

legal: A.ŠÀ *: TA-r[a-]* PRU 3 140f.:8

ú-ṭu n.?/adj.? "?"

econ.: KU6meš *:? ú-ṭu* RS 23.368:17' (PRU 6 p. 119 n. 1)

Nougayrol (ibid.) compared alphabetic *uṭ(m)* (see KTU 1.2 i 13; 1.5 i 5; 1.18 iv 3), the meaning of which remains uncertain (see Caquot-Sznycer-Herdner, Textes ougaritiques 128 n. j, 241 n. j).

ZI-ZA-ḫal-li-ma n. (m. pl.) (loanword?) "?" p. 400

legal: [*zaki/zakû*] PN *ù* P[N2] *ù* DUMUmeš*-šu a-di da-ri-ti iš-tu* KASKALmeš kur*mi-iṣ-ri ù iš-tu* KASKALmeš kur*ḫa-at-ti ù i-na : ZI-ZA-ḫal-li-ma (ana ekalli ... šipra mimma lā eppušū)* PRU 3 165f. r. 4'-6'

The clause may be rendered: "PN and PN_2 [are free] of the Egyptian and the Hittite corvée and of the z.'s." The word is marked as non-Akk. by the gloss sign. It apparently bears the Ugar. masc. pl. oblique */-īma/*, thus would be sg. */sisaḫallu/* or */zizaḫallu/*. The meaning and origin of the term remain obscure; see Sivan, Analysis 267; CAD S 321a. (Artzi's proposal, Bar-Ilan 1 37 n. 32, to read a compound noun ***sīsû*** + ***ḫallu*** "riding horse," is unlikely to be correct.)

x(-x)-DI-na-ma dual n. "?"

econ.: *2* [*(x?)* -]⌜*x*⌝-*DI*-⌜*na-ma*⌝ PRU 6 127:11 (list of garments)

The reading of the sign before *DI*, and whether a sign preceded that, are uncertain.

PART III

ORTHOGRAPHY AND GRAMMAR

CHAPTER 1. ORTHOGRAPHY

p. 400

A. The Ugarit Akkadian Syllabary

The syllabary employed to represent Ugaritic words in transcription is not discernibly different from that used to write the Akkadian of the texts in which the Ugaritic words are embedded. Since a thorough discussion of the Ugarit Akkadian syllabary would take us too far afield in the present study,[1] it will suffice here to note that the syllabary is essentially that found elsewhere in texts from the northern area of Western Peripheral Akkadian.[2] This syllabary, which had its origins in the Old Akkadian period, was heavily influenced by its transmission to the west through the Hurrian scribes who used and modified it, although there are overlays of other scribal traditions, including the contemporary Middle Assyrian and Middle Babylonian, in varying degrees as well.

1. Cv *Signs for Stops*

p. 400

Perhaps the most obvious characteristic of this syllabary is a marked confusion, or indiscriminateness, in the use of signs for stops and for sibilants, e.g., in Akkadian words in Ugarit texts: *qa-DU TU-un-ni-šu* for *qadu dunnīšu* (PRU 3 52f.:13); *ŠU-um-mu-uḫ* (PRU 3 58a:8) vs. *ZU-um-mu-uḫ* (PRU 3 113ff.:28), both for *summuḫ*, *i-ṢE/ZE-ʾe-er* for *izeʾʾer* (PRU 3 54ff.:8,18). This confusion is by no means as

[1]See my Akkadian of Ugarit.

[2]See the Introduction, pp. 4-5 with nn. 18-23. A partial bibliography on WPA syllabary, arranged chronologically: Böhl, Sprache der Amarnabriefe 1-26; Thureau-Dangin, Syllabaire accadien iv-v; Labat, Accadien de Boghaz-Köi 7-37; Berkooz, Nuzi Dialect passim; Speiser, IH 11-15; Nougayrol, PRU 3 pp. xxxv-xxxvi; Aro, AfO 18 144; Gamkrelidze, ArOr 406-18; Labat, Syria 39 14-19; Bush, GHL 15-33; Jucquois, Phonétique 60-71; Wilhelm, Ḫurro-Akkadisch 15-16; Moran, "Syrian Scribe" passim; von Soden-Röllig, AS[3] xxxv-xxxvii.

rampant in Ugarit Akk. texts as it is, for example, in texts from Mittanni[3] or even in texts found at Ras Shamra but written at Carchemish; in other words, in Ugarit Akk. texts, with greater regularity than at Mittanni or Carchemish, signs for stops and sibilants occur with the values we would expect in contemporary Mesopotamian texts (especially MB). Nevertheless, the lesser degree of confusion is only relative, and the fact that, e.g., the TA sign *may* be used for */tă/*, */dă/*, or */ṭă/* must always be borne in mind, for it often increases the difficulty of identifying the precise form of a suspected Ugaritic word with any real confidence.

The representation of the individual Ugaritic phonemes will be presented in detail further below (§E). Here and in the following section it will be convenient to present only a tabular summary of the individual *Cv* and *vC* signs attested for stops and for sibilants and other fricatives in Ugaritic words, and their values. The following table lists the *Cv* signs used for stops, with their phonemic values in Ugaritic words:[4]

Dentals				Velars				Labials		
sign	*/dv/*	*/tv/*	*/ṭv/*	sign	*/gv/*	*/kv/*	*/qv/*	sign	*/bv/*	*/pv/*
DA(335)[5]	x		x	GA(319)	x	x	x	BA(5)	x	x
DI(457)	x		x	GI(85)	x	x		BI(214)	x	x
DU(206)	x	x		GU(559)	x	x		BU(371)	x	x
TA(139)	x	x	x	KA(15)		x	x	PA(295)	x	x
TE(376)	x	x								
TI(73)	x	x		KI(461)		x	x			
TU(58)	x	x		KU(536)		x	x			
TUM(207)	x	x								
				QA(62)	x	x	x			
				QI(538)			x			
TU(595)			x	QU(191)			x			

☛ p. 400

The table indicates a fair degree of apparent randomness in the use of voiced, voiceless, and emphatic signs to represent the Ugaritic stops. There may, however, be more consistency than first meets the eye, at least in the use of the voiced signs. In a recent study in which he musters the available alphabetic evidence,[6] W. R. Garr concludes that voiceless consonants in Ugaritic were subject to voicing in a number of environments: (i) intervocalically; (ii) in contiguity to a voiced sonorant; (iii) before a

[3]See Adler, Das Akkadische des Königs Tušratta.

[4]For examples, see under the appropriate phonemes below in §E 1.

[5]Numbers in parentheses are those assigned to individual signs in Deimel, ŠL; Labat, Manuel d'épigraphie akkadienne[5]; Borger, ABZ[2].

[6]JNES 45 45-52.

voiced obstruant. If these conclusions are applied to the Ugaritic words in syllabic transcription, and the use of the signs for stops is considered according to the *phonetic* realizations of the words, rather than the phonemic (as in the chart above), the following interesting points emerge:

In all three occurrences of DU for */tu/*, the */t/* is intervocalic: *:ka-ar-ba-DU* = */karbātu/* = [karbādu] "twisted(?)" (KRB); *: ma-ad-da-DU* = */maddatu/* = [maddadu] "measurement" (MDD); *: ṣa-ma-DU* = */ṣamatū/* = [ṣamadū] "they are transferred" (ṢMT).

The use of GA and GI for */k/* occurs where the realization of */k/* ought to be [g]: *sí-GA-ni-ma* = */sikānīma/* = [sigānēma] "statues(?)" (SKN b); *:ta-am-GI* = */tamki/* = [tamgi] "?" (TMK). The use of GU for */ku/* appears in $^{\text{lú.meš}}$*GU-um*[, which is interpreted in the present study as */kumrū/* "(type of priest) (KMR), but with considerable reservation.

The only example of BA for */pa/*[7] appears in $^{\text{[d]ug!?}}$*ku?-BA-ra-tu*^{meš} = */kupārātu/?* = [kubārādu] "bowls(?)" (KPR).

In contrast, all of the voiceless signs (Tv, Kv, PA) occur where both voiceless and voiced phones are expected: e.g.,

TA in *at-TA* = */ʾattă/* = [ʾattă] "you (ms)" (ʾNT) and *: ṣa-ma-TA* = */ṣamata/* = [ṣamada] "is transferred" (ṢMT);

TE in *me-te* = */miʾtē/* = [meʾtē] "200" (Mʾ) and *mar-TE-im-tu* = */mardimtu/* = [mardemdu] "path(??)" (RDM);

TI in *TI-ib-nu* = */tibnu/* = [tibnu] "straw" (TBN) and *: na-ba-TI* = */naʾbadi/* = [naʾbadi] "flight" (ʾBD);

TU in *TU-un-na-nu* = */tunnanu/* = [tunnanu] "serpent" (TNN) and *ši-TU* = */šītu/* = [šīdu] "to place" (ŠYT);

TUM in *qa-aš-TUM* = */qaštu/* = [qaštu] "bow" (QŠT) and *ḫu-ul-ma-TUM* = */ǵulmatu/* = [ǵulmadu] "darkness" (ǴLM);

KA in *KA-as-pu* = */kaspu/* [kaspu] "silver" (KSP) and *da-KA-rù* = */dakaru/* = [dagaru] "male" (DKR^{1});

KI in $^{\text{d.giš}}$*KI-na-rù* = */kinnāru/* = [kennāru] "lyre" (DN; KNR) and ^{lú}*sà-KI-ni* = */sākini/* = [sāgene] "prefect" (SKN a);

KU in *KU-sú-mu* = */kussumu/* = [kussumu] "emmer" (KSM) and *ma-al-KU* = */malku/* = [malgu] "king" (MLK b);

PA in ^{túg}*PA-li-du-ma* = */palīdūma/* = [palēdūma] "(cloths)" (PLD) and *: ta-ar-PA-ṣí* = */tarbaṣi/* = [tarbaẓi] "stable" (RBṢ).

These observations may be plotted in tabular form as follows:

[7]While the use of the PA sign for *bá* is common in Ugarit Akk., the use of BA for *pá* is relatively rare.

Dentals				Velars				Labials		
sign	[dv]	[tv]	[ṭv]	sign	[gv]	[kv]	[qv]	sign	[bv]	[pv]
DA(335)	x		x	GA(319)	x		x	BA(5)	x	
DI(457)	x		x	GI(85)	x			BI(214)	x	x
DU(206)	x			GU(559)	x	(x?)		BU(371)	x	x
TA(139)	x	x	x	KA(15)	x	x	x	PA(295)	x	x
TE(376)	x	x								
TI(73)	x	x		KI(461)	x	x	x			
TU(58)	x	x		KU(536)	x	x	x			
TUM(207)	x	x								
				QA(62)	x	x	x			
				QI(538)			x			
ṬU(595)			x	QU(191)			x			

It will be noted that, apart from the signs BI and BU, for which no voiceless correspondents exist in this syllabary,[8] the voiced signs occur only for voiced and emphatic phones in Ugaritic words, not for voiceless phones, with one rather dubious exception. Conversely, the voiceless signs, as already noted, are used indiscriminately for voiceless, voiced, and emphatic phones. The signs for stops thus appear to reflect a bipartite system in which one set, the "voiceless" signs (and BI and BU), is unmarked for voice (or emphatic articulation), while another set, the "voiced" signs, is specifically marked as not voiceless. The number of examples is, however, too small to be certain that we are dealing with an actual system here, and not simply with coincidence. An analogous system is not discernible in the use of these signs in the writing of Akkadian words in these texts, nor in the signs used for writing Ugaritic (or Akkadian) sibilants and other fricatives (see 2, below); further, the origin of such an orthographic system within peripheral Akkadian would be difficult to pinpoint.[9] For these reasons it has seemed best, in our transliterations of the stops in Ugaritic words, to write either the basic value of the sign, in upper case, or the appropriate *phonemic* value of the stops. Thus, e.g., the word */maddatu/* "measurement," even though it may have been pronounced [maddadu], will be transliterated *ma-ad-da-DU*

[8]The PI sign is used in Ugarit Akk., except in a few instances in literary and lexical texts (but not in the S^{a} Voc. exemplars), only for *wv* and *yv*; see further below, n. 66.

[9]Neither the "marked" set nor the "unmarked" set coincides with Old Akkadian usage, where, for example, DA and DU are used for *da, ta* and *du, tu,* respectively, and BA, not PA, is used for *ba, pa.* The coincidence of usage between the "unmarked" set and the set of signs used by Hurrian scribes in the Mittanni letter EA 24 (see Bush, GHL 18-22) is higher, but again, not complete (e.g., DU, not TU, is used for *d/to/u*). It seems gratuitous to note that the use of the voiced signs for voiced phones corresponds to OB and MB usage.

or *ma-ad-da-tù,* but not *ma-ad-da-du.*[10]

The use of the *vC* signs for the stops (AD, ID, UD, AG, IG, UG, AB, IB, UB) is unremarkable. As was true throughout the history of Akkadian orthography, these signs do not distinguish among voiced, voiceless, or emphatic stops: e.g., AB in *ab-du* = /*ᶜabdu*/ "slave" (ᶜBD) and *ap-pu* = /*ˀappu*/ "nose" (ˀNP); AG in ITI *ma-ag-ma-r*[*i*] = /*magmari*/ (MN) and *: ma-aq-qa-du* = /*maqqadu*/ "grazing-rights(?)" (NQD).

2. Cv *and* vC *Signs for Sibilants and other Fricatives*

The following chart illustrates the use of *Cv* signs to represent the Ugaritic sibilants and other fricative phonemes:

sign	/ðv/	/zv/	/ẓv/	/sv/	/ṣv/	/šv/	/θv/
SA (104)				x		x	
SI (112)				x			
SU (7)				x			
ZA (586)		x		x	x		
ZI (84)	x	x		x	x		
ZU (6)	(x)	x	x	x	x		
ṢI (ZÉ 147)					x		
ṢU (ZUM 555)					x		
ŠA (353)						x	x
ŠÁ (597)						x	
ŠI (449)						x	x
ŠU (354)				x		x	x

With the exception of /ð/ (see below), the signs used to represent these Ugaritic phonemes fall consistently into two groups:

Z-signs to represent /z/, /ẓ/(?),[11] /s/, /ṣ/, with the occasional use of S-signs for /s/ and Ṣ-signs for /ṣ/;

Š-signs to represent /š/ and /θ/.

Among the former group, no pattern emerges when the possible phonetic realizations

[10]Furthermore, to take the opposite course, and write transliterations according to the possible *phonetic* value of the signs for stops, would result in a much larger number of cumbersome renderings, such as *da-ga*$_{14}$(KA)-*rù* for /*dakaru*/ ([dagaru]), *tu-gi*$_{5}$(KI)-*ii* for /*tōkīyi*/ ([tōgīyi]), *ḫal-la-dì* (TI) for /*ḥallati*/ ([ḥalladi]), etc.

[11]The sole possible example of /ẓ/ in the syllabic transcriptions, in *: ZU-ur-PI* = /*ẓurwu*/? "(aromatic) resin," may actually be /ṣ/ (/*ṣurwu*/?); see under ẒRW in the Glossary.

of the words are taken into account, unlike the situation with the signs for stops described above; thus, e.g., we find both SA and ZA for both [sa] and [za]: *SA-ap-lu* and *ZA-ap-lu* = /*saplu*/ = [sablu] "cauldron" (SPL); $^{\text{giš.meš}}$*ma-SA-wa-tu* = /*masawātu*/ = [mazawādu] "cypress(?) logs" (MSW); *ma-al-ZA-mu* = /*malsamu*/ = [malzamu] "course(?)/courier(?)" (LSM). There are two exceptions in the representation of these phonemes: ^{d}*SA-li-mu* for /*šalimu*/ (DN; ŠLM a) and *ŠU-KU-ru* for /*sug/kuru*/ "bolt" (SGR a). The former should be compared with SA for *ša* in Ugarit Akk. *SA-al(-)m[i,* for *šāl/šaʾal* "ask!" (EA 49:26),[12] and may reflect the OAkk. component of WPA orthography, since in OAkk. etymological **š* was normally written with S-signs;[13] the latter occurs between expected writings *ZU-KU-ru/ri,* and may therefore simply be a scribal error.[14]

The two examples of /*ð*/ are both written with Z-signs, so that /*ð*/ appears to fall in with the /*z*/, /*ẓ*/, /*s*/, /*ṣ*/ group. But the use of Z-signs in the two instances, a very small sample, may be coincidental, and other evidence, from the writing of names, indicates that /*ð*/ could be written with signs of either group, i.e., with either Z-signs or Š-signs. See §E 2, under /*ð*/.

The *vC* signs for sibilants and other fricatives have the following distribution among the syllabic transcriptions of Ugaritic words:

sign	/*vð*/	/*vz*/	/*vẓ*/	/*vs*/	/*vṣ*/	/*vš*/	/*vθ*/
AZ(131)				x			
IZ(296)					x		
UZ(372)							
ÁŠ(339)				x			x
AŠ(1)						x	x
IŠ(212)						x	
UŠ(211)							x

The few examples of these signs break down into the same groups as the corresponding *Cv* signs, with the notable exception of the ÁŠ sign, which occurs for /*as*/ in $^{\text{giš(.meš)}}$*ma-ÁŠ-wa-tu* = /*maswātu*/ "cypress(?) logs" (bis; vs. the biform $^{\text{giš.meš}}$*ma-SA-wa-tu* = /*masawātu*/; MSW), and probably for /*aθ*/ in *ma-ÁŠ-ḫa-ṭu-ma* = /*maθḫaṭūma*/? "(cloths)" (θḪṬ), but, interestingly, not for /*aš*/, which is only written with AŠ.[15]

[12]The reading is W.L. Moran's (private communication).

[13]Gelb, MAD 2^2 35-40.

[14]But note also Akk. *ŠU-um-mu-*[*uḫ*] for *summuḫ* (but see the copy: also a scribal error?), cited at the beginning of the preceding section.

[15]Note that ÁŠ also corresponds to alphab. *ð* in the GN ^{uru}*ÁŠ-da-di* = alphab. *aðdd*; see §E 2 a. The distribution and phonetic values of the ÁŠ sign in Ugarit Akk. require comment: it occurs

3. *Signs used for the Ugaritic Gutturals*

The representation of the Ugaritic gutturals is considered in detail below, §E 4. Here it will suffice to state generally that with few exceptions, the series of Ḫ-signs (ḪA, ḪÉ [KAN], ḪI, ḪU, AḪ) is used for Ugar. /ḥ/, /ḫ/, and /ǵ/, while the remaining three gutturals, /ʾ/, /h/, and /ʿ/, are either represented by the ʾ sign or by extra vowel-signs, or simply unexpressed in the writing.

4. CvC *Signs*

The *CvC* signs, of course, present all the difficulties of interpretation of both *Cv* and *vC* signs, but their use in the writing of Ugaritic words is otherwise unremarkable when compared with their occurrence in Ugarit Akk. texts in general. In not a few instances, the use of a *CvC* sign may be compared with a *Cv-vC* sequence with the same phonological value in another word, or even in the same word; as usual in matters of syllabic orthography, the choice of one writing over the other was apparently simply a matter of scribal whim. For the sake of completeness, all examples of *CvC* signs in the Ugaritic words are listed here, in the order of their sign number.[16]

2 ḪAL = *ḫal* in ITI *ḫal-la-t*[*u*]/*ti* = /*ḥallatu*/*i*/ (MN; ḤLL); *ZI-ZA-ḫal-li-ma* = /?/ "?" (see Appendix to Glossary)

12 TAR = *tar* in *: ti-tar-ḫ*[*u*] = /*tiʾ*/*ttarḫu*/ "she will hurry" (ʾRḪ); cf. *: ta-ar-bá-ṣí* = /*tarbaṣi*/ "stable" (RBṢ);
= *dar*$_6$?, in *TAR-QU* = /*darqu*/? "path" (DRQ); ^{túg}*pa-ḫa-TAR-ru* = /*paǵaddarru*/ "(garment)" (PǴ(N)DR);

74 MAŠ = *maš* in *maš-ka-ni* = /*maškani*/? "habitation(?)" (ŠKN); cf. *ma-aš-la-ḫa-ma* = /*mašlaḥāma*/ "(garments)" (dual; ŠLḤ); *ma-aš-nu-ú*? = /*mašnūʾu*/? "enemy(?)" (ŠNʾ);

88 KAB = *kab* in *mar-kab-te* = /*markabti*/? "chariot(?)" (RKB);

90 GAD note the pseudo-logogram MA.GAD for /*maqqadu*/ "grazing rights(?)" (cf. *: ma-aq-qa-du* = /*maqqadu*/; NQD);

111 GUR = *gur* in the possibly Ugar. *gur-bi-ZU* = /*gurbizū*/ "hauberk" (or Akk.?; GRBZ); cf. *gu*!-*ur*!-*bi-su* in PRU 6 140:1;

---

only rarely in Akk. words, and then only in lexical and literary texts and only with the value *áš*; in non-canonical texts, other than in the two Ugaritic words noted here, it occurs only in PN's, and never to denote /*aš*/ (for examples, see §E 2 b).

[16]See above, n. 5.

124 TAB = *dáb* in the Akkadianized form *ú-dáb-bi-qa-an-ni* "he put me together" (DBQ);

= *tap* in *tap-de*$_4$*-ti/tu*$_4$, vs. *: ta-ap-de*$_4$*-ti* = */tapdēti/u/* "exchange" (PDY);

129 NAB = *nab/p* in *naB-ku, naB-ki-ma,* vs. *: na-aB-ki-ma* = */nab/pku, -īma/* "spring"(NBK);

149 RAB = *rap* in *rap-⌜ú?⌝[* = */rapˀu/* "purification(?)" (RPˀ);

192 GAZ = *kàs* in *kàs-pu* = */kaspu/* "silver" (vs. *ka-as-pu* in the following line of the same text; KSP);

295k ŠAB = *šab/p* in *: šab-⌜li?-mi?⌝* = */šablimi/??* "retaining wall(??)" (BLM); *šap-ḫu* = */šapḫu/* "sprout, scion" (ŠPḤ);

307 MAR = *mar* in $^{\text{(lú(.meš))}}$*mar-ia(-an)-nu/ni(-ma)* = */maryannū/ī(ma)/* "charioteers" (MRYN); [^{túg}*m*]*ar-de*$_4$*-tu* = */mardētu/?* "(garment)" (RDY); *mar-de*$_4$*-em-tu* = */mardimtu/?* "path(?)" (RDM); *mar-ḫi-iš* = */marḫiš(u)/* "(a utensil)" (RḪŠ); *mar-kab-te* = */markabti/?* "chariot(?)" (RKB); *mar-za/zi-i* = [marza/iᶜi] "symposium" (RZḤ); with the last, cf. *ma-ar-zi-ḫi* = [marziḥi];

314 ŠID = *lak* in *pí-lak-ku* = */pilakku/* "spindle" (vs. Akk. *pí-la-ak-ku* in the same line; PLK^1);[17]

331e SAR = *sar* in *sar-rù* = */sarru/* "false" (SRR);

= *šar* in *ku-šar-ru* = */kōθaru/* (divine name; KθR);[18]

343 GAL = *qal* in *qal-lu,* vs. *qá-al-lu* = */qallu/* "small" (QLL);

355 LUL = *lip* in Akkadianized *lip-ḫu-dú-ma* "may they fear" (PḤ/ḪD);

401 ḪAR = *ḫar* in ^{túg}*šá-ḫar-tu* = */šaᶜartu/* "wool" (ŠᶜR b); vs. ^{urudu}*ḫa-ar-me-ša-tu* = */ḫarmiθātu/* "sickles(?)" (ḪRMθ); *ḫa-ar-ma-ni* = */ḥarmāni/* "sacred place(?)" (ḤRM b);

= *mur* in $^{\text{lú(.meš)}}$*mur-ú/i(-ma)* = */murˀu, -ū/īma/* "commander(s)(?)" (MRˀ);

= *ḫur* in *ḫur-ḫu-ra-ti* = */ḥurḥur(r)ati/* "(a plant)" (ḤRḤR);

554 SAL = *šal* in *šal-li-ma,* vs. *ša-li-ma* (same text) = */šallima/* "it paid, delivered" (ŠLM b);

575 UR = *lik* in ^{d}*ma-lik*^{meš} = */mālikūma/?* (DN; MLK c).[19]

[17]Note also 314 MES = RIT in the (pseudo-logogram) writing ^{lú}A.RIT (see HRT in the Glossary).

[18]For the doubly written *r*, see below, §D 2.

[19]Note also no. 143 KAN = *gan* in ^{d}*da-gan*, probably Akk. rather than Ugar. (DGN).

B. Determinatives

The use of determinatives with syllabically spelled words is relatively common in Ugarit Akkadian.[20] Among the Ugaritic words, roughly 15-20 percent[21] are furnished with a determinative which, with the exception of the plural marker ^{meš}, always precedes the word. As is generally true throughout the cuneiform tradition, the use of a determinative is optional, as several examples demonstrate (see, e.g., under ᵓZR, YṢR, KDD, Nᵓ, NGD, ǴMR). The following determinatives occur with the Ugaritic words:

1/m normally the determinative before men's (and, rarely, women's) names, $^{\text{l/m}}$ (a single vertical wedge, the DIŠ sign) also appears (three times), in addition to expected ^{lú} (also three times), before the word /*sākinu*/ "prefect" (SKN a);[22]

d before divine names in the god-lists Ug. 5 18, Ug. 5 170 (see under KNR; MLK c; ᶜNT; ŠLM a), but not in the polyglot god-list at the end of Ug. 5 137; also in a field designation (ᶜLY a);

dug before pots, jars; see under KDD, KPR, and *ki-ra-li-nu* in the Appendix to the Glossary;

giš before trees and items of wood; see under MSW, SGR a, ṢWᶜ, θǴR, θQD (and *ma-am-*[and *ni-ru*?/-*ú*?[in the Appendix to the Glossary);

íd before river/canal name; see under RḤB;[23]

lú before words denoting professions; see under BDL, BḤR, BRḤ, GLB, YṢR, YQŠ, KBS a, KMR, LBN², MD, MḪṢ a, MRᵓ, MRYN, NSK, NǴR a, SKN a, ᶜRB, ᶜŠR¹, ǴMR, ṢLL, θNN;

meš after either a determinative before the word (e.g., $^{\text{túg.meš}}$*ma-za-ru-ma*) or after the syllabic spelling of the word, with or without a determinative (e.g., ^{dug}*ka-du-ma*^{meš}, *qà-da-ru-ma*^{meš}), or both ($^{\text{túg.meš}}$*mu-ru-ú-ma*^{meš}, $^{\text{lú.meš}}$*ḫa-am-ru-ma*^{meš}, $^{\text{urudu.meš}}$*ma-ṣa-du-ma*^{meš}); see under ᵓZR, BDL, BḤR, YRᵓ, KDD, KMR, KSL, KPR, MD, MḪṢ b, MLK c, MSW, MRᵓ, MRYN, Nᵓ, NQB, SKK, ᶜṢD, ᶜRB, ᶜŠR¹, ǴMR, ṢWᶜ, QDR, QṬN;

mí/f the normal determinative before women's names; also before words denoting

---

[20]See the relevant section in my Akkadian of Ugarit.

[21]Because of the semantic nature of words that tend to attract determinatives, the majority of examples occur in economic texts, in lists of personnel, garments, vessels, and items of wood and metal.

[22]Other examples of ^{l} before forms other than PN's in Ugarit Akkadian texts are ^{l}*a-bi-šu* (PRU 3 32f.:6,9,15; apparently "his father" rather than a PN) and ^{l}MÍ.LUGAL-*ti* (PRU 3 51f.:16; = *šarrati* "queen," vs. ^{lf}PN MÍ.LUGAL-*tu*$_4$ ibid.:4).

[23]For ITI, which is probably a logogram rather than a determinative, see under ᵓθB, GMR, ḤLL, ḪYR. In the writing KI.MEŠ *ḫa-ar-ma-ni* (ḤRM b), it is unclear whether KI.MEŠ is a determinative or a logogram.

women's status or profession: see under BRḤ;[24]

túg before items of cloth or fabric; see under ʾZR, YRʾ, KND, KPθ, NGD, SKK, PLD, PǴ(N)DR, ᶜWR, Šᶜ R b (and *ib-lu* in the Appendix to the Glossary);

urudu before items of copper/bronze; see under HLM, ḪRMθ, MṢR, ᶜṢD.

Also a determinative, of sorts, is the gloss mark, which is considered in the next section.

C. The Gloss Mark[25]

The gloss mark, which we will indicate in transliteration by a colon (:), is normally composed of two small angled wedges (the GAM sign).[26] The many occurrences of the gloss mark in Ugarit Akkadian texts may be grouped under four general functions, as outlined below.[27] (For the gloss mark before Ugaritic words in particular, see 1 b, 3 b, and 4.) It should be noted that, regardless of its function, use of the gloss mark is entirely optional;[28] see further below.

1. *Word Divider*

a. To separate variant readings of a logogram in the Akkadian columns of a lexical text: only in MSL 14 143f. ii 25',26'.

b. To separate words in columned texts when a word in the left column breaks into the adjacent column to the right. Most examples occur in the polyglot S^a Vocabulary texts (and in the polyglot god-list attached to Ug. 5 137).[29] As it happens, this use of the gloss mark was necessary only between the third and

[24]Note also $^{mí/f}$ in ^{f}*a-ḫa-tu*$_4$*/ti*-LUGAL; see under ʾḪ.

[25]Although the indication of a following gloss is only one of the functions of the sign in question, it seems preferable to use the term "gloss mark" (or German "Glossenkeil") than to introduce a new term for it at this juncture.

[26]Already noted by Swaim, Grammar 72 n. 18, an exception occurs in PRU 3 169a:3, where the gloss mark is a single wedge.

[27]Only a summary of the uses is presented here, except as concerns the Ugaritic vocabulary; for more detailed discussion, see my Akkadian of Ugarit. Our presentation of the use of the gloss mark essentially follows Boyd's excellent treatment in Collection, 9-23; see also Kühne, UF 6 157-67 (esp. 158-59), 7 253-60; Swaim, Grammar 7-8.

[28]So also in the Canaanizing Amarna letters, in the Alalaḫ texts, and in Hittite texts from Boğazköy, as noted by Boyd, Collection 12; see also Artzi, Bar-Ilan 1 24-57.

[29]Exceptions are three instances in two bilingual (Sum.-Akk.) literary texts: Ug. 5 165:4',10'; 5 166:7'.

fourth columns, i.e., between some of the longer Hurrian entries and the Ugaritic entries that followed: e.g.,

ZA *a-mi-lu* *tar-⌜šu-wa-an⌝-ni* : *bu-nu-⌜šu⌝* Ug. 5 130 ii 5' (S^a Voc. no. 22.2).

Other examples in the polyglot vocabularies appear in Ug. 5 130 iii 4' (no. 32.4), 11' (no. 35/36.3), 16' (no. 37.4), 20' (no. 40.2); 5 131 7' (no. 51.2?), 8' (no. 53.4/54)?; 5 137 ii 35' (no. 189.2), 46' (no. 192.2), iii 36", 38" (both in god-list).

Since this use of the gloss mark does not indicate anything special about the word that follows it, but rather is simply part of the formatting of the texts in question, these instances of the gloss mark will not be indicated in the translitera-tion elsewhere in the present study.

3. To separate two unassociated logograms: only in *5 pu-ri-du₄* A.ŠÀ : GÍD.DA Ug. 5 5:6 (legal text).[30]

2. *Line Connector*

To mark material as part of the preceding line:

a. A word or part of a word at the end of a line, e.g., [10] ... *a-na* LUGAL [11]... : *be-li-šu* PRU 3 68f.:10-11; other examples: PRU 3 106f. r.2'-3'; 3 47f.:11-12,15-16, 20-21; 3 79ff.:15-16; 3 96ff.:35-36 (probably also ibid.:26-27).

b. A word or phrase comprising an entire line, probably to mark the line as a semantic unit with the preceding line,[31] e.g., [2] ... PN [3] : DUMU PN_2, Syria 16 194:2-3.

3. *Gloss Indicator after a Logogram*

a. Akkadian gloss:[32] e.g., [*qa*]-*du* É GIBIL : *eš₁₅*(IŠ)-*ši* PRU 3 119f.:4; other examples: PRU 3 47a:15; 3 47f.:11,13; 3 172b:2'; Ug. 5 24:14.

b. Ugaritic gloss: A.ŠÀ MUN$^{(meš)}$: *ZI-ṣú(-ú)-ma* (ṢYṢ); perhaps also $^{lú.meš}$DAM.GÀR^{meš} :*bi-da-lu-ma*[33] (BDL); ^{é}IM.D[Ù?.A?-*š*]*u*? : *šab-⌜li?-mi?⌝*

[30]Boyd, Collection 12.

[31]See Kühne, UF 6 158 n. 4. Normally, of course, no gloss mark appears at the beginning of a line, even if the preceding line ends in a preposition or a bound form, as in PRU 3 79ff.:31-32; 3 96ff.:18-19 (both texts in which several gloss marks appear); 3 143ff.:15-16; PRU 6 8:17-18.

[32]That the gloss mark is optional in such situations is shown, e.g., by ḪA.LA^{meš} *zi-te* PRU 3 54a:6; see further PRU 3 76a:5; 3 101f.:15; 3 102ff.:49; EA 45:32; 49:19.

[33]It is possible that Ugar. */bidălūma/* qualifies the logogram here, i.e., specifies a particular kind of merchant (see Alt, WO 2 338-42); but see Astour, ABAW NF 75 11-12.

(BLM); ^{túg}TÙN!? :!? *su-nu* (S'N); ⸢KID??⸣ : *pu-wa-ti*[34] (PWT); É KISLAḪ : *ta-am-kí* (TMK).

c. Hurrian gloss: ^{síg}SA$_5$: *ta-ba?-ri* TA 8 7f.:40; KI.BI.GAR.RA : *pu-ḫu-ga*$_{14}$*-ru-ši* PRU 3 51f.:7.

It is only in these examples that the sign under discussion functions as a true "gloss" mark, that is, as a sign of equivalence between the forms on either side of it.[35] Note that all of the examples gloss logograms. It has been suggested (e.g., Boyd, Collection 15) that the sign also appears before words in a few instances to mark glosses of preceding Akkadian words, and once to mark a gloss of a preceding Ugaritic word. But because of the rarity of such instances, and because each is subject to an alternate interpretation, it is unlikely that the sign was ever so used in Ugarit Akk. Thus, in PRU 3 137f.:4, where Nougayrol read [... *du-r*]*i* : *ḫa-me-ti,* with Akk. *dūri* "wall" glossed by Ugar. /*ḥāmīti*/ "wall" (ḤMY), the reading [*du-r*]*i* is only a possibility; the copy and the broken context also permit, e.g., [*š*]*a* or [*i-n*]*a*. In Ug. 5 3 r.10', Ugar. *ti-tar-ḫ*[*u*] = /*ti*'/*ttarḫu*/ "she will hurry" ('RḪ) does not gloss Akk. *tirḫuṣ* "she will(!) run," but rather qualifies it in hendiadys, "she will run quickly." In EA 48:8 Akk. *riq-qú* "aromatic substance" is followed by Ugar. : *ZU-ur-wu* "(aromatic) resin"; here too, I would suggest, the Ugaritic form qualifies more precisely the rather generic Akk. term, rather than actually glossing it. Finally, for PRU 6 56:4', where Boyd would see one Ugar. word glossed by another, see under b, above (BLM).

4. *"Foreign" Word Indicator*

As Boyd (Collection 11) has noted, the gloss mark precedes Akkadian words (and logograms) only in the situations outlined in 1 - 3, above. In all other instances, the function of the sign is to mark the following word as non-Akkadian. We may assume this to obtain even when the word exists in the Akkadian lexicon. Thus, for example, the gloss marks before *qú-bu-ri* in PRU 3 51f.:8,18 and before *ta-ar-bá-ṣí* in PRU 3 91f.:17 indicate that Ugaritic words (cf. alphabetic *qbr, trbṣ*; see QBR, RBṢ) rather than Akkadian *qubūru* and *tarbaṣu* are intended, since no other explanation for the occurrence of the gloss mark in these instances presents itself.

a. In one instance, the non-Akkadian word is probably Hurrian: É : *ku-na-ḫi* Ug. 5

[34]This word is probably a loan into Ugaritic, but since alphab. *pwt* is attested, we may consider it part of the Ugar. lexicon, and so list it here; see n. 37 of the Introduction.

[35]Nougayrol considered a number of other examples of the gloss mark before Ugaritic words to fall into this group; see, e.g., PRU 3 pp. 217-18 (on $^{(é)}$AN.ZA.GÀR), 225-26 (on ŠÀM.TIL.LA.BI.ŠÈ; see the Glossary above under ṢMT). In the majority, if not all, of these, however, the gloss sign serves to mark the following word as non-Akkadian; see under 4, below.

5:10,20.[36]

b. All other examples in our corpus of texts are Ugaritic words.[37] The majority of these occur in legal texts (often in designations of plots of land or other property, although such designations, like most syllabic transcriptions, more commonly appear without a gloss mark[38]); The few exceptions appear in economic texts (and are marked as such below). The following is a complete list:

: *na-ba-dì(-⌜šu-nu⌝)* = /*na*ʾ*badi*/ "escape" (ʾBD);
A.ŠÀ : *ad-ma-ni* = /ʾ*admāni*/ "red (soil)" (ʾDM);
: *ti-tar-ḫ[u]* = /*ti*ʾ/*ttarḫu*/ "she will hurry" (ʾRḪ);
[A.ŠÀ]ḫi.a : *ga-bi-ni* = /*gabīni*/? "hillock(?)" (GBN);
A.ŠÀḫi.a : *dì-ip-ra-ni-ma* = /*diprānīma*/ "junipers" (DPR);
A.ŠÀḫi.a : *mi-dá-ar-ú* = /*midar*ʿ*u*/? "seed-land" (DRʿ);
: *ḫa-me-ti* = /*ḥāmīti*/ "wall" (ḤMY);
AN.ZA.GÀR-*šu* : *ḫa-a-yi*, : *ḫi-i-yi(-šu)*, Éḫi.a : *ḫé-yi-ma* (but É *ḫe-e-ia*/*yu*, without gloss mark) = /*ḫāliyv*/ "vacant(?)" (ḪWY);
A.ŠÀḫi.a : *ma-aḫ-ZI-ZI* = /*maḫṣīṣi*/? "divide(?)" (ḪṢṢ);
É : *ḫi-ri-ti* = /*ḫirīti*/ "cemetary" (ḪRY);
: *ḫa-at-ni* = /*ḫatni*/? "son-in-law" (ḪTN);
: *ZU-ur-PI* = /*ẓurwu*/? (or /*ṣurwu*/?) "(aromatic) resin" (ẒRW)
A.ŠÀ : *ka(-an)-na-BI-PI* = /*kannăpīyv*/? "?" (KNP b);
Econ. : *ka-ar-ba-DU*[= /*karbātu*/? "twisted(?)" (KRB);
: *ma-ad-da-DU* = /*maddatu*/? "measurement" (MDD);
(A.ŠÀmeš) : *NAB*/*na-AB*/*ba*/*bá-ki-ma* = /*nab(a)kīma*/ "springs" (7 times, vs. one occurrence without gloss mark; NBK);
: *ma-aq-qa-du* = /*maqqadu*/ "grazing rights(?)" (vs. *mu-qa-dì-IM* = /*muqqādi*/?, without gloss mark; NQD);
A.ŠÀ : *sí-il-a* = /*sil*ʿ*a*/ "cliff(?)" (3 times, vs. once without gloss mark; SLʿ);
[AN.ZA].GÀR : *am-qa* = /ʿ*amqa*/ "stronghold(?)" (note also GN : [*am*?]-*qà*; ʿMQ[1]);
: *ma-a*ʾ*-ša-ri(-ša)* = /*ma*ʿ*šari*/ "tithe" (vs. *ma-ša-ra* = /*ma*ʿ*šara*/, without; ʿŠR[2]);
A.ŠÀḫi.a : *ḫu-li* = /*ġōli*/? "low ground(?)" (ĠWL);
: *ta-ap-de*$_4$*-ti* = /*tapdēti*/*u*/ "exchange" (but *tap-de*$_4$*-ti*/*tu*$_4$, without gloss mark; PDY);
A.ŠÀ(meš) : *ṣí-ib-bi-ri* = /*ṣibbīri*/ "collective land(?)" (twice, vs. *ṣí(-ib)-bi-ri*, without gloss mark, passim in PRU 6 55; ṢBR);

[36]See Nougayrol's comments, Ug. 5 p. 8 n. 1. The meaning of the term is unknown; in view of the sporadic alternation of *l* and *n* in Hurrian (Speiser, IH 27 §37), perhaps we should compare the (plural) form *kulaḫḫenna*, an epithet applied to gods (references in Laroche, GLH 151).

[37]The appearance of a gloss mark before a personal name in A.ŠÀ : [1]ÌR-DINGIR-*ti* (PRU 3 79ff.:5), discussed at some length by Kühne, UF 6 160-62, is in all probability simply a scribal error, occasioned by the use of the gloss mark before Ugaritic words in the following two lines.

[38]See above, pp. 10-11.

A.ŠÀ *: ṣa-i* = /*ṣāʿi*/ "basin" (once, vs. 9 times without gloss mark; ṢWʿ);
: ṣa-ma-ta = /*ṣamata*/, *: ṣa-ma-DU* = /*ṣamatū*/ "it was/they were transferred" (note also Akkadianized D *: ṣú-um-mu-ta*; vs. Akkadianized G forms *sa-mi-it* and *ṣa-ma-at*, passim; ṢMT);
É-*tu*₄ *: qú-bu-ri* = /*qubūri*/ "burial" (QBR);
É-*tu*₄ *: ta-ar-bá-ṣí* = /*tarbaṣi*/ "stable" (RBṢ);
A.ŠÀ(ḫi.a/meš) (íd)*(:) ra-aḫ-ba/bá-ni/na*[39] = /*raḥbāni/a*/ "wide place" (RḤB);
É KISLAḪ *: TA-am-GI* = /*tamki*/? "?" (TMK);
: ḫa-A[B-B]I = /?/ "?" (but *ḫa-AB-BU*, without gloss mark; see Appendix to Glossary);
(A.ŠÀmeš) *: ḫa-ar-ZA-ti* = /?/ "?" (see Appendix to Glossary);
: ra-⌜PA⌝-ni = /?/ "?" (see Appendix to Glossary);
Econ. *: ú-ṭu* = /?/ "?" (see Appendix to Glossary);
ZI-ZA-ḫal-li-ma = /?/ "?" (see Appendix to Glossary).[40]

D. The Indication of Consonant Doubling

1. *Expected Doubling*

As is well known, the indication of consonantal doubling is optional in Akkadian texts of all periods and dialects; thus, for example, a form such as *iparras* may be written either *i-pa-ar-ra-as* (or *i-par-ra-as*) or *i-pa-ra-as*. In Akkadian texts written at Ugarit, consonantal doubling is orthographically indicated, very approximately, in about half of the instances in which it is expected.[41] This is also true of the writing of Ugaritic words, as the following sample demonstrates:

a. Doubling indicated:
um-ma-ti = /*ʾummati*/? "clan(?)" (ʾMM); *ap-pu* = /*ʾappu*/ "nose" (ʾNP); *at-ta* = /*ʾattă*/ "you (ms)" (ʾNT); *⌜ba⌝-aḫ-ḫu-rù* = /*baḫḫuru*/ (or /*baḥḥuru*/) "youth" (BḪR); ITI *ḫal-la-ti/t[u?]* = /*ḥallati/u*/ (month name; ḤLL); *ḫe-en-ni-ṣu* = /*ḫinnīṣu*/? "piglet" (ḪNṢ); *: ma-ad-da-DU* = /*maddatu*/? "measurement" (MDD); *: ma-aq-qa-du* = /*maqqadu*/ "grazing rights(?)" (NQD); *sar-rù* = /*sarru*/ "false" (SRR); *pí-lak-ku* = /*pilakku*/ "spindle" (PLK¹).

[39]Note that the gloss mark appears after the determinative when both occur (PRU 6 56 r.2'); see Kühne, UF 6 159 with n. 12.

[40]See also PRU 3 96ff.:27; 3 140f.:8; 3 155f.:5-6.

[41]For example, one finds both *ur/ur*₅*-ra* (e.g., PRU 3 50f.:15; 3 99b:12) and *ú-ra* (e.g., PRU 3 77b:11) for *urra*; *a-nu-um-ma* (e.g., PRU 3 54ff.:21) and *a-nu-ma* (PRU 3 85f.:21) for *anumma*; *i-din* (e.g., PRU 3 47a:12) and *id-din* (e.g., PRU 3 45f.:9) for *iddin*; *i-la-aq-qè* (e.g., PRU 3 101f.:11)/*i-laq-qè* (e.g., PRU 3 45f.:15) and *i-la-qè* (e.g., PRU 3 73f.:14); and many other such examples; for details, see my Akkadian of Ugarit.

b. Doubling not indicated:[42]

bu-ri = /*burri*/? "(a bright metal?)" (BRR); [lú]*ga*5(QA)-*la-b*[*u*?] = /*gallăbu*/ "barber" (GLB); [*ḫ*]*a-ra-š*[*u*] = /*ḫar(r)ašu*/ "deaf(?)" (ḪRŠ); [dug]*ka-du-ma*[meš] = /*kaddūma*/ "jars" (KDD); *QA-QA-ra* = /*kakkara*/ "talent" (KKR); [d.giš]*ki-na-rù* = /*kinnāru*/ "lyre" (divine name; KNR); [lú]*la-*⌜*ba*?⌝*-nu* = /*labbănu*/ "brickmaker" (LBN[2]); *ma-qa-ḫa* = /*maqqaḥā*/ "pair of tongs" (LQḤ b); *pu-la-ṭu* = /*pullaṭu*/ "to save" (PLṬ); [lú]*ma-ṣi-lu* = /*maṣillu*/ "cymbalist" (ṢLL); *ra-ba-ti* = /*rabbati*/ "great" (RBB).

Note also the following sets of examples, in which the same word is written with and without graphic representation of a doubled consonant:

ú-nu-uš-ša and *ú-nu-ša* = /*ʾunuθθa*/ "estate tax" (ʾNθ); [lú.meš]*mar-ia-an-ni* = /*maryannī*/ and [(lú(.meš))]*mar-ia-nu(-ma)* = /*maryannu, -ūma*/ "charioteer(s)" (MRYN); *(:)ṣí-ib-bi-ri* and *ṣí-bi-ri* = /*ṣibbīri*/ "public land(?)" (ṢBR); *šal-li-ma* and *ša-li-ma* = /*šallima*/ "it paid, delivered" (ŠLM b).

The optional indication of doubling frequently results in uncertainty regarding the precise shape or morphological pattern of a word; note, e.g., the following:

: ti-tar-ḫ[*u*] = /*tiʾtarḫu*/ or /*tittarḫu*/ "she will hurry" (ʾRḪ or YRḪ)?
gu-wa-⌜*li*⌝ = /*guwăli*/ or /*guwwăli*/ (< **gaw(w)ăli*?) "circuit?" (GWL)?
[*ḫ*]*a-ra-š*[*u*] = /*ḫarašu*/ or /*ḫarrašu*/? "deaf(?)" (ḪRŠ)?
na-ḫa-li = /*naḫali*/ or /*naḫalli*/ "wadi" (NḪL)?
qà-da-ru-ma[meš] = /*qadarūma*/ or /*qaddarūma*/ "(containers)" (QDR)?

2. *Incorrect Doubling*

In Ugarit Akkadian texts, the occurrence of graphically doubled consonants that are phonologically or morphologically incorrect, such as *za-ak-ki* for expected *zaki* (PRU 3 110a:5), is not common.[43] Apart from a few Assyrian forms (see n. 43),

[42]Doubling is not indicated for /*w*/ or /*y*/, since the values *vw* and *vy* (for which, presumably, the PI sign would be used; see AS[3] no. 233) do not occur in the Ugarit Akkadian syllabary (but see §E 3 c, n. 101); thus, [*ḫ*]*u-wa-tu*4 = /*ḥuwwatu*/ "country" (ḤWW); *ḫu-PI-ú* = /*ḥuwwû*/ "to save" (ḤYY[1]/ḤWY[1] a); *ḫé-PI-ma* and *ḫi-*[*I*]*A?-ma* = /*ḥiyyūma*/ "life" (ḤYY[1]/ḤWY[1] b).

[43]There are a number of examples of *-itt* for expected *-īt* (e.g., *da-ri-it-ti* PRU 3 83f.:19) and *-utt* for *-ūt* (e.g., [*an*?*-n*]*u-ut-ti*? "these?" PRU 3 72f.:29; [lú.meš]DAM.GÀR-*ut-ti* "merchants" PRU 6 30:10; see also below, under c), but these are Assyrian forms, and thus not really instances of "incorrect" doubling; see von Soden, GAG §20d; idem, UF 11 748. It should be noted that several examples of incorrect doublings in Akkadian words are found in the Ugarit lexical texts, of the type in which many of our Ugaritic words appear; thus, for example, *za-am-ma-rù* for *zamāru* (= Ugar. *ši-i-ru* for /*šīru*/ [Ug. 5 137 iii 7]; see S[a] Voc. no. 197.2); others appear in the trilingual (no Ugar. column) S[a] Voc. text Ug. 5 135: *iz-zi-zu* for *izuzzu* (line 6'), *QI-en-nu* for *kīnu* (Ass. *kēnu*; line 7'), *pé-eṣ-ṣú* for *peṣû* (line 19'). For further details, see my Akkadian of Ugarit.

there is no clear evidence that consonantal doubling was used to indicate vocalic length (i.e., *vC:* for *v:C*).[44] The number of incorrect doublings in Ugaritic words is very small; apart from the few forms listed below, all instances of the graphic indication of doubling should be considered to reflect true phonological doubling.

a. The word */sākinu/*, a G active participle meaning roughly "prefect," occurs twice as (gen.) [lú/1]*sà-ki-ni* (PRU 3 38b:4; PRU 6 93:9), but three times with double *-nn-* indicated: [lú/1]*sà-ki-in-ni* (PRU 3 35f.:10; PRU 6 3:3; 6 8:1; probably also [1]*sà-ki-in<-ni>* in Ug. 5 54:1). The word also appears with a double *-nn-* in texts written elsewhere, viz., Carchemish (PRU 4 166ff.:8; 4 178a:8; PRU 6 35:2,4,8,r.3'), and Ušnatu (PRU 4 218b:1,4),[45] and in a Hittite text found at Ras Shamra, where the spelling is [lú]*za-ak-ki-in/en-ni(-iš(-ša))* (Ug. 5 pp. 769f.:1,9,14,17; see Kümmel, UF 1 160). Thus, the double writing of the */n/* is a phenomenon not confined to the Ugarit scribes, and it is possible that such writings, despite the transparent NWS pedigree of */sākinu/*, reflect learned spellings borrowed from the Hittite (or Hurro-Hittite) milieu.[46]

b. The DN */kōθaru/* is written *ku-šar-ru* in Ug. 5 137 iv a 19 (a polyglot god-list attached to S[a] Voc.; see KΘR), where a single */r/* is expected.[47] It seems likely that the scribe first wrote the form *ku-šar*, for */kōθar/*, without a case-ending as in the PN [1]*ku-šar-a-bi/bu* (PRU 3 154f.:5; PRU 3 72f.:21; Ug. 5 96:27), and then added the sign *ru* to express the case-ending, which each of the Ugaritic forms preserved in this god-list exhibits; cf. Akk. forms like *id-din-nu* for *iddinū* (PRU 3 58f.:18).

c. The form *qa-ad-šu-ut-ti* (PRU 3 140f.:7; see QDŠ c) reflects an abstract of Ugar. */*qadišu*/ "(a type of priest)" meaning "status of a *q*." (von Soden, UF 2 329-30), for which Ugar. */*qad(i)šūtu*/ is presumably expected. The double *-tt-* is in all likelihood due to the influence of Assyrian morphology, where the abstract ending is *-utt*, as in the following Akkadian form from Ugarit: *qal-lu-ut-ti* "servitude" (Ug. 5 49:5,8); cf. also the Akk. forms cited above in n. 43.

The following may also be instances of incorrect doubling, but other explanations of the gemination are in each case more likely:[48]

[44]As has been suggested, e.g., by Gröndahl, Personennamen 18 n. 16; Kühne, UF 6 165.

[45]Note also PRU 4 235:5; PRU 6 4:2; and RS 25.131:2 (cited CAD S 76b); and [lú]*sà-ak-ki-in-ni* (with double *-kk-* as well, as in the Hittite forms cited immediately following) in PRU 6 6:2; all texts of uncertain provenance.

[46]So also, perhaps, writings with double *-kk-*, i.e., [lú]*sà-ak-ki-ni*, in PRU 3 15f.:2; PRU 4 196f.:2.

[47]That the form is properly */kōθaru/*, with one */r/*, seems likely in view of the Greek transcription of the feminine counterpart in Phoenician as *Khoúsarthis*, probably for */kušart/* < **kawθar-t*; for the text, see Attridge-Oden, Philo of Byblos 100-1, 104 n. 4.

[48]For Nougayrol's *ma-qáb-bu* in PRU 6 168:9, read probably *ma-qá!-bu* = */maqqabu/*; see the Glossary under NQB, discussion.

d. The double *-ṣṣ-* in the S[a] Voc. (no. 34) form *iṣ-ṣú*["wood, tree(s)" (Ug. 5 130 iii 8'; see ᶜṢ) would, is the form were singular, be unexpected (PS **ᶜiḏ̣-*). It is likely, however, that the form is plural *iṣ-ṣú-[ma]* = */ᶜiṣṣūma/,* with doubling as in Akk. *iṣṣū* (vs., e.g., Hebrew *ᶜēṣîm*). For other non-lexical plurals in the S[a] Voc. texts, see nos. 37.2, 177.1, 189.3

e. The S[a] Voc. (no. 183.5) form *ma-aḫ-ḫa-[du]* "harbor" (Ug. 5 137 ii 21'; see ᵓḪD) probably represents a pronunciation [maḫḫadu] < **maᵓḫadu,* i.e., true phonetic gemination as the result of assimilation of the glottal stop to the following velar fricative.[49]

f. The form *: ka-an-na-pí-yv* (PRU 3 79ff.:7), which also occurs without double *-nn-* indicated, i.e., *: ka-na-pí-yv* (PRU 3 85f.:11), may be derived from the same root as */kanapu/* "wing, extremity" (Kühne, UF 7 253-56; see the Glossary under KNP a and b). Nevertheless, in view of the uncertain meaning of the term, apparently a nisba, it is not necessary to assume that it is formed directly from the base **kanap-* rather than another (admittedly unattested) base **kannăp-*.

E. The Representation of the Ugaritic Consonants

☛ p. 400

Listed here are the syllable sequences of the Ugaritic vocabulary, arranged by homorganic groups of Ugaritic consonantal phonemes,[50] with the signs used to represent those sequences; only *Cv* and, for some groups, *vC* signs are considered.[51] For rare signs or values, personal and geographical names (usually West Semitic) are cited as corroborative evidence, provided that such names may be equated, with a reasonable degree of certainty, with alphabetic attestations that indicate the consonant in question unambiguously.[52]

[49]See the S[a] Voc. commentary, and below, ch. 2 §A 2 b.

[50]For the possible distinction of allophonic variants in the representation of the consonants, especially among the stops, see above, §A 1. As noted there, the evidence is not free of ambiguity, and so the representation of the consonants is best treated here phonemically, a treatment that will also facilitate comparison with the usual alphabetic representation.

[51]Since many *CvC* signs do not distinguish voiced, voiceless, and emphatic sounds, even in normative Mesopotamian dialects of Akkadian, they furnish little information concerning the representation of the Ugar. consonants; a complete listing of *CvC* signs in syllabic transcriptions is given above, §A 4.

[52]See n. 39 of the Introduction.

1. *Stops*[53]

a. Dentals: */d/, /ṭ/, /t/*

/d/

/dă/ (a) with DA = *da*:

always in S^a Voc. texts: *a-da-nu* = */ʾadānu/* "father" (ʾDN); *da-ab-ḫu* = */dabḥu/* "sacrifice" (DBḤ); *da-ka-rù* = */dakaru/* "male" (DKR^1); *da-al!?-*⸢*lu*⸣ = */dallu/* "poor" (DLL); *d[a]-aq!?-qú* = */daqqu/?* "small(?)" (DQQ); in other texts: $^{(giš.meš)}$*bi-da-lu-ma/na* = */bidălūm/na/* "merchants" (BDL); *ku-bu-da-ti* = */kubuddāti/* "honoring gifts" (KBD b); *: ma-ad-da-DU* = */maddatu/?* "measurement" (MDD); *qà-da-ru-ma*^{meš} = */qad(d)arūma/* "(containers)" (QDR); note also perhaps *da-mu* = */damu/?* "blood" in Ug. 5 153 (DM).

(b) with TA = *dá*:

not in S^a Voc.; in other texts: *: mi-dá-ar-ú* = */midarʿu/?* "seed-land" (DRʿ).

Note the PN's *dá-li-li* (PRU 3 153f.:7; cf. ^{1}*da-li-li* PRU 3 53b:6,9; PRU 6 59:5') = alphab. *dll* (UT 385a no. 665); ^{1}*ḫu-dá-ši* (PRU 3 133f.:5; Syria 28 173f.:23; cf. ^{1}*ḫu-da-ši* ibid.:28; Ug. 5 95:4) = alphab. *bn ḥdθ* (UT 395a no. 843).

/dē/ with TE = *de*$_4$:

no S^a Voc. examples; in other texts: *tap-de*$_4$*-ti, : ta-ap-de*$_4$*-ti, tap-de*$_4$*-tu*$_4$ = */tapdēti/u/* "exchange" (PDY); perhaps [^{túg}*m*]*ar-de*$_4$*-tu* = */mardētu/?* "(garment)" (RDY).

/dĭ/ (a) with DI = *di*:

S^a Voc. *di-*[*k*]*a*$_4$*-ru* = */dikāru/* "bowl" (DKR^2); in other texts: note alphab. *d* = syll. *di* in KTU 5.14:5.

PN's and GN's: e.g., ^{1}*ya-ʾa-di-du* (PRU 3 119f. r.15'; 3 191f.:22, etc.; cf ^{1}*ia-ʾa-dì-dì*, under b) = alphab. *yʿdd* (UT 454a no. 1819); *ab-di-ḫa-ma-ni* (PRU 3 64f.:3) = alphab. *ʿbdḫmn* (UT 402b nol. 971); ^{uru}*áš-da-di* (PRU 6 156:3) = alphab. *aδdd* (KTU 4.709:2); ^{uru}*ḫal-bi kàr-ra-di* (PRU 3 189b:6'; 3 190a:11'; cf. ... *kar-ra-dì*, under b) = alphab. *ḫlb krd* (UT 402a no. 963); ^{uru}*raq*$_x$(ZUM)*-di*[54] (PRU 3 188f.:11'; 3 189b:16'; PRU 6 55:passim; Ug. 7 pl. 13:37; pl. 50:15'; cf. ^{uru}*raq*$_x$*-dì*, under b) = alphab. *rqd* (UT 485b no. 2351); gentilic ^{uru}*ma-ḫa-di-yu* (PRU 6 79:6) = alphab. *m(a/i)ḫdy* (UT 355a no. 130).

[53]Only *Cv* signs are listed for the stops; the *vC* signs, as expected, do not distinguish voiced, voiceless, or emphatic consonants, and are therefore unremarkable; see above, p. 199.

[54]On the reading *raq*$_x$, instead of Nougayrol's *ríq*, in this GN, see Gordon, UT 485b no. 2351; Rainey, IOS 5 21.

(b) with TI = *dì*:

not in Sᵃ Voc.; other texts: *: na-ba-dì(-⸢šu-nu⸣)* = */naʾbadi/* "escape" (ʾBD); *: dì-ip-ra-ni-ma* = */diprānīma/* "junipers" (DPR); perhaps also *mu-qa-dì-IM* = */muqqādi/?* "grazing rights(?)" (NQD); *qa-dì-iš* = Akkadianized *qadiš* (for */qadiša/*) "is sacred" (QDŠ a); note also *TI-ru* and *ša-TI-i,* perhaps for Ugar. */dīru/* and */šadî/,* in Ug. 5 153 (DYR, ŠDW).

PN's and GN's: e.g., ¹*ia-ʾa-dì-dì* (Ug. 5 12:2,3; cf. ¹*ya-ʾa-di-du,* under a); ¹ÌR-*dì* (PRU 3 79ff.; 3 81ff.; 3 83f.; 3 85f. passim) = alphab. *ʿbd* (UT 452b no. 1801); [ᵘʳᵘ*ḫal-bi*] *kar-ra-dì* (PRU 3 191a:7'; cf. ... *kàr-ra-di,* under a); ᵘʳᵘ*raqₓ*(ZUM)-*dì* (Ug. 5 9:3; 5 12:16; cf. ᵘʳᵘ*raqₓ-di,* under a).

(c) with TE = *de₄*:

not in Sᵃ Voc.; in other texts: perhaps *mar-de₄-em-tu* = */mardimtu/?* "path(?)" (RDM).

PN's: e.g., *da-de₄-ya* (PRU 3 196 ii 17'); = alphab. *ddy* (UT 384b no. 647); ¹*ša-de₄-ia-nu* (PRU 3 138f.:4) = alphab. *šdyn* (UT 488 no. 2387).

/dō/ no examples.

/dŭ̄/ (a) with DU = *du*:

in Sᵃ Voc.: *a-du-rù* = */ʾaduru/* "mighty" (ʾDR); *[a-ḫ]a-du* = */ʾaḥadu/?* "one" (ʾḤD); *du-ú* = */dū/* (determinative-relative pronoun; D); *⸢ḫu⸣-du-rù* = */ḥudŭ̄ru/* "room(?)" (ḤDR); *ma-a-du-ma* = */maʾ(a)dūma/* "much, many" (MʾD); *na-du* = */nādu/* "stela(?)" (ND); *ab-du* = */ʿabdu/* "slave" (ʿBD); *ša-du-ú* = */šadû/* "field" (ŠDW); in other texts: ᵈᵘᵍ*ka-du-ma*ᵐᵉˢ̌ = */kaddūma/* "jars" (KDD); ⁽ˡᵘ́⁾*mu-du(-ú/-ma)* = */mūdû(ma)/* "courtier(s)" (MD); *: ma-aq-qa-du* = */maqqadu/* "grazing rights(?)" (NQD); ⁽ᵘʳᵘᵈᵘ·ᵐᵉˢ̌⁾*ma-ṣa-du(-ma*ᵐᵉˢ̌*)* = */maʿṣadu, -ūma/* "adze(s)(?)" (ʿṢD); ᵗᵘ́ᵍ*pa-li-du-ma* = */palĭdūma/* "(garments)" (PLD); perhaps ᵍⁱˢ̌*šu-uq-du(-)ma*[= */θuqdu/* "almond" (θQD).

(b) with TU = *dú*:

not in Sᵃ Voc.; in other texts: perhaps *⸢ka?⸣-dú* =*/kaddu/?* "jar" (KDD); ᵗᵘ́ᵍ?*ka-na-TU* = */kan(n)ădu/?* "(type of garment)" (KND); ⁽ᵗᵘ́ᵍ⁾*na-AG?-TU/TU₄* = */nagdu/?* "(a linen garment)" (NGD).

Note perhaps the PN ¹*ša-TU-ya-na* (PRU 3 52f.:3), if = alphab. *šdyn* (unless this is ¹*ša-de₄-ia-nu*; see above under */di/*).

(c) with TUM = *du₄*:

in Sᵃ Voc.: *iš-du₄* = */ʾišdu/* "leg" (ʾŠD); in other texts: perhaps ⁽ᵗᵘ́ᵍ⁾*na-AG?-TU/TU₄* = */nagdu/?* "(a linen garment)" (NGD).

Cf. the PN ^{1}ÌR-*du*$_4$ (Ug. 5 4:10') = alphab. *ʿbd* (UT 452b no. 1801).[55]

/*ṭ*/

/*ṭă*/ (a) with DA = *ṭa*:

in S^{a} Voc.: *ṭa-bu* = /*ṭābu*/ "sweet" (ṬW/YB); in other texts: *na-ap-ṭa-ru* = /*napṭarū*/ "they exchanged(?)" (PṬR b).

(b) with TA = *ṭá*:

in S^{a} Voc.: probably *ba-TA-lu* = /*baṭalu*/? "false(hood)(?)" (BṬL); in other texts: *na-ap-ṭá-ra* = /*napṭara*/ "exchange(?)" (PṬR c).

Cf. the PN ^{1}*ṣa-ri-ṭá-na* (Ug. 7 pl. 2 r.6') = alphab. *ṣrṭn* (UT 476a no. 2195); perhaps also ^{1}*ia-ap-lu-ṭá-na* (PRU 3 37b:3), if = alphab. *ypṭln* (UT 468b no. 2048; but note also *ypltn*, ibid.); ^{f}*TA-la-ia* (PRU 3 61f.:8,17), if = alphab. *ṭly* (UT 406b no. 1037; but note also *dly*, UT 385a no. 663)?

/*ṭē*/ with ḪI/TÍ = *ṭé*:

not in S^{a} Voc.; in other texts: only alphab. *ṭ* = syll. *ṭé* (KTU 5.14:10). This writing, for the letter name */*ṭētu*/, is the only use of ḪI/TÍ to represent a Ugar. dental.[56]

/*ṭĭ*/ (a) with DI = *ṭi*:

no S^{a} Voc. examples; in other texts: only probably *qà?-ṭi-nu*[-*ma*?^{me}]$^{š?}$ = /*qaṭinnūma*/? "(implements)" (QṬN).

[Note the Hurrian PN ^{1}*pa-ṭi-še-ni* (PRU 6 73:15; 6 80:6; 6 90 r.1') = alphab. *pṭðn* (UT 468a no. 2038).]

[(b) with TI = *ṭì*:

only in the PN ^{1}DUMU-*ia-aš-pu-ṭì* (PRU 3 199ff. iii 13"), cf. alphab. *yθpṭ* (UT 506a no. 2727); perhaps also the GN ^{uru}TI-*ba/bá-qi/qí/qu* (PRU 3 61f.:7; 3 190a:12'; PRU 6 27:12,19; Ug. 7 pl. 13:44), which may correspond in alphab. to either *ṭbq* (UT 406a no. 1030) or *tbq* (UT 496b no. 2518).]

[55]For TUM = *du*$_4$ in Akk. words in Ugarit texts, cf., e.g., *pu-ri-du*$_4$ Ug. 5 5:6,7,13; *qa-du*$_4$ PRU 3 76b:5,6.

[56]For the sequence alphab. *ḥ*, *ṭ* = syll. KU, ḪI in KTU 5.14:9,10, Cross-Lambdin, BASOR 160 25-26 with n. 29 (following Albright), suggested that the value *ṭé* for ḪI would be unparalleled at Ugarit, and that the scribe of KTU 5.14 had reversed the syllabic equivalents for alphab. *ḥ* and *ṭ*; thus, they proposed ḪI for *ḥ* (not *ṭ*) and DI! rather than KU for *ṭ*. Speiser, BASOR 175 42-47, however, suggested that KU for /*ḥō*...../ was phonetically plausible. For the correspondence of alphab. *ṭ* and syll. ḪI, he accepted the unlikelihood of a value *ṭé*, and proposed instead ḪI = *ṭà*, for */*ṭayt*/, a form without contraction of a diphthong. This is unnecessary, however, since the value *ṭé* is in fact attested, albeit rarely, in Ugarit Akkadian texts (whereas the value *ṭà* is not), in *ṭé-ma* for *ṭēma* (Ug. 5 24:34; 5 49:20; 5 55 r.9') and probably also in the PN ^{1}*ši-ip-ṭé-yV* (PRU 6 54:8; cf. alphab. *θpṭy*[in KTU 4.140:2). Thus, the equation is alphab. *ṭ* = syll. *ṭé*, for */*ṭētu*/ (so also Cross, ErIs 8 24* n. 101).

[(c) with TE = *ṭe*$_4$:

perhaps in the PN [f]DUMU-*ši-IB-ṭe*$_4$ (Ug. 5 55:2), cf. alphab. *θbṭ* (UT 500b no. 2636)?; note also the GN [uru]*TE-ba-qu* (PRU 3 188f.:10'; 3 189b:15'), for which see under b.]

/*ṭō*/ no examples.

/*ṭŭ̄*/ (a) with ṬU = *ṭu*:

in S[a] Voc.: *ṭu-ú-ru* = /*ṭuhūru*/ "pure" (ṬHR); *pu-la-ṭu* = /*pullaṭu*/ "to save" (PLṬ); in other texts: note *ma-áš-ḫa-ṭu-ma* = /*maθḫaṭūma*/ "(cloths)" (θḪṬ); KU$_6$[meš] *ú-ṭu* = /?/ (see Appendix to Glossary).

[(b) with TU = *ṭú*:

perhaps in the PN [1]*qà-TU-na* (PRU 3 136f.:4), which may correspond in alphab. to either *bn qṭn* (UT 477b no. 2219) or *qṭn* (UT 481b no. 2289).]

[(c) with DU = *ṭù*:

only in the PN [1]*ia-aš-p*[*u*]*-ṭù* (PRU 3 195b A 1) = alphab. *yθpṭ* (UT 506a no. 2727).]

/*t*/

/*tă̄*/ (a) with TA = *ta*:

always in S[a] Voc.: *at-ta* = /*ʾattă̄*/ "you (ms)" (ʾNT); *aš-ta-ru* = /*ʿaθtaru*/ (divine name; ʿθTR); *ta-a-ma-tu*$_4$ = /*tahāmatu*/ "the deep" (THM); and probably [*z*]*u-ut-ta-ru* = /*zuttaru*/ "to go out(?)" (ZTR); *ta-*[*ma*?*-ru*?] = /*tamaru*/? "date palm(?)" (TMR); in other texts: *ḫi-nu-ta-me* = /*ḥinōtāmi*/? "2 'implements'" (ḤNW); *: ta-ap-de*$_4$*-ti* (and *tap-de*$_4$*-ti*/*tu*$_4$) = /*tapdēti*/*u*/ "exchange" (PDY); *: ṣa-ma-ta* = /*ṣamata*/ "it was transferred" (ṢMT); *: ta-ar-bá-ṣí* = /*tarbaṣi*/ "stable" (RBṢ); *ta-ba-ʾa* = /*tabaʿa*/ "he departed" (TBʿ); [lú]*ta-ri-ru-ma* = /*tărĭrūma*/ "(members of a profession)" (TRR); and probably *: TA-am-GI* = /*tamki*/? "?" (TMK).

[(b) with DA = *tá*:

perhaps in the (non-Sem.?) PN [1]*tá-ni-ia* (Ug. 5 5:4) = alphab. *tny* (UT 498b no. 2572).]

/*tē*/ (a) with TE = *te*:

no S[a] Voc. examples; in other texts: *me-te* = /*miʾtē*/ "200" (dual bound form; Mʾ).

(b) with TI = *ti* (*te*$_9$):

no S[a] Voc. examples; in other texts: perhaps *iš-ia-ti-mi* = /*ʿišyatēmi*/ "clamps(?)" (dual; ʿŠY).

/*tĭ̄*/ (a) with TI = *ti*:

always in S[a] Voc.: *ti-*[*n*]*a*?*-*[*t*]*u*$_4$ = /*tiʾnatu*/ "fig" (TʾN); *ti-ib-nu* =

/tibnu/ "straw" (TBN); in other texts: *um-ma-ti* = */ʾummati/*? "clan(?)" (ʾMM);*: ti-tar-ḫ[u]* = */tiʾ/ttarḫu/* "she will hurry" (ʾRḪ); *[ḫ]u-wa-tu*$_4$ = */ḥuwwatu/* "country" (ḤWW); ITI *ḫal-la-ti* = */ḥallati/* (month name; ḤLL); *: ḫa-me-ti* = */ḥāmīti/* "wall" (ḤMY); *ḫur-ḫu-ra-ti* = */ḥurḥur(r)ati/* "(a plant)" (ḤRḤR); *ḫu-up-pa-ti* = */ḫuppăti/* "shore(s)(?)" (ḪPP); *: ḫi-ri-ti* = */ḫirīti/* "cemetery" (ḪRY); *ku-bu-da-ti* = */kubuddāti/* "honoring gifts" (KBD b); *ku-ub-ZA-ti* = */kubsati/*? "laundering(?)" (KBS b); *:ta-ap-de*$_4$*-ti* = */tapdēti/* "exchange" (PDY); *: pu-PI-ti* = */puwwati/*? "madder(?)" (PWT); *ra-ba-ti* = */rabbati/* "great" (RBB); *am-ma-ti* = */?/* "?" (see Appendix to Glossary); *: ḫa-ar-ZA-ti* = */?/* "?" (see Appendix to Glossary).

(b) with TE = *te* (*ti*$_7$):

not in S^a Voc.; in other texts: perhaps *mar-kab-te* = */markabti/*? "chariot(?)" (unless for dual */markabtē/*; RKB).

Note the PN's *ma-at-te-nu* (PRU 3 199ff. iii 37) and *ma-te-nu* (PRU 6 54:2; 6 79:11; Ug. 5 95:2) = alphab. *mtn* (UT 416a no. 1169).

/tō/ with TU = *tu*:

no S^a Voc. examples; in other texts: *tu-ki-ii* = */tōkīyi/* "inner" (TWK); note also alphab. *t* = syll. *tu* (for the letter name */tō/*?[57]) in KTU 5.14:17.

/tŭ/ (a) with TU = *tu*:

in S^a Voc.: *tu-a-pí-[ku?]* = */tuhappiku/*? "to be upset(?)" (HPK); *šu-ḫu-ut-t[u?]* = */šuḥuttu/*? "bran, residue(?)" (ḤTT); *ši-tu* = */šītu/* "to place" (ŠYT); *tu-un-na-nu* = */tunnanu/* "serpent" (TNN); in other texts: ^{urudu}*ḫa-ar-me-ša-tu* = */ḫarmiθātu/* "sickles(?)" (ḪRMθ); *ku-ku-ba-tu* = */kukkubātu/* "vases" (KKB); *[k]a?-ma-ʾa-*⌜*tu*⌝ = */kamaʾātu/*? "truffles(?)" (KMʾ); $^{[d]ug!?}$*ku?-BA-ra-tu*^{meš} = */kupārātu/*? "bowls(?)" (KPR); $^{giš(.meš)}$*ma-ás/sa-PI-tu* = */mas(a)wātu/* "cypress(?) logs" (MSW); *ni-iʾ-tu* = sg. */niʾtu/*, $^{urudu.meš}$*ni-ʾa-tu* = pl. */niʾātu/* "(a tool)" (Nʾ); ^{túg}*ú-ra-tu* = */ᶜōrātu/* "hides(?)" (ᶜWR); $^{giš.meš}$*ṣa-ʾa-tu* = */ṣāᶜātu/* "(wooden) bowls" (ṢWᶜ); ^{túg}*šá-ḫar-tu* = */šaᶜartu/* "wool" (ŠᶜR b); perhaps also ^{urudu}*ul-ma-tu* = */hulmātu/*? "hammers" (HLM); *mar-de*$_4$*-em-tu* = */mardimtu/*? "path(?)" (RDM).

(b) with TUM = *tu*$_4$:

in S^a Voc.: ⌜*i*⌝*-ši-t[u*$_4$*]* = */ʾišītu/*? "fire" (ʾŠ); *ú-[P]I!?-[t]u*$_4$ = */huwătu/*? "word" (HW^2); *[ḫ]u-wa-tu*$_4$ = */ḥuwwatu/* "country" (ḤWW); *[ḫ]u-ul-ma-tu*$_4$ = */ḥulmatu/*? "strength(?)" (ḤLM); *ma-a-al-tu*$_4$ = */maᶜᶜaltu/*? "bolt(?)" (NᶜL); ^{d}*a-na-tu*$_4$ = */ᶜanatu/* (divine name;

[57]Cross-Lambdin, BASOR 160 24-25.

ᶜNT); *ḫu-ul-ma-tu₄* = /*ǵulmatu*/ "darkness(?)" (ǴLM); *qa-ri-t*[*u₄*] = /*qarītu*/ "town" (QRY); ⌜*qa*⌝-*aš-tu₄* = /*qaštu*/ "bow" (QŠ); *ša*?-*na*!?-[*t*]*u₄* = /*šanatu*/? "year" (ŠN); *ti*-[*n*]*a*?-[*t*]*u₄* = /*tiʾnatu*/ "fig" (TʾN); *ta-a-ma-tu₄* = /*tahāmatu*/ "the deep" (THM); probably also *IG-TU₄* = /*ʾiktu*/? "mortar" (ʾKT); *ku-ku-bá-t*[*u₄*] = /*kukkubatu*/? "vase" (KKB); in other texts: [*a*?-*ši*?-*r*]*a-tu₄* = /*ʾaθiratu*/? (note also perhaps ᵈ*aš-ra-tu₄* =/*ʾaθratu*/; divine name; ʾθR); ᵐⁱ*ba-ri-iḫ-tu₄* = /*bariḥtu*/ "fugitive(?)" (BRḤ); ⌜*vḫ*?⌝-*nu-tu₄* = /*ʾvḥnōtu*/? "(an implement)" (ḤNW); *tap-de₄-tu₄* = /*tapdētu*/ "exchange" (PDY); perhaps also [ᵗᵘ́ᵍ*m*]*ar-de₄-tu* = /*mardētu*/? "(garment)" (RDY); *ša-i-tu₄* = /*θāᶜittu*/? or /*θāᶜītu*/? "(a container)" (θᶜD/θᶜY); and note the (probable) PN ᶠ*a-ḫa-tu₄*-LUGAL = /*ʾaḫātu-*/ ("sister"; ʾḪ).

(c) with DU = *tù*:[58]

not in Sᵃ Voc.; in other texts: *: ma-ad-da-DU* = /*maddatu*/? "measurement" (MDD); *: ṣa-ma-DU* = /*ṣamatū*/ "they were transferred" (ṢMT); probably also *: ka-ar-ba-DU*[= /*karbātu*/? "twisted(?)" (KRB).

Note also the GN ᵘʳᵘ*ia-ar-tù* (PRU 3 190b:3; 3 191a:12'; cf. ᵘʳᵘ*ia-ar-tu₄* PRU 3 190a:7) = alphab. *yᶜrt* (UT 412b no. 1126).

b. Velars: /*g*/, /*k*/, /*q*/

/*g*/

/*gă*/ (a) with GA = *ga*:

in Sᵃ Voc.: *ga-ša-ru* = /*gaθaru*/ "strong" (divine name; GθR); perhaps also [*r*]*a*-[*g*]*a*?-[*zu*?] = /*ragāzu*/? "to be enraged(?)" (RGZ); *ra-g*[*a*?-*mu*?] = /*ragāmu*/? "to speak(?)" (RGM); in other texts: *: ga-bi-ni* = /*gabīni*/? "hillock(?)" (GBN); note also alphab. *g* = syll. *ga* in KTU 5.14:3.

PN *ga-ad-yi* (PRU 3 133f.:19), cf. alphab. *bn gdy* (UT 379a, no. 560); GN's ᵘʳᵘ*ú*/*u-ga-ri-it* (passim) = alphab. *ugrt* (UT 351 no. 69); ᵘʳᵘ*ga-li-li* (PRU 6 78:9) = alphab. *gll* (UT 380a no. 581).

(b) with QA = *ga₅*:

not in Sᵃ Voc.; in other texts: probably ˡᵘ́*QA-la-b*[*u*?] = /*gallăbu*/ "barber" (GLB).

Note the rare writing ᵘʳᵘ*u-ga₅-ri-*[*it*] (PRU 3 66a:24; vs. ᵘʳᵘ*ú*/*u-ga-ri-it* passim);

[58]See §A 1, above. In Akk. words in these texts, note, e.g., *an-nu-tù* PRU 3 90b:12; *tù-šab* PRU 3 54ff.:25; *i-tù-ur(-ni)* Ug. 5 6:17,22,26.

and the non-Sem. PN *ḫa-ra-QA-na* (PRU 3 199ff. ii 5; vs. *ḫar-GA-na* PRU 6 27:4,15) = alphab. *ǵrgn* (UT 465a no. 1987).

/*gē*/ no examples.

/*gĭ*/ (a) with GI = *gi*:

no Sᵃ Voc. examples; in other texts, note perhaps *sà-GI-ru* = /*sāg*/*kiru*/ "closing(?)" (SGR b); note also *iš-ši-KI, iš<-ši>-GI* = /?/ "?" (see Appendix to Glossary).

Cf. e.g., the GN ^{uru}*a-gi-mu* (PRU 3 189b:23'; Ug. 5 102:16') = alphab. *agm* (UT 351a no. 63).

(b) with KI = gi_5:

cf. *iš-ši-KI*, under a.

Note the Hurrian PN's *ta-KI-ša-na* (PRU 3 45f.:8) = alphab. *tgðn* (UT 496b no. 2526); ^{1}*a-KI*-^{d}IM/^{d}U (PRU 3 71f.:4,11; vs. ^{1}*a-gít*-^{d}IM/^{d}U, ibid.:5,7,16) = alphab. *agtθb* (UT 351b no. 70); perhaps also the PN ^{1}*ir-KI-ia-nu* (Ug. 5 12:47), cf. alphab. *irgy*? (UT 365b no. 339).

/*gō*/ no examples.

/*gŭ*/ (a) with GU = *gu*:

no Sᵃ Voc. examples; in other texts: *gu-wa-*⌜*li*⌝ = /*guw(w)ăli*/ "circuit(?)" (GWL)

Cf. the PN ^{1}*gu-ur-ba-nu* (PRU 6 150:1) = alphab. *grbn* (UT 381a no. 614); GN ^{uru}*gu-ub-li* (PRU 6 126:10) = alphab. *gbl* (UT 378 no. 551).

(b) with KU = gu_5:

not in Sᵃ Voc.; in other texts: note only ^{giš}*sú-KU*!(QI)-*ri* and *sú*/*ŠU-KU-ru*/*ri* = /*suguru*/*i*/ or /*sukuru*/*i*/ "bolt" (SGR).

Note the PN *na-KU-uz-ḫa-nu* (PRU 3 52f.:4) = alphab. *ngzḫn* (UT 441b no. 1606).

/*k*/

/*kă*/ (a) with KA = *ka*:

in Sᵃ Voc.: *da-ka-rù* = /*dakaru*/ "male" (DKR¹); *ka-bi-[du?]* = /*kabidu*/? "liver(?)" (KBD a); *ka-as-pu* = /*kaspu*/ "silver" (KSP); in other texts: ^{dug}*ka-du-ma*^{meš} = /*kaddūma*/ "jars" (KDD); *ku-re-ka-m[a?]* = /*kurēkāma*/?, *ku-re-ka-a[t?]* = /*kurēkāt*/ "(implements)" (KRK); note also *[k]a?-ma-ʾa-*⌜*tu*⌝ = /*kamaʾātu*/? "truffles(?)" (Kmʾ); ${}^{túg?}$*ka-na-TU* = /*kan(n)ădu*/? "(type of garment)" (KND); *: ka(-an)-na-BI-PI* = /*kannăpīyv*/? "?" (KNP b); *: ka-ar-ba-DU[* = /*karbātu*/? "twisted(?)" (KRB); *ma-ka-ri* = /*makāri*/? "to trade" (MKR); *maš-ka-ni* = /*maškani*/? "habitation(?)" (ŠKN).

(b) with QA = *ka4*:

in Sᵃ Voc.: probably *di-[k]a4-ru* = /*dikāru*/ "bowl" (DKR²);[59] in other texts: ˡᵘ*ka4-bi-s[ú]* = /*kābisu*/ "launderer" (KBS a); *ka4-ka4-ra* =/*kakkara*/ "talent" (KKR); *ZI-GA/QA-ni-ma* = /*sikānīma*/? "statues(?)" (SKN b).

Note the PN *ka4-bid-na-na* (PRU 3 121f.:4), cf. alphab. *bn kbd* (UT 417a no. 1187).

(c) with GA = *kà*:

note *ZI-GA/QA-ni-ma* = /*sikānīma*/? "statues(?)" (SKN b).

Cf. the gentilic LÚ ^[ur]u?^*ak*!-*kà-a-ii* "Akko-ite" (TA 8 7f.:33).

/*kē*/ no examples.

/*kĭ*/ (a) with KI = *ki*:

no Sᵃ Voc. examples; in other texts: ᵈ·ᵍⁱˢ̌*ki-na-rù* = /*kinnāru*/ "lyre" (divine name; KNR); *(:) NAB/na-AB/ba/bá-ki-ma* = /*nab(a)kīma*/ "springs" (NBK); ˡᵘ/¹*sà-ki(-in)-ni* =/*sākini*/ "prefect" (SKN); *tu-ki-ii* = /*tōkīyi*/ "inner" (TWK); note also *iš-ši-KI* (see under b).

(b) with GI = *kí*:[60]

no Sᵃ Voc. examples; in other texts: perhaps *: TA-am-GI* = /*tamki*/? "?" (TMK); *sà-GI-ru* = /*sāg/kiru*/ "closing(?)" (SGR b); note also *iš-ši-KI, iš<-ši>-GI* = /?/ "?" (see Appendix to Glossary).

Cf. perhaps the PN ᶠ*ma-l[i?]-GI-lu* (PRU 6 149 ii 5), if for /*mālik-ʾilu*/.

/*kō*/ with KU = *ku*:

only Sᵃ Voc. *ku-šar-ru* = /*kōθaru*/ (divine name; KθR).

Cf. the PN ¹*ku-šar-a-bi* (PRU 3 154f.:5), which may be compared with alphab. *kθrmlk* (UT 425a no. 1335).

/*kŭ*/ (a) with KU = *ku*:

always in Sᵃ Voc.: *a-na-ku* = /*ʾanākŭ*/ "I" (ʾNK); *ku-ku-ba-tu, ku-ku-bá-t[u4?]* = /*kukkubatu*/ "vase(s)(?)" (KKB); ⌜*ku*⌝-*sú-m[u]* = /*kussumu*/ "emmer" (KSM); *ma-al-ku* = /*malku*/ "king" (MLK b); *NAB-ku* = /*nabku*/ "spring" (NBK); *pí-lak-ku* = /*pilakku*/ "spindle" (PLK¹); probably also *[bi?]-ir?-ku* = /*birku*/? "knee(?)" (BRK); in other texts: *ku-bu-da-ti* = /*kubuddāti*/ "honoring gifts" (KBD b); *ku-ub-ZA-ti* = /*kubsati*/? "laundering(?)" (KBS b); *ku-re-ku* = /*kurēku*/? "(implement)" (KRK); perhaps also ⁿᵃ⁴*ku-s[ú?-li?-ma?]*ᵐᵉˢ̌ = /*kussŭlīma*/? "(kind of stone, pl.)" (KSL); ^[d]ug!?^*ku?-BA-ra-tu*ᵐᵉˢ̌ =

[59]For QA = *ka4* elsewhere in the Sᵃ Voc. exemplars, note Akk. [*z*]*a-QA-ru* = *zakāru* "to speak" (Ug. 5 130 iii 3' = no. 32.3).

[60]See §A 1, above. Note Akk. *:kí-ru-ú* PRU 3 47a:15; *kí-ib-ra-ti* Ug. 5 167:3 (cf. copy).

/kupārātu/? "bowls(?)" (KPR); túg⸢ZU/SU?-ku?-ma^{meš}⸣ = /sukkūma/? "(garments)" (SKK); $^{(giš)}$sú-KU-ru/ri = /suguru/i/? or /sukuru/i/? "bolt" (SGR a).

(b) with GU = ku_8:

not in S^a Voc.; in other texts: perhaps $^{lú.meš}$GU-um-[ru?(-šu?)] = /kumrū/ "(priests?)" (KMR).[61]

/q/

/qă/ (a) with QA = *qa*:

in S^a Voc.: *qa-ri-t*[u_4] = /qarītu/ "town" (QRY); ⸢*qa*⸣-*aš-tu*$_4$ = /qaštu/ "bow" (QŠ); perhaps also [*la*?-*q*]*a*?-*ḫu* = /laqāḥu/? "to receive(?)" (LQḤ a); in other texts: *ia-ar-qa-ni* = /yarqāni/ "yellow-green" (YRQ); *ma-qa-ḫa* = /maqqaḥā/ "pair of tongs" (dual bound form; LQḤ b); *ma-qa-bu-ma*^{meš} = /maqqabūma/ "hammers" (cf. *ma-qá-*[*bu-ma*], under c; NQB); *: ma-aq-qa-du* = /maqqadu/ "grazing rights(?)" (NQD); *: am-qa* = /ᶜamqa/ "stronghold" (cf. [*am*?]-*qà*? under b; ᶜMQ^1); perhaps also *mu-qa-dì-im* =/muqqādi(m)/? "grazing rights(?)" (NQD); *qa-dì-iš* = Akkadianized *qadiš* (for /qadiša/) "is sacred" (QDŠ a).

(b) with KA = *qà*:

in S^a Voc.: probably [*q*]*à*?-*ar-ṣú*? = /qarṣu/? "piece(?)" (QRṢ); in other texts: *qà-da-ru-ma*^{meš} = /qad(d)arūma/ "(containers)" (QDR); peⁿhaps also [*am*?]-*qà*? = /ᶜamqa/? (cf. *:am-qa*, under a; ᶜMQ^1); *qà*?-*ṭi-nu*-[*ma*?^{me}]$^{š?}$ = /qaṭinnūma/? "(implements)" (QṬN).

Note also the PN's ^{1}*qà-TU-na* (PRU 3 136f.:4) = alphab. *bn qṭn* or *qṭn* (UT 477b no. 2219, 481a no. 2289, resp.); ^{1}*bu-ra-qà-nu* (PRU 6 50:5,21), cf. alphab. *brqn* (UT 377a no. 524).

(c) with GA = *qá*:

not in S^a Voc.; in other texts: probably *ma-qá*!?-*bu* = /maqqabu/ "hammer" (vs. *ma-qa*-[*bu-ma*] in the same text; see also under a; NQB); perhaps also *qá-al-lu* = /qallu/ "small" (QLL).

Note ^{1}*ḫa-ZI-qá-ta-nu* (PRU 3 141f.:5; but ^{1}*ḫa-ZI-qa-ta-na* ibid.:9), cf. alphab. *bn ḥṣqt* (KTU 4.428:7); ^{uru}*ma*-⸢*qá*⸣-*bi* (PRU 3 40b:3; vs. ^{uru}*ma(-aʾ)-qa-bi/bu* ibdi.:2; PRU 3 190a:14'; 3 191a:15'; Ug. 7. pl. 13:31) = alphab. *mᶜqb* (UT 460b no. 1907).

/qē/ no examples.

[61] The only other occurrence of GU = ku_8 in Ugarit Akk. appears in a lexical text: [E].E = *i-ku*$_8$ *i-ku*$_8$ MSL 11 43ff. iv 49 (vs. E = *i-ku* ibid. iv 38).

/qĭ/ (a) with KIN = *qi*:

in Sª Voc.: probably [é?]⸢*qi?-id?-šu?*⸣, *qi-i*[*d-šu?*] = /*qidšu*/ "shrine" (QDŠ b); *qi-i-lu* = /*qiʿīlu*/ (less likely, /*qiʿlu*/) "vine-blossom(?)" (QʿL); in other texts: no examples.

PN: [1]*ša-ba-i-ni-qi* (PRU 6 55:12') = alphab. *θbʿnq* (UT 500b no. 2639); GN's: uru*ša-na-qi* (PRU 6 93:15; cf. *ša-na-qí*, under b; see ΘNQ in Glossary) = alphab. *θnq* (UT 505a no. 2712); uruTI-*ba-qi* (Ug. 7 pl. 13:44; cf. uru*TI-bá/ba-qí*, under b) = alphab. *ṭbq* (UT 406a no. 1030) or *ṭbq* (UT 496b no. 2518); uru*ša-ḫa-qi* (PRU 6 118:5') = alphab. *šḥq* (UT 488-89 no. 2398).

(b) with KI = *qí*:

not in Sª Voc.; in other texts: only lú*ia-qí-š*[*u*] = /*yāqišu*/ "fowler" (YQŠ).

Note the GN's *ša-na-qí* (PRU 3 199ff. iii 56'; cf. uru*ša-na-qi*, under a); uru*TI-bá/ba-qí* (PRU 3 61f.:7; PRU 6 27:12,19; cf. uruTI-*ba-qi*, under a); note also the RN (1)f*pí-ṣí-id-qí*[62] (PRU 3 50f.:2; 3 51f.:4).

/qō/ with KUM = *qu*:

no Sª Voc. examples; in other texts: only in alphab. *q* = syll. *qu* (for the letter name /*qōpu*/?[63]) in KTU 5.14:13.

/qŭ/ (a) with KUM = *qu*:

in Sª Voc.: *ḫé-qu* = /*ḥēqu*/ "lap" (ḤYQ); *qu-u*[*n?*]-*n*[*a?-nu?*] = /*qunnanu*/? "coiled(?)" (QNN); other texts: perhaps *a-mu-q*[*u*] = /*ʿamuqu*/ "deep (place)" (ʿMQ²); *TAR-QU* = /*darqu*/? "path" (DRQ).

PN's, GN's: 1*ṣa-du-qu* (PRU 6 79:7), cf. perhaps alphab. *ṣdq* (UT 472b no. 2147); 1*ia-qu-ri* (PRU 3 136b:11); [uru]*ša-ḫa-qu* (PRU 3 191a:7') = alphab. *šḥq* (UT 488-89 no. 2398).

(b) with KU = *qú*:

in Sª Voc.: *d*[*a*]-*aq!?-qú* = /*daqqu*/? "small(?)" (DQQ); in other texts: *: qú-bu-ri* = /*qubūri*/ "burial" (QBR); *KU-ul-KU-li* = /*qulqul(l)i*/? "cassia" (QLQL).

Note the PN 1*qú-ur-ḫa-nu* (PRU 6 78:21), cf. alphab. *qrḥ* (UT 480b no. 2274).

c. Labials: /b/, /p/

/b/

/bă/ (a) with BA = *ba*:

in Sª Voc.: ⸢*ba*⸣-*aḫ-ḫu-rù* = /*baḫḫuru*/ (or /*baḥḥuru*/) "youth" (BḪR);

[62]See Gröndahl, Personennamen 31, 55, 170.

[63]Cross-Lambdin, BASOR 160 25 with n. 24.

ba-TA-lu = /*baṭalu*/? "false(hood)(?)" (BṬL); *ba-a-lu(-ma)* = /*baᶜlu, baᶜ(a)lūma*/ "lord(s)" (BᶜL); in other texts: *: na-ba-dì(-⌈šu-nu⌉)* = /*naᵓbadi*/ "escape" (ᵓBD); [lú]*ba-ar-ḫu* = Akkadianized form *barḫu* and [mí]*ba-ri-iḫ-tu*₄ = /*bariḥtu*/ "fugitive, rustic(?)" (BRḤ); *ḫa-ba-li-ma* = /*ḥabalīma*/ "ropes, lots" (ḤBL); *mu-ba-li* = /*mōbali*/ "produce(?)" (YBL b); *ku-ku-ba-tu* =/*kukkubātu*/ "vases" (KKB); *la-ba-nu* = /*labanu*/ "white" (LBN[1]); *na-ba-ki-mi* = /*nabakīma*(!)/ "springs" (NBK); *ma-ba-ri* = /*maᶜbari*/ "pass" (ᶜBR); [lú].[meš]*ú-ru-ba-nu* = /*ᶜur(r)ŭb(b)ānū*/ "guarantors" (ᶜRB); [(íd)]*(:)ra-aḫ-ba-ni/na* = /*raḥbāni/a*/ "wide place" (see also under b; RḤB); *ta-ba-ᵓa* = /*tabaᶜa*/ "he departed" (TBᶜ); probably also *: ka-ar-ba-DU*[= /*karbātu*/? "twisted(?)" (KRB); [lú]*la-⌈ba?⌉-nu* = /*labbănu*/ "brickmaker" (LBN[2]); *ra-ba-ti* = /*rabbati*/ "great" (RBB).

(b) with PA = *bá*:

in Sᵃ Voc.: *ku-ku-bá-t*[*u*₄?] = /*kukkubatu*/ "vase" (cf. *ku-ku-ba-tu*, under a; KKB); in other texts: *na-bá-ki-ma* =/*nabakīma*/ "springs" (cf. *na-ba-ki-mi*, under a; NBK); *: ta-ar-bá-ṣí* = /*tarbaṣi*/ "stable" (RBṢ); [í]d*ra-aḫ-bá-ni/na* = /*raḥbāni/a*/ "wide place" (see also a; RḤB).

Note also [uru]*TI-bá-qí* (PRU 3 61f.:7; cf. [uru]*TI-ba-qi/qí/qu* PRU 3 190a:12'; PRU 6 27:12,19; Ug. 7 pl. 13:44) = alphab. *ṭbq* (UT 406a no. 1030) or *tbq* (UT 496b no. 2518); [uru]*ma(-aᵓ/aḫ)-ra-bá*[(ki)] (PRU 3 48f.:11; 3 65b:6; 3 102ff.:30,32,35; 3 150b r.6'; 3 151f.:5,7; 3 187d:3; 3 192f.:26,30; Ug. 7 pl. 13:24; cf. [uru]*ma-ra-ba* Ug. 5 12:1,13,14) = alphab. *mᶜrb(y)* (UT 461a no. 1915); perhaps also the PN [1]*ab-bá-na* (PRU 6 27:8, vs. [1]*ab-ba-na/nu* ibid.:15,20,25,26), cf. alphab. *abn* (UT 349b no. 32)?

/*bē*/ with BAD = *be*:

not in Sᵃ Voc.; in other texts: only in alphab. *b* = syll. *be* (for the letter name /*bētu*/[64] in KTU 5.14:2.

/*bĭ*/ always with BI = *bi*:

in Sᵃ Voc.: ⌈*bi*⌉*-i* (also *bi-*) = /*bi-*/ "in" (B); in other texts: [(giš.meš)]*bi-da-lu-ma/na* = /*bidălūm/na*/ "merchants" (BDL); [lú.meš]*b*[*i*]*-ḫi-ru* = /*biḥīrū*/? "elite (troops)" (BḤR[1]); [lú]*ka*₄(QA)*-bi-s*[*ú*] = /*kābisu*/ "launderer" (KBS a); *(:) ṣí(-ib)-bi-ri* = /*ṣibbīri*/ "collective land(?)" (ṢBR); probably also *: ga-bi-ni* = /*gabīni*/? "hillock(?)" (GBN); cf. perhaps *i-bi-la* for */*yabila*/? "it brought" (YBL a); also *(*[*i*]*a-)šu-bi-lu* = /*yašōbilu*/? "he will have brought(?)" or /*šōbilū*/? "have brought(?)" in Ug. 5 153 (YBL c).

/*bō*/ no examples.

/*bŭ*/ always with BU = *bu*:

64Cross-Lambdin, BASOR 160 25.

see ᵓYB, BNŠ, BRR, GLB, ḪYB, ṬW/YB, YθB b, KBD b, NQB, QBR.

/p/

/pă/ with PA = *pa*:

no Sᵃ Voc. examples; in other texts: ᵗᵘ́ᵍ*pa-li-du-ma* = */palĭdūma/* "(garments)" (PLD); ᵗᵘ́ᵍ*pa-ḫa-TAR-ru* = */paǵaddarru/* "(garment)" (PǴ(N)DR); probably also *ḫu-up-pa-ti* = */ḫuppăti/* "shore(s)(?)" (ḪPP); perhaps *pa-⌜si?⌝-la-nu* = */pasīlānu/*? "?" (PSL).

with BA = *pá*:

not in Sᵃ Voc.; in other texts: perhaps ⁽ᵈ⁾ᵘᵍ!?*ku?-BA-ra-tu*ᵐᵉˢ̌ = */kupārātu/*? "bowls(?)" (KPR); the writing may indicate a pronunciation [kubārādu], with intervocalic voicing of */p/* as [b].[65]

/pē/ no examples.

/pĭ/ always with BI = *pí*:[66]

in Sᵃ Voc.: *pí-iṭ-r[ù?]* = */piṭru/* "to loosen" (PṬR a); *pí-lak-ku* = */pilakku/* "spindle" (PLK¹); probably also ⌜*a*⌝-[*p*]*í*?-[*yu*?] = */ᵓāpiyu/*? "baker" (ᵓPY); *tu-a-pí-[ku?]* = */tuhappiku/*? "to be upset(?)" (HPK); *pí-i?-[tu₄?]* = */piᵓtu/*? "corner(?)" (Pᵓ); *pí-rù* = */pirru/*? "flight(?), separation(?)" (PRR); in other texts: *ḫa-pí-ri* = */ᶜapĭri/* "(a social class)" (ᶜPR); probably also *: ka(-an)-na-BI-PI* = */kannăpīyv/*? "?" (KNP b).

/pō/ no examples.

/pŭ/ always with BU = *pu*:

see ᵓNP, KNP a, KSP, ᶜPW(?), PWT, PLṬ, PRS(?); note also alphab. [*p*] = syll. [*p*]*u* in KTU 5.14:11.

2. *Sibilants and Other Fricatives*[67]

a. *Cv* sequences

/ð/

Only two words in our corpus contain */ð/*,[68] which is written with Z-signs in

[65]See above, §A 1, with n. 7.

[66]The PI sign has the value *pi* in Ugarit Akk. only in a few literary and lexical texts, which do not include the polyglot Sᵃ vocabularies; otherwise, */pĭ/* and */pĕ/* are always written with BI = *pí, pé* (in Ug. 5 12:27, the PN *PI-v*ᵓ*-TA-PI* is probably to be read *ya-a*ᵓ*-ta/dá-ya* (root ᵓ*-t-w* or ᶜ*-d-y*).

[67]See also §A 2, above.

[68]In most instances, of course, PS **ð* has merged with */d/*, as indicated clearly in the syllabic

both examples:

S^{a} Voc. *i-zi-ir-[tu$_4$?]* = /*ᶜiðirtu*/[69] "help" (ᶜðR);

ar-ra-⸢zu⸣ = Akkadianized durative *arraððu* "I grew weak" (RðY).

Since these two forms do not comprise a sample large enough for meaninful orthographic analysis, it may be helpful to consider the syllabic representation in Ugarit Akk. texts of proper names that are written with {ð} in alphabetic form, keeping in mind, of course, the problems associated with the analysis of names. (Since both the phonemic and the phonetic interpretations of the following examples are uncertain, *ðv* will not be enclosed between slashes or brackets at this point; see below.).

ða Ugar. words: no examples;

GN: alphab. ***amðy*** (UT 360b no. 222) appears as ^{uru}*am-mi-ZA* (PRU 3 189b:9'), ^{uru}*a-me-ZA* (PRU 3 190b:2), ^{uru}*am-mi-ZA-ú*[70] (PRU 3 191a:10'); but also ^{uru}*am-me-ŠA* (PRU 3 190a:20');

Hurrian PN's: ^{1}*a-na-ni-ZA-ar-ri* (PRU 3 199ff. iv 18) = alphab. ***annðr*** (UT 362a no. 256); EN-*mu-ZA* (PRU 3 91f.:8,16; 3 106f. r.2',3') = alphab. ***iw/brmð*** (UT 350b no. 47, 353b no. 116; see also under ***ði*** and ***ðu***); but *ta-gi$_5$-ŠA-na* (PRU 3 45f.:8) = alphab. ***tgðn*** (UT 496b no. 2526); ^{1}*iš-mi-ŠAR-ri* (PRU 3 138f.:8,10), probably = alphab. ***ḫðmðr*** (UT 401a no. 939).

ðe Ugar. words: no examples;

Hurrian PN's: ^{1}*a-dal/da-al-ŠE-ni* (see PRU 3 p. 242b) = alphab. ***adlðn*** (UT 352a no. 81); ^{1}*pa-ṭi-ŠE-ni* (PRU 3 73:15) = alphab. ***pṭðn*** (UT 468a no. 2038).

ði Ugar. word: S^{a} Voc. *i-ZI-ir-[tu$_4$]* = /*ᶜiðirtu*/ (ᶜðR);

WSem. PN's: alphab. ***yᶜðrn*** (UT 454b no. 1831) =^{1}*ia-ZI-ra-nu/na* (e.g., PRU 3 54ff.: 8,12,15,20[71]), but also ^{1}*ia-aʾ-ŠI-ra-nu* (ibid.:4), ^{1}*ia-ŠI-ra* (PRU 3 131a: 16); alphab. ***ðmrhd*** (UT 388b no. 727) = ^{1}*ZI-im-rad-du* (PRU 3 192f.:33), but note also ^{1}*ŠI-im-rad-du* in PRU 4 234b:16, provenance uncertain;[72] ^{1}*ZI-mi-ri-ya*

---

transcriptions: *da-ab-ḫu* = /*dabḫu*/ < ****ðabḫ***- (DBḪ); *da-ka-rù* = /*dakaru*/ < ****ðakar***- (DKR^{1}); : *mi-dá-ar-ú* = /*midarᶜu*/ < ****miðraᶜ***- (DRᶜ); perhaps also *TI-ru* = /*dīru*/? "foul(?)" (DYR). See Blau, JAOS 88 523-26. It will be noted that in the two examples of retained /*ð*/ in our corpus, both roots contain /*r*/ and one also has /*ᶜ*/, which may be involved in the lack of shift to /*d*/; see Gordon, UT 26-27 §5.3.

[69] That in *i-zi-ir-[tu$_4$]* = /*ᶜiðirtu*/ (ᶜðR) the /*ð*/ is the result of "fricativization" of *d* < ****ð*** intervocalically (Garr, JNES 45 50 n. 40) seems unlikely, since there is no other evidence for intervocalic spirantization/fricativization, either in our syllabic transcriptions or in alphabetic writings, apart from the few examples of etymological ****ð*** written with {ð} cited by Garr. But the latter are undoubtedly simply archaic spellings; if not, we would need to ask why, if ****ð*** and **d* had otherwise merged in all but a few forms, only the reflexes of the former would be subject to "fricativization."

[70] For the final -*ú*, see below, 3 c, with n. 106.

[71] The writings ^{1}*ia-ZI-ra-nu/na* also occur in PRU 3 67a:5; 3 79ff.:4; 3 106a:9,11; 3 146f.:6; 3 160f.:16; $^{(1)}$*ia-ZI-ra* in PRU 3 58f.:7; 3 146f.:13,16; 3 153f.:26.

[72] These variants were noted by Nougayrol, PRU 3 p. 262a, and associated with alphab. ***ð*** by Berger in WO 5 279.

(PRU 6 72:13') = alphab. *ðmry* (UT 388b no. 727); perhaps also [1]*qà-na-ZI* (PRU 6 38:20) = alphab. *qnð* (UT 479a no. 2248);

Hur. PN: [1]*ib-ra-mu-ZI* (PRU 3 130a:5,9,14) = *iw/brmð* (see under *ða*).

ðu Ugar. word: Akk. form *ar-ra-ZU* (RðY);

WSem. PN: [1]*ZU-uk-ri-ia-n[u]* (PRU 3 199ff. i 8"), which may be compared with alphab. *ðkry* (UT 388a no. 724);

Hur. word: note *tar-ŠU-wa-an-ni* "man" (often in the Sª Voc. texts; see the Glossary under BNŠ) as *trðwn(ð)* (Laroche, GLH 258);

Hur. PN: [1]EN-*mu-ŠU* (Ug. 7 pl. 50:11', r.8') = alphab. *iw/brmð* (see above under *ða*).

vð only in the GN [uru]*ÁŠ-da-di* (gen.) "Ashdod" (PRU 6 156:3), which corresponds to alphab. *aðdd* (KTU 4.709:2), gentilic *aðddy* (UT 353a no. 98).[73]

The vacillation between Z-signs and Š-signs in examples corresponding to alphab. {ð} is found in both WSem. and Hurrian forms.[74] The interpretation of alphab. {ð} in Hurrian forms is not entirely clear. It seems most likely, however, that {ð} represents the voiced allophone of a phoneme whose voiceless counterpart is usually written with {θ}, although the picture is confused by occasional writings with {ẟ}, the latter probably, in Hurrian forms, to be considered simply a graphic biform of {ð}, i.e., the voiced allophone.[75] The opinion that the pronunciation of this allophone was roughly [ž] seems plausible;[76] there being no signs that represented this sound precisely, Z-signs would accurately reflect the voiced quality, while Š-signs would more correctly reflect the place or manner of articulation (palatal? affricate?). Whether the Ugar. phone represented by {ð} was the same as the Hurrian cannot, of course, be demonstrated. But the similar alternation in syllabic forms between Z- and Š-signs suggests at least a similar pronunciation.

/z/

/ză/ with ZA = *za*:

no Sª Voc. examples; in other texts: (túg.meš)*ma-za-ru-ma* = */maʾzarūma/*? "loincloths(?)" (ʾZR); *mar-za-i* = [marzaʿi] "symposium" (RZḤ).

[73]It is not necessary to conclude, with Cross-Freedman, BASOR 175 48-50, that {ð} occurs in these alphab. forms because only {ð} represented an interdental (*/θ/* being a sibilant in their view). Rather, if the etymology of "Ashdod" is *θ-d-d*, as Cross-Freedman suggest, i.e, */ʾaθdād-/*, the writings *aðdd(y)* probably reflect the assimilatory voicing of */θ/* before */d/*. The appearance of ÁŠ in [uru]*ÁŠ-da-di* is not helpful here, since, as in other writings in which Š-signs correspond to alphab. {ð}, its use may indicate not voicelessness, but place of articulation (see below).

[74]Only a sample of the Hurrian names is cited above; see also, e.g., Gröndahl, Personennamen 206-7.

[75]We follow here Bush's analysis in GHL 61-71 §3.5; see also Laroche, Ug. 5 pp. 527-28. (Speiser, IH 31-35 §§44-46, proposed two phonemes, *s̄* and *z̄*.)

[76]See the studies cited by Garr in JNES 45 47 n. 21.

/zē/ no examples.[77]

/zĭ̄/ with ZI = *zi*:

in S[a] Voc.: *ḫu-zi-rù* = /*ḫuzīru*/ "pig" (ḪZR); in other texts: *ma-ar-zi-ḫi* and *mar-zi-i* = [marziḫi] and [marziˁi] "symposium" (RZḤ); note also perhaps *ar-zi-ma*[= /*ʾarzīma*/? "cedars(?)" in Ug. 5 153 (ʾRZ).[78]

/zō/ no examples.

/zŭ̄/ with ZU = *zu*:

in S[a] Voc.: perhaps [*z*]*u-ut-ta-ru* = /*zuttaru*/ "to go out(?)" (ZTR); in other texts: *ar-zu* = /*ʾarzu*/ "cedar" (ʾRZ); note also perhaps *gur-bi-ZU* = /*gurbizu*/? "hauberk" (GRBZ).

/ẓ/

/ẓă̄/, /ẓē/, /ẓĭ̄/, /ẓō/ no examples.

Note, however, the GN ^{uru}*ZA-ri-nu* (PRU 6 95:2; 6 111:4; Ug. 5 102:12') and its gentilic ^{uru}*ZA-ri-ni-yu* (PRU 6 138:4,7), which probably = alphab. *ẓrn* (UT 407b no. 1059); further, the PN's ^{1}*ZI-me-ni* (PRU 6 147:2) and ^{1}*ṢI-me-nu* (Ug. 7 pl. 50:2'), either of which may perhaps represent alphab. *ẓmn* (UT 407b no. 1055), although *ðmn* (UT 388a no. 726) should also be noted.

/ẓŭ̄/ with ZU:

no S[a] Voc. examples; in other texts, perhaps in *: ZU-ur-PI* = /*ẓurwu*/, "(aromatic) resin," although /*ṣurwu*/? is also possible (ẒRW).

/s/

/să̄/ (a) with SA = *sa*:

not in S[a] Voc.; in other texts: $^{giš.meš}$*ma-sa-wa-tu* = /*masawātu*/ "cypress(?) logs" (cf. $^{giš(.meš)}$*ma-ás-wa-tu* =/*maswātu*/; MSW); perhaps also *sa-ap-lu* = /*saplu*/? "cauldron" (more often *sà-ap-lu*; SPL).

Note also the PN ^{1}*sa-ḫu-ra-nu* (PRU 6 73:5; 6 78:22) = alphab. *sḫrn* (UT 449b no. 1749).

(b) with ZA = *sà*:

in S[a] Voc.: ⸢*ma*⸣*-al-sà-mu* = /*malsamu*/ "course(?)/courier(?)" (LSM); perhaps *pu-ru-s*[*à*?*-tu*$_4$?] = /*pur(r)ŭ̄s(s)atu*/? "division(?)"

[77]See the following note.

[78]Note also alphab. *z* = syll. *ZI* in KTU 5.14:8; since the early name of this letter is unknown, it is uncertain whether *ZI* here represents /*zĭ̄*.../ or /*zē*.../.

(PRS); in other texts: *ku-ub-ZA-ti* = */kubsati/*? "laundering(?)" (KBS b); *sà-GI-ru* = */sāg/kiru/* "closing(?)" (SGR b); $^{\text{lú/1}}$*sà-ki(-in)-ni* = */sākini/* "prefect" (SKN a); perhaps *sà-ap-lu* = */saplu/*? "cauldron" (once *sa-ap-lu*; SPL).

/sē/ no examples.

/sĭ/ (a) with SI = *si*:

no S^a Voc. examples; in other texts: only perhaps *pa-⌜si?⌝-la-nu* = */pasīlānu/*? "?" (PSL).

PN's: ^{1}*si-il-ʾa-nu* (PRU 6 72:12'; cf. *sí-il-a-*[*na*?] PRU 3 101f.:23), cf. alphab. *slʿy* (UT 450a no. 1765)?; ^{1}*píl-si-ya/ia* (PRU 6 72:14'; 6 109 A 3; cf. ^{1}*píl-sí-ya* PRU 3 194f.:2) = alphab. *plsy* (UT 468b no. 2053).

(b) with ZI = *sí*:

no S^a Voc. examples; in other texts: ^{lú}*na-s*[*í-ku*] = */nāsiku/* "metalsmith" (NSK); *(:) sí-il-a* = */silʿa/* "cliff(?)" (SLʿ).

PN's: note *sí-il-a-*[*na*?] and ^{1}*píl-sí-ya*, both cited under a; GN's: e.g., ^{uru}*sí-ia-an-ni* (PRU 6 45:8) = alphab. *syn* (UT 449b no. 1750); ^{uru}*sí-na-ru* (PRU 3 190a:10') = alphab. *snr* (UT 450b no. 1776).

/sō/ no examples.

/sŭ/[79] (a) with SU = *su*:

no S^a Voc. examples; in other texts: only perhaps *:!? su-nu* = */suʾnu/*? "hem" (SʾN).

Note the GN ^{uru}*ap-su-na* and its gentilic ^{uru}*ap-su-ni-yu-ma* (PRU 6 77:4,10), cf. alphab. *apsny* (UT 364b no. 310); PN ^{1}*su-su* (PRU 6 79:18) = alphab. *ss* (UT 450b no. 1779)?

(b) with ZU = *sú*:

in S^a Voc.: ⌜*ku*⌝*-sú-m*[*u*] = */kussumu/* "emmer" (KSM); in other texts: ^{lú}*ka*$_4$(QA)*-bi-s*[*ú*] = */kābisu/* "launderer" (KBS a); ^{giš}*sú-KU*!(QI)*-ri* and *sú-KU-ru/ri* =*/sug/kuri/u/* "bolt" (see also under c; SGR a); perhaps also $^{\text{na4}}$*ku-s*[*ú*?*-li*?*-ma*?]^{meš} = */kussŭlīma/*? "(kind of stone, pl.)" (KSL); note also alphab. *ś* = syll. *sú* in KTU 5.14:20.[80]

(c) with ŠU = *su*$_x$:[81]

only in *ŠU-KU-ru* = */suk/guru/* "bolt" (vs. *sú-KU-ru/ri* in preceding and following lines; SGR a); possibly a scribal error for ZU.

[79]Note also ^{túg}⌜*ZU/SU*?*-ku*?*-ma*^{meš}⌝ = */sukkūma/*? "(garments)" (SKK).

[80]See the recent study of Segert, UF 15 201-18, in which it is suggested that alphab. *ś* generally has the value */sŭ/*.

[81]See above, §A 2, with n. 14.

/*ṣ*/

/*ṣă*/ always with ZA = *ṣa*:

no S^a Voc. examples; in other texts: ^{urudu}*ma-am-ṣa-ar* = /*mamṣar(u)*/ "knife(?)" (MṢR); $^{\text{(urudu.meš)}}$*ma-ṣa-du(-ma*^{meš}*)* = /*maᶜṣadu, -ūma*/ "adze(s)(?)" (ᶜṢD); *(:) ṣa(-a)-i* = /*ṣāᶜi*/ and $^{\text{giš.meš}}$*ṣa-ʾa-tu* = /*ṣāᶜātu*/ "bowl(s)" (ṢWᶜ); *: ṣa-ma-ta/tù* = /*ṣamata/ū*/ "it is/they are transferred" (ṢMT); note also alphab. *ṣ* = syll. *ṣa* in KTU 5.14:12.

/*ṣē*/ with ZI = *ṣé*?:

no S^a Voc. examples; in other texts: perhaps *: ZI-ṣú(-ú)-ma* = /*ṣēṣūma*/ or /*ṣīṣūma*/ "salt fields" (ṢYṢ).

/*ṣĭ*/ (a) with ṢI = *ṣi*:

in S^a Voc.: *ṣi-il-PI*[= /*ṣilyatu*/ (or /*ṣilyu*/) "curse" (ṢLY); in other texts: ^{lú}*ma-ṣi-lu* = /*maṣillu*/ "cymbalist" (ṢLL); note also perhaps *([i]a-)ab-ṣi-ru* = /*y/ʾabṣiru*/? "he/I will cut down(?)" in Ug. 5 153 (BṢR).

Note the PN's ^{I}*ṣi-id-qa-na* (PRU 3 194f.:10,11,15; Ug. 5 12:4,5; cf. ^{I}*ṣí-id-qa-nu* PRU 3 196 ii 22) = alphab. *ṣdqn* (UT 472b no. 2147); ^{I}*ṣi-na-r[u]* (PRU 6 72:5') = alphab. *ṣnr* (UT 475 no. 2177); GN's ^{uru}*ba-ṣi-ri* (PRU 3 189b:29'; Ug. 7 pl. 13:3, etc.) = alphab. *bṣr* (UT 375-76 no. 500); ^{uru}*qi-im-ṣi* (PRU 6 78:11) = alphab. *qmṣ* (cf. UT 478b no. 2241).

(b) with ZI = *ṣí*:

no S^a Voc. examples; in other texts: $^{\text{(lú)}}$*ia-ṣí-ru-ma* = /*yāṣirūma*/ "potters" (YṢR); *(:) ṣí(-ib)-bi-ri* = /*ṣibbīri*/ "collective land(?)" (ṢBR); *: ta-ar-bá-ṣí* = /*tarbaṣi*/ "stable" (RBṢ); perhaps also *: ma-aḫ-ZI-ZI* = /*maḫṣīṣi*/? "divide(?)" (ḪṢṢ); see also under /*ṣē*/, above.

PN's: ^{I}*ṣí-id-qa-nu*, cited under a; RN $^{\text{(I)f}}$*pí-ṣí-id-qí*[82] (PRU 3 50f.:2; 3 51f.:4).

/*ṣō*/ no examples.

/*ṣŭ*/ (a) with ZUM = *ṣu*:

in S^a Voc.: *ar-ṣu* = /*ʾarṣu*/ "earth" (ʾRṢ); *ḫe-en-ni-ṣu* = /*ḫinnīṣu*/? "piglet" (ḪNṢ); in other texts: ^{lú}*ma-ḫi-ṣu* = /*māḫiṣu*/ "(a profession)" (MḪṢ a); $^{\text{[urudu.meš]}}$*me-ḫi-[ṣ]u-⸢ma⸣*^{meš} = /*miḫīṣūma*/ "(implements)" (MḪṢ b).

Note the gentilic ^{uru}*ṣu-ri-yu* "Tyrian" (PRU 6 79:6), cf. alphab. *ṣr* (UT 476a no. 2193); perhaps also the PN ^{I}*ṣu?-pa-ra-nu* (Ug. 5 86: 22), if = alphab. *ṣprn* (UT 475b no. 2186).

(b) with ZU = *ṣú*:

in S^a Voc.: *iṣ-ṣú-[ma?]* = /*ᶜiṣṣūma*/ "tree(s), wood" (ᶜṢ); probably

[82]See n. 62, above.

also *[q]à?-ar-ṣú?* = */qarṣu/?* "piece(?)" (QRṢ); in other texts: *u-ṣú-ru* and *ú-ṣú-ri* = */ᶜuṣṣūru/i/* "bird" (ᶜṢR); *:ZI-ṣú(-ú)-ma* = */ṣēṣūma/* or */ṣīṣūma/* "salt fields" (ṢYṢ); note also the Akk. form *:ṣú-um-mu-ta* "it is transferred" (ṢMT).

/š/

/šă/ (a) with ŠA = *ša*:

always in Sª Voc.: *:ša-du-ú* = */šadû/* (ŠDW; cf. perhaps *ša-TI-i* in Ug. 5 153, if for Ugar. */šadî/*); *ša-mu-ma* = */šamûma/* "sky" (ŠMY); *ša-ap-šu* = */šapšu/* "sun (god)" (ŠPŠ); probably also *ša?-na!?-[t]u₄* = */šanatu/?* "year" (ŠN); in other texts: *la-ša-nu* = */lašānu/* "tongue" (perhaps also *[l]a-ša-na-ia* in Ug. 5 153; LŠN); *ma-ša-ra, : ma-aʾ-ša-ri(-ša)* = */maᶜšara/i/* "tithe" (ᶜŠR²); *ša-li-ma* (and *šal-li-ma*) = */šallima/* "has delivered" (ŠLM b).

(b) with NÍG = *šá*:[83]

only in ᵗᵘ́ᵍ*šá-ḫar-tu* = */šaᶜartu/* "wool" (ŠᶜR b).

(c) with SA (= *ša₁₀*?):[84]

only in the DN ᵈ*SA-li-mu* = */šalimu/?* ("sound"; ŠLM a).

/šē/ no examples.

/šĭ/ always with IGI = *ši*:

in Sª Voc.: ⸢*i*⸣*-ši-t[u₄]* = */ʾišītu/?* "fire" (ʾŠ); ⸢*ši-i-ru*⸣ = */šiʾru/* "flesh" (ŠʾR); *ši-i-ru* = */šīru/* "song" (ŠYR); *ši-tu* = */šītu/* "to place" (ŠYT); *[š]i?-i-ru[* = */šiᶜīru/* "barley(?)" (ŠᶜR a); in other texts: ˡᵘ́⁽·ᵐᵉˢ̌⁾*a-ši-ru/ri-ma* = */ᶜăšīrū/īma/* "(royal officials)" (ᶜŠR¹); perhaps *ši-a-ru* = */šiharu/?* "crescent-shaped sickle(?)" (ŠHR).

/šō/ with ŠU:

note perhaps *([i]a-)šu-bi-lu* = */yašōbilu/?* "he will have brought(?)" or */šōbilū/?* "have brought(?)" in Ug. 5 153 (YBL c).

/šŭ/ (a) with ŠU = *šu*:

in Sª Voc.: *bu-nu-šu* = */bunŭšu/* "man" (BNŠ); *ḫa-ra-*⸢*šu?*⸣ = */ḥarrăšu/* "artisan" (ḤRŠ); *šu-ḫu-ut-t[u?]* = */šuḥuttu/?* "bran, residue(?)" (ḤTT); *[ḫ]a-ra-š[u]* = */ḫar(r)ašu/* "deaf(?)" (ḪRŠ); ⸢*na*⸣-

[83]The use of *šá* is considerably less common than the use of *ša* in Ugarit Akk., although it becomes more frequent in later, especially economic texts, particularly as the writing for the determinative-relative pronoun *ša*. In writings of PN's and GN's, *šá* usually corresponds to alphabetic *θ*; see below.

[84]See above, §A 2.

[*š*]*u-*⌜*ma*⌝ = /*našūma*/ "people" (NŠ); $^{\text{[é?]}}$⌜*qi?-id?-šu?*⌝ = /*qidšu*/ "sanctuary" (QDŠ b); *ša-ap-šu* = /*šapšu*/ "sun (god)" (ŠPŠ); in other texts: ^{lú}*ia-qí-š*[*u*] = /*yāqišu*/ "fowler" (YQŠ).

[(b) with ŠÚ = *šú*:

Note the GN ^{uru}*šu-ra-šú* (PRU 3 191a:19').[85]]

/*θ*/

All examples are written with Š-signs.[86]

/*θă*/ (a) with ŠA = *ša*:

in S^a Voc.: *ga-ša-ru* = /*gaθaru*/ "strong" (divine name; GθR); *mu-ša-bu* = /*mōθabu*/ "seat" (YθB b); in other texts: ^{urudu}*ḫa-ar-me-ša-tu* = /*ḫarmiθātu*/ "sickles(?)" (ḪRMθ); *ša-al-šu-ma* = /*θalθūma*/ "copper(?)" (pl.; θLθ); ^{lú}*ša-na-ni*, ^{lú}*ša-na-nu-ma* = /*θannăni, -ūma*/ "archer(s)(?)" (θNN); probably also *ša-i-tu₄* = /*θāᶜittu*/? or /*θāᶜītu*/? "(a container)" (θᶜD/θᶜY); perhaps *ša-ri-ma* = /*θarrīma*/? "small(?)" (θRR); note also alphab. *θ* = syll. *ša* in KTU 5.14:15.

PN's and GN's: *ḫu-ud*!*-ša-nu* (PRU 3 199ff. i 17") = alphab. *ḥdθn* (UT 395a no. 843); $^{\text{1}}$*ša-i-yv* (PRU 3 96ff.:4,5,7; 3 154f.:5) = alphab. *θᶜy* (UT 505a no. 2713); *ša-pí-DA-na* (PRU 6 30:6; 6 38:19; cf. *šá-pí-DA-na* under b), cf. alphab. *bn θpdn* (UT 505b no. 2724)?;[87] perhaps ^{uru}*mu-ur-ša-a* (PRU 6 78:7,8) = alphab. *mr*⌜*θ?ᶜ?*⌝ (see CTA 13:24, but KTU 1.13 reads *mrǵt*).

(b) with NÍG = *šá*:[88]

no S^a Voc. examples; in other texts, only perhaps ^{giš}*šá-*[*ḫ*]*a*!*?-*⌜*ru?*⌝*-*

[85]Although Nougayrol read *-ši*, the copy and the fact that nearly all of the GN's in PRU 3 191a are nominative both indicate that *-šú* is the more likely reading. This GN appears elsewhere as both ^{uru}*šu-ra-šu* (e.g., PRU 3 190b:5) and ^{uru}*šu-ra-ši* (e.g., PRU 3 188f.:12').

☛ p. 400

[86]A very small number of correspondences between alphabetic *θ* and syllabic writings with S-signs are attested in proper names: ^{uru}⌜*si?*⌝*-il-ḫa-na* (PRU 3 38b:2) = alphab. *θlḫny* (UT 502b no. 2681); $^{\text{1}}$*sa-an-ḫa-ra-na* (PRU 3 47f.:14) = alphab. *θnǵrn* (UT 504b no. 2711); note perhaps also the RN *ᶜmθtmr*, written $^{\text{1}}$*a(m)-mi-IS-tam-ri* (e.g., PRU 3 102ff.:2), although the use of IS in such examples (vs. IŠ in $^{\text{(1)}}$*am-mi-iš-tam-ra/ri*, e.g., PRU 3 53b:2) may reflect an optional partial assimilation (fronting, /*θ*/ > [s]) before the dental /*t*/ that is not reflected in the more conservative alphabetic spelling. In view of the rarity of /*θ*/ written with S-signs, and in view of the several other etymologies that may be proposed for *:ḫa-ar-ZA-ti* (PRU 3 95f.:11,20; see Appendix to Glossary), it seems unlikely that the latter reflects the root *ḥ-r-θ* "to plow," mentioned as orthographically possible by Kühne, UF 6 165-66 n. 57.

[87]Note also the Hurrian PN's $^{\text{1}}$DUMU-*ḫu-du-up-ša-ri* (PRU 3 199ff. ii 10) = alphab. *bn* [*ḫ*]*dpθr* (UT 400b no. 936); $^{\text{1}}$*a-na-ša-bu* (Ug. 7 pl. 50:7',r.7') = alphab. *annθb* (UT 362b no. 262).

[88]It is curious that *šá* occurs for /*θ*/ so often in names, and yet is rare for /*θ*/ in our corpus of Ugaritic vocabulary. Perhaps it was felt to be appropriate for the voiceless allophone of Hurrian /*θ*/ (Speiser's *š̄*), but less so for Ugaritic /*θ*/; as noted below, most of the names in which *šá* appears are non-Semitic.

ma = /*θaǵarūma*/? "door-leaves(?)" (θǴR).

Often in PN's and GN's, especially in economic texts; note that the majority of the following are non-Semitic: e.g., *šá-pí-DA-na* (Ug. 5 6:32; cf. *ša-pí-DA-na*, under a); ^{f}*šá-ru-me-li* (PRU 6 166:9), cf. perhaps alphab. *θrml* "alabaster" (UT 506-7 no. 2748; but note also ^{f}*šar-mi-la* PRU 3 85f.:5); *šá-qa-ba-ni* (PRU 6 90 r.8') = alphab. *θqbn* (UT 506a no. 2733); ^{1}*ku-šá-yv* (PRU 6 72:13') and ^{1}*ku-šá-ya-ni* (PRU 6 73:11), cf. alphab. *kθy* (UT 424b no. 1330; but note also ^{1}*ka-ši-yv* PRU 3 194f.:22); ^{1}*šá-ra-na* (PRU 6 73:20) = alphab. *θrn* (UT 507a no. 2752); ^{uru}*šá-am-ra-a* (PRU 6 77:7; 6 105:8') = alphab. *θmry* (UT 503b no. 2701); ^{uru}*šá-lur*$_x$(NIR)-*ba(-a)* [89] (PRU 6 105:3'; 6 134:7) and its gentilic ^{uru}*šá-lur*$_x$-*bi-yi/yu* (PRU 6 100:1; 6 138:19) = alphab. *θlrby* (UT 502-3 no. 2687).

/*θē*/ no examples.[90]

/*θĭ*/ with IGI = *ši*:[91]

no S^a Voc. examples; in other texts: *i-*⌜*ši?*⌝*-[bi?]* = /*ʾiθībi*/? (month name; ʾθB); *a-ši-ib* = /*ʾaθib*/ "let me dwell" (YθB a).

Note the PN ^{1}*ḫu-da/dá-ši* (PRU 3 133f.:5; Syria 28 173f.:23,28; Ug. 5 95:4) = alphab. *ḥdθ* (UT 395a no. 843); ^{1}*ši-pì-iṭ-*^{d}IM (Ug. 5 159:14), cf. alphab. *θpṭbʿl* (UT 506a no. 2727).[92]

/*θō*/ no examples.

/*θŭ*/ with ŠU = *šu*:

no S^a Voc. examples; in other texts: *ša-al-šu-ma* = /*θalθūma*/ "copper(?)" (pl.; θLθ); perhaps also ${}^{túg.me}$*ku-up-šu* = /*kupθu*/? "(a headdress)" (KPθ); ^{giš}*šu-uq-du(-)ma*[= /*θuqdu*/ "almond" (θQD).

PN's: ^{1}*šu-ub-am-mv* (PRU 3 56f.:15; 3 61f.:5,13; 3 64f.:3,9,15; 3 159f.:10; RA 38 5:15) and ^{1}*šu-ba-ʾa-mu* (PRU 6 72:10') = alphab. *θbʿm* (UT 501b no. 2661); ^{1}*ia-šu-ub-*DINGIR (PRU 6 39:8',18'), cf. alphab. *θbil* (UT ibid.).[93]

b. *vC* sequences

/*aC*/

/*að*/,[94] /*az*/, /*aẓ*/ no examples.

[89]For the reading of NIR as *lur*$_x$ in this GN, see Astour, UF 13 8 n. 49.

[90]For [θe] in Hurrian names, see the following note.

[91]In Hurrian names, ŠE often appears, corresponding to alphab. *θ* (the voiceless allophone of Hurrian /*θ*/): e.g., ^{1}*i-di-še-ni* (PRU 6 73:9) = alphab. *idθn* (UT 353a no. 97); ^{1}*ki-še-na* (PRU 6 150; but note also ^{1}*ki-ši-na*, next note) = alphab. *kθn* (UT 424b no. 1334).

[92]Other examples, probably all non-Semitic: ^{1}*ši-di-ia* (PRU 6 78:4,16) = alphab. *θdy* (UT 501a no. 2654); ^{1}*ki-ši-na* (Ug. 7 pl. 2 r.9'; but also ^{1}*ki-še-na*, previous note); ^{1}*ap-pí-*⌜*ši?*⌝ (Ug. 7 pl. 2:12') = alphab. *apθ* (UT 364b no. 315); ^{1}*du-[š]i?-na* (Ug. 7 pl. 2:13') = alphab. *dθn* (UT 387b no. 715).

[93]Note also the non-Semitic *šu-zi-ia-ya* (PRU 3 195b B ii 6) = alphab. *θðyy* (UT 501a no. 2659).

[94]Note the GN ^{uru}*ÁŠ-da-di* (gen.) "Ashdod" (PRU 6 156:3) = alphab. *aðdd* (KTU 4.709:2), cf.

/as/ (a) with AZ = *as*:

only in S[a] Voc. *ka-as-pu* = /*kaspu*/ "silver" (KSP).

(b) with ÁŠ = *ás*:[95]

only in $^{giš(.meš)}$*ma-ás-wa-tu* = /*maswātu*/ "cypress(?) logs" (cf. $^{giš.meš}$*ma-sa-wa-tu* = /*masawātu*/; MSW).

/aṣ/ no examples.

/aš/ with AŠ = *aš*:[96]

in S[a] Voc.: ⸢*qa*⸣-*aš-tu*$_4$ = /*qaštu*/ "bow" (QŠ); probably also *ma-aš-nu-ú*? = /*mašnǔʾu*/? "enemy(?)" (ŠNʾ); in other texts: *ma-aš-a-li* = /*mašʾali*/ "oracle(?)" (ŠʾL); *ma-aš-la-ḫa-ma* = /*mašlaḥāma*/ "(garments)" (dual; ŠLḤ).

/aθ/ (a) with AŠ = *aš*:

in S[a] Voc.: *aš-ta-ru* = /*ʿaθtaru*/ (divine name; ʿθTR); in other texts: perhaps *ma-aš-na* = /*maθnâ*/? (θNY).[97]

Note also the following PN's: ^{1}*aš-tar-a-bi* (PRU 3 141f.:3,8; cf. ^{1}DUMU-*aš-tar-mi* PRU 3 102ff.:29) = alphab. *ʿθtrab* (UT 462b no. 1941); ^{1}*ia-aš-ad-du/dì* (PRU 3 157:passim) = alphab. *yθʿd* (UT 416b no. 1179); ^{1}*ia-aš-p[u]-ṭù* (PRU 3 195b A 1) and ^{1}DUMU-*ia-aš-pu-ṭì* (PRU 3 199ff. i 13"), cf. alphab. *yθpṭ* (UT 506a no. 2727).

(b) with ÁŠ = *áš*:

no S[a] Voc. examples; in other texts: probably *ma-áš-ḫa-ṭu-ma* = /*maθḫaṭūma*/ "(cloths)" (θḪṬ).

Note also e.g., ^{uru}*áš-qu-lu-nu*<*-yu*> (PRU 6 79:9; root probably *θ-q-l*, as suggested by Cross-Freedman, BASOR 175 49); ^{1}*ta-áš-qú?-lu* (PRU 6 104:10; root *θ-q-l*?); ^{1}*áš-ta-bi*-LUGAL (PRU 6 77:5; 6 88:7'), cf. the alphab. writing of the Hurrian DN as *aθtb* (KTU 1.42:29,31; 1.116:15).

/iC/

/ið/, /iz/, /iẓ/, /is/ no examples.

/iṣ/ with GIŠ = *iṣ*:

only in S[a] Voc. *iṣ-ṣú-*[*ma*?] = /*ʿiṣṣūma*/ "tree(s), wood" (ʿṢ).

---

gentilic *aðdy* (UT 353a no. 98); see the discussion of /ð/ under a above.

[95]This is the only occurrence of ÁŠ with the value *ás* in the corpus of Akkadian texts from Ugarit; see §A 2, end, with n. 15.

[96]See n. 15, above.

[97]Note ^{d}*aš-ra-tu*$_4$ in Ug. 5 18:19, if the form represents Ugar. /*ʾaθratu*/; but Akk. *ašratu* is probably intended (see the Glossary under ʾθR).

/iš/ with IŠ = *iš*:

in Sª Voc.: *i-[r]i?-iš-[tu₄?]* = */ʾirištu/*? "request" (ʾRŠ); *iš-du₄* = */ʾišdu/* "leg" (ʾŠD); in other texts: perhaps *qa-dì-iš* = Akkadianized *qadiš* (for */qadiša/*) "is sacred" (QDŠ a); *mar-ḫi-iš* = */marḫiš(u)/* "(a utensil)" (RḪŠ).

/iθ/ no examples.[98]

/uC/

/uð/, /uz/, /uẓ/, /us/, /uṣ/, /uš/ no examples.

/uθ/ with UŠ = *uš*:

not in Sª Voc.; in other texts: *ú-nu(-uš)-ša* = */ʾunuθθa/* "estate tax" (ʾNθ); *uš-r[i-ia]-ni* = */ʾuθrīyāni/* "crown prince" (ʾθRYN).

3. *Sonorants*

a. Liquids: */l/, /r/*

/l/

/lă/ always with LA; see, e.g., ʾLN, GLB, L¹, LBN¹, LŠN.

/lē/ no examples.

/lĭ/ always with LI; see, e.g., GWL, HLNY, ḤBL, YBL b, L².

/lō/ no examples.

/lŭ/ once with LUM = *lu₄*, in Sª Voc. DINGIR-*lu₄* = */ʾilu/* "god, El" (but cf. also Sª Voc. ⌜*i?-lu?*⌝; ʾL); otherwise always with LU (see, e.g., BDL, BṬL, BᶜL, SPL, RGL).

/al/ always with AL; see, e.g., HLNY, LSM, MLK b.

/il/ with IL in *:sí-il-a* = */silᶜa/* (SLᶜ), Sª Voc. *ṣi-il-PI[* = */ṣilyatu/* or */ṣilyu/* "curse" (ṢLY).

/ul/ always with UL; see, e.g., ḤLM, ǴLM, QLQL.

/r/

/ră/ always with RA; see, e.g., ʾḪR, ʾθR, DPR, ḤRŠ, ḪRŠ, KKR; note also

[98]Note the syllabic spellings of the RN *ᶜmθtmr* (= */ᶜammiθtamrv/*), with both GIŠ = *is* and IŠ = *iš*, cited above in n. 86.

alphab. *r* = syll. *ra* in KTU 5.14:14.

/rē/ with RI, perhaps in *ku-RI-ku* = */kurēku/*? "(implement)" (KRK).

/rĭ/ always with RI; see, e.g., ᵓRŠ, BRḤ, GMR, ḤRM, ḪYR, ḪRY, RGL.

/rō/ no examples.

/rŭ/ in the Sᵃ Voc. text Ug. 5 137, word-final */-ru/* is written with AŠ = *rù* eight times (see ᵓDR, BḪR, DKR[1], ḤDR, NǴR b, SRR, PṬR a, PRR), with RU eight times, including four instances in the polyglot god-list at the end of the tablet (see GθR bis; ṬHR, KθR, ᶜWR, ᶜθTR, ŠYR, ŠᶜR); elsewhere AŠ = *rù* occurs word-finally only once, in the god-list Ug. 5 18 (see KNR); otherwise, only RU occurs, including word-finally: in Sᵃ Voc. texts: see DKR[2], ZTR, ṬHR, PRS, ŠᵓR; in other texts: see ᵓZR, BḤR[1], YṢR, YRᵓ, NW/YR, NǴR a, SGR a, SGR b, ᶜṢR, ᶜRB, ᶜŠR[1], ǴMR, PṬR b, PǴ(N)DR, QDR, ŠHR, TRR, θǴR.

/ar/ always with AR; see, e.g., ᵓRZ, ᵓRṢ, BRḤ, DRᶜ, ḤRM b, ḪRMθ, YRQ, KRB, MW/YR, MṢR.

/ir/ with IR; see BRK, ᶜðR, and *ir?-KU* in Sᵃ Voc. no. 48.2

/ur/ with UR in one example, *: ZU-ur-PI* = */ẓurwu/*? (or */ṣurwu/*?) "(aromatic) resin" (ẒRW); but with ÚR in $^{giš.meš}$*úr-nu* = */ᵓurnu/* "laurel(?)" (ᵓRN); cf. also ^{giš}ÚR.NU.UM and [^{giš}Ú]R.ZI.IN.NI in the Ugarit Akk. lexical text Syria 12 pl. 46ff. ii 49,53 (cf. MSL 5 112, notes to lines 237-264); the latter are the only attestations of *úr* (used syllabically) in the Ugarit Akk. texts (vs. *ur*, passim).

b. Nasals: */m/*, */n/*

/m/

/mă/ always with MA; see, e.g., ᵓDM, ᵓZR, ᵓMM, GMR, DPR, MᵓD.

/mē/ no examples

/mĭ/ with MI and ME; see §G 2, below.

/mō/ always with MU; see YBL b, YRᵓ, YθB b.

/mŭ/ always with MU; see, e,g., ḤRM, LSM, ᶜMQ[2], ǴRM, ŠMY.

/am/ with AM; see MṢR, ǴMR.

/im/ no examples.

/um/ UM, perhaps in $^{lú.meš}$*GU-um-*[*ru?(-šu?)*] = */kumrū/* "(priests?)" (KMR).

/n/

/nă/ always with NA; see, e.g., ʾBD, ʾNK, KND, KNR.

/nē/ perhaps *ni-r[u]* = */nēru/*? "lamp(?)," but */nīru/*? is also possible (NW/YR).

/nĭ/ always with NI; see §G 2, below.

/nō/ with NU, perhaps in *ḫi-nu-ta-me* = */ḥinōtāmi/*? and ⸢*vḫ?*⸣*-nu-tu*₄ = */ʾvḥnōtu/*? "(implement)" (ḤNW).

/nŭ/ always with NU; see, e.g., ʾDN, ʾNθ, ʾRN, BNŠ, LBN[1,2], LŠN.

/an/ with AN; see KNP b.

/in/ with EN and IN; see see §G 2, below.

/un/ with UN; see QNN, TNN.

3. Glides: */w/*, */y/*

/w/

The semivowel */w/* occurs only before vowels and before itself (i.e., */ww/*). The sequence */wv/* is normally written with the PI sign, regardless of the following vowel,[99] in Ugarit Akk. texts;[100] among the Ugaritic words, only the values *wa* and *wu* are attested. Note that since the vowel of PI = *wv* is ambiguous, the values assigned in the forms below are only *inferred,* on the analogy of morphologically similar forms. Doubled */ww/* is never explicitly indicated in Ugarit Akk. texts,[101] and so there are no examples of a sign with the value */vw/*.

/wă/ always with PI = *wa*:[102]

in Sᵃ Voc.: *ú-PI* = */huwa/* "he, it" (HW[1]); *[ḫ]u-PI-tu*₄ = */ḥuwwatu/*

[99]As is true of PI (and IA) for */yv/*; see below, n. 107.

[100]There are a few exceptions, especially for the indication of the diphthong *aw* (or *au*) in non-Semitic names, which is accomplished with the use of the Ú sign or a *uC* sign after a *Ca* sign: e.g., [1]*ta-ú-zi* (PRU 3 37a:12,14); [1]*a-up-šu/še* (PRU 3 170b:10'; PRU 6 79:10); note that the last example appears as alphab. *aupš/θ* (UT 348a nos. 6,7), in which the diphthong, if such it is, is reflected not by *w* but by aleph. (For the GN's [uru]*ḫu-pa-ta-ú,* [uru]*am-mi-za-ú* in PRU 3 191a:10',14', see below, n. 106.) In a few other examples, the sequence *vCwa* is written not *vC-wa,* but rather *v-Cu-a*: e.g., the gentilic [uru]*a-ru-a-di-yu* "Arwadite" (PRU 6 79:7,8; cf. [uru]*ar-wa-da* in EA 101:13,15, 105:12 [both Byblos], 149:59 [Tyre]); [1]*a-ru-a-nu* (PRU 6 79:16); note also [1]*su-a-nu-a-nu* (PRU 6 77:3).

[101]A possible exception is the PN [1]*ta-ú-wa-na* (PRU 6 29:4), if the form is to be read so (*/tawwăna/*?); but note alphab. *tiyn* (UT 496a no. 2506), which may suggest that the syllabic form is to be read [1]*ta-ú-ya-na.*

[102]Note also perhaps PI for the conjunction */wa-/* in Ug. 5 153 (see the Glossary under W).

"country" (ḤWW); probably also *ú-[P]I!?-[t]u*$_4$ = /*huwătu*/? "word" (HW^2); perhaps *P[I?-al/la?-d]u?* = /*waladu*/?? (or /*yaldu*/??) "child" (YLD); in other texts: *gu-PI-*⌜*li*⌝ = /*guw(w)ăli*/ "circuit(?)" (GWL); $^{\text{giš(.meš)}}$*ma-ás/sa-PI-tu* = /*mas(a)wātu*/ "cypress(?) logs" (MSW); *:pu-PI-ti* = /*puwwati*/? (PWT).

/*wē*/, /*wĭ*/ no examples.

/*wō*/ no vocabulary examples; note, however, perhaps alphab. *w* = syll. PI = *wu*? (for the letter name /*wō*/ < **waw*?[103]) in KTU 5.14:7.

/*wŭ*/ with PI = *wu*:[104]

in S^{a} Voc.: *ḫu-PI-ú* = /*ḥuwwû*/ < **ḥuwwayu*[105] (ḤYY^1/ḤWY^1); in other texts: *: ZU-ur-PI* = /*ẓurwu*/? (or /*ṣurwu*/?) "(aromatic) resin" (following Akk. nom. *riqqu*; ẒRW).

/*y*/

Like /*w*/, /*y*/ does not occur before consonants (other than itself, /*yy*/) in Ugaritic words. For the sequence /*yv*/, both the IA sign and the PI sign are used,[106] regardless

[103]Cross-Lambdin, BASOR 160 25.

[104]The value *wu* is otherwise attested in Ugarit Akk., apart from the possible example in the preceding paragraph, only in the lexical equation ḫa.wu.uz^{ki} = *ḫa-wu-*⌜*zu*⌝ MSL 11 43ff. iii 1 (cf. line 2; canonical [ḫa.b]u.uz^{ki}).

[105]See below, ch. 2 §E 3, with n. 107 there.

[106]It is likely that /*y*/ in Ugar. words and in WSem. PN's and GN's is indicated *only* by means of one of these two signs in Ugarit Akk. A reduplicated A sign occurs for *ayyv* and *āyv* in a few Akkadian words in literary texts, but never for non-Akk. forms. Syllabic writings of GN's and PN's ending in *-Ca-a* have been taken by some scholars to reflect final /*-āy(a)*/ or /*-ay(y)a*/, but more likely such writings have their usual significance, viz., /*-Câ*/; see below, §F 1 b; ch. 2 §E 3 n. 109.

It has also been suggested that the Ú sign occasionally represents /*-yu*/ (e.g., Kühne, UF 7 255 n. 9; Sivan, Analysis 179 n. 1), but the paucity of examples, for all of which alternative explanations are possible, renders this very doubtful. Rather, the Ú sign in WSem. forms, like other vowel signs, indicates either a long vowel (only when following a *Cu* sign, of course, as in *ša-du-ú* = /*šadû*/ "field" [ŠDW]; *ḫu-PI-ú* = /*ḥuwwû*/ "to save," not */*ḥuwwayu*/ [see below, ch. 2, §E 3; ḤYY^1/ḤWY^1 a]) or the presence of one of the gutturals /*ʾ*/, /*h*/, /*ʿ*/ (see below, under 4 b). The latter usage also obtains in the two GN's curiously written with final *-Ca-ú* in PRU 3 191a:10',14': ^{uru}*ḫu-PA-ta-ú* and ^{uru}*am-mi-za-ú*. These GN's appear elsewhere without final *-ú*: ^{uru}*ḫu-PA/BA-ta* (PRU 3 189b:21'; Ug. 5 102:15'; Ug. 7 pl. 13:47; ^{uru}*ḫa-PA-ta-yv* in PRU 3 190a:15, with *-a-* in the first syllable, is clearly a different town); ^{uru}*a(m)-mi/me-za/ša* (PRU 3 189b:9'; 3 190a:20'; 3 190b:2). The writings with *-ú*, I would suggest, are simply attempts by the scribe of PRU 3 191a to create nominative forms for these GN's that are normally monoptotic in /*-a*/ (note that in this list, all but two of the town names end in /*-u*/; the exceptions occur in lines 17',21'; in 7', read [^{uru}*ḫal-bu*] *kar-ra-di*, a genitive chain [cf. PRU 3 190a:11']; in 19', read $^{\text{[uru]}}$*šu-ra-šú*; in 26', read probably $^{\text{[uru]}}$*mu-a-*⌜*ru*⌝); the phonetic value of the final Ú sign, therefore, is probably simply /*-ʾu*/.

of the vowel; throughout this study, IA is transliterated as *ia, ie, ii, iu,* and PI as *ya, ye, yi, yu,*[107] though in normalizations of Ugaritic words only /y/ will appear, regardless of the sign. The IA sign is the more common of the two for */yă̄/*, while the PI sign is the more common for */yĭ̄/* and */yŭ̄/*. It should be noted that since both of these signs may represent /y/ plus any vowel (see n. 107), the values assigned in individual forms below, as with PI = *wv,* are entirely inferential; thus, the normalizations must, as far as the quality of the vowel after /y/ is concerned, be considered reconstructions. Such forms may not, therefore, be mustered as evidence in support of phonological processes, when our understanding of those processes (based on forms without /y/) has itself contributed to our normalization of those forms: e.g., the form *ia-ṣí-ru-ma* = */yāṣirūma/* (YṢR) may not be cited as evidence of the lack of a Canaanite shift in Ugaritic, since our transliteration of IA as *ia-* (rather than as *iu-*, for **/yōṣirūma/*) is itself due entirely to the prior observation that the shift has not occurred.

/yă̄/ (a) with IA:[108]

not in S^{a} Voc.; in other texts: acc. *ḫe-e-IA* = [ḫēya]? "vacant(?)" (vs. nom. *ḫe-e-PI*(*yu*) in the same text; ḪWY); ITI *ḫi-IA-*⌜*ri?*⌝ = */ḫiyyāri/* (month name; ḪYR); *IA-ar-qa-ni* = */yarqāni/* "yellow-green" (YRQ); $^{\text{(lú)}}$*IA-ṣí-ru-ma* = */yāṣirūma/* "potters" (YṢR); ^{lú}*IA-qí-š*[*u*] = */yāqišu/* "fowler" (YQŠ); $^{\text{(lú(.meš))}}$*mar-IA(-an)-nu/ni(-ma)* = */maryannu, -ū/ī(ma)/* "charioteer(s)" (MRYN); perhaps *iš-IA-ti-mi* = */ᶜišyatēmi/* "clamps(?)" (dual; ᶜŠY).

Gentilics: no examples.

PN's, GN's: passim, e.g., ^{1}*ia-ab-ni*-DINGIR (PRU 3 32f.:18; 3 52f.:4) and ^{1}*ia-a-ab-ni*-DINGIR (PRU 6 107:12, cf. ^{1}*ya-ab-ni*-DINGIR, ibid.:1) = alphab. *ybni*[*l*] (UT 373b no. 483); ^{1}*ia-an-ḫa-mu/mi* (PRU 3 113ff.:4,14,21) = alphab. *ynḥm* (UT 443a no. 1634); ^{1}*nu-ri-ia-nu/na* (e.g., PRU 3 45f.:passim) = alphab. *nryn* (UT 447b no. 1704); ^{uru}*ia(-a)-pa-rù/ru/ri* (PRU 3 190a:23'; 3 190b:4; 3 191a:16'; PRU 6 102:5) = alphab. *ypr* (UT 413a no. 1136).

[107]Following Gelb, Or. 39 537; see also Borger, ABZ^2 p. 97 no. 142a, p. 156 no. 383.

With rare exception, such as when required by a following *vC* sign (e.g., ^{1}*ye-eš-na* PRU 6 72:6',12'), Nougayrol consistently transliterated the PI and IA signs, when they have the value *y*+vowel, as *ya* and *ia*, respectively. That the sign could, however, have the values *ye, yi, yu* is demonstrated by the exceptions. Further, there is no evidence otherwise to suggest that in Ugaritic /y/ was invariably followed by */ă̄/*, so that we are certainly justified, e.g., in transliterating the obl. pl. form *: ḫé-PI-ma* (PRU 3 102ff.:15) as *: ḫé-yi-ma* (for [ḫēyīma]; see ḪWY), or the S^{a} Voc. form for "life" as nom. pl. *ḫé-yu-ma* (for [ḥeyyūma]; see ḤYY^1/ḤWY^1 b). Thus, in other forms, including gentilics, we are likewise justified in transliterating PI as *yv* and IA as *iv*, where *v* is the morphologically expected vowel; see Hillers, BASOR 200 18; Rainey, IOS 3 42.

[108]Note also IA in Ug. 5 153: [*i*]*a(-)ab-ṣi-ru* (line 1) and [*i*]*a(-)šu-bi-lu* (line 2), perhaps for 3ms forms */yabṣiru/*? "he will cut down(?)" and */yašōbilu/*? "he will have brought(?)" (see the Glossary under BṢR; YBL c), although the 1cs suffix may be intended instead, as probably in [*l*]*a-ša-na-ia* (r.4') = */lašāna-ya/* "my tongue" (see under -Y^2, LŠN).

(b) with PI:

in Sᵃ Voc.: probably *ṣi-il-PI*[= /*ṣilyatu*/ (less likely /*ṣilyu*/) "curse" (ṢLY); perhaps *al-li-ni-PI* = /*hallinīya*/? "here, now then" (HLNY); *P*[*I*?-*al*/*la*?-*d*]*u*? = /*yaldu*/?? (or /*waladu*/??) "child" (YLD);[109] in other texts: perhaps *ḫi-PI-ri* = /*ḫiyyāri*/ (month name; transiliteration only, no copy [vs. *ḫi-IA-*⌜*ri*?⌝ above]; ḪYR);

Gentilics: no examples.

PN's, GN's: e.g., ¹*ya-ab-ni*-DINGIR (PRU 6 107:1, cf. ¹*ia(-a)-ab-ni*-DINGIR, ibid.:12, etc., under a); ¹*ya-ap-lu-nu* (PRU 6 54:13) = alphab. *ypln* (UT 413a no. 1131); ¹*ša-dú-ya-na* (PRU 3 52f.:3), cf. alphab. *šdyn* (UT 488a no. 2387)?; ᵘʳᵘ*ya-a-li* (PRU 6 102:7).

☛ p. 400 /*yē*/ no examples.

Note, however, the GN ᵘʳᵘ*PI-na* (PRU 6 119:2), probably for /*yēna*/ < **yayn-* "vineyard," if the same town is also represented in ᵘʳᵘGEŠTIN-*na*, as suggested by Nougayrol, PRU 6 p. 163 n. 5. These forms probably correspond to alphab. *yny* (UT 412a no. 1114).

/*yĭ*/ (a) with IA:

no Sᵃ Voc. examples; in other texts: *tu-ki-IA* = /*tōkīyi*/ "inner" (TWK);

Gentilics: probably ˡᵘ́·⁽ᵘʳ⁾ᵘ!? *ak!-kà-a-ii* "Akko-ite" (TA 8 7f.:33).

PN's, GN's: no certain examples.

(b) with PI:

no Sᵃ Voc. examples; in other texts: gen. :*ḫa-a-PI* = [ḫāyi]?, :*ḫé-PI-ma* = [ḫēyīma]?, *ḫi-i-PI(-šu)* = [ḫīyĭ]? "vacant(?)" (ḪWY); ⌜ᵈ?*a*?⌝-*li-PI* = /ᶜ*ălĭyi*/? "ascendant" (ᶜLY a); ⌜*e*?⌝-*la-PI* = /ᶜ*ilāyi*/? "upper (part)(?)" (ᶜLY b); probably also *uḫ-ra-a-PI* = /ʾ*uḫrāyi*/ "destiny" (ʾḪR);

Gentilics (gen.): ᵘʳᵘ*šal-me-yi* (PRU 6 79:2,5) = alphab. *šlmy* (UT 490-91 no. 2424); ᵘʳᵘKI-*ba-a*ʾ-*li-yi* (PRU 6 79:4), cf. alphab. *aθrb*ᶜ*l* (UT 369a no. 424); ᵘʳᵘ*šá-lur*ₓ*-bi-yi*[110] (PRU 6 100:1) = alphab. *θlrby* (KTU 4.297:5); plural ᵘʳᵘ*ib*?-*na-li-yi-*[*m*]*a* (!) (PRU 6 113:6).[111]

PN's, GN's: possibly, e.g., ¹*la-i-yi* (PRU 3 45f.:4,9) = alphab. *liy* (UT 425a no. 1342); ¹*ša-i-yi* (PRU 3 96ff.:45; 3 154f.:5) = alphab. *θiy* (UT 500b no. 2629) or *θ*ᶜ*y* (UT 505a no. 2713).[112]

/*yō*/ [(a) with IA: no examples.]

(b) with PI:

probably Sᵃ Voc. *PI-mu*, most likely for /*yōmu*/ (less likely, /*yămu*/; YWM).

[109]For *PI-mu* "day," see under /*yō*/, below.

[110]See n. 89, above.

[111]For the reading, see the Glossary under MSW.

[112]It is unclear whether such forms were regularly declined as triptotes in /*-yu, -yi, -ya*/, or monoptotic, always ending in /*-ya*/.

/*yŭ*/ (a) with IA:

probably Sa Voc. *ḫi-[I]A?-ma* = /*ḥiyyūma*/ "life" (ḤYY^1/ḤWY^1 b);

Gentilics: probably ^{uru}*qa-ar-ti-i*[*u*] (PRU 6 148:18"; cf. ^{uru}*qar-ti-yu*, under b) = alphab. *qrty* (UT 481b no. 2278).

PN's: perhaps ^{1}*mu-ri-iu*, ^{1}*iz-zu-iu* (PRU 6 107:2,4); ^{1}*ku-ra-a-iu-ú*[(PRU 6 72:4').

(b) with PI:

in Sa Voc.: *ḫé-PI-ma* = /*ḥiyyūma*/ "life" (ḤYY^1 b); possibly also *ṣi-il-PI*, if for /*ṣilyu*/ "curse," but /*ṣilyatu*/ is more likely (ṢLY); in other texts: nom. *ḫe-e-PI* = [ḫēyu]? "vacant(?)" (vs. acc. *ḫe-e-IA* in the same text; ḪWY).

Gentilics (nom.):

in PRU 6 79: ^{uru}*ṣu-ri-yu* (line 6; = alphab. *ṣry* UT 496a no. 2196); ^{uru}*a-ru-a-di-yu* (7,8); ^{uru}*ma-ḫa-di-yu* (10; = alphab. *mḫdy* UT 432a no. 1453, and *maḫdy* and pl. *ma/iḫdym* UT 355a no. 130); ^{uru}SAG-*yu* (11,13; = alphab. *rišy(m)* UT 481b no. 2296[113]); ^{uru}*u-ga-ar-ti-yu* (15; = alphab. *ugrty* UT 351b no. 69); ^{uru}*a-ki-yu*[114] (18); ^{uru}*uš-na-ti-yu* (19); note also, with /*-ūyu*/, ^{uru}*a-ta-li-gu-yu* (17; = p. 400 alphab. *atlgy* UT 368b no. 410);

in PRU 6 138: ^{uru}*a-ru-ti-yu* (lines 1,14; cf. alphab. PN *arty* UT 367b no. 385); ^{uru}*ZA-ri-nu* (4,7; cf. alphab. GN *ẓrn* UT 407b no. 1059); ^{uru}*qar-ti-yu* (17; also ^{uru}⌜*qa*⌝*-ra-ti-yu*[115] PRU 6 78:1) and nom. pl. ^{uru}*qa-ra-ti-yu-ma* (25; = alphab. *qrty* UT 481b no. 2278); ^{uru}*šal-mi-yu* (18; = alphab. *šlmy* UT 490-91 no. 2424); ^{uru}*šá-lur$_x$-bi-y*[*u*][116] (19; cf. alphab. *θlrby*, gentilic in KTU 4.297:5);

also: note ^{íd}*na-aḫ-ra(-yv)* = alphab. *nhr(y)* (see under NHR in the Glossary); ^{uru}*ap-sú-na-yu* (PRU 3 37a:10), but pl. ^{uru}*ap-sú-ni-yu-ma* (PRU 6 77:10), cf. alphab. *apsny* (UT 364b no. 310); for PRU 6 78:1, see preceding paragraph.

PN's: perhaps, e.g., ^{1}*ša-i-yu* (PRU 3 96ff.:7) = alphab. *θiy* (UT 500b no. 2629) or *θ*ᶜ*y* (UT 505a no. 2713).

4. *Gutturals*[117]

There is a consistent distinction between the writing of /*ḥ*/, /*ḫ*/, and /*ġ*/ on the one hand, and of /ʾ/, /*h*/, and /ᶜ/ on the other. The former three phonemes are always indi-

[113]See Astour, JESHO 13 113-27, esp. 115 n. 4.

[114]Cf. $^{\text{lú.[ur]u!?}}$*ak!-kà-a-ii*, cited above under /*yĭ*/ a?

[115]What follows *-yu* at the end of the line is probably an erasure (vs. Nougayrol's *-m*[*a*]; see the copy); a pl. (in /*-ūma*/) is not expected here.

[116]See n. 89, above.

[117]On the indication of the West Semitic gutturals in personal names in Akkadian texts from Ras Shamra, see Gröndahl, Personennamen 12-13; Boyd, Collection 273-75, also presents the evidence of his list of Ugaritic words for the writing of the gutturals.

cated with Ḫ-signs,[118] while the latter, with very rare exception in the case of /ᶜ/, never are.[119]

a. /ḥ/, /ḫ/, /ǵ/

/ḥă/, /ḫă/, /ǵă/ always with ḪA:[120]

/ḥă/ in Sᵃ Voc.: [a-ḫ]a-du = /ʾaḥadu/? "one" (ʾḤD); ḫa-ri-mu = /ḥarĭmu/ "desecrated(?)" (ḤRM a); ḫa-ra-⸢šu?⸣ = /ḥarrăšu/ "artisan" (ḤRŠ); probably also la-ḫa-m[u] = /laḥămu/? "what is suitable" (LḤM); in other texts: ḫa-ba-li-ma = /ḥabalīma/ "ropes, lots" (ḤBL); : ḫa-me-ti = /ḥāmīti/ "wall" (ḤMY); ḫa-ar-ma-ni = /ḥarmāni/ "sacred place(?)" (ḤRM b); ma-qa-ḫa = /maqqaḥā/ "pair of tongs" (dual bound form; LQḤ b); ma-aš-la-ḫa-ma = /mašlaḥāma/ "(garments)" (dual; ŠLḤ).

PN's, GN's: e.g., ¹ia-an-ḫa-mu/mi (PRU 3 113ff.:4,14,21) = alphab. ynḥm (UT 443a no. 1634); ¹ḫa-ZI-qá/qa-ta-nu/na (PRU 3 141f.:5,9) = alphab. bn ḥṣqt (KTU 4.428:7); ᵘʳᵘša-ḫa-qi (PRU 6 118:5') = alphab. šḥq (UT 488-89 no. 2398).

/ḫă/ in Sᵃ Voc.: ma-aḫ-ḫa-[du] = [maḫḫadu] = /maʾḫadu/ "harbor" (ʾḪD); [ḫ]a-ra-š[u] = /ḫar(r)ašu/ "deaf(?)" (ḪRŠ); in other texts: :ḫa-a-yi = /ḫāyi/ "vacant(?)" (ḪWY); ᵘʳᵘᵈᵘḫa-ar-me-ša-tu = /ḫarmiθātu/ "sickles(?)" (ḪRMθ); : ḫa-at-ni = /ḫatni/? "son-in-law" (ḪTN); na-ḫa-li = /naḫal(l)i/? "wadi" (NḪL); probably ma-áš-ḫa-ṭu-ma = /maθḫaṭūma/ "(cloths)" (θḪṬ); note also alphab. ḫ = syll. ḫa in KTU 5.14:4.

PN's, GN's: e.g., ab-di-ḫa-ma-ni (PRU 3 64f.:3) = alphab. ᶜbdḫmn (UT 402b no. 971); ¹la-ḫa-sú-na (PRU 6 85:9',r. 15') = alphab. lḫsn (UT); gentilic ᵘʳᵘma-ḫa-

[118]Exceptions are the equation of alphab. ḥ with syllabic KU in KTU 5.14:9 (for which see below, on /ḥō/, with n. 125), and probably the PN ¹na-ʾ-PA-li (PRU 3 74b:6), perhaps corresponding to alphab. nḥbl (see the next n., and n. 127, below). Boyd, Collection 168,275, also cites the field designation :ra-⸢PA⸣-ni (PRU 3 140f.:26), which he and Nougayrol (ad. loc.) associate with the common form ⁽ⁱᵈ⁾(:)ra-aḫ-ba-ni/na = /raḥbāni/a/ (see RḤB); but :ra-⸢PA⸣-ni probably represents a different term; see the Appendix to the Glossary. On the lack of indication of /ḥ/ in the writings mar-zi/za-i, see Part III, ch. 2 §A 2 a.

[119]It should be noted at this point that the (syllabic) ʾ sign (i.e., ḫi+an, AS³ no. 233) is consistently distinguished from the AḪ sign (AS³ no. 234) in Ugarit Akkadian. The only confusions in the entire corpus of Akk. texts are the use of the ʾ sign for expected AḪ in the PN na-ʾ-PA-li (for which see further below, n. 127) and the use of AḪ for expected ʾ in the GN ᵘʳᵘma-AḪ-ra-bá ⁽ᵏⁱ⁾ and in the PN ¹ia-di-iḫ-DINGIRᵐᵉˢ̌; for these examples, and for the other instances of the writing of /ᶜ/ with Ḫ-signs, see below, §b 1 (see also there, n. 129, for the writing ma-aḫ-ḫa-[du] for expected /maʾḫadu/).

[120]Note also the ḪAL sign in ITI ḫal-la-t[u]/ti = /ḥallatu/i/ (ḤLL); also, e.g., in the GN ḫal-bi (e.g., Ug. 7 pl. 13:32) = alphab. ḫlb (UT 402a no. 963); and the Hurrian PN ¹a-ḫal-te-nu (e.g., PRU 3 199ff. i 2") = alphab. aǵltn (UT 363b no. 293).

di-yu (PRU 6 79:10) = alphab. *m(a/i)ḫdy* (UT 355a no. 130, 432a no. 1453).

/*ǵă*/ in Sª Voc.: perhaps *ḫa-ri-mu* = /*ǵarĭmu*/ "foe, adversary(?)" (ǴRM); in other texts: [l]lú*ḫa-ma-ru-ú*, lú*ḫa-*[*a*]*m-*[*r*]*u-ú* = sg. /*ǵam(a)ru-hŭ*/, (lú.meš)*ḫa-ma/am-ru-ma*meš = pl. /*ǵam(a)rūma*/ "apprentice(s)" (ǴMR); túg*pa-ḫa-TAR-ru* = /*paǵaddarru*/ "(garment)" (PǴ(N)DR);[121] note also alphab. *ǵ* = syll. *ḫa* in KTU 5.14:16.

PN's, GN's: 1*ḫa-ra-ga* 5*-na* (PRU 3 199ff. ii 5; also 1*ḫar-ga-na* PRU 6 27:4,16) = alphab. *ǵrgn* (UT465a no. 1985); 1*ḫa-zi-lu* (PRU 6 86 i 10), cf. alphab. *bn ǵzl* (note also the noun *ǵzlm* "spinners" [Nougayrol, PRU 6 p. 150]; UT 463b no. 1955); uru*a-ḫa-tu* (PRU 6 95:9; 6 105:6') = alphab. *aǵt* (UT 363b no. 295).

/*ḥē*/, /*ḫē*/, [/*ǵē*/] with KAN = *ḫé*, or with ḪI:[122]

/*ḥē*/ in Sª Voc.: *ḫé-qu* = /*ḥēqu*/ "lap" (ḤYQ); perhaps *ḫe?-e*[*-ru*] = /*ḥēru*/? "enclosure(?)" (ḤYR).

/*ḫē*/ in Sª Voc.: probably *ḫé-bu* and *ḪI-bu,* both for /*ḫēbu*/? "shame" (/*ḫību*/ is also possible, but less likely; ḪYB); for *ḫe-e-ia/yu, :ḫé-yi-ma,* see below, under /*ḫĭ*/.

/*ǵē*/ no examples.

/*ḥĭ*/, /*ḫĭ*/, /*ǵĭ*/ with ḪI, rarely with KAN = *ḫé*:[123]

/*ḥĭ*/ in Sª Voc.: *ḫi-*[*i*]*u?-ma* and *ḫé-yu-ma* = /*ḥiyyūma*/ "life" (ḤYY¹/ḤWY¹ b); in other texts: lú.meš*b*[*i*]*-ḫi-ru* = /*biḥīrū*/? "elite (troops)" (BḤR¹); *ma-ar-zi-ḫi* = [marziḥi][124] (RZḤ); perhaps also *ḫi-nu-ta-me* = /*ḥinōtāmi*/? "2 'implements'" (ḤNW).

PN: e.g., 1*mu-na-ḫi-mu* (PRU 3 122f.:22, and often) and 1*mu-na-ḫé-mu* (PRU 3 199f. edge ii 5) = alphab. *mnḥm* (UT 443a no. 1634).

/*ḫĭ*/ in Sª Voc.: *ḫe-en-ni-ṣu* = /*ḫinnīṣu*/? "piglet" (ḪNṢ); see also under /*ḫē*/, above; in other texts: *ḫe-e-yu/ia* = [ḫēyu/a]?, *:ḫé-yi-ma* = [ḫēyīma]?, *:ḫi-i-yi(-šu)* = [ḫīyĭ]?, all from /*ḫāyv*/? "vacant(?)" (ḪWY); ITI *ḫi-ia/ya-ri* = /*ḫiyyāri*/ (month name; ḪYR); *: ḫi-ri-ti* = /*ḫirīti*/ "cemetery" (ḪRY); lú*ma-ḫi-ṣu* = /*māḫiṣu*/ "(a profession)" (MḪṢ a); [urudu.meš]*me-ḫi-*[*ṣ*]*u-*⌜*ma*⌝meš = /*miḫīṣūma*/ "(implements)" (MḪṢ b).

PN: e.g., *a-ḫi-ia-a-nu* (PRU 6 90 r.5') = alphab. *aḫyn* (UT 354b no. 128).

[121]Perhaps also giš*šá-*[*ḫ*]*a!?-*⌜*ru?*⌝*-ma* = /*θaǵarūma*/? "door-leaves(?)" (θǴR), but the reading is very uncertain.

[122]See below, §G 2.

[123]See below, §G 2.

[124]Note also *mar-zi-i* and *mar-za-i(-ma)*; see ch. 2, §A 2 a.

/ǵĭ/ no Sª Voc. examples; in other texts: only ^lú^*na-ḫi-ru* = */nāǵiru/* "guard" (NǴR a).

/ḥō/, *[/ḫō/]*, */ǵō/* (see examples for the signs used):

/ḥō/ only in alphab. *ḥ* = syll. *ku* in KTU 5.14:9. The syllabic transcription *ku* is apparently intended to represent the first syllable of the letter name **/ḥōtu/*, as suggested by Speiser, BASOR 175 42-47. This is the only representation of [ḥ] by other than Ḫ-signs in our complement of Ugar. forms.[125]

/ḫō/ no examples.

/ǵō/ no Sª Voc. examples; in other texts: probably *: ḫu-li* = */ǵōli/*? "low ground(?)" (ǴWL).

/ḥŭ/, */ḫŭ/*, */ǵŭ/* always with ḪU:[126]

/ḥŭ/ in Sª Voc.: *da-ab-ḫu* = */dabḥu/* "sacrifice" (DBḤ); ⸢*ḫu*⸣*-du-rù* = */ḥudŭru/* "room(?)" (ḤDR); [*ḫ*]*u-wa-tu₄* = */ḥuwwatu/* "country" (ḤWW); *ḫu-PI-ú* = */ḥuwwû/* "to save" (ḤYY¹/ḤWY¹ a); [*ḫ*]*u-ul-ma-tu₄* = */ḥulmatu/*? "strength(?)" (ḤLM); *šu-ḫu-ut-t*[*u*?] = */šuḥuttu/*? "bran, residue(?)" (ḤTT); *šap-ḫu* = */šapḥu/* "sprout, scion" (ŠPḤ); perhaps also [*la*?*-q*]*a*?*-ḫu* = */laqāḥu/*? "to receive(?)" (LQḤ a); in other texts: ^lú^*ba-ar-ḫu* = Akkadianized form *barḫu* "fugitive, rustic(?)" (BRḤ); *ḫur-ḫu-ra-ti* = */ḥurḥur(r)ati/* "(a plant)" (ḤRḤR); perhaps also *ḫu-ma*?*-lu*? = */ḥumālu/*? "pity(?)" (ḤML).

Note, e.g., ^1^*ḫu-da/dá-ši* (PRU 3 133f.:5; Syria 28 173f.:23,28) = alphab. *ḥdθ*, and ^1^*ḫu-ud* (!)*-ša-nu* (PRU 3 199ff. i 17") = alphab. *ḥdθn* (UT 395a no. 843); *ḫu-ṣa-nu/na* (PRU 3 79ff.:4; 3 101f.:25) = alphab. *ḥṣn* (UT 398b no. 890).

/ḫŭ/ in Sª Voc.: *ḫu-zi-rù* = */ḫuzīru/* "pig" (ḪZR); *ḫu-r*[*a-ṣu*] = */ḫurāṣu/* "gold" (ḪRṢ¹); perhaps also ⸢*ba*⸣*-aḫ-ḫu-rù* = */baḫḫuru/* (or

[125] Speiser, loc. cit., adduced two examples of an alternation of *ḫ* and *k* in Hurrian words in Ugarit texts (one alphabetic, one syllabic); Speiser also noted examples of a sporadic *k* / *ḫ* interchange in Mesopotamian and Nuzi Akkadian (for which see also Knudsen, AOAT 1 147-55). A few instances also appear in the Akkadian of Ugarit, in lexical and literary texts: NA₄.UR₅.ZÌ.SAG = *taḫ-ḫa-sí* (MSL 10 37ff. A 205) and [ZÌ].SAG = *ta-ḫa-sí* (MSL 11 74f.:7), both for canonical *tak-ka-se-e* (MSL 11 76:23; see AHw 1307a); *GI-il-ṣa* (Ug. 5 162:12') for *ḫilṣa* or *ḫalṣa* (see Nougayrol, Ug. 5 p. 271; von Soden, UF 1 192; AHw 1558b); perhaps also *ḪU-rat* IM.RI.A // *qerub salāti* (Ug. 5 162:9'), if to be read *pak-rat* for *paḫrat* (von Soden, UF 1 191), although a scribal omission, *<pu->ḫu-rat*, is also possible.

[126] Note also the ḪAR sign with the value *ḫur* for */ḥur/* in *ḫur-ḫu-ra-ti* = */ḥurḥur(r)ati/* "(a plant)" (ḤRḤR).

/*baḫḫuru*/?) "youth" (BḪR); in other texts: *: ti-tar-ḫ[u]* = /*tiʾ/ttarḫu*/ "she will hurry" (ʾRḪ); *ḫu-up-pa-ti* = /*ḫuppăti*/ "shore(s)(?)" (ḪPP).

Note, e.g., [uru]*ḫu-ul-da* (PRU 3 133f.:7,11; 3 143ff.:19), cf. alphab. *gt ḫldy* (UT 402a no. 964).

/*ǵŭ̄*/ in Sa Voc.: *ḫu-ul-ma-tu₄* = /*ǵulmatu*/ "darkness(?)" (ǴLM).

Note also the GN [uru]*ḫu-be-li* (PRU 3 48f.:7; 3 76b:7; PRU 6 80:13; Ug. 5 49:9) = alphab. *ǵbl* (see Dietrich-Loretz-Sanmartín, UF 5 95).

/*vḥ*/, /*vḫ*/, /*vǵ*/ always with the AḪ sign:[127]

/*vḥ*/

/*aḥ*/ [(íd)]*(:) ra-aḫ-ba/bá-ni/na* = /*raḥbāni/a*/ "wide place" (RḤB).

/*iḥ*/ [mí]*ba-ri-iḫ-tu₄* = /*bariḥtu*/ "fugitive, rustic(?)" (BRḤ).

/*uḥ*/ no examples.

/*vḫ*/

/*aḫ*/ in Sa Voc.: note *ma-aḫ-ḫa-[du]*, probably for [maḫḫadu][128] < /*maʾḫadu*/ "harbor" (ʾḪD); perhaps also ⸢*ba*⸣*-aḫ-ḫu-rù* = /*baḫḫuru*/ (or /*baḥḥuru*/) "youth" (BḪR); in other texts: perhaps *: ma-aḫ-ZI-ZI* = /*maḫṣīṣi*/? "divide(?)" (ḪṢṢ).

/*iḫ*/ no examples.

/*uḫ*/ *uḫ-ra-a-yi* = /*ʾuḫrāyi*/ "destiny" (ʾḪR).

/*vǵ*/

/*aǵ*/ no examples.

/*iǵ*/ Sa Voc. *ni-iḫ-rù* = /*niǵru*/ "to guard" (NǴR b).

/*uǵ*/ no examples.

[127]A possible exception occurs in the PN *na-ʾ-PA-li* (PRU 3 74b:6), which may correspond to alphab. *bn nḥbl* (UT 442b no. 1632). If so, the writing contains the sole example in Ugarit Akk. texts of the use of the ʾ sign, otherwise consistently distinguished from AḪ (see above, n. 119), to represent a phoneme other than Akk. ʾ and Ugar. /ʾ/, /ʿ/; a scribal error, viz., the omission of the two final verticals of AḪ, should therefore not be ruled out.

Note the use of DAḪ with the value *taḫ* for /*taḥ*/ in the PN [1]DINGIR-*taḫ-mu* (e.g., PRU 3 113ff.:34) = alphab. *ilṯhm* (UT 351a no. 163).

[128]See the following note.

b. /ʾ/, /h/, /ᶜ/

(1) With Ḫ-signs

Of these three phonemes, only /ᶜ/ is ever written with a Ḫ-sign,[129] and then only very rarely; the following is a complete list:[130]

☛ p. 400

(i) *ḫa-pí-ri* = /ᶜapīri/ "(a social class)" (ᶜPR); the writing is probably a learned spelling of the Akkadianized form of the WSem. word;[131]

(ii) ᵗᵘ́ᵍ*šá-ḫar-tu* = /šaᶜartu/ "wool" (this is the most likely reading; see ŠᶜR b);

(iii) the GN ᵘʳᵘ*ma-aḫ-ra-bá* ⁽ᵏⁱ⁾ (PRU 3 102ff.:30,32), vs. ᵘʳᵘ*ma-ra-bá* in the same text (line 35) and passim in other texts,[132] for alphab. *mᶜrb(y)* (UT 461a no. 1915);

(iv) probably also the PN ¹*ia-di-iḫ*-DINGIRᵐᵉˢ̌ (Syria 59 204ff. colophon), if a form of *y-d-ᶜ* is represented; as in the case of *ḫa-pí-ri* above, the writing of this PN may be a learned (or archaizing) spelling.[133]

(2) With the ʾ sign[134]

The ʾ sign is used in the writing of Ugaritic words and WSem. proper names, as

[129]The Sᵃ Voc. spelling *ma-aḫ-ḫa-*[*du*] for expected /maʾḫadu/ may be a unique example of AḪ for /ʾ/, in view of the alphabetic spellings *miḫd* and *maḫd* for the harbor-town of Ugarit (UT 355a no. 130); note also the syllabic ᵘʳᵘ*ma-a-ḫa-di* (PRU 3 195b A 6), probably for /maʾḫadi/ (see below [3 b ii], for vowel-signs indicating syllable-closing guttural). More likely, however, *ma-aḫ-ḫa-*[*du*] reflects a pronunciation [maḫḫadu], with assimilation of /ʾ/ to the following /ḫ/, as also attested in the alphabetic writing of the gentilic *mḫdy* (UT 432a no. 1453); see Part III, ch. 2 §A 2 b.

Since Ugaritic /h/ is nowhere else written with Ḫ-signs, the GN ⁽ᶦ́ᵈ⁾*na-aḫ-ra(-yv)* (PRU 3 83f.:6; 3 127f.:7,17,22; 3 129a:13; cf. also PRU 3 140f.:10), also once written ᶦ́ᵈ*na-ḫa-ra* (PRU 3 89f.:4), undoubtedly reflects alphab. *nḫry*, as suggested by Nougaryol (PRU 3 p. 266b; see also Hillers, JNES 29 299-300), rather than *nhr* "river" (so Gröndahl, Personennamen 13; Sivan, Analysis 251); for the syll. writing of *nhr*, cf. probably the PN *ú-lu-na-a-ri* (PRU 3 199ff. iii 48) = alphab. *ulnhr* (UT 359b no. 195).

[130]The word *: ma-aḫ-ZI-ZI*, which Boyd, Collection 72-73, associates with the root *ᶜ-z-z*, more likely represents /maḫṣiṣi/; see under ḪṢṢ. Gröndahl, Personennamen 12-13, lists also the PN DUMU-DINGIR-*vḫ-ZI* (her *bin-ili-iḫ-zi*, following Nougayrol; PRU 3 196 i 16) and the GN ᵘʳᵘ⌜*si?*⌝*-il-ḫa-na* (PRU 3 38b:2) as examples of /ᶜ/ written with Ḫ-signs. She related the PN to the geminate root *ᶜ-z-z* (p. 112; not *ᶜ-z-y*, also posited by her), but this is morphologically difficult; the GN is probably to be compared with alphab. *θlḫny* (UT 502b no. 2681), despite the unusual correspondence of alphab. *θ* and syll. *si* (see above, n. 86).

[131]This is also Boyd's conclusion, Collection 274. See, e.g., CAD Ḫ 84-85, for examples in OA and OB texts, and MB Akk. texts from Nuzi, Alalaḫ, and Boğazköy.

[132]ᵘʳᵘ*ma-ra-bá* in PRU 3 48f.:11; 3 65b:6; 3 150b r.6'; 3 151f.:5,7; 3 187d:3; 3 192f.:30; Ug. 7 pl. 13:24; ᵘʳᵘ*ma-ra-ba* in Ug. 5 12:1,13,14; ᵘʳᵘ*ma-aʾ-ra-ba* in PRU 3 192f.:26. One wonders whether the writings with AḪ reflect an earlier form of the name, viz., /maǵrab-/; cf. Arabic.

[133] Cf. Amorite *ia-di-iḫ*-DINGIR (Gelb, et al., AS 21 p. 601 no. 3204).

[134]See above, n. 119.

in Akkadian words in texts from Ugarit and contemporary Mesopotamian sites, to indicate either a syllable-initial or a syllable-final guttural, followed or preceded by any vowel, respectively, i.e., for *ʾv* or *vʾ*.[135] Only /ʾ/ and /ʿ/ are represented by the ʾ sign, never /*h*/. Further, it should be remembered that the ʾ sign does not occur in any Ugar. words in the Sª Voc. texts.[136] The examples may be broken down as follows; note that each set is paralleled by a set of examples, usually larger, in which a *v*-sign or a *vC*-sign, rather than the ʾ sign, occurs for the guttural (see 3, below).

(a) Syllable-initial /ʾ/ and /ʿ/

All of the examples in Ugar. words reflect /ʾ/ or /ʿ/ plus /*ă*/; this is in all probability fortuitous, since the values *ʾi* and *ʾu* are attested in proper names.

(i) Word-initial:

No examples occur except in the second element of two closely related PN's: ¹*šub-ʾa-mu*[137] (Ug. 5 97:8) and ¹*šu-ba-ʾa-mu*[138] (PRU 6 72:10'), with which must be compared the much more frequent writings ¹*šu-ub-am-mv* (PRU 3 56f.:15; 3 61f.:5,13; 3 64f.:3,9, 15; 3 159f.:10) and ¹*šub-am-mu* (RA 38 5:15), all corresponding to alphab. *θbʿm* (UT 501b no. 2661).

(ii) Post-Consonantal:

No examples in Ugar. common words; note the PN's ¹*la-ab-ʾi-yu* (PRU 6 79:3) = alphab. *lbiy* (UT 426b no. 1347); ¹*sa-ar-ʾa-nu* (PRU 6 74:5'; alphab. unattested[139]); ¹*si-il-ʾa-nu* (PRU 6 72:12', cf. *si-il-a-[na?]* PRU 3 101f.:23; alphab. unattested); see also the PN's cited in the preceding paragraph. Finally, there is the PN ¹*ma-aʾ-ʾv-[B]I* (PRU 6 45:8), uniquely with two ʾ signs, which should probably be compared with alphab. *mab* (KTU 2.16:11), as suggested by Lipiński, OLP 12 97-98.

(iii) Intervocalic:

/ʾ/

plural *ni-ʾa-tu* = /*niʾātu*/ "(implements)" (vs. sg. *ni-iʾ-tu* = /*niʾtu*/, and *ni-it*; Nʾ); probably also [*k*]*a?-ma-ʾa-*⌈*tu*⌉ = /*kamaʾātu*/? "truffles" (KMʾ); and note *i-ṣa-ʾa* reflecting suff.-conj. */*yaṣaʾa*/ "it went out" (YṢʾ).

Note also the PN's ¹*tal-ma-ʾu/ʾi* (PRU 6 86 ii 9; 6 168:12) = alphab. *tlmu/i* (UT 498a no.

[135]Pace Berger, WO 5 279,281, who suggests that the sign is only used for *vʾ*. On the transliteration of the ʾ sign, see further Gelb, Or. 39 540. For the sign in Ugarit Akk., note, e.g., *ú-ma-ʾe-er* (PRU 3 79ff.:32), *i-zé/ze-ʾe-er* (PRU 3 54ff.:8,18, but *i-zé-er* line 12); literary *ma-aʾ-du* (Ug. 5 17:16); see also the next note. For other Akk. dialects, see AS³ no. 233.

[136]It does occur once in the Akk. column in *ru-uʾ-tu₄* (Ug. 5 135:15', Sª Voc. no. 60), and, strangely, once in the Hurrian column, in]*lu-ʾ*[(Ug. 5 137 ii 9', Sª Voc. no. 177.1).

[137]This is preferable to Nougayrol's ¹*ru-ʾ(?)-mu*; see Berger, UF 1 123.

[138]I.e., /*θūba-ʿammu*/, with an imperative in /*-a*/, vs. the more common short imperative in /*θub-ʿammu*/.

[139]The presence of the ʾ sign in this PN precludes associating it with the root *s-r-r* (so Sivan, Analysis 266) or the alphabetic PN *srn* (UT 452a no. 1797).

2557); ^{1}*ki-la-ʾe-e* (PRU 4 294:3), cf alphab. *kli* (UT 419a no. 1232)

/ʿ/

$^{giš.meš}$*ṣa-ʾa-tu* = */ṣāʿātu/* "(wooden) bowls" (ṢWʿ); *ta-ba-ʾa* = */tabaʿa/* "he departed" (TBʿ).

PN's, GN's: ^{1d}IM-*i-da-ʾa* (?) (PRU 6 79:1), cf. alphab. *bʿldʿ* (UT 375a no. 493); ^{1}*ya-a-pa-ʾu* (PRU 6 79:9; cf. ^{1}*ia-pa-ú* PRU 3 196 ii 18'), cf. alphab. *ypʿ* (UT 413a no. 1133);[140] ^{uru}*ṣa-ʾi* (PRU 6 78:13; cf. the noun *ṣa(-a)-i* = */ṣāʿi/* [ṢWʿ]), cf. alphab. *ṣʿ* (UT 475b no. 2178); ^{uru}*ku-mu-ri-ʾa* vs. [^{uru}*k*]*u-mu-ri-a* (PRU 6 164:4,10).

(b) Syllable-closing */ʾ/* and */ʿ/*

/ʾ/

only *ni-iʾ-tu* = */niʾtu/* (vs. pl. *ni-ʾa-tu* = */niʾātu/*; note also *ni-it*; Nʾ).

PN: *pí-iʾ-ta-yv* (Ug. 5 6:31), cf. alphab. *bn pity* (UT 465b no. 1994).

/ʿ/

Only *:ma-aʾ-ša-ri(-ša)* = */maʿšari/* "tithe" (cf. *ma-ša-ra* = */maʿšara/*; ʿŠR^{2}).

PN's, GN's: ^{1}*ia-aʾ-ŠI-ra-nu* (PRU 3 54ff.:4, vs. ^{1}*ia-ZI-ra-nu/na* in lines 8,12,15) = alphab. *yʿðrn* (UT 454b no. 1831);[141] ^{1}*ba-aʾ-lu-ú* (PRU 6 72:10); [^{1}*b*]*a-aʾ-la-TA-ni* (PRU 6 139:5), cf. alphab. *bʿldn* or *bʿltn* (UT 375a no. 493); perhaps ^{f}*i-nu-uʾ-mi* (PRU 3 60b:9,12);[142] ^{uru}*ma-aʾ-ra-bá* (PRU 3 192f.: 26, vs. ^{uru}*ma-ra-bá* in line 30, and passim in other texts [see n. 132, above], and ^{uru}*ma-aḫ-ra-bá*^{ki}, cited above under (1)) = alphab. *mʿrb* (UT 461a no. 1915); ^{uru}*ma-aʾ-qa-bu* (PRU 3 191a:15', vs. ^{uru}*ma-qa/⸢qá⸣-bi/bu* in PRU 3 40b:2,3; 3 190a:14'; Ug. 7 pl. 13:31) = alphab. *mʿqb* (UT 460b no. 1907); gentilic ^{uru}KI-*ba-aʾ-li-yi* (PRU 6 79:4), cf. alphab. *aθr bʿl* (UT 369a no. 424).

(3) Otherwise

(a) Syllable-initial

In open syllables,[143] *v*-signs appear for syllable-initial gutturals:

A for */ʾă/, /hă/, /ʿă/*
E for */ʾē/*
I, rarely E, for */ʾĭ/, /hĭ/, /ʿĭ/*

[140] Note also the PN ^{1}*iv-ʾ-di/dì-du/dì* (see PRU 3 p. 260a; further, PRU 6 31:27; Ug. 5 12:2,3) = alphab. *yʿdd* (UT 454a no. 1819), the interpretation of which is not clear: */yvʿdĭdu/*? */yvʿaddidu/*?

[141] See n. 72, above.

[142] I.e., */ʾī-nuʿmī/* "where-is-my-delight?" (cf. Berger, WO 5 281: "wo ist 'Naemi'"). Other possibilities are */ʿēn-ʾummi/* "mother's eye" (Sivan, Analysis 206), and */ʿēn-nuʿmi/* "eye-of-delight."

[143] Also in closed syllables when a doubled consonant follows and is written singly, as in the RN ^{1}*a-mis/mi-is-tam-rv* for */ʿamm-/*, vs. ^{1}*am-mi-is/iš-tam-rv* (both passim; alphab. *ʿmθtmr*).

Ú for /*hō*/ (?)

Ú, less often U,[144] for /*ʾŭ*/, /*hŭ*/, /*ʿŭ*/.[145]

In closed syllables, normally only *vC*-signs appear for syllable-initial gutturals, i.e., v_1C for /Gv_1C/; rarely, the sequence v_1-v_1C occurs.[146]

In word-initial position, the presence of one of /ʾ/, /h/, or /ʿ/ is invariably indicated simply by a *v*- or *vC*-sign,[147] as in *a-da-nu* = /*ʾadānu*/ "father" (ʾDN), *ap-pu* = /*ʾappu*/ "nose" (ʾNP).

After a consonant, the presence of /ʾ/, /h/, or /ʿ/ is signalled by a broken writing, i.e., *(C)vC-v(C)* for /*(C)vCGv(C)*/ (or, rarely, by the ʾ sign; see above, 2 ii), as in lú.meš*mur-ú-ma* = /*murʾūma*/ "commanders(?)" (MRʾ).[148]

Intervocalically, the presence of /ʾ/, /h/, or /ʿ/, when not indicated by the ʾ sign (see above, 2), is

(i) signalled by writings of the type Cv_1-$v_2(C)$ when the vowels on either side of the guttural differ,[149] e.g., in the GN uru*mu-a-ri* (e.g., PRU 3 189b:32') for alphabetic *mʿr* (UT 436a no. 1516);

(ii) not usually signalled explicitly when the vowels on either side of the guttural are the same, i.e., Cv_1-$v_1(C)$. When the guttural begins an open syllable, the writing is Cv_1-v_1, i.e., it has the appearance of a long vowel, as in *ta-a-ma-tu*$_4$ = /*tahāmatu*/ (THM);[150] when the guttural begins a closed syllable, the writing is simply Cv_1-v_1C,[151] i.e., it has the appearance of a single closed syllable, as in the GN uru*ia-ar-tu*$_4$ (PRU 3 190a:7') for alphabetic *yʿrt* (UT 412b no. 1126), i.e., /*yaʿartu*/ (not */*yartu*/).[152]

[144]The U sign is considerably less common than Ú in Ugarit Akk., but numerous examples of the former do occur, especially in initial and final position (very rare medially). (Ù occurs syllabically only in the writing of Akk. *u* "and.") See further below, n. 163.

[145]See also Jirku, ArOr. 38 (1970) 129-30.

[146]As in *ma-a-al-tu*$_4$ for /*maʿʿaltu*/ (see below, under /ʿ/); note also, in a lexical text, ída.am.mu.ra (glossed *ra-pí*) MSL 11 43ff. iv 11-14, for canonical ídḫa.am.mu.ra.pí (ibid. p. 26 §6:9').

[147]Once by ḪA; see under (1), above.

[148]So also for the indication of a post-consonantal glottal stop in Akkadian words in the Ugarit texts, e.g., *li-iš-al-šu* for *lišʾalšu* (PRU 3 83f.:28), *iš-a-am* for *išʾam* (Ug. 5 5:18); see GAG §23e.

A few examples of broken writings in Hurrian PN's, such as *ták-a-⌜an⌝* (PRU 3 67a:6), may be due to a Hurrian scribal practice of so indicating doubled consonants; cf. *ták-ka*$_4$*-na* (PRU 3 32f.:3).

[149]Such writings, i.e., Cv_1-$v_2(C)$, nearly always indicate the presence of /ʾ/, /h/, or /ʿ/ between the vowels, not the presence of /w/ or /y/ (see above n. 106). For a Ugarit Akk. example, note *tu-ma-er* (PRU 3 172b:5'); cf. *ú-ma-ʾe-er*, cited above in n. 135.

[150]Note the Akkadian infinitive *ša-a-li* (PRU 4 294:9), which may denote either *šaʾāli* or *šâli*.

[151]Except in a small number of instances, in which an extra vowel sign intervenes; see above, n. 146.

[152]Note the Ugarit Akkadian *i-zé-er* (PRU 3 54ff.:12) and *i-ze-er* (Syria 28 173f.:13), which may reflect either *izeʾʾer* or *izêr*. The former alternative is the more likely in the first instance, in view of *i-zé/ze-ʾe-er* in the same text (PRU 3 54ff.:8,18).

/ʾă/, /hă/, /ʿă/

/ʾă/ (a) with A:

in Sᵃ Voc.: *a-da-nu* = */ʾadānu/* "father" (ʾDN); *a-du-rù* = */ʾaduru/* "mighty" (ʾDR); *a-na-ku* = */ʾanākŭ/* "I" (ʾNK); ⌜*a*⌝-[*p*]*í*?-[*yu*?] = */ʾāpiyu/*? "baker" (ʾPY);[153] in other texts: ⌜*a*⌝-[*ši*?-*ra*?-*tu₄*?] = */ʾaθiratu/*? (divine name; ʾθR); *a-ši-ib* = */ʾaθib/* "let me dwell" (YθB a); perhaps *ma-aš-a-li* = */mašʾali/* "oracle(?)" (ŠʾL); note also alphab. *a* = syll. *a* in KTU 5.14:1.

Note also, e.g., ¹*rap-a-nu/na* (RA 38 5:14; Ug. 5 55:1) = alphab. *rpan* (UT 485 no. 2346); ᵘʳᵘ*ma-ri-a-te* (PRU 6 102:5) = alphab. *mrat* (UT 437b no. 1544)

(b) with *aC* signs:

in Sᵃ Voc.: *ap-pu* = */ʾappu/* "nose" (ʾNP); *at-ta* = */ʾattă/* "you (ms)" (ʾNT); *ar-ṣu* = */ʾarṣu/* "earth" (ʾRṢ); in other texts: *: ad-ma-ni* */ʾadmāni/* "red (soil)" (ʾDM); *al-la-an/ni* = */ʾallān(i)/* "oak" (ʾLN); *ar-zu* = */ʾarzu/* "cedar" (perhaps also pl. *ar-zi-ma*[= */ʾarzīma/*? in Ug. 5 153; ʾRZ).

Note also, e.g., the GN ᵘʳᵘIGI-*qáp-at* (PRU 3 188f.:6'; 3 189b:2'; 3 190a:6') = alphab. *ʿnqpat* (UT 458b no. 1887).

/hă/ (a) with A:

in Sᵃ Voc.: *tu-a-pí-*[*ku*?] = */tuhappiku/*? "to be upset(?)" (HPK); *ta-a-ma-tu₄* = */tahāmatu/* "the deep" (THM); in other texts: perhaps *ši-a-ru* = */šiharu/*? "crescent-shaped sickle(?)" (ŠHR).

PN: *ú-lu-na-a-ri* (PRU 3 199ff. iii 48) = alphab. *ulnhr* (UT 359b no. 195).

(b) with *aC* signs:

only Sᵃ Voc. *al-li-ni-PI* = */hallinīya/*? "here, now then" (HLNY).[154]

/ʿă/ (a) with A:

in Sᵃ Voc.: *ma-a-al-tu₄* = */maʿʿaltu/*? "bolt(?)" (NʿL);[155] in other texts: *a-mu-q*[*u*] = */ʿamuqu/* "deep (place)" (ʿMQ²); ᵈ*a-na-tu₄* =

[153]Perhaps also *ma-a-du-ma*, if for */maʾadūma/*; but */maʾdūma/* is also possible; see ch. 2 §B 1.

[154]In PN's in which the second element is the DN */Hadd-/*, aphaeresis of the */h/* and crasis are usually in evidence: ¹*na-qa-ma-du* (PRU 3 196 i 9) and ¹*níq-ma-*ᵈIM (passim), cf. alphab. *nqmd* (UT 447a no. 1698); ¹*zi-im-rad-da* (PRU 3 192f.:33) = alphab. *ðmrd* (KTU 4.682:10); ¹*ga-mi-rad-du/dì* (PRU 3 115f. r.8') and ¹*gi-im-ra-du* (PRU 3 199ff. iv 10), cf. alphab. *gmrd* (UT 380 no. 592). In these examples, it will be noted, the */h/* is also lacking in the alphabetic writings; occasionally, however, the more conservative alphabetic tradition preserves it: e.g., *gmrhd* (KTU 4.75 vi 7; 4.753:6). See further Gröndahl, Personennamen 131-33. Since many of these names reflect an earlier Amorite onomastic tradition, their significance for Ugaritic phonology is at best very limited.

[155]Perhaps also *ba-a-lu-ma*, if for */baʿalūma/*; but */baʿlūma/* is also possible; see ch. 2 §B 1.

/ᶜanatu/ (divine name; ᶜNT); lú(.meš)*a-ši-ru/ri-ma* = */ᶜăšĭrū/īma/* "(royal officials)" (ᶜŠR[1]); *(:) sí-il-a* = */silᶜa/* "cliff(?)" (SLᶜ); perhaps also ⌜d?*a*?⌝*-li-PI* = */ᶜălĭyi/*? "ascendant" (ᶜLY a).

PN's, GN's: e.g., (1)*a-zi-ra-na* (PRU 6 70:7; Syria 18 251ff.:11; root *ᶜ-δ-r*); see also n. 143, above; uru*u-bur-a* (PRU 3 188f.:4'; 3 189a:3'; 3 190a:1'; PRU 6 118:6'; Ug. 7 pl. 13:38) = alphab. *ubrᶜ* (UT 350b no. 50); uru*mu-a-ri* (PRU 3 189b:32'; 3 190a:28; Ug. 7 pl. 13:42) = alphab. *mᶜr* (UT 436a no. 1516); perhaps also uru*mu-ur-ša-a* (PRU 6 78:7,8) = alphab. *mr*⌜*θᶜ*⌝? (see CTA 13:24; but KTU 1.13 reads *mrǵt*).

(b) with *aC* signs:

in Sa Voc.: *ab-du* = */ᶜabdu/* "slave" (ᶜBD); *aš-ta-ru* = */ᶜaθtaru/* (divine name; ᶜθTR); in other texts: *: am-qa* = */ᶜamqa/* "stronghold(?)" (ᶜMQ[1]).

PN's, GN's: e.g., 1*šu-ub/šub-am-mv* (see under 2 a i, above); see also n. 143, above; uru*ba-aq-at* (PRU 3 189b:12') = alphab. *bqᶜt* (UT 376a no. 502); uru*ia-ar-ti/tu4/tù* (PRU 3 189b:23'; 3 190a:7'; 3 190b:3; 3 191a:12'; PRU 6 70:18) = alphab. *yᶜrt* (UT 412b no. 1126).

/ʾē/, [/hē/, /ᶜē/]

/ʾē/ with E:

only in Sa Voc. *e-bu* = */ʾēbu/* "enemy" (ʾYB).

/hē/ no examples.

/ᶜē/ with E:

perhaps in *e-*⌜*nu*?⌝ = */ᶜēnu/*? "eye(?)" in Ug. 5 153 (ᶜYN).

/ʾĭ/, /hĭ/, /ᶜĭ/

/ʾĭ/ (a) with I:

in Sa Voc.: ⌜*i*?*-lu*?⌝ = */ʾilu/* "god" (ʾL); *i-r[a?-tu4?]* = */ʾiratu/*? "chest(?)" (ʾR); *i-[r]i?-iš-[tu4?]* = */ʾirištu/*? "request" (ʾRŠ); ⌜*i*⌝*-ši-t[u4]* = */ʾišītu/*? "fire" (ʾŠ); in other texts: *i-*⌜*ši*?⌝*-[bi?]* = */ʾiθibi/*? (month name; ʾθB); lú.meš*mur-i* = */murʾī/* "commander(s)(?)" (MRʾ); note also alphab. ⌜*i*⌝ = syll. *i* in KTU 5.14:18.

PN's, GN's:[156] 1ÌR*-rap-i* (PRU 3 145f.:8), cf. alphab. *ᶜbdrpu* (UT 453a no. 1801); fDUMU.MÍ*-ra-ap-i* (PRU 3 64f.:4,12,14); DINGIR*-da-ab-i* (PRU 6 40:27), cf. alphab. *aḫdbu*[157] (UT 355b no. 132); 1*la-i-yv* (PRU 3 45f.:4,9; Syria

[156]Note also the following PN's, in which */ʾ/* is lost in crasis: 1*mi-il-ki-lu* (for */milkī-ʾilu/*, PRU 6 40:26); 1*i-ri-bi-li/la* (for **/yarib-ʾilv/*, PRU 3 64a:5,9,11; 3 70b:4).

[157]Cf. *dbat* (KTU 1.10 ii 21,22), possibly meaning "strength" (Loewenstamm, Comparative Studies 286 with n. 11), a meaning which would fit these names.

18 251ff.:34) = alphab. *liy* (UT 426a no. 1342); ^{uru}*na-ni-i* (PRU 3 189b:31'; Ug. 7 pl. 13:26) = alphab. *nni* (UT 444b no. 1657).

(b) with *iC* (rarely *eC*) signs:

in S^a Voc.: *iš-du*$_4$ = */ʾišdu/* "leg" (ʾŠD); perhaps also *IG-TU*$_4$ = */ʾiktu/*? "mortar" (ʾKT).

Cf. the GN ^{uru}*ma-ra-el*[158] (PRU 3 190b:10) = alphab. *mril* (UT 437b no. 1545).

/hĭ/ no examples.

Note, however, the GN ^{uru}*iz-pu/pí* (PRU 6 70:11; 6 131:7; Ug. 5 102:13'; 5 104:3'; Ug. 7 pl. 13:23; 7 pl. 62b:5) = alphab. *hzp* (UT 389-90 no. 757).[159]

/ʿĭ/ (a) with I:

in S^a Voc.: *i-zi-ir-[tu*$_4$*?]* = */ʿiðirtu/* "help" (ʿðR); [*š*]*i?-i-ru*[= */šiʿīru/* "barley(?)" (ŠʿR a); perhaps also *i-pu-ú* = */ʿipû/*? "destruction(?)" (ʿPW); *qi-i-lu* = */qiʿīlu/* (less likely, */qiʿlu/*) "vine-blossom(?)" (QʿL); in other texts: *ṣa-i, ṣa-a-i* = */ṣāʿi/* "basin" (ṢWʿ); perhaps also *ša-i-tu*$_4$ = */θāʿītu/*? or */θāʿittu/*? "(a container)" (θʿD/θʿY);[160]

PN's, GN's: note ^{1}*ša-i-yv* (PRU 3 59f.:4; 3 96ff.:4,5,7; 3 154f.:5), cf. alphab. *θʿy* (UT 505a no. 2713); $^{[1]}$*ša-ba-i-ni-qi* (PRU 6 55:12') = alphab. *θbʿnq* (UT 500b no. 2639); ^{uru}DINGIR-*iš-tam-i* (PRU 3 108f.:6; 3 189b:13'; PRU 6 131 r.1') = alphab. *ilštmʿ* (UT 358a no. 163).

(b) with E:[161]

no S^a Voc. examples; only ⌜*e?*⌝*-la-PI* = */ʿilāyi/*? "upper (part)(?)" (ʿLY b).

(c) with *iC* signs:

in S^a Voc.: *iṣ-ṣú-[ma?]* = */ʿiṣṣūma/* "tree(s), wood" (ʿṢ); in other texts: perhaps *iš-ia-ti-mi* = */ʿišyatēmi/* "clamps(?)" (dual; ʿŠY).

Note the PN ^{1}*il-pí-yv* (PRU 3 196 i 19) = alphab. *ʿlpy* (UT 457a no. 1859).

[*/ʾō/*], */hō/*, */ʿō/*

/ʾō/ no examples

/hō/ with Ú?:

note perhaps alphab. *h* = syll. *ú* in KTU 5.14:6, for the letter name */hō/* or */hū/*(?).[162]

158Cf. ^{uru}*ma-ra*-DINGIR (or *-il*) in PRU 6 78:23,24; Ug. 7 pl. 13:17.

☛ p. 400

159Perhaps also the PN ÌR-*mi-ir* (PRU 3 96ff.:14), cf. alphab. *ilmhr* (UT 357b no. 163); but whether the second element *-mi-ir* reflects */mihir/* or */mīr/* (< **mihr*) cannot be demonstrated.

160Note also *mar-zi-i* and *mar-za-i* = [marzi/aʿi] (RZḤ); see ch. 2 §A 2 a.

161See below, §G 2.

162See Cross-Lambdin, BASOR 160 25. See also the next note.

/ʿō/ with Ú?:

^{túg}*ú-ra-tu* = /ʿōrātu/ "hides(?)" (ʿWR).

Note perhaps the (Canaanite) PN ^{1}*ša-am-ú-na* (= /šamʿōna/ < **šamʿān-*; Ug. 5 12:29), cf. alphab. *šmʿn* (UT 492a no. 2441).

/ʾŭ/, /hŭ/, /ʿŭ/

/ʾŭ/ (a) with Ú:

in S^a Voc.: *rap-*⌜*ú*?⌝[= /rapʾu/ "purification(?)" (RPʾ); *ma-aš-nu-ú*? = /mašnŭʾu/? "enemy(?)" (ŠNʾ); in other texts: *ú-nu(-uš)-ša* = /ʾunuθθa/ "estate tax" (ʾNθ); $^{\text{lú(.meš)}}$*mur-ú-ma* =/murʾūma/ "commanders" (MRʾ); perhaps $^{\text{túg.meš}}$*mu-ru-ú-ma*^{meš} = /mōruʾūma/? "(garments)" (YRʾ).

PN's, GN's: ^{1}*ú-la-nu* (PRU 6 70:14), cf. alphab. *uln* (UT 359a no. 195)?; ^{1}*ma-aš-šu-ú* (PRU 3 199ff. iii 7) = alphab. *mšu* (UT 439a no. 1560); ^{uru}*na-nu-ú* (PRU 3 190a:27) = alphab. *nnu* (UT 444b no. 1657); ^{uru}*ú-ga-ri-it* (passim; also with *u-*, see under b) = *ugrt* (UT 351 no. 69).

(b) with U:

no S^a Voc. examples; in other texts: ^{lú}*mur-u* = /murʾu/ (gen.!) "commander(?)" (MRʾ); note also alphab. *u* = syll. *u* in KTU 5.14:19.[163]

Note also the GN's ^{uru}*u-ga-ri-it* (PRU 3 59f.:3, and often, though less common than *ú-*; see under a); ^{uru}*u-bur-a* (PRU 3 188f.:4'; 3 189a:3'; 3 190a:1'; PRU 6 118:6'; Ug. 7 pl. 13:38) = alphab. *ubrʿ* (UT 350b no. 50); ^{uru}*u-bu-sú/sí* (PRU 3 190b:11; 3 191b:1) = alphab. *ubš̀* (UT 350a no. 36).

(c) with *uC* signs:

no S^a Voc. examples; in other texts: *uḫ-ra-a-yi* = /ʾuḫrāyi/ "destiny" (ʾḪR); *um-ma-ti* = /ʾummati/? "clan(?)" (ʾMM); $^{\text{giš.meš}}$*úr-nu* = /ʾurnu/ "laurel(?)" (ʾRN); *uš-r*[*i-ia*]*-ni* = /ʾuθrĭyāni/ "crown prince" (ʾθRYN).

PN's, GN's: $^{[1?]}$*ul-lu-pí* (PRU 3 194a:11), cf. alphab. *ulp* "chief" (UT 359b no. 202); ^{uru}*ul-la-mi/me* (see PRU 3 p. 267b; also Ug. 5 99:4; Ug. 7 pl. 13:16) = alphab. *ulm* (UT 359a no. 187); $^{[\text{uru}]}$*uš-ka-ni* (PRU 6 70:6) = alphab. *uškn* (UT 368a no. 398).

/hŭ/ (a) with Ú:

in S^a Voc.: *ú-PI* = /huwa/ "he, it" (HW^{1}); *ú-*[*P*]*I*!?-[*t*]*u*$_4$ = /huwătu/?

[163]It is difficult to know whether any significance is to be attached to the fact that alphab. *h* is equated with syll. *ú* while alphab. *u* is equated with syll. u_1 in KTU 5.14. Note, however, that in the forms cited in this section, including proper nouns, whereas Ú occurs to represent each of /ʾŭ/, /hŭ/, and /ʿŭ/, U is largely restricted to representing /ʾŭ/, with a few notable exceptions. The distinction between U for /ʾu/ and Ú for /hō/ or /hū/ in KTU 5.14 conforms to this tendency.

"word" (HW[2]); *ṭu-ú-ru* = /*ṭuhūru*/ "pure" (ṬHR); in other texts: *-ú* = /*-hŭ̄*/ (suffix; -H); see also above, under /*hō*/.

PN's, GN's: perhaps [1]*ba-aʾ-lu-ú* (PRU 6 72:10'), i.e., /*baᶜluhŭ̄*/?; perhaps some of the instances of the GN written uruÚ-*ra-a* are the same as uru*u-ra-a* (see under b), and correspond to alphab. *hry* (UT 392a no. 795).[164]

[(b) with U:

Perhaps in the GN uru*u-ra-a* (Ug. 5 100:1), if = alphab. *hry* (see under a).]

(c) with *uC* signs:

no Sa Voc. examples; in other texts: perhaps urudu*ul-ma-tu* = /*hulmātu*/? "hammers" (HLM).

/*ᶜŭ̄*/ (a) with Ú:

no Sa Voc. examples; in other texts: *: mi-dá-ar-ú* = /*midarᶜu*/? "seed-land" (DRᶜ); *ú-ṣú-ri* =/*ᶜuṣṣūri*/ "bird" (cf. *u-ṣú-ru,* under b; ᶜṢR); [lú].meš*ú-ru-ba-nu* = /*ᶜur(r)ŭ̄b(b)ānū*/ "guarantors" (ᶜRB); perhaps also *ú-lu* = /*ᶜūlu*/? "young (animal)(?)" (ᶜWL).

PN: [1]*ia-pa-ú* (PRU 3 196 ii 18'; cf. [1]*ya-a-pa-ʾu* PRU 6 79:9), cf. alphab. *ypᶜ* (UT 413a no. 1133).

(b) with U:

no Sa Voc. examples; other texts: only *u-ṣú-ru* = /*ᶜuṣṣūru*/ "bird" (cf. *ú-ṣú-ri,* under a; ᶜṢR).

PN: perhaps [1]*ia-aš-mu-u* (Ug. 5 81:45), cf. alphab. *bn yšmᶜ* (UT 492a no. 2441).

[(c) with *uC* signs: no examples.

Note the PN [1]*uz-zi-nu/na* (PRU 3 33f. r.10'; 3 35f.:6') = alphab. *ᶜzn* (UT 455a no. 1837).[165]]

(b) Syllable-closing

If not indicated by the ʾ sign (see above, 2b),[166] the presence of a syllable-closing /ʾ/ or /ᶜ/ (no examples of /*h*/) may be either[167]

[164]The writing uruÚ-*ra-a* occurs in PRU 3 33f. r.6'; PRU 6 80:10; 6 78:10; 6 95:5; 6 134:4. It is likely that in the last three of these, uru*šam-ra-a* is intended, since other towns in those lists correspond to a fair degree with those in PRU 6 105, where uru*šá-am-ra-a* appears in line 8, and with those in PRU 6 111, with uru*šà[m]-r[a-a]* in line 6; cf. also the towns in the alphabetic texts KTU 4.49; 4.68; 4.244; 4.308, in which *θmry* appears. In one or both of the other instances of uruÚ-*ra-a,* however, the town intended may be the same as that written uru*u-ra-a.*

[165]The PN *ḫu-ZI-na* (PRU 6 83 iii 3), which Sivan, Analysis 208, lists under *ᶜuzzu,* is probably to be associated instead with alphab. *ḫsn* (UT 403b no. 985; i.e., a *qutayl* form, /*ḫusēna*/).

[166]For AḪ for expected syllable-closing /ʾ/ and /ᶜ/, see above under (1).

[167]It is possible that both of the possibilities listed below may indicate the quiescence of the guttural and concommitant lengthening of the preceding vowel (especially of /*vʾC*/ > /*v̄C*/, a common phenomenon in Semitic), e.g., uru*bi-i-ri* for /*bīri*/ rather than /*biʾri*/. But such a change is

(i) unrepresented in the script, as in *ma-ša-ra* for */maʿšara/* (ʿŠR^2); or

(ii) indicated by an extra vowel-sign, as in ⸢*ši-i-ru*⸣ for */šiʾru/* (ŠʾR); the attested signs are:

A for */aʾ/*, */aʿ/*;
I for */iʾ/*, */iʿ/* (and E for */iʾ/* in a PN?);
(Ú for */uʿ/* in a PN).

(i) No indication of the guttural:

/vʾ/ in S^{a} Voc.: *ti-*[*n*]*a*?-[*t*]*u*$_4$ = */tiʾnatu/* "fig" (TʾN); in other texts: *: na-ba-dì(-*⸢*šu-nu*⸣*)* = */naʾbadi/* "escape" (ʾBD); $^{\text{(túg.meš)}}$*ma-za-ru-ma* = */maʾzarūma/*? "loincloths(?)" (ʾZR); *me-te* = */miʾtē/* "200" (Mʾ); :!? *su-nu* = */suʾnu/*? "hem" (SʾN); perhaps also *ti-tar-ḫ*[*u*], if for */tiʾtarḫu/* rather than */tittarḫu/* (ʾRḪ).[168]

Note perhaps the gentilic ^{uru}*ma-ḫa-di-yu* (PRU 6 79:6); cf. alphab. *ma/iḫdy(m)* (UT 355a no. 130), but note also *mḫdy* (UT 432a no. 1453); see above, n. 129.

/vʿ/ no S^{a} Voc. examples; in other texts: *ma-ba-ri* = */maʿbari/* "pass" (ʿBR); $^{\text{(urudu.meš)}}$*ma-ṣa-du(-ma*^{meš}*)* = */maʿṣadu, -ūma/* "adze(s)(?)" (ʿṢD); *ma-ša-ra* = */maʿšara/* "tithe" (cf. *ma-aʾ-ša-ri(-ša)* under 2b above; ʿŠR^2).

PN's, GN's: ^{1}*ia-ZI-ra-nu/na* (e.g., PRU 3 54ff.:8,12,15,20; cf. also ^{1}*ia-aʾ-ŠI-ra-nu* ibid.:4) and ^{1}*ia-ŠI-ra* (PRU 3 131a:16) = alphab. *yʿðrn* (UT 454b no. 1831); ^{1}*ba-la-az-ki* (MSL 10 149ff. colophon), i.e., */baʿl-/* (cf. $^{\text{1d}}$IM-*la-az-ki* PRU 3 169a:23; ^{d}U-*la-az-ki* PRU 6 49:19'); ^{1}*nu-ma-ri-ša-ip* (Ug. 5 98:2), if for */nuʿm-/*; ^{uru}*ma-ra-ba/bá* $^{\text{(ki)}}$ (PRU 3 48f.:11; 3 65b:6; 3 102ff.:35 [but ^{uru}*ma-aḫ-ra-bá* $^{\text{(ki)}}$ in lines 30,32]; 3 150b r.6'; 3 151f.:7; 3 187d i 3; 3 192f.:30 [but ^{uru}*ma-aʾ-ra-bá* in line 26]; Ug. 5 12:1,13,14; Ug. 7 pl. 13:24) = alphab. *mʿrb* (UT 461a no. 1915); ^{uru}*ma-qa/*⸢*qá*⸣*-bi/bu* (PRU 3 40b:2,3 3 190a:14'; Ug. 7 pl. 13:31; but ^{uru}*ma-aʾ-qa-bu* PRU 3 191a:15') = alphab. *mʿqb* (UT 460b no. 1907).

---

not supported by the evidence of the alphabetic texts. It is also possible that such writings reflect the presence of an echo vowel, i.e., */biʾĭri/* (cf., e.g., Hebrew *yeʾĕsōr*), and should thus be placed under the discussion of intervocalic gutturals, above (under a); the same may likewise obtain in some examples of the use of the ʾ sign for expected syllable-closing */ʾ/* and */ʿ/* (e.g., in the PN ^{1}*ba-ʾa-lu-ú* [PRU 6 72:10] for */baʿăluhǔ/* rather than ^{1}*ba-aʾ-lu-ú* for */baʿluhǔ/*; cf. Hebrew *naʿărô*). But the possibility that an echo vowel is represented in such forms in ultimately untestable, given the limitations of the syllabic writing system; certainly such vowels would have non-phonemic status, in view of parallel forms in which the */ʾ/* and */ʿ/* (and therefore any following echo vowel) are simply not indicated in writing (type i, below), and of parallel forms in which syllable-closing */ʿ/* is written with AḪ (see under 1, above).

[168]Note also the form *ni-it* (Ug. 5 84:12), without a case-ending, for */niʾt/*?, */niʾit/*? (Nʾ).

(ii) With an extra vowel-sign:

/vʾ/ in Sª Voc.: ⸢*ši-i-ru*⸣ = /*šiʾru*/ "flesh" (ŠʾR); *pí-i*?-[*tu*₄?] = /*piʾtu*/? "corner(?)" (Pʾ); perhaps also *ma-a-du-ma,* if for /*maʾdūma*/ rather than /*maʾadūma*/[169] (MʾD); other texts: no examples.

PN's, GN's: ^uru^*bi-i-ri* (PRU 3 93b:7; = ^uru^PÚ in ibid.:10) = alphab. *bir* (UT 370 no. 437); ^uru^*ma-a-ḫa-di* (PRU 3 195b A 6), cf. alphab. gentilic *mi*/*aḫdym* (UT 355a no. 130; see above, n. 129); note also perhaps the PN ^1^*ie-e-*[*d*]*a-ra* (PRU 6 72:16), which probably reflects the root *ʾ-d-r* (rather than *ᶜ-ð-r*, as suggested by Nougayrol, PRU 6 p. 144b), i.e., a shortened form of */*yiʾdarānu*/ or */*yiʾdar*-DN/ (cf. alphab. *adrdn,* UT 353a no. 94a), with /*i*/ = [e] (i.e., [yeʾdar-] because of the preceding /*y*/ (see §G 2).

/vᶜ/ in Sª Voc.: *ba-a-lu* = /*baᶜlu*/ "lord" and perhaps pl. *ba-a-lu-ma,* if for /*baᶜlūma*/ rather than /*baᶜalūma*/[170] (BᶜL); perhaps *qi-i-lu,* if for /*qiᶜlu*/ rather than /*qiᶜīlu*/ (though the latter is more likely; QᶜL); in other texts: no examples.

PN's: ^1^*ba-a-la-nu* (Ug. 5 86:18) = alphab. *bᶜln* (UT 375a no. 493); ^1^*nu-ú-ma-ya(-nu)* (Ug. 5 98:1,3), cf. alphab. *bn nᶜmyn* (UT 445a no. 1665).

F. The Indication of Vowel Length[171]

The representation of vowel length in the syllabic writings of Ugaritic words closely follows the conventions of contemporary Akkadian, especially Babylonian, orthography.[172] In particular, the following may be observed.[173]

1. The explicit indication of a long vowel by means of an extra vowel-sign is normal only at word end, and only under two conditions:

[169] In view of the existence of at least sporadic pretonic vowel syncope in Ugaritic (see ch. 2 §B 1), the precise phonological interpretation of this form and of *ba-a-lu-ma* (see below, under /*v*ᶜ/), both plurals of *qatl* nouns for which *qatalūma* is expected, must remain uncertain: either /*maʾadūma*/ or > /*maʾdūma*/; either /*baᶜalūma*/ or > /*baᶜlūma*/.

[170] See the preceding note.

[171] In our phonemic and phonetic transcriptions of Ugaritic words throughout this study, following the usual practice in transcribing Akkadian forms, both long vowels inherited from Proto-NWS and vowels resulting from the contraction of diphthongs are indicated with a macron. Vowels resulting from the contraction of triphthongs, and of syllable-initial *w, y* and a following vowel (see below, 1 b), conversely, are indicated with a circumflex.

[172] See, e.g., von Soden, GAG §7e; Aro, Studien 26-28.

[173] The only example in which a long vowel may be indicated by the doubling of the following consonant (i.e., *vC:* for *v:C*; so Gröndahl, Personennamen 18 n. 16; Kühne, UF 6 165) is the form *qa-ad-šu-ut-ti* for expected /*qad(i)šūti*/. But here the abstract ending *-utt* probably reflects Assyrian morphology; see above, §D 2, with n. 43.

a. In monosyllabic forms:[174] *du-ú* = /*dū*/ (determinative-relative pronoun; D); *la-a* (bis) = /*lā*/ "not" (L¹).[175] An extra vowel sign also appears on the two attested monosyllabic forms in which the vowel is underlyingly short:[176] *le-⌜e⌝* = [lē][177] = /*li*/ "to" (L²); ⌜*bi*⌝-*i* = [bī] = /*bi*/ "in" (B). These forms occur in succession as Sª Voc. nos. 32.5 and 32.6 (Ug. 5 130 iii 5',6'). In all probability the vowel is written (and pronounced) long in these two normally proclitic forms precisely because they are in a lexical list, where they are out of any context, and thus uniquely not proclitic to anything.[178] The same phenomenon is also attested for Akkadian proclitics in Mesopotamian lexical lists.[179]

b. For final vowels long from contraction of triphthongs: *ḫu-wu-ú* = /*ḥuwwû*/ < **ḥuwwayu* "to live" (ḤYY¹/ḤWY¹ a); :*ša-du-ú* = /*šadû*/ < **śadawu* "field" (ŠDW);[180] the PN ᶠ*mi-il-ka-a* (PRU 3 54ff.:21), for /*milkâ*/ < **milkāya*. Note also *i-pu-ú* = /*ᶜipû*/? "destruction(?)," in which /-*û*/ is probably from a contraction of post-consonantal *-*wu*, i.e., **ᶜipwu*? (ᶜPW). These examples are discussed in greater detail below, ch. 2 §E 3. The extra vowel-sign in such forms probably indicates at least a phonetic distinction between long vowels that result from triphthong contraction (*v̂*) and long vowels either inherited from PNWS or that result from diphthong contraction (*v̄*; cf. *me-te* = /*miʾtē*/ < **miʾtay* under 2, below). But the evidence is too sparce and ambiguous to ascertain whether a phonemic distinction existed or, if it did, its nature.[181] They will nevertheless be distinguished from other long vowels by means of a circumflex (even in our phonemic transcription), to indicate their historical origin (see n. 171).

[174]Cf., e.g., the usual writings of Akkadian *šū* and *šī* as *šu-ú*, *ši-i*; *kī* as *ki-i*; and in Ugarit Akk. and other dialects, the common writing of *lā* as *la-a* (alongside *la*).

[175]Note that possible examples of Ugar. /*lā*/ are written simply *la* 4 times, but *la-a* once, in Ug. 5 153.

[176]See the commentary on Sª Voc. no. 32.5 in Part I.

[177]On the quality of the vowel, see below, §G 2.

[178]Compare the probable occurrence of /*bi*/ without an extra vowel-sign in proclisis in Sª Voc. no. 47.3: *bi-RU*-[. (/*bi*-/ may also occur, likewise written simply *bi*, in Ug. 5 153 r.6',7'.)

[179]See Part I, in the commentary on Sª Voc. no. 32.5, with n. 8.

[180]Cf. perhaps *ša-TI-i*, if for Ugar. /*šadî*/, in Ug. 5 153 r.6'.

[181]What, for example, would be the distinction, if any, between */*banū*/ "sons of" and */*banû*/ < **banayū* "they built"? In Akkadian, of course, forms analogous to the latter underwent a stress shift (*banû́* < **bániyū*), but the same claim may not simply be transferred to Ugaritic without some internal evidence to support it. An alphab. form such as *aḫ* "papyrus thicket" (< Egyptian; see UT 355a no. 129; Rainey, UF 3 169), if for */*ʾaḫû*/ < **ʾaḫwu* (cf. Heb. *ʾāḥû*), may indicate that stress did not shift in Ugar. forms, i.e., */*ʾáḫû*/, since an unstressed /*a*/ in this form should have assimilated to the *u*-vowel of the following syllable in accordance with the rule discussed below in ch. 2 §A 1 d.

2. Other final long vowels, including /ē/ < *ay, are unmarked:

/-ā/ : the dual nom. bound form *ma-qa-ḫa* = /maqqaḥā/ "pair of tongs" (LQḤ b).[182]

/-ē/ (< *ay): in the bound dual oblique form *me-te* = /miʾtē/ "200" (Mʾ).

/-ī/ : the bound pl. oblique forms lú.meš*mur-i*[183] = /murʾī/ "commanders(?)" (MRʾ); lú.meš*mar-ia-an-ni* = /maryannī/ "charioteers" (MRYN).

/-ū/ : the pl. nom. bound forms lú.meš*b[i]-ḫi-ru* = /biḥīrū/ "elite (troops)" (BḤR); lú.meš*mur-ú* = /murʾū/ "commanders" (MRʾ); lú(.meš)*mar-ia-nu* = /maryannū/ "charioteers"(MRYN);

the 3 m. pl. suffix-conj. forms *na-ap-ṭa-ru* = /napṭarū/ "they exchanged(?)" (PṬR b); *: ṣa-ma-DU* = /ṣamatū/ "they were transferred" (ṢMT); probably also *ḫa-ba-ṭu* = /?/ (see the Appendix to the Glossary).[184]

3. Medial long vowels are not usually written with an extra vowel-sign, even vowels long from contractions of di- and triphthongs, as in *ḫé-qu* = /ḥēqu/ < *ḥayqu "lap" (ḤYQ); *ša-mu-ma* = /šamûma/ < *šamayūma "sky" (ŠMY; see ch. 2 §E 3). Out of roughly a hundred forms with medial long vowels, only the following examples are written with an extra vowel-sign:[185]

uḫ-ra-a-yi = /ʾuḫrāyi/ "destiny" (ʾḪR); *ḫe?-e[-ru]* = /ḥēru/? "enclosure(?)" (ḤYR); *:ḫa-a-yi* = /ḥāyi/, and *ḫe-e-ia/yu* = [ḫēya/u] and *:ḫi-i-yi(-šu)* = [ḫīyī], vs. *:ḫé-yi-ma* = [ḫīyīma] "vacant(?)" (ḪWY); *ma-a-⌜ar?⌝* = /mār(a)/ "it was exchanged" (Akkadianized; MW/YR); *ṣa-a-i* (5 times) vs. *(:)ṣa-i* (6 times) = /ṣāʿi/ "basin" (note also the pl. giš.meš*ṣa-ʾa-tu* = /ṣāʿātu/; ṢWʿ); *:ZI-ṣú-ú-ma* (once) vs. *:ZI-ṣú-ma* (bis) = /ṣīṣūma/ or /ṣēṣūma/ "salt fields" (ṢYṢ); *ši-i-ru*[186] = /šīru/ "song" (ŠYR; cf. *ši-tu* = /šītu/ "to place" [ŠYT]).

The very rare explicit indication of long vowels results in ambiguity concerning

[182]Note also *at-ta* = /ʾattă/ (ʾNT). The final vowel of PS *ʾantă "you (m.s.)" is anceps; whether the reflexes of anceps vowels in Ugaritic were long or short cannot be determined on the basis of the evidence available.

[183]The use of a vowel-sign here and in similar writings (e.g., lú.meš*mur-ú*, below), after a syllable-closing consonant, does not indicate vowel length, but rather the presence of one of the gutturals /ʾ/, /h/, /ʿ/; see above, §E 4 b (3a).

[184]Note also *a-na-ku* = /ʾanākŭ/ (ʾNK), the final vowel of which, like that of /ʾattă/ (see above, n. 182), is anceps in PS.

[185]Other occurrences of medial vowel signs, such as *ṭu-ú-ru* and *ma-a-al-tu₄*, signal the presence of one of the gutturals /ʾ/, /h/, /ʿ/: /ṭuhūru/ (ṬHR), /maʿʿaltu/ (NʿL); see also the next n. See the discussion of the gutturals, above, §E 4 b (3).

[186]Note also the identical spelling in two other Sᵃ Voc. words, where the I sign indicates the presence of a guttural rather than a long vowel: /šiʾru/ (ŠʾR); /šiʿīru/ (ŠʿR a).

vowel length, and thus morphological pattern, in a large number of forms: e.g., the adjective *ḫa-ri-mu* = /*ḥarĭmu*/ "desecrated(?)" (ḤRM a; *qatil* or *qatīl*?); the noun of occupation *ḫa-ra-*⌜*šu*?⌝ = /*ḥarrăšu*/ "artisan" (ḤRŠ; *qattal* or *qattāl*?); the noun *bu-nu-šu* = /*bunŭšu*/ "man" (BNŠ; *qutul* or *qutūl*?). For further discussion and additional examples, see below, ch. 3 §C 2.

G. The Representation of the Individual Vowels[187]

1. /*a*/, /*ā*/

Short /*a*/ participates in several phonological processes, in which it undergoes assimilation to a following glide or following stressed or long vowel. These processes are described below in ch. 2 §A 1 b - e.

Long /*ā*/ is subject to raising (assimilation) before /*y*/; see ch. 2 §A 1 e. Otherwise, /*ā*/ remains unchanged in all attested examples. There is no evidence of the Canaanite shift of **ā* > *ō* in any of the words in our corpus.[188] A representative sample:

> *a-da-nu* = /*ʾadānu*/ "father" (ʾDN); *a-na-ku* = /*ʾanākŭ*/ "I" (ʾNK); *uḫ-ra-a-yi* = /*ʾuḫrāyi*/ "destiny" (ʾḪR); ⌜*a*⌝-[*p*]*i*?-[*yu*?] = /*ʾāpiyu*/? "baker" (ʾPY); *: ḫa-me-ti* = /*ḥāmīti*/ "wall" (ḤMY); *ṭa-bu* = /*ṭābu*/ "sweet" (ṬW/YB); lú*ka4-bi-s*[*ú*] = /*kābisu*/ "launderer" (KBS a); d.giš*ki-na-rù* = /*kinnāru*/ "lyre" (divine name; KNR); *la-ša-nu* = /*lašānu*/ "tongue" (LŠN); (*:*) *ṣa*(*-a*)*-i* = /*ṣāʿi*/, pl. giš.meš*ṣa-ʾa-tu* = /*ṣāʿātu*/ "bowl(s)" (ṢWʿ); *ta-a-ma-tu4* = /*tahāmatu*/ "the deep" (THM); for other examples see under G participles and under the affix /*-ān*/ in ch. 3 §C 2 e and n.

2. /*ē*/,[189] /*i*/, /*ī*/

The cuneiform syllabary is only partly able to manifest a distinction between the vowels *e* and *i*, specifically, with the signs E and I and with a few *Cv* and *vC* signs, such as TE and TI (vs., e.g., LI for both *le* and *li*) and EL and IL (vs., e.g., IM for both *em* and *im*).[190] Nevertheless, in those cases in which such a graphic distinction

[187]For the vowels /*â*/, /*î*/, /*û*/ resulting from triphthong contraction, see ch. 2 §E 3.

[188]Cf. Gordon, UT 31 §5.17; Sivan, Analysis 25-29, §5.1. The *ā* > *ō* shift is, however, attested in a number of PN's and GN's, all of which thus reflect dialects other than that represented by the syllabic transcriptions of actual Ugar. words; see under /*ō*/, /*u*/, /*ū*/ (below, 3).

[189]See n. 171 above.

[190]Not all dialects of Akkadian, of course, distinguish between *i* and *e* to the same extent. See, in

between *e* and *i* is possible,[191] a fairly consistent pattern can be discerned in the writing of Ugaritic words, as the following analysis shows.

a. The Reflex of **ay*[192]

The vowel that is the Ugaritic reflex of syllable-final **ay* is normally written with the E sign or with *Ce* signs:[193]

E: *e-bu* = */ʾēbu/*[194] "enemy" (ʾYB); perhaps also *ḫe?-e*[*-ru*] = */ḥēru/*? "enclosure(?)" (ḤYR).

BE (BAD): note alphab. *b* = syll. *be* in KTU 5.14:2, reflecting the letter name **/bētu/*.[195]

---

general, AS[3]; further, Gelb, MAD 2[2] 123-26; Hecker, Grammatik 24 §14; Finet, L'accadien 8 §5k; Aro, Studien 43-45, 72-73; Mayer, Untersuchungen 15 §9; Jucquois, Phonétique 95-110.

[191]Viz., in our texts, between E and I, BE (BAD) and BI; ḪÉ (KAN) and ḪI (see below); EL and IL; ME and MI; EN and IN; ŠE and ŠI; EŠ and IŠ; TE and TI. We will see below, however, that the contrast between EL and IL, ME and MI, EN and IN, is effectively neutralized by the lowering of */ĭ/* to [ĕ] around sonorants (see n. 211).

Since the NE sign is virtually unused in the Ugarit Akk. syllabary (only in the PN ᶠ⌜NE⌝-*ši-ta* [RA 38 5:3; cf. alphab. *nθt*, UT 448b no. 1722?] and as *ṭè* in the literary *ṭè-em* [Ug. 5 164:21', vs. *ṭe-em* ibid.:27',43']), a contrast between NE and NI is effectively not possible.

☛ p. 401

There is a tendency in peripheral Akk. dialects to use, alongside the ḪI sign with both the value *ḫi* and the value *ḫe*, the KAN sign with the specific value *ḫé* (see AS[3] pp. 19 and 3*, no. 105; Jucquois, Phonétique 97). Since ḪI can represent *ḫe* as well as *ḫi*—as evidenced in the Ugar. words *:ḪI-e-ia/yu* (see ḪWY), *ḪI-en-ni-ṣu* (ḪNṢ), *ḪI*?*-e*[*-ru*?] = */ḥēru/*? (ḤYR), and *ḪI-bu* as a variant writing of *ḫé-bu* (in Sª Voc. no. 47.2; see ḪYB), for all of which see further below—whereas KAN seems to indicate only *ḫé* (not *ḫí*), the contrast between these two signs is not precisely the same as that between, e.g., TI and TE, *each* of which seems, as we will see below, to represent only one vocalic phone in Ugar. words, viz., TI = *ti* and *dì* (but not te_9 or de_9), TE = *te* and de_4 (but not ti_7 or di_{12}). The use of KAN for *ḫé* in peripheral Akk. dialects is undoubtedly due to the same practice in some Hurrian and Hittite orthographies; see Bush, GHL 20; Riemschneider, FS Otten 281 [ḪI for *ḫi* and *ḫe*, KAN only for *ḫé*]; Melchert, Studies 83). (The same orthographies attest a contrast in vowels for GI and KI, viz., GI for *g/ke* vs. KI for *g/ki* [± *g/ke*]; see Berkooz, Nuzi Dialect 10-11; Bush, GHL 22,41; Riemschneider, FS Otten 276-81. This contrast, however, is not evident in Ugarit Akk. texts in either Ugaritic forms [see above, §E 1 b] or Akk. forms, except for the common use of GI for *qè* in forms of *leqû*.)

[192]On the phonological process involved, see also below, ch. 2 §A 1 e, end.

[193]Possible examples of */ē/* written with ambiguous *Ci/e* signs are the following: *ku-RI-ku* = */kurēku/*? and *ku-RI-ka-m*[*a*?] = */kurēkāma/*? "(implement)" (see KRK); *ni-r*[*u*] = */nēru/*? or */nīru/*? "lamp(?)" (NW/YR); *:ZI-ṣú(-ú)-ma* = */ṣīṣūma/* or */ṣēṣūma/* "salt fields" (ṢYṢ).

No examples of *eC* signs for */ēC/* are expected, since Ugar. */ē/* < **ay* could not occur in a closed syllable.

[194]A stative participle (verbal adj.), < **ʾayib-* (cf. Hebrew *mēt, gēr*); see Albright, BASOR 89 32 n. 26.

[195]See Cross-Lambdin, BASOR 160 24-25.

ḪÉ (KAN):[196] *ḫé-qu* = */ḥēqu/* "lap" (ḤYQ); probably also *ḫé-bu,* alongside *ḪI-bu,* both = */ḫēbu/*?[197] "shame(?)" (ḪYB).

TE: = *te* for */tē/*: *me-te* = */miʾtē/* "200" (bound dual oblique; Mʾ);

= *de*$_4$ for */dē/*:[198] *(:)tap/ta-ap-de*$_4$*-tu*$_4$*/ti* = */tapdētu/i/*[199] "exchange" (PDY); perhaps also [^{túg}*m*]*ar-de*$_4$*-tu* = */mardētu/*? "(garment)" (RDY).

Only one likely exception, with a *Ci* sign, is attested:

TI: *iš-ia-ti-mi* = */ᶜišyatēmi/*? (dual oblique; ᶜŠY).

See the discussion below.

b. The Reflexes of **i* and **ī* [200]

These are usually written with the I sign or with *Ci* or *iC* signs; there is, however, a significant set of exceptions, with E, *eC,* or *Ce* :

i-signs

I: ⸢*i?-lu?*⸣ = */ʾilu/* "god" (ʾL); *i-r*[*a?-tu*$_4$*?*] = */ʾiratu/*? "chest(?)" (ʾR); *i-*[*r*]*i?-iš-*[*tu*$_4$*?*] = */ʾirištu/*? "request" (ʾRŠ); ⸢*i*⸣*-ši-t*[*u*$_4$] = */ʾišītu/*? "fire" (ʾŠ); ⸢*bi*⸣*-i* =*/bi/* "in" (B); $^{lú.meš}$*mur-i* = */murʾī/* "commanders(?)" (MRʾ); *i-zi-ir-*[*tu*$_4$*?*] = */ᶜiðirtu/* "help" (ᶜðR); *i-pu-ú* = */ᶜipû/*? "destruction(?)" (ᶜPW); *i-pu-ú* = */ᶜipû/*? "destruction(?)" (ᶜPW); *(:) ṣa(-a)-i* = */ṣāᶜi/* "basin" (ṢWᶜ); *qi-i-lu* = */qiᶜīlu/* (less likely, */qiᶜlu/*) "vine-blossom(?)" (QᶜL); *mar-zi-i* and *mar-za-i* = [marzi/aᶜi] "symposium" (RZḤ); ⸢*ši-i-ru*⸣ = */šiʾru/* "flesh" (ŠʾR); *ši-i-ru* = */šīru/* "song" (ŠYR); [*š*]*i?-i-ru*[= */šiᶜīru/* "barley(?)" (ŠᶜR a); *ša-i-tu*$_4$ = */θāᶜittu/*? or */θāᶜītu/*? "(a container)" (θᶜD/θᶜY).

BI: ⸢*bi*⸣*-i* = */bi/* "in" (B); $^{(giš.meš)}$*bi-da-lu-ma/na* = */bidălūm/na/* "merchants" (BDL); $^{lú.meš}$*b*[*i*]*-ḫi-ru* = */biḥīrū/*? "elite (troops)" (BḤR^1); *: ga-bi-ni* = */gabīni/*? "hillock(?)" (GBN); *ka-bi-*[*du?*] = */kabidu/*? "liver(?)" (KBD a); ^{lú}*ka*$_4$(QA)*-bi-s*[*ú*] = */kābisu/* "launderer" (KBS a); *(:) ṣí(-ib)-bi-ri* = */ṣibbīri/* "collective land(?)" (ṢBR).

[196] See above, n. 191.

[197] The forms *ḫé-bu* and *ḪI-bu* are variants in Sᵃ Voc. no. 47.2. Since there is nothing to condition a realization of */i/* as ⸢ē] (see below), the former must represent */ḫēbu/*, i.e., a *qatl* noun. The latter may be read *ḫi-bu* = */ḫību/*, a *qīl* adjective or noun, but it seems unlikely that two distinct forms are reflected by the variant writings; thus, we should read *ḪI-bu* as *ḫe-bu* (see above, n. 191), i.e., also as the *qatl* form */ḫēbu/*.

[198] The use of TE for *de*$_4$ is not due to the common Hurrian or WPA confusion of stops, but rather is a relic of the Old Akkadian syllabary, which distinguishes */di/* and */de/*; see Moran, "Syrian Scribe" 161 n. 34.

[199] I.e., a *taqtal* form (Gt verbal noun), which is more likely semantically than a D verbal noun *taqtīl* (**/tapdītu/*, with TE = *di*$_{12}$).

[200] For */ī/* as a reflex of P(NW)S **iy*, see ch. 2 §E 1 b.

ḪI[201]: $^{lú.meš}$*b*[*i*]-*ḪI-ru* = /*biḫīrū*/ "elite (troops)" (BḤR^1); *ḪI*-[*i*]*u?-ma* (but also *ḫé-yu-ma* = /*ḥiyyūma*/ "life" (ḤYY^1/ḤWY^1 b); *ḪI-nu-ta-me* = /*ḥinōtāmi*/? "(implements, du.)" (ḤNW); :*ḪI-i-yi(-šu)* = [ḫīyi̊] and *ḪI-e-ia/yu* = [ḫēya/u] "vacant(?)" (also :*ḫé-yi-ma* = [ḫēyīma] and :*ḫa-a-yi* = [ḫāyi]; ḪWY); *ḪI-ya/ia-ri* = /*ḥiyyāri*/ (month name; ḤYR); *ḪI-en-ni-ṣu* = /*ḫinnīṣu*/ "piglet" (ḪNṢ); :*ḪI-ri-ti* = /*ḫirīti*/ "cemetery" (ḪRY); ^{lú}*ma-ḪI-ṣu* = /*māḫiṣu*/ "(a profession)" (MḪṢ a); $^{[urudu.meš]}$*me-ḪI*-[*ṣ*]*u*-⌜*ma*⌝^{meš} = /*miḫīṣūma*/ "(implements)" (MḪṢ b); ^{lú}*na-ḪI-ru* = /*nāǵiru*/ "guard" (NǴR a); *ma-ar-zi-ḪI* = /*marziḥi*/ "symposium" (RZḤ); *mar-ḪI-iš* = /*marḫiš(u)*/ "(a utensil)" (RḪŠ).[202]

IL: (:) *sí-il-a* = /*silᶜa*/ "cliff(?)" (SLᶜ); *ṣi-il-PI*[= /*ṣilyatu*/ (or/*ṣilyu*/) "curse" (ṢLY).

MI: : *šab*-⌜*li?-mi?*⌝ = /*šablimi*/?? "retaining wall(??)" (BLM); : *mi-dá-ar-ú* = /*midarᶜu*/? "seed-land" (DRᶜ); *iš-ia-ti-mi* = /*ᶜišyatēmi*/ "clamps(?)" (dual; ᶜŠY); *a-ra-mi-ma* = /?/ (see Appendix to Glossary).

IN: no examples.

ŠI: *a-ši-ib* = /*ʾaθib*/ "let me dwell" (YθB a); $^{lú(.meš)}$*a-ši-ru/ri-ma* = /*ᶜāšīrū/īma*/ "(royal officials)" (ᶜŠR^1); *ši-a-ru* = /*šiharu*/? "crescent-shaped sickle(?)" (ŠHR); *ši-tu* = /*šītu*/ "to place" (ŠYT); and *ši-i-ru* three times (see above, under the I sign).

IŠ: *i*-[*r*]*i?-iš*-[*tu₄*?] = /*ʾirištu*/? "request" (ʾRŠ); *iš-du₄* = /*ʾišdu*/ "leg" (ʾŠD); *iš-ia-ti-mi* = /*ᶜišyatēmi*/ "clamps(?)" (dual; ᶜŠY); *mar-ḫi-iš* = /*marḫiš(u)*/ "(a utensil)" (RḪŠ).

TI: for /*ti*/: : *ti-tar-ḫ*[*u*] = /*tiʾittarḫu*/ "she will hurry" (ʾRḪ); *ti*-[*n*]*a?*-[*t*]*u₄* = /*tiʾnatu*/ "fig" (TʾN); *ti-ib-nu* = /*tibnu*/ "straw" (TBN); for final /*-ti*/: e.g., : *ḫa-me-ti* = /*ḥāmīti*/ "wall" (ḤMY); *ra-ba-ti* = /*rabbati*/ "great" (RBB); and passim.

for /*di*/: : *na-ba-dì*(-⌜*šu-nu*⌝) = /*naʾbadi*/ "escape" (ʾBD); : *dì-ip-ra-ni-ma* = /*diprānīma*/ "junipers" (DPR); *mu-qa-dì(-IM?!)* = /*muqqādi*/? "grazing rights(?)" (NQD); *qa-dì-iš* = Akkadianized *qadiš* (for /*qadiša*/) "is sacred" (QDŠ a).

e-signs

E: *ḪI-e-ia/yu* = [ḫēya/u] "vacant(?)" (also *ḪI-i-yi(-šu)* = [ḫīyi̊], :*ḫé-yi-ma* = [ḫēyīma], and :*ḫa-a-yi* = [ḫāyi]; ḪWY); *le*-⌜*e*⌝ = /*li-*/ "to" (L^2); ⌜*e?*⌝-*la-PI* = /*ᶜilāyi*/? "upper (part)(?)" (ᶜLY b).[203]

[201]See n. 191, above.

[202]For *ḪI-bu*, see above, n. 197.

[203]Perhaps also ⌜^{giš}*e?-la-mu*⌝ = /?/ (see Appendix to Glossary), if the form is *qitāl*.

BE (BAD) : no examples.

ḪÉ (KAN) : *ḫé-yu-ma* = /*ḥiyyūma*/ "life" (also *ḪI*-[*i*]*u*?-*ma*; ḤYY[1]/ḤWY[1] b); :*ḫé-yi-ma* = [ḫēyīma] "vacant(?)" (also *ḪI-e-ia/yu* = [ḫēya/u], *ḪI-i-yi(-šu)* = [ḫīyĭ], and :*ḫa-a-yi* = /*ḫāyi*/; ḪWY).

EL: no examples.

ME: : *ḫa-me-ti*[204] = /*ḥāmīti*/ "wall" (ḤMY); *ḫi-nu-ta-me* = /*ḥinōtāmi*/? "2 'implements'" (ḤNW); [urudu]*ḫa-ar-me-ša-tu* = /*ḫarmiθātu*/ "sickles(?)" (ḪRMθ); *me-te* = /*miʾtē*/ "200" (Mʾ); [urudu.meš]*me-ḫi-*[*ṣ*]*u-*⸢*ma*⸣[meš] = /*miḫīṣūma*/ "(implements)" (MḪṢ b).

EN: *ḫe-en-ni-ṣu* = /*ḫinnīṣu*/? "piglet" (ḪNṢ).

ŠE: no examples.

EŠ: no examples.

TI: for /*ti*/: only *mar-kab-te* = /*markabti*/? "chariot(?)" (RKB);
for /*di*/: probably *mar-de₄-em-tu* = /*mardimtu*/? "path(?)" (RDM).[205]

The foregoing examples indicate a clear preference for writing the Ugaritic reflexes of **i* and **ī* with *i*-signs and the Ugaritic reflex of **ay* with *e*-signs. Since the writing of Ugaritic words in syllabic cuneiform was not a part of the scribal tradition imported from Mesopotamia, we may assume that most of the Ugaritic forms are ad hoc writings rather than learned spellings (as is often true of the writing of Akk. words; see e.g., n. 205, above). The consistent distinction in the use of *i*- and *e*-signs, therefore, leads to two significant conclusions. First, the general scholarly consensus that the reflex of **ay* was /*ē*/, and thus differed form the reflex of **ī* as /*ī*/,[206] is confirmed.[207] Second, we must conclude that the scribes considered the various *i*- and *e*-signs to have phonetically distinct values, in other words, that a given sign *Ci* for which there existed a contrasting *Ce* sign properly had the value [Cĭ] but not [Cĕ]. These conclusions are not vitiated by the set of exceptions cited above in which the reflexes of **i* and **ī* are written with *e*-signs. For an examination of those exceptions reveals that all but one of them occur in a well-defined phonological environment, namely, before or after the sonorants /*l*/, /*m*/, /*n*/, and /*y*/.[208] In view of the

[204]Originally **ḥāmiyt*-, rather than /*ḥāmēti*/ < **ḥāmiyat*- (so Boyd, Collection 88-89). The triphthong /*iya*/ seems usually to be retained in Ugaritic; see ch. 2 §E 3.

[205]The writing of the Akk. loanword /*mūdû*/ in the bound pl. oblique as [(lú.meš)]*mu-de₄* (see MD) is a learned spelling (reflecting Akk. sg. *mūde*).

[206]As in nearly all of the Semitic languages in which **ay* contracted; a notable exception, of course, is Babylonian, where **ay* > *ī*, and merged with *ī* < **ī*.

[207]Thus, the common opinion that the alphabetic aleph-*i* sign represents, in addition to vowelless /ʾ/, /ʾ/ plus two distinct vowel qualities, /*ē*/ and /*i*/, /*ī*/, also finds support. Similarly, therefore the alphabetic *u*-aleph probably represents both /ʾ*ō*/ and /ʾ*u*/, /ʾ*ū*/; see further below.

[208]The sole exception is *mar-kab-te* (PRU 3 96ff.:28), apparently for /*markabti*/, unless dual

consistent use of *i*-signs for /*i*/ and /*ī*/ in all other environments, we may therefore propose that those phonemes had allophones, [e] and [ē] respectively, in the neighborhood of a sonorant:[209]

$$/\check{\bar{\imath}}/ \;=\; [\check{\bar{e}}] \;//\; \underset{[+\text{sonor}]}{C} \quad .^{210}$$

Note that the presence of a sonorant does not invariably trigger the writing of /*ĭ*/ with an *e*-sign, as several examples show: e.g., ⸢*i*?-*lu*?⸣ = /*ʾilu*/ "god" (ʾL); *: mi-dá-ar-ú* = /*midarᶜu*/? "seed-land" (DRᶜ). Thus, the allophones [e] and [ē] may be written with either *e*-signs (phonetic spellings) or with *i*-signs (phonemic spellings),[211] as in the variant forms *ḪI-e-ia/yu* = [ḫēya/u] and *:ḫé-yi-ma* = [ḫēyīma] vs. *:ḪI-i-yi(-šu)* = /*ḫīyĭ*/ ("vacant(?)"; ḪWY).[212]

The evidence for the lowering of /*ĭ*/ to [ĕ] around sonorants in Ugaritic words is admittedly rather sparse. The evidence of proper nouns, as was noted in the Introduction (pp. 8-9), may not be included in a linguistic analysis since the dialect of any given name is not ultimately ascertainable, and thus may neither confirm nor contradict more reliable dialectal data. Nevertheless, it should be pointed out at this juncture that in West Semitic names in the Ugarit Akkadian texts, when etymology suggests an original **i* or **ī*, that vowel is usually written with *i*-signs; when *e*-signs appear for expected **ĭ*, it is predominantly in the neighborhood of a sonorant. A representative sample:

I and E:

ˡ*i-li-*[*ia*] (Ug. 5 95:3) for /*ʾilīya*/; *i-li-na* (PRU 6 83 iv 15) for /*ʾilīna*/; but *e-li-ia-ya* (Syria 18 253f.:5) for /*ʾilīyāya*/; ˡ*ye-e-*[*d*]*a-ra* (PRU 6 72:16), which probably represents [yeʾdar-] = /*yiʾdar-*/ (short for /*yiʾdarānu*/ or /*yiʾdar-* DN/), i.e., a prefix-conj. form of *ʾ-d-r* (cf. alphab. *adrdn*, UT 353a no. 94a).[213]

/*markabtē*[*mi*]/ is intended. But "chariots" is difficult in context; see the Glossary under RKB.

It is curious that no examples of *e*-signs for /*ĭ*/ occur around the sonorant /*r*/; instead, we find, e.g., *ši-i-ru* = /*šīru*/ "song" (ŠYR) and for /*šiᶜīru*/ "barley" (ŠᶜR a); *(:) ṣí(-ib)-bi-ri* = /*ṣibbīri*/ "collective land(?)" (ṢBR); ˡᵘ́⁽·ᵐᵉˢ̌⁾*a-ši-ru/ri-ma* = /*ᶜăšīrū/īma*/ "(royal officials)" (ᶜŠR¹). There is too little evidence to determine whether the nonoccurrence of *e*-signs around /*r*/ is fortuitous (i.e., all examples are phonemic writings; see below) or indicates that /*r*/ did not have the lowering effect on /*ĭ*/ that the other sonorants did.

[209] This is, I believe, the most likely explanation of the writing *le-*⸢*e*⸣ in Sᵃ Voc. no. 32.5: it reflects the normal pronunciation of phonemic /*li*/ as [le], lengthened to [lē] out of context; for the vowel length, see above, §F 1 a.

[210] Thus, /*ī*/ = [ē] around sonorants, a pronunciation perhaps close enough to that of /*ē*/ (< **ay*) to level the contrast between the two. This levelling of contrast is the most likely explanation for the single occurrence of an *i*-sign to indicate /*ē*/, viz., in dual oblique *iš-ia-ti-mi* = /*ᶜišyatēmi*/ "clamps(?)" (ᶜŠY); the TI sign in this form, in other words, may be the result of a hypercorrection, a misanalysis of [ᶜišyatēmi] as */*ᶜišyatīmi*/ (= [ᶜišyatēmi]) because of the following sonorant /*m*/.

[211] Note that this means that EL (unattested) and IL, ME and MI, and EN and IN (unattested) are in completely free variation in the writing of Ugaritic words.

[212] These forms derive from /*ḫāyu*/, with *ă* > *ĭ* / *y*; see below, ch. 2 §A 1 e. The original form is preserved in *:ḫa-a-yi* (see ḪWY).

[213] The E sign here indicates a syllable-final guttural; see above, p. 254. If our interpretation of this name is correct, it is interesting to note that even in the common verbal prefix /*yi-*/, the vowel /*i*/

BI and BE (BAD):

^{1}*a-bi-yv* and ^{1}*a-be-yv* (PRU 3 187a:4,9) for */ʾabīyv/*; ^{1}*kal-bi-yv* (PRU 3 131f.:4; 3 145f.:4,11) and ^{1}*kál-be-yv* (PRU 3 96ff.:6,11,30,33; 3 154f.:7) for */kalbīyv/*.[214]

ḪI and ḪÉ (KAN):

^{1}*mu-na-ḫi-mu* (PRU 3 122f.:22, and often) and ^{1}*mu-na-ḫé-mu* (PRU 3 199f. edge ii 5) for */munaḥḥimu/*; ^{1}*i-ḫi-ia-nu/na* (PRU 3 54a:5,10; Ug. 5 5:25) and ^{1}*e-ḫé-ia-nu* (PRU 3 192f.:28) for */ʾiḫīyānu/*.[215]

IL and EL:

^{1}*mi-il-ki-lu* (PRU 6 40:26) for */milkī-(ʾi)lu/*; ^{f}*mi-il-ka-ia* (PRU 3 66a:5) and ^{f}*mi-il-ka-a* (PRU 3 54ff.:21) for */milkăya, -kâ/*; but ^{uru}*ma-ra-el* (PRU 3 190b:10) for */marra-ʾil/*?[216]

MI and ME:

$^{(1)}$*ia-ri-mi* (PRU 3 137b r.9'; 3 165f. r.19') and ^{1}*ia-ri(-im)-me* (PRU 3 122f.:22; 3 125:21'; 3 137f. r.4'; 3 151f. r.7'; 3 155f.:24) for */yarim-mi/*?;[217] ^{1}*šu-mi-y[a-n]a* (PRU 3 106a:5) and *šu-me-ia-na* (colophons in Syria 12 235; MSL 13 128ff. [for the colophon, see Syria 12 pl. 44]) for */šumīyāna/*; note also the names with *mi-il-*, cited under IL/EL above.

IN and EN:

no clear examples of either sign.[218]

ŠI and ŠE:

^{1}*ši-ip-⸢ṭí⸣-yv* (PRU 6 54:8);[219] no clear examples of ŠE.

---

was lowered in proximity to the /y/ (i.e., [ye-]).

[214]If the first part of the name *ši-BE-ID*-^{d}IM (Ug. 5 159:14) reflects */θipiṭ-/*, the writing is an unusual instance of an unconditioned *e*-sign (BE) for /i/. The GN BE-*ka-ni* (PRU 3 188f.:7'; 3 189b:4'; 3 192f.:1; 3 194f.:8) must be left out of consideration, since the form is uncertain. A derivation from the root *b-k-y* "to weep" (*/bikyānu/*; see Sivan, Analysis 211) seems phonologically and semantically unlikely; a connection with **/biqᶜ-/* "valley, rift," while semantically attractive, is also unlikely since it would be unusual for the syllable-initial /ᶜ/ not to have some indication in the writing. Astour, UF 13 7-8 and n. 39, suggests a reading *úš-ka-ni*, comparing alphab. *uškn*, but the value *úš* for BAD is otherwise unknown in Akk. texts written at Ugarit.

[215]The pronunciation of this name is apparently [ʾeḫēyānu], phonemically */ʾiḫīyānu/*, from **ʾaḫīyānu*; cf. alphab. *iḫyn* (and *aḫyn*, UT 354-55 no. 128). The [ē] of the second syllable is the allophone of /ī/ before /y/; the [e] of the first syllable is due to a different phonological process, according to which an unstressed **a* assimilates to a following long or stressed vowel (in this case /ī/ = [ē]) when a guttural intervenes; see below, ch. 2 §A 1 c.

[216]Cf. ^{uru}*ma-ra*-DINGIR (PRU 6 78:23,24; Ug. 7 pl. 13:17) and alphab. *mril* (UT 437b no. 1545).

[217]Note that spellings with both MI and ME occur in texts written by the scribe Munaḫḫimu, the son of Yarim-mi. In view of the spellings with double *-mm-* (note also nominative ^{1}*ia-ri-im-mu* PRU 3 61f.:21), this name is probably to be analyzed as the verbal form */yarim/* plus enclitic *-m*; see Sivan, Analysis 125-26, 266. An alternative possibility is to see in it a hypocoristic form involving a root *r-m-m* "to bellow" (cf. Akk. *ramāmu*), short for **/yarimmu-Haddu/* (or sim.) "Haddu-bellows."

[218]The analysis of each of following names is uncertain: ^{1}*mi-il-ki-in-a-ri* (Ug. 5 10 r.5'; */milkī-(yi)nᶜar/*?); ^{f}*ḫa-am-mi-en-na-yv* (PRU 6 55:5'); ^{1}*ni-en-na* (PRU 4 202f. r.7').

[219]Note also the (abbreviated?) form in ^{f}DUMU-*ši-ip-ṭe₄* (Ug. 5 55:2).

IŠ and EŠ:

uruDINGIR-*iš-tam-i* (PRU 3 108f.:6, and often; cf. alphab. *ilštmᶜ* UT 358a no. 163) for /ʾ*ilī-(yi)štamᶜi*/??; no clear examples of EŠ.[220]

TI (= *ti, dì*) and TE (= *te, de*₄):

¹*ša-dì-ia* (PRU 3 40b r.2') and ¹*ša-de*₄*-ya*, ¹*ša-de*₄*-ia-nu* (PRU 3 18f.:4; Syria 18 251ff.:33) for /*šadīyā(nu)*/; PN ÌR-*dì* (often in PRU 3 79a; 3 79ff.; 3 81ff.; 3 83f.; 3 85f.) for /ᶜ*abdi*/; PN's *ma-te-nu* and *ma-at-te-na* (PRU 3 199ff. iii 37; PRU 6 54:2; 6 79:11; 6 107:5; Ug. 5 95:2) for /*mattinu/a*/.[221]

3. /*ō*/, /*u*/, /*ū*/

The monophthongized reflex of **aw* is generally assumed to be [ō] as in other West Semitic languages, rather than [ū] as in Akkadian, and thus retained as distinct from the phoneme /*ū*/ < **ū*. The evidence of the syllabic transcriptions neither supports nor refutes this assumption directly; all examples of the reflex of **aw* are perforce written with *u*-signs, since Akkadian has no *o*-vowel.[222] Nevertheless, since the reflex of **ay* is represented in the syllabic transcriptions as a vowel distinct from /*ī*/ (the reflex of **ī*), viz., the lower vowel /*ē*/, it is reasonable on grounds of symmetry to assume that **aw* likewise contracted to a vowel the quality of which was lower, /*ō*/, than that of /*ū*/ < **u*.

The following are all of the examples:

mu-ba-li = /*mōbali*/ < **mawbali* "produce(?)" (YBL b);[223]
mu-ša-bu = /*mōθabu*/ < **mawθabu* "seat" (YΘB b);
tu-ki-ii = /*tōkīyi*/ < **tawkīyi* "inner" (TWK);

[220]The composition of the PN *eš-ma-aʾ-nu* (PRU 6 72:8) is not clear; "Amoritish" tradition for /*yišmaᶜ-nŭ*/?

[221]Note also, however, the PN's ᶠMU-*a-da-te* and ⁽ᶠ⁾*um-mi-a-da-te* (PRU 6 107:6,7), in which the second element apparently reflects /ʾ*adat(t)i*/, thus with the TE sign for unconditioned /*-ti*/; so also in the GN uru*qa-ra-te* for /*qarati*/ (PRU 6 175:9) vs. expected uru*qa-ra-ti* (Ug. 5 12:17,22). The West Semitic origin of each of the following GN's with TE is open to question: uru*ma-ri-a-te* (PRU 6 102:3); uru*pa-šá-ra-te* (ibid.:1); uru*a-ru-te* (ibid.:8,10; PRU 6 150:6?); é*du-me-te* (GN?; PRU 6 122:2).

[222]In some Hurrian orthographies, particularly that of the Mittanni letter (EA 24), the Hurrian vowels *u* and *o* are consistently distinguished, either by the use of different *Cv* signs, as in KU for *g/ko* vs. GU for *g/ku*, or by the use of the U sign for *o* vs. the Ú sign for *u*, as in *-šu-u-* for *-šo-* vs. *-šu-ú-* for *-šu-*; see Speiser, IH 23-25 §§29-31; Bush, GHL 41-42 §3.112. This system is not in evidence in our corpus, however: we find KU for /*kō*/ (probably) in *ku-šar-ru* = /*kōθaru*/ (DN; KΘR) and for /*kŭ*/ in *a-na-ku* = /ʾ*anākŭ*/ "I" (ʾNK); and extra vowel-signs, viz., U or Ú, do not occur in any of the examples that originally contained **aw*.

[223]Cf. perhaps *([i]a-)šu-bi-lu* in Ug. 5 153, if for /*yašōbilu*/? "he will have brought(?)" or /*šōbilū*/? "have brought(?)" (YBL c).

probably or possibly also

ḫi-nu-ta-me = /*ḥinōtāmi*/? < **ḥinawtāmi*? and ⌜*vḫ*⌝*-nu-tu₄* = /*ʾvḥnōtu*/? < **ḥinawtu*? "(implement)" (ḤNW);

túg.meš*mu-ru-ú-ma*meš = /*mōruʾūma*/? < **mawraʾūma?* "(garments)" (YRʾ);

ku-šar-ru[224] = /*kōθaru*/ < **kawθaru*?[225] (divine name; KθR);

túg*ú-ra-tu* = /*ᶜōrātu*/ < **ᶜawrātu*? "hides(?)" (ᶜWR);

: *ḫu-li* = /*ǵōli*/? < **ǵawli*? "low ground(?)" (ǴWL);

finally, note also *PI-mu*, which probably reflects /*yōmu*/ < **yawmu* (less likely, /*yằmu*/; YWM).

[A vowel [ō] is also represented by *u*-signs in PN's and GN's that reflect dialects in which the Canaanite **ā* > *ō* shift has occurred (not Ugaritic; see under /*a*/, /*ā*/, above, p. 257).[226] Whether this vowel has the same quality and/or quantity as Ugaritic /*ō*/ < **aw* cannot be determined. Some examples:

¹*a-du-ni-*ᵈU (for [ʾadōnī-], PRU 3 196 ii 20'; vs. Ugar. *a-da-nu* = /*ʾadānu*/ [ʾDN]) uru*áš-qu-lu-nu*<*-yu*?> (for [ʾaθqolōn-], PRU 6 79:9; cf. 6 96:4'); ¹*bu-ra-qu-nu* (for [buraqōnu], PRU 3 195b B i 9; vs. ¹*bu-ra-qà-nu* PRU 6 50:5,27); ¹*ú-lu-ni* (for [ʾūlōni], PRU 3 194f.:19; vs. ¹*ú-la-nu* PRU 6 70:14).]

The reflexes of P(NW)S **u* and **ū* undergo no obvious phonological changes as Ugar. /*u*/ and /*ū*/.[227] Note, however, that some instances of /*u*/ derives from **a*, the result of assimilation to a following *u*-vowel or /*w*/; see ch. 2 §A 1 b - e.

[224]On the double writing of *r*, see above, §D 2 b.

[225]See the comments in the Glossary under KθR.

[226]See Sivan, Analysis 28-29 (though some of the names are interpreted differently here); and, for additional examples, Gröndahl, Personennamen 22 §18.

[227]It is possible that, like short /*a*/ and /*i*/, short /*u*/ was susceptible to the rules of syncope described below, ch. 2 §B, but we may point to no certain examples. It is also possible that, like /*i*/ and /*ī*/ (see above), /*u*/ and /*ū*/ had lower allophones [o] and [ō] in the neighborhood of sonorants (or in other environments); but unlike the case of /*i*/, /*ī*/, the syllabic writing system of Ugarit Akk. renders the detection of such allophones of /*u*/, /*ū*/, if they existed, impossible; see further, ch. 2 §A 1 e.

CHAPTER 2. PHONOLOGICAL PROCESSES

Presented here is a set of phonological rules and other observations[1] that represents an attempt to account for forms that deviate from the shape expected for them on the basis either of similar forms in syllabic transcription or of comparative Semitic phonology and morphology. The observations proceed from an assumption that the syllabic transcriptions reflect a single dialect, and can, therefore, be expected to display a consistent phonology, with sound rules that operate regularly. Where possible, I have tried to include examples in alphabetic form[2] that appear to exhibit the same processes, and, of course, to ensure that the observations apply consistently to both syllabic and alphabetic examples at our disposal,[3] i.e., that no counterexamples to the rules are attested in either syllabic or alphabetic form (unless so noted).[4] It must be admitted, however, that the number of syllabic transcriptions is too few, and the interpretation of many too uncertain, to expect what follows to be definitive. Moreover, the alphabetic evidence is clearly not linguistically uniform; the literary texts, especially, are rife with the type of archaic and archaizing forms associated with epic and religious poetry (as in Mesopotamia), and seem to defy, for the present, consistent analysis.[5]

Many of the observations that appear below are not new (see nn. 1-3), and what is intended here is not a complete presentation of Ugaritic phonology, which would take us too far afield of the syllabic transcriptions. Rather, it is hoped that what emerges is a more consistent and economical[6] formulation of Ugaritic phonological

[1]See also ch. 1 of Sivan's Analysis, where some of the processes described below were first noted. Boyd also presents a brief review of phonology in Collection 260-71.

[2]See, e.g., Fronzaroli, La fonetica ugaritica, which appeared when only a few of the Akkadian texts written at Ugarit had been published; further, ch. 5 of Gordon's UT, where little use is made of the syllabic transcriptions.

[3]In only a few discussions of Ugaritic phonology are both sources of evidence taken into account, e.g., Rainey, UF 3 151-72; Segert , Basic Grammar, passim.

[4]The opinion expressed in the Introduction concerning proper nouns bears repeating here; a name exhibiting a divergent phonology may not be cited as a counterexample to a process that is relatively well documented in common words, in either syllabic or alphabetic form, since it cannot be established that the name reflects the same dialect as the common words.

[5]See, e.g., below §E 3, on the behavior of triphthongs.

[6]It might be objected that the rules and observations that follow are rather too numerous or too complicated to sustain a claim of economy. Several points should be noted, however: Ugaritic was not Proto-Semitic, but a spoken language; in view of the limited evidence at our disposal, we should undoubtedly assume that the phonological situation was actually still more complicated; the number of processes delineated herein is in any case fewer than must be posited to describe the morphophonemics of most of the Semitic languages.

processes, as exhibited by the syllabic forms and their alphabetic analogues, than has hitherto been possible.

Comparison of our syllabic transcriptions with the alphabetic evidence for the Ugaritic vowels necessarily involves assumptions concerning the nature of the three aleph signs, which have been the subject of much discussion.[7] The hypothesis that best fits the evidence of the syllabic transcriptions, in my opinion, is Ginsberg's:

a-sign:	/ʾa/, /ʾā/
i-sign:	/ʾi/, /ʾī/, /ʾē/, /vʾ/
u-sign:	/ʾu/, /ʾū/, /ō/.

Only the *i*-sign, in other words, is used for syllable-final /ʾ/, regardless of the preceding vowel, as in *mizrtm,* which may be compared with syllabic ^(túg.meš)^*ma-za-ru-ma* = /*maʾzarūma*/? "loincloths(?)" (ʾZR),[8] and in *sin,* which probably corresponds to :!? *su-nu* = /*suʾnu*/? "hem" (SʾN); conversely the *a*-sign and the *u*-sign, with a few exceptions, indicate only the vowel following /ʾ/.[9]

Several of the rules discussed below also involve presuppositions about the underlying position of stress in Ugaritic words. Essentially, non-phonemic stress patterns like those of Akkadian and Arabic were assumed, viz., (i) stress does not fall on the ultima; (ii) stress falls on the first syllable back from the ultima that is closed or contains a long vowel; (iii) if there are no such long syllables, stress falls on the first syllable. No forms are encountered that provoke a reconsideration of these presuppositions, and several phenomena are neatly explained by them. Nevertheless, it should be remembered that all arguments that proceed from the basis of reconstructed stress patterns are tenuous at best.

A. Assimilation

1. *Vowels*

a. Forms without Assimilation

The majority of forms in syllabic transcription show no vowel assimilation; some examples:

[7]See, e.g., Ginsberg, Or. 5 175-76; Gordon, UT 18-19 §4.4,6-8; Marcus, JANES 1 50-60; Blau-Loewenstamm, UF 2 19-33; Segert, Basic Grammar 22-23 §21.4. The most thorough review of the problem is that of Verreet, UF 13 223-58.

[8]Note that this form contradicts the sound rule proposed by Harris, JAOS 57 151-57 (see also his Development 36 §8), to account for instances of the *i*-sign when /*a*/ is expected, viz., *a* > *e* / _ ʾ*C*; note also *na-ba-dì* = /*naʾbadi*/ (ʾBD); *ma-a-du-ma*, if = /*maʾdūma*/ rather than /*maʾadūma*/ (MʾD).

[9]It is the exceptions, of course, that stir the debate. A few of these are discussed below, n. 58.

short /*a*/ : (túg.meš)*ma-za-ru-ma* = /*ma*ʾ*zarūma*/? "loincloths(?)" (ʾZR);
[mí]*ba-ri-iḫ-tu*$_4$ = /*bariḥtu*/ "fugitive, rustic(?)" (BRḤ);
ḫa-ba-li-ma = /*ḥabalīma*/ "ropes, lots" (ḤBL);
⸢*na*⸣-[*š*]*u*-⸢*ma*⸣ = /*našūma*/ "people" (NŠ);
(urudu.meš)*ma-ṣa-du(-ma*[meš]*)* = /*ma*ʿ*ṣadu, -ūma*/ "adze(s)" (ʿṢD);
[lú]*ma-ṣi-lu* = /*maṣillu*/ "cymbalist" (ṢLL);
qà-da-ru-ma[meš] = /*qad(d)arūma*/ "(containers)" (QDR);
qa-ri-t[*u*$_4$] = /*qarītu*/ "town" (QRY);
ša-mu-ma = /*šamûma*/ "sky" (ŠMY);

short /*i*/ : *i-r*[*a*?-*tu*$_4$?] = /ʾ*iratu*/? "chest(?)" (ʾR);
di-[*k*]*a*$_4$(QA)-*ru* = /*dikāru*/ "bowl" (DKR[2]);
ḫi-nu-ta-me = /*ḥinōtāmi*/? "2 'implements'" (ḤNW);
i-pu-ú = /ʿ*ipû*/? "destruction(?)" (ʿPW);

short /*u*/ : *ḫu-zi-rù* = /*ḫuzīru*/ "pig" (ḪZR);
ḫu-r[*a-ṣu*] = /*ḫurāṣu*/ "gold" (ḪRṢ[1]);
pl. *ku-ku-ba-tu* = /*kukkubātu*/ "vase(?)" (KKB);
[d]ug!? *ku?-BA-ra-tu*[meš] = /*kupārātu*/? "bowls(?)" (KPR).

Forms that do exhibit vowel assimilation reflect the results of several distinct phonological processes, described in the following sections.

b. *qattv̄*$_1$*l* > *qv*$_1$*ttv̄*$_1$*l*

p. 401

Note the following forms:

ḫe-en-ni-ṣu = /*ḫinnīṣu*/? "piglet" (ḪNṢ);
(:) ṣí(-ib)-bi-ri = /*ṣibbīri*/ "collective land(?)" (ṢBR);
iš-ši-KI, iš<-ši>-GI? = /?/ (see Appendix to Glossary).

Since the pattern *qittīl* (and *qittil*) is rare, indeed probably nonexistent, in PS, these forms may be considered reflexes of PS **qattīl*. And since there are no forms among the syllabic transcriptions with first vowel /*a*/ and second vowel /*ĭ*/ in which the middle radical is written double, it may be suggested that PS **qattīl* > Ugar. *qittīl* generally.[10] The following alphabetic forms probably attest the same phenomenon:

ibr = */ʾ*ibbīru*/ < *ʾ*abbīr*-[11] "bull" (UT 350a no. 39; Heb. ʾ*abbîr*);

[10]So also in Arabic; see Barth, Nominalbildung 51 §35a, 139 §87a; Brockelmann, Grundriss 1 363 §155.

[11]The stem *ibr* in names such as the RN *ibrn* is probably not */ʾ*ibbīr*-/ "bull." The fact that *ibrn* invariably appears in syllabic orthography as (1)*i-bi-ra-nv*, never with double *-bb-*, indicates that */ʾ*ibīrānv*/ is the correct normalization. The base of the name is thus more likely */ʾ*ibīr*-/ < *ʾ*abīr*- "strong," i.e., originally *qatīl* like Heb. *ʾ*ābîr* (cst. ʾ*ăbîr*); */ʾ*ibīr*-/ < *ʾ*abīr*- reflects a

irby = */*ʾirbīyu*/ < **ʾarbīy*- "locusts" (UT 365b no. 332; vs. Heb. *ʾarbe* < **ʾarbiy*-).[12]

The form *irby*, if normalized correctly */*ʾirbīyu*/, indicates that the medial consonants could be a cluster C_1C_2 as well as geminate C_1C_1.[13]

No syllabic transcriptions provide evidence of an analogous development of PS **qattūl* > Ugar. *quttūl*. Nevertheless, at least one alphabetic form suggests such a development:

ulp = */*ʾullūpu*/ [14] < **ʾallūp*- "chief" (UT 359b no. 202; cf. Heb. *ʾallûp*).[15]

We may therefore formulate a more general rule of regressive assimilation:

$a > v_1$ / __$CC\acute{v}_1$ (i.e., essentially, **qattīl* > *qittīl*, **qattūl* > *quttūl*).

Note that more than one consonant must intervene between **a* and the following vowel; the rule thus does not apply to *qatīl* or *qatūl* forms, which remain unchanged,[16] unless they are II-guttural[17] (see under c, below) or I-ʾ (see under d,). Further, we may observe that the rule does not operate across certain morpheme boundaries; cf., e.g., ${}^{\text{dug}}$*ka-du-ma*${}^{\text{meš}}$ = /*kaddūma*/ (not */*kuddūma*/; KDD); *ša-ri-ma* = /*θarrīma*/? (not */*θirrīma*/; ΘRR).

Since it is not affected by this rule, the form ⌜*ba*⌝-*aḫ-ḫu-rù* "youth" (BḪR) must reflect a *qattul* form, i.e., /*báḫḫuru*/, in contrast to *qat(t)ūl* in the Hebrew cognate *bāḥûr* < **baḥūr*-, pl. *baḥûrîm* < **baḫḫūr*-.[18]

---

different sound rule than the one under discussion here; see below under d.

[12]Contrast the forms *aliy(n)* (epithets of Baʿl; UT 426a no. 1342), in which the second vowel must be short, */*ʾalʾiy(ān)u*/. Another possible example with assimilation is *iqnu/i* = */*ʾiqnīʾu/i*/ "lapis lazuli" (UT 365a no. 323). If Akk. *uqnû*, *uqniātum* (AHw 1426-27) exhibits a more primitive first vowel, Ugar. */*ʾiqnīʾu*/ would be the result of a rare assimilation of **u* to /*ī*/.

[13]Note also alphab. *izml* = */*ʾizmīlu*/ < **ʾazmīlu* (< **ʾazamīlu*); see below, n. 67. Cf. $C_1aC_2C_3\bar{v}_1C_4 > C_1v_1C_2C_3\bar{v}_1C_4$ in Arabic; Brockelmann, Grundriss, 1 181 §68 b *e*.

[14]Cf. the PN]*ul-lu-pí* (PRU 3 194a:11).

[15]For another possible alphabetic example of this phenomenon, see below, n. 31.

[16]Cf. Arabic, where **qattīl* > *qittīl* (see above, n. 10), but *qatīl* remains unchanged. There are very few forms among the syllabic transcriptions which we may identify with certainty as *qatīl* or *qatūl* (vs. *qatil*, *qatul*); note, however, probably *: ga-bi-ni* = /*gabīni*/? "hillock(?)" (GBN); a form with the same surface shape, which likewise does not undergo vowel assimilation, is *qa-ri-t*[*u4*] = /*qarītu*/ "town" (QRY). (The form *: ḫi-ri-ti* = /*ḫirīti*/ "cemetery" [ḪRY] is an Akk. loanword.)

[17]Since roots II-guttural exhibit a rule $*qaG\bar{v}_1l > qv_1G\bar{v}_1l$, and all roots undergo $*qatt\bar{v}l > qv_1tt\bar{v}_1l$, the pattern of some forms II-guttural is uncertain; e.g., *ṭu-ú-ru* "pure" (ṬHR) may reflect /*ṭuhūru*/ < **ṭahūr*- or /*ṭuhhūru*/ < **ṭahhūr*-; ${}^{\text{[urudu.meš]}}$*me-ḫi-*[*ṣ*]*ú*-⌜ma⌝${}^{\text{meš}}$ "(implements)" (MḪṢ b) may reflect /*miḫīṣūma*/ < **maḫīṣ*- or /*miḫḫīṣūma*/ < **maḫḫīṣ*-. In the majority of these instances, comparative and internal reconstruction suggests that a single medial radical is more likely (see below, nn. 21, 22), but certainty is of course impossible.

[18]Similarly, in *a-du-rù* "mighty" (ʾDR), the vowel of the second syllable must be short, even if the middle radical is double, viz., /*ʾádduru*/; a single /*d*/ is more likely, however: /*ʾáduru*/.

☛ p. 401

c. Vowel Harmony around Gutturals

There is a clear tendency for like vowels to appear on either side of a guttural. Thus, e.g., all *qitīl* forms attested among the syllabic transcriptions are II-guttural; conversely, no *qatīl* forms II-guttural occur. Since the pattern *qitīl* is at best rare in Semitic,[19] we may deduce the existence of a vowel harmony rule around gutturals,[20] viz., regressive assimilation. There are exceptions, however:

tu-a-pí-[*ku*?] = /*tuhappiku*/? "to be upset(?)" (HPK);
⌜*ba*⌝-*aḫ-ḫu-rù* = /*baḫḫuru*/ (or /*baḥḥuru*/) "youth" (BḪR);
ši-a-ru = /*šiharu*/? "crescent-shaped sickle(?)" (ŠHR);
gen. (:) *ṣa*(*-a*)*-i* = /*ṣāᶜi*/ "basin" (ṢWᶜ);
^{lú}*ma-ḫi-ṣu* = /*māḫiṣu*/ "(a profession)" (MḪṢ a);
^{lú}*na-ḫi-ru* = /*nāǵiru*/ "guard" (NǴR a).

Thus, this assimilation rule did not affect /*u*/, stressed vowels, or long vowels, and may be formulated more precisely as follows (*G* = guttural):

$$\underset{\text{[-stress]}}{a, i} > v_1 \;/\; \_\_Gv_1 \;.$$

In most of the examples, assimilation is to a following stressed or long vowel:[21]

$^{\text{lú.meš}}$*b*[*i*]*-ḫi-ru* = /*biḥīrū*/? < **baḥīr-* "elite (troops)" (pl. bound form; BḤR^1);
ṭu-ú-ru = /*ṭuhūru*/ < **ṭahūr-*[22] "pure" (ṬHR);
probably pl. $^{\text{túg.meš}}$*mu-ru-ú-ma*^{meš} = /*mōruʾūma*/? < **mawraʾūma*? "(garments)" (less likely *maqtūl*; YRʾ);
pl. $^{\text{[urudu.meš]}}$*me-ḫi-*[*ṣ*]*ú-*⌜*ma*⌝^{meš} = /*miḫīṣūma*/ < **maḫīṣ-* "(implements)" (MḪṢ b);
qi-i-lu = /*qiᶜīlu*/ < **qaᶜīl-* "vine-blossom(?)" (less likely, /*qiᶜlu*/; QᶜL);
[*š*]*i*?*-i-ru* = /*šiᶜīru*/ < **šaᶜīr-* "barley" (ŠᶜR a);
ta-a-ma-tu$_4$ = /*tahāmatu*/ < **tihāmatu* "the deep" (THM);

[19]See Brockelmann, Grundriss 1 356 §139, where only Hebrew forms are listed, most of them, in all likelihood, loans from Aramaic. For the similarly rare *qitil*, see ibid. 338 §121.

[20]Cf. the similar phenomenon in Ethiopic (Geᶜez), e.g., *lehiq* < **lahīq*; *yaḥawwer* < **yiḥawwvr*; see Lambdin, Introduction 10.

[21]It is possible that some, or even all, of the forms listed below as *qitīl* and *qutūl* may instead have doubled middle radicals, *qittīl, quttūl*, and reflect the effects of the rule discussed above, under b; see also n. 17. Since the remaining examples of the rule under discussion are also susceptible of other interpretations, no absolute proof of the existence of the rule may be offered. Nevertheless, the circumstantial evidence is great enough, I believe, to leave little doubt. If the rule did not exist, we would have to assume, for example, that no *qatīl* or *qatūl* forms II-guttural occur in our corpus, a most unlikely coincidence; further, the number of Ugar. proto-forms that differed from their cognates (e.g., **ṭahhūr-*, **šaᶜᶜīr-*, **tahhāmat-*) would increase significantly.

[22]As in Arabic *ṭahūr*, vs. Hebrew *ṭāhōr* < **ṭahur-*.

note also *šu-ḫu-ut-t*[*u*?] = /*šuḥúttu*/? "bran(?)," the original form of which may be **šuḥuttu* or **šaḥuttu* (ḤTT).

Two additional examples suggest that the following vowel need not be stressed or long, however;[23] unfortunately, neither example is free of uncertainty regarding its underlying form:[24]

gen. *ma-ar-zi-ḫi* and *mar-zi-i* = [márziḥ/ʿi], probably < **marzaḥi* (RZḤ), as suggested by the biform *mar-za-i* = [márzaʿi], which should probably be regarded as a quasi-phonemic spelling; Hebrew *marzēaḥ,* of course, suggests an original *maqtil* form rather than *maqtal,* but if the underlying Ugar. form were /*marziḥ-*/, the form [marzaʿi] would be inexplicable;[25] thus, the more likely original Ugar. form is **marzaḥ*;[26]

ma-aš-nu-ú? "enemy(?)" (ŠNʾ); if this word is correctly interpreted, the pattern may be *maqtal,* with vowel harmony around the /ʾ/, i.e., /*mašnuʾu*/ < **mašnaʾu*. For *maqtal* as a form for agent nouns, note alphab. *mlak* = */*malʾaku*/ "messenger" (perhaps also ⌜*ma*⌝*-al-sà-mu* = /*malsamu*/ [LSM] the meaning of which is uncertain: "course(?)" or "courier(?)"). It is also possible, however, that *ma-aš-nu-ú*? instead reflects /*mašnūʾu*/, i.e., a *maqtūl* form ("hated"), despite the rarity of the pattern *maqtūl* in NWS.

The only form which does not conform to this rule among the syllabic transcriptions (other than [marzaʿi], cited above) is the fem. plural *ni-ʾa-tu* = /*niʾātu*/ (Nʾ). Evidently the rule did not necessarily operate across certain morpheme boundaries.[27] It did operate, apparently optionally, across others, however,[28] as shown by variant alphabetic writings of *aḫ* = */*ʾaḫu*/ "brother," viz., *iḫ(h/y), uḫ(h/y),* which must be

[23]Cf. the vowel harmony rule in Assyrian, where, generally, any unstressed *a* in an open syllable assimilates to the vowel of the following syllable (not conditioned by an intervening guttural, as in Ugar.), as in the declension of "queen": *šarrutu, šarrete, šarrata*; see von Soden, GAG §10e.

[24]Note also ᵘʳᵘ*na-nu-ú*, gen. ᵘʳᵘ*na-ni-i* (PRU 3 189b:31'; 3 190a:27) = alphab. *nnu*/*nni*, i.e., /*nanv*$_1$*ʾv*$_1$/ (UT 444b no. 1657); perhaps ¹*ia-aš-mu-u* (Ug. 5 81:45), if for /*yašmuʿu*/ < **yašmaʿu*.

[25]There is no other evidence, for example, for the operation of a sound rule within Ugaritic which lowers /*i*/ to [a] before a guttural. Such a rule did operate, at least in closed syllables, at some point in the history of Hebrew, and may account for the form of *mirzaḥ* in Amos 6:7; i.e., *mirzaḥ* may derive from either **marzaḥ* or **marziḥ*. (Verbs II- and III-guttural with theme-vowel *a* do not reflect a Ugaritic sound rule, as suggested by Segert, Basic Grammar 37 §38.41, but rather a much earlier, i.e., PNWS change, since the same phenomenon is found in all NWS dialects.)

[26]It is possible, in fact, that the entire phrase *bêt marzēaḥ* in Jeremiah 16:5 is a loan of the genitive chain /*bētu marzaḥi*/, pronounced in the loaning dialect [bētu marziḥi], as in Ugar.

[27]Also not across the /*h*/ of third person suffixes: e.g., *mẓah* = */*maẓvʾa-hŭ*/ "he reached him" KTU 1.12 ii 50,51; *lksih* = */*li-kvssiʾi-hŭ*/ (or /*-hĭ*/ as in Arabic?). The operation of the Ethiopic vowel harmony rule around gutturals, mentioned above in n. 20, is also restricted at certain morpheme boundaries.

[28]Including perhaps the masc. pl. marker, if the form /*mōruʾūma*/ cited above is correctly interpreted as a *maqtal* form.

attributed to a rule of vowel harmony around gutturals;[29] note the following examples:

nom. sg. bound *uḫ* = */ʾuḫū/*[30] (KTU 4.643:13); contrast gen. sg. bound *aḫ* = */ʾaḫī/* (4.103:5);

nom. sg. *uḫh* = */ʾuḫū-hŭ/* (KTU 4.80:10; 4.759:4); *uḫy* = */ʾuḫū-ya/* (2.4:19; 2.41:20); contrast *aḫy* = */ʾaḫū-ya/* (2.14:10,15);

gen. sg. *iḫh* = */ʾiḫī-hŭ/* (KTU 4.123:23), *iḫy* = */ʾiḫī-ya/* (2.41:18; 2.44:2); contrast *aḫh* = */ʾaḫī-hŭ/* (5.9:10), *aḫy* = */ʾaḫī-ya/* (2.14:3; 2.38:2).[31]

The biforms may represent free variation in actual speech; alternatively, perhaps only the forms which show the assimilation reflect the true pronunciation, and the forms with initial *a* are morphophonemic writings.

d. Assimilation of *a* after Word-initial /ʾ/

p. 401

Two forms are not accounted for by either of the preceding two rules:

i-[*r*]*i*?*-iš-*[*tu*$_4$?] = /*ʾirištu*/ "request" (ʾRŠ);

ITI *i-*⌜*ši*?⌝*-*[*bi*?] = /*ʾiθību*/? (month name; ʾθB).

The first form corresponds to alphab. *iršt* (UT 367a no. 379), and is cognate with the Heb. hapax *ʾărešet* (Psalm 21:3), Akk. *erištu,* and Eblaite *ì-rí-sa-tum* (MEE 4 225 no. 234; see below, n. 32). The pattern of the Ugar. form, *qitil-t,* while common in Akk., is abnormal in West Semitic (the Heb. form, of course, reflects *qvtvl-t,* where either *v* may have been *a* or *i*). If the Ugar. and Heb. forms are not borrowings, an unlikely possibility,[32] then we may suggest that both Ugar. /*ʾirištu*/ and Heb. *ʾărešet*

[29]They may not be attributed to the initial /ʾ/ of the root, which is involved in another rule to be discussed presently (see under d below), since that rule did not operate in circumstances analogous to those in the forms *iḫ(-), uḫ(-)* to produce variant forms of *ab* "father."

[30]The evidence of nearly all Semitic languages shows that the vowels of the case-endings of the sg. bound forms of PS **ʾaḫ-* "brother" (and of **ʾab-* "father" and **ḥam-* "father-in-law"), before both genitive nouns and pronominal suffixes, were long: **ʾaḫū/ʾaḫī/ʾaḫā* (see Huehnergard, "Three Notes" §2 with nn. 45,46). It should be assumed that this also obtains in Ugar., since we have no evidence for positing a shortening of these vowels (pace Segert, Basic Grammar 37, §38.41).

[31]Note also the following pl. forms, in which we may assume that the second radical *ḫ* is doubled, as in Akk. *aḫḫū,* Heb. *ʾaḥîm* (< **ʾaḫḫīma*): obl. *aḫm* = */ʾaḫḫīma/* (KTU 1.22 i 5); with suffixes, nom. *aḫh* = */ʾaḫḫū-hŭ/* (1.12 ii 48), obl. *aḫh* = */ʾaḫḫī-hŭ/* (1.4 vi 44; 1.17 i 19,20). I am unable to account for the apparently nom. pl. *iḫh* in KTU 1.24:35, except to suggest that perhaps it reflects a *partial* assimilation (raising) of /*a*/ to the following /*ū*/, i.e., *[ʾiḫḫū-hă] < **ʾaḫḫū-hă.*

[32]In his discussion of Eblaite *ì-rí-sa-tum,* Krebernik, ZA 73 10, following Gelb, MAD 3 67 and citing Arabic *ʿarūs* "bride," suggests that the root of the Eblaite form and of Akk. *erištu, erēšu,* where **a* has become *e,* is *ʿ-r-š,* and that the Ugar. and Heb. forms with initial *ʾ* must therefore be loanwords. (The Ugar. verb *ʾ-r-š* "to request" would thus have to be considered either another borrowing or a denominative of /*ʾirištu*/.) It seems unlikely, however, that Arabic *ʿarūs* is cognate with the root under discussion. Further, there are other examples in Akk. in which expected **a*

reflect an earlier **ʾariš-tv,* i.e., a substantivized fem. verbal adj. (*qatil-t*; i.e., "desired (thing)").

The form */ʾiθību/,* if read and interpreted correctly,[33] exhibits a *qitīl* pattern, which is at best rare in Semitic,[34] and may therefore reflect an original *qatīl* pattern, i.e., **ʾaθību.*

Thus, */ʾirištu/* and */ʾiθību/* would exhibit the effect of a sound rule by which unstressed **a* in an open syllable assimilated to a following vowel. Since, however, forms such as ^{mí}*ba-ri-iḫ-tu*$_4$ = */bariḥtu/* "fugitive, rustic(?)" (BRḤ) and *qa-ri-t*[*u*$_4$] = */qarītu/* "town" (QRY) do not exhibit assimilation, it would seem that the initial /ʾ/ of */ʾirištu/* and */ʾiθību/* is a crucial part of the conditioning environment.[35] The rule may thus be formulated as follows:

$a > v_1 \,/\, ʾ \_\_ C\acute{v}_1$.[36]

Although only */ʾirištu/* and */ʾiθību/* among our syllabic transcriptions exhibit this rule, the shape of several alphabetic examples, likewise not attributable to other rules, may provide confirmation of its existence; unfortunately, the interpretation of each of these is somewhat uncertain:[37]

imt = */*ʾimittu*/? < **ʾamíntu*? "truth(?)" (KTU 1.5 i 18bis,19; cf. Heb. *ʾĕmet,* likewise < **ʾamíntu*; see Caquot-Sznycer-Herdner, Textes ougaritiques 242 n. s);

iwl = */*ʾiwīlu*/? < **ʾawílu* "noble(?)" (KTU 4.46:2; note also, however, *awl*

---

became *e* without one of the gutturals **ḥ*, **ʿ*, **ǵ* as conditioning factor, but rather, apparently, a neighboring sonorant (as in *erṣetu*; see GAG §9b; note also the OAkk. PN *la-te-ni-iš* [Gelb MAD 3 54], the root of which must be associated with Heb. *ʾ-n-š* "be(come) weak" [pace Gelb, ibid.]). Thus, Akk. ***erištu*** may, like the Ugar. and Heb. forms (see below), instead reflect **ʾarišt-*. (Alternatively, Akk. *erištu* may reflect **ʾirišt-*, with *e* < *i* before *r* [cf. GAG §9h]; the precise form of Eblaite *ì-rí-sa-tum,* because of the vagaries of Eblaite orthography, is uncertain: */ʾirišatum/, /ʾirištum/,* or */ʾiršatum/* [cf. Fronzaroli, QS 13 143].)

[33]An alternative possibility is to normalize */ʾiθθību/,* the form of which would reflect the operation of the rule described in b, above. But writings in which *v-Cv* appears for initial *ʾ/h/ʿvCCv-* are not common (note, however, *u/ú-ṣú-ru/ri* = */ʿuṣṣūru/i/* [ʿṢR]); rather, we find, e.g., *ap-pu* = */ʾappu/* (ʾNP); *um-ma-ti* = */ʾummati/* (ʾMM); *al-li-ni-ya* = */hallinīya/* (HLNY).

[34]See n. 19 above.

[35]The word */ʿiδirtu/* (ʿδR), unlike */ʾirištu/,* does not reflect an original *qatil-t* form, but rather *qitl-at*; see §C below.

[36]The rule as written affects only **a,* since there are no clear examples of the assimilation of original **i* or **u* in this environment. Note, however, alphab. *uṭb* (UT 355b no. 140), which may be a loan of Akk. (< Sum.) *ed/ṭa/uppu* "hem(?)" (AHw 185a; CAD E 22; see Virolleaud, PRU 5 p. 125; Dietrich-Loretz, BiOr 23 129a); perhaps *uṭb* = */*ʾuṭubbu*/ < **ʾiṭubbu* (Akk. *eṭuppu*?). If the rule did apply to all short vowels in open syllables after initial /ʾ/, however, we should consider the possibility that our evidence for the quality of the prefix-vowel of the D and Š prefix-conjugations, viz., the use of the *a*-aleph in 1cs forms, may be misleading; for in the forms *ʾvqáttil-* (D) and *ʾvšáqtil* (Š), any underlying *v* would become /*a*/ by this rule.

[37]Note also the names with */*ʾibīr-*/ < **ʾabīr-* "strong"; see above, n. 11.

in KTU 1.12 ii 56; cf. Akk. *awīlum*/*amīlu*);[38]

uzr = */ʾuzūru/? < *ʾazū́ru? "girded(?)" (KTU 1.17 i 2-22; i.e., passive ptcpl.; see Sanmartín, UF 9 369-70; Dietrich-Loretz, UF 10 65-66);

urbt = */ʾurubbatu/ < *ʾarúbbatu? "window" (UT 365a no. 329; cf. Heb. *ʾărubbâ* < *ʾarubbatu?; see Gordon, UT 31 §5.19[39]).

Since forms of */ʾabu/ "father" are consistently written with the *a*-aleph when the word has a pronominal suffix (e.g., *abh* = nom. */ʾabūhŭ̄/, gen. */ʾabīhŭ̄/), this rule did not operate across at least some morpheme boundaries; contrast the behavior of */ʾaḫu/ "brother" with suffixes, discussed in the preceding section.

The form *a-du-rù* "mighty" (ʾDR) is not affected by this rule; thus, for the sake of consistency, we must conclude that the form is a *qatul* (not *qatūl*) adjective, in which the initial syllable is stressed: /ʾáduru/;[40] cf. *a-mu-q[u]* = /ᶜamuqu/ "deep (place)," corresponding to Heb. *ᶜāmōq*, Akk. *emuq-*, both < *ᶜamuq-.

e. Raising of *ă̄* before /w/ and /y/

The forms of several words, when compared with their cognates in other languages, indicate that before the glides /w/ and /y/, the original vowels *a and *ā were raised to homorganic vowels. Before /y/, *a was pronounced [e], and thus realized as an allophone of /i/ (see ch. 1 §G 2); *ā was pronounced [ē], and realized either as the phoneme /ē/ < *ay or, more likely, as an allophone of /ī/. Before /w/, *a (no examples with *ā) was realized as an allophone of /u/.[41] Whether it was pronounced [u] or [o] cannot be ascertained, but [o] seems more likely given the pronunciation [e] before /y/.

ú-[w]a!?-[t]u₄ = /huwătu/ "word" ([howătu]?; HW[2]); cf. Akk. *awătum*/*amătu* "word";

[ḫ]u-wa-tu₄ = /ḫuwwatu/ "land" ([ḫowwatu]?; ḪWW); cf. Heb. *ḥawwôt*

[38]See further under e below.

[39]The form *udm* cited by Gordon in the same paragraph probably reflects */ʾudum-/, i.e., a *qutul* form, which developed in Hebrew into *ʾidum- (> *ʾĕdōm*) by the regular dissimilation of two *u*-vowels.

[40]Also possible, though less likely, is a *qattul* form: /ʾadduru/. If the alphab. fem. *adrt* (see, e.g., Sanmartín, UF 9 371-73; Macdonald, UF 10 161-73) reflects the same word, the form is probably */ʾad(u)ratu/, i.e., with ending /-at/; if the fem. ending is simple /-t/, we might expect */ʾudurtu/ < *ʾadúrtu (unless paradigmatic pressure from the masc. form prevented the operation of the rule; so also with the masc. pl. *adrm* = */ʾad(u)rūma/; on the possible syncope of the second vowel in */ʾad(u)ratu/, */ʾad(u)rūma/, see §B below).

[41]Cf. the assimilation of *a > *u* before a labial consonant evidenced in some PN's, as described by Sivan, Analysis 19-20, §3.1.

"tent-villages";[42]

ḫé-yu-ma and *ḪI-[i]u?-ma* = [ḥeyyūma] = /*ḥiyyūma*/ "life" (ḤWY¹/ḤYY¹ b); cf. Heb. *ḥayyîm*, Aram. *ḥayyin*;

: ḫa-a-yi = /*ḫāyi*/, *ḫe-e-ia/yu* = [ḫēya/u], *: ḫé-yi-ma* = [ḫēyīma], *: ḫi-i-yi(-šu)* = /*ḫīyĭ*/ "vacant(?)" (ḪWY); originally probably a *qāl* adjective.[43]

In the last set of examples, the writing *: ḫa-a-yi* exhibits the original form of the word; one wonders whether it is a dialectal biform (but see also below, on alphabetic forms).

Since the second /*a*/ of the pl. form ^giš.meš^*ma-sa-wa-tu* = /*masawātu*/ (MSW) did not undergo the change under discussion, it may be that the rule only operated on initial syllables. Thus, a possible formulation is:

☛ p. 401 *ā* > [+hi] / #*C*__ {*w,y* }.

Note that this rule, unlike the others considered thus far, is not restricted in its operation to unstressed **a* (and **ā*): **ḥáwwatu* > /*ḥuwwatu*/; /*ḫā́yu*/ > [ḫēyu].

An alphabetic form that probably shows the effect of this rule is the interrogative adverb *iy* "where?" (UT 356a no. 143), apparently for **/ʾiyyv̈/* < **ʾayyv̌* (cf. Heb. *ʾayyē, ʾayy-, ʾê-*). But a number of other forms that fit the conditions of the rule exhibit no change of **a* in the first syllable:

ay = (gen.) **/ʾayyi/*? "which?, any(?)"[44] (KTU 1.23:6bis; cf. 1.17 vi 3); cf. Akk. *ayyu*, Arab. and Eth. *ʾayy*;

pl. *aylm* = (acc.) **/ʾayyalīma/* "bucks" (KTU 1.6 i 24) and fem. *aylt* = (sg.? acc.?) **/ʾayyal(a)ta/* (1.92:11), (pl. obl.) **/ʾayyalāti/* "doe(s)" (1.1 v 19; 1.5 i 17; 1.133:8); cf. Akk. *ayyalu*, Heb. *ʾayyāl(â)*;

note also the form *awl* in KTU 1.12 ii 56, variously rendered "first" (e.g., Aistleitner, Wörterbuch 10 no. 108), "prince" (Caquot-Sznycer-Herdner, Textes ougaritiques 350 n. z), based on comparision with Arab. *ʾawwal* "first"; the same word may appear as *iwl* in an economic text, KTU 4.46:2, in which case the underlying form is not **/ʾawwalu/* but rather **/ʾawīlu/* (cf. Akk. *awīlum/amīlu*), with *iwl* reflecting **/ʾiwīlu/* according to the rule discussed in the preceding section.

The reason for the failure of the rule to operate in these forms is unclear. The initial

[42]Perhaps also *gu-wa-⌜li⌝* = /*guw(w)ăli*/ "circuit" ([gow(w)ăli]?; GWL), but the original shape of this word (*qat(t)ăl* or *qut(t)ăl*) is uncertain.

[43]Note also the month name *ḫi-ia/ya-ri* = /*ḫiyyāri*/ = (ḪYR), which is probably related to Akk. *ayyāru* (> Arab. *ʾayyār*, Heb. and Syr. *ʾiyyār*). Since, however, ITI *ḫi-a/ia-ri(-i/e)* also shows up in texts from Alalaḫ and Nuzi (see AHw 342b), the *i*-vowel of the first syllable may not be the result of a Ugar. sound rule (as I suggested in JAOS 107), but simply part of the form in which the word found its way into Ugar., probably via Hurrian.

[44]So, e.g., Gordon, UT 355b no. 142; less likely is "island, coast" or an interjection (cf. Caquot-Sznycer-Herdner, Textes ougaritiques 369 with n. d).

/ʾ/ is not likely to be the restricting feature, given alphab. *iy* "where?" and the operation of the rule after similar consonants (/*h*/, /*ḥ*/, /*ḫ*/) in syllabic forms.[45] Must we label all of these examples historical spellings of archaic poetic forms?

We should note finally that the contraction of the diphthongs **ay* and **aw* to /*ē*/ and /*ō*/, respectively,[46] is probably in part the result of a phonological process similar to that described above. Thus, as elsewhere in the language, **ay* > [ey] and **aw* > [ow]; when these sequences were syllable-final, the glides were lost, with compensatory lengthening of the vowel:[47] i.e.,

**ḥayqu* > *[ḥeyqu] > /*ḥēqu*/ "lap" (ḤYQ);
**tawku* > *[towku] > /*tōku*/ (in /*tōkīyu*/ "inner"; TWK).

f. Lowering of /*ĭ*/ to [ĕ] around Sonorants

Still another phonological process that should probably be mentioned under the rubric of assimilation is that which results in the pronunciation of the phonemes /*i*/ and /*ī*/ as [e], [ē] in the neighborhood of sonorants (discussed in ch. 1 §G 2). Since the precise phonetic quality of neither the allophones transcribed here as [e], [ē] nor the sonorant consonants is known, however, the mechanics of the process (lowering and/or backing? untensing?) cannot be determined.

2. *Consonants*

a. Assimilatory Voicing and Devoicing

As was noted above in our discussion of the syllabary, W. R. Garr[48] has attempted to show recently that consonants in Ugaritic were subject to the following rules of voicing and devoicing, which are, in effect, processes of assimilation:

(a) voiceless consonants were voiced (i) intervocalically; (ii) in contiguity to a voiced sonorant; (iii) before a voiced obstruant;
(b) voiced obstruents were devoiced before voiceless obstruents.

[45]It might be suggested that the rule operated *only* after these consonants, i.e., only after back fricatives (assuming then that /*guw(w)ăli*/, cited above in n. 42, is not the result of this rule). But this strikes me as an unlikely restriction for the environment of a vowel-raising rule.

[46]See ch. 1 §G 2, 3.

[47]Before /*w*/ and /*y*/, i.e., when the glides were doubled, it is unlikely that this second step occurred: thus, e.g., **ḥawwatu* > [ḥowwatu] (= /*ḥuwwatu*/), but (probably) not > */*ḥōwatu*/; **ḥayyūma* > [ḥeyyūma] (= /*ḥiyyūma*/), but (probalby) not > */*ḥēyūma*/; the sequences -*ww*- and -*yy*- are quite stable in Semitic.

[48]JNES 45 45-52.

Since nearly all *vC* signs fail to distinguish voiced, voiceless, and emphatic phones, the devoicing of voiced phonemes (b) cannot, a priori, be detected in the syllabic orthography in most instances. The only phoneme for which devoicing would be discernible is /ᶜ/,[49] the voiceless counterpart of which is [ḥ], and which we would expect to be written with Ḫ-signs;[50] but it is not clear from the alphabetic evidence that /ᶜ/ was subject to devoicing.[51] In the only instance in our corpus of /ᶜ/ before a voiceless obstruent, devoicing is not indicated: *ma-ša-ra* and *ma-a*ᵓ*-ša-ri(-ša)* = /*ma*ᶜ*šara*/*i*/ (ᶜŠR²).[52]

It was noted earlier (ch. 1 §A 1) that voicing intervocalically and in the neighborhood of a sonorant might explain the examples in which voiceless phonemes are represented by voiced signs, e.g., in *ka-ar-ba-DU* = /*karbātu*/ = [karbādu] "twisted(?)" (KRB); *: ta-am-GI* = /*tamki*/ = [tamgi] "?" (TMK), since the latter occur otherwise only for voiced phonemes. But the paucity of examples, and other difficulties, cast doubt on the validity of such an interpretation. Analogous to the devoicing of /ᶜ/, just considered above, we should also expect the voicing of /*ḥ*/ to [ᶜ] to be discernible in the syllabic transcriptions, since [ḥ] is normally written with Ḫ-signs, while [ᶜ] is not. The following are the instances in which /*ḥ*/ ought to be voiced:

> lú*ba-ar-ḫu* = Akkadianized form *barḫu* "fugitive, rustic(?)" (BRḤ);
> *ḫur-ḫu-ra-ti* = /*ḥurḥur(r)ati*/ "(a plant)" (ḤRḤR);
> *la-ḫa-m*[*u*] = /*laḥămu*/? "what is suitable" (LḤM);
> [*la*?*-q*]*a*?*-ḫu* = /*laqāḥu*/? "to receive(?)" (LQḤ a);
> *ma-qa-ḫa* = /*maqqaḥā*/ "pair of tongs" (dual bound form; LQḤ b);
> *mar-za-i* = [marzaᶜi], *mar-zi-i* = [marziᶜi], *ma-ar-zi-ḫi* = [marziḥi] (RZḤ).

Only in the last set of examples is the intervocalic voicing of /*ḥ*/ reflected in the orthography, in two out of three instances. If voicing had occurred in the other examples, we must assume that the spellings are phonemic rather than phonetic.[53]

[49] The retention of a voiced pronunciation of /*ð*/ (rather than voiceless [θ]) would be discernible if written with Z-signs, which are not used for /*θ*/ (see below, n. 53). The issue is moot here, however, since no instances of /*ð*/ before a voiceless obstruent occur among the syllabic transcriptions.

[50] On the representation of the Ugaritic guttural consonants in syllabic transcription, see ch. 1 §E 4.

[51] Garr, JNES 45 51.

[52] Note that /*b*/ is devoiced before /*š*/ in alphab. *lpš*, a biform of *lbš* "garment"; see ibid., 46,51. It is unclear whether we should expect devoicing of /ᶜ/ before the emphatic phoneme /*ṣ*/ in (urudu.meš)*ma-ṣa-du(-ma*meš*)* = /*ma*ᶜ*ṣadu, -ūma*/ "adze(s)(?)" (ᶜṢD).

☛ p. 401

[53] The phonetic realizations of /*ð*/, /*š*/, and /*θ*/, and their relationships to one another, remain unclear; see ch. 1 §E 2 a. On the basis of the alphabetic biforms *tkšd* and *kðd*, Garr, JNES 45 47, suggests that the grapheme {ð} could represent the voiced counterpart of {š} in Ugaritic, i.e., *tkšd* for [takšudu], and *kðd* for [kažada]. (An alternative, though less attractive, possibility is that {š} and {ð} in these forms are simply graphic variants, as occasionally in Hurrian names; see ch. 1 §E 2 a.) If Garr is correct, we might expect the voiced allophone of /*š*/ to be written with Z-signs on occasion in the syllabic transcriptions, since Z-signs correspond to alphab. {ð} in /ᶜ*iðirtu*/ (see ᶜðR)

b. Assimilation of ʾ to a following Guttural

p. 401

The most plausible explanation of the writing *ma-aḫ-ḫa-*[*du*] for expected /*maʾḫadu*/ "harbor, quay" (ʾḪD), unless it is a scribal error (AḪ for the ʾ sign[54]), is that it represents a pronunciation [maḫḫadu]. If so, /ʾ/ has assimilated to the following guttural /*ḫ*/. There are no alphabetic examples of this form as a common noun. The name of the harbor area of Ugarit, however, is the same word, and one alphabetic writing of the latter, the gentilic *mḫdy* (KTU 4.635:17), probably reflects the same phenomenon. More commonly, we find an aleph sign: twice with the expected *i*-sign for syllable-final /ʾ/,[55] in gentilic pl. *miḫdym* (KTU 4.383:1; 4.611 i 1); but elsewhere with the *a*-sign: directive(?) *maḫdh* (KTU 4.149:5), gentilic sg. *maḫdy* (KTU 4.181:3) and pl. *maḫdym* (KTU 4.263:5). The writings with the *i*-sign may be historical spellings; note, however, the syllabic ^{uru}*ma-a-ḫa-di* (PRU 3 195b A 6), in which the syllabic A sign probably reflects the pronunciation of /ʾ/, i.e., /*maʾḫadi*/,[56] perhaps indicating that the assimilation of /ʾ/ to /*ḫ*/ was sporadic rather than consistent, and that the pronunciations [maʾḫadu] and [maḫḫadu] were in free variation.[57] The alphabetic writings with the *a*-sign are more difficult to understand; it is conceivable that in these the appearance of *an* aleph sign reflects historical orthography, while the non-pronunciation of an actual /ʾ/ (i.e., [maḫḫadu]) has resulted in the representation of the *vowel* of the syllable, /*a*/, rather than the appropriate *i*-sign.[58]

---

and (Akk. form) *ar-ra-zu* (RðY) and in some WSem. and Hurrian names (also discussed above, ibid.). But Ugar. /*š*/ is invariably written with Š-signs, even when a voiced allophone is expected, as in ⸢*i*⸣-*ši-t*[*u*$_4$] = /*ʾišitu*/? "fire" (ʾŠ); *bu-nu-šu* = /*bunŭšu*/ "man" (BNŠ); *ḫa-ra-šu* = /*ḥarrăšu*/ "artisan" (ḤRŠ) and /*ḫar(r)ašu*/ "deaf(?)" (ḪRŠ); ^{lú}*ia-qí-šu* = /*yāqišu*/ "fowler" (YQŠ); *la-ša-nu* = /*lašānu*/ "tongue" (LŠN); ⸢*na*⸣-[*š*]*u*-⸢*ma*⸣ = /*našūma*/ "men" (NŠ); $^{lú(.meš)}$*a-ši-ru/ri-ma* = /*ʿăšīrū/īma*/ "(officials)" (ʿŠR¹). The phoneme /*θ*/ is also always written with Š-signs, even when a voiced allophone might occur (as opposed to the voiced allophone of Hurrian *θ*, which is written with both Z- and Š-signs; see above, ibid.): *ga-ša-ru* = /*gaθaru*/ "strong" (divine name; GθR); ^{urudu}*ḫa-ar-me-ša-tu* = /*ḫarmiθātu*/ "sickles(?)" (ḪRMθ); *a-ši-ib* = /*ʾaθib*/ "let me dwell" (YθB a); *mu-ša-bu* = /*mōθabu*/ "seat" (YθB b); *ša-al-šu-ma* = /*θalθūma*/ "copper(?)" (pl.; θLθ).

[54] Since the AḪ sign is not used elsewhere in the syllabic transcriptions to represent /ʾ/, a transliteration *ma-áʾ-ḫa-*[*du*] is unlikely.

[55] See the discussion on the significance of the aleph signs, above, p. 268.

[56] See ch. 1 §E 4 b (3 b ii), p. 254.

[57] The writing of the gentilic ^{uru}*ma-ḫa-di-yu* (PRU 6 79:6) is ambiguous; it may represent [maʾḫadīyu] or [maḫḫadīyu].

[58] Among the most notorious instances of unexpected aleph signs in alphabetic forms are the verbs *t/yuḫd* (KTU 1.2 i 40[bis]; 1.4 iv 16) and *yuhb* (1.5 v 18), where *t/yiḫd* and *yihb* are expected (*t/yiḫd* do occur elsewhere). It will be noted that *t/yuḫd* derive from the same root as **maʾḫadu*, while *yuhb* is likewise II-Guttural. If the suggestion here concerning alphab. *maḫd* is correct, then, since we also have in syllabic transcriptions evidence of the assimilation of **a* to following vowels (see above, §A), perhaps it may likewise be proposed that *t/yuḫd* and *yuhb* reflect the pronunciations [t/yuḫḫud-] < [t/yaḫḫud-] < /*t/yaʾḫud-*/ and [yuhhub-] < [yahhub-] < /*yaʾhub-*/ (although the latter is

c. Assimilation of *n* to a following Consonant

The complete assimilation of an etymological **n* to an immediately following consonant is always reflected in the relevant forms in syllabic transcription:

ap-pu = /*ʾappu*/ < **ʾanpu* "nose" (ʾNP);
at-ta = /*ʾattă̄*/ < **antă̄* "you (ms)" (ʾNT);
ma-a-al-tu$_4$ = /*ma*^{cc}*altu*/? < **man*^{c}*altu* "bolt(?)" (N^{c}L);
ma-qá!?-bu and *ma-qa-bu-ma*$^{(\text{meš})}$ = /*maqqabu, -ūma*/ < **manqab-* "hammer" (NQB);
: *ma-aq-qa-du* = /*maqqadu*/ < **manqadu* and *mu-qa-dì-IM* = /*muqqādi*/? < **munqādi* "grazing-rights(?)" (NQD);
loanword ^{túg}*pa-ḫa-dar*$_6$*-ru* = /*paǵaddarru*/ < Hur. *paǵandarri* "(garment)" (alphab. both *pǵdr* and *pǵndr*; PǴ(N)DR).

In /*ma*^{cc}*altu*/, if our interpretation is correct, **n* has assimilated to a following guttural, /^{c}/ (see N^{c}L in the Glossary).

Note also the assimilation of *l* in *ma-qa-ḫa* = /*maqqaḥā*/ "pair of tongs" (dual bound form; LQḤ b), as in prefix-conj. forms of the verb *lqḥ*; contrast Hebrew *mal elqāḥayim*.

B. Syncope

1. *Pretonic*

A large number of forms attest to the general preservation of short vowels in open syllables; some examples:

a-du-rù = /*ʾaduru*/ "mighty" (ʾDR);
i-r[a?-tu$_4$*?]* = /*ʾiratu*/? "chest(?)" (ʾR);
ga-ša-ru = /*gaθaru*/ "strong" (divine name; GθR);
da-ka-rù = /*dakaru*/ "male" (DKR^1);
la-ba-nu = /*labanu*/ "white" (LBN^1);
a-mu-q[u] = /^{c}*amuqu*/ "deep (place)" (^{c}MQ^2).

---

a-stem, **yiʾhab-*, in Hebrew). The *u*-sign, present in the forms as a quasi-historical spelling or morphographemic device (i.e., to indicate that the root is underlyingly I-ʾ), would then represent not /ʾ/, which was no longer pronounced, but simply the vowel of the first syllable. It should be noted, however, that the assimilation of *a* to a following vowel is otherwise restricted to unstressed *a*, while the changes [t/yaḫḫud-] > [t/yuḫḫud-] and [yahhub-] > [yuhhub-] would seem to involve stressed *a*.

There are, however, several forms that suggest the existence of a rule of vowel syncope; note the following two pairs of examples:

pl. $^{\text{giš.meš}}$*ma-sa-wa-tu* = /*masawātu*/ (once) and $^{\text{giš(.meš)}}$*ma-ás-wa-tu* = /*maswātu*/ (twice) "cypress(?) logs" (MSW); both of these biforms (each with $^{\text{gis.meš}}$) occur in the same text;

pl. *: na-bá-ki-ma* = /*nabakīma*/ [59] and *(:) na-AB/NAB-ki-ma* = /*nabkīma*/ "springs" (NBK).

In both of these sets of examples, plurals of sg. *qatl* forms (assumed in the case of */*maswatu*/) exhibit both the expected base *qatal* and, against expectation, an apparent base *qatl*.[60] It is possible that the pl. forms with base *qatl* are simply analogical innovations, in which the external markers of plurality are added onto the singular base, as is the case for most nouns and adjectives in the language.[61] It is more likely, however, that these forms reflect instead the operation of an optional rule of syncope, also evidenced in the following examples, which cannot be explained as plurals formed on a singular base:

pl. [*ḫ*]*a-ma-ru-m*[*a*$^{\text{(meš)}}$] = /*ǵamarūma*/ and $^{\text{lú.meš}}$*ḫa-am-ru-ma* = /*ǵámrūma*/ "apprentices" (ǴMR; the sg. is a *qatal* form, /*ǵamaru*/; see below, §2);

fem. pl. *: ka-ar-ba-tù*[= /*karbātu*/? < **karvbātu* "twisted(?)" (KRB);[62]

note also the GN ^{uru}*la-bi-nu-ma* = /*labinūma*/, literally "bricks"[63] (PRU 3 190a:24), which also occurs as [^{uru}*l*]*a-ab-nu-ma* (PRU 3 191a:28') and (obl.) ^{uru}*la-ab-ni-ma* (PRU 3 166f.:6,8,10; 3 190b:6; Ug. 7 pl. 13:18), i.e., /*labnū/īma*/;[64] further, the gentilic pl. ^{uru}*qa-ra-ti-yu-ma* = /*qaratīyūma*/ (PRU 6 78:25) and sg. ^{uru}*qar-ti-yu* (PRU 6 138:17), ^{uru}*qa-ar-ti-i*[*u*] (PRU 6 148:15',18") = /*qartīyu*/.[65]

[59]Also *na-ba-ki-mi*, probably an error for *na-ba-ki-ma*; less likely dual formed on pl. base /*nabak-*/.

[60]Note also perhaps *ar-zi-ma*[in Ug. 5 153, if for Ugar. /*ʾarzīma*/? < **ʾarazīma* "cedars" (ʾRZ); the pl. *qutl* forms $^{\text{lú(.meš)}}$*mur-ú/i(-ma)* = /*murʾū/ī(ma)*/, presumably < **muraʾūma* "commanders(?)" (MRʾ), and ^{urudu}*ul-ma-tu*, if for pl. /*hulmātu*/ < **hulamātu* rather than sg. /*hulmatu*/ (HLM).

[61]See, e.g., Sivan, Analysis 81 n. 6.

[62]Perhaps also *: ḫa-ar-ZA-ti* (see Appendix to Glossary), if the form is fem. pl. of a *qatvl* adj.; but a sg. *qatl-at* form is also possible. Note also *qa-ad-šu-ut-ti* (QDŠ c), which may represent a Ugar. abstract /*qadšūti*/ < **qadišūti* (with incorrect *-tt-*) or an Akkadianized (Assyrian) form *qadšutti*.

[63]Alphab. *lbnm* (UT 426-27 no. 1350). The form is the pl. of *lbnt*, which occurs as a common noun, "brick(work)," and is undoubtedly sg. */*labinatu*/; cf. Heb. *ləbēnâ*, pl. *ləbēnîm*, Syr. *lbe(n)tā*, pl. *lebne*, Arab. sg. *labina*. (Note also the syllabic transcription of the Ugar. agent noun ^{lú}*la-*⌜*ba*?⌝*-nu* = /*labbănu*/ "brickmaker"; see the Glossary under LBN^{2}.)

[64]The writing ^{uru}*la-ib-ni-ma* in Ug. 5 12:7 is simply a scribal error for either *la-bi-* or *la-ab-*.

[65]Alphab. *qrty* (UT 481 no. 2278). The base of this GN is surely /*qar-at-*/, i.e., a biradical *qal* form with fem. *-at*, not /*qarât-*/, as suggested by Sivan, Analysis 36; syncope of a long, and presumably stressed, vowel would be most unexpected. (Similarly, the gentilic ^{uru}*u-ga-ar-ti-yu* [PRU 6 79:15, also ^{uru}*u-ga-ar-ti*<*-yu*> in line 16], also noted by Sivan, ibid., indicates not that long

It will be noted that in all of these examples, the vowel that is subject to syncope is the second of two short vowels in open syllables, and precedes the tonic syllable;[66] the rule may therefore be expressed as follows:[67]

$$\breve{v} > \phi \;/\; \breve{v}C\_\_C\acute{v} \;.$$

The pairs */masawātu/* and */maswātu/*, */nabakīma/* and */nab/pkīma/*, */ǵamarūma/* and */ǵamrūma/* (and the GN and gentilic forms cited above) are apparently biforms in free variation. The rule of pretonic syncope was, therefore, optional. It did not occur in the few other forms in our corpus in which its application was possible:

ḫa-ba-li-ma = */ḥabalīma/* "ropes, lots" (ḤBL);
[*k*]*a*?-*ma*-*ˀa*-⌜*tu*⌝ = */kamaˀātu/*? "truffles(?)" (KMˀ).[68]

2. *Post-tonic*

☛ p. 401

The writings

[l]^(ú)*ḫa-ma-ru-ú*["his apprentice" and
^(lú)*ḫa-*[*a*]*m-*[*r*]*u-ú* "his apprentice," ^(lú)*ḫa-am-ru*<-*šu*>-*nu* "their apprentice" (ǴMR),

which occur in the same text (PRU 6 79), all represent the same sg. noun, nominative, with a pronominal suffix (*-ú* for Ugar. */-hŭ̄/* in the first two instances, Akk. *-šunu* in the third).[69] The most economical way to account for the biforms */ǵamaru-hŭ̄/* and */ǵamru-hŭ̄/* (and */ǵamru/-šunu*), I would suggest, is to propose that the noun is lexically a *qatal* form, */ǵamaru/*,[70] and that the form */ǵámru-hŭ̄/* < */ǵamaru-hŭ̄/* is

---

vowels could be dropped, but rather that the third vowel of the name Ugarit must be short, */ˀugărit(u)/*.)

[66]Cf. Aramaic where, after the shift of stress to final or penultimate syllables, pretonic vowel reduction occurred at some point; as in our Ugar. examples, reduction was to ø in the second of two short pretonic syllables: e.g., **malakín* > **malakín* > *malk̲ín*. Note also, of course, the syncope of short vowels in Akkadian (**parisum* > *parsum*) and, especially in bound forms, in Hebrew (**malakay* > *malk̲ê*).

[67]Cf. Sivan, Analysis 34-36, who refers to "dropped vowels as a result of stress shift." An alphabetic example that may exhibit the effects of both this rule and our first rule of vowel assimilation (see above, §A 1 b) is *izml* "sack" (UT 354a no. 122), a loanword of (or related to) Akk. *azamillu/azamīlu* (Dietrich-Loretz, OLZ 62 536; cf. Ugarit Akk. *a-za-me-la-te* in PRU 6 155:8); the Ugar. form will have undergone the following developments: **ˀazamīlu* > **ˀazmīlu* (syncope) > **/ˀizmīlu/* (**a* > v_1 / _ $CC\acute{v}_1$; cf. **/ˀirbīyu/* < **ˀarbīyu*).

[68]Also perhaps ^(túg)*šá*-[*ḫ*]*a*!?-⌜*ru*?⌝-*ma*, if for */θaǵarūma/* ? "door-leaves(?)" (θǴR), but the reading is uncertain. Two forms II-guttural are orthographically ambiguous with regard to sycope: *ba-a-lu-ma* = */baˁalūma/* or */baˁlūma/* (BˁL); *ma-a-du-ma* = */maˀadūma/* or */maˀdūma/* (MˀD).

[69]See Rainey, IOS 3 43, who also first proposed the emendation in the third form.

[70]Vs. the Arabic cognate *ǵum(u)r*, for which see Bravmann, JCS 7 27. Rainey's normalization of the form as *ǵam(m)aru* (IOS 3 43) suggests the possibility of a doubled middle radical; it would be

the result of a second, likewise optional, rule of syncope by which a sequence of four open syllables with short vowels (the ultima may be long or short), presumably stressed on the first,[71] is reduced to three syllables with the deletion of the first post-tonic vowel; i.e.,

v̆ > *ø* / *v̆́C__Cv̆Cv̆̄* (or, *Cv̆́Cv̆Cv̆Cv̆̄* > *Cv̆́CCv̆Cv̆̄*).

While such a rule seems phonologically plausible, there are unfortunately no other clear examples among the syllabic transcriptions that might illustrate its operation. A possible instance is the writing ^{d}*aš-ra-tu*$_4$ in Ug. 5 18:19 (ʾΘR), in contrast to the writing ⸢*a*⸣[*-ši?-ra?-tu*$_4$?] which, though mostly reconstructed, nevertheless indicates the expected open first syllable, i.e., */*ʾaθiratu*/ (cf. Heb. *ʾăšērâ*). It is likely that the writing ^{d}*aš-ra-tu*$_4$ is simply the Akk. form of this goddess's name, *ašratu,* since many of the DN's in the god-list in which it occurs (Ug. 5 18), even though it parallels precisely an alphab. list (see KTU 1.47; 1.118), are Akk. rather than Ugar.[72] In view of the rule of syncope just described, however, we may at least point out the possibility, however small, that ^{d}*aš-ra-tu*$_4$ instead represents Ugar. /*ʾáθratu*/ [73] < */*ʾáθiratu*/, with the post-tonic short vowel deleted as in /*ǵamru-hū̆*/ < /*ǵamaru-hū̆*/.

Still another form in our corpus, if correctly interpreted, evidences a similar process of syncope:

: *ti-tar-ḫ*[*u*] = /*tiʾtarḫu*/ < **tiʾtariḫu* (ʾRḪ; or /*tittarḫu*/ < **tittariḫu,* if YRḪ).

This form is best taken, in my view, as a Gt *yaqtulu* (i.e., imperfective), the underlying base of which is presumably *yíqtatil-*. With the addition of the modal /*-u*/, apparently, syncope may occur: *yíqtatilu* > *yíqtatlu.* Here, the vowel immediately following the stressed initial syllable may not be deleted, since the first syllable is already closed, and so the next vowel is dropped instead; i.e.,

v̆ > *ø* / *v̆́CCv̆C__Cv̆̄* (or, *Cv̆́CCv̆Cv̆Cv̆̄* > *Cv̆́CCv̆CCv̆̄*).

The developments illustrated by /*ǵamaru-hū̆*/ > /*ǵamru-hū̆*/ and **tiʾtariḫu* > /*tiʾtarḫu*/ bear more than a surface resemblance to one another. In all likelihood, they are manifestations of a single process of syncope, which may be restated as follows: In a sequence of three (or more?) post-tonic open syllables with short vowels (ultima may be long), the first structurally amissable vowel[74] is subject to optional deletion.[75]

---

very difficult to account for the deletion of the second /*a*/ if that were true, however, without positing that two distinct bases, and thus two distinct words, underlie these writings, all of which, as noted, occur in a single text (as do the plural forms /*ǵam(a)rūma*/ discussed in the preceding section).

[71] See above, p. 268.

[72] See above, pp. 9-10.

[73] See also below, §C, with n. 81.

[74] I.e., a vowel that may be deleted without causing the creation of a structurally unacceptable syllable (e.g., beginning or ending with two consonants).

[75] This rule will, of course, be somewhat difficult to detect in alphabetic forms. One alphabetic

C. Vocalic *ṛ*

The forms

i-zi-ir-[*tu*₄?][76] = /*ᶜiðirtu*/ "help" (ᶜðR);
ᵗᵘ́ᵍ*šá-ḫar-tu* = /*šaᶜartu*/ "wool" (ŠᶜR b)

differ from their cognates elsewhere in Semitic, *ᶜ*iðrat-*[77] and **śaᶜrat-*,[78] in having a bisyllabic base rather than a monosyllabic *qvtl*. Since the pattern *qitil-t* exhibited by /*ᶜiðirtu*/ is rare in Semitic,[79] apart from Akkadian, it is likely that these Ugar. forms are secondary developments from original *qvtl-at* forms, as suggested by Sivan, Analysis 59, §8.2.1. Since *qvtl-at* is generally stable otherwise in Ugar. (see ch. 3 §C 1 c), it would seem that the third radical *r* is responsible for the changes, perhaps as follows:

$$ra > \underset{\circ}{r} = v_1r \;/\; v_1C\_\_C \;.$$

In other words, the unstressed sequence *ra* apparently developed into a vocalic *ṛ* when post-consonantal: i.e., $q\acute{v}_1tratv > q\acute{v}_1t\underset{\circ}{r}t$; the latter was pronounced (and written) $q\acute{v}_1tv_1rt$, with the vowel quality of *ṛ* dependent on that of the preceding syllable:

*ᶜ*iðratu* > *ᶜiðṛtu* = /*ᶜiðirtu*/;
**śaᶜratu* > *šaᶜṛtu* = /*šaᶜartu*/.

---

form may, in fact, be a counterexample to the rule as stated here, viz., *ylt* in KTU 1.23:53(bis), 60(bis), which is usually and, it must be admitted, most reasonably taken to be a suffix-conj. 3 f dual, i.e., */*yalattā*/ < **yaladtā* (so, e.g., Gordon, UT 70 §9.7). If that is correct, comparison with the 3 f dual perfect in Arabic, *qatalatā*, would suggest that syncope of the second post-tonic vowel of an original **yaladatā* has occurred, whereas our rule, deleting the first such vowel, would generate an unattested form **yaldatā* (written **yldt* rather than *ylt*). There are several alternative explanations, however. First, it may be suggested that the P(NW)S 3 f dual form was simply **qataltā*, so that Ugar. */*yalattā*/ would not be the result of syncope; Arab. *qatalatā* could be an innovation based on 3f sg. *qatalat*. (The OAkk. 3 f dual form *śalimtā* "the two of them are fine" [Gelb, MAD 3 272] is of no help here, since it may reflect either **šalimtā* or **šalimatā*.) It is also possible that *ylt* is not a suffix-conj. form, but rather a participle, perhaps sg. */*yālittu*/ < **yālidtu*, as must be true of *ylt* in KTU 1.17 i 41 (and is presumably what Caquot-Sznycer-Herdner, Textes ougaritiques 376-77, have in mind in their rendering of KTU 1.23:53,60 as "'La femme, ô El, a enfanté'. 'Qu'a-t-elle enfanté'?" since in no way can *ylt* be taken as suffix-conj. if it is sg. [*/*yaladat*/]), or perhaps dual construct */*yālittā*/ < **yālidtā* (i.e., *ylt mh ylt yldy*/*ilmy* "Bearing what? Bearing the children/gods").

[76]The restoration of a broken final -*tu*₄ sign, for which there is room on the copy, is quite certain; see the commentary on Sᵃ Voc. no. 33 in Part I.

[77]Cf. Heb. *ᶜezrâ*.

[78]Cf. Heb. *śaᶜărâ*, Syr. collective *saᶜrā*, Arab. *šaᶜr(a)*.

[79]For the word /*ʾirištu*/, see above, §A 1 d.

In addition to these two forms, note the GN ^{uru}*ia-ar-tv*[80] = /*ya*ᶜ*artv*/ (cf. alphab. *y*ᶜ*rt,* UT 412b no. 1126), < **ya*ᶜ*ratu* (cf. Syr. *ya*ᶜ*rā,* Heb. *ya*ᶜ*ar* "woods" < **ya*ᶜ*r-*).[81]

The form : *mi-dá-ar-ú* = /*midar*ᶜ*u*/ (DRᶜ), originally **midra*ᶜ*u,* differs from those discussed above in that the new vowel before the *r* does not mimic the vowel of the preceding syllable. Perhaps the /*a*/ is due to the following /ᶜ/.

D. Prothesis

One form may exhibit a prothetic /ʾ/, viz., ⌜*vḫ?*⌝*-nu-tu*₄. As Nougayrol suggested,[82] this word, if its first sign is indeed AḪ, may be a biform of /*ḥinōtu*/ "(an implement)," attested in the dual *ḫi-nu-ta-me* = /*ḥinōtāmi*/ (ḤNW).[83] Since the vowel represented by AḪ is ambiguous, we are unfortunately prevented from knowing the precise shape of the prothetic syllable: /ʾ*vḥnōtu*/. Alphabetic examples of prothetic /ʾ/ exhibit the full range of vowels: *udm*ᶜ*t* "tears" (UT 386a no. 676); the month name *yrḫ ib*ᶜ*lt* (KTU 1.119:1), probably to be compared with Phoenician *yrḥ p*ᶜ*lt* (Xella, Testi rituali 27-28); *azmr* "twigs" (KTU 1.41:51; see de Moor, UF 1 177). In the development /*ḥinōtu*/ > /ʾ*vḥnōtu*/, a short /*i*/ followed by a sonorant and a long vowel was lost and the resulting initial sequence */*ḥn*/ resolved with the addition of a preceding vowel. A similar environment probably obtained in *azmr* (i.e., **zi*/*umāru* > */ʾ*azmāru*/; cf. Heb. *zəmôrâ* < **zi*/*umār-*) and *udm*ᶜ*t*.[84]

E. The Behavior of /*w*/ and /*y*/ [85]

1. *Syllable-final: Diphthongs*

a. The Diphthongs **aw* > /*ō*/ and **ay* > /*ē*/

Conforming to the alphabetic evidence, all forms in syllabic transcription show

80PRU 3 189b:23'; 3 190a:7'; 3 190b:3; 3 191a:12'; PRU 6 70:18.

81Sivan, Analysis 59 §8.2.2; the PN's ᶠ*dá-la-ap-tu*₄ (PRU 3 52f.:6,20) and ¹ʔDUMU-*ka-bar-ta-a* (PRU 6 28 r. 3'), also noted by Sivan, probaby reflect original *qatal-t* forms. Note, however, the form *a-šar-ti* in PN's in PRU 3 205b:5; Ug. 5 9:20; if the DN */ʾ*aθiratu*/ had a biform /ʾ*aθratu*/ as a result of syncope, as suggested above in §B 2, another biform /ʾ*aθartu*/ might also have developed from the latter by the process under discussion here.

82Ug. 5 p. 178 n. 4.

83Although forms with prothetic /ʾ/ are attested in alphab. forms (see below), there are, to my knowledge, no other Ugaritic words attested both with and without the prothetic syllable; see also the next note, however.

84Note also, e.g., Heb. ʾ*ezrôa*ᶜ as a rare biform of *zərôa*ᶜ, both from **ðirā*ᶜ*-*.

85For the assimilation of **a* to a following consonantal /*w*/ or /*y*/, see above, §A 1 d.

the unconditional contraction of the original diphthongs **aw* and **ay* to simple vowels. The examples have already been cited above, and need not be repeated here.

For **aw* > */ō/*, see ch. 1 §G 3.

For **ay* > */ē/*, see ch. 1 §G 2.

See also in this chapter, §A 1 e, end.

b. **iy* > */ī/*

As expected, the reflex of P(NW)S **iy* before a consonant is */ī/*, as in the fem. nouns *qa-ri-t*[*u*$_4$] = */qarītu/* < **qariy-tu* (alphab. *qrt*;[86] QRY), and (G participle) *:ḫa-me-ti* = */ḥāmīti/* < **ḥāmiy-ti* (ḤMY);[87] for the latter, compare the alphab. sg. form *ḥmt* with the plural *ḥmyt* = **/ḥāmiyātu/* (UT 397b no. 876), in which consonantal */y/* is preserved in the triphthong */iyā/*.[88] Other examples are *qitl* (verbal) nouns of roots II-y: ⸢*ši-i-ru*⸣ = */šīru/* (< PS **šiyr-*; ŠYR); *ši-tu* = */šītu/* (< PS **šiyt-*; ŠYT).[89]

c. **uw* > */ū/*

Note perhaps *ú-lu* = */ᶜūlu/*? < P(NW)S **ᶜuwl* "young (animal)(?)" (ᶜWL).

☛ p. 401

[86] The various biforms of this vocable for "town" in West Semitic are rather bewildering. Some forms are based on a biradical root *q-r*, viz., fem. **qar-t*: Targumic Aram. *qartā* (but pl. *qirwayyā*), Hebrew *qeret* (rare; note perhaps also the GN *qartâ*?), Phoenician *qrt* = **qart*. Others are derived from a triradical root III-y; these are either *qutl-at*, as in Syriac *quryā* (> emphatic *qritā*); or *qatl-at*, as in Arabic *qarya* (pl. *qur-an* < **quray-un*); note also Hebrew *qiryâ* and Bib./JAram. *qiryā* (emph. *qiryətā*), both < **qary-at* (or reflecting still another base, *qitl-at*?). The Ugar. form */qarītu/* < **qariy-tu*, it will be noted, deviates from all of these. In alphab. texts, we find both *qrt* and *qryt* for the sg. (UT 480-81 no. 2278). Thus, Ugaritic, like Hebrew (*qiryâ* and *qeret*) and some Aramaic dialects (*qartā* and *qiryā*), had at least two biforms for "town." The writing *qryt* clearly represents **/qaryatu/*; whether *qrt* in all instances represents */qarītu/*, corresponding to the syllabic transcription, or sometimes a third form, with biradical base, **/qar-(a)tu/* is, of course, difficult to determine. The GN ^{uru}*qa-ra-tu/ti/te* = */qaratv/* (PRU 6 95:1; 6 134:9; 6 175:9; Ug. 5 12:17,22; gentilic ^{uru}*qa-ra-ti-yu(-ma)* = */qaratīyu, -ūma/* PRU 6 78:1,25, and, with pretonic syncope [see above, §B 1], ^{uru}*qar-ti-yu*, ^{uru}*qa-ar-ti-i*[*u*] = */qartīyu/* PRU 6 138:17; 6 148:15',18") may or may not reflect the local Ugaritic idiom. The alphab. plural *qrht*, however, probably is based on a biradical sg. form, like other plurals in *-h* elsewhere in West Semitic (including Ugar.; cf. *amht* "female slaves," *ilhm/t* "god(desse)s"), i.e., **/qarăhātu/*, from sg. **/qar(a)tu/* (though it is possible that the latter sg. form had since fallen out of the language). (Whether Hebrew *qîr* "wall" is related to these forms [i.e., the biradical root *q-r*; or **qīr* < **qiyr* < **qiry* by metathesis?] requires further study; note also Moabite *qr* "town.")

[87] Note also perhaps the participial form *ša-i-tu*$_4$, the root of which may be III-y, thus */θāᶜītu/* < **θāᶜiy-tu* (θᶜY); but */θāᶜittu/* < **θāᶜid-tu* is also possible.

[88] As elsewhere; see under 3, below. The noncontraction of */iyă/* in Ugar. shows that *:ḫa-me-ti* does indeed represent */ḥāmīti/* from **ḥāmiy-tv*, and not **/ḥāmēti/* < **hāmiy-atv*. The syllabic writing actually does indicate the pronunciation [ḥāmēti], but the [ē] is an allomorph of */ī/*, due to the preceding sonorant */m/*; see above, ch. 1 §G 2.

[89] Perhaps also *ni-r*[*u*], if for */nīru/* (cf. Heb. *nîr*), but */nēru/* (cf. Heb. *nēr*) is also possible (NW/YR). The form */ḫirītu/* "grave," is probably an Akkadian loanword; see the Glossary under ḪRY.

2. *Word-initial and Post-consonantal*[90]

a. Word-initial

/w/: A possible example is the form *P[I-x-d]u*, perhaps meaning "child," if our reconstruction is correct; in view of alphab. *wld* (and cf. Hebrew *wālād*), it may be that *w[a-la-d]u* = /*waladu*/ is intended rather than *y[a-al-d]u* = /*yaldu*/.[91]

/y/: Note, e.g., *PI-mu* = /*yōmu*/ "day" (less likely, /*yămu*/; YWM); (lú)*IA-ṣí-ru-ma* = /*yāṣirūma*/ "potters" (YṢR); for other examples, see under Y in the Glossary. For the curious writings *i-bi-la* and *i-ṣa-ʾa*, probably for */*yabila*/(?) and */*yaṣaʾa*/, respectively, see under YṢʾ in the Glossary.

b. Post-consonantal

/w/: Note the *qutl* form : *ZU-ur-PI* = /*ẓurwu*/? (or /*ṣurwu*/?) "(aromatic) resin" (ẒRW; cf. Hebrew *ṣŏrî*), corresponding to alphab. *ẓrw*; cf. alphab. *thw*, probably for */*tuhwu*/ "wasteland" (KTU 1.5 i 15; Hebrew *tṓhû*).

Other examples are the two instances of pl. giš(.meš)*ma-ás-wa-tu* = /*maswātu*/, vs. one of giš.meš*ma-sa-wa-tu* = /*masawātu*/ "cyrpess(?) logs" (MSW), the former having undergone pretonic vowel syncope (see above, §B 2); no strictly analogous forms occur in alphab. writing.[92]

The form *i-pu-ú* may reflect an original *qitl* noun III-*w*, i.e., /*ᶜipû*/ < **ᶜipwu* (ᶜPW), in which the consonantal *w* has been lost, rather than retained as in /*ẓurwu*/ above, in a development analogous to that exhibited by the alphabetic writings of *qitl* nouns III-*y*, viz., **qityu* > *qitû* (see below under /y/ in this section). (Note also perhaps the alphab. *qatl* (?) form *aḫ* = /*ʾaḫû*/? < **ʾaḫwu*? "papyrus thicket(?)" [UT 355a no. 129; see Rainey, UF 3 169].)

Doubled /ww/ occurs in [*ḫ*]*u-wa-tu₄* = /*ḥuwwatu*/ (ḤWW); *ḫu-wu-ú* = /*ḥuwwû*/ (ḤYY¹/ḤWY¹ a); probably in *pu-wa-ti* = /*puwwati*/ (PWT); and perhaps in *gu-wa-⌜li⌝* = /*guw(w)ăli*/ (GWL).

/y/: The Sᵃ Voc. form *ṣi-il-PI*[ ] "curse" (ṢLY) may represent a simple *qitl* noun, /*ṣilyu*/. Since, however, most expected *qitl*'s of roots III-*y* in alphabetic writings

[90]Consonantal /w/ followed by any vowel is written with the PI sign, while /y/ followed by any vowel is written with either PI or IA (all examples are presented above in Part I, §E 3 c, pp. 235-39); the ambiguity inherent in these conventions results in uncertainty in the interpretation of some examples.

[91]Note also perhaps the PI sign for the Ugar. conjunction /*wa-*/? in Ug. 5 153 (see under W in the Glossary).

[92]The alphab. form *bnwt* "creatures" (KTU 1.6 iii 5,11) almost certainly represents */*banūwātu*/ < **banūyātu*, with /w/ < **y* after /*ū*/; see Sivan, UF 14 216 with n. 137.

appear without *y*, apparently reflecting a change **qityu* > **qitû*,[93] it is more likely that the form is instead fem. *ṣi-il-ya*[*-tu*$_4$] = /*ṣilyatu*/. Note also perhaps dual *iš-ia-ti-mi* = /*ᶜišyatēmi*/? (ᶜŠY); further, the loanword (lú(.meš))*mar-ia(-an)-nu*/*ni* = /*maryannŭ*/*ĭ*/ (MRYN).

Doubled /*yy*/ occurs in *ḫé-yu-ma* and *ḫi-*[*i*]*u*?*-ma* = /*ḥiyyūma*/ "life" (ḤYY¹/ ḤWY¹ b); ITI *ḫi-ia*/*ya-ri* = /*ḫiyyāri*/ (month name; ḪYR).

3. *Intervocalic: Triphthongs*

The problem of contraction vs. retention of original triphthongs in Ugaritic has been the subject of several recent detailed studies by D. Sivan[94] and E. Verreet.[95] Sivan's conclusion that these sequences exhibit "no systematic behavior"[96] is, in my opinion, not entirely warranted by the data. I find Verreet's conclusions concerning III-weak verbs to be closer to the mark, though with some reservations. Verreet suggests that in singular forms, final triphthongs contracted when the vowels on either side of the glide were the same, but remained uncontracted otherwise,[97] i.e.,

$$-v_1 w/y v_1 > -\hat{v}$$

$$\text{but } -v_1 w/y v_2 = \text{unchanged.}$$

In plural and energic forms, however, Verreet finds that contracted and uncontracted forms occur in virtually free variation.[98] Such widespread variation, or flouting of apparent phonological rules, however, is unexpected in normal language (unless the sound changes being observed—contraction of triphthongs, in this case—are at their inception). Furthermore, the nature of the alphabetic texts makes it likely that we have to reckon, on the one hand, with several chronological phases of the language, and, on the other, since the texts are poetic and religious, with a tendency for the scribes to use, inconsistently, archaic and archaizing forms.[99] We should probably

93E.g., *pr* = */*pirû*/ < **piryu* "fruit" (UT 470b no. 2105); perhaps also some or all of the following verbal nouns: *bk* = */*bikû*/ < **bikyu* "weeping" (UT 372a no. 464); *hg* = */*higû*/ < **higyu* "counting" (UT 389a no. 747); *hr* = */*hirû*/ < **hiryu* "conception" (UT 392a no. 794); *ṣp* = */*ṣipû*/ < **ṣipyu* "viewing" (UT 475b no. 2183). (See also the discussion on /*ᶜipû*/ immediately above.) Conversely, it should be noted, *qatl* forms III-*y* apparently remained unchanged: e.g., *ary* = */*ʾaryu*/ "kinsman" (UT 366a no. 349); *gdy* = */*gadyu*/ "kid" (UT 378b no. 560); *ẓby* = */*ẓabyu*/ "gazelle" (UT 407a no. 1045).

94UF 14 209-18 (nominal forms); 16 279-93 (verbs III-weak).

95UF 16 312-16; 17 330-41.

96UF 14 218; cf. 16 293.

97UF 16 316.

98UF 17 341.

99A conceptually analogous situation obtains in the literary dialects of Akkadian, viz., Standard Babylonian and the so-called Hymno-Epic style of Old Babylonian. In these, forms reflecting the

also recognize the existence of morphographemic spellings, i.e., spellings in which a *y* or *w* appears, even though unexpected on phonological grounds, to indicate either the root or the aspect (e.g., *yaqtulu* vs. *yaqtul*) of a form. It is likely, therefore, that a more consistent linguistic reality in the spoken language underlies the confusion of variant forms attested in the alphabetic texts. While a thorough review of the examples is not possible here, and would undoubtedly necessitate some modifications, the following set of rules may be proposed, with all due reservation, to account for the majority of forms attested in both alphabetic texts[100] and syllabic transcription; examples and discussion follow below.

-awv̄̆$_1$ and *-ayv̄̆*$_1$	> *-v̂*$_1$[101]
-uwū̆	> *-û*
-uwā̆	no change[102]
-iyv̄̆	no change
-v̄wv̄̆ and *-v̄yv̄̆*	no change

a. **-awv̄̆*$_1$ and **-ayv̄̆*$_1$ > /*-v̂*/ [103]

Note the following forms in syllabic transcription:[104] *ša-du-ú* = /*šadû*/ < **śadawu*[105] (alphab. invariably *šd*; ŠDW);[106] *ḫu-PI-ú* = /*ḥuwwû*/ < **ḥuwwayu*[107] p. 401

contemporary spoken dialect appear side-by-side with noncontemporary forms that result from the scribes' attempts to contrive a more elevated, archaic language. The two levels of language in these dialects thus yield inconsistent descriptions when such texts are subjected to a synchronic linguistic analysis. As an example, one that is strictly analogous to the problem of the Ugaritic triphthongs, note that the prologue to the Code of Ḫammurapi exhibits, inter alia, both "spoken" *ib-bu-ú* "they named" (i 49) and *ša-me-e* "of the sky" (i 4,22) and archaizing *ib-bi-ù* (i 17) and *ša-ma-i* (ii 31).

[100]That is, apart from those that must be attributed to either archaizing or morphographemic spelling. In addition, there are undoubtedly some forms that must be seen as artificial innovations on the part of the scribes within the archaizing process.

[101]On the phonetic and phonemic significance of these vowels, see ch. 1 §F 1 b, with n. 181 there.

[102]I know of no examples in which the triphthong **-uwi* (with short *i*) might be expected. Note, however, that **-uwī* (long *ī*) apparently became /*-î*/ in the fem. sg. imperatives *li* = */*l(v)ʾî*/ < **l(v)ʾuwī* "be strong"; *di* = */*d(v)ʾî*/ < **d(v)ʾuwī* "fly"; see Verreet, UF 16 315.

[103]These rules do not apply word-initially; rather, **ă* is raised to /*u*/ before /*w*/ and to /*i*/ before /*y*/ in such situations, resulting in the stable triphthongs /*uwā̆*/ and /*iyā̆*/, as in *ú*-[*P*]*I*!?-[*t*]*u*$_4$ = /*huwā̆tu*/? < **hawā̆tu* "word" (HW²); see above, §A 1 e. Note, too, that these rules do not operate across a significant morpheme boundary such as the acc. sg. marker /*-a*/ followed by the 1cs suffix /*-ya*/ = /*...-a-ya*/; see Gordon, UT 36 §6.6. A possible syllabic example is [*l*]*a-ša-na-ia*, if for Ugar. acc. /*lašāna-ya*/, in Ug. 5 153 (see -Y² in Glossary).

[104]Other syllabic transcriptions that may reflect contracted triphthongs are *ma-aš-nu-ú*?, if for /*maθnû*/ < **maθnayu* "repetition"; *mu-ru-ú-ma*, if for /*mō̆/ūrûma*/ < *...*-vyūma*. Both of these words are probably derivatives of roots III-guttural, however; see under ŠNʾ and YRʾ, respectively, in the Glossary.

[105]Both Old Akkadian and Old Assyrian *šadwum* "mountain" (see Gelb, MAD 2² 122; MAD 3 263-64; AHw 1124) and OSA *s²dw* "mountain?" (Beeston et al., Sabaic Dictionary 131) indicate,

(ḤYY^1/ḤWY^1 a); note also /-*û*-/ < *-*ayū* in *ša-mu-ma* = /*šamûma*/ < **šamayūma*[108] (ŠMY). Note also perhaps *ma-aš-na,* which may reflect an adverbial accusative ("secondly") of the *maqtal* noun written *mθn* ("repetition") in alphab. texts; if so, the writing, for expected */*maθnâ*/ < **maθnaya,* either is the result of a scribal error (i.e., *ma-aš-na*<-*a*>), or exhibits a curious, ad hoc shortening of the final contracted vowel.[109]

An exception is the form $^{\text{giš.meš}}$*ma-sa-wa-tu* = /*masawātu*/ "cypress(?) logs"

---

against Hebrew *śāday,* that this word was originally III-*w*. Old Babylonian *šadûm* (gen. *šadîm*) and Hebrew *śāde* (and *śāday*) attest to an original *qatal* pattern.

[106]Cf. perhaps the writing *ša-TI-i,* if for Ugar. gen. /*šadî*/, in Ug. 5 153.

[107]The following points should be noted concerning this form. (a) Since the Ú sign is not used elsewhere in our corpus for /*yu*/ (see above, pp. 236-37 with n. 106), it is most unlikely that *ḫu-PI-ú* represents /*ḥuwwayu*/, as suggested by Sivan, Analysis 179 n. 1; nor is there any reason to expect a form III-ʾ, as suggested by Blau-Greenfield's normalization *ḫuwwāʾu* in BASOR 200 17. (b) Medial /-*ww*-/ is more likely than /-*yy*-/ (i.e., /*ḥuyyû*/) for the D stem of this root; see Marcus, JSS 17 76-82. (c) Finally, since triphthongs in which the first vowel is long remain uncontracted in all other syllabic examples (see parag. e below), we must conclude that the original form of /*ḥuwwû*/ was **ḥuwwayu,* not **ḥuwwāyu*; thus, the D infinitive had the pattern *quttal,* with short *a* in the second syllable (cf. Rainey, IEJ 19 108, who notes that the *quttal* forms of Amarna Canaanite must contain short *a,* since long *ā* in **quttāl* would have yielded unattested **quttōl*).

☛ p. 402

[108]Most of the cognates (e.g., Akk. *šamāʾū*/*šamê,* Eth. *samāy,* Arab. *samāʾ*) indicate that the root of "sky" was originally III-weak (in Hebrew, apparently, **šamayīm* underwent an ad hoc change > **šamaym*).

[109]Here mention should be made of the various GN's written in syllabic texts with final *Ca-a,* such as ^{uru}*šá-lur*$_x$*-ba-a* (PRU 6 105:3'). Many of these GN's appear in alphabetic texts with final *y,* as in *θlrby* (UT 502b no. 2687); see Richardson, JSS 23 298-315. Thus, Rainey (IOS 3 40-41) and Kühne (UF 7 255 and n. 9) suggest that the final -*Ca-a* in syllabic forms represents /-*āy(a)*/ or /-*ay(y)a*/. This interpretation is difficult to accept, however. First, -*Ca-a* does not indicate -*Cāy(v)* elsewhere in Ugarit Akkadian, but only -*Câ* (only a *reduplicated* A sign indicates *ayyv* or *āyv,* in several Akkadian forms, all of which occur in literary texts: e.g., *da-a-a-nu*/*n*[*i*$_7$] Ug. 5 162:4'; Ug. 6 394ff. iii 9'; vetitive *a-a-iṭ-ḫa-šum-ma* Ug. 5 17:38; cf. ibid. r.22'; Ug. 5 168:33',34'; *pu-ru-sa-a-a* Ug. 5 162:3', cf. 7',17'; see AS^3 62 no. 315; GAG §22b). Secondly, several of the GN's in -*Ca-a* are also written simply with final -*Ca* in syllabic form: e.g., ^{uru}*šá-lur*$_x$*-ba* (PRU 6 134:7), while still other GN's with final *y* in alphab. form appear *only* with final -*Ca* (not -*Ca-a*) in syllabic form: e.g., ^{uru}*ḫu-ul-da* (PRU 3 133f.:7; 3 143ff.:19), alphab. *ḫldy* (UT 402a no. 964). Finally, some of the alphabetic GN's in *y* also appear in biforms without the *y*; see Richardson, JSS 23 304-7. The most likely interpretation of these data is that the GN's in question originally ended in *-*aya,* which contracted to /-*â*/ according to the sound rule under discussion here. The syllabic spellings in -*Ca-a* thus probably reflect the contracted pronunciation, as do the alphab. spellings without *y,* whereas the alphab. spellings with *y* should be seen as learned (historical) spellings reflecting the earlier pronunciation (so also Richardson, JSS 23 314-15). The syllabic spellings in -*Ca,* without -*a,* apparently exhibit a shortening of the final vowel of /-*Câ*/ that is difficult to explain.

A few PN's also exhibit final -*Ca-a* in syllabic spelling: e.g., ZA-*al-la-a* (PRU 3 119f.:16); ^{f}*mi-il-ka-a* (PRU 3 54ff.:16,21). It seems likely that these are to be interpreted in the same way as the analogous GN's, i.e., as forms ending in /-*â*/ < *-*aya*. Note, however, that the sound change did not apply consistently, as is often true of names; thus, e.g., with ^{f}*mi-il-ka-a* above, compare $^{\text{1f}}$*mi-il-ka-IA* (PRU 3 66a:5).

(MSW), which occurs in the same text as the biform $^{giš.meš}$*ma-á*[*s-w*]*a-tu* = /*maswātu*/. These plural forms of the (unattested) sg. */*maswatu*/[110] are probably to be explained as analogical (paradigmatic) restorations of the original *qatal-āt* (> *qatl-āt*, with syncope; see above, §B 1) plural pattern. They contrast with the alphabetic plurals *qnm* = */*qanûma*/ < **qanawūma*[111] "reeds" (UT 479a no. 2244), *gdm* = */*gadûma*/ < **gadayūma* "kids(?)"[112] (cf. sg. *gdy* = */*gadyu*/; UT 378b no. 560).[113]

b. *-*uwŭ̄* > /-*û*/

No syllabic examples illustrating this triphthong occur. For alphabetic examples, such as *tdu* = */*tadʾû*/ < **tadʾuwu* "she flies" (KTU 1.16 vi 6,7), see Verreet, UF 16 313-16; 17 338.

c. *-*uwă̄*: no change

Note the independent pronoun *ú-wa* = /*huwa*/ (HW); *ú-*[*w*]*a*!?-[*t*]*u*$_4$ = /*huwătu*/, originally **hawătu* (HWW); another possible example is *gu-wa-*⌜*li*⌝ = /*guw(w)ăli*/ (GWL), but the pattern of this form is uncertain (*qutăl* or *quttăl*, either possibly *qat(t)ăl* originally; see above, §A 1 e).

For alphabetic examples, see Verreet, UF 16 313-16.

d. *-*iyv̆̄*: no change[114]

The only syllabic example is uncertain because of the broken text: in S^a Voc. no. 34.2, Nougayrol read *a*[(?)-]*p*[*u* (?)] for the G participle "baker." But in view of the alphabetic spellings *apy*, pl. *apym* (UT 364a no. 303), and, indeed, of the fact G participles of verbs III-*y* are consistently written with *y* in the alphabetic texts, attesting to the stability of the triphthongs /-*iyv̆̄*/, we should undoubtedly read instead ⌜*a*⌝-[*p*]*í*-[*yu*] = /ʾ*āpiyu*/ (ʾPY).[115]

[110]Cf. Syriac *msutā* < **mvswat-* "cypress."

[111]Or **qanuwūma*? Cf. Eblaite ^{giš}GI = *qá-nu-wu*, [*qá*]-*nu-um*; see Krebernik, ZA 73 16.

[112]Other interpretations are possible for this form; see Caquot-Sznycer-Herdner, Textes ougaritiques 157 n. d.

[113]As other alphabetic examples of the contraction of -*awv* and -*ayv*, we may point to the numerous *maqtal* nouns of roots III-weak, nearly always written without final *w* or *y*, e.g., *mᶜn* = */*maᶜnû*/ < **maᶜnayu* "response" (UT 458a no. 1883); see Sivan, UF 14 214, for other examples.

Exceptions are verbs such as suffix-conj. *ᶜly* = */*ᶜalaya*/ "he went up" (KTU 1.4 i 23); *yaqtulu*-form *ibǵyh* = */ʾ*ibǵayu-hŭ̄*/ "I will show him" (KTU 1.3 iii 29). As suggested above, such forms are probably archaisms; cf., in contrast, *ᶜl* = */*ᶜalâ*/ (= */*ᶜalaya*/, above; KTU 1.3 i 21).

[114]The form /*mūdû*/ (< **mūdeu*) should not be considered an exception, since the word is a loan from Akkadian.

[115]It is notable that even the triphthongs *-*iyi* and *-*iyī* seem usually to be preserved: e.g., gen. sg. (cst.) *rᶜy* = */*rāᶜiyi*/ "shepherd" (KTU 4.618:3), gen. pl. *rᶜym* = */*rāᶜiyīma*/ (KTU 4.378:1); fem. sg. imperative *kry* = */*k(v)riyī*/ "dig" (KTU 1.12 i 23); and other examples, for which see

e. *-v̄wv̆ and *-v̄yv̆: no change

No examples of triphthongs -v̄wv̆ occur in the syllabic transcriptions.[116]

*-āyv̆ is illustrated by the following: *uḫ-ra-a-yi* = /ʾuḫrāyi/ "destiny" (cf. Syriac (ʾ)ḥrāyā; ʾḪR); *:ḫa-a-yi* = /ḫāyi/ "vacant(?)" (ḪWY); ⸢*e*?⸣-*la-PI* = /ʿilāyi/? "upper (part)(?)" (ʿLY b); note also the gentilics [uru]*ap-sú-na-yu* = /ʾapsŭnāyu/ "Apsunaean" (PRU 3 37a:10) and (probably) [lú.[ur]u!?]*ak!-kà-a-ii* = /ʾakkāyi/ "Akko-ite" (TA 8 7f.:33).[117]

*-īyv̆ occurs in the writings *ḫe-e-ia/yu* = [ḫēya/u], *:ḫé-yi-ma* = [ḫēyīma], *:ḫi-i-yi(-šu)* = [ḫīyĭ] "vacant(?)" (ḪWY); probably also in *al-li-ni-PI* = /hallinīya/? "here, now then" (HLNY), although we may not be certain that the ending is not /-iya/ instead; the same is true of the adj. ⸢d?*a*?⸣-*li-PI* = /ʿălīyi/? "ascendant" (ʿLY a); note also the nisba form *tu-ki-ii* = /tōkīyi/ "inner" (TWK), and the many gentilics in /-īyu/, pl. /-īyū/īma/, cited above, ch. 1 §E 3 c (pp. 237-39).

*-ūyv̆ is found only in the curious gentilic [uru]*a-ta-li-gu-yu* = /ʾatalligūyu/ (PRU 6 79:17).

Verreet, UF 17 339.

At least some of the exceptions to the preservation of *-*iyĭ* noted by Sivan, UF 14 213, are susceptible of other explanations. Thus, e.g., the adjective *dw* = */dawû/ "sick" (UT 384b no. 652) was probably *qatal*, i.e., **dawayu*, rather than *qatil* originally (so also Gordon, UT 59 §8.25). The adjective *θn* "scarlet" (UT 503-4 no. 2702) does not necessarily reflect the same pattern as Hebrew *šānî* < **θanīyu*; cf. the instances in which the syllabic transcriptions show a Ugaritic form to differ from its Hebrew cognate, noted throughout this study (see above, pp. 14-15 of the Introduction). The numeral "eight" is more difficult to explain. The various Semitic languages indicate an original form **θamāniyu*, and yet Ugaritic consistently has *θmn*, without a final *y* (UT 45 §7.16; 503b no. 2698). A possible explanation, offered with all due reservation, is that in Ugaritic, as in Akkadian (GAG §139f), numerals may normally have had no case-ending; for "eight," then, we would have *θmn* = */θamānī/ < **θamāniy*.

[116]See above, n. 92, on alphab. *bnwt* "creatures."

[117]A significant set of exceptions would appear to be the *qatāl* infinitives of verbs III-*y*, which frequently occur without final *y* in the alphabetic texts; see, e.g., Verreet, UF 17 339 with n. 126. I am unable to account for these examples if they are in fact *qatāl* forms. Perhaps, however, such examples reflect instead the pattern *qitl*, a common infinitive pattern in Ugaritic (see, e.g., below, ch. 3 §D 2 a; there is no reason not to assume that some, or even many, verbal roots in Ugaritic had more than one infinitive pattern); for roots III-*w/y*, the patterns *qityu/qitwu* became *qitû*, which appears without indication of the third radical in alphab. writing (see above, n. 93). (The form *la* in the difficult expression *la šmm* "the heavens ...-ed(?)" [KTU 1.3 v 18; 1.4 viii 22-23; 1.6 ii 25] cannot be so explained, of course, and if it is an infinitive, it must reflect */laʾâ/ < **laʾāwu*, a very unusual sound change [see Sivan, UF 16 292; Verreet, UF 16 315]. Perhaps, therefore, despite the plural subject (*/šamûma/), the form is simply suffix-cong. 3ms */laʾâ/ < **laʾawa*; cf. Rainey, IEJ 19 109.)

CHAPTER 3. MORPHOLOGY

A. Pronouns

1. *Personal*

a. Independent::

1cs *a-na-ku* = /*ʾanākŭ*/ (ʾNK)
2ms *at-ta* = /*ʾattă*/ (ʾNT)
3ms *ú-PI* = /*huwa*/ (HW).

b. Suffixal

(1cs *ia* = /*-ya*/, possibly in [*l*]*a-ša-na-ia*, if for Ugar. acc. /*lašāna-ya*/ "my tongue" in Ug. 5 153 [-Y^2; LŠN])
3ms *-ú* = /*-hŭ*/, in [l]ú*ḫa-ma-ru-ú*, lú*ḫa-*[*a*]*m-*[*r*]*u-ú* = sg. /*ǵam(a)ru-hŭ*/ "his apprentice" (-H; ǴMR).

p. 402

2. *Determinative-relative*

masc. sg. nom. *du-ú* = /*dū*/ (D)

B. Numerals

The following are the only forms attested:

[*a-ḫ*]*a-du* = /*ʾaḥadu*/ "one" (ʾḤD);
me-te = /*miʾtē*/ "two hundred" (dual bound obl.; Mʾ).

C. Nouns and Adjectives

1. *Inflection*

a. Summary of Noun and Adjective Inflectional Endings

	masculine		feminine	
	unbound	bound	unbound	bound
sg. nom.	*-u*	*-u*	*-(a)tu*	*-(a)tu*
gen.	*-i*	*-i*	*-(a)ti*	**-(a)ti*
acc.	*-a*	*-a*	*-(a)ta*	**-(a)ta*
du. nom.	**-āmi, -āma*	*-ā*	*-(a)tāmi, *-(a)tāma*	**-(a)tā*
obl.	*-ēmi, *-ēma*	**-ē*	*-(a)tēmi, *-(a)tēma*	*-(a)tē*
pl. nom.	*-ūma*	*-ū*	*-ātu*	*-ātu*
obl.	*-īma*	*-ī*	**-āti*	*-āti*

b. Mimation

As is to be expected from the evidence of the alphabetic texts, the forms in syllabic transcription do not exhibit mimation (except for */-ma/* on the masc. pl.; see below). Certain word-final signs, which in the early periods of Akkadian (OAkk., OA, OB) had values *Cvm,* were usually transliterated as such by Nougayrol, e.g., *da-ka-rum* and [*ḫ*]*u-wa-tum*. But these signs continued in use word-finally in Akkadian texts even after the loss of mimation in that language, as a traditional spelling practice, thereby acquiring values Cv_x; as indicated by both the alphabetic forms and the majority of syllabic transcriptions of Ugaritic words, written with final *Cv* signs, it is these latter values, Cv_x, that are intended in the forms in which such signs occur,[1] thus, *da-ka-rù,* [*ḫ*]*u-wa-tu*$_4$, etc.[2]

An apparent exception to the observations made above is the form *mu-qa-dì-IM,* evidently for */muqqādi/,* a biform of */maqqadu/* "grazing rights(?)" (NQD). If the form is not the result of a scribal error (read *mu-qa-dì*$^{hi.a!}$?), the indication of mimation is unexplained.

[1]So also, of course, in many examples in Akkadian words in the texts written at Ugarit. See my Akkadian of Ugarit, especially the Signlist.

[2]See also Rainey, IEJ 19 107.

c. Gender: the Markers of the Feminine Singular[3]

Two markers of the feminine singular, */-at/* and */-t/*, occur on the Ugaritic words in our corpus.

/-at/ is perforce the only allomorph found after bases ending in a consonant cluster (*CC-*) and in a long vowel plus a consonant (*v̄C-*):

(1) base in *CC-*:

um-ma-ti = */ʾummati/*? "clan(?)" (ʾMM); [*ḫ*]*u-wa-tu*$_4$ = */ḥuwwatu/* "country" (ḤWW); ITI *ḫal-la-ti/t*[*u*?] = */ḥallati/u/* (month name; ḤLL); [*ḫ*]*u-ul-ma-tu*$_4$ = */ḥulmatu/*? "strength(?)" (ḤLM); *ku-ub-ZA-ti* = */kubsati/*? "laundering(?)" (KBS b); *: ma-ad-da-DU* = */maddatu/*? "measurement" (MDD); *iš-ia-ti-mi* = */ʿišyatēmi/* "clamps(?)" (dual; ʿŠY); *ra-ba-ti* = */rabbati/* "great" (RBB); *ḫu-ul-ma-tu*$_4$ = */ǵulmatu/* "darkness(?)" (ǴLM); *ti-*[*n*]*a?-*[*t*]*u*$_4$ = */tiʾnatu/* "fig" (Tʾ N).

(2) base in *v̄C-*:

ta-a-ma-tu$_4$ = */tahāmatu/* "the deep" (THM).

When the occurrence of */-at/* is not phonologically necessary,[4] the two allomorphs occur in free variation, a situation also clearly evidenced by the alphabetic data.[5] Note, however, that in the syllabic transcriptions, at least, */-t/* is much more common than */-at/*.

(1) */-at/*:

i-r[*a?-tu*$_4$?] = */ʾiratu/*? "chest(?)" (ʾR); *ku-ku-ba-tu* = */kukkubatu/*? (KKB); note also the divine name ^{d}*a-na-tu*$_4$ = */ʿanatu/* (ʿNT), the origin and form of which are uncertain; further, *ša?-na!?-*[*t*]*u*$_4$ = */šanatu/*? "year" (ŠN).[6] p. 402

(2) */-t/*:

i-[*r*]*i?-iš-*[*tu*$_4$?] = */ʾirištu/*? "request" (ʾRŠ); ^{mí}*ba-ri-iḫ-tu*$_4$ = */bariḥtu/* "fugitive, rustic(?)" (BRḤ); *: ḫa-me-ti* = */ḥāmīti/* < **ḥāmiytu* "wall" (ḤMY);

[3]It is likely that some of the forms in syllabic transcription that do not have an overt feminine marker */-(a)t/* are nevertheless fem., e.g., */šapšu/*, */kurēku/* (see Gordon, UT 423a no. 1030, and note the pl. *ku-re-ka-a*[*t*?] = */kurēkāt/*; see under KRK). But the syntactic conditions of connected text, which permit the recognition of such forms, are lacking in the case of most of the syllabic transcriptions, which generally occur in isolation.

[4]The phonological shape of the base of a few fem. sg. words is uncertain: gen. *ḫur-ḫu-ra-ti* = */ḥurḥur(r)ati/* (ḤRḤR); fem. *pu-ru-s*[*à?-tu*$_4$?] = */pur(r)ŭsatu/*? */purussatu/*? (PRS).

[5]See Gordon, UT 52-53, §8.3. The free variation of original **-at* and **-t* also obtains in Hebrew, of course, in some instances even yielding biforms of the same word (e.g., *maṣṣēbâ* < **manṣibat-* vs. *maṣṣebet* < **manṣibt-*). In most of the other Semitic languages, the two allomorphs have generally been reduced to one, either by levelling (as in Arabic), or as the result of phonological changes (as in Akkadian, Aramaic).

[6]For *ú-*[*P*]*I!?-*[*t*]*u*$_4$ = */huwătu/*? "word" (HW^2), see below, n. 25.

perhaps dual *ḫi-nu-ta-me* = /*ḥinōtāmi*/?, sg. (with prothetic /ˀ/) ⌜*vḫ*⌝*-nu-tu*$_4$ = /ˀ*vḥnōtu*/? < **ḥinawtu*? "implement" (ḤNW); dual bound obl. *me-te* = /*miˀtē*/ "200" (Mˀ); *ma-a-al-tu*$_4$ = /*maᶜᶜaltu*/? "bolt(?)" (NᶜL); *pí-i?-*[*tu*$_4$?] = /*piˀtu*/? "corner(?)" (Pˀ); *tap-de*$_4$*-ti*, *:ta-ap-de*$_4$*-ti*, *tap-de*$_4$*-tu*$_4$ = /*tapdēti*/*u*/ < **tapdayt-* "exchange" (PDY); *qa-ri-t*[*u*$_4$] = /*qarītu*/ < **qariytu* "town" (QRY); ⌜*qa*⌝*-aš-tu*$_4$ = /*qaštu*/ "bow" (QŠ); perhaps [^{túg}*m*]*ar-de*$_4$*-tu* = /*mardētu*/? < **mardaytu*? "(garment)" (RDY); *mar-de*$_4$*-em-tu* = /*mardimtu*/? "path(?)" (RDM); *mar-kab-te* = /*markabti*/? "chariot(?)" (RKB); *ša-i-tu*$_4$ = /*θāᶜītu*/ < **θāᶜiytu* or /*θāᶜittu*/ < **θāᶜidtu* "(vessel)" (θᶜY/θᶜD);[7] note also two forms ending in /*-vrtu*/ < **-ratu*: *i-zi-ir-*[*tu*$_4$?] = /ᶜ*iðirtu*/ (= [ᶜiðr̥tu]?) < *ᶜ*iðratu* "help" (ᶜðR); ^{túg}*šá-ḫar-tu* = /*šaᶜartu*/ (= [šaᶜr̥tu]?) < **śaᶜratu* "wool" (ŠᶜR b).

The form ⌜*i*⌝*-ši-t*[*u*$_4$] "fire" (ˀŠ) is uncertain; since the PS base of "fire" was simply *ˀ*iš-*, the most likely possibility is that ⌜*i*⌝*-ši-t*[*u*$_4$] represents a form with a suffix **-īt*, i.e., /ˀ*išītu*/.[8]

For the form of the fem. pl., see the next section.

d. Number

(1) Masculine plurals

nominative	/*-ūma*/,	bound form	/*-ū*/
oblique	/*-īma*/,	bound form	/*-ī*/

(a) nominative unbound forms:

☛ p. 402

$^{\text{(túg.meš)}}$*ma-za-ru-ma* = /*maˀzarūma*/? "loincloths(?)" (ˀZR); *ba-a-lu-ma* = /*baᶜ(a)lūma*/ "lord" (BᶜL); *ḫé-PI-ma* and *ḫi-*[*i*]*u?-ma* = /*ḥiyyūma*/ "life" (ḤYY¹/ḤWY¹ b); $^{\text{(lú)}}$*ia-ṣí-ru-ma* = /*yāṣirūma*/ "potters" (YṢR); $^{\text{túg.meš}}$*mu-ru-ú-ma*^{meš} = /*mōruˀūma*/? "(garments)" (YRˀ); ^{dug}*ka-du-ma*^{meš} = /*kaddūma*/ "jars" (KDD); *ma-a-du-ma* = /*maˀ(a)dūma*/ "much, many" (MˀD); ^{lú}*mu-du-ma* = /*mūdûma*/ "courtiers(?)" (MD); $^{\text{[urudu.meš]}}$*me-ḫi-*[*ṣ*]*u-*⌜*ma*⌝^{meš} = /*miḫīṣūma*/ "(implements)" (MḪṢ b); ^{lú}*mur-ú-ma* = /*murˀūma*/ "commanders(?)" (MRˀ); ^{lú}*mar-ia-nu-ma* = /*maryannūma*/ "charioteers" (MRYN); *ma-qa-bu-ma* $^{\text{(meš)}}$ = /*maqqabūma*/ "hammers" (NQB); ⌜*na*⌝*-*[*š*]*u-*⌜*ma*⌝ = /*našūma*/ "people" (NŠ); ^{túg}⌜*ZU*/*SU?-ku?-ma*^{meš}⌝ = /*sukkūma*/? "(garments)" (SKK); $^{\text{urudu.meš}}$*ma-ṣa-du-ma*^{meš} = /*maᶜṣadūma*/ "adzes(?)" (ᶜṢD); $^{\text{lú(.meš)}}$*a-ši-ru-ma* = /ᶜ*ăšīrūma*/ "(officials)" (ᶜŠR¹); [*ḫ*]*a-ma-ru-*

[7]Probably also the sg. forms written *ni-ˀ-tu*: i.e., *ni-iˀ-tu* = /*niˀtu*/ (not *ni-ˀa-tu* = /*niˀatu*/; see Nˀ); cf. the alphab. *nit*. Plural forms are probably to be read *ni-ˀa-tu* = /*niˀātu*/.

[8]See the commentary on Sᵃ Voc. no. 48.1 in Part I.

m[*a*$^{(meš)}$] and $^{lú.meš}$*ḫa-am-ru-ma*^{meš} = /*ǵam(a)rūma*/ "apprentices" (ǴMR); ^{túg}*pa-li-du-ma* = /*palĭdūma*/ "(garments)" (PLD); *qà-da-ru-ma*^{meš} = /*qad(d)arūma*/ "(containers)" (QDR); *ša-mu-ma* = /*šamûma*/ < **šamayūma* "sky" (ŠMY); *ma-áš-ḫa-ṭu-ma* = /*maθḫaṭūma*/ "(cloths)" (θḪṬ); ^{giš}*šá*-[*ḫ*]*a*!?-⌜*ru*?⌝-*ma* = /*θaǵarūma*/? "door-leaves(?)" (θǴR); *lu-ḫu-ma* = /?/ (see Appendix to Glossary).

(b) nominative bound forms:

$^{lú.meš}$*b*[*i*]-*ḫi-ru* = /*biḥīrū*/? "elite (troops)" (BḤR[1]); $^{lú(.meš)}$*mur-ú* = /*murʾū*/ "commanders(?)" (MRʾ); $^{lú(.meš)}$*mar-ia-nu* = /*maryannū*/ "charioteers" (MRYN). p. 402

(c) oblique unbound forms:

: *dì-ip-ra-ni-ma* = /*diprānīma*/ "junipers" (DPR); *ḫa-ba-li-ma* = /*ḥabalīma*/ "ropes, lots" (ḤBL); : *ḫé-yi-ma* = /*ḫīyīma*/ "vacant(?)" (ḪWY); $^{lú.meš}$*a-ši-ri-ma* = /*ʿăšĭrīma*/ "(officials)" (ʿŠR[1]); *ZI-GA*/*QA-ni-ma* = /*sikānīma*/? "statues(?)" (SKN b); *a-ra-mi-ma* = /?/ and :*ZI-ZA-ḫal-li-ma* = /?/ (see Appendix to Glossary).

(d)oblique bound forms:

$^{lú.meš}$*mur-i* = /*murʾī*/ "commanders(?)" (MRʾ); $^{lú.meš}$*mar-ia-an-ni* = /*maryannī*/ "charioteers" (MRYN); perhaps also the suffixal form : *ḫi-i-yi*(-*šu*), if pl., = /*ḫīyī*/, but the form may be sg. /*ḫīyi*/ ("vacant(?)"; ḪWY).

In addition to the above, note also the unique form $^{[lú.m]eš}$*bi-da-lu-na* = /*bidălūna*/ "merchants" with which compare the normative : *bi-da-lu-ma* = /*bidălūma*/ (BDL). The former is associated by Dietrich-Loretz-Sanmartín, UF 5 90-91, with the alphab. form *kšmn* "emmer" (KTU 4.269:4). It seems likely that we are dealing in both of these forms with dialectal biforms of the external masc. plural morpheme, /*-ūna, -īna*/,[9] attested in several first-millennium NWS dialects;[10] given the rare occurrence of the biform, it undoubtedly reflects the dialect(s) of individuals not native to the city of Ugarit, and should not be considered normative.[11]

[9]A Hurrian pl. ending, suggested by Alt, WO 2 342, seems unlikely.

[10]See, e.g., Harris, Development 9; Garr, Dialect Geography 89-91.

[11]The writing *na-ba-ki-mi* for expected pl. /*nabakīma*/ (cf. the several examples of :*NAB*/*na-AB-ki-ma*) is probably simply a scribal error (-*mi* for -*ma*); less likely, a dual /*nabakēmi*/ formed on the plural base /*nabak-*/.

(2) Feminine plurals[12]

nominative (unbound and bound) */-ātu/*
oblique (unbound and bound) */-āti/*.

(a) nominative unbound forms:

perhaps ^{urudu}*ul-ma-tu* = */hulmātu/*? "hammers(?)" (HLM); [*k*]*a-ma-ʾa-tu* = */kamaʾātu/* "truffles(?)" (KMʾ); : *ka-ar-ba-tù*[= */karbātu/*? "twisted(?)" (KRB); $^{\text{giš(.meš)}}$*ma-ás/sa-wa-tu* = */mas(a)wātu/* "cypress(?) logs" (MSW); ^{túg}*ú-ra-tu* = */ᶜōrātu/* "hides(?)" (ᶜWR).[13]

(b) oblique unbound forms:

no examples.

For bound forms, see under f, below.

(3) Dual forms

nominative */-āma/* and */-āmi/*, bound form */-ā/*
oblique */-ēmi/*, bound form */-ē/*.

☛ p. 402

The */a/* of allomorph with */-āma/* (and presumably also unattested oblique */*-ēma/*) is of course unexpected on basis of Arabic *-āni/-ayni*, but is attested in syllabic transcriptions of NWS dual forms in other Akkadian text corpora (see Sivan, Analysis 111-12). If the forms with final */-mi/* and the Arabic endings reflect the shape of allomorph inherited from P(NW)S, we may suggest that the innovative Ugar. and other NWS forms with final */-ma/* arose via an analogy with masc. pl. forms, based on the bound forms, viz:

/-ū/, /-ī/ : */-ā/, /-ē/* :: */-ūma/, /-īma/* : *X* = */-āma/, /-ēma/*.

(a) nominative unbound forms:

/-āma/: probably 2 *ku-re-ka-m*[*a*?] = */kurēkāma/*? "(implements)" (KRK);
probably *ma-aš-la-ḫa-ma* = */mašlaḥāma/* "(garments)" (ŠLḤ);
note also 2 [(*x-*)?]⌜*x*⌝-*DI*-⌜*na-ma*⌝ (see Appendix to Glossary, end).

[12]It should be noted that these endings are identical with those of the contemporary Akk. dialect (of MB/MA in general, and of Ugarit in particular), so that the actual Ugar. endings may not be isolated absolutely.

[13]See also n. 7 above.

/-āmi/: probably 2 *ḫi-nu-ta-me* = */ḥinōtāmi/*? "implements" (ḤNW).

(b) nominative bound forms:

ma-qa-ḫa = */maqqaḥā/* < **malqaḥā* "tongs" (LQḤ b).

(c) oblique unbound forms:

/-ēmi/: probably fem. *iš-ia-ti-mi* = */ᶜišyatēmi/* "clamps(?)" (ᶜŠY); possibly also *na-ba-KI-mi,* if for */nabakēmi/*, a dual formed on the pl. base */nabak-/*, although a scribal error for the oft-attested pl. */nab(a)kīma/* is more likely; also, *mar-kab-te*[, if "chariot" is intended (broken context), may be dual */markabtē*[*mi*]*/*, or bound */markabtē/* (RKB).

(d) oblique bound forms:

fem. *me-te* = */miʾtē/* "200" (Mʾ).

The rarity of the dual in our corpus of forms stems in part from the fact that it was not necessarily used after the numeral "2"; rather, the plural follows "2" in several instances:[14] see the Glossary under ʾZR, YRʾ, ḪRMθ, ᶜWR, ṢWᶜ, QDR, QṬN.

e. Case

(1) Triptotic singulars

As expected, the vast majority of sg. Ugar. nouns in syllabic transcription exhibit three case-endings: nom. */-u/*, gen. */-i/*, acc. */-a/*. Since these endings, when they occur on unbound forms, correspond exactly with those of the contemporary dialect of the Akkadian texts in which they occur (MB/MA, Ugarit Akk.), however, we may not isolate them as a specifically Ugaritic morphological feature.

(2) Diptotic singulars

Two forms exhibit genitives in */-a/*, i.e., are diptotic: *(:) sí-il-a* = */silᶜa/* "cliff(?)" (SLᶜ); and ⁽ⁱᵈ⁾*(:) ra-aḫ-ba/bá-na* = */raḥbāna/* "wide place," which occurs along with ⁽ⁱᵈ⁾*ra-aḫ-ba/bá-ni* (note both ⁱᵈ*ra-aḫ-bá-ni/na* in PRU 3 72f.:8,11). As noted by Liverani, RSO 38 131-60, diptotic endings (genitive in */-a/*) are common on proper nouns in the Ugarit Akkadian texts, especially on forms in */-ān/*.

[14]See Sivan, Analysis 112-13.

(3) A very small number of examples are written without case-endings:[15]

The form ^{d}*ma-lik*^{meš} in the "Ugarit Pantheon" list Ug. 5 18 is apparently the result of scribal caprice in which the pl. morpheme (*/-ūma/*; cf. alphabetic *mlkm*) is indicated with the plural determinative ^{meš} rather than syllabically.[16] The writing *ni-it* for expected */niʾtu/*, which contrasts with *ni-iʾ-tu* in other texts, may be intended to reflect the absolute form of Akkadian; it occurs in a text (Ug. 5 84:13) that also attests one of the few bound forms without a case ending (*ma-ar-ḫi-iš*, line 10). For the latter, see the end of the next section.

f. The Bound Form of the Singular and the Feminine Plural

Corroborating the alphabetic evidence provided by words ending in /ʾ/, for which three signs were available to distinguish the appropriate vowel,[17] the syllabic transcriptions show clearly that the short case-vowels of the sg. and of the fem. pl. were retained in the bound form, contrary to the situation in Akkadian, where the ending of bound forms was determined not by case but by the phonological shape of the base:[18]

(acc.) *ú-nu-ša* É^{meš} "tax on the estate" (ʾNθ);
(fem. pl. nom.) *2* ^{urudu}*ḫa-ar-me-ša-tu* ^{giš}MÁ^{meš} "2 marine 'sickles(?)'" (ḪRMθ);
(gen.) *: ḫa-at-ni* PN "PN's father-in-law" (ḪTN);
(fem. pl. obl.) *ku-bu-da-ti* LUGAL "honoring-gifts for the king" (KBD b);
(acc.) *x ka₄-ka₄-ra* GUŠKIN/KÙ.BABBAR-*pí* "x talents of gold/silver"[19]

[15]Note also the pseudo-logogram MA.KAD, vs. *: ma-aq-qa-du* = */maqqadu/* (NQD).

[16]For other forms in this list, some of them possibly Ugaritic, like ^{d}*da-gan*, also without a case-vowel, see the Introduction, p. 10.

[17]See G. Tuttle, "Case Vowels" 253-68. A contrary conclusion concerning the significance of the three alephs at the end of bound forms is reached by Z. Zevit, JSS 28 225-32. Zevit suggests, on the basis of exceptions to the rule, "that no case endings were indicated in the juncture between a noun in status constructus and its following genitive" (229); rather, the appearance of the various alephs is the result of conflicting orthographic conventions. I find Zevit's arguments unconvincing; the exceptions are very few in number, and some of them are probably not exceptions (*mri* in KTU 1.22 i 13 is probably a scribal error, as shown by the corrected *mria* in 1.4 vi 41; I would take *ṣbu* in 1.14 ii 33 as nominative); the personal names mentioned by Zevit, 230-31 and n. 15, as has been maintained throughout this study, should not be compared with the contemporary local language (in any event, some of the names cited by Zevit may be explained in other ways: for **kunap-ili*, read probably */kūna-pī-ʾili/*; sandhi in the case of *bi-DI-ʾi-lu* [Qadeš]; diverse dialects; etc.). Finally, an appeal to variant orthographic practices only for word-final items seems forced. (Although their dates of publication would indicate otherwise, the JCS 33 [1981] article cited below and Zevit's [1983] appeared at roughly the same time, so that neither writer had access to the other's results.)

[18]Note also the PN (or title?) nom. ^{f}*a-ḫa-tu₄*(-)LUGAL, gen. ^{f}*a-ḫa-ti*(-)LUGAL "king's-sister" (ʾḪ).

[19]These examples, and *1* GUN (= Akk. *bilta* or Ugar. */kakkara/*) KÙ.BABBAR-*pí* ... *i-din* "he

(KKR);

(nom.) *la-ša-nu* UR.GI$_7$ "hound's tongue" (LŠN);

(fem. nom.) *: ma-ad-da-tù* É *: ku-na-ḫi* "the measurement of a/the *kunaḫi*-house" (MDD);

(nom.) ⌜^{lú}⌝*ma-ḫi-ṣu ub-x*["a */māḫiṣu/* of x(?)" (MḪṢ a);

(nom.) ^{lú}*mur-ú* ^{1}*i-bi-ra-na* "commander(?) of ᵓIbīrānu" (MRᵓ; sg. in PRU 6 93:16);

(fem. sg. nom.) *1 ni-iᵓ-*⌜*tu* ŠU⌝^{meš} and (pl. nom.) *5* $^{\text{urudu.meš}}$*ni-ᵓa-tu* ŠU^{meš} "1 (5) hand-*/niᵓtu/*('s)" (Nᵓ);

(gen.) *ma-ba-ri* GN "the pass of/at GN" (ᶜBR);

(fem. nom.) *tap-de$_4$-tu$_4$* A.ŠÀ^{meš} "exchange of field" (PDY); the acc. forms *(:) tap/ta-ap-de$_4$-ti* A.ŠÀ, where **/tapdēta/* is expected, are apparently the result of sandhi with the following *eqli*;

(fem. pl. nom.) *2* $^{\text{giš.meš}}$*ṣa-ᵓa-tu* É "two wooden bowls for the house" (ṢWᶜ).

Note also the following writings, in which the nom. case-ending is indicated before a pronominal suffix: $^{\text{[l]ú}}$*ḫa-ma-ru-ú*, ^{lú}*ḫa-*[*a*]*m-*[*r*]*u-ú* = sg. */ǵam(a)ru-hū̆/* "his apprentice(s)" (-H; ǴMR). Further, perhaps, [*l*]*a-ša-na-ia* in Ug. 5 153, if for Ugar. acc. */lašāna-ya/* "my tongue" (-Y^{1}; LŠN).

Only four bound forms without a case-ending occur; in view of the much larger set of forms that do bear a case-ending, these few examples must be viewed as imitating Akkadian practice (see §G 2, on Akkadianized forms):

A.ŠÀ^{meš} $^{(1)}$*al-la-an* (-)$^{(1)}$*še-er/ri-DA/TA(-an)-ni* "fields of 'the oak-of-Šer(i)dannu'" (ᵓLN);

ku-re-ka-a[*t*?] ⌜*x*⌝*-ṣi* "(implements for ...)" (KRK);

2 ^{urudu}*ma-am-ṣa-ar bu-li* "2 animal knives(?)" (MṢR);

1 mar-ḫi-iš iš-ia-ti-mi "1 pan(?) with clamps(?)" (RḪŠ).

Note, finally, that many Akkadian words in the Ugarit texts also bear a case-ending when in the bound form, both before a genitive noun and before a pronominal suffix; these case-endings are, as noted above, at variance with normative Akkadian grammar, and undoubtedly reflect the underlying Ugar. dialect of the scribes.[20]

---

gave ... 1 talent of silver" PRU 3 54a:17-19, indicate that the construction involving number, measure, and thing measured differed in Ugaritic from its counterpart in Akkadian. In Akkadian, the measure is normally in the absolute state, while the thing measured derives its case from context: e.g., *1 bilat kaspa* for acc. "1 talent of silver"; see von Soden, GAG §62d. In Ugaritic, however, at least in these few examples, the measure derives its case from context, and is bound to the thing measured, which is therefore always genitive: (acc.) *1 kakkara kaspi*. See JCS 33 205.

[20] See JCS 33 199-205.

2. *Patterns*

In the lists below, forms appear under the assumed *singular*, whether attested or not, according to their synchronic Ugaritic shape rather than their (probable) PNWS form (e.g., *qatalūma* plurals of *qatl* forms appear under *qatl*; /*šiʿīru*/ < **šaʿīru* appears under *qitīl* rather than *qatīl*).[21] Fem. forms with /-*t*/ or /-*at*/ and forms with afformatives (such as /-*ān*/ and /-*īy*/) are listed under the corresponding form without ending (the latter also in special sections, however; see m - o, below, pp. 315-16).

a. *qv̆l*

☛ p. 402

qal :[22] probably *a-da-nu* = /*ʾadānu*/ < PS **ʾad* + -*ān*[23] "father" (ʾDN);
(^{f}*a-ḫa-tu*$_4$/*ti-* = /*ʾaḫātu*/ "sister" [probably in PN; ʾḪ]);
pl. ⸢*na*⸣-[*š*]*u*-⸢*ma*⸣ = /*našūma*/ "people" (NŠ);
fem. ⸢*qa*⸣-*aš-tu*$_4$ = /*qaštu*/ "bow" (QŠ);
fem. *ša*?-*na*!?-[*t*]*u*$_4$ = /*šanatu*/? "year" (ŠN).

qil: ⸢*i*?-*lu*?⸣ = /*ʾilu*/ "god" (ʾL);
fem. *i-r*[*a*?-*tu*$_4$?] = /*ʾiratu*/? "chest(?)" (ʾR);
fem. dual bound obl. *me-te* = /*miʾtē*/ "200" (Mʾ);
fem. *ni-iʾ*/*ʾa-tu* = /*niʾtu*/, pl. /*niʾātu*/ "(utensil)" (Nʾ);
fem. *pí-i*?[-*tu*$_4$?] = /*piʾtu*/? "corner(?)" (Pʾ);
note also the difficult form ⸢*i*⸣-*ši-t*[*u*$_4$] = /*ʾišītu*/? "fire," apparently PS **ʾiš*- with an ending /-*īt*/ (ʾŠ).[24]

qul: only *qul* < *qal*, in fem. *ú*-[*w*]*a*!?-[*t*]*u*$_4$ = /*huwătu*/ < **hawătu*?[25] "word"

[21] It should go without saying that the classification of many forms is nevertheless based in large part on comparative Semitic evidence.

[22] Note also *da-mu* in Ug. 5 153, if for Ugar. /*damu*/ "blood" (DM). See also below, under *qul*.

[23] See the commentary on Sª Voc. no. 24.3, with n. 2 there.

[24] For *iṣ-ṣú*["wood," for which sg. */*ʿiṣu*/ is expected, read probably pl. *iṣ-ṣú-*[*ma*] = /*ʿiṣṣūma*/, listed under *qitl*, under c below.

[25] The form must be compared with its only cognate, Akk. *awătum*, the shape of which is disputed (von Soden: *awātum*; CAD: *awatum*; Goetze, Or. 16 244-45: *āwatum*). It seems likely that the base of the word for "word" was originally biradical, **haw* (the Akk. verb *awûm* is probably denominative, as suggested by von Soden, AHw 91a), and that biforms existed already in PS: a form with the common fem. marker *-*at*, i.e., **haw-at-* (cf. e.g., **ʾam-at-* "female slave"), and a form with an alternate fem. sg. ending, *-*āt*, i.e., **haw-āt-*; the latter ending appears on a few other fem. sg. forms of biradical roots, e.g., **ʾaḫāt* "sister," **ḥam-āt* "mother-in-law," **ʾiš-āt* "fire" (though not in Ugar.; see under *qil* above); for the latter, see Blau, IOS 2 62-65; in general, Brockelmann, Grundriss 1 409-10.

(HW²).[26]

b. *qv̄l*

qāl: gen. *: ḫa-a-yi* = /*ḫāyi*/ "vacant(?)" (ḪWY; see also under *qīl*); p. 402
ṭa-bu = /*ṭābu*/ "sweet" (ṬW/YB);
na-du = /*nādu*/ "stela(?)" (loanword; ND);
gen. *(:) ṣa(-a)-i* = /*ṣāᶜi*/, pl. ^giš.meš^*ṣa-ʾa-tu* = /*ṣāᶜātu*/ "bowl, basin" (ṢWᶜ).

qēl[27] < **qayl*: *e-bu* = /*ʾēbu*/ (originally *qatil*) "enemy" (ʾYB);
ḫé-qu = /*ḥēqu*/ < **ḥayq-* "lap" (ḤYQ);
perhaps *ḫe?-e[-ru]* = /*ḥēru*/? < **ḥayr-*? "enclosure(?)" (ḤYR);
ḫé/ḫe-bu = /*ḫēbu*/? < *ḫayb-*? "shame(?)" (ḪYB);
also *e-*⌜*nu*?⌝ in Ug. 5 153, if = Ugar. /*ᶜēnu*/ < **ᶜayn-* "eye(?)" (ᶜYN).[28]

qīl: *ši-i-ru* = /*šīru*/ "song" (ŠYR);
ši-tu = /*šītu*/ "to place" (ŠYT);[29]
perhaps also *TI-ru* in Ug. 5 153, if for Ugar. /*dīru*/ "foul(?)" (DYR);
note also [qēl] = *qīl* < *qāl* in *ḫe-e-yu*, acc. *ḫe-e-ia* [ḫēyv], gen. *:ḫi-i-yi(-šu)* = /*ḫīyv*/, pl. obl. *:ḫé-yi-ma* = [ḫēyīma] "vacant(?)" (ḪWY; see also under *qāl*).[30]

qōl < **qawl*: *PI-mu* = /*yōmu*/ < **yawm-* "day" (less likely, /*yămu*/; YWM);
gen. *: ḫu-li* = /*ǵōli*/? < **ǵawl-* "low ground(?)" (ǴWL);
probably ^túg^*ú-ra-tu* = /*ᶜōrātu*/ < **ᶜawr-* "hides(?)" (note also the sg. [*ú*?]-*ru*; ᶜWR);
*/*tōku*/ < **tawk-*, in gen. *tu-ki-ii* = /*tōkīyi*/ "inner" (TWK).

qūl: perhaps *ú-lu* = /*ᶜūlu*/? "young (animal)(?)" (ᶜWL).[31]

[26]Another possible example is the unidentified (adj.?) *lu-ḫu-ma* (see Appendix to Glossary); but it seems more likely that the form is II-*w* or geminate.

[27]For [qēl], see also under *qīl*, below.

[28]Note also *NI-r[u]* "lamp(?)" and *: ZI-ṣú(-ú)-ma* "salt fields" for either *qēl* < **qayl* forms /*nēru*/ and /*ṣēṣūma*/ or *qīl* forms /*nīru*/ and /*ṣīṣūma*/ (NW/YR; ṢYṢ).

[29]Both /*šīru*/ and /*šītu*/, of course, may also be considered *qitl* forms of roots II-*y*; another possible, albeit unlikely, example, but from II-*y*, is *mi-ti(-šu-nu)*, if the form is Ugar. /*mītī*/? (MWT). See also the preceding note.

[30]These forms result from the assimilation of **ā* to /*ī*/ before /*y*/; see ch. 2 §A 1 e, pp. 275-77.

[31]Note also the unidentified forms *lu-ḫu-ma* (pl.) and *: ú-ṭu*, which may reflect either II-*w* or geminate roots; see the Appendix to the Glossary.

c. *qvtl*

qatl, pl. base *qatal* and, with pretonic syncope,[32] *qatl*:

(1) Sound roots:[33]

gen. : *ad-ma-ni* = /*ʾadmāni*/ "red (soil)" (ʾDM);
ar-zu = /*ʾarzu*/ "cedar" ; note also perhaps pl. *ar-zi-ma* in Ug. 5 153, if for Ugar. /*ʾarzīma*/ < **ʾarazīma* (ʾRZ);
ar-ṣu = /*ʾarṣu*/ "earth" (ʾRṢ);
ba-a-lu = /*baʿlu*/ "lord," pl. *ba-a-lu-ma* = /*baʿalūma*/ or /*baʿlūma*/[34] (BʿL);
da-ab-ḫu = /*dabḥu*/ "sacrifice" (DBḤ);
perhaps *TAR-QU* = /*darqu*/? "path" (DRQ);
(*/*ḥablu*/?, in) pl. obl. *ḫa-ba-li-ma* = /*ḥabalīma*/ "ropes, lots" (ḤBL);
gen. *ḫa-ar-ma-ni* = /*ḥarmāni*/ "sacred place(?)" (ḤRM b);
perhaps gen. : *ḫa-at-ni* = /*ḫatni*/ (unless Akkadianized form;[35] ḪTN);
gen. *ia-ar-qa-ni* = /*yarqāni*/ "yellow-green" (YRQ);
(*/*kamʾ(at)u*/?, in) pl. [*k*]*a-ma-ʾa-tu* = /*kamaʾātu*/? "truffles(?)" (KMʾ);
kàs-pu and *ka-as-p*[*u*] = /*kaspu*/ "silver" (KSP);
(*/*maʾdu*/?, in) pl. *ma-a-du-ma* = /*maʾadūma*/ or /*maʾdūma*/[36] (MʾD);
ma-al-ku = /*malku*/ "king" (MLK b);
NAB-ku = /*nabku*/ [napku], pl. obl. *(:) NAB/na-AB/ba/bá-ki-ma/mi* = /*nabakīma*/ and /*nabkīma*/ (NBK);
☛ p. 402
$^{\text{(túg)}}$*na-AG?-TU/*TU_4 = /*nagdu*/? "(a linen garment)" (NGD);
sà/sa-ap-lu = /*saplu*/? "cauldron" (SPL);
ab-du = /*ʿabdu*/ "slave" (ʿBD);
acc. : *am-qa* = /*ʿamqa*/ "stronghold(?)" ($ʿMQ^1$);
[*q*]*à?-ar-ṣú?* = /*qarṣu*/? "piece(?)" (QRṢ);
gen. $^{\text{(íd)}}$*(:) ra-aḫ-ba/bá-ni/na* = /*raḥbāni/a*/ "wide place" (RḤB);
perhaps *rap-*⌜*ú?*⌝[= /*rapʾu*/ "purification(?)" (RPʾ);
šap-ḫu = /*šapḥu*/ "sprout, scion" (ŠPḤ);
ša-ap-šu = /*šapšu*/ "sun (god)" (ŠPŠ);
gen. : *TA-am-GI* = /*tamki*/? "?" (TMK);
(*/*θalθu*/, in) pl. *ša-al-šu-ma* = /*θalθūma*/? "copper" (θLθ);
perhaps (*/*θaǵru*/, in) pl. ^{giš}*šá-*[*ḫ*]*a!?-*⌜*ru?*⌝*-ma* = /*θaǵarūma*/? "door-leaves(?)" (θǴR).

[32]See ch. 2 §B 1, pp. 280-82.

[33]For III-*r* /*šaʿartu*/ < **śaʿrat-*, see d below, under *qatal*.

[34]See p. 282 n. 68.

[35]See the Glossary under ḪTN, and below, §G 2.

[36]See p. 282 n. 68.

(2) Geminate and II-*n* (*qall*):

ap-pu = /*ʾappu*/ < **ʾanpu* "nose" (ʾNP);
da-al!?-⸢*lu*⸣ = /*dallu*/ "poor" (DLL);
d[*a*]-*aq*!?-*qú* = /*daqqu*/? "small(?)" (DQQ);
fem. ITI *ḫal-la-ti*/*t*[*u*?] = /*ḥallati*/*u*/ (month name; ḤLL);
⸢*ka*⸣-*dú* = /*kaddu*/? and pl. ^{dug}*ka-du-ma*^{meš} = /*kaddūma*/ "jar(s)" (KDD);
fem. *: ma-ad-da-DU* = /*maddatu*/? "measurement" (MDD);
sar-rù = /*sarru*/ "false" (SRR);
qal-lu and (acc.!) *qá-al-lu* = /*qallu*/? "small" (QLL);
GAL-*bu*,]*ra-bu* = /*rabbu*/? and fem. gen. *ra-ba-ti* = /*rabbati*/ "great" (RBB);
perhaps pl. obl. *ša-ri-ma* = /*θarrīma*/? "small(?)" (θRR).[37]

(3) II-*w*: **qawl* > *qōl*, listed above under b.

(4) II-*y*: **qayl* > *qēl*, listed above under b.

(5) III-*w*:

(fem. */*maswatu*/, in) pl. $^{\text{giš(.meš)}}$*ma-ás*/*sa-wa-tu* = /*masawātu*/ and /*maswātu*/ "cypress(?) logs" (MSW)).

(6) III-*y*:

no examples.

qitl: (1) Sound roots:[38]

perhaps *IG-TU*$_4$ = /*ʾiktu*/? "mortar" (ʾKT);
iš-du$_4$ = /*ʾišdu*/ "leg" (ʾŠD);
[*bi*?]-*ir*?-*ku* = /*birku*/? "knee(?)" (BRK);
pl. obl. *: dì-ip-ra-ni-ma* = /*diprānīma*/ "junipers" (DPR);
ni-iḫ-rù = /*niǵru*/ "to guard" (NǴR b);
gen. *(:) sí-il-a* = /*silʿa*/ "cliff(?)" (SLʿ);
pí-iṭ-r[*ù*?] = /*piṭru*/ "to loosen" (PṬR a); p. 402
[$^{\text{é?}}$]⸢*qi*?-*id*?-*šu*?⸣ and *qi-i*[*d-šu*?] = /*qidšu*/ "sanctuary" (QDŠ b);
ri-i[*g*]-*lu* = /*riglu*/ "foot" (RGL);
⸢*ši-i-ru*⸣ = /*šiʾru*/ "flesh" (ŠʾR);
fem. *ti*-[*n*]*a*?-[*t*]*u*$_4$ = /*tiʾnatu*/ "fig" (TʾN);
ti-ib-nu = /*tibnu*/ "straw" (TBN).[39]

[37]Note also unidentified fem. gen. *am-ma-ti*; *ḫa-AB-BU* and gen. *: ḫa-A*[*B-B*]*I*; see the Appendix to the Glossary.

[38]See also below d, under *qitil-t*, for III-*r* /*ʿiðirtu*/.

[39]Note further ^{túg}*IB-lu* GAL^{meš} and *i*[*r*]-*KU*, for which see the Appendix to the Glossary; also *qi-i-lu* which may reflect a *qitl* form /*qiʿlu*/, although a *qitil* (< **qatil*) form /*qiʿilu*/ is more likely

(2) Geminate (*qill*):

pl. *ḫi-[i]u?-ma* and *ḫé-yu-ma* = /*ḥiyyūma*/ < **ḥayyūma*[40] "life" (ḤYY^1/ḤWY^1 b);

(note probably the pl. *iṣ-ṣú-[ma?]* = /*ᶜiṣṣūma*/? vs. unattested sg. *qil* form */*ᶜiṣu*/? (ᶜṢ));

pí-rù = /*pirru*/? "flight(?), separation(?)" (PRR).

(3) II-*y*:

see b above, under *qil*.

(4) III-*w*:

perhaps *i-pu-ú* = /*ᶜipû*/? < **ᶜipwu*? "destruction(?)" (ᶜPW).

(5) III-*y*:

perhaps fem. dual obl. *iš-ia-ti-mi* = /*ᶜišyatēmi*/? (ᶜŠY);

ṣi-il-PI[= fem. /*ṣilyatu*/?, less likely masc. /*ṣilyu*/?, "curse" (ṢLY).

qutl: (1) Sound roots:[41]

gen. *uḫ-ra-a-yi* = /*ʾuḫrāyi*/ "destiny" (ʾḪR);

$^{giš.meš}$*úr-nu* = /*ʾurnŭ*/ "laurel(?)" (ʾRN);

perhaps pl. ^{urudu}*ul-ma-tu* = /*hulmātu*/? < **hulamātu* "hammers" (possibly sg. /*hulmatu*/ intended; HLM);

fem. [*ḫ*]*u-ul-ma-tu*$_4$ = /*ḥulmatu*/? "strength(?)" (ḤLM);

fem. gen. *ku-ub-ZA-ti* = /*kubsati*/? "laundering(?)" (KBS b);

perhaps (pl. cst.) $^{lú.meš}$*GU-um-[ru?(-šu?)]* = /*kumrū*/? "(priests)" (KMR);

$^{túg.me}$*ku-up-šu* = /*kupθu*/? "(a headdress)" (KPθ);

^{lú}*mur-ú*, pl. $^{lú.meš}$*mur-ú-ma*, etc., = /*murʾu*/ pl. /*murʾūma*/ < **muraʾūma*? "commander(s)" (MRʾ);

☛ p. 402 :!? *su-nu* = /*suʾnu*/? "hem" (SʾN);

fem. *ḫu-ul-ma-tu*$_4$ = /*ġulmatu*/ "darkness(?)" (ĠLM);

pl.(?) ^{giš}*šu-uq-du(-)ma* = /*θuqdūma*/? "almonds" (θQD).

(2) Geminate (*qull*):

fem. gen. *um-ma-ti* = /*ʾummati*/? "clan(?)" (ʾMM);

gen. *bu-ri* = /*burri*/? "(a bright metal?)" (BRR);

fem. [*ḫ*]*u-wa-tu*$_4$ = /*ḥuwwatu*/ < **ḥawwatu*[42] "country" (ḤWW);

(QᶜL).

[40]See ch. 2 §A 1 e, pp. 275-77.

[41]Note also the noun /*ʾuθrīyānu*/, for which see the Glossary under ʾθRYN.

[42]See ch. 2 §A 1 e, pp. 275-77.

fem.(?)/pl.(?) *ḫu-up-pa-ti* = /*ḫuppăti*/ "shore(s)(?)" (ḪPP);
pl. ^{túg}⌜*ZU/SU?-ku?-ma*^{meš}⌝ = /*sukkūma*/? "(garments)" (SKK).[43]

(3) III-*w*:

: *ZU-ur-PI* = /*ẓurwu*/? (or /*ṣurwu*/?) "(aromatic) resin" (ẒRW).

d. *qv̆t(t)v̆l*[44]

qat(t)ăl:

(1) *qatal*:[45]

probably (numeral) [*a-ḫ*]*a-du* = /*ʾaḥadu*/[46] "one" (ʾḤD);
probably *ba-TA-lu* = /*baṭalu*/? "false(hood)(?)" (BṬL);
ga-ša-ru = /*gaθaru*/ "strong" (divine name; GθR);
da-ka-rù = /*dakaru*/ "male" (DKR1);
[*ka-n*]*a-pu* = /*kanapu*/? "wing(?)" (KNP a);
la-ba-nu = /*labanu*/ "white" (LBN1);
perhaps gen. *na-ḫa-li* = /*naḫali*/? (or /*naḫalli*/?) "wadi" (NḪL);
(divine name ^{d}*a-na-tu*$_4$ = /*ᶜanatu*/ (ᶜNT));
sg. $^{\text{[l]ú}}$*ḫa-ma-ru-ú* = /*ǵamaru-hŭ*/ and, with post-tonic syncope,[47] ^{lú}*ḫa-*[*a*]*m-*[*r*]*u-ú*, ^{lú}*ḫa-am-ru<-šu>-nu* = /*ǵamru(-hŭ)*/ "his(/their) apprentice"; pl. [*ḫ*]*a-ma-ru-m*[*a*$^{\text{(meš)}}$] = /*ǵamarūma*/ and, with pretonic syncope,[48] $^{\text{lú.meš}}$*ḫa-am-ru-ma*^{meš} = /*ǵamrūma*/ "apprentices" (ǴMR);
III-*w* *ša-du-ú* = /*šadû*/ < **śadawu* "field"; note perhaps also *ša-TI-i* in Ug. 5 153, if for Ugar. /*šadî*/ (ŠDW);
III-*y* pl. *ša-mu-ma* = /*šamûma*/ < **šamayūma* "sky" (ŠMY);
^{túg}*šá-ḫar-tu* = /*šaᶜartu*/ (= [šaᶜr̥tu]?) < **śaᶜratu*[49] (ŠᶜR b).

(2) *qatāl*: p. 402

note *a-da-nu* = /*ʾadānu*/ (< PS **ʾad* + *-ān*) "father" (ʾDN);

[43]Note also (gen.?) : *pu-wa-ti* = /*puwwati*/ "madder(?)" (PWT), the Semitic origin of which is uncertain.

[44]Because of the ambiguity of the syllabic writing system in the representation of both vowel length and consonant gemination (see above, pp. 13-14), the precise pattern of many forms cannot be determined with certainty. Bisyllabic bases in this section are listed such that forms with *v̆*, indicating that the length of the relevant vowel is uncertain, follow forms in which the length of the vowel is more certain (*v̆* and *v̄*), i.e., in the following order: *qvtv̆l, qvtv̄l, qvtv̆l, qvttv̆l, qvttv̄l, qvttv̆l, qvt(t)v̆l*.

[45]See also the *qatal* base plurals of *qatl* forms, listed under c above.

[46]Note, however, that the corresponding Hebrew forms in the sg., *ʾeḥād*, fem. *ʾaḥat*, derive from *qattal*, viz., **ʾaḥḥad-*.

[47]See ch. 2 §B 2, pp. 282-83.

[48]See ch. 2 §B 1, pp. 280-82.

[49]See ch. 2 §C, pp. 284-85.

p. 402

perhaps [*la*?-*q*]*a*?-*ḫu*? = /*laqāḥu*/? "to receive" (LQḤ a);
la-ša-nu = /*lašānu*/[50] "tongue" (LŠN);
perhaps *ma-ka-ri* = /*makāri*/? "to trade" (MKR);
perhaps [*r*]*a*-[*g*]*a*?-[*zu*?] = /*ragāzu*/? "to be enraged(?)" (RGZ);
perhaps *ra-g*[*a*?-*mu*?] = /*ragāmu*/? "to speak(?)" (RGM);
fem. *ta-a-ma-tu*$_4$ = /*tahāmatu*/ < **tihāmatu*[51] "the deep" (THM).

(3) *qatăl*:

la-ḫa-m[*u*] = /*laḥămu*/? "(what is) suitable(?)" (LḤM).

(4) *qat(t)ăl*:[52]

[*ḫ*]*a-ra-š*[*u*] = /*ḫar(r)ašu*/ "deaf(?)" (ḪRŠ);
pl. *qà-da-ru-ma*^{meš} = /*qad(d)arūma*/[53] "(containers)" (QDR);

(5) *qattāl*:

gen. *al-la-an/ni* = /ʾ*allān(i)*/ "oak" (ʾLN).

(6) *qattăl*:[54]

^{lú}*ga*$_5$-*la-b*[*u*] = /*gallăbu*/ "barber" (GLB);
ḫa-ra-⌜*šu*?⌝ = /*ḥarrăšu*/ "artisan" (ḤRŠ);
: *ka(-an)-na-BI-PI* = /*kannăpīyv*/? "?" (KNP b);
^{lú}*la-*⌜*ba*?⌝*-nu* = /*labbănu*/ "brickmaker" (LBN²);
gen. ^{lú}*ša-na-ni* = /*θannăni*/, pl. nom. ^{lú}*ša-na-nu-ma* = /*θannănūma*/ "archer(s)(?)" (θNN).

qat(t)ĭl:

(1) *qatil*:[55]

fem. *qa-ri-t*[*u*$_4$] = /*qarītu*/ < **qariytu* "town" (QRY);
^{d}*SA-li-mu* = /*šalimu*/? "sound" (divine name; ŠLM a).

[50]Originally (pre-PS) a biradical, to which *-*ān* is added; cf. Egyptian *ns*, Coptic *las*, Berber *irs* < *ils*.

[51]See ch. 2 §A 1 c, pp. 271-73.

[52]For /*kakkaru*/, see below, g (Reduplicated forms).

[53]It is possible that this is pl. of a *qatl* form; see the comments in the Glossary under QDR.

[54]Comparative evidence for the vowel of the second syllable of agent/occupation nouns *qattăl* is inconsistent. Aramaic dialects generally have *qattāl*, as in *ṭabbāḥā* "butcher," whereas Hebrew, as in *ṭabbāḥ*, normally has *qattal* (not *qattāl*, pace, Barth, Nominalbildung 49-50 §33e, and others); Akkadian forms are usually normalized as *qattāl* (see, e.g., GAG §55o), but at least some forms exhibit Assyrian vowel harmony, as in *šarruqum* "thief," and so must be *qattal*. (Arabic examples such as *ṭabbāḫ* probably reflect Aramaic influence.)

[55]Note the Akkadianizing form ^{lú}*ba-ar-ḫu*, and the fem. ^{mí}*ba-ri-iḫ-tu*$_4$; the latter may reflect Akk. or Ugar. /*bariḥtu*/. See also below, under *qitil*, for I-ʾ /ʾ*irištu*/.

perhaps the fem. divine name ⸢*a*⸣-[*ši?-ra?-tu*$_4$?], [*a?-ši?-r*]*a-tu*$_4$ = /*ʾaθiratu*/?, possibly also, with post-tonic syncope,[56] ᵈ*aš-ra-tu*$_4$ = /*ʾaθratu*/ (ʾθR);

(2) *qatīl*:[57]

: *ga-bi-ni* = /*gabīni*/? "hillock(?)" (GBN);
pa-⸢*si?*⸣*-la-nu* = /*pasīlānu*/? "?" (PSL).

(3) *qatĭl*:[58]

ḫa-ri-mu = /*ḥarĭmu*/ "desecrated(?)" (ḤRM a);
gen. *ḫa-pí-ri* = /*ᶜapĭri*/ "(a social class)" (ᶜPR);
ḫa-ri-mu = /*ǵarĭmu*/ "foe, adversary(?)" (ǴRM);
pl. ᵗᵘ́ᵍ*pa-li-du-ma* = /*palĭdūma*/ "(garments)" (PLD).

(4) *qattil*:

no examples.

(5) **qattīl* > *qittīl* (q.v., below).

qat(t)ŭl:

(1) *qatul*:

a-du-rù = /*ʾaduru*/ (less likely, /*ʾadduru*/) "mighty" (ʾDR);
a-mu-q[*u*] = /*ᶜamuqu*/ "deep (place)" (ᶜMQ^2).

(2) *qatūl*:[59]

no examples.

(3) *qattul*:

⸢*ba*⸣*-aḫ-ḫu-rù* = /*baḫḫuru*/ (or /*baḥḥuru*/) "youth" (BḪR).

[(4) **qattūl* > *quttūl*: no examples.]

qit(t)ăl:

(1) *qital*:

perhaps dual *ḫi-nu-ta-me* = /*ḥinōtāmi*/?, sg. (with prothetic /ʾ/) ⸢*vḫ*⸣*-nu-tu*$_4$ = /*ʾvḥnōtu*/? < **ḥinawtu*? "(implement)" (ḤNW);

[56]See ch. 2 §B 2, pp. 282-83.

[57]The form (pl.) ˡᵘ́*ta-ri-ru-ma* (TRR) may reflect *qatīl* or participial *qātil*. For *qatīl* forms of roots II-guttural, see below, under *qitīl*.

[58]The forms ⸢ᵈ?*a?*⸣*-li-yi* (ᶜLY a) and (pl.) ˡᵘ́⁽·ᵐᵉˢ̌⁾*a-ši-ru*/*ri-ma* (ᶜŠR^1) may reflect *qatĭl* or participial *qātil*.

[59]For *qatūl* forms of roots II-guttural, see below, under *qutūl*.

perhaps *ši-a-ru* = /*šiharu*/? "crescent-shaped sickle(?)" (ŠHR).

(2) *qitāl*:[60]

di-[*k*]*a*$_4$(QA)-*ru* = /*dikāru*/ "bowl" (DKR^2);
perhaps *ZI-GA/QA-ni-ma* = /*sikānīma*/? "statues(?)" (SKN b);
⸢*e*?⸣-*la-PI* = /*ᶜilāyi*/? "upper (part)(?)" (ᶜLY b).

(3) *qitǎl*:[61]

pl. $^{\text{([lú.m]eš)}}$*(:) bi-da-lu-ma/na* = /*bidǎlūm/na*/ "merchants" (BDL);

(4) *qittāl*:

ITI *ḫi-ia/ya-ri* = /*ḫiyyāri*/ (month name; ḪYR);
$^{\text{d.giš}}$*ki-na-rù* = /*kinnāru*/ "lyre" (divine name; KNR).

qit(t)ǐl:

(1) **qitil*, in fem. *qitil-t*:[62]

(a) < *qatil-t*, I-ʾ:[63] *i*-[*r*]*i*?-*iš*-[*tu*$_4$?] = /*ʾirištu*/? < **ʾarištu* "request" (ʾRŠ);

(b) < *qitl-at*, III-*r*:[64] *i-zi-ir*-[*tu*$_4$?] = /*ᶜiðirtu*/ (= [ᶜiðṛtu]) < **ᶜiðratu* "help" (ᶜðR).

(2) *qitīl* < *qatīl*:

(a) I-ʾ:[65]

i-⸢*ši*?⸣-[*bi*?] = /*ʾiθību*/? (month name; ʾθB);

(b) II-guttural:[66]

pl. bound form $^{\text{lú.meš}}$*b*[*i*]-*ḫi-ru* = /*biḥīrū*/? < **baḥīr*- "elite (troops)" (BḤR^1);

pl. $^{\text{[urudu.meš]}}$*me-ḫi*-[*ṣ*]*u*-⸢*ma*⸣^{meš} = /*miḫīṣūma*/ < **maḫīṣ*-"(implements)" (MḪṢ b);

probably *qi-i-lu* = /*qiᶜīlu*/ < **qaᶜīl*- (less likely, /*qiᶜlu*/) "vine-blossom(?)" (QᶜL);

[*š*]*i*?-*i-ru*[= /*šiᶜīru*/ < **šaᶜīr*- "barley(?)" (ŠᶜR a).

[60]For II-guttural, see also above under *qatāl*.

[61]Note also the unidentified ⸢^{giš}*e*?-*la-mu*⸣; see the Appendix to the Glossary.

[62]Note also the Akk. loanword *: ḫi-ri-ti* = /*ḫirīti*/ "cemetery" (ḪRY).

[63]See ch. 2 §A 1 d, pp. 273-75; see also (2) immediately below.

[64]See ch. 2 §C, pp. 284-85.

[65]See also (1 a) above, with n. 63.

[66]See ch. 2 §A 1 c, pp. 271-73.

(3) *qittīl* < **qattīl*:[67]

ḫe-en-ni-ṣu = /*ḫinnīṣu*/? "piglet" (ḪNṢ);
gen. *(:) ṣí(-ib)-bi-ri* = /*ṣibbīri*/ "collective land(?)" (ṢBR).

qut(t)ăl:[68]

(1) *qutal*:

no certain examples.

(2) *qutāl*:

ḫu-r[*a-ṣu*] = /*ḫurāṣu*/ "gold" (ḪRṢ[1]);
perhaps pl. [d]ug!?*ku*?-*BA-ra-tu*meš = /*kupārātu*/? "bowls(?)" (KPR).

(3) *qută̄l*:

ḫu-ma?-*lu*? = /*ḥumă̄lu*/? "pity(?)" (ḤML).

(4) *quttal*:[69]

perhaps [*z*]*u-ut-ta-ru* = /*zuttaru*/ "to go out(?)" (ZTR);
ḫu-PI-ú = /*ḥuwwû*/ < **ḥuwwayu* "to live" (ḤYY[1]/ḤWY[1] a);
pu-la-ṭu = /*pullaṭu*/ "to save" (PLṬ);
probably *qu-u*[*n*?]-*n*[*a*?-*nu*?] = /*qunnanu*/? "coiled(?)" (QNN).
probably *tu-un-na-nu* = /*tunnanu*/ "serpent" (TNN).

(5) *qut(t)ă̄l*:

gen. *gu-wa-*⌜*li*⌝ = /*guw(w)ă̄li*/ (possibly < **gaw(w)ă̄li*) "circuit(?)" GWL).

qutēl < **qutayl*:

probably *ku-RI-ku* = /*kurēku*/, du. nom. *ku-RI-ka-m*[*a*] = /*kurēkāma*/, pl. bound *ku-RI-ka-a*[*t*] = /*kurēkāt(u)*/ "(implement)" (KRK).

qutīl: *ḫu-zi-rù* = /*ḫuzīru*/ "pig" (ḪZR).

qut(t)ŭ̄l:

(1) *qutul*:

probably (giš)*sú-KU-ru*/*ri* = /*sug*/*kuru*/*i*/? "bolt" (SGR a).

(2) *qutūl*:

(a) gen. *: qú-bu-ri* = /*qubūri*/ "burial" (QBR);;
(b) < *qatūl*, II-guttural:[70] *ṭu-ú-ru* = /*ṭuhūru*/ < **ṭahūru* "pure" (ṬHR).

[67]See ch. 2 §A 1 b, pp. 269-70.
[68]For /*huwătu*/ "word," see a above, under *qul*.
[69]For *quttal* as the form of the D infin./v.n., see above, p. 290 n. 107.
[70]See ch. 2 §A 1 c, pp. 271-73.

(3) *qutŭl*:

bu-nu-šu = /*bunŭšu*/ "man" (BNŠ);
⸢*ḫu*⸣-*du-rù* = /*ḥudŭru*/ "room(?)" (ḤDR).

(4) *quttul*:[71]

⸢*ku*⸣-*sú-m*[*u*] = /*kussumu*/ "emmer" (KSM).

(5) *quttūl*:

u-ṣú-ru, ú-ṣú-ri = /ᶜ*uṣṣūru/i*/ "bird" (ᶜṢR);

(6) *qut(t)ŭl*:

pl. obl. $^{\text{na}_4}$*ku-s*[*ú?-li?-ma?*]^{meš} = /*kussŭlīma*/? "(kind of stone)" (KSL);
Akk. form pl. $^{\text{[lú].meš}}$*ú-ru-ba-nu* = /ᶜ*ur(r)ŭb(b)ānū*/ "guarantors" (ᶜRB).[72]

☛ p. 402

e. *qv̄tv̆l*

qātil (G participle):[73]

⸢*a*⸣-[*p*]*í*?-[*yu*?] = /ʾ*āpiyu*/? "baker" (ʾPY);
III-*y* fem. gen. : *ḫa-me-ti* = /*ḥāmīti*/ < **ḥāmiyt-* "wall" (ḤMY);
pl. $^{\text{(lú)}}$*ia-ṣí-ru-ma* = /*yāṣirūma*/ "potters" (YṢR);
^{lú}*ia-qí-š*[*u*] = /*yāqišu*/ "fowler" (YQŠ);
^{lú}*ka*$_4$(QA)-*bi-s*[*ú*] = /*kābisu*/ "launderer" (KBS a);
^{lú}*ma-ḫi-ṣu* = /*māḫiṣu*/ "(a profession)" (MḪṢ a);
perhaps ^{d}*ma-lik*^{meš}, if for /*mālikūma*/? "counsellors(?)" (divine name; MLK c);
^{lú}*na-s*[*í-ku*] = /*nāsiku*/ "metalsmith" (NSK);
^{lú}*na-ḫi-ru* = /*nāǵiru*/ "guard" (NǴR a);
sà-GI-ru = /*sāg/kiru*/ "closing(?)" (SGR b);
gen. $^{\text{lú/1}}$*sà-ki(-in)-ni* = /*sākini*/ "prefect" (SKN a);
ša-i-tu$_4$, perhaps for III-*y* /*θā*ᶜ*ītu*/ < **θā*ᶜ*iytu* or for /*θā*ᶜ*ittu*/ < **θā*ᶜ*idtu* "(vessel)" (θᶜY/θᶜD).

qōtal < **qawtal*:

divine name *ku-šar-ru*[74] = /*kōθaru*/? (KθR).

[71]See also g below (Reduplicated forms), for fem. /*kukkubatu*/.

[72]See also n. 4 above.

[73]See also the forms cited above in nn. 57, 58.

[74]On the doubling of the /*r*/, see ch. 1 §D 2 b, p. 210; on the form in general, see under KθR in the Glossary.

f. *qvtvll*

qatall: perhaps gen. *na-ḫa-li*, if for /*naḫalli*/ rather than (*qatal*) /*naḫali*/ "wadi" (NḪL).

qitall: loanword *pí-lak-ku* = /*pilakku*/ "spindle" (PLK^1).

qutull:[75] (loanword?) acc. *ú-nu(-uš)-ša* = /*ʾunuθθa*/ "estate tax" (ʾNθ); fem. pl. bound obl. *ku-bu-da-ti* = /*kubuddāti*/ "honoring gifts" (KBD b).

g. Reduplicated forms

qalqal: acc. *ka$_4$-ka$_4$-ra* = /*kakkara*/ < **karkar-* "talent" (KKR).

qulqul(l): fem. gen. *ḫur-ḫu-ra-ti* = /*ḥurḥur(r)ati*/ "(a plant)" (ḤRḤR); fem. *ku-ku-ba-tu*, *ku-ku-bá-t*[*u$_4$*?] = /*kukkubatu*/, pl. /*kukkubātu*/, "vase(?)" (KKB); gen. *KU-ul-KU-li* = /*qulqul(l)i*/? "cassia" (QLQL).

h. Preformative ʾ-

Only in ⌜*vḫ*?⌝-*nu-tu$_4$* = /*ʾvḥnōtu*/?, with prothetic /ʾ/;[76] cf. dual ob. *ḫi-nu-ta-me* = /*ḥinōtāmi*/? (ḤNW).

i. Preformative *m-*

maqtal:

(1) Sound roots:

pl. $^{\text{(túg.meš)}}$*ma-za-ru-ma* = /*maʾzarūma*/? "loincloths(?)" (ʾZR);
ma-aḫ-ḫa-[*du*] = /*maʾḫadu*/ > [maḫḫadu] "harbor, quay" (ʾḪD);
gen. ITI *ma-ag-ma-r*[*i*] = /*magmari*/ (month name; GMR);
⌜*ma*⌝-*al-sà-mu* = /*malsamu*/ "course(?)/courier(?)" (LSM);
dual bound *ma-qa-ḫa* = /*maqqaḥā*/ < **malqaḥ-* "pair of tongs" (LQḤ b);
^{urudu}*ma-am-ṣa-ar* = /*mamṣar(u)*/ "knife(?)" (MṢR);
gen. *ma-ba-ri* = /*maᶜbari*/ "pass" (ᶜBR);
ma-ṣa-du /*maᶜṣadu*/, pl. $^{\text{urudu.meš}}$*ma-ṣa-du-ma*^{meš} = /*maᶜṣadūma*/ "adze(s)(?)" (ᶜṢD);

[75]Note also the forms listed in d above, under *qut(t)ŭl*; see also n. 4 above.

[76]See ch. 2 §D, p. 285.

gen. *ma-a*ʾ*-ša-ri(-ša),* acc. *ma-ša-ra* = /*ma*ᶜ*šari/a*/ "tithe" (ᶜŠR^2);
gen. *mar-za-i* = [marzaᶜi], also, with assimilation, *ma-ar-zi-ḫi* and *mar-zi-i* = [marziḥ/ᶜi][77] "symposium" (RZḤ);
perhaps fem. gen. *mar-kab-te* = /*markabti*/? "chariot(?)" (RKB);
gen. *ma-aš-a-li* = /*maš*ʾ*ali*/ "oracle(?)" (ŠʾL);
perhaps gen. *maš-ka-ni* = /*maškani*/? "habitation(?)" (ŠKN);
dual *ma-aš-la-ḫa-ma* = /*mašlaḥāma*/ "(garments)" (ŠLḤ);
pl. *ma-áš-ḫa-ṭu-ma* = /*maθḫaṭūma*/ "(cloths)" (θḪṬ).

(2) I-*w* (*mōtal* < **mawtal*):

gen. *mu-ba-li* = /*mōbali*/ "produce(?)" (YBL b);
mu-ša-bu = /*mōθabu*/ "seat" (YθB b);
see also under (4), immediately below.

(3) I-*n* (*mattal* < **mantal*):[78]

fem. *ma-a-al-tu*$_4$ = /*ma*ᶜᶜ*altu*/? "bolt(?)" (NᶜL);
ma-qá!?*-bu* = /*maqqabu*/, pl. *ma-qa-bu-ma*$^{(\text{meš})}$ = /*maqqabūma*/ "hammer(s)" (NQB);
: *ma-aq-qa-du* = /*maqqadu*/ "grazing rights(?)" (note also the pseudo-logogram MA.KAD; NQD).

(4) III-guttural (*maqtuGu* < *maqtaGu*?):[79]

probably I-*w* pl. $^{\text{túg.meš}}$*mu-ru-ú-ma*^{meš} = /*mōru*ʾ*ūma*/? < **mawra*ʾ*ūma*? "(garments)" (or *maqtūl*?; YRʾ);
perhaps *ma-aš-nu-ú* = /*mašnu*ʾ*u*/? "enemy(?)," if < **mašna*ʾ*u,* but perhaps the form is *maqtūl* (ŠNʾ).

(5) III-*y* (**maqtû* < **maqtayu*; fem. *maqtē-t* < **maqtay-t*):

perhaps [^{túg}*m*]*ar-de*$_4$*-tu* = /*mardētu*/? < **mardayt-*? "(garment)" (RDY);
perhaps acc. *ma-aš-na* = /*maθna*/*â*/? < **maθnaya* "second(ly)" (θNY).

maqtil:

(1) Sound roots:[80]

perhaps fem. *mar-de*$_4$*-em-tu* = /*mardimtu*/? "path(?)" (RDM);
mar-ḫi-iš = /*marḫiš(u)*/ "(a utensil)" (RḪŠ).

(2) Geminate (**maqlil* > *maqill*):

^{lú}*ma-ṣi-lu* = /*maṣillu*/ "cymbalist" (ṢLL).

[77]See ch. 2 §1 c, p. 272.

[78]See also /*maqqaḥā*/ < **malqaḥā*, under (1).

[79]See ch. 2 §1 A c, pp. 271-73.

[80]For [marziḥ/ᶜi] "symposium," see above under *maqtal*.

maqtīl: gen. *: ma-aḫ-ZI-ZI* = /*maḫṣīṣi*/? "divide(?)" (ḪṢṢ).

maqtul: see the possible examples of *maqtul* < *maqal*, III-guttural, cited under *maqtal* (4) above.

maqtūl: possible examples are cited under *maqtal* (4) above.

miqtal: *: mi-dá-ar-ú* = /*midarᶜu*/ < **midraᶜu*[81] "seed-land" (DRᶜ).

muqtāl: perhaps *mu-qa-dì(-IM?)* = /*muqqādi*/? "grazing rights(?)" (NQD).

j. Preformative *n*-

naqtal (N stem infin./v.n.):

: na-ba-dì(-⸢šu-nu⸣) = /*naᵓbadi*/ "escape" (ᵓBD);
na-ap-ṭá-ra = /*napṭara*/ "exchange(?)" (PṬR c).

k. Preformative *š*-[82]

šaqtil: perhaps gen. *: šab-⸢li?-mi?⸣* = /*šablimi*/?? "retaining wall(??)" (BLM).

šuqtul (or *šaqtul*, I-guttural), geminate, > *šuqull*:

šu-ḫu-ut-t[*u*?] = /*šuḥuttu*/?, possibly < **šaḥuttu* "bran, residue(?)" (ḤTT).

l. Preformative *t*-

taqtal: Gt infin./v.n. III-*y tap-de₄-ti*, *: ta-ap-de₄-ti*, *tap-de₄-tu₄* = /*tapdēti*/*u*/ "exchange" (PDY);
gen. *: ta-ar-bá-ṣí* = /*tarbaṣi*/ "stable" (possibly a loanword; RBṢ).

taqattil: perhaps *ta-ga-bi-ra(-yv)* = /*tagabbir-*/? "?" (GBR).

tuqattil: tD infin/v.n. *tu-a-pí-*[*ku*?] = /*tuhappiku*/? "to be upset(?)" (HPK).

m. Afformative -*y*

/-*āy*/: gen. *uḫ-ra-a-yi* = /ᵓ*uḫrāyi*/ "destiny" (ᵓḪR);
gentilics: *ta-ga-bi-ra(-yv)* = /*tagabbirāy-*/? (GBR); ^uru^*ap-sú-na-yu* (PRU 3 37a:10), but also pl. ^uru^*ap-sú-ni-yu-ma* (PRU 6 77:10, from GN ^uru^*ap-sú-na(-a)*, e.g., PRU 6 134:13; 6 137:0); probably also ^lú.[ur]u!?^*ak*!*-kà-a-ii* (TA 8 7f.:33).

[81]See ch. 2 §C, pp. 284-85.

[82]For alphabetic forms, see p. 96 n. 62.

/-*īy*/: gen. *tu-ki-ii* = /*tōkīyi*/ "inner" (TWK);[83]

gentilics: e.g., ^{uru}*ṣu-ri-yu* (PRU 6 79:6); pl. ^{uru}*qa-ra-ti-yu-ma* (PRU 6 138:25); and many others, for which see above, pp. 238-39.

/-*ūy*/: only gentilic ^{uru}*a-ta-li-gu-yu* (PRU 6 79:17; from GN ^{uru}*a-tal-lig*$^{(ki)}$, e.g., PRU 3 102ff.:38,41,44; Ug. 5 12:15; Ug. 7 pl. 13:15).

n. Afformative -*n*

/-*ān*/:[84] gen. *: ad-ma-ni* = /*ʾadmāni*/ "red (soil)" (ʾDM);
probably *a-da-nu* = /*ʾadānu*/ (PS *ʾ*ad* + -*ān*) "father" (ʾDN);
perhaps gen. *uš-r*[*i-ia*]-*ni* = /*ʾuθrĭyāni*/ "crown prince" (ʾθRYN);
pl. obl. *: dì-ip-ra-ni-ma* = /*diprānīma*/ "junipers" (DPR);
gen. *ḫa-ar-ma-ni* = /*ḥarmāni*/ "sacred place(?)" (ḤRM b);
gen. *ia-ar-qa-ni* = /*yarqāni*/ "yellow-green" (YRQ);
Akk. form pl. $^{[lú].meš}$*ú-ru-ba-nu* = /*ʿur(r)ŭb(b)ānū*/ "guarantors" (ʿRB);
pa-⸢*si?*⸣*-la-nu* = /*pasīlānu*/? "?" (PSL).
gen. $^{(íd)}$*(:) ra-aḫ-ba/bá-ni/na* = /*raḥbāni/a*/ "wide place" (RḤB).

o. Afformative *t*-

/-*īt*/?: perhaps in ⸢*i*⸣*-ši-t*[*u*$_4$] = /*ʾišītu*/? (< PS *ʾ*iš* + -*īt*?)[85] "fire" (ʾŠ).

3. *Loanwords*

a. Akkadian (and Sumerian via Akkadian):

a-ia-ku = /*ʾayyakku*/? (divine name; ʾYK), Akk. *ayyakku*;
perhaps gen. *a-la-ḫi-ni* = /*ʾalaḫḫini*/ "miller" or a PN (ʾLḪN); the origin of Akk. *alaḫḫinu* is unclear;
perhaps ^{lú}*ga*$_5$*-la-b*[*u*] = /*gallăbu*/ "barber" (GLB), Akk. *gallābu*;
perhaps *di-*[*k*]*a*$_4$(QA)*-ru* = /*dikāru*/ "bowl" (DKR^2), possibly via an unknown intermediary language; cf. Akk. *diqāru*;
perhaps *a-ri-tu*$_4$ = /*harītu*/? "shield" (HRT), Akk. *arītu*; Akk. form probably intended;
: ḫi-ri-ti = /*ḫirīti*/ "cemetery" (ḪRY), Akk. *ḫirītu*;
perhaps fem. *ku-ku-ba-tu, ku-ku-bá-t*[*u*$_4$?] = /*kukkubătu*/ "vase(?)"

[83] Possibly also gen. *uš-r*[*i-ia*]*-ni* = /*ʾuθrĭyāni*/ "crown prince"; see under ʾθRYN in the Glossary.

[84] See also above, n. 50, on /*lašānu*/; note also the unidentified gen. *ra-*⸢*PA*⸣*-ni*, for which see the Appendix to the Glossary.

[85] See the commentary on S^a Voc. no. 48.1, p. 63.

(KKB), Akk. *kukkubu*;

$^{(\text{lú})}$*mu-du(-ú)*, pl. ^{lú}*mu-du-ma* (also obl. bound $^{(\text{lú.meš})}$*mu-de*$_4$) = /*mūdû*, -*ûma*/ "courtier(s)(?)" (MD), Akk. participle of *idû* "to know";

na-du = /*nādu*/ "stela(?)" (ND), Akk. *nadû*/*nādu* < Sum. na.rú/dù.a;

perhaps gen. *KU-ul-KU-li* = /*qulqul(l)i*/? "cassia" (QLQL), Akk. *qulqullânu*;

perhaps *qu-u*[*n*?]-*n*[*a*?-*nu*?] = /*qunnanu*/? "coiled(?)" (QNN), Akk. *qunnunu*;

perhaps gen. : *ta-ar-bá-ṣí* = /*tarbaṣi*/ "stable" (RBṢ), Akk. *tarbāṣu*.

(b) Hurrian:

perhaps *IG-TU*$_4$ = /ʾ*iktu*/? "mortar" (ʾKT), Hur. *itki*;

perhaps acc. *ú-nu(-uš)-ša* = /ʾ*unuθθa*/ "estate tax" (ʾNθ), Hur. unattested;

perhaps gen. *uš-r*[*i-ia*]-*ni* = /ʾ*uθrīyāni*/ "crown prince" (ʾθRYN), Hur. unattested;

$^{(\text{lú})}$*mar-ia-nu*, pl. ^{lú}*mar-ia-nu-ma* (obl. bound $^{\text{lú.meš}}$*mar-ia-an-ni*) = /*maryannu*, -*ūma*/ "charioteer(s)" (MRYN), Hur. *mari(y)anni* (< Indo-European);

^{túg}*pa-ḫa-TAR-ru* = /*paǵaddarru*/ "(garment)" (PǴ(N)DR), Hur. *paǵandarri*;

perhaps *qà*?-*ṭi-nu*-[*ma*?^{me}]$^{\text{š?}}$ = /*qaṭinnūma*/? "(implements)" (QṬN), (Hur. *kadinni*?, unattested in Hur. texts). p. 403

(c) unknown origin:

perhaps *gur-BI-ZU*^{meš} = /*gurbizu*/ "hauberk" (GRBZ); but Akk. *gurpisu* probably intended;

perhaps pl. ^{urudu}*ḫa-ar-me-ša-tu* = /*ḫarmiθātu*/ "sickles(?)" (ḪRMθ);

pí-lak-ku = /*pilakku*/ "spindle" (PLK^1);[86]

^{dug}*KI-ra-li-nu* (see Appendix to Glossary);

pl. obl. : *ZI-ZA-ḫal-li-ma* (see Appendix to Glossary).

Appendix: *Proper Nouns*

(a) Divine names:

a-ia-ku = /ʾ*ayyakku*/ ? (ʾYK);

⌜*i*?-*lu*?⌝ = /ʾ*ilu*/? (ʾL);

⌜*a*⌝-[*ši*?-*ra*?-*tu*$_4$?], [*a*?-*ši*?-*r*]*a-tu*$_4$ = /ʾ*aθiratu*/? (ʾθR); perhaps also ^{d}*aš*-

[86]See the commentary to S^{a} Voc. no. 184.1, p. 83, with n. 40.

ra-tu$_4$, if for Ugar. /*ʾaθratu*/, with vowel syncope, but Akk. *ašratu* is probably intended;
ba-a-lu = /*baʿlu*/ (pl. *ba-a-lu-ma* = /*baʿ(a)lūma*/; BʿL);
g[a]-ša-ru = /*gaθaru*/ (GθR);
(Akk. ^{d}*da-gan* = /*dagan*/ [DGN]);
ku-šar-ru = /*kōθaru*/ (KθR);
$^{d.giš}$*ki-na-rù* = /*kinnāru*/ (KNR);
^{d}*ma-lik*^{meš}, perhaps for pl. /*mālikūma*/? (MLK c);
(epithet) gen. ⸢$^{d?}$*a?*⸣*-li-yi* = /*ʿălīyi*/? (ʿLY a);
^{d}*a-na-tu*$_4$ = /*ʿanatu*/ (ʿNT);
aš-ta-ru = /*ʿaθtaru*/ (ʿθTR);
^{d}*SA-li-mu* = /*šalimu*/ (ŠLM a);
ša-ap-šu = /*šapšu*/ (ŠPŠ).

The following also appear in the polyglot Weidner list at the end of Ug. 5 137:
PI-mu = /*yōmu*/ (less likely, /*yămu*/) "day" (YWM);
$^{[é?]}$⸢*qi?-id?-šu?*⸣, *qi-i[d-šu?]* = /*qidšu*/ "shrine" (QDŠ b);
ša-mu-ma = /*šamûma*/ "sky" (ŠMY);
ta-a-ma-tu$_4$ = /*tahāmatu*/ "the deep" (THM).

b. Month names:

ITI *i-*⸢*ši?*⸣*-[bi?]* = /*ʾiθibi*/? (ʾθB);
gen. ITI *ma-ag-ma-r[i]* = /*magmari*/ (GMR);
fem. ITI *ḫal-la-t[u?]/ti* = /*ḥallatu/i*/ (ḤLL);
gen. ITI *ḫi-ia/ya-ri* = /*ḫiyyāri*/ (ḪYR).

D. Verbs

1. *Summary of Verbal Forms*

	G	Gt	N	D	tD	Š
Suff.-Conj.						
3ms	*qatvla*			*qattila*		
3mp	*qatvlū*		*naqtalū*			
Pref.-Conj.						
yaqtul						
1cs	*ʾaqtil*					
yaqtulu						
1cs/3ms	(*ʾ/yaqtilu*?)[87]					(*yvšaqtilu*?)[87]
3fs		*tiqtatlu*				
Imperative						(*šaqtil*?)[88]
Vbl. Noun	*qitlu* *qatālu*?	*taqtalu*?	*naqtalu*	*quttalu*	*tuqattilu*? (*taqattil-*?)	(*šaqtilu*?) (*šuqtulu*/ *šaqtulu*?)
Act. Ptcpl.	*qātil*,					
Vbl. Adj.	*qatal*, *qatĭl*, *qatŭl*; *maqtūlu*?				*quttalu*?	

p. 403

p. 403

2. *Attested Forms*

Forms are arranged here by stem/conjugation; a synopsis appears at the end of this section:

G Suffix-conj.

3ms: *: ṣa-ma-ta* = /*ṣamata*/ "it was transferred"; note also the partly Akk. forms *ṣa-ma-at*, and the fully Akk. forms *ṣa-mi-it*; cf. also the 3mp form cited below (ṢMT);

ta-ba-ʾa = /*tabaʿa*/ "he departed" (TBʿ);

[87]Note the following in Ug. 5 153, which may be a Ugar. text: *([i]a-)ab-ṣi-ru*, perhaps for G 3ms /*yabṣiru*/ or 1cs /*ʾabṣiru*/ (BṢR); *([i]v-)šu-bi-lu*, perhaps for Š *yaqtulu* 3ms /*yvšōbilu*/ or imperative mp /*šōbilū*/ (YBL c).

[88]Note the form *([i]a-)šu-bi-lu*, cited in the preceding note.

Akk. forms, without /*-a*/:

II-*w*/*y* *ma-a-⸢ar?⸣* for /*mār(a)*/ "it was exchanged" (MW/YR);
qa-dì-iš = Akkadianized *qadiš* (for /*qadiša*/) "is sacred" (QDŠ a);
see also the first entry above; note also the curious I-*y* (**w*) forms *i-bi-la* "it brought" and *i-ṣa-ʾ* "it went out," perhaps for */*yabila*/ and */*yaṣaʾa*/, resp. (YBL a; YṢʾ).

3mp: *: ṣa-ma-tù* = /*ṣamatū*/ "they were transferred" (ṢMT);
probably also /*ḫa-ba-ṭu*/ = /?/ (see Appendix to Glossary).

Prefix-conj.:[89]

1cs *yaqtul* (jussive) I-*y* (**w*): *a-ši-ib* = /*ʾaθib*/ "let me dwell" (YθB a).

p. 403 Akk. forms:

durative 3ms *i-ma-li-ik* = *imallik* "he wil have authority" (MLK a);
precative 3mp *lip-ḫu-dú-ma* = *lipḥ/ḫudū-ma* "let them fear" (PḤ/ḪD).

Verbal nouns:

qitl:[90] *ni-iḫ-rù* = /*niǵru*/ "to guard" (NǴR b);
pí-iṭ-r[*ù*?] = /*piṭru*/ "to loosen" (PṬR a);
geminiate *pí-rù* = /*pirru*/? "flight(?), separation(?)" (PRR);
II-*y* *ši-tu* = /*šītu*/ "to place" (ŠYT).[91]

qatāl: perhaps [*la*?-*q*]*a*?-*ḫu* = /*laqāḥu*/? "to receive(?)" (LQḤ a);
perhaps *ma-ka-ri* = /*makāri*/? "to trade," if Ugar. (MKR);
perhaps [*r*]*a*-[*g*]*a*?-[*zu*?] = /*ragāzu*/? "to be enraged(?)" (RGZ);
p. 403 perhaps *ra-g*[*a*?-*mu*?] = /*ragāmu*/? "to speak(?)" (RGM).

Active Participle:

qātil: many examples are listed above, §C 2 e (p. 312).

Verbal Adjective/Passive Participle:

See above, §C 2 b, c, d: noun patterns *qāl, qēl, qīl, qatl* geminate, *qatal, qatĭl, qatŭl*.

p. 403 Note also perhaps the form *ma-aš-nu-ú*? "enemy," if for /*mašnūʾu*/, i.e., a *maqtūl* form, "hated" (ŠNʾ); but the form may be *maqtal* instead; see §C 2 i above.

Gt Prefix-Conj.:

p. 403 3fs *yaqtulu* (imperfective) *:ti-tar-ḫ*[*u*] = I-ʾ /*tiʾtarḫu*/ (or I-*y* [**w*]

[89] Note also the form ([*i*]*a-*)*ab-ṣi-ru*, cited above in n. 87.

[90] See Blau-Greenfield, BASOR 200 17; Sivan, Analysis 168.

[91] See n. 29 above.

/tittarḫu/) < **tiʾtariḫu* (or **tittariḫu*), with post-tonic syncope[92] (ʾRḪ or YRḪ).

Verbal Noun *taqtal* (?):

Cf. perhaps the forms

III-*y* (:) *tap/ta-ap-de*$_4$*-tu*$_4$*/ti* = */tapdētu/i/* < **tapdaytv* "exchange" (PDY);

: *ta-ar-bá-ṣí* = */tarbaṣi/* "stable" (unless a loanword; RBṢ).

N Suffix-Conj.:

3mp: *na-ap-ṭa-ru* = */napṭarū/* "they exchanged(?)" (PṬR b).

Prefix-Conj.:

Akk. form:

durative 1cs III-*y*: *ar-ra-⸢zu⸣* = *arraððu* "I grew weak" (RðY).

Verbal Noun *naqtal*:

: *na-ba-dì(-⸢šu-nu⸣)* = */naʾbadi/* "escape" (ʾBD);

na-ap-ṭá-ra = */napṭara/* "exchange(?)" (PṬR c).

D Suffix-Conj.:

3ms: *šal-li-ma* and *ša-li-ma* = */šallima/* "it paid/delivered" (ŠLM b).

Akk. form:

verbal adj. (predicative, "stative"), with Ugar. suffix-conj. 3ms marker */-a/* (?): : *ṣú-um-mu-ta* "it was transferred" (ṢMT).

Prefix-Conj.:

Akk. form: p. 403

preterite 3ms *ú-dáb-bi-qa-an-ni* = Akkadianized form *udabbiqannī* "he put me together" (DBQ).

Verbal Noun *quttal*:[93]

perhaps [*z*]*u-ut-ta-ru* = */zuttaru/* "to go out(?)" (ZTR);

III-*y* *ḫu-PI-ú* = */ḥuwwû/* < **ḥuwwayu* "to live" (ḤYY^{1}/ḤWY^{1} a);

pu-la-ṭu = */pullaṭu/* "to save" (PLṬ).

Verbal Adj. *quttal* (?):

perhaps *qu-u*[*n*?]-*n*[*a*?-*nu*?] = */qunnanu/*? "coiled(?)" (QNN);

Cf. also *tu-un-na-nu* = */tunnanu/* "serpent" (TNN)?

Akk. form. with Ugar. suffix-conj. marker */-a/*: see above, under

[92]For post-tonic syncope, see above, pp. 282-83; for the Gt in general, see most recently Verreet, UF 16 319-21.

[93]For *quttal* as the form of the D infin./v.n., see above, p. 290 n. 107.

suffix-conj.

☛ p. 404

tD Verbal Noun *tuqattil*:

tu-a-pí-[*ku*?] = /*tuhappiku*/? "to be upset(?)" (HPK); (but note also perhaps the forms *ta-ga-bi-ra(-yv)* = /*tagabbir-*/? [GBR]).

Š Prefix-conj. or Imperative(?): see n. 87 above.

Verbal Nouns(?): note the following forms:

šaqtil: perhaps *:šab-*⌜*li*?*-mi*?⌝ = /*šablimi*/?? "retaining wall(??)" (BLM);

šuqtul (or *šaqtul*, I-guttural), geminate > *šuqull*: *šu-ḫu-ut-t*[*u*?] = /*šuḥuttu*/?, possibly < **šaḥuttu* "bran, residue(?)" (ḪTT).

Synoptic Table of Attested Forms (Akk. forms omitted)

	G	Gt	N	D	tD	Š
Suff.-Conj.						
3ms	*ṣamata*			*šallima*		
	tabaᶜa					
	**yabila*?					
	**yaṣaʾa*?					
3mp	*ṣamatū*		*napṭarū*			
	ḫa-ba-ṭu					
Pref.-Conj.						
yaqtul						
1cs	*ʾaθib*					
yaqtulu						
1cs/3ms	(*ʾ/yabṣiru*?)					(*yvšōbilu*?)
☛ p. 404 — 3fs		*tiʾtarḫu*/ *tittarḫu*				
Imprtv (mp)						(*šōbilū*?)
☛ Vbl. Noun	*niǵru*	*tapdētu*?	*naʾbadu*	*zuttaru*?	*tuhappiku*?	(*šablimu*)
	piṭru	*tarbaṣu*?	*napṭaru*	*ḫuwwû*	(*tagabbir*-?)	(*šuḥuttu*)
☛	*pirru*?			*pullaṭu*		
	šītu					
☛	*laqāḥu*?					
☛ p. 404	*ragāzu*?					
	ragāmu?					
Act. Ptcpl.	*qātil*, passim					
Vbl. Adj.	(*qatal*,*qatvl*, *qvl*, etc.)				*qunnanu*?	
	mašnūʾu?				*tunnanu*?	

E. Adverbs

al-li-ni-PI = /*hallinīya*/? "here, now then" (HLNY);
la-a = /*lā*/ "not" (L^1);[94]
perhaps *ma-aš-na* = /*maθna*/*â*/? "secondly(?)" (θNY).

F. Prepositions

⸢*bi*⸣-*i* (also *bi-*) = /*bi-*/ "in" (B);
le-⸢*e*⸣ = /*li-*/ "to(ward)" (L^2).

G. Akkadianized Forms

A number of forms which reflect Ugaritic roots exhibit not Ugaritic morphology, but rather the morphology of the Akkadian dialect of the texts in which they occur.[95] These are collected here for convenience of reference.

1. *Pronominal Suffixes*

A Ugaritic pronominal suffix is attested only in the forms cited above, §A 1 b (p. 293). More often, Ugar. forms are furnished with Akkadian suffixes, including, probably, an example from the same text as the one in which Ugar. /*ǵam(a)ru-hŭ*/ "his apprentice" occurs:

lú*ḫa-am-ru*<*-šu*>*-nu* = /*ǵamru*/*-šunu* "their apprentice."

Other examples:

gen. : *na-ba-dì-*⸢*šu-nu*⸣ = /*naʾbadi*/*-šunu* "their flight" (ʾBD);
gen. : *ḫi-i-yi-šu* = /*ḫīyĭ*/*-šu* "its vacant area(s)" (ḪWY);
perhaps *mi-ti-šu-nu,* if for Ugar. /*mīti*/*-šunu* "their death" (MWT);
gen. *ma-aʾ-ša-ri-ša* = /*maᶜšari*/*-ša* "its tithe" (ᶜŠR^2);
note also the Akk. form verb, with an Akk. 1cs acc. suffix: *ú-dáb-bi-qa-an-ni* = *udabbiq-annī* "he put me together" (DBQ).

2. *Nouns and Adjectives*

The sg. vbl. adj. lú*ba-ar-ḫu* "fugitive, rustic" (BRḤ) reflects Akk. *parsu* rather than Ugar. *qatvlu* (the corresponding fem. mí*ba-ri-iḫ-tu*$_4$ may reflect either Akk. or Ugar. /*bariḥtu*/). So also perhaps the sg. noun : *ḫa-at-ni* for expected Ugar.

[94] Also *la* and *la-a* in Ug. 5 153, if for Ugar. /*lā*/.
[95] See above, p. 15.

*/ḫatanu/ (ḪTN).

Four sg. bound forms which do not exhibit a case-vowel, contrary to the majority of examples in syllabic transcription, are in imitation of Akk. morphology; the forms are cited above, §C 1 f.

The few examples of unbound forms which do not exhibit a case ending, cited above, §C 1 e (3) (p. 300), probably reflect the Akk. absolute form of the noun.

Some or all of the following may be plural; if so, they exhibit the Akk. masc. plural ending *-ū* rather than Ugar. */-ūma/*: $^{giš.meš}$*úr-nu* = */ʾurnŭ/* "laurel(?)" (ʾRN); $^{[lú].meš}$*ú-ru-ba-nu* = */ʿur(r)ŭb(b)ānū/* "guarantors" (ʿRB); note also *3 gur-BI-ZU*^{meš} "hauberks" (GRBZ).

3. *Verbs*

Three of the four Ugar. forms that appear in literary texts are verbs that exhibit completely Akkadian morphology:[96]

preterite 3ms *ú-dáb-bi-qa-an-ni* = *udabbiq-annī* "he put me together" (DBQ);
precative 3mp *lip-ḫu-dú-ma* = *lipḥ/ḫudū-ma* "may they fear" (PḤ/ḪD);
durative 1cs *ar-ra-zu* = *arrazzu* "I was becoming weak" (RðY).

Other thoroughly Akkadian forms are the following:

durative 3ms *i-ma-li-ik* = *imallik* "will have (no) authority" (MLK a);
predicative vbl. adj. ("stative") *ṣa-mi-it* = *ṣamit* "is transferred," which contrasts with the Ugar. *: ṣa-ma-ta* = */ṣamata/* and the mixed forms *ṣa-ma-at* and D *: ṣú-um-mu-ta,* for which see below (ṢMT).

Still other forms are mixed:

the 3ms forms *ṣa-ma-at* exhibit a Ugar. base, like *:ṣa-ma-ta* = */ṣamata/,* but the endingless form of the Akk. predicative (viz., *paris-ø*) vs. the Ugar. suffix-conj. ending */-a/* (*qatvl-a*), like the fully Akk. forms *ṣa-mi-it* (ṢMT); so also the II-weak form *ma-a-*⌜*ar*⌝ "is exchanged" (MW/YR); the form *qa-dì-iš* (QDŠ) probably also belongs here, i.e., a Ugar. *qatil* base */qadiš-/* with the Akk. ending *-ø* (for Ugar. **/qadiša/*), but it may also, of course, be considered to exhibit thorougly Akk. morphology (*paris*);
conversely, the form *: ṣú-um-mu-ta* (ṢMT) exhibits an Akk. base (D verbal adjective) with the Ugar. ending */-a/*;
the difficult forms *i-bi-la* and *i-ṣa-ʾa* apparently have essentially Ugaritic bases, for **/yabila/*? and **/yaṣaʾa/* (YBL a, YṢʾ), but the initial **/ya-/*

[96]For the fourth form, see the Glossary under ḤML.

of each has been replaced with a more "Akkadian-like" *i*-;[97]
finally, the N verbal noun : *na-ba-dì(-⸢šu-nu⸣)* = /*naʾbadi*/ (ʾBD), while formally reflecting Ugar. morphology (*naqtalu*, vs. Akk. *naprusu*), probably owes its conjugation to Akk. N *nābutu*/*naʾbutu*.[98]

[97]Kühne, UF 5 188-89.
[98]Boyd, Collection 35-37.

Bibliography of Works Cited

Aartun, K.

"Neue Beiträge zum ugaritischen Lexicon I," *UF* 16 (1984) 1-52.

"Neue Beiträge zum ugaritischen Lexicon (II)," *UF* 17 (1985) 1-47.

Adler, H.-P.

Das Akkadische des Königs Tušratta von Mitanni. (AOAT 201, 1976).

Aistleitner, J.

Wörterbuch der ugaritischen Sprache, 4th ed. (ed. O. Eissfeldt; Berichte über die Verhandlungen der Sächsischen Akademie der Wissenschaften zu Leipzig, Philologisch-historische Klasse, 106/3; Berlin: Akademie, 1974).

Albright, W.F.

"An Archaic Hebrew Proverb in an Amarna Letter from Central Palestine," *BASOR* 89 (1943) 89-92.

Alt, A.

Review of *PRU 3*, *ZA* 52 (1957) 328-33.

Arnaud, D.

"La culture suméro-accadienne," in article "Ras Shamra," in *Supplément au Dictionnaire de la Bible* (ed. H. Cazelles, A Feuillet; Paris: Letouzey & Ané) 9/52-53 (1979) 1348-59.

"Les textes cunéiformes suméro-accadiens des campagnes 1979-1980 à Ras Shamra-Ougarit," *Syria* 59 (1982) 199-222.

"La lettre Hani 81/4 et l'identification du site de Ras Ibn Hani (Syrie)," *Syria* 61 (1984) 15-23.

Arnaud, D.; Kennedy, D.

"Les textes en cunéiformes syllabiques découverts en 1977 à Ibn Hani," *Syria* 56 (1979) 317-24.

Aro, J.

Studien zur mittelbabylonischen Grammatik (StOr 20, 1955).

Review of *PRU 3*, *AfO* 18 (1957-58) 143-44.

Artzi, P.

"The 'Glosses' in the el-Amarna Tablets," *Bar-Ilan* 1 (1963) 24-57 (English summary, xiv-xvii).

Astour, M.C.

"The Origin of the Terms 'Canaan,' 'Phoenician,' and 'Purple,'" *JNES* 24 (1965) 346-50.

"Some New Divine Names from Ugarit," *JAOS* 86 (1966) 277-84.

"Maʾḫadu, the Harbor of Ugarit," *JESHO* 13 (1970) 113-27.

"A Letter and Two Economic Texts," in Fisher, ed., *AnOr* 48 23-35.

"The Merchant Class of Ugarit," in *Gesellschaftsklassen im Alten Zweistromland und in den angrenzenden Gebieten* — XVIII. Rencontre assyriologique internationale, München, 29. Juni bis 3. Juli 1970 (ed. D.O. Edzard; ABAW NF 75, 1972) 11-26.

"Les frontières et les districts du royaume d'Ugarit," *UF* 13 (1981) 1-11.

Attridge, H.W.; Oden, R.A., Jr.

Philo of Byblos, The Phoenician History: Introduction, Critical Text, Tranlation, Notes (Catholic Biblical Quarterly Monograph Series, no. 9; Washington: Catholic Biblical Association, 1981).

Barth, J.

Die Nominalbildung in den semitischen Sprachen, 2nd ed. (Leipzig: Hinrichs, 1894).

Beeston, A.F.L.; Ghul, M.A.; Müller, W.W.; Ryckmans, J.

Sabaic Dictionary (Louvaine-la-Neuve: Peeters, 1982).

Berger, P.-R.

"Die Alašia-Briefe Ugaritica 5, Noug. Nrn. 22-24," *UF* 1 (1969) 217-21; 2 (1970) 357.

"Zu den Wirtschafts- und Rechtsurkunden Ugaritica V," *UF* 1 (1969) 121-25; 2 (1970) 355-56.

Review of Gröndahl, *Personennamen, WO*5 (1969-70) 271-82.

"Zu den 'akkadischen' Briefen Ugaritica V," *UF* 2 (1970) 285-93.

"Zum ugaritischen Wörterbuch, 1.," *UF* 2 (1970) 339-40.

"Zur Bedeutung des in den akkadischen Texten aus Ugarit bezeugten Ortsnamens *Ḫīlu* (*Ḥl*)," *UF* 2 (1970) 340-46.

Bergmann, E.

Codex Ḫammurabi: Textus Primigenius, 3rd ed. (Rome: Pontificium Institutum Biblicum, 1953).

Berkooz, M.

The Nuzi Dialect of Akkadian: Orthography and Phonology (Supplements to *Language* 23; Philadelphia: Linguistic Society of America, University of Pennsylvania, 1937).

Biella, J.C.

Dictionary of Old South Arabic: Sabaean Dialect (HSS 25; Chico, Calif.: Scholars, 1982).

Birot, M., ed.

Archives royales de Mari 14: Lettres de Yaqim-Addu Gouverneur de Sagarātum (Paris: Musée du Louvre, 1974).

Blau, J.

"On Problems of Polyphony and Archaism in Ugaritic Spelling," *JAOS* 88 (1968) 523-26.

"Marginalia Semitica II," *IOS* 2 (1972) 57-82.

Blau, J.; Greenfield, J.C.

"Ugaritic Glosses," *BASOR* 200 (1976) 11-17.

Blau, J.; Loewenstamm, S.E.

"Zur Frage der scriptio plena im Ugaritischen und Verwandtes," *UF*2 (1970) 19-33.

"Ugaritic *ṣly* 'to curse,'" *Lĕšonénu* 35 (1970-71) 7-10.

Böhl, F.M.T.

Die Sprache der Amarnabriefe mit besonderer Berücksichtigung der Kanaanismen (Leipzig: Hinrichs, 1909).

Borger, R.

"Zu Ugaritica V, Nr. 18 und 138," *RA* 63 (1969) 171-72.

Assyrisch-babylonische Zeichenliste, 2nd ed. (AOAT 33/33A, 1981).

Boyd, J.L. III

"A Collection and Examination of the Ugaritic Vocabulary Contained in the Akkadian Texts from Ras Shamra" (PhD. Dissertation, University of Chicago, 1975).

Bravmann, M.M.

"An Arabic Cognate of Ugaritic *ğmrm,* " *JCS* 7 (1953) 27.

Brockelmann, C.

Grundriss der vergleichenden Grammatik der semitischen Sprachen, 2 vols. (Berlin, 1908-13; repr. Hildesheim: Olms, 1961).

Lexicon Syriacum, 2nd ed. (Halle/Saale: Niemeyer, 1928).

Brown, F.; Driver, S.R.; Briggs, C.A.

A Hebrew and English Lexicon of the Old Testament with an Appendix containing the Biblical Aramaic based on the Lexicon of William Gesenius as translated by Edward Robinson (Oxford: Clarendon, 1907).

Buccellati, G.

"Due note ai testi accadici de Ugarit (1. ZUR = *ṣar*$_x$ 2. MAŠKIM = *sākinu*)," *OA* 2 (1963) 223-28.

Bush, F.W.

"A Grammar of the Hurrian Language" (PhD. Dissertation, Brandeis University, 1964; Univ. Microfilms no. 64-12852).

Caquot, A.

"La lettre de la reine Puduḫepa," in *Ug*.7 121-34.

Caquot, A.; Sznycer, M.; Herdner, A.

Textes ougaritiques 1: Mythes et légendes (Littératures anciennes du proche-orient; Paris: Cerf, 1974).

Cathcart, K.J.

"Notes on Some Hebrew Words for Vessels and their Cognates," *RSO* 47 (1972) 55-58.

Cazelles, H.

Review of *PRU 3*, *VT* 6 (1956) 218-23.

Cohen, H.; Sivan, D.

Ugaritic Hippiatric Texts: A Critical Edition (New Haven: American Oriental Society, 1983).

Cross, F.M.

"Yahweh and the God of the Patriarchs," *HTR* 55 (1962) 225-59.

"The Origin and Early Evolution of the Alphabet," *ErIs* 8 (1967) 8*-24*.

Canaanite Myth and Hebrew Epic: Essays in the History of the Religion of Israel (Cambridge, Mass.: Harvard, 1973).

Cross, F.M.; Freedman, D.N.

"The Name of Ashdod," *BASOR* 175 (1964) 48-50.

Cross, F.M.; Lambdin, T.O.

"A Ugaritic Abecedary and the Origins of the Proto-Canaanite Alphabet," *BASOR* 160 (1960) 21-26.

Dahood, M.

"Canaanite-Phoenician Influence in Qoheleth," *Biblica* 33 (1952) 30-52, 191-221.

"Hebrew and Ugaritic Equivalents of Accadian *pitū purīdā*," *Biblica* 39 (1958) 67-69.

"Hebrew-Ugaritic Lexicography VIII," *Biblica* 51 (1970) 391-404.

de Moor, J.C.

"Studies in the New Alphabetic Texts from Ras Shamra II," *UF* 1 (1969) 167-88; 2 (1970) 303-27.

"Ugaritic Lexicography," in *Studies on Semitic Lexicography* (ed. P. Fronzaroli; QS 2; Florence: Istituto de Linguistica e di Lingue Orientali, 1973) 61-102.

Deimel, A.

Šumerisches Lexikon, 3rd ed.; 4 vols. (Rome: Pontificium Institutum Biblicum, 1928-50).

Del Olmo Lete, G.

"The Ugaritic War Chariot: A New Translation of *KTU* 4.392 (*PRU V,* 105)," *UF* 10 (1978) 47-51.

Dhorme, E.

"Petite tablette accadienne de Ras Shamra," *Syria* 16 (1935) 194-95.

Diakonoff, I.M.

"Some Remarks on I568," *ArOr* 47 (1979) 1 40-41.

Dietrich, M.; Loretz, O.

"Die soziale Struktur von Alalaḫ und Ugarit. I. Die Berufsbezeichnungen mit der hurritischen Endung *-ḫuli,*" *WO* 3 (1966) 188-205.

"Der Vertrag zwischen Šuppiluliuma und Niqmandu: Eine philologische und kulturhistorische Studie," *WO* 3 (1966) 206-45.

"Zur ugaritischen Lexikographie (I)," *BiOr* 23 (1966) 127-32.

"Zur ugaritischen Lexikographie (II)," *OLZ* 62 (1967) 533-52.

"Untersuchungen zur Schrift- und Lautlehre des Ugaritischen (I): Der ugaritische Konsonant *ǵ*," *WO* 4 (1967-68) 300-315.

"Zur ugaritischen Lexikographie (III)," *BiOr* 25 (1968) 100-1.
"*pilku* = *ilku* 'Lehenspflicht,'" *UF* 4 (1972) 165-66.
"Die ug. Gewandbezeichnungen *pǵndr, knd, kndpnṯ*," *UF* 9 (1977) 340.
"Bemerkungen zum Aqhat-Text. Zur ugaritischen Lexikographie (XIV)," *UF* 10 (1978) 65-71.
"Einzelfragen zu Wörtern aus den ugaritischen Mythen und Wirtschaftstexten. Zur ugaritischen Lexikographie (XV)," *UF* 11 (1979) 189-98.
"Kennt das Ugaritische einen Titel *aḫat-milki* = *šar-elli* = *ṯryl* 'Schwester des Königs'?" *UF* 15 (1983) 303.
Dietrich, M.; Loretz, O.; Sanmartín, J.
"Zur ugaritischen Lexikographie (VII): Lexikographische Einzelbemerkungen," *UF* 5 (1973) 79-104.
"Zur ugaritischen Lexikographie (VIII): Lexikographische Einzelbemerkungen," *UF* 5 (1973) 105-17.
"Zur ugaritischen Lexikographie (XI): Lexikographische Einzelbemerkungen," *UF* 6 (1974) 19-38.
"Zur ugaritischen Lexikographie (XIII)," *UF* 7 (1975) 157-69.
Die keilalphabetischen Texte aus Ugarit einschliesslich der keilalphabetischen Texte ausserhalb Ugarits 1: Transkription (AOAT 24, 1976).
Dillmann, C.F.A.
Lexicon Linguae Aethiopicae cum indice latino, 4 vols. (Leipzig, 1865; repr. New York: Ungar 1955).
Driver, G.R.
Canaanite Myths and Legends (Old Testament Studies 3; Edinburgh: Clark, 1956).
Durham, J.W.
"Studies in Boğazköy Akkadian" (PhD. Dissertation, Harvard University, 1976).
Ebeling, E.
Keilschrifttexte aus Assur religiösen Inhalts (Leipzig/Berlin, 1919-23).
Ebeling, E.; Meissner; et al.
Reallexicon der Assyriologie (Berlin/Leipzig, 1932-)..
Finet, A.
L'accadien des lettres de Mari (Brussels: Palais des Académies, 1956).
Fisher, L.R., ed.
The Claremont Ras Shamra Tablets (AnOr 48, 1971).
Freilich, D.; Pardee, D.
"{ẓ} and {ṭ} in Ugaritic: a Re-examination of the Sign-Forms," *Syria* 61 (1984) 25-36.
Friedrich, J.
"Churritisch-Ugaritisches und Churritisch-Luwisches," *AfO* 14 (1944) 329-31.

Fronzaroli, P.
La fonetica ugaritica (Sussidi Eruditi 7; Rome: Edizioni di Storia e Letteratura, 1955).
"Per una valutazione della morfologia eblaita," *Studi Eblaiti* 5 (1982) 93-120.
"Eblaic Lexicon: Problems and Appraisal," in *Studies on the Language of Ebla* (ed. idem; QS 13; Florence: Istituto di Linguistica e di Lingue Orientali, 1984) 117-57.

Fronzaroli, P., ed.
Studies on Semitic Lexicography (QS 2; Florence: Istituto de Linguistica e di Lingue Orientali, 1973).
Studies on the Language of Ebla (QS 13; Florence: Istituto di Linguistica e di Lingue Orientali, 1984).

Gamkrelidze, T.V.
"The Akkado-Hittite Syllabary and the Problem of the Origin of the Hittite Script," *ArOr* 29 (1961) 406-18.

Garr, W.R.
Dialect Geography of Syria-Palestine, 1000-586 B.C.E. (Philadelphia: University of Pennsylvania, 1985).
"On Voicing and Devoicing in Ugaritic," *JNES* 45 (1986) 45-52.

Gaster, T.H.
"The Harrowing of Baal. A Poem from Ras Shamra," *Acta Or.* 16 (1938) 41-48.
"The Canaanite Epic of Keret," *JQR* 37 (1946-47) 285-93.
"Ugaritic Philology," *JAOS* 70 (1950) 8-18.

Gelb, I.J.
Glossary of Old Akkadian (MAD 3; Chicago: University of Chicago, 1957).
Old Akkadian Writing and Grammar, 2nd ed. (MAD 2; Chicago: University of Chicago, 1961).
"Comments on the Akkadian Syllabary," *Or.* 39 (1970) 516-46.

Gelb, I.J.; et al.
The Assyrian Dictionary of the Oriental Institute of the University of Chicago (Chicago: Oriental Institute, 1956-).

Gelb, I.J.; et al.
Computer-Aided Analysis of Amorite (AS 21; Chicago: Oriental Institute, 1980).

Ginsberg, H.L.
"The Rebellion and Death of Ba^{c}lu," *Or.* 5 (1936) 161-98.

Goetze, A.
"Short or Long *a*? (Notes on Some Akkadian Words)," *Or.* 16 (1947) 239-50.
"Hittite courtiers and their titles," *RHA* 12 (54) (1952) 1-14.

Gordon, C.H.
"Observations on the Akkadian Tablets from Ugarit," *RA* 50 (1956) 127-33.
"Ugaritic *ḫrt*/*ḫirîtu* 'cemetery,'" *Syria* 33 (1956) 102-3.
Ugaritic Textbook: Grammar, Texts in Transliteration, Cuneiform Selections,

Glossary, Indices (AnOr 38, 1965).
Gordon, C.H.; Lacheman, E.R.
"The Nuzu Menology," *ArOr* 10 (1938) 51-64.
Görg, M.
"Die Priestertitel *kmr* und *khn*," *BN* 30 (1985) 7-14.
Gray, J.
The Krt Text in the Literature of Ras Shamra: A Social Myth of Ancient Canaan, 2nd ed. (Leiden: Brill, 1964).
Greenfield, J.C.
"Ugaritic Lexicographical Notes," *JCS* 21 (1967) 89-93.
"The *marzeaḥ* as a Social Institution," *Acta Antiqua Academiae Scientiarum Hungaricae* 22 (1974) 451-55.
"*našû-nadānu* and its Congeners," in *Memoirs of the Connecticut Academy of Arts and Sciences* 19 (Finkelstein Memorial Volume, ed. M. deJong Ellis; 1977) 87-91.
Gröndahl, F.
Die Personennamen der Texte aus Ugarit (Studia Pohl 1; Rome: Pontificium Insitutum Biblicum, 1967).
Güterbock, H.G.; Jacobsen, T., eds.
Studies in Honor of Benno Landsberger on his Seventy-fifth Birthday, April 21, 1965 (AS16; Chicago: University of Chicago, 1965).
Haas, V.; Thiel, H.J.
Die Beschwörungsrituale der Allaituraḫ(ḫ)i und verwandte Texte (Hurritologische Studien 2; AOAT 31, 1978).
Haas, V.; Wilhelm, G.
"Zum ḫurritischen Lexikon I," *Or.* 41 (1972) 5-10.
Hallo, W.W., ed.
Essays in Memory of E.A. Speiser (American Oriental Series 53; New Haven: American Oriental Society, 1968).
Harris, Z.S.
"A Conditioned Sound Change in Ras Shamra," *JAOS* 57 (1937) 151-57.
The Development of the Canaanite Dialects (American Oriental Series 16; New Haven, 1939).
Hecker, K.
Grammatik der Kültepe-Texte (AnOr 44, 1968).
Held, M.
"The Root ZBL/SBL in Akkadian, Ugaritic and Biblical Hebrew," in Hallo, ed., *Essays Speiser* 90-96.
Heltzer, M.
"The Word *ṣṣ* in Ugaritic (About the occurence of salt-taxes in Ugarit)," *AION* 18 (1968) 355-61.

"Zur Bedeutung des Ausdrucks «die *ṣibbiru*-Felder» in Ugarit," *OLP* 8 (1977) 47-55.

Herdner, A.

Corpus des tablettes en cunéiformes alphabétiques découvertes à Ras Shamra-Ugarit de 1929 à 1939 (Mission de Ras Shamra 10; Paris: Imprimerie Nationale, 1963).

"Nouveaux textes alphabétiques de Ras Shamra — XXIVe campagne, 1961," in *Ug*. 7 1-74.

Hillers, D.R.

Review of Gröndahl, *Personennamen*, *JNES* 29 (1970) 298-300.

"A Hebrew Cognate of *unuššu/ʾunṯ* in Is.33:8," *HTR* 64 (1971) 257-59.

"Additional Note," *BASOR* 200 (1976) 18.

Hoffner, H.A., Jr.

"Ugaritic *pwt* : A Term from the Early Canaanite Dyeing Industry," *JAOS* 87 (1967) 300-3.

Huehnergard, J.

"The Akkadian Dialects of Carchemish and Ugarit" (Ph.D Dissertation, Harvard University, 1979).

"Akkadian Evidence for Case-Vowels on Ugaritic Bound Forms," *JCS* 33 (1981) 199-205.

"Five Tablets from the Vicinity of Emar," *RA* 77 (1983) 11-43.

"A Dt Stem in Ugaritic?" *UF* 17 (1985) 402.

"On Verbless Clauses in Akkadian," *ZA* 76 (1986) 218-49.

"Northwest Semitic Vocabulary in Akkadian Texts," *JAOS* 107/4 (1987).

The Akkadian of Ugarit (HSS forthcoming).

"RS 15.86 (PRU 3, 51f.)," *UF* forthcoming.

"Three Notes on Akkadian Morphology," in *Working with No Data: Egyptian and Semitic Studies Presented to Thomas O. Lambdin* (ed. D. Golomb; Winona Lake, Ind.: Eisenbrauns, forthcoming).

Izre'el, Š.

"The Gezer Letters of the el-Amarna Archive — Linguistic Analysis," *IOS* 8 (1978) 13-90.

"On the Use of the So-Called Ventive Morpheme in the Akkadian Texts of Amurru," *UF* 16 (1984) 83-92.

"The Akkadian Dialect of the Scribes of Amurru in the 14th-13th Centuries B.C." (PhD. Dissertation, Tel-Aviv University, 1985).

Jirku, A.

"Die Umschrift ugaritische Laryngale durch der akkadischen Buchstaben Ú," *ArOr* 38 (1970) 129-30.

"Ugaritic *mswn* and Ugaritic *maswatu*," *JNSL* 3 (1974) 34.

Johnstone, T.M.

Ḥarsūsi Lexicon and English-Ḥarsūsi Word-List (London: Oxford University, 1977).

Jibbāli Lexicon (Oxford: Oxford University, 1981).

Jucquois, G.

Phonétique comparée des dialectes moyen-babyloniens du nord et de l'ouest (Bibliothèque du Muséon 53; Louvain: Institut Orientaliste, 1966).

Kaufman, S.A.

The Akkadian Influences on Aramaic (AS 19; Chicago: University of Chicago, 1974).

Kennedy, A.R.S

"Cooking and Cooking Utensils," in *Encyclopædia Biblica: A Critical Dictionary of the Literary, Political and Religious History, the Archæology, Geography and Natural History of the Bible* (ed. T.K. Cheyne, J. Sutherland Black; London: Black, 1899) 1 887-892.

Knudsen, E.E.

"Spirantization of Velars in Akkadian," in *lišān mitḫurti: Festschrift Wolfram Freiherr von Soden zum 19.VI.1968 gewidmet von Schülern und Mitarbeitern* (ed. W. Röllig with M. Dietrich; *AOAT* 1, 1969) 147-55.

Knudtzon, J.A.

Die El-Amarna-Tafeln mit Einleitung und Erläuterungen, 2 vols. (Leipzig: Hinrichs, 1915; repr. Aalen: Zeller, 1964).

Kraemer, J.; Gätje, M.; Ullman, M., ed.

Wörterbuch der klassischen arabischen Sprache (Wiesbaden: Harrassowitz, 1957-).

Kraus, F.R.

"Akkadische Wörter und Ausdrücke, IX," *RA* 69 (1975) 31-40.

"Akkadische Wörter und Ausdrücke, X-XI," *RA* 70 (1976) 165-72.

Kraus, F.R., ed.

Altbabylonische Briefe (Leiden: Brill, 1964-).

Krebernik, M.

"Zur Syllabar und Orthographie der lexikalischen Texte aus Ebla," *ZA* 72 (1982) 178-236; 73 (1983) 1-47.

Krecher, J.

"Glossen," *RlA* 3 (1969) 431-40.

"Schreiberschulung in Ugarit: Die Tradition von Listen und sumerischen Texten," *UF* 1 (1969) 131-58.

Krotkoff, G.

"*laḥm* 'Fleisch' und *leḥem* 'Brot,'" *WZKM* 62 (1969) 76-82.

Kühne, C.

"Randnotizen zu PRU VI," *UF* 5 (1973) 185-89.

"Mit Glossenkeilen markierte fremde Wörter in akkadischen Ugarittexten," *UF* 6 (1974) 157-67; 7 (1975) 253-60.

"Eine analytische Liste der akkadischen Ugarittexte," *UF* 6 (1974) 129-56; "Nachträge und Berichtigungen," 7 (1975) 515-16.

Kümmel, H.M.

"Ugaritica Hethitica," *UF* 1 (1969) 159-65.

Labat, R.

L'Akkadien de Boghaz-Köi: Étude sur la Langue des Lettres, Traités et Vocabulaires Akkadiens trouvés à Boghaz-Köi (Bordeaux: Delmas, 1932).

"Le rayonnement de la langue et de l'écriture akkadiennes au deuxième millénaire avant notre ère," *Syria* 39 (1962) 1-27.

Manuel d'épigraphie akkadienne, 5th ed. (revised and corrected by F. Malbran-Labat; Paris: Geuthner, 1976).

Lambdin, T.O.

"Egyptian Loanwords in the Old Testament," *JAOS* 73 (1953) 145-55.

"Egyptian Words in Tell El Amarna Letter No. 14," *Or.* 22 (1953) 362-69.

Introduction to Classical Ethiopic (Ge^{c}ez) (HSS 24; Missoula, Mont.: Scholars, 1978).

Lambert, W.G.

"Götterlisten," *RlA* 3 (1969) 473-79.

Landsberger, B.

"Assyrische Königsliste und 'Dunkles Zeitalter,'" *JCS* 8 (1954) 31-45, 47-73, 106-33.

Landsberger, B.; et al.

Materials for the Sumerian Lexicon (Rome: Pontifical Biblical Institute, 1937-).

Lane, E.W.

An Arabic-English Lexicon, derived from the best and the most copious Eastern Sources, &c., 8 vols. (London: Williams and Norgate, 1863-93).

Laroche, E.

"Documents en langue hourrite provenant de Ras Shamra," in *Ug. 5* 447-544.

"Études de linguistique anatolienne, III," *RHA* 28 (1970) 22-71.

"RS 20.189," *UF* 11 (1979) 477-80.

Glossaire de la langue hourrite (Paris: Klincksieck, 1980).

Leslau, W.

"Observations on Semitic Cognates in Ugaritic," *Or.* 37 (1968) 347-66.

Levy, J.

Neuhebräisches und Chaldäisches Wörterbuch über die Talmudim und Midraschim, 4 vols. (Leipzig: Brockhaus, 1876-89).

L'Heureux, C.E.

Rank among the Canaanite Gods El, Ba^{c}al, and the Repha$^\supset$im (HSM 21; Missoula, Mont.: Scholars, 1979).

Lichtenstein, M.H.
"Psalm 68:7 Revisited," *JANES* 4 (1972) 97-112.
Lipiński, E.
"*skn* et *sgn* dans le sémitique occidental du nord," *UF* 5 (1973) 191-207.
"Aḫat-Milki, reine d'Ugarit, et la guerre du Mukiš," *OLP* 12 (1981) 79-115.
Liverani, M.
"Antecedenti del diptotismo arabo nei testi accadici di Ugarit," *RSO* 38 (1963) 131-60.
"Le chêne de Sherdanu," *VT* 27 (1977) 212-16.
Loewenstamm, S.E.
"Lexicographical Notes on 1. *ṭbḫ*; 2. *hnny/hlny*," *UF* 5 (1973) 209-11.
Comparative Studies in Biblical and Ancient Oriental Literatures (AOAT 204, 1980).
Loretz, O.
"Ugaritisches *ṣamātu* und hebräisches *ṣm(y)tt*," *BiZ* 6 (1962) 269-79.
Macdonald, J.
"The Unique Ugaritic Personnel Text KTU 4.102," *UF* 10 (1978) 161-73.
Marcus, D.
"The Three Alephs in Ugaritic," *JANES* 1 (1968) 50-60.
"The Verb 'To Live' in Ugaritic," *JSS* 17 (1972) 76-82.
Margulis, B.
"The *Kôšārôt/kṯrt*: Patroness-saints of Women," *JANES*4 (1972) 52-61.
"Of Brides and Birds: a Reply to M. Lichtenstein," *JANES*4 (1972) 113-17.
Mayer, W.
Untersuchungen zur Grammatik des Mittelassyrischen (AOATS 2, 1971).
"*mardatu* 'Teppich,'" *UF* 9 (1977) 173-89.
Meier, G.
"Ein akkadisches Heilungsritual aus Boğazköy," *ZA* 45 (1939) 195-215.
Melchert, H.C.
Studies in Hittite Historical Phonology (Göttingen: Vandenhoeck & Ruprecht, 1984).
Miller, P.D., Jr.
"The *mrzḥ* Text," in Fisher, ed., *AnOr* 48 37-48.
Moran, W.L.
"A Syntactical Study of the Dialect of Byblos as Reflected in the Amarna Tablets" (PhD. Dissertation, Johns Hopkins University, 1950).
"The Use of the Canaanite Infinitive Absolute as a Finite Verb in the Amarna Letters from Byblos," *JCS* 4 (1950) 169-72.
"New Evidence on Canaanite *taqtulū(na)*," *JCS* 5 (1951) 33-35.
"Ugaritic *ṣîṣûma* and Hebrew *ṣîṣ*, " *Biblica* 39 (1958) 69-71.
"Early Canaanite *yaqtula*, " *Or.* 29 (1960) 1-19.

"The Hebrew Language in its Northwest Semitic Background," in *The Bible and the Ancient Near East: Essays in honor of William Foxwell Albright* (ed. G.E. Wright; Garden City, N.Y.: Anchor/Doubleday, 1961) 59-84.

"The Syrian Scribe of the Jerusalem Amarna Letters," in *Unity and Diversity* (ed. H. Goedicke, J.J.M.Roberts; Baltimore: Johns Hopkins, 1975).

"Putative Akkadian *šukammu*," *JCS* 31 (1979) 247-48.

"Note brève (*sūnu*)," *RA* 77 (1983) 93-94.

Nougayrol, J.

Le Palais royal d'Ugarit 3: Textes accadiens et hourrites des Archives Est, Ouest et Centrales (Mission de Ras Shamra 6; Paris: Imprimerie Nationale, 1955).

Le Palais royal d'Ugarit 4: Textes accadiens des Archives Sud (Archives internationales) (Mission de Ras Shamra 9; Paris: Imprimerie Nationale, 1956).

"'Vocalises' et 'syllabes en liberté' à Ugarit," in *AS* 16 29-39.

"Textes suméro-accadiens des archives et bibliothèques privées d'Ugarit," in *Ug. 5* 1-446.

"La Lamaštu à Ugarit," in *Ug. 6* 393-408.

"Nouveau 'Silbenvokabular A' d'Ugarit," *RA* 63 (1969) 83-85.

Le Palais royal d'Ugarit 6: Textes en cunéiformes babyloniens des Archives du Grand Palais et du Palais Sud d'Ugarit (Mission de Ras Shamra 12; Paris: Imprimerie Nationale, 1970).

Nougayrol, J.; Laroche, E.; Virolleaud, C.; Schaeffer, C.F.A.

Ugaritica 5: Nouveaux textes accadiens, hourrites et ugaritiques des Archives et Bibliothèques privées d'Ugarit, commentaires des textes historiques (Mission de Ras Shamra 16; Paris: Imprimerie Nationale, 1968).

Owen, D.I.

"An Akkadian Letter from Ugarit at Tel Aphek," *TA* 8 (1981) 1-17.

Pardee, D.

"A Further Note on PRU V, no. 60, Epigraphic in Nature," *UF* 13 (1981) 151-56.

"Ugaritic," *AfO* 29/30 (1983-84) 321-29.

Pettinato, G.

Materiali epigrafici di Ebla 4: Testi lessicali bilingui della Biblioteca L. 2769 (Seminario di Studi Asiatici, Series maior 4; Naples: Istituto Universitario Orientale, 1982).

Rabinowitz, J.J.

"A Biblical Parallel to a Legal Formula from Ugarit," *VT* 8 (1958) 95.

Rainey, A.F.

"Family Relationships in Ugarit," *Or.* 34 (1965) 10-22.

"The Military Personnel of Ugarit," *JNES* 24 (1965) 17-27.

"LÚMAŠKIM at Ugarit," *Or.* 35 (1966) 426-28.

"Notes on the Syllabic Ugaritic Vocabularies," *IEJ* 19 (1969) 107-9.
"The Scribe at Ugarit: His Position and Influence," *Proceedings* of the Israel Academy of Sciences and Humanities (Jerusalem) 3 (1969) 126-47.
"Linguistic Method—May They Preserve it," *Lĕšonénu* 35 (1970-71) 11-15.
"Observations on Ugaritic Grammar," *UF* 3 (1971) 151-72.
"Verbal Forms with Infixed *-t-* in the West Semitic el-Amarna Letters," *IOS* 1 (1971) 86-102.
"Gleanings from Ugarit," *IOS* 3 (1973) 34-62.
"Reflections on the Suffix Conjugation in West Semitized Amarna Tablets," *UF* 5 (1973) 235-62.
"More gleanings from Ugarit," *IOS* 5 (1975) 18-31.
"Morphology and the Prefix-Tenses of West Semitized el-ᶜAmarna Tablets," *UF* 7 (1975) 395-426.

Richardson, M.E.J.
"Ugaritic Place Names with Final *-y*," *JSS* 23 (1978) 298-315.

Riemschneider, K.K.
"Zur Unterscheidung der Vokale *e* und *i* in der hethitischen Orthographie," in *Festschrift Heinrich Otten* (ed. E. Neu, C. Rüster; Wiesbaden: Harrassowitz, 1973) 273-81.

Röllig, W.; Dietrich, M., eds.
lišān mitḫurti: Festschrift Wolfram Freiherr von Soden zum 19.VI.1968 gewidmet von Schülern und Mitarbeitern (AOAT 1, 1969). .

Salonen, A.
Die Hausgeräte der alten Mesopotamier nach sumerisch-akkadischen Quellen; 2 vols. (AASF, Series B 139, 144; Helsinki, 1965-66)

Sanmartín, J.
"Ug. *uzr* und Verwandtes," *UF* 9 (1977) 369-70.
"Zu ug. *adr* in KTU 1.17 VI 20-23," *UF* 9 (1977) 371-73.

Schaeffer, C.F.A., ed.
Ugaritica 3: Sceaux et cylindres hittites, épée gravée du cartouche de Mineptah, tablettes chypro-minoennes et autres découvertes nouvelles de Ras Shamra (Mission de Ras Shamra 8; Paris: Geuthner, 1956).
Ugaritica 4: découvertes des xviiie et xixe campagnes, 1954-1955, fondements préhistoriques d'Ugarit et nouveaux sondages, études anthropologiques, poteries grecques et monnaies islamiques de Ras Shamra et environs (Mission de Ras Shamra 15; Paris: Imprimerie Nationale, 1962).

Scullion, J.J.
"Some difficult texts in Isaiah cc.56-66 in the light of modern scholarship," *UF* 4 (1972) 105-28.

Segert, S.
"The Last Sign of the Ugaritic Alphabet," *UF* 15 (1983) 201-18.
"Polarity of Vowels in the Ugaritic Verbs II/ʾ/," *UF* 15 (1983) 219-22.

A Basic Grammar of the Ugaritic Language with selected texts and glossary (Berkeley: University of California, 1984).
A Grammar of the Ugaritic Language, part 2 (Manuscript).
Sivan, D.
"Final Triphthongs and Final *yu/a/i — wu/a/i* Diphthongs in Ugaritic Nominal Forms," *UF* 14 (1982) 209-18.
"Diphthongs and Triphthongs in Verbal Forms of Verba Tertiae Infirmae in Ugaritic," *UF* 16 (1984) 279-93.
Grammatical Analysis and Glossary of the Northwest Semitic Vocables in Akkadian Texts of the 15th-13th C.B.C. from Canaan and Syria (AOAT 214, 1984).
Sjöberg, A., ed.
The Sumerian Dictionary of the University Museum of the University of Pennsylvania (Philadelphia: University Museum, 1984-).
Speiser, E.A.
Introduction to Hurrian (AASOR 20; New Haven: American Schools of Oriental Research, 1941).
"Akkadian Documents from Ras Shamra," *JAOS* 75 (1955) 154-65.
"The Syllabic Transcription of Ugaritic [*h*] and [*ḥ*]," *BASOR* 175 (1964) 42-47.
Steinkeller, P.
Review of H. Limet, *Textes sumeriens de la IIIe dynastie d'Ur, JCS* 35 (1983) 244-50.
"A Note on sa-bar = sa-par4/pàr 'Casting Net,'" *ZA* 75 (1985) 39-46.
Stol, M.
"Zum altmesopotamischen Bierbereitung," *BiOr* 28 (1971) 167-71.
Swaim, G.
"A Grammar of the Akkadian Tablets found at Ugarit" (PhD. Dissertation, Brandeis University, 1962; Univ. Microfilms no. 63-5831).
Thiel, W.
"Zur gesellschaftlichen Stellung des mudu in Ugarit," *UF* 12 (1980) 349-56.
Thureau-Dangin, F.
Le Syllabaire accadien (Paris: P. Geuthner, 1926).
"Vocabulaires de Ras-Shamra," *Syria* 12 (1931) 225-66.
"Nouvelles fragments de vocabulaires de Ras-Shamra," *Syria* 13 (1932) 234-41.
"Trois contrats de Ras-Shamra," *Syria* 18 (1937) 245-55.
Tsumura, D.T.
"The Verba Primai WAW, WLD, in Ugaritic," *UF* 11 (1979) 779-82.
Tuttle, G.A.
"Case Vowels on Masculine Singular Nouns in Construct in Ugaritic," in *Biblical and Near Eastern Studies: Essays in Honor of William Sanford LaSor* (ed. Tuttle; Grand Rapids, Mich.: Eerdmans, 1978) 253-68.

Van Selms, A.

"The Root *k-ṯ-r* and its Derivatives in Ugaritic Literature," *UF* 11 (1979) 739-44.

Van Soldt, W.H.

"Hurrian *utte,* 'emmer,'" *RA* 75 (1981) 93.

Vargyas, P.

"Le *mudu* à Ugarit. Ami du roi?" *UF* 13 (1981) 165-79.

Verreet, E.

"Das silbenschliessende Aleph im Ugaritischen," *UF* 15 (1983) 223-58.

"Beobachtungen zum ugaritischen Verbalsystem," *UF* 16 (1984) 307-21.

"Beobachtungen zum ugaritischen Verbalsystem II," *UF* 17 (1985) 319-44.

Virolleaud, C.

(Séance du 18 novembre 1959) *GLECS* 8 (1959) 65-66.

von Schuler, E.

"Hurritische Nomina Actoris," *RHA* 19 (68) (1961) 19-23.

von Soden, W.

Akkadisches Handwörterbuch, unter Benutzung des lexikalischen Nachlesses von Bruno Meissner (Wiesbaden: Harrassowitz, 1965-81). .

"Kleine Beiträge zum Ugaritischen und Hebräischen," in *Hebräische Wortforschung: Festschrift zum 80. Geburtstag von Walter Baumgartner* (Leiden: Brill, 1967) 291-300.

"Bemerkungen zu einigen literarischen Texten in akkadischer Sprache aus Ugarit," *UF* 1 (1969) 189-95.

Grundriss der akkadischen Grammatik samt Ergänzungsheft (AnOr 33, 47; Rome: Ponfificium Institutum Biblicum, 1969). .

"Zur Stellung des 'Geweihten' (*qdš*) in Ugarit," *UF* 2 (1970) 329-30.

"Assyriasmen im Akkadischen von Ugarit und das Problem der Verwaltungssprache im Mitannireich," *UF* 11 (1979) 745-51.

von Soden, W.; Röllig, W.

Das akkadische Syllabar, 3rd ed. (AnOr 42, 1976).

Waschow, H.

Babylonische Briefe aus der Kassitenzeit (MAOG 10/1 Gräfenhainichen: Heine, 1936).

Wehr, H.

Arabic-English Dictionary, 3rd ed. (ed. M.J. Cowan; Ithaca, N.Y.: Spoken Languages Services, 1976).

Weidner, E.F.

"Altbabylonische Götterlisten," *AfK* 2 (1924-25) 1-18, 71-82.

Weippert, M.

"^{lú}AD.DA.A.NI in den Briefen des Abduḫeba von Jerusalem an den Pharao," *UF* 6 (1974) 415-19.

Wesselius, J.W.

"Two Notes on Ugaritic Toponyms," *UF* 15 (1983) 315.

Wilhelm, G.

Untersuchungen zum Ḫurro-Akkadischen von Nuzi (AOAT 9, 1970).

"Der hurritische Ablativ-Instrumentalis */ne/*," *ZA* 73 (1983) 96-113.

Das Archiv des Šilwa-Teššup 3: Rationenlisten 2 (Wiesbaden: Harrassowitz, 1985).

"Hurritische Lexikographie," *Or.* 54 (1985) 487-96.

"Marginalien zu Herodot, Klio 199," in *Festschrift W.L. Moran* (ed. I.T. Abusch, J. Huehnergard, P. Steinkeller; Harvard Semitic Studies; forthcoming).

Wiseman, D.J.

The Alalakh Tablets (Occasional Publications 2; London: British Institute of Archaeology at Ankara, 1953).

Xella, P.

I testi rituali di Ugarit 1 (Pubblicazioni del Centro di Studio per la Civiltà Fenicia e Punica 21; Studi Semitici 54; Rome: Consiglio Nazionale delle Ricerche, 1981).

Zaccagnini, C.

"Note sulla terminologia metallurgica di Ugarit," *OA* 9 (1970) 315-24.

Zevit, Z.

"The Question of Case Endings on Ugaritic Nouns in Status Constructus, " *JSS* 28 (1983) 225-32.

Indices

A. Corpus of Ugarit Akkadian Texts

1. *By Place of Publication of Transliteration.*

AnOr 48 26 (RS 1957.3)
AnOr 48 27 (RS 1957.4)

AS 16 29ff.:1-37 (RS 20.125 side A)
AS 16 29ff.:1-4,... (RS 25.455*+)
AS 16 29ff.:7-25,... (RS 22.225 side B)
AS 16 29ff.:27-44 (RS 20.155 side A)
AS 16 31ff.:11-54,... (RS 20.125 side B)
AS 16 31ff.:27-40,... (RS 24.77)
AS 16 31ff.:30-41,... (RS 20.215)
AS 16 31ff.:40-48,... (RS 22.220 i-ii)
AS 16 31ff.:55-68 (RS 5.X)
AS 16 31ff.:109-24 (RS 25.133)
AS 16 33ff. A 1-22 F 1'-17' (RS 17.41)
AS 16 33ff. B 1-40,... (RS 22.222)
AS 16 33ff. B/C E 1-14 (RS 22.411)
AS 16 33ff. C 1-13 D 27'-37' (RS 22.435)
AS 16 33ff. C 31-41 D 10'-13' (RS 22.215)
AS 16 33ff. D 21'-32' (RS 20.155 side B)
AS 16 39 (RS 20.11)

EA 45 (Berlin 1692)
EA 46 (Berlin 1694)
EA 47 (Berlin 1693)
EA 48 (Berlin 1690)
EA 49 (Cairo 4783)

KTU 4.165 rev. (RS 15.76)
KTU 4.381 obv. (RS 18.102)
KTU 5.14 (RS 19.159)

MSL 4 122f. (no RS no.)
MSL 5 30-37 (V_5) see Syria 12 pl. 49
MSL 5 51-80 (V_1) see Syria 13 237+12 236ff.
MSL 5 68ff. (V_3) (RS 17.250)
MSL 5 71-72, 75 (V_2) see Syria 12 231ff.
MSL 5 93-137 (RSh I,II) see Syria 12 pl. 46ff.
MSL 5 119-20 (RSh IV) see Syria 10 pl. 77 6
MSL 5 131 (RSh III) see Syria 10 pl. 77 5
MSL 5 158 (V_5) see Syria 10 pl. 77 5
MSL 5 173-80 (V_2) see Syria 12 228ff.
MSL 5 175-83 (V_3-V_4) see Syria 12 pl. 46ff.
MSL 6 28ff. (RS) (RS 17.98)
MSL 6 36-39 (V_1) see Syria 12 pl 46ff.
MSL 6 36-39 (V_{1a}) see Syria 13 235
MSL 7 136ff. (RS) (RS 17.336)
MSL 8/1 100ff. (RS 17.40)
MSL 8/2 96ff. (RŠ a) (RS 20.32 i 1 - iv 45)
MSL 8/2 96ff. (RŠ b) (RS 17.03 obv.(?))
MSL 10 37ff. (A) (RS 22.346+ 349)
MSL 10 37ff. (B) (RS 25.415)
MSL 10 37ff. (C) (RS 25.454)
MSL 10 37ff. (D) (RS 22.337)
MSL 10 37ff. (E) (RS 21.06B)
MSL 10 37ff. (F) (RS 20.129A)
MSL 10 37ff. (G) (RS 26.144)
MSL 10 37ff. (H) (RS 26.137)
MSL 10 37ff. (S1) (RS 20.222A)
MSL 10 107ff. (A) (RS 22.346+ 349)
MSL 10 107ff. (D) (RS 22.337)
MSL 10 107ff. (E) (RS 20.218)
MSL 10 107ff. (F) (RS 20.171)
MSL 10 127ff. (RS) (RS 25.519)
MSL 10 149ff. (A) (RS 20.32 iv 46ff.)
MSL 10 149ff. (B) (RS 17.03 r.?)
MSL 10 149ff. (C) (RS 20.167)
MSL 11 43ff. (A) (RS 23.82+ 364)
MSL 11 43ff. (B) (RS 20.179A + rev. ii-iii)
MSL 11 43ff. (C) (RS 22.217C)
MSL 11 50ff. (A) (RS 20.192)
MSL 11 50ff. (B) (RS 20.201)
MSL 11 74f. (frag. h) (RS20.181c)
MSL 11 169 a (RS 20.156)
MSL 11 169 b (RS 25.419)
MSL 13 126 (RS 25.454E (?))
MSL 13 128ff. (no RS no.)
MSL 14 143f. (no. 22) (RS 25.457 + 26.150*)
MSL 17 18f.,21 (U) (RS 26.139A)
MSL 17 44b (RS 25.425)

PRU 2 116 (p. 49) see KTU 4.165

PRU 3 4b (RS 16.112)
PRU 3 32f. (RS 16.129)
PRU 3 33f. (RS 16.114)
PRU 3 34b (RS 8.207)
PRU 3 35a (RS 15.37)
PRU 3 35f. (RS 15.182)
PRU 3 36c (RS 15.180)
PRU 3 37a (RS 15.81)
PRU 3 37b (RS 16.287)
PRU 3 38b (RS 15.41)
PRU 3 39a (RS 16.61)
PRU 3 40b (RS 15.173)
PRU 3 45f. (RS 16.140)
PRU 3 47a (RS 16.150)
PRU 3 47f. (RS 16.166)
PRU 3 48f. (RS 16.248)
PRU 3 49b (RS 16.263)

PRU 3 50a (RS 16.275)
PRU 3 50f. (RS 16.277)
PRU 3 51f. (RS 15.86)
PRU 3 52f. (RS 15.85)
PRU 3 53b (RS 15.89)
PRU 3 54a (RS 15.90)
PRU 3 54ff. (RS 15.92)
PRU 3 56f. (RS 15.120)
PRU 3 58a (RS 15.146+161)
PRU 3 58f. (RS 15.Z)
PRU 3 59f. (RS 16.133)
PRU 3 60b (RS 16.141)
PRU 3 61f. (RS 16.156)
PRU 3 62b (RS 16.158)
PRU 3 62f. (RS 16.167)
PRU 3 63b (RS 16.174)
PRU 3 64a (RS 16.190)
PRU 3 64f. (RS 16.200)
PRU 3 65b (RS 16.247)
PRU 3 66a (RS 16.252)
PRU 3 66b (RS 16.254A)
PRU 3 67a (RS 16.255A+E)
PRU 3 67b (RS 16.262)
PRU 3 68f. (RS 16.269)
PRU 3 69f. (RS 16.276)
PRU 3 70b (RS 16.279)
PRU 3 70f. (RS 16.295)
PRU 3 71f. (RS 16.356)
PRU 3 72f. (RS 16.371)
PRU 3 73f. (RS 16.385)
PRU 3 74b (RS 16.283)
PRU 3 75a (RS 16.344)
PRU 3 75b (RS 15.91)
PRU 3 76a (RS 16.144)
PRU 3 76b (RS 16.160)
PRU 3 77a (RS 16.278)
PRU 3 77b (RS 16.142)
PRU 3 78 (RS 15.Y)
PRU 3 79a (RS 16.254D)
PRU 3 79ff. (RS 16.239)
PRU 3 81ff. (RS 16.143)
PRU 3 83f. (RS 16.157)
PRU 3 85f. (RS 16.250)
PRU 3 86ff. (RS 15.119)
PRU 3 88b (RS 15.88)
PRU 3 89a (RS 15.123+ 16.152)
PRU 3 89f. (RS 16.135)
PRU 3 90b (RS 16.147)
PRU 3 91a (RS 16.170)
PRU 3 91f. (RS 16.189)
PRU 3 93a (RS 16.208)
PRU 3 93b (RS 16.244)
PRU 3 94f. (RS 16.245)
PRU 3 95f. (RS 16.246)
PRU 3 96ff. (RS 16.249)
PRU 3 98f. (RS 16.260)
PRU 3 99b (RS 16.284)
PRU 3 100a (RS 16.368)
PRU 3 101f. (RS15.138+ 16.393B)
PRU 3 102ff. (RS 15.109+ 16.296)
PRU 3 106a (RS 16.206)
PRU 3 106f. (RS 16.285)
PRU 3 107f. (RS 16.238)
PRU 3 108f. (RS 16.251)
PRU 3 109b (RS 16.207)
PRU 3 110a (RS 16.267)
PRU 3 110f. see Syria 18 253f.
PRU 3 112a (RS 15.126)
PRU 3 112f. (RS 15.114)
PRU 3 113ff. (RS 16.353)
PRU 3 115f. (RS 16.148+ 254B)
PRU 3 117 (RS 15.143+164)
PRU 3 118 (RS 15.155)
PRU 3 119f. (RS 16.204)
PRU 3 121f. (RS 15.136)
PRU 3 122f. (RS 15.145)
PRU 3 124 (RS 15.167+163)
PRU 3 125 (RS 15.147)
PRU 3 126 (RS 16.162)
PRU 3 127f. (RS 16.154)
PRU 3 129a (RS 16.343)
PRU 3 129b (RS 8.098)
PRU 3 130a (RS 15.70)
PRU 3 130b (RS 15.100)
PRU 3 131a (RS 15.118)
PRU 3 131f. (RS 15.122)
PRU 3 132b(+)133a (RS 15.127 (+?)15.131)
PRU 3 133a see PRU 3 132b (+) 133a
PRU 3 133f. (RS 15.132)
PRU 3 134f. (RS 15.137)
PRU 3 135f. (RS 15.140)
PRU 3 136b (RS 15.141)
PRU 3 136f. (RS 15.168)
PRU 3 137b (RS 15.190)
PRU 3 137f. (RS 16.86)
PRU 3 138f. (RS 16.131)
PRU 3 140f. (RS 16.132)
PRU 3 141f. (RS 16.134)
PRU 3 142b (RS 16.136)
PRU 3 143a (RS 16.137)
PRU 3 143ff. (RS 16.138)
PRU 3 145f. (RS 16.139)
PRU 3 146f. (RS 16.153)
PRU 3 147b (RS 16.171)
PRU 3 147c (RS 16.172)
PRU 3 148a (RS 16.178)
PRU 3 148f. (RS 16.182+199)
PRU 3 149f. (RS 16.184)
PRU 3 150b (RS 16.188)
PRU 3 150f. (RS 16.197)
PRU 3 151f. (RS 16.201)
PRU 3 152f. (RS 16.202)
PRU 3 153f. (RS 16.205+192)
PRU 3 154f. (RS 16.242)
PRU 3 155f. (RS 16.243)
PRU 3 156f. (RS 16.253)
PRU 3 157b (RS 16.254C+ 255C)
PRU 3 158a (RS 16.254F)
PRU 3 158b (RS 16.255D)
PRU 3 159a (RS 16.256)
PRU 3 159f. (RS 16.261+)
PRU 3 160f. (RS 16.282)
PRU 3 161b (RS 16.281)
PRU 3 161f. (RS 16.286)
PRU 3 162f. (RS 16.348)
PRU 3 163f. (RS 16.363)
PRU 3 164b (RS 16.383)
PRU 3 165a (RS 16.384)
PRU 3 165f. (RS 16.386)
PRU 3 166b (RS 16.413)
PRU 3 166f. (RS 15.139)
PRU 3 168a (RS 16.186)
PRU 3 168b (RS 16.198B)
PRU 3 168c (RS 15.113)
PRU 3 169a (RS 16.145)
PRU 3 169f. (RS 16.163)
PRU 3 170b (RS 8.279)
PRU 3 171a (RS 15.150)
PRU 3 171b (RS 16.173)
PRU 3 172a (RS 16.175)
PRU 3 172b (RS 16.191A)
PRU 3 172c (RS 16.191B)
PRU 3 173a (RS 16.240)
PRU 3 173b (RS 16.254E)
PRU 3 173c (RS 16.255B)
PRU 3 174a (RS 16.255G)
PRU 3 174c (RS 16.280)
PRU 3 175a (RS 16.311)
PRU 3 176a (RS Pt. 383G)
PRU 3 187a (RS 15.43)
PRU 3 187b (RS 16.357)
PRU 3 187c (RS 15.154)
PRU 3 187d (RS 16.125)
PRU 3 188a (RS 16.126A)
PRU 3 188b (RS 16.151)
PRU 3 188c (RS 16.290)
PRU 3 188f. (RS 10.044)
PRU 3 189b (RS 11.790)
PRU 3 190a (RS 11.800)
PRU 3 190b (RS 11.830)
PRU 3 191a (RS 11.841)
PRU 3 191b (RS 15.20)
PRU 3 191c (RS 15.179)
PRU 3 192a (RS 15.183)
PRU 3 192b (RS 16.313)
PRU 3 192f. (RS 12.34+43)
PRU 3 194a (RS 11.787)
PRU 3 194f. (RS 11.839)
PRU 3 195b (RS 15.09)
PRU 3 196 (RS 15.42+110)
PRU 3 197b (RS 16.181)
PRU 3 198a (RS 16.291)
PRU 3 198b (RS 16.359B)
PRU 3 199ff. (RS 16.257+)
PRU 3 204f. (RS 15.172)
PRU 3 205b (RS 16.155)
PRU 3 206a (RS 16.274)
PRU 3 206b (RS 16.294)
PRU 3 206f. (RS 15.135)
PRU 3 207b (RS 16.187B (!))
PRU 3 208b (RS 16.110)
PRU 3 209a (RS 16.359C)
PRU 3 209b (RS 16.292A)
PRU 3 210a (RS 16.292B)
PRU 3 210b (RS 15.X)

PRU 3 211f. (RS 12.47)
PRU 3 212b (RS 13.53)
PRU 3 213b see Ug. 5 118
PRU 3 213c (RS 15.54)
PRU 3 213f. obv. (RS 16.364)
PRU 3 214b (RS 16.416)
PRU 3 311f. (RS 15.10)

PRU 4 78b see PRU 3 91a
PRU 4 201 (RS 18.02)
PRU 4 202f. (RS 18.20+ 17.371)
PRU 4 294 (RS 19.70)

PRU 5 34A (p. 48) see KTU 4.381

PRU 6 3 (RS 17.455)
PRU 6 8 (RS 17.239)
PRU 6 21 (RS 17.331)
PRU 6 22 (RS 17.363)
PRU 6 23 (RS 17.376+377)
PRU 6 24 (RS 18.53)
PRU 6 25 (RS 17.53)
PRU 6 27 (RS 17.01)
PRU 6 28 (RS 17.39)
PRU 6 29 (RS 17.147)
PRU 6 30 (RS 18.500)
PRU 6 31 (RS 19.98)
PRU 6 32 (RS 19.128)
PRU 6 33 (RS 17.408)
PRU 6 34 (RS 17.410)
PRU 6 37 (RS 17.88)
PRU 6 38 (RS 17.356)
PRU 6 39 (RS 17.358)
PRU 6 40 (RS 17.360)
PRU 6 42 (RS 18.280)
PRU 6 43 (RS 17.77)
PRU 6 44 (RS 18.267)
PRU 6 45 (RS 18.21)
PRU 6 46 (RS 17.350B)
PRU 6 47 (RS 17.322)
PRU 6 49 (RS 17.378A)
PRU 6 50 (RS 17.388)
PRU 6 51 (RS 17.426)
PRU 6 52 (RS 19.78)
PRU 6 53 (RS 27.53)
PRU 6 54 (RS 19.33)
PRU 6 55 (RS 18.22)
PRU 6 56 (RS 17.121)
PRU 6 59 (RS 17.333)
PRU 6 65 (RS 18.264)
PRU 6 66 (RS 18.274)
PRU 6 68 (RS 17.84)
PRU 6 69 (RS 17.329)
PRU 6 70 (RS 17.50)
PRU 6 71 (RS 17.432)
PRU 6 72 (RS 19.65)
PRU 6 73 (RS 19.107A)
PRU 6 74 (RS 19.120)
PRU 6 75 (RS 19.121)
PRU 6 76 (RS 17.361C)
PRU 6 77 (RS 19.32)
PRU 6 78 (RS 19.41)
PRU 6 79 (RS 19.42)
PRU 6 80 (RS 19.111)
PRU 6 81 (RS 19.182)
PRU 6 82 (RS 17.242)
PRU 6 83 (RS 17.430)
PRU 6 84 (RS 19.30)
PRU 6 85 (RS 19.79)
PRU 6 86 (RS 19.82)
PRU 6 88 (RS 19.94)
PRU 6 89 (RS 19.110)
PRU 6 90 (RS 19.114)
PRU 6 91 (RS 19.132)
PRU 6 92 (RS 19.173A)
PRU 6 93 (RS 17.131)
PRU 6 95 (RS 19.74)
PRU 6 96 (RS 19.91)
PRU 6 97 (RS 19.118)
PRU 6 98 (RS 18.101B)
PRU 6 99 (RS 19.09)
PRU 6 100 (RS 19.51)
PRU 6 101 (RS 19.130)
PRU 6 102 (RS 19.12)
PRU 6 103 (RS 19.173B)
PRU 6 104 (RS 19.43)
PRU 6 105 (RS 19.117)
PRU 6 106 (RS 19.119)
PRU 6 107 (RS 19.25)
PRU 6 108 (RS 19.83)
PRU 6 109 (RS 19.131)
PRU 6 110 (RS 19.88)
PRU 6 111 (RS 19.129)
PRU 6 112 (RS 17.99)
PRU 6 113 (RS 19.26)
PRU 6 114 (RS 19.71)
PRU 6 115 (RS 17.37)
PRU 6 116 (RS 17.64)
PRU 6 117 (RS 17.136)
PRU 6 118 (RS 18.116)
PRU 6 119 (RS 19.69)
PRU 6 120 (RS 19.116)
PRU 6 121 (RS 19.141)
PRU 6 122 (RS 21.203)
PRU 6 123 (RS 17.328)
PRU 6 125 (RS 19.10)
PRU 6 126 (RS 19.28)
PRU 6 127 (RS 19.57)
PRU 6 128 (RS 19.104)
PRU 6 129 (RS 19.133A)
PRU 6 130 (RS 19.X)
PRU 6 131 (RS 19.35A)
PRU 6 132 (RS 19.85)
PRU 6 133 (RS 19.152)
PRU 6 134 (RS 19.19A)
PRU 6 135 (RS 17.134)
PRU 6 136 (RS 17.240)
PRU 6 137 (RS 19.27)
PRU 6 138 (RS 19.46)
PRU 6 139 (RS 19.139)
PRU 6 140 (RS 19.92)
PRU 6 141 (RS 19.112)
PRU 6 142 (RS 19.135)
PRU 6 143 (RS 21.200)
PRU 6 144 (RS 19.38)
PRU 6 145 (RS 19.08)
PRU 6 146 (RS 19.77)
PRU 6 147 (RS 19.127)
PRU 6 148 (RS 17.97)
PRU 6 149 (RS 17.354)
PRU 6 150 (RS 18.101A)
PRU 6 151 (RS 18.266)
PRU 6 152 (RS 18.270)
PRU 6 153 (RS 18.271)
PRU 6 154 (RS 19.05)
PRU 6 155 (RS 19.07)
PRU 6 156 (RS 19.20)
PRU 6 157 (RS 19.23)
PRU 6 158 (RS 19.24)
PRU 6 159 (RS 19.35B+E)
PRU 6 162 (RS 19.36)
PRU 6 163 (RS 19.64)
PRU 6 164 (RS 19.90)
PRU 6 165 (RS 19.93)
PRU 6 166 (RS 19.99)
PRU 6 167 (RS 19.124)
PRU 6 168 (RS 21.199)
PRU 6 170 (RS 19.34)
PRU 6 172 (RS 19.140A)
PRU 6 175 (RS 21.202)
PRU 6 p. 99c see KTU 4.165

RA 38 5 (RS 11.856)
RA 38 7ff. see PRU 3 194f.
RA 38 10f. see PRU 3 194a
RA 38 12 (RS 8.043)
RA 63 83f. (RS 29.103)

Syria 10 pl. 77 4a-c (no RS no.)
Syria 10 pl. 77 5 (no RS no.)
Syria 10 pl. 77 6 (no RS no.)
Syria 12 226 (Text 1) see MSL 4 122f.
Syria 12 226 (Text 2) see MSL 13 128ff.
Syria 12 228ff. (no RS no.)
Syria 12 231ff. (no RS no.)
Syria 12 236ff. see Syria 13 237 + 12 236ff.
Syria 12 pl. 46ff. (no RS no.)
Syria 12 pl. 49 (no RS no.)
Syria 13 234 (no RS no.)
Syria 13 235 (no RS no.)
Syria 13 237+12 236ff. (no RS no.)
Syria 16 194 (RS 6.345)
Syria 18 249f. (RS 8.145)
Syria 18 251ff. (RS 8.213)
Syria 18 253f. (RS 8.208)
Syria 21 124 see PRU 3 190b
Syria 21 125f. see PRU 3 189b
Syria 21 126f. see PRU 3 190a
Syria 21 127f. see PRU 3 191a
Syria 21 129f. see PRU 3 188f.
Syria 28 49ff. see PRU 3 192f.
Syria 28 173f. (RS 14.16)
Syria 59 201 (RS 1979.22)

Syria 59 204ff. (RS 1979.24+ 1980.388)
Syria 59 208 no. 3 (RS 1980.386)
Syria 59 208 no. 4 (RS 1980.385)
Syria 59 209ff. (RS 1979.25)
Syria 59 217 (RS 1979.26)
Syria 59 218f. (RS 1980.389)
Syria 59 220f. (RS 1980.383)

TA 8 7f. (Aphek 52055/1)

UF 11 479 (RS 20.189A+B)

Ug. 5 1 (RS 17.65)
Ug. 5 2 (RS 17.21)
Ug. 5 3 (RS 17.33)
Ug. 5 4 (RS 17.20)
Ug. 5 5 (RS 17.22+87)
Ug. 5 6 (RS 17.149)
Ug. 5 7 (RS 17.36)
Ug. 5 8 (RS 17.38)
Ug. 5 9 (RS 17.61)
Ug. 5 10 (RS 17.67)
Ug. 5 11 (RS 17.19)
Ug. 5 12 (RS 17.150+34)
Ug. 5 13 (RS 17.465)
Ug. 5 14 (RS 17.332)
Ug. 5 14bis see PRU 6 123
Ug. 5 15a (RS 17.10)
Ug. 5 15b (RS 17.80)
Ug. 5 16 (RS 17.81)
Ug. 5 17a (RS 17.155)
Ug. 5 17b (RS 15.152)
Ug. 5 18 (RS 20.24)
Ug. 5 19 (RS 20.06)
Ug. 5 21 (RS 20.168+195P)
Ug. 5 24 (RS 20.238)
Ug. 5 28 (RS 20.184)
Ug. 5 29 (RS 20.200C)
Ug. 5 49 (RS 20.13)
Ug. 5 54 (RS 20.23)
Ug. 5 55 (RS 20.178)
Ug. 5 81 (RS 21.230)
Ug. 5 82 (RS 20.226)
Ug. 5 83 (RS 20.146)
Ug. 5 84 (RS 20.235)
Ug. 5 85 (RS 20.236)
Ug. 5 86 (RS 20.176)
Ug. 5 87 (RS 20.203B)
Ug. 5 88 (RS 21.07A)
Ug. 5 89 (RS 20.214B)
Ug. 5 90 (RS 20.252A)
Ug. 5 95 (RS 20.01)
Ug. 5 96 (RS 20.12)
Ug. 5 97 (RS 20.20)
Ug. 5 98 (RS 20.07)
Ug. 5 99 (RS 20.425)
Ug. 5 100 (RS 20.04)
Ug. 5 101 (RS 20.131)
Ug. 5 102 (RS 20.207A)
Ug. 5 103 (RS 20.143B)
Ug. 5 104 (RS 20.144)
Ug. 5 105 (RS 20.211A.B+)
Ug. 5 106 (RS 20.220)
Ug. 5 107 (RS 20.180B)
Ug. 5 108 (RS 20.251)
Ug. 5 109 (RS 21.03E)
Ug. 5 110 (RS 21.210 obv.)
Ug. 5 111 (RS 20.177)
Ug. 5 112 (RS 22.220 iii-v)
Ug. 5 113 (RS 20.135)
Ug. 5 114 (RS 20.139 iii-vi)
Ug. 5 115 (RS 22.218)
Ug. 5 116 (RS 20.196C)
Ug. 5 117 (RS 21.63C)
Ug. 5 118 (RS 14.128)
Ug. 5 120 (RS 20.195A)
Ug. 5 121 (RS 23.495)
Ug. 5 122 (RS 17.85)
Ug. 5 123 (RS 24.309)
Ug. 5 124 (RS 22.344+23.24)
Ug. 5 125 (RS 5.302 side A)
Ug. 5 126 (RS 20.175)
Ug. 5 127 (RS 20.136 side A)
Ug. 5 128 (RS Fragment B)
Ug. 5 129 (RS Fragment C)
Ug. 5 130 (RS 20.149)
Ug. 5 131 (RS 20.426G+ 201G)
Ug. 5 132 see UF 11 479
Ug. 5 133 (RS 23.493A)
Ug. 5 134 (RS 20.426D)
Ug. 5 135 (RS 21.62)
Ug. 5 136 (RS 21.63D)
Ug. 5 137 i 1-iii 32" (RS 20.123+)
Ug. 5 137 iii 33"ff. (RS 20.123+)
Ug. 5 138 (RS 20.426B)
Ug. 5 143 (RS 20.160N)
Ug. 5 144 (RS 21.10)
Ug. 5 145 (RS 20.196A)
Ug. 5 146 (RS 20.161D)
Ug. 5 147 (RS 21.05D)
Ug. 5 148 (RS Pt. 1844)
Ug. 5 149 (RS 20.14)
Ug. 5 150 (RS 21.63A)
Ug. 5 151 (RS 21.07H)
Ug. 5 152 (RS 6.X)
Ug. 5 157 (RS 20.208B)
Ug. 5 159 (RS 17.86+)
Ug. 5 160 (RS 17.102)
Ug. 5 161 (RS 17.325)
Ug. 5 162 (RS 25.460)
Ug. 5 163 (RS 22.439)
Ug. 5 164 (RS 25.130)
Ug. 5 165 (RS 23.34(+))
Ug. 5 166 (RS 25.424)
Ug. 5 167 (RS 22.421)
Ug. 5 168 (RS 22.219+398)
Ug. 5 170 (RS 26.142)
Ug. 5 172 (RS 25.438C)
Ug. 5 173 (RS 25.511B)

Ug. 6 394ff. (RS 25.456A+)
Ug. 6 401ff. (RS 25.459)
Ug. 6 403b (RS 25.513)
Ug. 6 404 (RS 25.457)

Ug. 7 pl. 1a (RS 34.21)
Ug. 7 pl. 2 (RS 34.36)
Ug. 7 pl. 3 (RS 34.62)
Ug. 7 pl. 4a (RS 34.70)
Ug. 7 pl. 10 (RS 34.127)
Ug. 7 pl. 13 (RS 34.131)
Ug. 7 pl. 46 (RS 34.166)
Ug. 7 pl. 50 (RS 34.169)
Ug. 7 pl. 56 (RS 34.178)
Ug. 7 pl. 62b (RS 34.180i)
Ug. 7 pl. 64 (RS 34.180l)

Unpublished texts:

RS 12.227A (see CAD N/1 336b, s.v. *naqû* lex.)
RS 17.154 (see CAD E s.v. *ebbu* 1a4', *ēdiššu* lex.)
RS 20.426 (mentioned MSL 13 127)
RS 22.227B+ (see see MSL 14 395)
RS 22.431A+ (see Ug. 5 p. 290)
RS 23.368 (see see PRU 6 p. 119 n. 1, p. 155 n. 5, p. 156 n. 3)
RS 25.428 (see PRU 6 p. 150 n.3)
RS 25.456 (see Ug. 5 p. 227)

2. *Cross-index by RS (Excavation) Number*

The cross-reference is to Index A 1, above.

RS 22.439 see Ug. 5 163
RS 23.82+ see MSL 11 43ff. (A)
RS 23.34(+) see Ug. 5 165
RS 23.368 see Index A 1, end
RS 23.493A see Ug. 5 133
RS 23.495 see Ug. 5 121
RS 24.77 see AS 16 31ff.:27-40,...
RS 24.309 see Ug. 5 123
RS 25.130 see Ug. 5 164
RS 25.133 see AS 16 31ff.:109-24
RS 25.415 see MSL 10 37ff. (B)
RS 25.419 see MSL 11 169 b
RS 25.424 see Ug. 5 166
RS 25.425 see MSL 17 44b
RS 25.428 see Index A 1, end
RS 25.438C see Ug. 5 172
RS 25.454 see MSL 10 37ff. (C)
RS 25.454E(?) see MSL 13 126
RS 25.455*+ see AS 16 29ff.:1-4,...
RS 25.456 see Index A 1, end
RS 25.456A+ see Ug. 6 394ff.
RS 25.457(?!) see Ug. 6 404
RS 25.457(?!)+26.150* see MSL 14 143f. (no. 22)
RS 25.459 see Ug. 6 401ff.
RS 25.460 see Ug. 5 162
RS 25.511B see Ug. 5 173
RS 25.513 see Ug. 6 403b
RS 25.519 see MSL 10 127ff.(RS)
RS 26.137 see MSL 10 37ff. (H)
RS 26.139A see MSL 17 18f.,21 (U)
RS 26.142 see Ug. 5 170
RS 26.144 see MSL 10 37ff. (G)
RS 27.53 see PRU 6 53
RS 29.103 see RA 63 83ff.
RS 34.21 see Ug. 7 pl. 1a
RS 34.36 see Ug. 7 pl. 2
RS 34.62 see Ug. 7 pl. 3
RS 34.70 see Ug. 7 pl. 4
RS 34.127 see Ug. 7 pl. 10
RS 34.131 see Ug. 7 pl. 13
RS 34.166 see Ug. 7 pl. 46
RS 34.169 see Ug. 7 pl. 50
RS 34.178 see Ug. 7 pl. 56
RS 34.180i see Ug. 7 pl. 62b
RS 34.180l see Ug. 7 pl. 64
RS 1957.3 see AnOr 48 26
RS 1957.4 see AnOr 48 27
RS 1979.22 see Syria 59 201
RS 1979.24+1980.388 see Syria 59 204ff.
RS 1979.25 see Syria 59 209ff.
RS 1979.26 see Syria 59 217
RS 1980.383 see Syria 59 220f.
RS 1980.385 see Syria 59 208 no. 4
RS 1980.386 see Syria 59 208 no. 3
RS 1980.389 see Syria 59 218f.
RS Fragment B see Ug. 5 128
RS Fragment C see Ug. 5 129
RS Pt. 383G see PRU 3 176a
RS Pt. 1844 see Ug. 5 148

RS texts without excavation numbers:

see MSL 4 123
MSL 13 128ff.
Syria 10 pl. 77 4a-c
Syria 10 pl. 77 5
Syria 10 pl. 77 6
Syria 12 228ff.
Syria 12 231ff.
Syria 12 pl. 46ff.
Syria 12 pl. 49
Syria 13 234
Syria 13 235
Syria 13 237 + 12 236ff.

B. Texts Cited

1. *Ugarit Akkadian Texts*

RA

Syria

TA 8 7f.

UF 11 479

Ugaritica 5

2. *Other Sumero-Akkadian Texts*

3. *Alphabetic Ugaritic Texts*

Text and line numbers according to *KTU*.

C. Forms Cited

1. *Ugaritic*

☛ p. 404

Syllabic transcriptions are listed by root, which appears in upper case roman; roots are followed by phonemic normalizations of the forms, between slashes. References to the syllabic transcriptions cited as examples in the section on the representation of the consonants (Part III, ch. 1 §E, pp. 211-54) do not appear below, since inclusion of them would crowd the index to no purpose.

Alphabetic forms are listed under the form cited in the monograph (not by root), in lower case italic.

Unidentified Ugaritic forms in syllabic transcription (Glossary, pp. 189-94) appear at the end of the list (p. 364).

Unidentified Forms

2. *Sumerian (Signs)*

3. *Akkadian*

4. Hurrian

5. Arabic

6. *Aramaic (including Syriac)*

7. *Eblaite*

ar-za-tum = /ʾarzatum/ 109
ì-rí-sa-tum = /ʾir(i)š(a)tum/ 273,273n, 274n
ì-sa-du = /ʾišātu(m)/? 63
ba-da-lum = /bad(d)ălum/? 112
ʾà-du-ru$_{12}$/lu-um = /ḥadru(m)/? 78n
a-a-mu-mu = /(l)aḥămum/? 81n
li-sa-nu = /lišānu(m)/ 143
qá-nu-wu, [qá]-nu-um = /qanuwum/? 291n
ra/la-da-mu(-mu) = /radāmum/? 177
sa-ʾà-lum/a-um = /śah(r)um/ 180
ti-ì-tum/du = /tiʾittum/? 51
ti-ʾà-ma-tum = /tihāmatum/ 185
wa-zi-lu-um = /wāṣirum/ 134

8. *Ethiopic (Geʿez)*

lehiq 271n
leḥma 81n
lesān 143
yaḥawwer 271n
ḥayq 72
marḥa 149
šāhr 180
reḥba 179
samāy 290n
tasannana 187
berur 115
baṭala 88
tamr, tamart 76
ḫarawa 130
ḫadara 78n
ʾaḥadu 67
ʾesāt 63
ʾayy 276
karabā 140
karaya 130
kafar 139
wald 77
morāʾ/moreʾ 134
ʿalawa 57n
zebḥ 97

9. *Hebrew*

ʾābâ 91
ʾebyôn 91,91n
ʾabbîr, ʾābîr 269,269n
ʾădāmâ, ʾadmônî 104
ʾĕdōm 275n
ʾādôn 48
ʾaddîr 87
ʾ-h-b (yeʾĕhab) 280n
ʾāḥ, pl. ʾaḥîm 273n
ʾeḥād, fem. ʾaḥat 67,307n
ʾāḥû 255n
ʾayyē, ʾayy-, ʾê- 276
ʾayyāl(â) 276
ʾiyyār 129,276n
ʾēlôn, ʾallôn 107
ʾallûp 270
ʾĕmet 274
ʾ-n-š 274n
ʾărubbâ 275
ʾarbe 270
ʾōren 110
ʾărešet 60,110,273
ʾiššô 63
ʾăšērâ 283
ʾēt 150
bōr 115
bāḥar 113
bāḥûr, pl. baḥûrîm 84
bāṭal 88
bāṣar 114
bārûr 115
məbaśśēr 94
gabnunnîm, gibbēn 115
gôlān 116
gēr 57, 258n
gallāb 116
gilgāl 174
d-b-r (nidbarnû) 167
derek 120
halmût 121
hāpak 84
wālād 77
zebaḥ 97
z-b-l 94n
z-w/y-r 118
zākār 96
zəmôrâ 285
zərôaʿ, ʾezrôaʿ 285n
ḥeder 78
ḥawwôt 78,127,275
ḥāzîr 84
ḥayyîm 60,127,276
ḥêq 72
ḥ-l-m II 99
ḥāmal, ḥumlâ 125
ḥōp 129,190
ḥuppâ 129
ḥāṣaṣ 129
ḥōr 130
ḥāram 90
heḥĕrîm 89
ḥermôn 126
ḥarmēš 130
ḥārûṣ 76
ḥērēš 100
ḥātān 131
ṭabbāḥ 308n
ṭāhōr 58,271n
yôm 67
yeled 77
yaʿar 285
ṣē(ʾ)t 15n
yōṣēr 134
môqēd 154
y-r-ʾ 134
yarqôn 134
môšāb 102
kābēd 62
kəbu(w)ddâ 135
kəbārâ 139
k-b-r II 140

10. *Modern South Arabian dialects*

Ḥarsūsi

Jibbāli

11. *Old South Arabian dialects*

Addendum

After this study had gone to press there came to my attention a recent publication in which a number of Ugarit Akkadian lexical texts appear. The volume is *Materials for the Sumerian Lexicon, Supplementary Series* vol. 1 (*MSL SS1*), by M. Civil, O.R. Gurney, and D.A. Kennedy (Rome: Pontificium Institutum Biblicum, 1986); pages 75-89 contain an edition of a Ugarit version of a two-column (Sum.-Akk.) Middle Babylonian Grammatical Text in 16 exemplars, most of them published for the first time, by Kennedy (text pp. 78ff.). While no new Ugaritic vocabulary appears in these exemplars, a few of the entries are relevant at some points in the discussion above, especially in Part I. The following brief comments and notices are keyed to the pages above.

P. 12 and n. 53. The number of Ugarit Akkadian texts increases by 13 to 578 on 570 tablets. Three of the 16 exemplars were published or noted previously: text C, RS 22.227A, is undoubtedly the same as the text referred to as RS 12.227A in CAD N/1 336b s.v. *naqû* lex.; text E = Syria 12 p. 226 (pl. 47), discussed in MSL 4 123; text N = PRU 3 211f.

P. 46 no. 21. Note lines 207-208 of the grammatical text, exemplar G: UZU, ZU = *ši-i-ru* (text E: UZU, KA = [ ]).

P. 47 no. 22.1. Note lines 2-4 of the grammatical text: ZA.E.ME.EN = *a*[*t-ta*]; GÁ.E ZA.E = *a-na-ku* [*ù at-ta*]; ZA.E GÁ.E = *at-*[*ta ù a-n*]*a-ku.*

P. 48 no. 24.1. Line 12: NU = *la-a.*

P. 49 no. 25.3. Line 15: NA = MIN(.MIN) (= *la-a*).

Pp. 52-53 nos. 32.5, 32.6. It is worth noting that although 17 Sumerian forms are equated with *ina* and *ana* in lines 35-68, MU does not appear among them.

P. 55 no. 35/36.2. Note line 193: GÁ.GÁ = *ša-ka*$_4$*-nu.*

P. 56 no. 35/36.4. See above on p. 47 no. 22.1.

P. 61 no. 45.4. Note line 122 of the grammatical text: DINGIR = MIN.MIN (= *šar-ru*).

P. 68 no. 63.4. The proposal that the Sum. and Akk. columns here had UD and *anumma* finds support now in line 162 of the grammatical text: UD = *a-nu-um-ma.*

P. 69 no. 63.6?. Cf. line 254 UD.DA = *a-ṣu/ṣú-ú* (but also UD.DA = *ṣītum* "emergence, etc." line 250; = *abālu* "to dry up" 251; = *qatû* "to end"? 252; = *šumma* "if" 253).

P. 69 no. 62.1. Note in line 144: UD.ZALA[G].GA = MIN.MIN (= UD-*mu na-me-er-tu*$_4$).

P. 72 no. 158.2 and p. 73 no. 159.2. Note lines 203, 205: ÚR = *na-ṣa-ru,* URU$_3$ = MIN.MIN.

Pp. 76-77 nos. 176.x, 176.y. Line 150: DUMU = *ma(-a)-rù.*

P. 84 no. 185. Line 217: ŠUL = *eṭ-lu*$_4$.

P. 86 no. 187.1. Line 6: LÚ = MIN.MIN (= *šu-ú*).

P. 87 no. 188.1. Line 123: LUGAL = MIN.MIN (= *šar-ru*).

P. 87 no. 189.3. Line 244: MAḪ = MIN.MIN (= *ma-du*)

P. 93 no. 193.1. Line 192: ÍL.LÁ = *ša-qú-ú*; line 211: ÍL = *ša-qú-ú*.

P. 100 no. 198.10. This entry of the S^a Voc. text should be restored as (Sum.) IDIM = (Akk.) *šarru* = (Hur.) *ewirni* = (Ugar.) *ma*!-*al-ku*; cf. line 114 of the grammatical text: IDIM = MIN(.MIN) (= *šar-ru*). (Note also [IDIM i-di-im = *ša*]*r*!-*ru* = Hittite LUGAL-*uš* in a Boğazköy text [Izi], MSL 13 144 r. 9'.)

Pp. 347-350. Note the following additions and changes in RS numbers:

RS 12.47 = MSL SS1 78ff. N
*RS 12.227A = RS 22.227A (below)
RS 20.148+21.60 = MSL SS1 78ff. D
RS 20.165C+171,3+222C+228B = MSL SS1 78ff. B
RS 20.166A+B = MSL SS1 78ff. F
RS 20.214A = MSL SS1 78ff. L
RS 20.230 = MSL SS1 78ff. A
RS 20.241A+B = MSL SS1 78ff. J
RS 22.227A = MSL SS1 78ff. C
RS 22.396 = MSL SS1 78ff. P
RS 25.433 = MSL SS1 78ff. I
RS 25.442 = MSL SS1 78ff. H
RS 25.459A+B = MSL SS1 78ff. G
RS 25.526C = MSL SS1 78ff. M
RS 25.526D = MSL SS1 78ff. K
RS 26.160 = MSL SS1 78ff. O
no RS no.: change "see MSL 4 123" to "see MSL SS1 78ff. E"

Additions and Corrections

This volume has been out of print for some time, and a revised edition was promised several years ago. It has, however, proved impossible to carry out a thorough revision of the text, and so I have settled on reissuing the book in its original form with an addendum listing major corrections and additions. Many of these were first noted in some of the longer reviews of the book, and I am very grateful to those reviewers for their insightful comments: D. Pardee (1991), S. Parker (1989), D. Sivan (1989), M. Smith (1989), and especially W.H. van Soldt (1990). A number of changes are based on texts written at Ugarit that have been published in the last twenty years.

I cannot claim that the following set of additions is complete; it consists simply of the notes and marginalia that I have collected since the book first appeared in 1987. But I hope that these will nevertheless be of use to readers.

This addendum will also be published online at eisenbrauns.com (thanks to the good offices of Jim Eisenbraun), so that users of the original form of the book may likewise have access to it.

The list follows, and is keyed to, the pagination of the first printing of the book.

I wish, finally, to thank Michael Coogan and Jo Ann Hackett for their good advice and their careful reading of these notes, and for saving me from many errors.

Carlisle, Mass.
July 2008

p. 12. A number of reviewers, especially van Soldt (1990: 733), have added more question marks to the interpretation of text Ug. 5 153 as Ugaritic. Thus the forms in that text should probably be treated even more circumspectly. It is worth repeating, however, that at least some of the text cannot be read as Akkadian.

p. 17. In the list of publications, at Syria 16 194, read Dhorme (not Virolleaud).

pp. 22–23. Major improvements in the arrangement and interpretation of the Polyglot S^a Vocabulary texts were presented by van Soldt in his reviews of Sivan 1984 and of the present book (van Soldt 1989; 1990). In van Soldt's careful reconstruction there are six manuscripts, including two represented by unpublished texts. These are, together with the S^a Vocabulary sign numbers covered by each:

Text A_1:	Ug. 5 130(+)134(+)131+138: nos. 20–25, 32–44, 46–48, 61–(64?)
Text A_2:	Ug. 5 136: nos. 66–(69?)
Text A_3:	Ug. 5 137: nos. 150–154, 157–160, 173–211
Text B:	Ug. 5 135: nos. 50–65, 142–161
Text C:	Ug. 5 133: nos. 39–46, 170–174a
Text D:	RS 20.429 (unpublished): nos. 18–38
Text E:	Ug. 5 132; UF 11 479: nos. 24–48
Text F:	RIH 77/5 (unpublished): nos. 11–27

Texts A_1, A_2, and A_3 comprise three tablets of a single manuscript A, each with two columns on each side. Texts B and C "are probably one-column tablets which contain the whole text. Texts D, E, and F are excerpts" (van Soldt 1990: 729). Van Soldt's improvements naturally result in a number of new readings.

A new trilingual S^a Vocabulary text was discovered at Ras Shamra in 1994 and published by B. André-Salvini and M. Salvini (1998, with new and additional readings in André-Salvini and Salvini 1999). This large tablet, RS 94.2939, shows the Akkadian and Hurrian readings current in the Ugarit scribal curriculum for a large number of the S^a signs that are broken in the quadrilingual manuscripts.

Copies of the S^a Vocabulary also appear among Akkadian texts from the city of Emar (Arnaud 1985–88, vol. 4, plates 139–142; see also Cohen 2003); these have also allowed some improved readings of the Ugarit versions.

pp. 24–25, S^a Voc. No. 22.1. In the Hurrian column, read *ši-ni-am* rather than *ši-ni-*⌜*bi*⌝ (van Soldt 1990: 732).

S^a Voc. No. 23. In the Ugaritic column, van Soldt's collation suggests that the first sign is partially visible, and possibly *ú*, thus ⌜*ú*?⌝-*ru*.

S^a Voc. Nos. 26–28. In the Akkadian column of these lines, unpublished Ugarit S^a Vocabulary texts have the following forms (van Soldt 1990: 731); unfortunately the Ugaritic column of the lines is broken.

No. 26 BA = *suppinnu* ‘(a tool used in brick-making and spinning)’
No. 27 ZI = *nupultu* ‘person’
No. 28 GI = *qanû* ‘reed’

S^a Voc. No. 30.1. In the Hurrian column, read with van Soldt (1990: 731) *i-t[i]n-ni*.

S^a Voc. No. 32.1. The Ugaritic form is *ša-⸢an⸣-[t]u$_4$*, not *ša-na-tu$_4$* (van Soldt 1990: 731). See below, ad p. 51, no. 32.1.

pp. 26–27, S^a Voc. No. 34. This line also appears in UF 11 479: 13 (van Soldt 1989: 651), which preserves only the Ugaritic form: *i-ṣú* ‘wood’; see below, ad p. 54.

S^a Voc. No. 35/36.1. In the Akkadian column an Emar S^a Voc. exemplar here has *pisannu* ‘container, box’.

S^a Voc. No. 37.3. In the Akkadian column, van Soldt (1990: 733) suggests *ná]k$^?$-ru* ‘enemy’ rather than our proposed *z]é$^?$-ru*.

pp. 28–29, S^a Voc. No. 41.4. The Ugaritic form is *[x]-iZ-ḫu* rather than *[la-q]a-ḫu*, according to van Soldt’s collation (1989: 650). See below, ad p. 59.

S^a Voc. No. 44.2. Van Soldt (1989: 651) notes that collation confirms our proposed reading of the Ugaritic form: *i-[r]i-iš-[t]u$_4$*. The new trilingual S^a Voc. RS 94.2939 supplies the Hurrian *ta-ri-iš-še$^!$* for ‘request’.

pp. 28–31, S^a Voc. Nos. 45–51. In light of the collations and studies of van Soldt (1989, 1990), these lines may now be read as follows; lines attested in the new trilingual S^a Voc. RS 94.2939 are also given here.

S^a #	Sign	Akkadian	Hurrian	Ugaritic	Meaning	Reference
45.1	[A]N	*ša-mu-⸢ú⸣[*		]	sky	Ug. 5 133 i 12'
	[		*ḫa]-bur-ni*	*⸢ša-mu⸣-ma*		UF 11 479 29
	AN	*ša-mu-ú*	*ḫa-ur-ni*			RS 94.2939 ii 6
45.2	AN	*e-nu [*		]	An, El,	Ug. 5 133 i 13'
	[		*]⸢e⸣-ni*	*⸢i-lu-ma⸣*	god(s)	UF 11 479 30
	AN	*a-nu*	*a-ni*			RS 94.2939 ii 7
45.3	AN	*i-lu [*		]	god, El	Ug. 5 133 i 14'
	[	]	*e-ni*	*i-lu*		UF 11 479 31
	AN	*i-lu*	*e-ni*			RS 94.2939 ii 8

45.4	AN	*šar-ru* [		]	king	Ug. 5 133 i 15'
45.5	[A]N	*šar-ra-nu* [		]	kings	Ug. 5 133 i 16'
46.1	[ḪA]L	*ḫal-l*[*u*		]	crotch,	Ug. 5 133 1 17'
	[ ]		*zi-ia-ni*	[*ḫ*]*u*$^?$-*ṣa*-[*nu*$^?$]	lap$^?$	UF 11 479 32
	ḪAL	*ḫal-lu*	*zi-ia-an-ni*			RS 94.2939 ii 9
46.2	[ḪAL]	*b*[*a-ru-ú*		]	diviner	Ug. 5 133 1 18'
	[ḪAL	*ba-ru*]-⌜*ú*⌝$^?$	*pu-ru-li-ni*	*pu-r*[*u-li-nu*]		UF 11 479 33
	[		*p*]*u-ru-l*[*i-ni*	]		Ug. 5 131 1'
	ḪAL	*ba-a-ru*	*wu-ru-ul-li-ni*			RS 94.2939 ii 10
47.1	[UR	*kalbu*]	*ir-bi*	*ka-a*[*l-bu*]	dog	UF 11 479 34
	[	]	*ir-wi* [	]		Ug. 5 131 2'
	UR	*kál-bu*	*ir-wi*			RS 94.2939 ii 11
47.2	UR	⌜*ba*⌝-*a*[*š-tu*$_4$	*in-n*]*i*	*ḫe*-⌜*bu*⌝	shame?	UF 11 479 35
	[		]*in-ni*	*ḫé-bu*		Ug. 5 131 3'
	UR	*bá-aš-tu*	*in-ni*			RS 94.2939 ii 12
47.3	[UR]	*mi-it-*[*ḫ*]*a-ri-i*[*š*	]	*pí-ru*	equally/	UF 11 479 36
	[UR	*mitḫāriš*]	*pí-ir-ri*	*ir-ku*	elephant$^?$	Ug. 5 131 4'
	UR	*mi-it-ḫa-ri-iš*	*pì*-⌜*ir*⌝-*ri*			RS 94.2939 ii 13
48.1	NE	*i-ša-tu*$_4$ [		]*i-ši-t*[*u*$_4$]	fire	UF 11 479 37
	NE	*i*-⌜*ša*⌝-*tu*	*ta-a-ri*			RS 94.2939 ii 14
48.2?	[NE$^?$	*perʾu*	*ḫ*]*í-iš-ši*	*šap-ḫu*	scion	Ug. 5 131 5'
48.3?	[NE$^?$	*napištu*$^?$	*š*]*u-ḫu-ur-ni*	*ḫé-yu-ma*	life	Ug. 5 131 6'
48.4	NE	*pè-em-tu*	*šul-li*		charcoal	RS 94.2939 ii 15
48.5	NE	*ṭì-ik-me-nu*	*šal-mi*		ashes	RS 94.2939 ii 16
48.6	NE	*nu-ru*	*ta-gi*		light	RS 94.2939 ii 17
49	GIBIL	*eš-šu*	⌜*šu-ḫé*⌝		new	RS 94.2939 ii 18

missing in the quadrilingual S^a Voc. texts

50	[KA]	*ši-⸢in⸣-nu*	[	]	tooth	Ug. 5 135 2'
51.1	[SA]G	*qa-qa-du*	*pa-[a-ḫi*	]	head	Ug. 5 135 3'
51.2	[SAG	*amīlu*	*tar-š]u-wa-an-ni*	*: bu-nu-šu*	man	Ug. 5 131 7'

(52–63.3 as on pp. 30–33)

pp. 32–33, Sª Voc. No. 63.4. The question marks after sign UD and Akk. *anumma* are unnecessary in view of the equation of those terms in the Ras Shamra grammatical text *MSL SS1*, as noted in our Addendum to the original book.

Sª Voc. No. 63.6. A more likely reading of this line is as follows; see below, ad p. 69.

63.6	[UD?	*šaḫāṭu?*	?	*]ḫu?-ut-ta-ru*	to attack	Ug. 5 138 7'

pp. 34–35, Sª Voc. Nos. 156–160. The new trilingual text RS 94.2939 allows us to restore these lines with more confidence. See further below, ad pp. 72–74.

156	AR	*na-ma-ru*	*ḫi-⸢x-x-x⸣[*	]	to shine	Ug. 5 135 r. 14'
	AR	*⸢ki⸣-i-nu*	*ḫi-iš-na-a[r?-*]		true	RS 94.2939 iv 5'
157	⸢MUŠ⸣	*ṣi-i-ru*	*ap-ši?[*	]	serpent	Ug. 5 135 r. 15'
	MUŠ	*ṣí-ru*	*⸢ap-še⸣*			RS 94.2939 iv 6'
	[			*]tu-un-na-nu*		Ug. 5 137 i 8'
158.1	[Ú]R	*[s]u?-nu*	*⸢ḫu⸣-ri![*	]	lap	Ug. 5 135 r. 16'
	⸢ÚR⸣	*sú-ú-nu*	*ḫu-ri*			RS 94.2939 iv 7'
	[		]	*ḫé-qu*		Ug. 5 137 i 9'
158.2	⸢ÚR⸣	*⸢na?-[ṣ]a!?ru*	*⸢x⸣-ru-[*	]	to guard	Ug. 5 135 r. 17'
	ÚR	*na-ṣa-ru*	*ut-ru-um-mi*			RS 94.2939 iv 8'
158.3	⸢ÚR⸣	*pè-nu*	*ur!-n[i?*	]	foot	Ug. 5 135 r. 18'
	ÚR	*pè-e-ni*	*ur-ni*			RS 94.2939 iv 9'
	[		]	*ri-i[g]-lu*		Ug. 5 137 i 10'
159.1	ŠEŠ	*a-ḫu*	*še-e-n[i?*	]	brother	Ug. 5 135 r. 19'
	ŠEŠ	*a-ḫu*	*še-in-ni*			RS 94.2939 iv 10'
159.2	ŠEŠ	*na-ṣa-r[u*		]	to guard	Ug. 5 135 r. 20'
	ŠEŠ	*na-ṣa-ru*	*ut-ru-um-mi*			RS 94.2939 iv 11'
	[		]	*ni-iḫ-rù*		Ug. 5 137 i 11'

159.3	ŠEŠ	*ma-r[a-ru*		]	to be	Ug. 5 135 r. 21'
	ŠEŠ	*ma-ra-ru*	*ma-la-še*		bitter	RS 94.2939 iv 12'
160.1	IB	*ú-r[a*$^?$*-šu*$^?$		]	unclean	Ug. 5 135 r. 22'
	IB	*ú-ra-šu*	*i-še-na*		garment$^?$	RS 94.2939 iv 13'

pp. 36–37, S^{a} Voc. No. 173.1. Cf. BAD = *BI-TUM* in the Emar S^{a} Voc.

S^{a} Voc. No. 173.3. Cf. BAD = *ba-la-ṭu*$_4$ in the Emar S^{a} Voc.

S^{a} Voc. No. 173.4. In the Ugaritic column, read perhaps [*u*]*z-zu*; see below, ad pp. 74–75.

S^{a} Voc. No. 173.6. Cf. BAD = *la-BI-TUM* in the Emar S^{a} Voc.

pp. 38–39, S^{a} Voc. No. 176.y. In the Akkadian column, rather than our proposed *šerru*, the Emar S^{a} Voc. here equates TUR with *la*ʾ*û* 'small child', *ṣeḫru* 'young, small', and *māru* 'son'.

S^{a} Voc. No. 180.1. In the Akkadian column, the Emar S^{a} Voc. here has *qatnu* 'thin, fine'; see below, ad p. 79.

S^{a} Voc. No. 180.3/181. This line is to be read as follows (Wilhelm 1992); see below, ad p. 80.

180.3	[SIG	*šāqûtu*	*t*]*ap-ša-ḫal-še*	*ma-aš-q*[*u-ú*$^?$]	office of cupbearer	Ug. 5 137 ii 15'

S^{a} Voc. No. 182. The Emar S^{a} Voc. has TE = *me-nu*, apparently for *mīnu* 'what?' (see CAD M/2 89b).

S^{a} Voc. No. 183.1. Cf. KAR = *e-ṭe*$_4$*-rù* in the Emar S^{a} Voc.

pp. 40–43, S^{a} Voc. Nos. 186–198. In these lines too the new trilingual text RS 94.2939 allows more certain restorations and interpretations. See further below, ad pp. 84–100.

186.1	[ŠA]Ḫ	*še-ḫu-ú*	*ú-ḫe*	*ḫu-zi-rù*	pig	Ug. 5 137 ii 25'
185.2	ŠÁḪ	⸢*še-ḫu-ú*	*ú-ḫé*⸣			RS 94.2939 v 3'
186a?	[ŠAḪ.TU]R?	*kur-ku-za-nu*	—	*ḫe-en-ni-ṣu*	piglet	Ug. 5 137 ii 26'
186.2	[ŠAḪ	]⸢*x*⸣*-rù*	*šu-ra-at-ḫe*	*qi-i-lu*	anus?	Ug. 5 137 ii 27'
185.3	⸢ŠÁḪ⸣	*šu*$^?$*-bu-ru*	*zu-*⸢*ra-at*$^?$⸣*-ḫé*			RS 94.2939 v 4'
187.1	[LÚ	*šu-ú*]	*ma-an-ni*	*ú-wa*	he	Ug. 5 137 ii 28'
	LÚ	*šú-ú*	*ma-an-ni*			RS 94.2939 v 6'
187.2	[LÚ	*ša?*]	*a-PI*	*du-ú*	(relative pronoun)	Ug. 5 137 ii 29'

187.3	[LÚ	*bēlu*	]⌜*e*$^{?}$⌝-*we-ri*	*ba-a-lu-ma*	lord	Ug. 5 137 ii 30'
187.4	[LÚ	*amīlu*	*tar-š*]*u-wa-ni*	*bu-nu-šu*	man	Ug. 5 137 ii 31'
	LÚ	*a-mi-lu*	*ta-a-e*			RS 94.2939 v 5'
188.1	[LUGAL	*šarru*	*e-we-e*]*r-ni*	*ma-al-ku*	king	Ug. 5 137 ii 32'
	LUGAL	*šar-ru*	*e-we-er-ni*			RS 94.2939 v 7'
188.2	[LUGAL	*bēlu*	*eweri*	*b*]*a*-⌜*a-lu-ma*⌝	lord	Ug. 5 137 ii 33'
189.1	[MAḪ	*ṣīru*	]⌜*x*⌝	*a-du-rù*	noble	Ug. 5 137 ii 34'
	MAḪ	*ṣe-e-ru*	⌜*a-mu-mi-ia-aš-še*⌝			RS 94.2939 v 9'
189.2	[MAḪ	*ṣēru*	*a-wa-a*]*r-re*	: *ša-du-ú*	plain, field	Ug. 5 137 ii 35'
189.3	[MAḪ	*mādu*/*ma*ʾ*du*	]-*ši*	*ma-a-du-ma*	much, many	Ug. 5 137 ii 36'
189.4	MAḪ	*ra*-⌜*bu-ú*⌝	*ta-la-am-e*		large	RS 94.2939 v 8'
189.5/ 190.1	[MAḪ/ [ḪUL	*rubû*$^{?}$/ *sarru*$^{?}$/*ṣabru*$^{?}$	]-*ri*	*š*/*sar-rù*	prince$^{?}$/ false$^{?}$	Ug. 5 137 ii 37'
190.2	[ḪUL	*masku*	*ni-ru*]-*ba-de*	*ba-ṭá-lu*	bad	Ug. 5 137 ii 38'
	ḪUL	*ma-às-ku*	⌜*ni-ru*⌝-*pa-te*			RS 94.2939 v 11'
190.3	[ḪUL	*zāmânu*$^{?}$	]-⌜*x*⌝	*ḫa-ri-mu*	foe$^{?}$	Ug. 5 137 ii 39'
190.4	[ḪUL	*lemnu*	*šu*]-*bi*	*ḫa-ri-mu*	evil	Ug. 5 137 ii 40'
	ḪUL	*lem-nu*	*šu-be*			RS 94.2939 v 10'
190.5$^{?}$	[ḪUL	*zīru*$^{?}$	*TA*]*R*$^{?}$-*du-bar-ri*	*ma-aš-nu-ú*$^{?}$	enemy$^{?}$	Ug. 5 137 ii 41'
190.6	ḪUL	*a*-⌜*ša*$^{?}$⌝-*x*	⌜*šú*$^{?}$⌝-*ni-te*		?	RS 94.2939 v 12'
190.7	ḪUL	*lum*-⌜*nu*⌝	[*x*]-*ḫa*-ʾ*u-ú-ni*		harm	RS 94.2939 v 13'
191.1	[GUL	*lemnu*$^{?}$]	*šu-bi*	*ḫa-ri-mu*	evil	Ug. 5 137 ii 42'

191.2$^{?}$	[GUL	*ubbutu*$^{?}$]	*na-ak-di*	*i-pu-ú*	obliter-ation$^{?}$	Ug. 5 137 ii 43'
191.3$^{?}$	[GUL	*pīru*$^{?}$]	*pí-i-ri*	*pí-rù*	eleph-ant	Ug. 5 137 ii 44'
	⸢GUL⸣	*pí-ru*	*pí-ri*			RS 94.2939 v 14'
192.1	[ÁŠ	*ku-na*]*-šu*	*ut-te*	⸢*ku*⸣*-sú-m*[*u*]	emmer	Ug. 5 137 ii 45'
	⸢ÁŠ⸣	*ku-un-šu*	*ut-te*			RS 94.2939 v 15'

(192.2–193.4 as on pp. 40–43)

194.1	G[AB	*irtu*	*n*]*e-ḫé-er-ni*	*i-r*[*a*$^{?}$*-tu*$_{4}^{?}$]	chest	Ug. 5 137 ii 53'
	GAB	*i-ir-tu*	*né-ḫé-er-ni*			RS 94.2939 v 21'

(194.2–197.2 as on pp. 42–43)

198.1	IDIM	*na*[*b-qu*$^{?}$]	⸢*tar*⸣*-m*[*a-n*]*i*	*naB-ku*	spring	Ug. 5 137 iii 8
	IDIM	*na-ag-bu*	*tar-ma-ni*			RS 94.2939 v 25'

pp. 42–43, S^{a} Voc. No. 198.5. Following collation, van Soldt (1989) notes that the signs of the Ugaritic column look like [*r*]*a-m*[*u*] rather than our proposed [*r*]*a-*[*g*]*a*$^{?}$-[*zu*$^{?}$] or Nougayrol's [*r*]*a-n*[*u*$^{?}$; thus read probably:

198.5	[IDIM	*kabtu*	?	*r*]*a-m*[*u*]	exalted	Ug. 5 137 iii 13'

S^{a} Voc. No. 198.8. The equation of IDIM with Akkadian *ekletu* 'darkness' now appears in the Emar S^{a} Voc.

S^{a} Voc. No. 198.10. See the Addendum above, p. 374, for reading this line as follows; the equation IDIM = *šarru* also appears in the Emar S^{a} Voc.

198.10	[IDIM	*šarru*	*ewirni*]	*ma-al-ku*	king	Ug. 5 137 iii 17'

p. 49, no. 25.2. Van Soldt (1990: 732) prefers to understand the line as 'waterskin' rather than 'stela' because the form *nādu* for the latter is "a late variant of the only lexically attested *nadû*"; but as noted on p. 49, another Ugarit lexical text does give the form *na-du* for 'stela', so the word in that form was known to the Ugarit scribes.

p. 50, no. 30.x/30a.x. Van Soldt (1989: 651; 1991: 307) proposes to read the Ugaritic form *ri-gi-mu* as an unusual writing for /rigmu/ (with an epenthetic vowel), a *qitl* infinitive meaning 'to speak'$^{?}$ (see also Tropper 2000: 169). But given the irregular writing that must be assumed and the fact that neither no. 30 GIM nor no. 30a BAN denotes 'to speak', the suggestion is difficult to accept.

p. 51, no. 31. Van Soldt (1990) reads the Ugarit form as *ti-*[*i*]*t-tu*$_4$, which would presumably reflect a form /tittu/ as in Akkadian, with loss of /ʾ/ and assimilation of /n/. Since loss of /ʾ/ is relatively rare in Ugaritic, however (Tropper 2000: 157–59), the reading *ti-*[*n*]*a-tu*$_4$ remains more likely.

p. 51, no. 32.1. As noted by van Soldt (1990), the Ugaritic word for 'year' is written *ša-*⸢*an*⸣-[*t*]*u*$_4$, not *ša-na-tu*$_4$ as expected. The writing reflects a pronunciation [šantu], the result of syncope of the medial unaccented *a* of the underlying form /šánatu/, a form that also accounts for the non-assimilation of *n*. Other instances of post-tonic syncope are cited above, pp. 282–83. Were the original or underlying form of the word **šantu* in Ugaritic, of course, we would expect the *n* to have assimilated, yielding a form **šattu* as in northern Hebrew, Moabite, Phoenician, and some dialects of Aramaic.

p. 54, no 34. The Ugaritic form *i-ṣú* in UF 11 479: 13 represents the singular /ʿiṣu/, alongside the plural /ʿiṣṣūma/ reflected in the writing *iṣ-ṣú-*[*ma*] of Ug. 5 130 iii 8'.

p. 59, no. 41.4. Since collation reveals the signs of the Ugaritic column to be [*x*]*-iZ-ḫu* rather than [*la-q*]*a-ḫu*, the proposed infinitive /laqāḥu/ is obviously to be deleted above, pp. 143, 320. The writing [*x*]*-iZ-ḫu* is probably another *qitl* infinitive (see p. 320), perhaps [*ni*]*-iṣ-ḫu* for /niṣḥu/ 'to be(come) pure', thus another instance of S[a] Voc. No. 40 (40.4), EL = *el(ē)lu* '(to be) pure'. The root *n-ṣ-ḥ* meaning 'be pure' is attested in Arabic and Gəʿəz, although in Northwest Semitic, including alphabetic Ugaritic (*nṣḥ*, DUL 647), the root has instead the meaning 'succeed, endure, shine'. If our identification is correct, it would mean that text UF 11 479 lacked sign no. 41 IGI (as well as no. 42 IGI-*gunû* = SIG_7).

p. 61, no. 45.1. Van's Soldt's collation shows that the reading of the Ugaritic word as *ša-mu-ma* is fairly certain.

p. 61, no. 45.2. Nougayrol's suggestion that Akkadian *e-nu* was written for expected *a-nu* 'An' is confirmed by RS 94.2939 ii 7. Van Soldt's collation (1990: 731) of UF 11 479 shows that line 30 is to be placed here rather than at no. 45.3, and that the Ugaritic column has the plural form ⸢*i-lu-ma*⸣ = /ʾilūma/; compare the plural (of majesty) /baʿalūma/ in the Ugaritic column of no. 37.2.

p. 61, no. 45.3. Van Soldt's collation (1990: 731) of UF 11 479 shows that in line 31 the Hurrian form is *e-ni* 'god' rather than *ta-ni* as suggested by Laroche's copy, and that the Ugaritic form is *i-lu* for /ʾilu/ 'god'. This line thus goes here rather than at no. 45.4.

p. 61–62, no. 45.4. With the adjustments just noted to nos. 45.2 and 45.3, this line now appears only in Ug. 5 133 i 15'.

pp. 61–62, nos. 45.5, 46.1. I read UF 11 479: 32 as [*b*]*a*?-*a*-[*lu*?-*ma*?] 'lords', i.e., sign no. 45.5 corresponding to Akkadian *šarrānū* 'kings' in Ug. 5 133 i 16'. With van Soldt 1990: 732, however, we should equate UF 11 479: 32 with sign no. 46.1 ḪAL = Akkadian *ḫallu* = Hurrian *zianni* 'crotch' (thus no. 45.5 now only appears in Ug. 5 133 i 16'). Further, van Soldt's collation shows that the medial sign of the Ugaritic word is *ZA*. With reservation, I propose to read [*ḫ*]*u*-*ṣa*-[*nu*] for /ḫuṣănu/ 'lap', cognate with Hebrew *hṓṣen*, Arabic *ḥiḍn*, Gəʿəz *ḥəśn*, for which see Militarev and Kogan 2000: 117–18. The proposed Ugaritic form is not attested in alphabetic texts.

p. 62, no. 46.2. See van Soldt 1989a for the correct reading of this line as ḪAL = Akkadian *bārû* 'diviner', corresponding to Hurrian *purulini*, which in turn is the source of the Ugaritic form *pu*-*r*[*u*-*li*-*nu*], attested in alphabetic texts as *prln* (see DUL 680).

p. 62, no. 47.1. It is now well established that Hurrian *irvi* means 'dog' (corresponding thus to sign UR and Akkadian *kalbu*), so that the Ugaritic word is to be read *ka*-*a*[*l*-*bu*] as tentatively suggested on p. 62.

p. 63, no. 47.3. In the new trilingual S^{a} Voc. RS 94.2939 ii 13, Hurrian *pì*-⌜*ir*⌝-*ri* is equated with Akkadian *mitḫāriš* 'equally' at sign no. 47.3; thus, Hurrian [*p*]*í*-*ir*-*ri* in Ug. 5 131 4' must also belong here, and that in turn gives us the meaning of the Ugaritic form *ir*-*KU* in the latter. Ugaritic *ir*-*KU* must therefore be a *qitl* noun with adverbial -*u*. Perhaps we may suggest, with all due reservation, /ʿirku/, which, if we may compare Hebrew *ʿḗrek* 'row', might literally mean something like 'in a row', hence 'equally'(?); note alphabetic *ʿrk* 'list' (DUL 182), presumably < 'row'.

In UF 11 479: 36, I would suggest, the Ugaritic form *BI*-*ru* denotes not, as I originally proposed, the preposition /bi-/ plus the beginning of a noun, but rather the word /pīru/ 'elephant', the scribe having misconstrued Hurrian *pirri* 'equally' as the noun *piri*, equivalent to Akkadian *pīru* 'elephant', as in no. 191.3, for which see below, ad pp. 91–92.

p. 64, no. 48.2. Our original 48.2 NE? = Hurrian [*p*]*í*-*ir*-*ri* = Ugaritic *ir*-*KU* is now to be read as another instance of no. 47.3; see the preceding entry.

p. 64, no. 49.1. The line we originally placed at sign no. 49 GIBIL must now be placed at no. 48.2, for it seems that no. 49 GIBIL was missing from the quadrilingual vocabularies. Thus read NE = BIL for BÌL (giš + gibil) = Akkadian *perʾu* 'shoot, scion' and the Hurrian *ḫešši* and Ugaritic /šapḥu/ as before. (Van Soldt [1989a, 1990:

732] reads this line and the next two lines of Ug. 5 131, viz. lines 5'–7', as additional instances of sign no. 47 UR; but that seems unlikely since none of the Hurrian or Ugaritic words in those lines fit well as glosses of UR.)

p. 64, no. 50.2??. Since it is still difficult to connect any of the values of no. 50 KA or no. 51 SAG with the meaning 'life' of the Hurrian and Ugaritic columns, perhaps we may suggest instead, with all due reservation, that Ug. 5 131 6' is another instance of no. 48 NE, the scribe having misconstrued the value NE = IZI as ZI = *napištu*. In this case signs 50 and 51 would be missing from Ug. 5 131 (as well as no. 52 and perhaps no. 53; see the following paragraph).

p. 66, no. 53.4/54. This line, Ug. 5 131 8', is placed by van Soldt (1989, 1990) at sign no. 48 NE 'fire'; he thus reads the Ugaritic column as *iš-tu*$_4$, a variant of *i-ši-tu*$_4$, discussed on p. 63 at no. 48.1. But a form *ʾ*ištu* for 'fire' is unprecedented in Semitic; all languages that show the feminine ending have long *ā* before *t* (Akkadian, Aramaic, Ethiopic; pace Tropper 2000: 185). Thus the original identification of the Ugaritic word as *iš-du*$_4$ for /ʾišdu/ 'leg' remains more likely, as does the original placement of the line at sign no. 53 DU or 54 SUḪUŠ (with sign 52 or signs 52 and 53 missing from Ug. 5 131). (Note that if van Soldt is correct that Ug. 5 131 5'–7' should be placed at no. 47 UR—though as noted just above this seems unlikely—we may still read line Ug. 5 131 8' as /išdu/ by proposing another instance of no. 47 UR, in this case UR for ÚR, which is also used as a logogram for Akkadian *išdu* 'foundation', and which appears in the S^a Voc. at no. 158, where it is equated with, inter alia, Ugaritic /riglu/ 'foot' [no. 158.3].)

p. 68, no. 63.4. As noted in the Addendum to the original publication of this book (p. 374), the proposed reading of the line as no. 63 UD = Akkadian *anumma* 'now (then), here' is confirmed by the Ugarit version of the MB grammatical text.

p. 69, no. 63.6. It was noted on p. 69 that an intransitive D verb (/zuttaru/$^?$ 'to go out') was problematic (see also Tropper 2000: 564). Further, alphabetic *ztr* in KTU 1.17 i 28, ii 17 is most likely a noun (see *DUL* 1001–2). If the first, broken sign of the Ugaritic form may be read as *ḫu* rather than *zu*, the form may represent a D verb /ǵuttaru/ 'to attack', corresponding to alphabetic *ǵtr* in KTU 1.103+:39 (see DUL 327f.), and to sign UD, for UD.DU = È = Akkadian *šaḫāṭu*.

p. 72, no. 156. RS 94.2939 offers Akkadian *kīnu* 'true', an otherwise unattested equation, rather than *namāru* 'to shine' as in Ug. 5 135.

p. 72, no. 158.1. The reading of the Akkadian as *sūnu* 'lap' is now confirmed by RS 94.2939 iv 7'.

p. 72, no. 158.2. The reading of the Akkadian as *naṣāru* is now confirmed by RS 94.2939 iv 8', which also offers the Hurrian infinitive *utr=ummi*, which also glosses ŠEŠ = *naṣāru* three lines later in the same text (RS 94.2939 iv 11'); the Hurrian root *utr-* is otherwise unattested (André-Salvini and Salvini 1998: 22).

p. 72, no. 158.3. RS 94.2939 iv 9' gives the Hurrian for 'foot' as *urni*, so that we are undoubtedly to read *ur*$^{!}$-*n*[*i*$^{?}$] in Ug. 5 135 r. 18' as well. As noted by André-Salvini and Salvini (1998: 21), this word is undoubtedly the same as *uri* 'foot' attested in a bilingual S^{a} Voc. from Boğazköy, with the individualizing suffix *-ni*. The distinction between the two Hurrian words for 'foot', *ugri* and *ur(n)i*, is unclear.

p. 73, no. 160.1. RS 94.2939 iv 13' confirms Nougayrol's original reading of the Akkadian as *urāšu*, meaning perhaps 'something dirty, unclean garment' (see André-Salvini and Salvini 1998: 13).

pp. 74–75, no. 173.4. Van Soldt 1991: 304 follows Nougayrol in reading the Ugaritic, tentatively, as [*ku-u*]*s-sú* for the D verb /kussû/ < **kussawu*. But our objections to this reading remain valid. Perhaps the scribe considered Akkadian *katāmu* in its meaning 'to overwhelm' (see CAD K 300b), in which case the Ugaritic may simply be [*u*]*z-zu* for /ʿuzzu/ 'strength, power', alphabetic *ʿz* (I) (DUL 195–96).

p. 77, no. 176.y. See above on the Emar S^{a} Voc. Akkadian equivalents of sign 176 TUR here, any of which could correspond to Ugaritic /wal(a)du/ 'child'.

p. 77, nos. 177.1, 177.2. The readings proposed here had already been suggested by J. W. Wesselius in 1979, in a study unfortunately overlooked by me.

pp. 78–79, no. 178. See Pardee 1984: 219 with n. 27 for a possible Ugaritic root *ḫdr* meaning 'to stay inside' (KTU 2.33:15), which might also be the root of Ugaritic ⸢*ḫu*⸣*-du-rù* here, rather than *ḥdr*.

p. 79, no. 180.1. Akkadian *qatnu*, as in the Emar S^{a} Voc. here, corresponds well with our proposed Ugaritic /daqqu/.

p. 80, no. 180.3?/181?. Wilhelm (1992) has shown that the Hurrian column offers an abstract noun *tapšaġalže* meaning 'office of cupbearer', from *tapšaġi* 'cupbearer', and corresponding to Akkadian *šāqûtu*; as Wilhelm notes, the sign SIG has apparently been either interpreted as SAGI (= *šāqû* 'cupbearer') or related to the lexical (Diri) equation DUG.A.SIG = *mašqû* 'watering place, drinking vessel'. Thus the Ugaritic form is undoubtedly /mašqû/ (< **mašqayu*), i.e., a *maqtal* form of the root *š-q-y* 'to give to drink', with which Wilhelm rightly compares Hebrew *mašqe*, which on at least one occasion (Genesis 40: 21) denotes 'office of cupbearer'. Note alphabetic *mšq* in *mšq mlkt* 'the queen's cup' (KTU 4.265: 1; see DUL 593), which may be the same word and thus, like Hebrew *mašqe*, denote both 'drink' and 'office of cupbearer'.

Sign no. 181 SIG$_5$ is thus missing in Ug. 5 137 (as also in the Emar S^a Voc.).

p. 82, no. 183.2. The Akkadian writing *la-sà-mu* probably represents the adjective *lasmu*, here substantivized in the meaning 'runner'; see Huehnergard 1989: 117 with n. 66 for the (probably) epenthetic second vowel of the writing.

p. 82, no. 183.3. Hurrian *puḫḫi* 'nose' is also attested as *punḫi*; see Wegner 1995: 123.

p. 82, n. 37. Correct the cross-reference at the end of this note to n. 107 (p. 290).

p. 83, no. 183.5. Van Soldt (1989: 649) points out that the scribe of Ug. 5 137 did not use the ʾ sign, and so the writing *ma-AḪ-ḫa-du* for the Ugaritic word might indeed denote *ma-áʾ-ḫa-du* for /maʾḫadu/, rather than our proposed [maḫḫadu] with assimilation of ʾ to the following *ḫ*.

pp. 83–84, no. 184.2. For the Hurrian infinitive *tapš=oġ=umme* corresponding to Akkadian *nabalkutu* 'to cross, exceed, turn upside down', see Wilhelm 1992: 252f. The reading of the Ugaritic form as /tuhappiku/ was also suggested by van Soldt (1989: 651; 1991: 303) and by Lambert (1988).

p. 84, no. 185. Alphabetic *bḫr* (KTU 1.15 v 22) is also glossed 'lad' in DUL 219.

pp. 84–85, no. 186.1. On alphabetic *ḫzr* 'assistant, auxiliary', which is not related to the syllabic form *ḫu-zi-rù* here, see further DUL 417–18.

p. 85, no. 186.2. André-Salvini and Salvini (1998) read the Akkadian of RS 94.2939 v 4' as no. 185 ŠÁḪ = *šuburru* 'anus, buttocks'. Sign no. 186 ŠAḪ is similarly equated with *šuburru* in the Emar S^a Vocabulary. André-Salvini and Salvini (1998: 24) state that the Hurrian of RS 94.2939 v 4', *zu-⸢ra-at/ap⸣-ḫé*, is previously unattested; but it is close enough to *šu-ra-at-ḫe* in Ug. 5 137 ii 27' that the two writings undoubtedly denote the same word. Thus Ugaritic *qi-i-lu* must also denote 'anus, buttocks'; no root *q-x-l* (with *x* = *w/y/ʾ/ʿ/h*) suggests itself, however.

p. 86, no. 187.1. The restoration of the sign and the Akkadian as LÚ = *šu-ú* is now confirmed by the Ugarit grammatical text (as noted in our original Addendum, p. 373) and by RS 94.2939 v 6'.

p. 86, no. 187.4. The trilingual S[a] Voc. RS 94.2939 v 5' offers a different Hurrian word for 'man', *ta-a-e* (which is usually written *taḫe*), than *taršuwanni* found elsewhere in these texts; see André-Salvini and Salvini 1998: 17–18.

p. 87, no. 189.1. For Hurrian ⸢*a-mu-mi-ia-aš-še*⸣ in RS 94.2939 v 9', see André-Salvini and Salvini 1998: 9, who identify it as an adjective based on the noun *amummini* 'administrator' < 'high-placed'. This adds weight to the identification of the Ugaritic form *a-du-rù* as 'noble' or the like.

p. 87, no. 189.3. Syllabic /maʾadūma/ 'many' corresponds to alphabetic *mad* in KTU 1.14 ii 35; DUL 511. Alphabetic *mid* (also once *mud*) instead reflects the noun /muʾdu/ 'abundance' (also used adverbially, 'much, greatly', like Hebrew *məʾōd*; see DUL 512). See also the next paragraph.

p. 87, new S[a] Voc. no. 189.4. It is possible that Akkadian *rabû* and Hurrian *talme* 'large' in RS 94.2939 v 8' correspond to Ugaritic *ma-a-du-ma* 'much, many' in Ug. 5 137 ii 36' (thus, no. 189.3; see the preceding paragraph), but it is more likely that these are distinct entries for sign no. 189.

p. 88, new S[a] Voc. no. 189.5?. See the following paragraph.

p. 88, no. 190.1. This line is unfortunately not in the newly published trilingual S[a] Voc. RS 94.2939. Nougayrol's original proposal to read Ug. 5 137 ii 37' as ḪUL = Akkadian *sarru* = Ugaritic *sar-rù* = /sarru/ 'false; liar', which I also adopted, remains possible. (The Akkadian column may have had *ṣabru*, as in the corresponding S[a] Voc. from Emar, rather than *sarru*.) But it is equally possible to interpret Ug. 5 137 ii 37' as another instance of sign no. 189 MAḪ, which is equated in one lexical text (a commentary on Enūma Eliš vii 96; see CAD R 396a) with Akkadian *rubû* 'prince', in which case the Ugaritic may be read *šar-rù* = /šarru/ 'prince', alphabetic *šr* (cf. Hebrew *śar*; cognate with Akkadian *šarru* 'king'), and the Hurrian, perhaps, as another instance of *eweri* 'king'.

p. 88, no. 190.2. RS 94.2939 v 11' shows that in Ug. 5 137 ii 38' we are to read sign no. 190 ḪUL = Akkadian *masku* = Hurrian *nirubade*, all meaning 'bad' (for the Hurrian form, see André-Salvini and Salvini 1998: 14). Our interpretation of Ugaritic *ba-TA-lu* as /baṭalu/, a *qatal* adjective cognate with Arabic *baṭala* 'to be false, vain, worthless' (still unattested alphabetically) thus remains likely.

pp. 89–90, nos. 190.3, 190.4, 191.1. RS 94.2939, unfortunately, has no line corresponding to Ug. 5 137 ii 39'; I still consider my proposal to read the Ugaritic of no. 190.3 as /ǵarĭmu/ 'foe' to be plausible.

RS 94.2939 v 10' shows that Hurrian *šu-be* in nos. 190.4 and 191.1 corresponds to Akkadian *lemnu* 'evil' rather than *šulputu* as I had suggested; *lemnu* in turn provides the meaning of Ugaritic *ḫa-ri-mu* in Ug. 5 137 ii 40' and 42'. It still seems likely to me that the Ugaritic word is /ḥarĭmu/ originally meaning 'desecrated, unholy', as proposed on pp. 89–90, but having shifted semantically to the broader sense 'evil'.

p. 90, no. 190.5. Evidence for a passive *maqtūl* participle in Ugaritic remains sparse at best (Tropper 2000: 476–76). Thus our alternative suggestion to take the syllabic form *ma-aš-nu-ú*? as a *maqtal* noun with vowel assimilation around the ᵓ, i.e., [mašnuᵓu] for /mašnaᵓu/, is to be preferred. Other Ugaritic *maqtal* nouns denoting persons are /malᵓaku/ 'messenger' and /malsamu/ 'runner'.

p. 91, no. 191.2. In the Akkadian column, the Sᵃ Voc. from Emar at sign no. 191 GUL has, inter alia, the D form *ubbutu* 'destroyed; to destroy', which lends support to our proposal that the Ugaritic *i-pu-ú* reflects a *qitl* verbal noun /ᶜipû/ 'obliteration'.

pp. 91–92, no. 191.3. The new trilingual text RS 94.2939 v 14' has sign no. 191 GUL/SÚN, which is equated with Akkadian *BI-ru*, which the editors André-Salvini and Salvini (1998: 15) reasonably identify as *pīru* 'elephant', an identification accepted in CAD (P 418b), although the equation seems to be unattested otherwise (see CAD ibid.). The Ugaritic word for 'elephant' is not yet attested in alphabetic texts; we might expect it to be /pīlu/ as elsewhere in West Semitic (and occasionally in Akkadian); if the identification of the Akkadian *pí-ru* as 'elephant' is correct, the Ugaritic /pīru/ (like the Hurrian *piri*) may be a loan from Akkadian, or simply a north Syrian Wanderwort.

As an alternative, we may note that GUL = SÚN corresponds to Akkadian *rīmtu* 'wild cow', and suggest that the scribe wrote a semantically similar word, *bīru* 'bull; young cattle (regardless of sex)'. The Ugaritic *bi-rù* might then reflect /biᶜru/, unattested alphabetically, but cognate with Gəᶜəz *bəᶜr* 'ox' and Aramaic/Hebrew *bəᶜîr* 'cattle' (and, probably, Akkadian *bīru* itself).

p. 93, no. 193.1. The Akkadian of RS 94.2939 v 18' is *še-qu-*⸢*ú*⸣, which confirms our emendation to *še*!*-qu-ú* in Ug. 5 137 ii 49'.

pp. 94–95, no. 194.1. RS 94.2939 v 21' confirms the Akkadian column as *irtu* 'chest'; the Hurrian word is *neḫerni* (see Wegner 1995: 121 for other instances).

Note, in an Sᵃ Voc. text from Emar, the West Semitic form *ri-i-ú* for /riᵓu/ 'lung' (glossing ḪAR), a masculine form corresponding to feminine *riᵓa* in Arabic and *rēᵓā* in post-biblical Hebrew; see Cohen 2002.

p. 95, no. 194.3. An alphabetic form *pṭr* occurs in KTU 1.16 vi 8, and is glossed 'aperture' in DUL 687, probably related to the root meaning 'to loosen, separate'. Note also the form *pẓr* 'to loosen' in KTU 1.107: 34, with <ẓ> as a hypercorrect spelling for <ṭ> (see DUL 690).

p. 96, no. 194.4. For other Ugaritic forms with *š*-prefix, see now Tropper 2000: 600–2.

p. 97, no. 198.1. Note that the new trilingual RS 94.2939 has the expected form *nagbu* in the Akkadian column.

p. 98, no. 198.5. Ugaritic [*r*]*a-m*[*u*], if that is indeed the reading as van Soldt suggests, probably represents the adjective /răāmu/ = alphabetic *rm*, 'high, exalted' (DUL 741), corresponding to Akk. *kabtu*, which is equated with sign 198 IDIM in the Emar S^a Voc. and which may likewise mean 'honored, important'. The length of the base vowel of /răāmu/ is uncertain; note Hebrew *rām* < **ram-* vs. Aramaic *rām* < **rām-*.

p. 100, no. 198.10. The reading of the Ugaritic as *ma-al-ku* is confirmed by the equation of IDIM = *šarru* in the Ugarit grammatical text. For IDIM = *kabtu*, as I had proposed originally, see instead the preceding paragraph.

p. 104, new root ᵓBᶜLT.

/ᵓibᶜalatu/ n. month name.

econ.: (gen.) *ib-a-la-ti* RS 25.455A+ iii 4' (van Soldt 1991: 303).

Alphabetic: *ibᶜlt* KTU 1.119: 1, 11 (DUL 5).

p. 107, root ᵓL. Add the plural form /ᵓilūma/. See above, ad p. 61, no. 45.2.

p. 108, root ᵓNθ. The Hurrian word *unuššum* is now attested in Old Assyrian; see Günbattı 2004: 252 line 79; further, Márquez-Rowe 2006: 292–93.

p. 109, root ᵓRḪ. Delete this root. Van Soldt's collation of a cast of Ug. 5 3 indicates that after the gloss sign in r. 10' we have either *ti-tar-*⌜*ḫu-Za*⌝ or *ti-tar-*⌜*ri-Za*⌝. The former is difficult to parse as any meaningful form. The latter, however suggests a D *yaqtula* form of a root *trZ*, /titarriZa/; could this be denominative from the noun *trẓẓ*, 'light march, speed' (DUL 880), itself a derivative of the verb *rwẓ* 'to run'? This would certainly fit the context, viz., a Ugaritic gloss of the Akkadian *tirḫuṣ* 'she will run quickly'.

p. 112, root BDL. A more accurate translation of Ugaritic *bdl* is 'substitute, proxy'; see DUL 217; Schloen 2001: 226–30. (The Hurrian etymology discussed in the latter, following a suggestion of I. Márquez Rowe, seems unlikely; a Hurrian form with an initial labial stop should be imported into Semitic with /p/, not /b/.)

See also below, ad p. 167, root PṬR.

p. 113, root BLM. Van Soldt's collation of the line reads *qa-du* É IM X DI/KI : *šaB-*⸢*li-mi*⸣, in which X "is a horizontal at the bottom of the line" (1990: 733). My proposal to read a *šaqtil* form of a root *blm* should probably be discarded, although I have no other explanation of the form after the gloss mark, except to return to Boyd's suggestion that it represents a form of the root *špl*, either a noun /šaplu/ 'low place' or an adjective /šapalu/ 'low' (with post-tonic syncope; see pp. 282–83) plus enclitic *-mi* (which does occur sporadically in Ugarit Akkadian in contexts where it is not expected; see Huehnergard 1989: 210).

p. 114, root B^{c}L. See also above, ad p. 104, for the new root ˀB^{c}LT.

p. 114, new root B^{c}R$^{?}$. See above, ad p. 91–92, no. 191.3, for the following possible reading:

/bi^{c}ru/$^{?}$ n. '(a bovine)'$^{?}$.

p. 122, root ZTR. Delete this root; see above, ad p. 69, no. 63.6.

p. 122, new root ḤBṬ$^{?}$.

/ḥabaṭū/$^{?}$ v. G suffix-conj. 'they were lost'$^{?}$.

legal: (garments) ŠU PN *ki ḫa-ba-ṭu* '(garments) in the custody of PN, though they have been lost' PRU 6 128.

Alphabetic: *tḥbṭ* (DUL 354).

The alphabetic form *tḥbṭ* in KTU 1.82: 25, a list of incantations, is glossed 'to be beaten' by Caquot (1988: 40; 1989: 68) and others, including DUL 354. The meaning 'to beat' is based on comparison with the root *ḥbṭ* 'to beat' in Hebrew and Aramaic, and a verb *ḥabaṭa* in Arabic, which, Caquot noted, can mean 'périr'. But the Arabic verb that is cognate with the Hebrew and Aramaic root is actually *ḫabaṭa* 'to beat', and so a Ugaritic cognate to those roots should also have *ḫ* as its first root consonant (note also *ḫbṭ* 'to beat, strike' in Sabaean). Thus *tḥbṭ* in KTU 1.82 is indeed probably cognate to Arabic *ḥabaṭa*, and means 'may you/they be lost/perish'. That in turn suggests the meaning of *ḫa-ba-ṭu* in PRU 6 128: 7, viz., 'to be(come) lost, go missing', as originally suggested by Nougayrol in the editio princeps ("quand (?) ils ont disparu (??)").

p. 125, root ḤLL. In the first text, read probably genitive *ḫal-la-t*[*e*] with van Soldt (1989: 651), who also notes that the month name occurs as well in RS 25.455A+B iii 6'.

p. 126, new root ḪṢN[?]. See above, ad pp. 61–62, nos. 45.5, 46.1 for the following possible reading.

/ḫuṣănu/$^?$ ‘crotch, lap’.

lex.: (Sum.) [ḪAL] = (Akk.) [*ḫallu*] = (Hur.) *zi-ia-ni* = (Ugar.) [*ḫ*]*u*$^?$-*ṣa*-[*nu*$^?$] UF 11 479: 32 ((polyglot vocab.)

S^a Voc. no. 46.1.

Alphabetic: unattested.

p. 126, root ḪRḪR. Perhaps to be deleted; as noted by van Soldt (1990:733), both of the forms cited here may be Akkadian rather than Ugaritic.

p. 127, new root ḪDR$^?$. See above on pp. 78–79, no. 178.

pp. 128–29, root ḪYR. The month name /ḫiyyāru/ occurs in a number of other Ugarit Akkadian texts; see van Soldt 1991: 340.

p. 129, new root ḪLR$^?$.

/ḫullūru/$^?$ n. ‘chickpea(s)’.

letter: GÚ.GAL *ḫu-ul-lu-ru* ‘chickpea(s)’ PRU 6 18: 14.

Alphabetic: unattested.

The Akkadian word for ‘chickpea’ is *ḫallūru*. The form in PRU 6 18, with the pattern *quttūl* rather than *qattūl*, may thus be Ugaritic; see pp. 269–70. Note, however, that the provenance of PRU 6 18 is not certain and, further, that the form *ḫullūru* also occurs once in an Akkadian text from Nuzi.

p. 131, root ẒRW. On Sabaean *ḍrw* and other Semitic cognates, see Sima 2000: 269–70.

p. 133, root YṢʾ. Note the similar form *i-ṣa-ma* (with enclitic *-ma*) in RS 25.423, cited by van Soldt (1989: 650); in the latter instance, however, the form, as translated by van Soldt (‘he will go out’) is not perfective.

p. 135, root KBD. Delete entry (a) /kabidu/. The S^a Voc. line 47.1 denotes ‘dog’, and the Ugaritic form is to be read *ka-a*[*l-bu*] = /kalbu/; see above, ad p. 62, sign 47.1.

Entry (b) /kubuddatu/ is probably also to be deleted; the form [*k*]*u-bu-ut-ta-tu*$_4^{meš}$ has now appeared in a text written in Egypt (Lackenbacher 1995: 81 and n. 28), where a Ugaritic word is unlikely, and so the form in PRU 3 98f. is probably also simply a (peripheral) Akkadian term. But see also Márquez-Rowe 2006: 220–21.

p. 136, root KLB. This root, and the Ugaritic word /kalbu/ 'dog', are now confirmed in S[a] Voc. 47.1; see above on p. 62, sign 47.1.

pp. 140–141, root KRK. Note Egyptian Arabic *kurēk* 'shovel', which is said to derive from Turkish *kürek* (Littmann 1954: 124; Badawi and Hinds 1986: 744); it is possible, however, that the Turkish, Arabic, and Ugaritic words all descend from an early Anatolian word.

p. 143, root LQḤ. Delete entry (a) /laqāḥu/. See above, ad p. 59, no. 41.4.

pp. 145–46, root MW/YR. This root should probably be deleted. Márquez-Rowe (2006: 233 n. 41), on the basis of his collation, suggests that PRU 3 51f.: 9 should be read simply *a-na* PN$_2$-*ma a-di* ⸢*da*⸣-[*ri-ti*]. This seems preferable to my proposal based on my own collation of the line (see Huehnergard 1986: 170). If Márquez-Rowe's reading is correct, lines 8–9 are to be translated 'The burial-ground of PN$_1$ belongs only to PN$_2$ forever'. For similar examples of enclitic *-ma* in a verbless clause, see Huehnergard 1989: 205.

p. 146, root MḪṢ. Entry (a) /māḫiṣu/ probably means 'weaver; beater'; see DUL 541–42.

pp. 147–48, root MSW. Vita 1995 proposes an alternative interpretation of the forms $^{\text{giš(.meš)}}$*ma-ás/sa-wa-tu* as 'oars', corresponding to alphabetic *mθṭ* and Hebrew *māšôṭ/miššôṭ*. There are several difficulties with this suggestion, however, that make it highly unlikely: (a) PRU 114 is a list of trees or types of wood, in which a manufactured item such as 'oars' is out of place; (b) the value $ša_{10}$ for *SA* is very rare in Ugarit Akkadian; and (c) the consonantal *w* of the syllabic forms should also appear in an alphabetic writing of this word and in a Hebrew cognate.

p. 150, new root -N.

/-nā/ pron. suff. 1cp 'our'.

legal: LUGAL EN-*na-a* 'the king our lord' PRU 3 41ff.: 19.

Alphabetic: *-n*.

The Ugarit Akkadian text PRU 3 41ff. (RS 16.270) was not included in our corpus because it seemed possible that it was written at Amurru. Several scholars have, however, convincingly argued that it was indeed written at Ugarit (Kühne 1973: 183; Izre'el 1991: 22–23; 1992: 169; Márquez-Rowe 2000). Thus the writing *-na-a*, which in context is obviously the 1cp suffix 'our', provides the vocalization of that suffix in Ugaritic (with the same vowel as in Arabic, Aramaic, and Ethiopic, vs. Hebrew *-nû*, Akkadian *-ni*).

p. 150, root N'. Additional cognates of Ugaritic /ni'tu/ have come to light: note Mari Akkadian ^{giš}*ne-e-tum* 'ax' (see DUL 612) and Eblaite *ne-a-tum/ni-a-ti* 'ax' (Archi 2005).

p. 153, root NSK. Note the following additional example, construct plural /nāsikū/:

econ: ⌜*na-sí-ku*⌝ URUDU 'bronze-smiths' PRU 3 195b B 1 (van Soldt 1991: 306).

Syllabic ⌜*na-sí-ku*⌝ URUDU corresponds to the frequent alphabetic *nsk θlθ*, i.e., /nāsikū θalθi/ (see DUL 911).

p. 153, new root NṢḪ. See above, ad p. 59, no. 41.4, for the following:

/niṣḫu/? G v.n./infin. 'to be(come) pure'?.

lex.: (Sum.) [EL] = (Akk.) [*elēlu*?] = (Hur.) [ ] = (Ugar.) [*ni*]-*IZ-ḫu* UF 11 479: 24 (polyglot vocab.)

S^{a} Voc. no. 40.4.

Alphabetic: Cf. *nṣḥ* 'to be victorious' (DUL 647).

p. 155, new root NTK?.

*/nutku/?, pl. (Akkadianized) /nutkū/ n. '(a glass paste)'.

letter: *ù lu-ú-me-e šu-bu-lu-um-ma la-a tu-še-ba-la ù* NA_4 *ka-am-ma : nu-ut-ki la-a ta-na-aš-ši-ma la-a tu-še-ba-la* 'do not under any circumstances do this kind of sending; do not collect and send such stone : *nutku*' PRU 4 221ff. (RS 17.383): 23–25.

Alphabetic: *ntk* (DUL 653).

PRU 4 221ff. is a letter sent to the king of Ugarit by his ambassador Taguḫlu, and so it was almost certainly not written at Ugarit, and was not included in our original corpus. But Taguḫlu's use of the form *nutku*, rather than the form *nitku* attested once in a core MB text (see CAD N/2 299b), may reflect his native Ugaritic pronunciation. See Sanmartín 1992 for the meaning 'glass paste/beads' (used as a substitute for lapis lazuli), for the likely connection of *nutku* with alphabetic *ntk* with the same meaning (DUL 651–52), and for the derivation of the noun from the Akkadian and Northwest Semitic root *ntk* 'to spill, pour (out)'.

p. 155, new root NθK?.

/naθku/? n. 'bite'.

lit.: *ina* ÚŠ.MEŠ *na-aš-ki-ša* 'with the blood of her bite' Ug. 5 17 r. 7'.

Alphabetic: *nθk* (DUL 653).

Since Akkadian for 'bite' is *nišku*, the writing in this literary text probably represents the Ugaritic form. The same line contains the Akkadianized Ugaritic verb *li-ip-ḫu-dú*, for which see p. 166.

pp. 156–57, roots SKK, SKN. It is now quite clear from examples at Emar and Mari that the word *sí-kà/ka₄-ni-ma* in Ug. 5 96 represents the oblique pl. of /sikkānu/, with double *-kk-*, and thus a *qitlān* form of the root *skk* rather than a form of the root *skn*. Further, the meaning of the word is 'stela, standing stone'. For surveys of bibliography see Pentiuc 2001: 156–59; DUL 759; Durand 2005.

p. 158, root SRR. See above, ad p. 88, no. 190.1, for the possibility that this line denotes 'prince' rather than 'false', thus Ugaritic *šar-ru* = /šarru/ rather than *sar-ru* = /sarru/.

p. 159, new root ᶜZZ. See above, ad pp. 74–75, no. 173.4 for the following possible reading.

/ᶜuzzu/? n. 'strength, power'?.

lex.: (Sum.) BAD = (Akk.) *katāmu* = (Hur.) *ḫu-x*[ ] = (Ugar.) [*u*]*z*?-*zu* Ug. 5 137 i 21" (polyglot vocab.)

Sᵃ Voc. no. 173.4.

Alphabetic: *ᶜz* (DUL 195–96).

p. 160, root ᶜMQ. In the second entry we are perhaps to read ᵘʳᵘ*ku-um-ba* : ⸢*at*?⸣-*qà*; see below, ad p. 164, new root ᶜTQ.

p. 161, root ᶜṢ. Note the singular form, also found in an Sᵃ Voc. text (van Soldt 1989: 651).

/ᶜiṣu/, pl. /ᶜiṣṣūma/? n. 'tree(s), wood'.

lex.: (Sum.) [GIŠ] = (Akk.) [*iṣu*] = (Hur.) *ta-li* = (Ugar.) *i-ṣú* UF 11 479: 13 (polyglot vocab.)

(Sum.) [GIŠ] = (Akk.) [*iṣṣū*?] = (Hur.) [*tali*] = (Ugar.) *iṣ-ṣú-*[*ma*] Ug. 5 130 iii 8' (polyglot vocab.)

Sᵃ Voc. no. 173.4.

Alphabetic: *ᶜṣ*, pl. *ᶜṣm* (DUL 186–87).

p. 162, root ᶜṢR. Note also the form *uṣ-ṣu-ur* in an Emar lexical text; see Cohen 2003: 184.

p. 162, root ᶜRB. On the form ⁽ˡᵘ́⁾·ᵐᵉˢ̌*ú-ru-ba-nu*, see Hoftijzer and van Soldt 1991.

p. 162, new root ᶜRB².

/yiᶜrabu/ v. G *yaqtulu* 3ms 'he will enter'.

legal: *i-ṣa-ma iḫ-ra-bu* 'he will exit and enter' RS 25.423: 13 (van Soldt 1989: 650).

Alphabetic: *y^{c}rb* (DUL 179–80).

(This form is not, despite our normalization, evidence for the Barth–Ginsberg rule, since the first sign could also be transliterated *a$\underline{h}$*.)

p. 162, new root ^{c}RK$^{?}$. See above, ad p. 63, no. 47.3, for the following possible reading.

/^{c}irku/$^{?}$ n. as adverb 'equally'.

lex.: (Sum.) [UR] = (Akk.) [*mit$\underline{h}$ariš*] = (Hur.) *pí-ir-ri* = (Ugar.) *ir-ku* Ug. 5 131 4' (polyglot vocab.)

S^{a} Voc. no. 47.3.

Alphabetic: *^{c}rk* (DUL 182).

p. 163, root ^{c}ŠR^{1}. On the etymology of this term for an official, see now the bibliography cited in DUL 189, and add Dietrich and Loretz 1991.

p. 164, new root ^{c}TQ$^{?}$. See Márquez-Rowe 2006: 214–15 with n. 10 for this root and the interpretation of the following.

/^{c}at(v)qu/$^{?}$ adj. 'ruined, abandoned'$^{?}$.

legal: *it-ta-ši* ... URU *at-qà ša-ak-na* 'took ... the ruined city Šakna' PRU 3 112f.: 4–6.

it-ta-ši ^{uru}*ku-um-ba* : ⌜*at*$^{?}$⌝*-qà* 'took the ruined city of Kumba' PRU 3 152f. 3.

Alphabetic: Cf. the verb *^{c}tq* 'to pass', N 'to become old, age' (DUL 191–92).

The form [^{c}atqu] would be the result of post-tonic syncope (see above, pp. 282–83), for an underlying *qatvl* adjective.

p. 165, new root ǴTR$^{?}$. See above, ad p. 69, no. 63.6, for the following possible reading.

/ǵuttaru/$^{?}$ D v.n./infin. 'to attack'$^{?}$.

lex.: (Sum.) [UD$^{?}$] = (Akk.) [*ša$\underline{h}$āṭu*$^{?}$] = (Hur.) [ ] = (Ugar.)]*$\underline{h}$u*$^{?}$*-ut-ta-ru* Ug. 5 138 7 (polyglot vocab.)

S^{a} Voc. no. 63.6.

Alphabetic: *ǵtr* (DUL 327–28).

p. 165–66, new root PGR.

/pagrūma/ n. month name.

econ.: (gen.) *pag-ri-ma* RS 25.455A+ iii 1 (van Soldt 1991: 306).

Alphabetic: *pgrm* (DUL 665–66).

p. 167, root PṬR. For entry (b), Tropper (2000: 532–33) remarks that the meaning given here, viz., 'to exchange' (lit. 'to release to one another'?) is unlikely for the root *pṭr* in West Semitic. He thus proposes instead to read the form as *na-ab-da-lu*! = /nabdalū/, again N suffix-conj. 3mp, but from *bdl*, the root of the noun /bidalūma/ 'substitutes'. While semantically attractive, the proposal is difficult to accept, since a verbal root *bdl* is otherwise unattested, and since an emendation is required for the new reading. Thus Nougayrol's original reading and our interpretation of the form as /napṭarū/ seem preferable.

p. 169, new root PR. For the following readings, see above, ad p. 63 no. 47.3 and pp. 91–92, no. 191.3.

/pīru/? n. 'elephant'?.

lex.: (Sum.) [GUL] = (Akk.) [*pīru*?] = (Hur.) *pí-i-ri* = (Ugar.) *pí-rù* Ug. 5 137 ii 44' (polyglot vocab.)

(Sum.) [UR] = (Akk.) *mit*[*ḫ*]*āri*[*š*] = (Hur.) [*piri*?] = (Ugar.) *pí-ru* UF 11 479: 36.

Sa Voc. nos. 47.3, 191.3?.

Alphabetic: Unattested.

p. 169, new root PRLN. See van Soldt 1989a for the following.

/purulin(n)u/ n. 'diviner'.

lex.: (Sum.) [ḪAL] = (Akk.) [*ba-ru*]-*ú*? = (Hur.) *pu-ru-li-ni* = (Ugar.) *pu-r*[*u-li-nu*] UF 11 479: 33 (polyglot vocab.)

Sa Voc. no. 46.2.

Alphabetic: *prln* (DUL 680).

p. 169, root PRS. Delete this root; for the reading of the Ugaritic, see under the new root PRLN just above.

p. 169, root ?PRR. Delete this root; for the reading, see above, new root PR.

p. 171–72, root ṢMT. In Huehnergard 1989: 68 (and n. 142) I suggested that this verb was better understood to mean 'to devolve (of property)'. It should be noted that my interpretation of the forms listed under ṢMT as Ugaritic remains a minority view (see, e.g., Márquez-Rowe 2006: 227–28), most scholars preferring to see them as examples of the verbal adjective of Akkadian *ṣamādu* 'to join'. But the latter view, in my opinion, presents insurmountable difficulties: (a) it is unusual in these texts for Akkadian verbal forms to take on Ugaritic morphology, as in the form *ṣa-ma-ta* (unlike Canaanizing forms in Amarna texts; but see below, ad p. 320, on *ti-tu-ru-na*, and ad p. 321, on *te-ṣa-bi-tu*$_4$); (b) the gloss mark preceding two instances of these forms would remain unexplained; (c) as noted on p. 171, Akkadian *ṣamādu* is not used of the transfer of property.

p. 174, root QṬN. This root should perhaps be deleted, and the form read instead *ka-di-nu*, i.e., *katinnu*, the Hurro-Akkadian word for a work implement or weapon, as proposed by Heltzer 1989 and Vita 1996. The writing with medial *DI* may reflect Hurrian intervocalic voicing. The equation of the form with Ugaritic *qṭn* is accepted, however, by Pentiuc 2001: 145–46.

p. 175, root Qᶜ L. The root of Ugaritic *qi-i-lu* 'anus, buttocks' is uncertain; see above, ad p. 85, no. 186.2.

p. 176, root RGZ. Delete this root; see instead below, ad pp. 177–78, new root RWM.

p. 177, root RGM. See above, ad p. 50, no. 30.x/30a.x. for *ri-gi-mu* as a possible (but unlikely) writing of /rigmu/ 'word'.

p. 177–78, new root RWM?. See above, ad p. 98, no. 198.5, for the following.

/rằmu/? adj. 'high, exalted'?.

lex.: (Sum.) [IDIM] = (Akk.) [*kabtu*?] = (Hur.) [ ] = (Ugar.) [*r*]*a-m*[*u*] Ug. 5 137 iii 13' (polyglot vocab.)

Sᵃ Voc. no. 198.5.

Alphabetic: *rm* (DUL 741).

pp. 177–78, new root RWẒ. See below, ad p. 186, new root TRẒ.

p. 179. Between ?RKM and ?RᶜB, add a cross reference:

?RM: see RWM (above, ad pp. 177–78).

p. 180, root Šʾ L. Correct the text reference: PRU 3 56f.: 5 (Clemens 2002: 221).

p. 182, root ŠN. As noted above, ad p. 51, no. 32.1, the Ugaritic form here is written *ša*-⌜*an*⌝-[*t*]u_4, not *ša-na-tu*$_4$.

p. 183, new root ŠPL?. See above, ad p. 113, root BLM, for the following:

/šaplu/? n. 'low place'? or /šapalu/? adj. 'low'?.

legal: *qa-du* É IM X DI/KI : *šaB*-⌜*li-mi*⌝ 'with the low? ... house' PRU 6 56: 4'.

Alphabetic: Cf. verb *špl* (DUL 836).

p. 184, new root ŠQY. See above, ad p. 80 for the following.

/mašqû/ n. 'office of cupbearer'.

lex.: (Sum.) [SIG] = (Akk.) [*šāqûtu*] = (Hur.) [*t*]*ap-ša-ḫal-še* = (Ugar.) *ma-aš-q*[*u-ú*$^?$] Ug. 5 137 ii 15' (polyglot vocab.)

S^a Voc. no. 180.3.

Alphabetic: Cf. *mšq* (DUL 593).

p. 184, new root ŠRR. See above, ad p. 88, no. 190.1, for the possibility that that entry may denote 'prince' rather than 'false', thus Ugaritic *šar-ru* = /šarru/ rather than *sar-ru* = /sarru/.

p. 185, root TMR. For the alphabetic form *tmry* in RIH 83/2 see Bordreuil apud Pardee 1991: 306.

p. 186, new root TRẒ$^?$. See above, ad p. 109, for the suggestion that *ti-tar-ri*$^?$*-ZA* in Ug. 5 3 r 10' may denote Ugaritic /titarriẓa/ 'she must hasten', a D *yaqtula* form of a root TRẒ, denominative of *trẓẓ* 'light march, speed'.

p. 186, new root TRN$^?$.

/tarnu/$^?$ n. 'mast (of a ship)'.

letter: *aš-šum* ^{giš}*ta-ar-ni* GAL 'concerning the large mast' PRU 6 19: 4'.

Alphabetic: *trn* (DUL 879).

Cf. Hebrew *tōren* 'mast'. The word *tarnu* is not otherwise attested in Akkadian texts (AHw 1331a; CAD T 239b). Note, however, that the provenance of PRU 6 19 is uncertain; Nougayrol (ad loc. p. 21 n. 1) pointed out that certain features of the writing resemble those of Ug. 5 no. 22, a letter from Cyprus.

p. 186, root θḪṬ. The alphabetic form *mθṭm* in KTU 4.689: 3 probably means 'oars' (see above, ad pp. 147–48), and so should not be compared with the syllabic form *ma-ÁS-ḫa-ṭu-ma*. Thus the root of the latter is uncertain: *ð/s/ṣš/θ/z/ẓ-ġ/ḥ/ḫ-ṭ*.

p. 189: *am-ma-ti*. Márquez-Rowe (2006: 247–48) wonders "whether the (presumably Ugaritic) word could be connected with Hurrian *ammade* ... meaning 'grandfather, ancestor', and denoting then in the Ugarit deeds something like 'inherited sonship'."

p. 190: *ḫa-AB-BI/BU*. Compare perhaps alphabetic *ġb* '(sacrificial) pit'$^?$ (DUL 316).

p. 190: *ḫa-ba-ṭu*. See above, ad p. 125, new root ḤBṬ.

p. 191: *ir*$^?$*-KU*. See above, ad p. 63, no. 47.3, and ad p. 162, new root ^{c}RK.

p. 191: [*I*]*i*$^?$/[*U*]*Z*$^?$*-ZU*. See above, ad pp. 74–75, no. 173.4, and ad p. 159.

p. 192: *ma-aš-*⸢*x*⸣[. See above, ad pp. 80, 184 (root ŠQY).

p. 193: *ra-*⸢*PA*⸣*-ni*. See van Soldt 2005: 40–41 with n. 349, who agrees with Nougayrol that this form is another instance of /raḫbānu/ (see above, pp. 178–79).

p. 193: *ri/tal-GI-mu*. See above, ad p. 50.

p. 193: *ZI-ZA-ḫal-li-ma*. A number of scholars have proposed that this word is derived from *sisû* 'horse', thus perhaps 'couriers'. See Márquez-Rowe 2006: 239 n. 95.

pp. 195–265, Part III, Chapter 1. Orthography. A number of minor corrections could be made to this chapter on the basis of the new and corrected readings offered in the preceding pages, but the basic presentation would not be affected, so a detailed list seems unnecessary.

pp. 195–202. As shown by van Soldt, the "confusion" in the writing of stops pertains only "to the older layer of texts written at Ugarit. The younger texts tend to write the stops much more in accordance with Mesopotamian practice" (van Soldt 1990: 734; see also van Soldt 1991: passim).

pp. 196–99. Van Soldt (1990: 734–35), perhaps rightly, challenges our proposal that certain syllabic writings reflect a surface intervocalic voicing rule in Ugaritic.

pp. 211–65. Note the 1978 study of Segert on the syllabic representation of Ugaritic phonemes, which I unfortunately overlooked.

p. 230, n. 86. On the various syllabic writings of the royal name ^{c}*mθtmr*, see now Hutton 2003.

p. 238. On the use of the PI sign for /yē/, note also, in a trilingal lexical fragment from Aphek, [GEŠTI]N.MEŠ = (Akk.) *ka-ra-nu* = *PI-nu*, i.e., /yēnu/ 'wine' (Rainey 1983: 137 line 3).

p. 239. For gentilics in *-ūyu*, compare the alphabetic writing *qnuym* = (pl.) /qanʾūyū-ma/ in RS 17.434+: 39', noted by Pardee (1991: 306).

p. 244. Another instance of a Ḫ-sign for /^{c}/ is the writing *iḫ-ra-bu* for /yi^{c}rabu/; see above, ad p. 162, new root ^{c}RB^{2}.

p. 250, n. 159. Syllabic *mi-ir* in the PN ÌR-*mi-ir* undoubtedly represents /mihīr/ < **mahīr* (with assimilation around the guttural; see pp. 271–73); cf. Hebrew *māhîr* 'skilled', Syriac *mhirā* 'practiced scribe'.

p. 258, n. 191. In the second paragraph of the note, delete the reference to alphabetic *nθt*, which is to be read ⸢*a*⸣*θt* (Pardee).

pp. 269–70. Another possible example of the assimilation $qatt\bar{v}_1 l > qv_1 tt\bar{v}_1 l$ is /ḫullūru/ < **ḫallūru*; see above, ad p. 129.

pp. 271–73. As noted above, ad p. 90, no. 190.5, the normalization [mašnuˀu] for /mašnaˀu/, with short [u] in the second syllable due to assimilation, now seems more likely. See also above, ad p. 250, n. 159, on the form /mihīr/ < **mahīr*. Note, finally, that a similar assimilation is attested in a number of Amarna Canaanite passive suffix-conj. forms with the shape *qitil* for expected *qatil*, all with a guttural as the medial consonant; see Rainey 1996: 2.306.

Sivan (1989: 361–62) and Tropper (2000: 171) prefer to see *mrzḥ* as a *maqtil* noun, despite the paucity of evidence for vowel lowering before gutturals in Ugaritic (see my n. 25 on p. 272). But my explanation of Hebrew *marzēaḥ* as a frozen loan (ibid. n. 26) should probably be abandoned.

pp. 273–75. Additional alphabetic examples of the assimilation of an unstressed vowel in an open syllable after initial /ˀ/ are listed by Tropper 2000: 174–75, who generalizes the rule to affect any short vowel, thus $v_1 > v_2$ / ˀ__$C\acute{v}_2$ (see also my n. 26 on p. 274).

p. 276. The beginning of the formula for the sound rule given about one-third of the way down the page contains an unfortunate typo, *ā* for intended *ă*; i.e., it should read *ă* > [+hi] / #*C*__ {*w*,*y*}.

p. 278, n. 53. Pardee (1991: 306) notes that a verb *kðd* probably does not exist (read instead *k-ðd* 'like a herd of ...').

p. 279. As noted above, ad p. 83, the writing *ma-AḪ-ḫa-du* may not in fact indicate the assimilation of ˀ to the following *ḫ*, i.e., it may denote *ma-áˀ-ḫa-du* for /maˀḫadu/. Thus, much of the discussion on this page may be moot.

pp. 282–83. Other instances of post-tonic syncope have been noted in the preceding pages: [šantu] < /šánatu/ (see ad p. 51, no. 32.1); [ˁatqu] < /ˁátvqu/ (see ad p. 164); perhaps also [šaplu] < /šápalu/ (see ad p. 113).

p. 286, n. 86. On alphabetic *qrt* and syllabic /qarītu/ and their Semitic cognates, see also Nöldeke 1910: 130 and van Soldt 2005: 182–83.

pp. 289–90. Monophthongization of *-ayu* has also occurred in the form /mašqû/ <

**mašqayu*; see above, ad p. 80. Much more detail on the reflexes of original triphthongs is given by Tropper (2000: 194–200).

p. 290, n. 108. Note the archaic/archaizing writing *šmym* = /šamayūma/ (KTU 1.19 iv 24, 30), in which the original triphthong is preserved.

p. 293, A.1.b. Add 1cp suffix *-na-a* = /-nā/ 'our'; see above, ad p. 150, new root -N.

p. 295, near end. Note that the syllabic writing of 'year' is *ša-⸢an⸣-[t]u*$_4$, for [šantu] < /šanatu/; see above, ad p. 51, no. 32.1.

p. 296, d (1) (a). Add ⸢*i-lu-ma*⸣ = /ʔilūma/ 'god(s)'; see above, ad p. 61, no. 45.2.

p. 297, d (1) (b). Add ⸢*na-sí-ku*⸣ URUDU = /nāsikū θalθi/ 'bronze-smiths'; see above, ad p. 153, root NSK.

p. 298 (3) Dual forms. The allomorph of the dual ending with *-a*, in *-āma*, is probably original, the *i* of *-āmi* and of Arabic *-āni* undoubtedly the result of dissimilation (the *i* then spreading to the oblique *-ēmi* and Arabic *-ayni*); see Brockelmann 1908–13 1.253 §94b. (Note also the masc. dual *yaqtulu* verb *ti-eš-ma-na*, presumably for /tišma^{c}āna/ 'they listen', in EA 103:22.)

pp. 302–3. The length of the base vowel in the form [*r*]*a-m*[*u*] = /rā̆mu/ 'exalted' is uncertain, so it is unclear whether it belongs under *qal* or *qāl*.

p. 304. Add to the list of *qatl* forms *na-aš-ki-ša* = /naθki/$^{?}$ 'bite'; see above, ad p. 155.

p. 305. Add to the list of *qitl* forms [*ni*]-*is-ḫu* = /niṣḫu/$^{?}$ 'to be(come) pure'$^{?}$; see above, ad pp. 152–53.

p. 306. Add to the list of *qutl* forms *nu-ut-ku* = /nutku/$^{?}$ '(a glass paste)'; see above, ad p. 155, new root NTK$^{?}$.

p. 307. Under *qatal* add perhaps *šap-li-mi* for [šapli]$^{?}$ < /šapali/ 'low'$^{?}$; see above, ad p. 113.

p. 308, top. Delete from the list of *qatāl* forms [*la*?-*q*]*a*?-*ḫu*? (see above, ad p. 59, no. 41.4) and [*r*]*a*-[*g*]*a*?-[*zu*?] (see above, ad pp. 177–78, new root RWM).

p. 312. Add under *quttūl* perhaps *ḫu-ul-lu-ru* = /ḫullūru/$^{?}$ 'chickpea(s)'; see above, ad p. 129.

p. 317. Add to the Hurrian loanwords *pu-r*[*u-li-nu*] = /purulin(n)u/ 'diviner'; see above, ad p. 169, new root PRLN.

p. 319. In the summary of verbal forms:

Add G *yaqtulu* 3ms *yiqtalu*.
Delete probably G Vbl. Adj. *maqtūlu*.
Delete Gt *yaqtulu* 3fs *tiqtatlu*.
Add D *yaqtula* 3fs *tiqattila*?.

p. 320. Under G Prefix-conj.:

Add *yaqtulu* 3ms *iḫ-ra-bu* = /yi^{c}rabu/ 'he will enter' (RS 25.423: 13); see above, ad p. 162 (^{c}RB^{2}).

Note the 3mp form *ti-tu-ru-na* '(if) they return' (RS 22 .399+: 17), in which the Akkadian verb *târu* is supplied with the Ugaritic 3mp prefix *t-* and with the *yaqtulu* 3mp ending *-ūna*; the form is cited by van Soldt 1991: 432 and Tropper 2000: 459.

Under G Verbal nouns:

Delete geminate *pí-rù* = /pirru/; see above, ad p. 169, new root PR.
Add perhaps [*ni*]-*IZ-ḫu* = /niṣḫu/$^{?}$ 'to be(come) pure'$^{?}$; see above, ad pp. 152–53.
Delete [*la*?-*q*]*a*?-*ḫu*? = /laqāḫu/; see above, ad p. 59, no. 41.4.
Delete [*r*]*a*-[*g*]*a*?-[*zu*?] = /ragāzu/; see above, ad pp. 177–78, new root RWM.

Under G Verbal Adjective/Passive Participle:

Delete probably the form *ma-aš-nu-ú*, which is more likely a *maqtal* noun; see above, ad p. 90, no. 190.5.

pp. 320–21. Delete the Prefix-Conj. 3fs *yaqtulu* form *:ti-tar-ḫ*[*u*]; see above, ad p. 109, and below, ad p. 321, D Prefix-Conj.

p. 321. Under D Prefix-Conj., add perhaps 3fs *yaqtula* form *ti-tar-ri*$^{?}$*-ZA* = /titarriẓa/ 'she must hasten'; see above, ad pp. 109 and 186. This interpretation is offered with much reservation. If it is correct, however, it indicates that the prefix vowel of the D stem in *yaqtul-* forms was *i* rather than *u* or *a*, i.e., *yiqattil-*. The *a* vowel in the prefix of 1cs forms, i.e., *ʾaqattil-*, which is well documented in a number of alphabetic examples written <aqtl>, would thus be the result of vowel harmony after initial ʾ, for which see above, ad pp. 273–75. Supporting evidence for *i* as the prefix vowel of the D is the 3mp form *te-ṣa-bi-tu*$_4$ '(if) they seize' in PRU 6 50: 16, for expected *iṣabbatū* or *iṣbatū* (see Huehnergard 1989: 160); although the root of the latter form is Akkadian, the morphology can be considered purely Ugaritic, especially the prefix *t* for 3mp, i.e., D *yaqtul* 3mp *tiqattilū*. Whether the prefix vowel in the D participle might also have changed from the original *u* to *i* (i.e., *muqattil* to *miqattil*) is difficult to ascertain; certain PN's show the form *muqattil* (see Tropper 2000: 562), but we cannot be sure, of course, that these reflect Ugaritic morphology.

Under D Verbal Noun, instead of [*z*]*u-ut-ta-ru* = /zuttaru/, read perhaps *ḫu*$^{?}$*-ut-ta-ru* = /ǵuttaru/$^{?}$ 'to attack'$^{?}$; see above, ad p. 69, no. 63.6, and p. 165, new root ǴTR.

p. 322. The form of the tD verbal noun /tuhappiku/ may be compared with the form of the Eblaite Dt infinitive, *tuptarris*, as noted by Lambert (1988); on the form see further Tropper 2000: 574.

In the synoptic table of attested forms:

- In G Suff.-Conj., for *ḫa-ba-ṭu*, read perhaps 3mp *ḥabaṭū*.
- Add G Pref.-Conj. *yaqtulu* 3ms form *yiᶜrabu*; also in G Pref.-Conj., note (Akk.) *ti-ta-ru-na*, with 3mp *yaqtulu* ending *-ūna*.
- Delete G Vbl. Noun forms *pirru*, *laqāḥu*, *ragāzu*; add *niṣḥu*$^{?}$.
- Delete G Vbl. Adj. *mašnūᵓu*.
- Delete Gt Pref.-Conj. *yaqtulu* 3fs *tiᵓtarḫu*/*tittarḫu*.
- Add perhaps D Pref.-Conj. *yaqtula* 3fs *titarriẓa*.
- Change D Vbl. Noun *zuttaru*$^{?}$ to *ǵuttaru*$^{?}$.

pp. 358–64. Delete the following roots from the index of Ugaritic forms:

ᵓRḪ p. 390	?KBD /kubuddatu/ p. 392	PRR /pirru/ p. 397
BLM p. 391	LQḤ /laqāḥu/ p. 393	?QṬN /qaṭinnu/ p. 398
ZTR /zuttaru/ p. 391	MW/YR /mār(a)/ p. 393	RGZ /ragāzu/ p. 398
?ḤRḤR p. 392	SKN /sikānu/ p. 395	?θḪṬ /maθḫaṭu/ p. 399
KBD /kabidu/ p. 392	PRS /pur(r)ū̆s(s)atu/ p. 397	

Add the following roots to the index of Ugaritic forms:

ᵓBᶜLT /ᵓibᶜalatu/ p. 390	NTK /nutkū/ p. 394	PGR /pagrūma/ p. 396
ᵓL /ᵓilūma/ (pl.) p. 390	NθK /naθku/ p. 394	PR /pīru/ p. 397
BᶜR /biᶜru/ p. 391	SKK /sikkānu/ p. 395	PRLN /purulin(n)u/ p.397
ḤBṬ /ḥabaṭū/ p. 391	ᶜZZ /ᶜuzzu/ p. 395	RWM /rā̆mu/ p. 398
ḤṢN /ḥuṣā̆nu/ p. 392	ᶜṢ /ᶜiṣu/ (sg.) p. 395	ŠPL /šap(a)lu/ p. 398
ḪLR /ḫullūru/ p. 392	ᶜRB^{2} /yiᶜrabu/ pp. 395–96	ŠQY /mašqû/ p. 398
KLB /kalbu/ p. 393	ᶜRK /ᶜirku/ p. 396	ŠRR /šarru/ p. 399
-N /-nā/ p. 393	ᶜTQ /ᶜat(v)qu/ p. 396	TRẒ /titarriẓa/ p. 399
NṢḤ /niṣḥu/ p. 394	ǴTR /ǵuttaru/ p. 396	TRN /tarnu/ p. 399

Bibliography Cited in the Additions and Corrections

André-Salvini, Béatrice and Mirjo Salvini. 1998. Un nouveau vocabulaire trilingue sumérien-akkadien-hourrite de Ras Shamra. Pp. 3–40 in D. Owen and G. Wilhelm, eds., *Studies on the Civilizaton and Culture of Nuzi and the Hurrians*, vol. 9 (Bethesda, MD: CDL).

André-Salvini, Béatrice and Mirjo Salvini. 1999. Note brevi. *Studi Micenei ed Egeo-Anatolici* 41: 145–48.

Archi, Alfonso. 2005. Minima Eblaitica 22: The Symbolism of the Axe (*niʾtum*) in the Oath. *NABU* 2005/69.

Arnaud, Daniel. 1985–88. *Emar VI/1–4*. 4 volumes. Paris: Éditions Recherche sur les Civilisations.

Badawi, El-Said and Martin Hinds. 1986. *A Dictionary of Egyptian Arabic: Arabic–English*. Beirut: Librairie du Liban.

Caquot, André. 1988. Un recueil ougaritique de formules magiques: KTU 1.82. *SEL* 5: 31–43.

Caquot, André and Jean-Michel de Tarragon. 1989. *Textes ougaritiques*, vol. 2: *Textes religieux et rituels*. LAPO 14. Paris: Cerf.

Clemens, D.M. 2002. Review of *Handbook of Ugaritic Studies*. *JNES* 61: 221–23.

Cohen, Yoram. 2002. The West Semitic/Peripheral Akkadian Term for "Lung." *JAOS* 122: 824–27.

Cohen, Yoram. 2003. Studies in the Literary Texts from Emar. Ph.D. dissertation, Harvard University.

Dietrich, M. and O. Loretz. 1991. Ugaritisch *ʿšr, āširūma* und äthiopisch *ʿaššara*. Pp. 309–27 in Alan S. Kaye, ed., *Semitic Studies in Honor of Wolf Leslau on the Occasion of His Eighty-fifth Birthday*. 2 volumes. Wiesbaden: Harrassowitz.

DUL = G. del Olmo Lete and J. Sanmartín. 2004. *A Dictionary of the Ugaritic Language in the Alphabetic Tradition*. Translated by W.G.E. Watson. 2d ed. 2 volumes. Leiden: Brill.

Durand, Jean-Marie. 2005. *Le Culte des pierres et les monuments commémoratifs en Syrie amorrite*. Florilegium Marianum 8. Paris: Éditions Recherche sur les Civilisations.

Günbattı, Cahit. 2004. Two Treaty Texts Found at Kültepe. Pp. 249–68 in J.G. Dercksen, ed., *Assyria and Beyond: Studies Presented to Mogens Trolle Larsen*. Leiden: NINO.

Heltzer, Michael. 1989. Akkadian *katinnu* and Hebrew *kīdōn*, "Sword." *JCS* 41: 65–68.

Hoftijzer, J. and W.H. van Soldt. 1991. Texts from Ugarit concerning Security and Related Akkadian and West Semitic Material. *UF* 23: 189–216.

Huehnergard, John. 1986. RS 15.86 (PRU 3, 51f.). *UF* 18: 169–71.

Huehnergard, John. 1989. *The Akkadian of Ugarit*. HSS 34. Atlanta: Scholars.

Hutton, Jeremy M. 2003. An Areal Trend in Ugaritic and Phoenician and a New Translation of KTU 1.15 I 3. *UF* 35: 243–58.

Izre'el, Shlomo. 1991. *Amurru Akkadian: A Linguistic Study*. 2 volumes. HSS 40–41. Atlanta: Scholars.

Izre'el, Shlomo. 1992. Review of Huehnergard 1989. *BiOr* 49: 168–80.

Kühne, Cord. 1973. Ammistamru und die Tochter der 'Grossen Dame'. *UF* 5: 175–84.

Lackenbacher, Sylvie. 1995. Une correspondance entre l'administration du pharaon Merneptah et le roi d'Ougarit. Pp. 77–83 in M. Yon et al., eds., *Le pays d'Ougarit autour de 1200 av. J.-C.* Ras Shamra–Ougarit XI. Paris: Éditions Recherche sur les Civilisations.

Lackenbacher, Sylvie. 2002. *Textes akkadiens d'Ugarit: Textes provenant des vingt-cinq premières campagnes.* LAPO 20. Paris: Cerf.
Lambert, Wilfred G. 1988. A Further Note on *tōhû wābōhû*. *UF* 20: 135.
Littmann, Enno. 1954. Türkisches Sprachgut im Ägyptisch-Arabischen. Pp. 107–27 in Fritz Meier, ed., *Westöstliche Abhandlungen: Rudolf Tschud zum siebzigsten Geburtstag überreicht von Freunden und Schülern.* Wiesbaden: Harrassowitz.
Márquez Rowe, Ignacio. 2000. The King of Ugarit, His Wife, Her Brother, and Her Lover: The Mystery of a Tragedy in Two Acts Revisited. *UF* 32: 365–72.
Márquez Rowe, Ignacio. 2006. *The Royal Deeds of Ugarit: A Study of Ancient Near Eastern Diplomatics.* AOAT 335. Münster: Ugarit-Verlag.
Militarev, Alexander and Leonid Kogan. 2000. *Semitic Etymological Dictionary*, vol. 1: *Anatomy of Man and Animals.* AOAT 278/1. Münster: Ugarit-Verlag.
Nöldeke, Theodor. 1910. *Neue Beiträge zur semitischen Sprachwissenschaft.* Strassburg: Trubner.
Pardee, Dennis. 1991. Review of *UVST*. *JNES* 50: 304–6.
Parker, Simon B. 1989. Review of *UVST*. *JBL* 108: 320–22.
Pentiuc, Eugen. 2001. *West Semitic Vocabulary in the Akkadian Texts from Emar.* HSS 49. Winona Lake, IN: Eisenbrauns.
Rainey, Anson F. 1976. A Tri-lingual Cuneiform Fragment from Tel Aphek. *TA* 3: 137–40.
Rainey, Anson F. 1996. *Canaanite in the Amarna Tablets.* 4 volumes. Leiden: Brill.
Sanmartín, Joaquín. 1992. RS-akk. *nutku* und ug. alph. *ntk* «Glaspaste, -perle(n)». *NABU* 1992/111.
Schloen, J. David. 2001. *The House of the Father as Fact and Symbol: Patrimonialism in Ugarit and the Ancient Near East.* Winona Lake, IN: Eisenbrauns.
Segert, S. 1978. Rendering of Ugaritic Phonemes by Cuneiform Syllabic Signs in the Quadrilingual Vocabularies from Ras Shamra. Pp. 257–68 in vol. 2 of B. Hruška and G. Komoróczy, eds., *Festschrift Lubor Matouš.* Budapest.
Sima, Alexander. 2000. *Tiere, Pflanzen, Steine und Metalle in den altsüdarabischen Inschriften.* Wiesbaden: Harrassowitz.
Sivan, Daniel. 1984. *Grammatical Analysis and Glossary of the Northwest Semitic Vocables in Akkadian Texts of the 15th–13th C.B.C. from Canaan and Syria.* AOAT 214. Kevelaer/Neukirchen–Vluyn: Butzon & Bercker/Neukirchener.
Sivan, Daniel. 1989. A New Study of Ugaritic Words in Syllabic Transcription. *UF* 21: 357–64.
Smith, Mark S. 1989. Review of *UVST*. *CBQ* 51: 718–20.
Soldt, W.H. van. 1989. Review of Sivan 1984. *BiOr* 46: 645–51.
Soldt, W.H. van. 1989a. *ʾAtn prln*, "ʾAttānu the Diviner." *UF* 21: 365–68.
Soldt, W.H. van. 1990. Review of *UVST*. *BiOr* 47: 728–36.
Soldt, W.H. van. 2005. *The Topography of the City-State of Ugarit.* AOAT 324. Münster: Ugarit-Verlag.
Tropper, Josef. 2000. *Ugaritische Grammatik.* AOAT 273. Münster: Ugarit-Verlag.
Vita, Juan-Pablo. 1995. Acadio *maswatu*, ugarítico *mṯṯ* "remo". Préstamo ugarítico al acadio de Ugarit. *AuOr* 13: 139–41.
Vita, Juan-Pablo. 1996. La herramienta *katinnu* en el texto de Ugarit RS 19.23. *Sefarad* 46: 439–43.
Wegner, Ilse. 1995. Die hurritische Körperteilbezeichnungen. *ZA* 85: 116–26.
Wesselius, J.W. 1979. New and Old Ugaritic Words. *AIUON* 39: 105–6.
Wilhelm, Gernot. 1992. Zum viersprachigen Vokabular aus Ugarit. *Studi Micenei ed Egeo-Anatolici* 29: 249–53.